Autobiography
of
Beverly Franklin

Racial Inequality in New England USA, and beyond,
1933-2022

Beverly Franklin

MAPLE
PUBLISHERS

Autobiography of Beverly Franklin

Author: Beverly Franklin

Copyright © 2023 Beverly Franklin

The right of Beverly Franklin to be identified as author of this work has been asserted by the author in accordance with section 77 and 78 of the Copyright, Designs and Patents Act 1988.

First Published in 2023

ISBN 978-1-83538-064-2 (Paperback)
        978-1-83538-065-9 (Hardback)
        978-1-83538-066-6 (E-Book)

Book Cover Design and Book Layout by:
        White Magic Studios
        www.whitemagicstudios.co.uk

Published by:
        Maple Publishers
        Fairbourne Drive, Atterbury,
        Milton Keynes,
        MK10 9RG, UK
        www.maplepublishers.com

A CIP catalogue record for this title is available from the British Library.

Acknowledgements

Beverly died on the 24th of December 2022. She had completed her autobiography except for the acknowledgements and title.

We are so pleased that she finished it because she always said it was for the family that she was writing it. Beverly was part of the U3A, (University of the Third Age) in Hampstead, "Write Your Memoirs" class for over 10 years. She made wonderful friends there and had great support and encouragement to complete her autobiography.

As a family we remember her relating to us all these events that happened in her life. We are so proud that she managed to write it all down for future generations.

CONTENTS

PART ONE

INTRODUCTION

MY PARENTS

My father, John Robert Allen, was born on the 20th of September 1900 in Hampton, Virginia, USA. His parents were Susan Clark and Thomas Allen.

According to my Uncle Thomas, my father's brother, their family history was most unusual. Given the exceptional circumstances, unfortunately, the facts he related can never be corroborated or confirmed.

Susan Clark, their mother, was the offspring of a white mother and a black father. During the Civil War (1861-1865), Susan's grandmother was killed by Union soldiers. Her abandoned baby was either found by a black family who decided to look after her or the baby was brought to the black family in the hopes that they would care for her. In either case, the white baby was raised by a black family. Many years later, she married a black man and produced my grandmother, Susan Clark.

Susan Clark married Thomas Allen. He was born in the West Indies and worked as an engineer in the British Navy. Later, he migrated to Virginia, USA where he met my grandmother. Thomas's father, who was white, had married a black woman from Montserrat so Thomas was what would be considered mixed race.

If these facts are true, both my paternal grandparents were half black and half white.

My grandfather, Thomas Allen, died at the age of forty-two. My grandmother was left with a family of six children to raise and absolutely no means of support.

As a result, my father who was the eldest in the family, was forced to relinquish his education as he was about to enter his fourth and last year of high school. His aim had been to pursue further education at a college or university when he completed his high school studies.

His inability to attain the education he so desired remained a deep source of regret. To compensate for this loss, he was often observed engaged in activities which he deemed could "improve his mind", like mathematical problems and crossword puzzles. He often claimed that chess and bridge, pastimes in which he took great delight, were beneficial for stimulating the growth of grey matter in the brain.

My mother, Juanita Pearl Fowler, was born on the 20th of August 1900 in Nova Scotia, Canada. Her parents were Annie Jenkins and James Fowler. They owned a farm in Broad Cove, Annapolis, Nova Scotia where they raised eleven children.

I know nothing of my grandfather, James Fowler's, ancestry but it is obvious from his wedding picture that he is of mixed race.

I know only marginally more about my grandmother's ancestry, but I do know that I inherited Native American ancestry as well as black and white ancestry from her.

My mother and her sister, Myrtle, trained to be teachers in Nova Scotia. In 1835, compulsory school attendance became mandatory in Nova Scotia for children from seven to twelve years old, except for those who lived two miles from their nearest state school.

But, for families living in the countryside, farming would always take precedence over schooling. People's livelihoods, particularly in remote areas, were totally dependent on work on the farm or in the fisheries.

One room schoolhouses were built to educate children who lived in rural areas. A single teacher, usually a woman, taught children of all ages in the one schoolroom available. The basic subjects were taught reading, writing, arithmetic, as well as history and geography. Ability, not age, was the dominant factor in promotion to the next level of learning.

My mother taught in a one room schoolhouse in Nova Scotia and became a well-known and accomplished teacher. I do not know when she emigrated to the United States, but I do know that she was greatly disappointed that she was not allowed to teach there. Her Canadian credentials were not considered valid. She could only teach with American qualifications and would be required to retrain at an American Teacher Training College. Whatever money she earned at whatever jobs she could find was required for her own maintenance. She never earned enough money to retrain as a teacher in the United States.

I do not know how or where my parents met but they were married on the fourth of July 1932 in New Haven, Connecticut, USA. Not only my mother, but various members of her family had moved from Canada to the USA. From their marriage certificate, I can see that the witnesses at the wedding were her brother, Leon, from Canada, and her sister, Lena, who had settled as a married woman in New Haven, Connecticut. Lena's daughter, Esther Morrow, was also a witness at the wedding.

When my parents were married, my father's occupation on the marriage certificate was recorded as elevator operator. They had married only three years after the Great Depression had started. The Great Depression lasted from 1929 to 1939 and was considered the most disastrous economic recession in the history of the industrialised world.

Rapid financial decline resulted in a sharp increase in unemployment. Finding a job of any kind was a challenging proposition.

My father really wanted a secure job that would provide him with a reasonable pension. He passed the exams to become a Port Patrol Officer in the Civil Service and remained in this occupation for the rest of his working life, until he retired.

THE BEGINNING

After my parents married, they rented an apartment in Cambridge, MA. which was directly across the road from a primary school.

My mother told me that I was constantly running to the sitting room windows to watch the children walking to school, constantly pestering her about when I could attend.

I was probably about four years old, far too young to attend school in the US. Pre-school (kindergarten) commences at 5 years old.

In exasperation, my mother eventually took me to the headmaster to ask if I could be enrolled in school. My mother, who had been a teacher, thought I might be ready for this experience, despite my age. Though surprised at her request, he said he would need a private interview with me to decide whether or not this was a feasible proposition.

When we both emerged from his office, he said that he would be delighted to enter me in the kindergarten class.

None of these events do I remember, nor do I remember the apartment in which we lived.

My entering school meant that not only would my mother be liberated from my incessant pestering, but also that she would have more time to spend with my younger brother who was only 15 months younger than I was.

With two such young and lively children, I'm sure that she must have been prone to feelings of tiredness and exhaustion. Any small respite would undoubtedly, have been welcomed.

As my father had always wanted to own his own house, they decided to leave their apartment and look for a house in a different part of Cambridge. My father, who was of medium brown complexion, visited many houses advertised for sale, only to be told, as soon as the door opened, that it was unfortunate, but the house had just been sold to the previous viewer.

Upon seeing him as a prospective buyer, the house owner's immediate response was always negative, and my parents knew why. Their reactions were a blatant expression of racial prejudice.

To overcome this impenetrable barrier to purchasing property, my mother, who looked totally white, would ring for an appointment to view the same property that had just "been sold". She would be invited to view the property, be graciously shown round, and asked to inform them whether or not she wished to purchase it.

In the 1940's, 1950's and 1960's, there was no legislation to protect any minority group from discrimination in the housing market. Mortgage companies often implemented a practice known as redlining, i.e., marking out specific areas occupied by minority groups as undesirable and, therefore, not worthy of any kind of investment. People living in these areas were refused mortgages to buy houses and loans to improve their own houses. If black individuals did receive a mortgage or a loan, it was often at a higher rate than their white counterparts would have paid for a similar dwelling.

My father always maintained that his mortgage, his house insurance, and his life insurance were exorbitantly priced. I actually heard him ask the life insurance salesman if black people paid more for their insurance than white people. Of course, it was denied, the companies that offered insurances and loans and the people who worked for them always refuted the idea of any discriminatory practices. As they were not prepared to reveal their records, no case could ever be established against them.

As the applications of minority individuals were usually rejected, they were meant to consider themselves fortunate if they acquired any documents or policies and, in gratitude, never to complain.

My parents somehow overcame all the obstacles placed in their way and eventually acquired a mortgage to purchase a house in Cambridge, MA. It was situated on Chilton Street, about a mile from Harvard Square. Two-story, detached clapboard houses lined both sides of the street. In front of every house was a small garden and a much larger one in the rear.

The area in which we lived was not racially exclusive as both black and white families had settled there, sometimes living next door to each other. Our neighbours to the right of our house were Italians and the house facing us was populated by an Irish family.

My father rented the ground floor of our house to an Irish family with five children. When we were young, the two girls in the family were our constant playmates. Their father was a policeman. In fact, there were three Irish families on our street whose fathers were policemen. We were friendly with the children in two of these families but the children in the third family never associated with us.

SCHOOL

I attended kindergarten again in a new school, though there was some reluctance to allow my entry, as I was only 4 years of age. The only two activities that I can recall about kindergarten were trying to solve puzzles and best of all, the entire class taking turns to beat cream into butter in a large wooden churn.

At five, I entered first grade, Miss Anderson's class. On the last day of kindergarten, we were ushered into our classrooms for the next year, Miss Anderson read us a story about some beautiful creatures who lived at the bottom of the sea. Two of them had started to argue. I was totally engrossed. I'd always loved stories but suddenly, in the middle of the narrative, she stopped abruptly, saying; "Time is up." She would see us all next year and we were dismissed, ready to go home. I left feeling a great sense of injustice. "It wasn't fair. You can't stop a story in the middle of the most exciting part."

I wondered what first grade would be like and prayed that we would be allowed to finish any story we were reading. On the first day of school, I set out with great anticipation, anxiously hoping to hear the end of the story.

The first class that day was phonetics, no mention of the story at all. As the day progressed, it became clear that Miss Anderson wasn't about to read our story. There were too many other things to do, like numbers and writing letters the correct way and making sure that we sat up straight at our desks (it was good for our posture) and not talking unless we raise our hands and never talking unless she called our name and lunchtime and recess and time to go to the toilet. By the end of the day, I had to accept that she would never have time to finish our story because she was always teaching us too many new things.

Despite my initial trepidation about stories ending properly, I loved first grade. On Fridays, Miss Anderson often read a poem and when she asked if anyone knew the poem she was about to read, my hand often shot into the air. Anyone who knew the poem had to stand in front of the class and repeat the poem from memory.

I remember reciting 'My Shadow' by Robert Louis Stevenson:

"I have a little shadow that goes in and out with me and

What can be the use of him is

More than I can see.

He is very like me from

The heels up to the head

And I see him jump before me

When I jump into my bed.

There are 12 more lines in this poem. I think that I included most of them in my recitation that day.

Another day, I recited 'The Cow':

The friendly cow all red and white

I love with all my heart

She gives me cream with all her might

To eat with apple tart.

There were numerous poems I seemed to know: 'The Swing', 'The Wind', 'At the Sea-Side', etc. - all by Robert Louis Stevenson. At no time, can I remember memorising these poems. My mother always read to me, and it may have been with her encouragement that I learned them or just unconsciously absorbed the rhymes and rhythms.

Looking at the number of poems I could recite, I concluded that my mother must have fallen in love with the poems of Robert Louis Stevenson. In addition, I remember reciting 'The Night Before Christmas':

"T'was the night before Christmas

When all through the house

Not a creature was stirring

Not even a mouse.

The stockings were hung by the

Chimney with care

In hopes that St. Nicholas

Soon would be there

I'm shocked at the length of the poem, 14 four-line verses. If I recited all of them, I am impressed. If so, it is evidence of a youthful brain functioning very well. I would not like my memory to be tested now on the recitation of these or any other poems.

When I was about six or seven, the school sent someone whom I remember thinking was a totally unremarkable woman, to give me an IQ test. I think, because it was such an important occasion, that I thought the person sent would be in some way outstanding or different.

There was some discussion of giving me a "double promotion", that meant I would be moved up to the class above me. It would have been a "double promotion" as I was already in a class a year beyond my age.

I was never promoted to a class two years above my age and can only presume that I did not exceed expected limits on the IQ test. I was doing exceptionally well in school and in retrospect, am grateful that I remained where I was. Otherwise, I might have been left struggling both academically and socially.

CHURCH

As both my parents were Baptists, when we were very young, my brother and I first attended Sunday school every week at the Baptist Church not far from where we lived. The neighbourhood was predominantly white, as was the church congregation where only a few black families attended service every Sunday.

I distinctly remember being required to memorise the names of all the books in the Bible, both the Old and New Testament, the 23rd Psalm and John, chapter 3 verse 16.

"For God so love the world, that he gave his only begotten Son, that whosoever believeth in him, should not perish, but have everlasting life."

There were numerous other verses that I don't recall that we were expected to recite verbatim every Sunday. What memories do remain of my early experiences at Sunday school relate more to hymns, which I always sang with great enthusiasm.

"If you're happy and you know it,
Clap your hands
"If you're happy and you know it
Clap your hands.
If you're happy and you know it
Your life will surely show it
If you're happy and you know it
Clap your hands.

Two verses followed in a similar vein, with the refrain of "Stamp your feet," and the last one was "Shout Amen."

Another was "We are climbing Jacob's ladder
We are climbing Jacob's ladder
We are climbing Jacob's ladder
Soldiers of the cross.

The one I recall with great fondness is "Jesus loves me." I had not sung this hymn for at least 35 years when, as a mature student at Bedford College, I met someone who became a very close friend. She had attended chapel every Sunday in Wales, sometimes two or three times a day at boarding school. To our astonishment, we realized that we had learned the same hymn as five-year-olds, ten years apart.

It became our "party piece." We would shock our mostly agnostic, college friends by suddenly bursting into song, lustily emitting in dulcet tones:

"Jesus loves me, this I know
For the Bible tells me so
Little ones to Him belong
I am weak but He is strong.

Yes, Jesus loves me
Yes, Jesus loves me
Yes, Jesus loves me-For the Bible tells me so.

Even after we moved to our new house in another part of Cambridge, we all continued to attend the same Baptist Church, in spite of the fact that it was much farther away.

One summer, my brother and I begged our parents to allow us to go to a revival meeting. It was August. We were bored and desperate to do something new and exciting, particularly when our friends weren't available for play.

As I was considered very responsible, meaning that I could reliably look after my younger brother, and the streets were considered very safe, my mother, under great pressure from me, finally relinquished her opposition and permitted us to attend.

A huge circular tent, furnished with an altar and rows of seats for the choir and the expected congregation, welcomed all worshippers. Our assumption was that there would be lots of hymn-singing which we both enjoyed and preaching, of course, but that was of much less interest to us. But neither of us had ever attended church, only Sunday School, so had never been exposed to Baptist preaching.

As the day progressed, the blazing rays of the sun permeated the khaki canvas. enveloping us all in a pale-yellow glow. We grew warmer and warmer and began to perspire but this was of no concern, as all our eyes were firmly fastened on the minister and his fervent sermon which engulfed the entire space of the tent.

As the sermon developed, the minister's voice lyrically rose and fell, undulating rhythmically and eventually burst forth in a great crescendo.

Tiny beads of perspiration slowly trickled down his pale, white cheeks. He began to turn a lurid pink as he implored us to abandon our wayward behaviour and confront our sins.

One by one, people approached the altar and knelt before him. With hands outstretched, he gently lay his palms on their heads and prayed for Jesus to accept them into his kingdom.

The choir and the minister alternated their appeals. As the choir sang "Come to Jesus and live", the minister responded with the words "Let Him fill your life."

Choir   - "Sing to Jesus and live"

Minister - "Let Jesus be your Saviour."

Choir   - "Fly to Jesus and live"

Minister - "Now your burdens are lifted.

              Let Jesus wipe away your sins."

As I listened, I felt his words were aimed directly at me. I wanted to walk those special steps to the altar. I willed myself to make the journey but, to my distress, my knees remained steadfastly fastened in place, glued to the communal bench on which I knelt. The conflict between my sincere desires and my body's immobility, reflected how frightened I was to act on these new uplifting, overwhelming feelings.

I longed to embrace a new and holy life (with no knowledge of what that entailed) but my body resisted and would not let me proceed. Needless to say, I felt a total failure for not having the courage to follow my sudden impulse to approach the altar and be saved forever.

Over time, I became reconciled to my shameful reluctance. When I later thought about this event, I recalled that no children had approached the altar on that fateful day. My guilt was somewhat alleviated. I convinced myself that I was carried away by the heightened emotion that the entire congregation was experiencing and decided that "being saved" was an onerous decision, so serious that it should be made only by adults.

On even later consideration, I realised that I was particularly vulnerable. The emotive side of Baptist sermons had never been part of my life experience. I had only attended Sunday school and that was a straightforward teaching experience about Bible stories, no emotions involved.

My faith was not dimmed or seriously disturbed by this experience. The following summer found me selling packets of seeds to our neighbours. With the proceeds collected slowly throughout the summer months, I purchased a new Bible.

CHANGING CHURCHES

I was not at all unhappy at the Baptist Church but thought that it would be more interesting to go to Sunday school with my friends every week. So, I asked my parents if I could attend the Episcopalian Church. Instead of walking to church with only my brother as a companion, I envisaged an exciting social time, particularly with one of my special friends.

For me, another important fact was that the journey to the Episcopalian Church was much shorter. I gave great prominence to this line of reasoning when asking my parents to consider my proposition, never mentioning the social aspect which seemed to me to be of much greater importance.

Initially, my parents were shocked that I would not be a member of the church to which they both belonged. After much careful thought, they relinquished their resistance, reasoning that I would still remain a Christian, even though the rituals at church services might be very different.

I was overjoyed. Thereafter, from the age of 12, I first attended Sunday School every week and after confirmation. At Christ Church, I learned to follow the church services following the Book of Common Prayer. The church was situated just over a mile from our house and only a 2-minute walk from the centre of Harvard Square.

The original Book of Common Prayer was the one used by the British when they established the Church of England in America. In 1789, The Episcopalian Church officially separated from the Church of England, relinquishing allegiance to the king and the royal family. In every other aspect, the Episcopalian version of the Book of Common Prayer is the same as the one in common use in Anglican services in England.

THE BIBLE

The only other activities in which I had engaged were singing in the choir, going to the church summer camp for 2 weeks and once, being the narrator for the Christmas Pageant. The Christmas reading remained a very fond memory.

I stood in the pulpit, reading from the lectern, the specified verses about the birth of Christ. The old King James version of the Bible was still in use. In my attempt to reveal the underlying metre of the lines, I tried to project my voice emphatically, with some sort of vigour and expression.

The role definitely appealed to any latent acting desire that I possessed. Reading quotations from the Bible was the part of the service which I particularly enjoyed. The quotations always preceded the reading of the sermon which was meant to be more relevant to everyday life, but here, I often found my concentration wandering.

I was more absorbed in the language of the Bible which seemed to fall into a definite rhythm evoked by the sound of the spoken verses. I regret its passing, the old King James version, now having been translate into a more familiar, but more static form of language. Practicality has been substituted for elegance.

Along with many others, I have concluded that the newer version of the King James Bible has undoubtedly lost its poetic voice and dynamic cadence.

CONFIRMATION

I had already been baptised in the Baptist church when I was a baby.

At 13, I decided to become confirmed as an Episcopalian. After a year of preparation, during which we studied the Old and New Testament, the history and doctrines of the Episcopalian Church and the Book of Common Prayer.

For the confirmation service, I wore my new, white broderie anglaise dress which my mother had purchased for my June graduation from the Russell Grammar School. As it was now midsummer, I had turned 13 when I was received into the Episcopalian Church with the Bishop's official laying of hands. The bishop placed his hands on the heads of all those who were confirmed. Performing his act, meant that he served as an instrument of God who blessed His children and established them as official members of the Episcopalian Church.

In attendance were my very proud parents, whose initial reservations about my joining the Episcopalian Church, had now completely vanished.

MY PARENTS' CHURCH

It was decided one Easter Sunday that the entire family would go to the Easter service at the Baptist Church in Boston which my parents attended.

My brother and I wore our new Easter outfits - he, his dark brown corduroy jacket with slightly lighter brown trousers and I, my new pale blue dress of fine cotton with puffed sleeves and a line of 4 pink cotton roses in the centre of the bodice, covered with a light wool coat of a deeper shade of blue.

My father appeared in a smart felt hat which he always wore when wearing a suit. My mother and I donned hats and gloves, necessities in the 1950's, to create the finishing touch to any outfit.

As we travelled on public transportation, by bus and the underground and a ten-minute walk at the end, it took us at least an hour to reach our destination. The church was populated by a black congregation and a black minister. My brother and I had never attended a church composed entirely of black people.

When we were very young, we had attended Sunday School at the local Baptist Church. The composition of the church, with three or four exceptions, was totally white as was the minister. The same could be said of the congregation and the minister of the Episcopalian Church which we attended after we had moved to a different area in Cambridge.

We all settled into our pews to hear the morning service. My brother and I were accustomed to the service at the Episcopalian Church. Readings from the Book of Common Prayer with designated communal responses, subdued, spoken almost in a chant, a ritual without emotion. While the sermon could often be fervent and intense, it was delivered in a calm and solemn manner.

Although the Episcopalian and Baptist minister were of the same Christian persuasion, they took very divergent paths in the presentation of their beliefs to their respective congregations.

The Baptist minister commenced the sermon with conversational prose and slowly changed to a more rhythmic tonal chant. The inflection of the minister's voice and the cadence of the preaching, combined with appropriate interjections of the choir singing hymns, resulted in heightened emotion in the congregation.

This dynamic interaction produced uninhibited one- and two-word responses in those listening. The onset of this behaviour in a few, initiated similar behaviour in others. I noted that my parents remained silent throughout this period.

The rhythmic sounds, the animated sermon, the alternating preaching, and hymn singing encompassed us. My brother and I turned our heads simultaneously and stared into each other's eyes. The current experience was an acknowledgement and recognition of a very potent memory. Our first and only observation of such dramatic sermons occurred during the day we had gone to the Revival meeting in the tent at our first Baptist Church meeting.

As we sat in my parents' church, mesmerised once again by the rhythms and the sounds, there was a sudden shout and quite suddenly, a woman fainted. She fell to the floor before our startled eyes. We watched in amazement and shock as four ushers rushed to her seat, picked her up, put her on a stretcher and carried her down the aisle to the church exit, hopefully to recover in a less heated and intense atmosphere. When I glanced at my parents, they looked surprised and appeared to be as shocked as we were.

My parents never approved of any sort of loud outburst or very heightened reaction to either pain, pleasure, or surprise. I assumed that such an emotional outburst and in such a public place had met with serious disapproval on their part.

The choir continued to sing but from a state of reverence and awe, we were unexpectedly hurtled into a state of bewilderment and fear. The spell was broken, we were no longer entranced but sat rigidly on the edge of our seats, worried that the minister's exhortations might provoke an overwhelming response in yet another member of the congregation. In addition, we were secretly more than a little concerned that our parents attended a church where such unexpected events could occur.

Although we found Baptist charismatic preaching appealing as it engaged all our emotions, at the time, we were pleased to return to the predictable, less flamboyant preaching of the Episcopalian church. It was formal and familiar and designed to produce only restrained and predictable responses from the congregation.

ADDENDUM

Having grown up in predominantly "white churches", neither my friends nor I were acquainted with the rich musical heritage that black Americans had bequeathed to the world.

In the 1950's, radio broadcasts were the main transmitters of ideas and sounds that were different from those in our accustomed environment. It was through listening to recordings played on the radio that I became acquainted with the famous black, internationally recognised, bass singer and actor, Paul Robeson. I fell in love with the resonances of his deep, bass sounds. I later came to appreciate the performances of numerous black church choirs, so exultant and full of fervour and conviction.

Around the year 2010, a white friend of mine insisted that I should accompany her to a concert in London. The Harlem Gospel Singers were performing. She had admired them for years. I was totally unfamiliar with their music.

Once again, I was overwhelmed by the power and strength of this kind of singing. There seemed an authoritative command in their message to reform and "follow Jesus".

I allowed myself to wonder --if I had grown up, from a very young age, in a church with such music, would I still be a church member? This kind of music was compelling and engaged my emotions immediately, but I had to come to terms with my inability to believe in the doctrines which the music and the church espoused.

I had relinquished my Christian beliefs when I was a teenager-- a few years after my confirmation at 13 in the Episcopalian Church. I would just have to settle for valuing and appreciating the music which produced such a persistently powerful and emotive reaction in me.

AFTER SCHOOL ACTIVITIES

DANCING

Aside from learning the piano, the other consistent activity in which I seriously engaged was tap dancing. Ballet was the preferred option, but as the classes were oversubscribed, with strong adult disapproval, I was eventually allowed to settle for tap dancing.

I'm sure that my mother was possessed of an irrational fear that, if exposed to this type of dance, I might slowly descend into a life of debauchery and immoral pleasure. After all, tap dancers were to be seen in clubs where smoking, drinking and the over-consumption of alcohol were rampant and unrestrained.

Although these fears were not openly expressed, I believe that these irreverent thoughts were the foundation of her vociferous objections to my desire to tap dance.

It was only with considerable persuasion from my best friend's mother that my mother's fears were allayed, and I was finally allowed to attend these classes.

At the dance school, acrobatics were considered a useful adjunct to any type of dancing--to limber the muscles and produce more flexible joints. Sadly, for me there was never an accretion of skills in this sphere. I remained forever in awe of those who, after a few weeks of stretching at the bar, could perform the splits and contort their bodies into unbelievable and miraculous shapes.

Over time, my tap-dancing skills improved as my steps became more nimble and rhythmic, but I did not possess the natural talent to move with either great elegance or grace. No need for any anxious concern that I would flee to the chorus line or take to the stage at all!!

What impelled us to continue the incessant daily practice of the difficult dance steps was the giddy expectation of appearing in the final recital. The overwhelming appeal of the ultimate performance was not just the entertainment itself, where we could exhibit our hard-won skills. One of the greatest attractions was actually displaying our glorious, tailor-made costumes.

Multicoloured sequins crisscrossed our bodices and were more liberally sprinkled around the very top layer of our many, multi-layered chiffon skirts. We believed ourselves ecstatically beautiful as we danced across the stage emitting tiny flashes of light under strategically placed spotlights, irrespective of the proficiency of our performance.

Though mesmerised by our glittering outfits, on the night of the performance, most of us were filled with a certain level of trepidation and anxiety at the thought of performing before a huge audience of parents, friends, and well-wishers in an enormous hall in the centre of Boston.

ACTING

Another infrequent, but much-loved pastime during my teenage years was that of acting. Amateur dramatic clubs and a few church groups occasionally sought young people to take part in their productions.

I was an eager participant and was told on many occasions that I was convincing in the part that I had undertaken. Although my acting experience was brief (It lasted only two to three years), I longed to be asked to participate in new productions.

One year, I was asked to join a teen-age club which was established to carry out projects to help the elderly. For two years, I paid fortnightly and sometimes weekly visits to what we called an Old Folks Home. We spent time talking to many different individuals, performed any small tasks that they requested and usually wrote letters for them. When I started working after school, I no longer, had time to continue these activities so decided to resign from the club.

THE GIRL SCOUTS

For many years, I was an ardent member of the Girl Scouts and even at senior level, diligently continued to earn badges in craft, music, outdoor activities and sewing. Both my parents were highly encouraging and supportive of my scout membership—particularly, as I was involved in worthy social pursuits as well as healthy outdoor activities.

What I truly delighted in was the fact that I was allowed to go camping. With the exception of the occasional sleepover at a friend's house, I, never, ever left home. Weekends away with the Scouts meant that I could briefly escape parental supervision and engage in more exciting ventures.

Some of us learned to make a fire with the dry, brittle wood we had gathered from the forest floor and spent many evenings cooking simple meals over the flames.

The most desirable skill to acquire was that of melting marshmallows. Placed on a spindly twig, we had to turn them until they were transformed from pallid white to a crispy brown. Sadly, many marshmallows thwarted our best attempts to sear them by suddenly turning black, splitting, and dripping and then falling in slow descent into the voracious fire.

All these wonderfully engaging activities took place as we sat under the sweet and pungent smelling pine trees, singing songs we had learned at our weekly meetings.

AFTER SCHOOL ACTIVITIES – THE PIANO

At the age of nine or ten, I started piano lessons. As it was a novel activity, I applied myself vigorously and enthusiastically to everything that I was expected to learn. Although my ardent zeal began to wane when it came to practising scales and arpeggios, I persevered, in at least an hour of continual practise. These included the desirable and undesirable assignments as well as one or two complicated tunes.

It was always a delight when the stark and boldly individual black and white keys mingled harmoniously together and metamorphosed into a simple, recognisable melody.

I had lessons for six or seven years with Miss Wild who came to our house once a week. She was imperturbable, calm, and composed, never lost her temper, and proved a constant source of encouragement. Any learning that ensued could be attributed to her endless patience, even at those times when I hadn't practised sufficiently for the lesson.

She instilled in me an awareness and sensitivity to intricacies of sound which were intrinsic to the music. Entire phrases and movements began to exude levels of feeling and passion that I never anticipated the music possessed.

One summer, while she was teaching me and other children in the neighbourhood, she was hired as a teacher at the prestigious New England Conservatory in Boston, MA. It was one of the most eminent music colleges i8n New England.

I assumed that she would dispense with our lessons as the fees paid by my parents were minimal compared to those of the Conservatory students. In addition, I was not training to become a professional musician. Teaching the Conservatory students had to be a more interesting and challenging proposition.

Miss Wild and I had travelled a long journey together from my beginnings as a pre-pubescent primary school student to a now unsure and sometimes opinionated adolescent. She had moulded, encouraged, challenged, coaxed, and exposed me to the multiple sides of music, to its myriad frustrations, joys, and rewards. I was pleasantly surprised when she informed my parents that she would continue to teach me and was pleased to do so.

As our old piano was constantly going out of tune, she must have been in despair that I would ever develop a sense of proper pitch for any note, white or black. She once passed me off as a student at the Conservatory so that I could test out the sound and touch of different types of pianos on the premises.

On Sunday afternoon, she organised many informal recitals at the homes of her pupils. The parents willingly took turns to provide a collation of tea, sandwiches, and cakes, after all the pupils had dutifully displayed their burgeoning talents to the proud and beaming audience.

For a marked sensitivity to sound and rhythm and an enduring appreciation of classical music, I will always owe her a debt of gratitude.

OTHER RECITALS

Aside from home recitals, our only public appearances were at various church social gatherings and school assemblies. Pupils who studied an instrument of any sort or could recite a poem were in demand at both these institutions.

With the encouragement and tutelage of Miss Wild, I was often found performing my latest piano accomplishment and in addition, eagerly reciting a piece of poetry.

OUR LIFE AT HOME

Between church, school and outside activities, my brother and I were constantly engaged in worthwhile pursuits.

My brother was unbelievably enthusiastic about his swimming lessons at the YMCA. In lieu of dancing lessons, which he never had any desire to undertake, he received a bicycle and often went on short, brisk excursions around the neighbourhood.

We were fortunate because we usually received the toys that we most desired at Christmas and were always given books to read. My parents were avid believers in the value of a good education, impressing us with the fact that reading was an essential basis for acquiring knowledge in any subject.

Despite the fact that money was sparse, we were always well dressed. Both my parents were very careful with money. But, at no time did they ever have enough money to take us on a holiday. We did not feel deprived and thought that our friends who went on holiday were just more privileged as they had more money.

My mother often made my dresses when I was in the early years of primary school. I was transformed into a mannequin, standing rigid and inflexible, while she held up newspapers to cut her own patterns for cotton and occasionally velvet dresses. Initially she used a treadle Singer sewing machine and later an electric one to produce garments that looked professionally made.

Being very prudent, my parents saved every penny to put unto a special bank account to ensure that my brother and I would have some money to go to university.

Over the years, their main expense was the monthly payment for the mortgage. My father was determined that he would own his own house.

My mother had a series of brown envelopes, all labelled and kept in a metal box. For every bill, she duly placed the requisite payment into a specific envelope whenever my father received his salary.

She did allow us to have the occasional treats of ice-cream or lollipops, especially on journeys to visit my father's relatives in Boston or sometimes when we visited my mother's Canadian friends who had settled in the US, in Lynn, MA, a much longer trip than going to Boston.

As we had no car, we travelled on buses and usually made one or two changes on the underground to reach what seemed to my brother and me, an interminable destination. These visits were always on Sundays as Saturday was my father's weekly shopping day for food at Fanueil Hall Market in Boston. This imposing market building was home to many merchants.

Its fame relates to the fact that in 1764, at Fanueil Hall, the colonists protested about the Sugar Act, proclaiming to the British that there was to be: "No taxation without representation."

The cacophony of the numerous hawkers becomes overwhelming as one meanders through the endless rows of stalls. Italians, Armenians, Russians, Czechs, Irish, Poles and many other nationalities could be heard insistently calling and entreating everyone to purchase their fresh meat, fish, poultry, fruit and vegetables.

My father maintained that they had all developed sleight of hand because, inevitably, they inserted into his brown paper bag, at least one piece of fruit or vegetable that was withered or bruised. No matter how hard he concentrated or how intently he gazed, he never perceived anyone slipping in the undesirable article.

On Friday nights, on his way home from work, he always bought freshly caught fish. As Boston and Cambridge had many Catholic immigrants, there was always a plethora of fresh fish, as Friday was, for many, a fasting day from meat.

PRESERVING FRUIT AND VEGETABLES

My mother and I spent many long hours preserving the produce from our garden. My mother sterilised Mason Jars and lined them up on the counter. All households used this type of jar as they had proved so reliable for preserving food. They were made of glass and had a zinc cap which completely sealed the lid.

The process began with my washing the fruit or vegetables and placing them in a pan for parboiling. They were then placed in the jars and covered with boiling water, leaving a space between the surface of the food and the top of the jar. Salt had been added to the cooking water of the vegetables, or sugar if it was fruit.

With a damp, clean cloth, I wiped round the top rim of the jar. The sterilised cap was then screwed on and the outside of the jar wiped clean.

Our cellar shelves were full to bursting with peaches, cherries, plums, pears, beans, carrots, beets, pickled onions and cucumber, tomato relish, spicy apple and nutmeg spread, and raspberry and strawberry jam.

My father often commented that, in her endeavours to feed the family, my mother was working far too hard and had produced enough food to feed the entire neighbourhood.

Such observations in no way deterred my mother from her pursuits. Much of the excess was given to friends and neighbours, and especially to friends who were old or ailing.

On the other side of the cellar, far removed from the shelves laden with food, was the coal shed, where coal was periodically delivered for the furnace and our kitchen stove.

Both my parents found the coal stove a great convenience. The oven cooked evenly all around, and it created a cosy, warm area when we all congregated around the kitchen table.

But the coal stove was also an anathema to them. There was the incessant need to remove the ashes from behind the grate, with all the consequent dust which that produced. They had always planned to buy a new gas stove, but the arrival of the war in 1941, destroyed any hopes of that desire being fulfilled.

No new machines of any sort would be generally available for the next five or six years, at least two years after the war ended.

As soon as it was feasible and affordable, my parents purchased a new gas stove, and a Bendix top-loading washing machine.

SATURDAYS

Every day my brother and I shared the tasks of setting the dinner table and washing and drying the dishes. These tasks completed, we always disagreed about whose turn it was to clean the stove and sweep the floor. My mother always intervened to settle the matter fairly and we were forbidden to discuss the matter further.

Saturdays was our real workday. We both had our allotted jobs to perform. The day started with tidying and cleaning our respective bedrooms and then continued with work inside and outside the house.

My brother emptied all the wastebaskets and carried the kitchen refuse bag to empty in the outside bins. He swept the front and back stairs, the paths around the side and front of the house and helped my father with the gardening. If we ran out of anything, usually bread or flour, he was sent to the local corner shop which was run by Italian immigrants. My mother always objected to the prices charged, but then as now, the corner shop was conveniently open when other shops were not.

I dry-mopped around the carpets in the dining room and sitting room and then vacuumed the carpets. The worst job was the dusting, particularly the piano. The top was covered with numerous photographs of family members and friends. Each had to be removed in order to dust the top of the piano and then replaced in the order in which they stood. The small upright piano fitted neatly into one corner of the sitting room. I loved playing it but cleaning it was hardly enjoyable, not only because of all the photos but also due to the endless number of entwined curlicues on each leg.

No grand swoop over the surface with a duster would suffice. Each curlicue required an individual rub inside and out. It was entirely too fussy and finicky a job and hastened my impetus to finish the task as soon as possible.

After this, I helped my mother with the cooking, which meant washing all the leafy vegetables picked from the garden three times. That was my father's rule. He insisted that the soil in which they grew could only be completely removed if washed in clean water three times. Even though I often declared them clean after two rinses, I never succeeded in convincing him to change his mind.

Chopping vegetables was far too repetitious to be interesting. I preferred measuring different ingredients, usually for a cake or pudding. I stirred the dry and liquid ingredients together until they formed a sticky mass, which, at intervals, when my mother's gaze was averted, I secretly tasted with a clean, silver spoon.

Pouring it into a shiny buttered container was a great delight because I was then genuinely allowed to scrape the bowl to eat any of the remaining batter, before my mother placed the entire concoction in the oven.

On Saturdays, an essential part of the time was taken up with preparing our clothes for Sunday school. Cleaning shoes was requisite. As my Sunday shoes were made of patent leather, a touch of petroleum jelly on the surface and then buffed with a soft cloth, created a brilliant, gleaming shine.

My brother's leather shoes required the application of a hard wax polish which had to dry before being brushed, a much messier job than mine.

My mother allotted the steaming of men's trousers to my father and brother. They were experts at creating a crisp, straight crease down the front of each trouser leg.

If necessary, in the summertime, I ironed a dress or blouse and skirt. In the wintertime, woollen clothes took less preparation as they were chemically cleaned and pressed at the dry cleaners.

CHESS

Every Saturday morning, my father, invariably, played chess with his friends in our sitting room. How my brother and I resented this activity. So as not to interfere with their concentration, we were expected to make no noise. As our shoes clicked on the wooden floors, the edges not covered with carpet, we were forced to walk on tiptoe and spoke in incessant whispers.

My father and his cohorts, sat like immobile, immovable statues, eyes glued to the chess board. The games seemed to consist of endless silences, punctured with occasional outbursts of joy or exasperation, depending on who had won or lost a piece.

We were eternally grateful that they took it in turns to visit each other's houses. So, on some Saturday mornings, normality reigned, and we could return to our occasionally rambunctious behaviour.

Sadly, the claustrophobic atmosphere associated with chess conditioned my attitude toward the game forever. I announced to everyone that I would never learn to play chess and never have. Now, many years later, I bear no malice of thought towards the chess pieces and could probably be enticed to participate.

My brother, on the other hand, became a superb player, was a member of the chess club in high school, and replicated the same silent scenes, playing chess with my father on a regular basis.

SATURDAY FILMS

Occasionally, we were allowed to attend the Saturday morning films. Some of my friends attended frequently but we were permitted to view only those films which passed my mother's approval.

In order to see any film, we had to complete all our Saturday jobs before 9am, with hopes of not being late for the local 10 am viewing. We carefully perused the advertisements, choosing only the ones we thought my mother would think were appropriate, mostly Disney films or the ones featuring the child star, Shirley Temple.

My mother always stated that it was better to read a book than to fill our heads with worthless rubbish. Little did she know of the "rubbish" which accompanied the approved film. The short cliff-hangers at the end of the feature film were meant to guarantee our return the following week. They were crammed full of violence and very abusive individuals.

The theme was always the same. A cruel despot, utilising the most terrifying and painful methods, tried to obtain dominion over peaceful powers and innocent citizens. Once attacked, these innocent citizens and peaceful powers instantly transformed into hostile and aggressive opponents. And thus, the saga continued in one blood-curdling scene after the other, until the evil tyrant was ultimately defeated.

As we attended infrequently, we, initially, couldn't follow the plot. But that fact remained irrelevant as our eyes were glued to the screen. We sat silently in breathless anticipation, waiting to be enthralled and horrified by the evil-doer's next horrendous spine-chilling deed.

By deliberate omission, we carefully shielded our mother from the morbid reality of cliff-hangers. We feared she might collapse from the shock of realising that her innocent young children had been exposed to such a brutal, evil world and would prohibit our Saturday morning ventures forever.

SATURDAY EVENINGS

On most Saturday evenings, my parents played bridge with various friends. So involved were they that on Sunday mornings we could overhear the passionately heated discussions which emerged from behind their bedroom door.

They were reconstructing the entire game, move by move, criticising various players in turn. If only the crucial cards had been played, there would have been a more challenging and totally different outcome.

Neither my brother or I fully appreciated the reasons why they felt compelled to carry on a game which had ended the previous night, forgetting completely our own animated and extremely heated discussions over who was right or had even cheated, when playing various board games.

My parents' avid enthusiasm for bridge left me with a reluctance to ever learn the game. In my burgeoning imagination, they seemed to be enthralled by a game which appeared to take possession of them. I had no intention of imitating my parents' zealous behaviour.

Many years later, when I was at college, I was invited to join a bridge club and promptly resisted. I was seriously concerned that if I agreed to participate, I would be fighting for time to write my essays and complete my lab reports.

SUNDAYS

On Sunday mornings, my brother and I furtively sipped the lemon and lime mixer which had probably been added to some sort of alcoholic drink the night before. We preferred it to the tasteless tonic water.

Knowing that the left-over hors-d'oeuvres would be safely tucked away in the fridge, we opened the door and proceeded to nibble a bit of everything in sight, small green olives with red pimientos, dill pickles, slices of ham and salty beef, crunchy carrots and celery sticks, a variety of delectable spreads for crispy crackers and even a few wilting potato crisps that had inadvertently come into contact with the cream cheese. The Saturday night collation became our clandestine first course before breakfast.

Sunday was a day considered sacrosanct in our household. My father always ended the bridge game and stopped consuming any alcohol at the stroke of midnight. No amount of persuasion on his friends' part would convince him to do otherwise.

As a religious man, he felt that Sunday demanded two things from everyone, the first, that we should all attend church or Sunday school and the second, that we should engage in no work.

If I queried the reason for this, my paternal grandmother, also a devout Christian, always quoted Exodus, chapter 20, verses 9 and 10. "Six days shalt thou labour and do all they work. But the seventh day is the Sabbath of the Lord thy God: in it thou shalt not do any work."

The reason that Saturday was such a work-oriented day was suddenly revealed: It was decreed by God. The vegetable chopping, braising, and cooking meat, baking pies, cakes, and puddings; all this food preparation was meant to avoid any unnecessary work on a Sunday. Somehow this rule did not apply to Sunday morning breakfasts, though we children never recognised the anomaly.

On Sunday, my father always prepared the first meal of the day—fresh orange juice or half a grapefruit, tasty Parker House rolls that smelled of yeast and spicy sausages, or bacon with scrambled or poached eggs and sometimes pancakes with maple syrup.

With great aplomb, my father would assert that he was a very good cook and would commence cooking. We loved his breakfasts, and he loved creating them.

But wasn't this work, cooking on a Sunday? If cooking dinners was prohibited, why weren't breakfasts? Shouldn't we have eaten uncooked dry cereal with milk or have a piece of fresh fruit and possibly a piece of toast with butter and jam? Or would even making a piece of toast be regarded as work if we were strictly following the Scriptures?

My brother and I were much too delighted with our Sunday morning breakfasts to ever question whether or not my father should indulge us in this manner. And I do think that my father's joy in his creations completely obliterated any thought of them being classified as work of any kind.

GARMENTS and WINTER ACTIVITIES

The heaviest layers of clothing were always reserved for winter and all vests, socks, hats, scarves, mittens, and coats were usually made of wool. The rubber boots worn, fitted over the shoes with four or five metal buckle closures on the front.

Girls wore heavy cotton lisle stockings, over which woollen knee socks could be pulled. As they were an unattractive muddy brown colour, I disliked them intensely, but my mother insisted that I wear them for warmth as I was prone to bouts of bronchitis every winter.

Snow would often cling to our woollen coats and form hard, encrusted icy lumps which were difficult to pull from the fibres. Synthetic fabrics had not yet been used in the manufacture of children's clothes.

In Massachusetts, we had the most glorious winter snowstorms. If a deluge of snow had completely blocked the roads and transportation appeared impossible, school was sometimes cancelled, but it was a very rare occurrence.

If a huge snowstorm had descended everywhere, my mother, brother and I would be glued to the radio, listening intently for the announcement which informed us whether or not the Russell Grammar School would be closed for the day. I loved school and found it exciting so I often prayed that school would remain open.

But if we couldn't attend and were allowed to play outside, we would have a whole day to abandon ourselves to all the pleasures that could be derived from newly fallen snow.

If you could hear tinkling and clinking when the wind swept over the trees, it meant that all the branches were coated with ice, and those enticing sounds were an indication that it was bitterly cold.

We spent many happy days engaging in snowball fights or creating a mammoth snowman. With wooden sleds and toboggans, my friends and

I would trudge well over a mile to the very highest hills. If a sled was not available, a tea tray would suffice and was always faster than a sled with two heavy metal runners.

I loved the sudden wave of excitement and sometimes fear that engulfed me as I whooshed down the hill with the biting wind attacking my face, turning it rigid from cold.

But my favourite winter past-time was really ice-skating. The highly skilled performance of the Danish skater, Sonja Henie, totally entranced me.

After winning numerous Olympic and World titles, she was lured to Hollywood and became a famous film star. Her film career lasted from 1937 to 1958.

Every winter, a new ice rink was created for us. When the temperature was intensely cold, long, coiled hoses spewed enormous sprays of water onto the black paved area of our playground. Before our eyes, the unremarkable, gravelly area transformed into a smooth, crystal-clear sheet of ice.

We all rushed hastily to be the first to christen the pristine surface with our unique and original patterns and designs. Ice crystals leapt wildly in the air as each blade made its distinguishing mark. Within minutes, notches, hollow spaces, and elongated indentures obliterated the gleaming, uppermost layer of ice as we attempted to demonstrate our burgeoning ice-skating skills. But most of our sustained efforts were directed towards learning to glide across the ice gracefully and come to an effortless stop.

Every year, I practised diligently, trying to emulate Sonja Henie's magnificent spin which constantly increased in speed at the end of every performance. Despite high expectations, with very basic skating skills and weak ankles, I was never in a position to perfect such a complicated feat.

Once I accepted that I would not become a skating star, I began to relax and take pleasure in the skills I had acquired.

Attempting to take a more measured approach to my expectations was a wiser decision than I had realised. I could take pride in my accomplishments, even if not so great, and also avoid the inevitable defeat of unrealistic expectations.

CLOTHES CARE

With the arrival of winter, I performed a weekly chore which I absolutely detested, assisting my mother to hang washing on the clothesline outside.

In the freezing cold, we carefully pegged each article of clothing to the outstretched line on our back porch. We hung the wet washing with cold, damp fingers, in an atmosphere so cold that my every breath turned white on exhalation. As the day progressed, the temperature would fall and the intensely cold water in the clothes transformed every garment into a solid sheet of ice.

When we removed the clothes from the line, our fingers stuck firmly to each and every surface and slowly became stiff and numb with little movement and no feeling.

When the laundry was draped over the hot radiators, each article slowly unfroze and returned to its original limp, dry state.

Each cotton garment was sprinkled with water and then rolled into a long cylinder to spread the moisture evenly in preparation for ironing. Starching the collars and cuffs of my father's white shirts every week was my next task.

Powdered starch was dissolved with cold water to remove any lumps. Boiling water thickened the starch, turning it opaque. The collars and cuffs were dipped into this concoction, set aside and later ironed until they were rigid and stiff.

Every summer my mother undertook the tedious task of starching all my cotton dresses, but most mothers reserved starched dresses for special occasions only.

MOTHBALLS

When winter had ended, all winter clothes and blankets were cleaned, placed in bags or containers, and stored in cedar chests, lined with moth balls.

The mothballs contained naphthalene which changes from a solid into a gas and releases fumes which could kill moths and moth larvae. They were very effective in preventing moths from eating wool and creating great holes in precious fabrics.

With the widespread use of synthetic fabrics, the demand for mothballs has slowly receded. Today, they are no longer in common use as they were found to be toxic for human beings and other animals.

MEDICATION

COD LIVER OIL

Due to the winter sun shining infrequently and not very intensely, my mother insisted that we consume Cod Liver Oil to supplement the low doses of Vitamin D we were receiving.

As my mother was Canadian, from Nova Scotia, she grew up in an area where cod was plentiful so had no need to consume oil or pills to obtain the requisite amount of Vitamin D.

My brother and I vociferously objected to swallowing the pale yellow, oily liquid with a fishy taste. "It is not a matter for debate. It's for your health, particularly your bones", my mother would declare, with a full spoon poised at my lips and then my brother's. Down it went and we were each given a peppermint to remove any lingering taste.

We were both very sceptical. "Could only one teaspoon full of oil really help your bones to grow?"

Recent scientific articles have clarified the situation and dispelled any doubts about the efficacy of Cod Liver Oil. If you live in North America at latitudes above the thirty-seventh parallel, you may be receiving little or no Vitamin D at all, especially during the winter months when the sun sinks lower into the southern hemisphere.

As both Nova Scotia and Massachusetts, where we lived, are above the thirty-seventh parallel, my mother's health concerns were completely justified.

COLDS

If I had developed a serious cough, at bedtime, my chest was rubbed with a fine coating of Vicks Vapour Rub and covered with a warm piece of flannel to avoid smearing my pajamas and sheets. For a stuffy nose, I sniffed menthol drops which had been dispersed on a clean white handkerchief.

I was given hot milk with ginger to ease congestion in my chest. The addition of ginger to the milk, particularly if I felt nauseous, was meant to settle my stomach.

After any illness, eggnog with a hint of vanilla and nutmeg were offered, to stimulate my appetite and provide some nourishment. Another memorable drink that we imbibed after any illness, was malted milk. Malt is a sweet powder made from barley. Its extract is a good source of iron, niacin and potassium. My mother always insisted that it was a restorative, fortifying tonic. As it was sweet and easily digested, we needed no persuasion to drink it.

The very worst, most repugnant medicine that we were required to take was castor oil. It is a very potent laxative which my mother used infrequently and only when necessary. At the sight of the bottle filled with the pale yellow liquid, my brother and I stood rigid and anxious in anticipation of what was yet to come.

No amount of reasoning on my mother's part would stop us from recoiling and retching at the thought of ingesting this dreadful oily liquid. As the spoon was placed upon our lips, we would hold our noses, hoping to swallow without detecting the strong, bitter taste. It became a battle between retching and swallowing. It was better to swallow to avoid going through the same procedure all over again. If successful, we ate oranges to remove the bitter taste from our mouths and sometimes a sweet peppermint, as well.

CHILDHOOD DISEASES

When I was an infant, pertussis, or whooping cough, as it is more commonly called was rampant and I eventually succumbed to it. I recovered but it was an experience that traumatised my mother.

She described the uncontrollable fits of coughing, followed by a high-pitched "whoop sound" as I struggled to breathe afterwards. With every whoop, she was convinced that I would not survive. As many children who caught the disease died every year, her fears were well-founded.

The introduction of the pertussis vaccine in the 1950's, usually given in combination with tetanus, diphtheria, polio, and influenza B immunisations, has prevented the high incidence of this disease.

In the 1940's, in order to attend school in the United States, it was compulsory for parents to produce a certificate which indicated that their child had received a smallpox injection. This requirement for school entry ceased in 1972. WHO, the World Health Organisation, wiped out all known smallpox viruses from the world in 1980 and recommended that all countries stop vaccinating for smallpox.

My brother survived a serious case of polio, but for no apparent reason, I never caught it. We both caught mumps, measles and chicken pox but never caught either scarlet fever or rheumatic fever. Rheumatic fever, a streptococcus infection, is still common worldwide and is responsible for many cases of damaged heart valves. Scarlet fever terrified us as any child who caught it was quarantined and remained isolated for long periods of time. As the mortality rate was 15 to 20%, it was a disease to be avoided. With the advent of antibiotics, this disease has become much less severe, and the dangerous complications are usually prevented.

SCHOOL LUNCHES

In the United States, the tradition of materially successful parents sending their children to private schools does exist but is not so widespread as it is in England.

In most state schools (known as public schools in the U.S.), there are usually a proportion of students from professional families. In my eighth-grade class, the list of highly qualified fathers' occupations were listed as a doctor, a judge, a town-planner, and a senator. These educated families had usually been resident in the United States for many generations.

As well as the more permanently established families, there were also more recent arrivals, immigrants from Italy, Ireland, Greece, Armenia, and Scandinavia. Their children were in the majority in most classrooms.

In most cases, their fathers earned their living in less lucrative, more practical employment. They often worked in factories or were engaged in activities that involved construction or repair. Some were policemen and post men; others worked in shops. One Italian father sold ice cream from his van to the passing schoolchildren every day. In our school, all the teachers were Irish Catholics while the student body was composed of a mixture of Irish and Italian Catholics, Protestants and the occasional Jewish or Greek Orthodox student.

As the school did not provide hot lunches, we all carried our multicoloured tin lunchboxes to school every day. My lunch box epitomised a first-class example of a well-balanced, healthy diet. In the 1940's, my mother, already a devotee of healthy eating, attended the lectures of Gayelord Hauser, an American nutritionist, originally from Germany.

He promoted the "natural way of eating" and advocated eating foods rich in vitamin B and discouraged the consumption of sugar and white flour. Although he was not a doctor, he was criticised by the American Medical Association and attacked by the flour and sugar companies. The press treated him as an eccentric oddity. Although he is now considered an original founder of the natural food movement, it was not until the 1970's that scientific research proved that his approach to nutrition was valid and officially acceptable.

PRAYERS AND EASTER

As there is a separation of church and state in the United States, no prayers were ever recited in school. Many of the first settlers in the United States had fled religious persecution under the reign of King Charles the First in England.

The memory of England's harsh, repressive history, no doubt, inspired the writing of the First Amendment of the United States Constitution. It guarantees freedom of religion, speech, assembly, and the press. It also protects the right to peaceful protest and to petition the government.

While prayers were never recited in school, Catholics who were required to attend Mass on holy days, were allowed to attend church, prior to attending school. On that day, the five or six non-Catholic pupils left in the classroom waited for twenty or twenty-five pupils to return. It was only then that the daily lessons could begin.

Ash Wednesday was a memorable holy day. All Catholics returned to the classroom with a mark of black ash in the shape of a cross imprinted on their forehead. Protestants celebrated many of the same holy days, but their forms of public worship were different.

Both Protestants and Catholics considered Ash Wednesday a day of repentance for their sins. It is the beginning of Lent, the forty days set aside for reflection before the celebration of Easter and is marked by fasting.

We were expected to abstain from eating at least, one type of food that we particularly desired. I often relinquished chocolate. We were also expected to refrain from any kind of overindulgence. The fast lasted until Easter Sunday when we all went to church to celebrate the resurrection of Christ.

Easter Sunday was a day of rejoicing on many levels. My brother and I would be outfitted in new clothes and shoes: a summer coat and a new dress for me and new shirt, jacket and trousers for him. When I was older, gloves, a hat and a handbag completed the ensemble.

The whole neighbourhood was on display. Each family secretly proud of their ostentation as they paraded down the street to attend their respective churches. After dutifully attending the Easter service, the children could hardly wait to reach home.

Part of the day's excitement related to the eagerly anticipated Easter egg hunt. After forty days of relinquishing our favourite sweets, we were delighted to be searching everywhere for them and being allowed to eat them without any associated guilt.

We were never allowed to eat the entire hoard of sweets we had found immediately. Ever sensible, my parents always encouraged us to put some aside for a consumption at a later date.

THE PLEDGE OF ALLEGIANCE

Every morning before lessons commenced, the entire class made an oath of loyalty to the national flag and to the United States of America. In unison, we all recited The Pledge of Allegiance.

"I pledge allegiance to the flag of the United States of America and to the republic for which it stands; one nation indivisible with liberty and justice for all."

It was performed standing and was accompanied by a salute with the arm and hand outstretched towards the flag. Because of its similarity to the Nazi salute, in 1942, President Roosevelt altered the salute to a hand gesture over the heart.

I began to wonder why and for what purpose did we engage in this daily performance. I knew of no other democratic country where swearing an oath of allegiance to the nation was a school requirement.

Upon investigation, I discovered that the pledge of allegiance was written in 1892 by Frances Bellamy, a Baptist minister, and a Christian socialist. He viewed the pledge as an "inoculation that would protect those who were insufficiently patriotic Americans from the virus of radicalism and subversion."

He had initially wanted to insert the words "equality and fraternity" but on further consideration, eliminated them because, he knew that there were people on his committee who did not believe in equality for women or for African Americans.

In 1954, the phrase, "under God" was included in the pledge which resulted in criticism and disapproval. After much debate, the inclusion was declared legal because the phrase means that the government endorsed religion as desirable but did not support any specific religious belief.

Most states in the USA recite the pledge; only Vermont, Wyoming and Hawaii abstain.

It does seem ironic that a democratic country whose constitution is founded on the right to dissent, and freedom of speech should expect its citizens to swear loyalty to it continually.

CHILTON STREET

With the exception of the family in the house facing ours, no-one on our part of Chilton Street ever displayed any signs of racial prejudice towards us. Sonny and Billy, the Irish twins, who lived across the street were the only children who engaged in racial taunts. When they were together, they would bully my brother and sometimes physically attack him. These incidents occurred only when the twins were together. When they were on their own, they never had the courage to attack him, proving what cowards they actually were.

Chilton Street was divided into two sections. We lived at the lower end. To reach the upper part, we had to cross Vassal Lane, a larger road at right angles to us. Mainly Irish people and a few, new immigrant families lived on the upper part of Chilton Street. It was longer than our part of the street and formed a hill which led to Huron Avenue, the broad, busy road along which we all walked to school.

Sometimes, when coming home from school, not long after we had entered the upper part of Chilton Street, a group of Irish children would form a gang and taunt us with racially abusive names and remarks.

For protection, all the black children remained together as a group and walked down the middle of the road. Our parents had taught us never to retaliate to such abuse physically. They were worried that these incidents could escalate into violent behaviour and that someone would inevitably, be injured.

We had no inclination or desire to fight anyone so didn't really need convincing. Such wise advice turned out to be very practical as any form of physical attack would have been totally pointless as we were always so greatly outnumbered.

Our only retaliation was to chant in unison, "Sticks and stones may break my bones, but names will never harm me".

As they pursued us, their provocative behaviour continued at high pitch. Receiving no seriously antagonistic or violent responses from us, as we neared our end of the road, their disturbing, abusive behaviour slowly diminished as, one by one, they left the gang to return to their homes.

These Irish gangs never behaved violently towards us and when alone, none of these Irish children ever tried to confront or attack us in any way. Many of the black children often decided to take a longer route home to avoid the racial abuse we encountered from the children we deemed as "poor white trash".

In school, the one racial incident that shocked everyone, occurred when someone in our eighth-grade class was called a "dirty Jew".

The principal took swift action, visiting every classroom to state that no racism or prejudice towards other pupils would be tolerated in the Russell Grammar School. His words were reassuring and his actions commendable.

Throughout the education system, we were never subjected to overt racial abuse, from either the teachers or the students. But, because racism was never clearly apparent or demonstrably expressed, those who did not belong to minority groups generally believed that racial prejudice did not really exist.

THE FIELD

Especially in summer, my brother and I had but one aim, to escape the confinement of our house and the parental restrictions at home. What a feeling of freedom we experienced as we ran down the back stairs and rushed headlong into the garden.

At the height of summer, we plucked the sweet, juicy fruit from our prolifically producing peach tree. In late summer, growing in large clusters on well-trained vines were dusky purple Concord grapes. When young, we devoured them until we could eat no more and then relinquished the rest to the birds.

Aside from the daffodils, irises and tulips that grew along the fences in the rear garden and the rose bushes in the front, the garden spaces were entirely ours to play in, areas where we could give vent to all our pent-up energy.

During the Second World War, the government encouraged everyone to plant Victory Gardens to help the war effort. To our dismay, our father planted every vegetable imaginable in the rear garden.

Although we benefitted from eating fresh, organic produce, we were not overjoyed at the idea of losing some of our precious play space. My father explained that we were living in exceptional times. The country was at war with Germany. Victory Gardens were meant to address the potential food shortage and as food produced at home required no transportation, it also conserved fuel.

But we were hardly deprived of play space as nearly directly across the road from us was a sprawling field which all the local children visited daily. There was an abundance of long grass which we ran through with wild abandon, forcing all the grasshoppers to flee in haste.

Scattered everywhere were a variety of flowering shrubs, lilac, lavender, wild roses, and some with red berries which the girls mashed into meals to feed their dolls. There were buttercups, daisies, black-eyed Susan's and wild poppies blowing in the breeze. Dotted about were small crab apple trees with delicate, pink buds which slowly turned into soft, white flowers before producing their tiny, sour fruit. In late summer, tall spikes of goldenrod appeared. Having been told that it caused hay fever, we always gave it a wide berth.

Bees, beetles, butterflies, crickets, grasshoppers, grass snakes and many varieties of ants appeared in great profusion. One of my friends collected fireflies in a jar. A small group of us stood in awe as a corner of her dark garden was suddenly illuminated by their cool, bioluminescent glow.

Watching orderly rows of ants carrying bits of food to the mounds they had built and seeing them unite to fiercely attack any foreign invaders, were events that completely absorbed our attention for hours on end. We were always desperate to catch butterflies so that we could observe their entire life cycle. It was only in books that we had seen the egg change to larvae and then metamorphose from pupae to the magnificent butterfly, beating its wet wings to eventually escape into the surrounding foliage. Despite many hours of concentrated pursuit, we never caught a butterfly so never achieved our desired objective.

Until we were teenagers, the field remained a constant playground and a place for exploration for the entire neighbourhood. And then, one day, it began to disappear almost overnight. Two houses with large gardens suddenly appeared in its place.

The magical land that aroused curiosity and investigation of everything animate and inanimate that resided there had been transformed into a viable, profitable, commercial venture. The disappearance of our very small nature reserve was a great loss to everyone, but especially to all the curious and inquisitive minds who wished to investigate and rejoice in its wild plants and trees and to observe untamed creatures in their treasured natural habitats.

THE SECOND WORLD WAR

Since September 1939, World War Two had been raging in Europe. Despite providing unrestricted material aid to the allies, the USA pursued an isolationist policy. President Roosevelt did not wish to cause ructions to those in the American populace who were reluctant to enter the war directly (especially after the devastating effects of World War One).

On December the 7th 1941, the Japanese attacked Pearl Harbor, the American naval base in Hawaii, taking the Americans completely by surprise. This act effectively ended America's strong isolationist movement.

Congress declared war on Japan the following day. On the 11th of December, Italy and Germany declared war on the United States and the US government reciprocated without delay.

Despite the fact that no bombs had fallen on the US mainland, the entire economy was propelled into war preparations and war production. Consumer goods were no longer considered a priority. Military goods took precedence and nation-wide rationing began almost immediately.

War ration books were issued to each family. Coal, petrol, tires, sugar, butter, meat, milk, nylon stockings and shoes were all subject to the limitations of rationing.

With valid shoe stamps, anyone could purchase one pair of shoes. Stamps were not available to purchase shoes for recreation or sports use and two-tone leather shoes were barred completely. Only solid plain colours were permitted.

My brother and I were growing rapidly and frequently changing shoe sizes, far too frequently for my mother's liking. One morning, I entered the kitchen to see my mother in despair, carefully cutting out what she considered a very resilient piece of cardboard, to cover an incipient hole in the sole of my shoe.

In exasperation and great haste, she was forced to rush to the local Ration Board to urgently request another book of stamps for children's shoes. In our household, it was always shoes that caused the most consternation, as the rationed stamps seemed insufficient to keep up with our demands. Everyone appeared to accept the restriction of all other rationed items as part of their contribution to the war effort.

Of particular consideration was the rationing of tea. Whereas most Americans drank coffee, my mother was Canadian and drank tea. Every day commenced with not too strong a cup for both my parents.

I don't recall our tea ration ever running out, but my parents did attempt to extend the supply by substituting other beverages. Hot water and a slice of lemon was my father's favourite concoction. He continued to drink this until the day he died., claiming that as it was full of vitamin C, it cleansed the body. My mother's preference was for mint tea, made from dried or fresh mint leaves from the garden.

In the 1940's, TV was not yet a widespread, War news and public announcements were relayed by radio and newspapers.

One of the government's main concerns was centered around the production and conservation of food. Any spare space around or behind a dwelling was converted into a "Victory Garden". Everyone we knew carefully tended and cultivated fruit and vegetables grown from seed or small seedlings.

There were many War Bond Drives encouraging the public to buy bonds to generate revenue for the war effort. When I was eleven, I started saving money every week to eventually purchase one.

CLOTHING DURING THE WAR

As many materials were rationed during the war, styles in clothing for both men and women altered considerably. The emphasis was on thrift. The aim was to use as little material as feasible.

Many women were now working in factories. Wearing skirts was deemed unacceptable as they were thought to be a hazard when working with machinery. The women readily relinquished their skirts for very practical trousers.

Button and zipper fastenings were exchanged for elastic waistbands. The problem of sizing was therefore reduced as nearly everyone could fit into a garment with an expandable waist.

Both men's and women's outfits were curtailed and reduced on all sides. Men's jackets were shorter, and the patch pockets removed. Trousers were created without cuffs. The only indulgence allowed was the introduction of shoulder pads. Shoulders became more prominent as they grew in size and width. Surrounded by a plethora of trim, dark austere outfits, this small lenience was a slight nod in the direction of a fashionable female shape. Women's skirts and dressed were reduced in length and for the first time in the history of fashion, women's legs were on display.

As women's legs could now be exhibited, stocking sales should have expanded, but silk was requisitioned by the government for the manufacture of parachutes. Only stockings made of cotton or rayon were available and they tended to droop and completely lose their desired shape.

Wearing short socks in shoes became a popular custom with women and especially teenagers who designate them as "bobby socks."

As no attractive stockings were available, women began to paint their legs with make-up. They drew seams up the back of their legs with eye-liner.

But it was soon realised that painted stockings produced serious pitfalls. If you crossed your legs, the seams would smear. And, if it rained, the stockings would run and eventually vanish forever.

Stockings were held up with garter belts which later transformed into pantyhose and tights made from nylon and lycra.

Nylon stockings were not available to the general public until after the war, in 1946. When they appeared, the shops were mobbed, and the merchandise disappeared in a hysterical crush of nanoseconds.

Another light-hearted touch was added to wartime clothing when the zoot suit appeared. Photographs in magazines introduced us to these outrageous outfits, worn mainly by musicians. The trousers consisted of very wide legs with very tight cuffs and a long coat with wide padded shoulders.

We found them strange, ridiculous, and amusing. Only once did I ever see the genuine article, worn by a group of rowdy teenagers, standing at a street corner. They were very noisy, no doubt, to attract attention to their ostentatious gear.

None of our male friends or acquaintances would ever have dreamt of wearing such pretentious outfits. We and they were far too conservative to appreciate or engage in such sartorial exhibitionism.

AIR RAID PRACTISE

Air raid drills were instigated to train everyone to respond properly to the air raid alarm signal. At specific times, all streetlights were turned off. Those at home were required to reduce all light to a very low intensity. Any light might alert an observant enemy plane which could result in gunfire or bombing.

To enforce everyone's compliance, air raid wardens walked along every street and road to check that no light emerged from any dwelling.

When we heard the alarm, my brother and I were instantly alarmed as it was a distinct warning of danger. We then sat rigidly and silently, scared and suddenly frightened at the sound of any unexpected noise.

As my father turned out the house lights, my mother would simultaneously pull down the blackout blinds. They were literally black blinds which ensured that no light escaped.

We sometimes dared to peek through the crack at the edge of the blind where it bowed out slightly from the window. Shrouded in total darkness, we peered into a startlingly bright, glowing sky full of brilliant beams crisscrossing each other. Searchlights were scattered in different directions, visually tracking the sky for any unexpected, foreign planes.

To my knowledge, no-one ever detected an enemy plane on any part of the eastern coast of the US. But there were   false alarms, accompanied by the inevitable blackouts which left my brother and me in abeyance, always expecting some disaster to befall.

As the war progressed, we slowly realised that no great misfortune had befallen anyone, anywhere in the United States. Our fears slowly receded. We were no longer overwhelmed by an imminent sense of danger when the pulsating air-raid siren sounded, though, to be honest, a residual anxiety always remained with me.

WAR FILMS

Many films produced during the war were openly propagandist in their efforts to denigrate our enemies, particularly Japan and Germany. Though the Italians were, at one point, our enemies also, I don't remember any propaganda being directed against them in films.

The Japanese were depicted as foreign villains, completely uncivilised and incapable of reasoning while the Germans were regimented, fanatical and ruthless.

On Saturday mornings, at the cinema. we saw that simple cartoon characters, Popeye and even Bugs Bunny could defeat these wicked evildoers, on their own, never requiring any assistance. Their actions demonstrated how inadequate and incompetent these malevolent creatures were.

How we cheered when the "good guys" had won and completely crushed those who would destroy us and the entire world. We onlookers were approximately ten to fifteen years old.

Pearl Harbor was always referred to as a "sneak attack" and an infamous act. "Remember Pearl Harbor" became the phrase constantly repeated to foster allegiance to US engagement in World War 2.

In newspapers and comic books, the concept of the "yellow peril" was widely promulgated. The term had generally referred to Asians whose origins were Chinese or Japanese. It was assumed that they were planning to insidiously weaken or destroy Western civilisation directly through war or by utilising more devious methods, entering host countries through immigration.

Posters were inscribed with the words: "We here highly resolve that these dead shall not have died in vain." with the American flags waving valiantly in the wind.

The government's used every type of media to promote its wartime messages certainly produced its desired effect on us children. We all became very patriotic and considered it our urgent duty to loyally support our country.

Drives were organised to recycle various household products. Girl Scouts were expected to support the war effort and we did so with great enthusiasm. With my Scout uniform on display and my sturdy, red metal wagon, I went from house to house collecting newspapers, rubber, tin cans and kitchen fats which were used as raw materials for explosives.

JAPANESE INTERNMENT

In 1942, President Roosevelt interned the 110,000 Japanese Americans residing on the western coast of the United States--despite the fact that many were American citizens and their American born children were also deemed to be American citizens.

The Japanese, having perpetrated an "unprovoked attack" on American territory were unrelentingly categorised as intrinsically evil. Being fervent patriots, we children never questioned Japanese internment, considering it the consequences of their nation's belligerent behaviour.

Though there were protestors against Japanese interment, in the main, the majority of the American public concurred with this viewpoint.

My parents seemed to be unnerved by the government's actions, by the fact that US residents could be forced to leave their homes to be incarcerated in undesirable camps.

My mother was Canadian and not a naturalised American citizen. Without doubt, she had no reason to fear similar treatment. But it was at this time that she hastily applied for and acquired American citizen ship.

It was with great regret and sorrow that she publicly relinquished her allegiance to Canada which she had always seen as her true homeland.

PRESIDENT ROOSEVELT and DISCRIMINATION IN THE 1940'S

During the Great Depression of the 1930's, President Roosevelt had instituted what were termed "New Deal Housing and employment projects". They were public works programmes that provided loans, jobs and wages which stimulated a seriously depressed economy.

While these new policies proved beneficial for everyone, discrimination against some minority groups persisted especially black Americans. These discrepancies remained in existence in every area in which these "New Deal Projects" were implemented.

Despite these problems, Roosevelt was perceived as someone who was concerned about the plight of the poor and underprivileged and was considered to hold more favourable views than previous presidents towards the problems of minority groups.

Traditionally, black Americans had always voted Republican but in support of Roosevelt, they altered their habitual patterns and began to vote for the Democrats

During the war, most factory workers had been recruited into the military, leaving many new job vacancies available to the general public. The employers habitually followed along, practised policy of hiring white unemployed workers before considering unemployed black candidates. As a result, few black men had access to defense jobs.

It was only in 1941, when A. Philip Randolph, a labour leader, informed Roosevelt that there would be a march of 100,000 people on Washington to demand equality in war-related jobs and all units in the military that Roosevelt attempted to alter the situation.

Under order 8802, he created the FEPC, the Fair Employment Practice Committee, which prohibited "discrimination in the employment of workers in the government and defense industries, because of race, creed, colour or national origin."

In 1943, a new executive order, number 9436, was announced, stating that all government contracts must have a non-discrimination clause.

It was at this point that fair employment policies finally began to be seriously enforced. The FEPC was used to great advantage in the north but due to strong resistance against its implementation, the south never truly enforced these policies.

WAR RECRUITMENT

One of my uncles, too old to enter the army, my father's brother, Thomas, worked in a defense factory throughout the war. He helped to manufacture specialised parts of aeroplane motors.

Another uncle, Bill, and a first cousin, Howard, were enlisted in the army.

The majority of black Americans willingly entered the military service, but there were few who were less enthusiastic about a patriotic summons to war. They were skeptical about what their allotted roles would be and what type of treatment they would receive. They deliberately presented themselves as frenzied individuals with disordered thoughts, hoping to be classified as "not of sound mind".

Some suggested that they could not participate in a "white man's war" as white people had consistently mistreated them. They declared that they would be likely to shoot any white man they saw, unable to distinguish between a white enemy and a white compatriot.

The jazz musicians, Dizzy Gillespie and Thelonious Monk, as well as Malcolm X, made similar claims. All were deemed unsuitable or unfit for service. Malcolm X was rejected on the grounds of being mentally unfit.

Although those who resisted conscription were very few in number compared to those who were active participants, their fears about treatment within the military establishment proved to be justified.

THE MILITARY and SEGREGATION

Prior to World War Two, the US military had always maintained racially segregated units. Despite the fact that nearly one million black

Americans had joined the forces, this policy was maintained throughout the war.

Black soldiers were always supervised by white officers and generally relegated to menial tasks within the support services such as: cooks, cleaners, drivers, and cargo handlers. One of the most significant restrictions they were forced to endure was that they were prohibited from engaging in combat.

Due to the exigencies of war, a first exception was made in 1949, during the Battle of the Bulge. General Eisenhower, desperately requiring more support, temporarily desegregated the army to allow black units to join the battle. Both units were awarded citations for heroism.

The second exception occurred when, in an attempt to prove that black soldiers could perform as well as their white counterparts, civil rights leaders convinced those in power to create all-black combat units.

For the first time, black recruits were trained as pilots. In 1944, the Tuskegee Airmen were so successful that not one of their bombers was ever lost in battle. After completing many successful attacks, in 1944 and 1945, they began accompanying white pilots in Italy. They protected the harbours and American bombers from assaults by German fighter pilots, and as a result, earned many distinguished citations.

In spite of the government's initial resistance, the War Department finally altered its policy of banning black nurses from the army. In 1944, the first black nurses arrived in England.

Although President Roosevelt had established two Fair Employment Committees, one in 1941 and a second in 1943, desegregation in the army was never effectively put into practice.

President Harry Truman, in 1948, signed executive order, 9981, to fully integrate the armed services. Similar to the previous executive orders, it did not eliminate segregated military units in the US. All black fighting units existed in the Korean War, (from 26July 1950 to 27 July 1953), but attempts were instigated during this time to include both black and white soldiers in integrated units.

It was not until 1954 that all black units had been eliminated within the US military services.

THE END OF WORLD WAR TWO

On the 8th of May 1945, the war in Europe ended when Nazi Germany surrendered, but the war in the Pacific continued.

The United States, the Republic of China and the United Kingdom signed The Potsdam Declaration on the 26th of July 1945, threatening Japan with "prompt and utter destruction". As the Japanese disregarded this ominous warning, on the 6th of August 1945, the US dropped the first atomic bomb on Hiroshima, followed by a second atomic bomb dropped on Nagasaki on the 9th of August.

After these lethal attacks, Emperor Hirihito, speaking for the first time on radio, broadcast the news to the Allies that the Japanese had surrendered. The American government always maintained that, despite thousands of civilian casualties in both cities, that dropping these bombs was a necessity. It brought the war to a rapid end and saved the lives of many in the Allied Zone.

In some communities, there were public celebrations, parties with exuberant, high-spirited singing and dancing. There were no such celebrations in our neighbourhood, only a feeling of general relief that the war had ceased with many animated discussions about the devastation and destruction involved and the tragedy of all the lives that had been lost. Everyone seemed to have friends or relatives who had become the casualties of the war.

THE GERMAN DEATH CAMPS

It was not until the last three or four months of the war that the Allied troops discovered the existence of the German death camps, and the full horror of the Holocaust was revealed. Newspapers continually reported the dreadful news but no picture or even the printed word could convey the overpowering malevolence of the German atrocities.

We were all stunned into disbelief when we saw the newsreels at our local cinema. In open pits, there were starved, emaciated men, women and children with despairing, sunken eyes, callously and deliberately thrown on top of one another, forming enormous piles of dead bodies. The ones that remained were walking skeletons with limbs like sticks and protruding, bulging joints, barely alive.

Who were the human beings who could perpetrate such heinous acts? The whole world was incredulous and reacted with revulsion to these revolting revelations. Even the war did not condone such gruesome and degrading treatment of one human being towards another.

THE NUREMBERG TRIALS

In November 1945, the first international trial for war crimes took place in the German city of Nuremberg. Twenty-four major war criminals were indicted for numerous crimes including the newly created crime of genocide. Three, Adolph Hitler, Goebbels and Himmler committed suicide before the trial. Twelve were sentenced to death, one in absentia. Three were acquitted and the rest were given prison sentences from seven years to life imprisonment. One, Herman Goring, committed suicide the night before his execution.

There were twelve additional trials from December 1945 to April 1949. These included judges and lawyers who implemented Eugenics laws which supported Hitler's plans to produce racial purity and led to the annihilation of at least six million Jews.

Other trials dealt with army officers and German industrialists who were indicted for using slave labour and violent treatment towards prisoners in concentration camps.

Medical experiments on camp inmates led to the Doctors' trial for crimes against humanity. Seventy-one went to prison for varying lengths of time. Eight individuals were sentenced to life imprisonment and twelve defendants received death sentences.

There is no doubt that the Nuremberg trials led to the advancement of the definition and interpretation of international law. In 1948, the Universal Declaration of Human Rights and the United Nations Genocide Law were established. In 1949, a further law was instituted, the Geneva Convention on the Laws and Customs of War.

These advancements in international law were created as a result of the Nuremberg Trials and remain extant to this day.

AFTER THE WAR

HOUSING

In 1945, there was an urgent need for reasonably priced family homes. William Leavitt, with his rapidly constructed, mass produced housing units responded to this demand by producing affordable houses in suburban areas. These units would become the most popular sort of housing purchased for many generations.

There was one plan from which line after line of these units were constructed. Pete Seeger created a song which reflected what many thought about these units:" Little boxes on the hillside,

Little boxes made of ticky tacky

Little boxes

Little boxes

Little boxes all the same.

There's a green one and a pink one

And a blue one and a yellow one

And they're all made out of ticky tacky

And they all look just the same." Etc.

Although the houses were dull and uniform in appearance, the demand for new housing increased consistently, allowing Leavitt to increase production of his "Leavittowns", as they were commonly described.

The Federal Housing Authority (the FHA) supported a policy of low-interest loans for veterans, but only for those developments which were owned 100% by white people. Due to this policy, segregation was legally encouraged by the FHA in public housing.

Neither black nor Jewish families were allowed to purchase these homes. Despite the fact that he was Jewish, Leavitt stated that his business interest was a priority and his most Important consideration. If whites desired to live in exclusive, non-mixed developments, he chose not to sell homes to Jewish families.

This legacy of racial segregation spread to other developers and helped to create the wide discrepancy in home ownership that still exists between the races today.

Sadly, only one to two percent of FHA loans ever went to non-whites regardless of an individual's military rank.

EDUCATION

The 1944 GI Bill did not prove advantageous for non-whites in advancing home loans nor did it succeed in producing university places for them at reasonable prices. Some veterans could not gain access to university due to their totally inadequate secondary education.

Most white universities, at the time, enforced official and unofficial quotas, so black Americans were usually excluded. They applied to southern colleges and universities, set up exclusively for black students. Due to underfunding, these institutions could not cope with the thousands of applications they received and had no choice but to reject more than half of these prospective students.

My uncle, Bill, was one of the fortunate few who was able to take advantage of the offer of further education. He had been educated in the north, in Boston MA, where educational standards were consistently higher than those in the south. In addition, he had completed his high school education with reasonable grades. As a result, he was accepted for a four year course of study at Boston University, from which he received a BSc degree.

RUSSELL GRAMMAR SCHOOL

When the war ended in May 1945, I was nearly twelve years old, only one year left before I departed forever from the Russell Grammar School.

In the eighth grade (the last year of this school), we were presented with our first male teacher, Mr. Brennan, who taught us algebra. The formidable Miss Coyne was the main class teacher.

Both were Irish Catholics, as were all my teachers, with one exception, my French teacher in high school.

In Miss Coyne's class, the two activities which seemed to consume enormous amounts of time were: parsing sentences and memorising and reciting poems. I mention these topics as teachers in the present day no longer expect students to engage in either of these pursuits.

Every student was required to memorise a poem of his or her choice on the weekend and to recite it before the entire class on Monday morning. We had one book of poetry at home by the author, William Wordsworth. I often chose one of his poems to memorise for recitation.

Other poems, we learned in class and memorised were: Henry Wadsworth Longfellow's, "The Village Smithy" and "The Wreck of the Hesperus", as well as Alfred Noyes's, "The Highwayman.

So long are some of these poems, it is possible that we didn't memorise them in their entirety. But, it is to be noted, that they are all rhyming poems. I am sure that the similarity of sound at the endings of the lines facilitated the memory process.

The second of these activities, the parsing of sentences died out between my childhood and that of my children's, never to be heard of again. I state this emphatically as when I attempted to help one of my children with her French homework, she was totally bewildered when I commented: "You can't say that. Only adjectives can modify nouns." I was suddenly a person speaking a foreign language . She had never been taught the different parts of speech and was totally unaware of the existence of articles, adverbs, adjectives, nouns and verbs.

Learning these parts of speech meant that one could identify them   and explain their function in a sentence.

Having parsed many sentences and understood how the parts of speech worked stood me in good stead when I went to High School. My first English teacher told my mother that I never made grammatical mistakes and understood very clearly how sentences were constructed.

I also clearly remember how boring parsing sentences was. What kept me alert was fear of failure. If I made one or possibly two mistakes, our teacher, Miss Coyne, would be sure to order me to move, in total disgrace, to a different row, one of lower rank. To remain in the first row, we had to maintain consistently high marks. Better to pay attention than to suffer the humiliating degradation of forced removal from a prime position.

In June 1945, I graduated from Russell Grammar School. I was still twelve years old but would turn thirteen in early July. Ever practical, my parents (it was really my father's idea) presented me with a typewriter as a graduation present.

Typewriting would be a time saving device for my high school homework, and a very practical asset for my future jobs. My father was already planning for the summer holidays when I would be looking for employment to earn money for my college tuition.

SUMMER HOLIDAYS

In the United States, there are long summer holidays, usually from the end of June to early September. When the United States consisted mainly of farming communities, children were required to work on the farm in the summer months to pick the ripened fruit and vegetables. Hence, the long summer holidays which some now see as an undesirable relic from the past.

None of our parents made any effort to entertain us during these prolonged holidays. It was assumed that we would help our parents by performing jobs they assigned us and in our own spare time, we were expected to entertain ourselves.

We were not gainfully employed every minute of every day. I am sure that the boredom we sometimes experienced spurred us on to find friends to play with and encouraged us to occupy the vacant spaces constructively.

Although lessons were discontinued during the summer, I was still expected to practise my piano lessons, including the dreadful scales and arpeggios. As my dance routines were meant to be perfect for the September class, I continued to practice my tap-dance steps. I also attempted to complete work on various badges for the Girl Scouts.

My great escape was reading. I borrowed as many books as I could carry each week from the public library and completely immersed myself in the words on the page. I loved being transported to different places and far away countries and really enjoyed venturing inside someone else's mind.

We spent our free time playing card games, marbles, hopscotch skipping rope and "pick up sticks". Everyone possessed myriad board games. Most are still in existence today: Checkers, Parcheesi, Cluedo, Monopoly and the controversial Ouija Board.

We were warned that the Ouija Board could prove dangerous. An individual, simply by moving a small wooden object around the board, might gain access to the spirit world and persons long dead might be encouraged to speak.

I was simultaneously suspicious and somewhat gullible. My best friend was often the star of the show. She would become totally rigid, eyes noticeably enlarged, staring straight ahead and breathing rapidly while a spirit guided her hand around the surface of the board.

I was amazed, astonished, and full of desire to believe, but also frightened to enter this spirit world. What would I find there? I didn't want to meet dead people. But shouldn't I be courageous enough to at least, peer into this new realm?

I did believe that when we died, we all went to heaven. (We all believed that). Wasn't Heaven a sort of good spiritual world? Where did these other spirits reside? Was there a world outside of Heaven? How did she contact these strange spirits?

My friend was very convincing in her role as a guide to an unknown world, inhabited by amorphous creatures, but I was not quite ready to completely suspend my disbelief.

When I dared to share my reservations and asked numerous questions, she responded by totally rejecting my friendship. Apparently, our relationship was defined by unquestioned acceptance of what she defined as truth, without doubt of any sort being part of the equation. "But this was my best friend. How could she treat me like this?"

At the time, the overpowering devastation and despair that my friend's rejection caused, seemed to me, beyond measure. Unfortunately, as I proceeded through childhood, I encountered more of these distressing situations with my friends and occasionally with others.

But where would I be if I had not learned to relinquish my naivety and totally accepting stance towards others who felt they could control our relationship? What kind of friendship was so fragile that legitimate questions could make it crumble? As I learned not to engage in such imbalanced relationships, I began to establish my own standards of what constituted true friendship.

OUR OWN ENTERTAINMENT

Occasionally, some of us produced our own form of entertainment which to which we invited the general public. We always thought that we would reach a wide audience but, in reality, those who attended our events were well-known acquaintances, parents and friends.

We recited poetry, danced and then had an interval at which Kool Aid, a fruit-flavoured sugary drink could be purchased for five cents. After fifteen minutes, the entertainment commenced again.

The two who were really talented somersaulted vigorously across the grass, one somersaulting forwards and the other backwards. They both ended dramatically and hopefully at the same time, doing the splits.

At the end, we all gathered to sing a few well-rehearsed songs, such as: "She'll Be Coming Around the Mountain When She Comes", "I'm Looking Over a Four Leaf Clover", Singing Polly Wally Doodle All the Day", leaving two of our very favourites until last—"Accentutate the Positive" and "Mairzy Doats and Dozy Doats".

Accentuate the Positive by Johnny Mercer

You've got to accentuate the positive

Eliminate the negative

Latch on to the affirmative

But don't mess with mister in-between

You've got to spread joy up to the maximum.

Bring gloom down to the minimum

Have faith, a pandemonium

Liable to walk upon the scene.

To illustrate my last remark

Jonah in the whale, Noah in the ark

What did they do

Just when everything looked dark.

They said we better accentuate the positive

Eliminate the negative

Latch on to the affirmative

But don't mess with mister in-between.

The other song which we never tired of singing was Mairzy Doats.

Glancing at the words, they seem to make no sense.

"Mairzy doats and dozy doats and liddle lambzy divey

A kiddley divey too, wouldn't you"?

"If the words sound queer and funny to your ear, a little bit jumbled and jivey,

Sing "Mares eat oats and does eat oats and little lambs eat ivy,

A kid will eat ivy too, wouldn't you?"

HOLIDAY ACTIVITIES

Although some of my friends went to different states on holiday, my family never managed to do so. It was simply not on their agenda. There was no money to spare for such activities. We knew of children who spent a few weeks or even longer at Camp Atwater, the only camp for well-off coloured teen-agers.

Those who attended were often children whose parents were from the professional classes, doctors, lawyers, or dentists. Their salaries were undoubtedly far more lucrative than those of the coloured families in my neighbourhood.

The predominant concern of the families with whom we were acquainted was to pay off the mortgage. This obligation left little to spend on long summer holidays and certainly could not be extended to pay for even one week at the highly esteemed but outrageously expensive Camp Atwater.

During the summer, we did have long sojourns to Revere Beach in Boston. We straddled the horses on the Merry-Go Round and tried to convince our parents to let us jump on any rides that weren't too frightening or stomach-churning.

We ate sticky, melt-in-the-mouth cotton candy, consumed, drowned in mustard, hot dogs and fizzy soda pop, which we considered exciting as we never indulged in such unhealthy food at home.

FREAK SHOWS

As we meandered in leisurely fashion along the promenade, our senses were unrelentingly assaulted. Although the sea was not yet in sight, the pungent, penetrating smell of salty sea air began to encompass us, while the blistering sun permeated every exposed surface on our bodies.

The discordant cacophony of the stall holders attacked us on every side, entreating everyone to: "Hook the peg with a ring", "Shoot the moving object", "Break the balloon with a dart", "Hit the bullseye".

Did anyone really want any of those cheap, tawdry prizes on offer: key rings, a plastic doll, a tiny goldfish, a very small fuzzy bear? Probably not, but we pestered our parents incessantly to let us try to win something.

Our parents sensibly guided us away from the pleas of the stall holders and past the alarming pictures of strange people on billboards, advertising the freak show.

Those on display were described as human oddities: "The Bearded Lady", "The Man with Elastic Skin", "The Armless Lady", "Dwarves", "Albinos", "The Man with Three Legs. Their conditions resulted from faulty genes and malformations of the embryo or even disease. One of the most famous was Joseph Merrick, the Elephant Man. In 1884, he was displayed with a variety of extreme deformities.

Becoming part of the circus show was often their only means of earning a living. While most were exploited, a few made their circus owners rich, became independent, travelled widely and met the famous in foreign lands.

We were never allowed to enter the freak show tents. My parents were adamant that these poor individuals should be cared for with compassion and should never be put on display to be gawked at with horror and disgust.

Thank goodness, these shows no longer exist. As the public became more educated about the causes of these physical differences, people began to be treated with more sympathy and understanding. Freak show then disappeared entirely as a form of human entertainment.

As we were carefully led away from these disturbing pictures, we proceeded slowly on our way, avoiding any new sellers of merchandise. To avoid cramps, we were forced to wait an hour after eating before being allowed to swim. At the appointed time, we would run wildly and with great abandon into the mouth-shuddering, spine-tingling Atlantic Ocean. Fortunately, after a few minutes, our bodies adjusted to the temperature, and we were then prepared to remain in the freezing water forever.

We loved every minute of being there, nipping in and out of the frantically waving brown branches of seaweed, inadvertently scratching ourselves on the stiffened pale sea grass, pausing to peer into still, sun-warmed pools on the rocks, collecting snails in buckets of water to watch their fluid, soft bodies move in and out of their firm, hard shells.

We spent hours throwing stones on the sand, waiting for a huge squirt to emerge from the soft, damp surface. This eruption would instantly instigate a frenzied, mad scramble, everyone digging frantically with hands used as shovels, to reach the buried treasure beneath, the clam that had ejected the powerful jet and revealed its secret hiding place.

We built endless sandcastles on the beach, waiting and watching for the moment when the ferocious, in-coming tide would wash away all our magnificent constructions in one fell swoop.

We always returned home happy and contented, but weary and exhausted, ready for a good night's sleep.

TEEN AGE YEARS

I finally became a teenager in 1946. In July, 2 months before my entry to high school, I turned 13. In the late 1940's, adolescents were, for the first time, called "teenagers" and I now officially, acquired this label.

I do not know why the short, cotton socks (often white), which everyone wore were given the nondescript title of "bobby socks". They were the fashion rage across the entire country. I wore them, initially, with saddle shoes, two-toned brown lace-ups, and later with moccasins, flat soft leather, unadorned shoes.

Sweaters were very popular and always made of wool. At one time, long, baggy sweaters called "Floppy Joes", became the fashion and were worn with skirts of one solid colour or tartan-pleated ones.

I acquired a large collection of twin sets of various hues. My plaid skirts were always worn with a blouse or a set of sweaters which closely matched one of the colours in the pattern of the skirt.

Dresses were generally worn mid-calf length. They slowly shortened and eventually crept up the leg to rest just below the knee.

As I was over a year younger than all of my friends, my parents declared that it was inappropriate for me to attend their occasional parties and dances. I felt that I suffered unjustifiably for nearly the first three years of my teen age life, especially on weekends, as I remained at home alone while my friends were enjoying themselves at parties.

All of my friends became what I call earnest supplicants on my behalf, one, Joyce, ended up on bended knees, begging and pleading with my mother to allow me to go to their latest party. As I heard her earnestly trying to convince my mother to change her mind, my hopes would soar. But such endeavours were always to no avail.

My mother was adamant. She responded concisely and succinctly, "She is far too young.". I spent most of my weekends feeling sad and tearful, sitting dejected in my bedroom. I considered my parents outmoded in their attitudes. They always knew best. Their rules were strict and must be adhered to. There was no room for negotiation.

Within my brother's vocabulary and mine, the words "why" and "no" were never uttered in response to a parent's demands. Both parents were resolute in their agreed outlook on life. Their parents had insisted on complete obedience, without question and were not lenient or indulgent. As a result, they had become moral, upright, hard-working individuals and hoped that they were providing the same sort of structure for us to replicate their behaviour.

I spent most weekends feeling angry with my parents for forcing me to follow their unreasonable, and uncompromising rules, but it was no fun feeling so miserable for days on end. I had always thought that reading would be a great escape from the reality of my intensely unhappy state of mind. But, if I were very distraught, I could not even engage in this form of consolation.

Trying to dispel my unhappy feelings, I became involved in serious displacement activity, diligently applying myself to cleaning my bedroom, ironing clothes or polishing my shoes for church, all jobs that I had to do on weekends anyway but they were now done with enforced vigour.

Given the clash between my desire for more independence and my parents authoritarian rules, I remained intransigent in my belief that they were over-protective and oppressive. Over time, my anger did become less intense, and I was able to live most weekends without unrelenting feelings of resentment and indignation.

In their defence, both of my parents were born in 1900. Their ideas of childhood were formed by attitudes and beliefs that were genuinely Victorian. Strong parental control and strict rules governing child-rearing were what they had experienced and these were the principles they continued to put into practise with us.

At the time, consumed with my own desires, I never accorded them any credit for trying to protect me and keep me from harm at a time when I was a very young, inexperienced, and vulnerable adolescent.

DATES

One month before my sixteenth birthday, I was finally allowed to go to parties and to go on my very first date. After my date was parentally approved, I went to a film in the afternoon with a seventeen-year-old high school student.

I was overjoyed by the prospect of going on a date, more than with the date himself. He was not bad looking, had a pleasant manner, and was intelligent enough, but I didn't fancy him in any way. The greater part of my excitement related to the fact that I could act like my friends, be a normal teenager, and go out on weekends, legitimately, with the opposite sex.

Boys always came to a girl's house to pick them up and were expected to bring them home at an agreed time.

My father felt it was his duty to interrogate every young man who ever asked to date me. "Was he planning a college education?" If not. "What kind of further education would he pursue?" "What kind of a job was he hoping to attain?" If already studying at college, "What subjects did he prefer? What career was he planning to follow"?

The doorbell would ring. I would usher in an unsuspecting, prospective date, introduce him to my father and leave him to experience the onslaught of questions.

Not a very auspicious beginning for an enjoyable evening out. I was always in fear that, after the encounter with my father, the boy I dated would decide that it was too much of an ordeal to go out with me and that this was the first and last time that I would ever see him.

I was constantly embarrassed by my father's treatment of these young men, so much so that I felt compelled to apologise for my father's invasive questioning.

Before every date, I would loudly proclaim to my father: "Dad, remember, he's only asked me out for the evening. He's not planning to marry me." But my words fell on deaf ears as my father felt he had a moral obligation to assess the worthiness of all boyfriends, however fleeting their presence.

PARTIES

Ever since my sister-in-law took my children to see the film "Grease" with John Travolta and Olivia Newton-John enacting teen-age life and love, I've had great difficulty portraying the reality of my teenage existence.

Although the entire story is an imaginative fantasy, as it was set in the USA, my children were convinced that it was a true depiction of my adolescent years.

There were two dances of the day: one was spirited and lively, the other was very slow and evenly paced. The jitterbug displayed in the film bears no resemblance to the fast dance in which we engaged. We were never so agile or nimble.

The boy's hand always rested on the girl's back. His right hand held his partner's left hand to guide her movements. That is the only similarity with which I can identify. Our male partners swung the girls round and drew them in again. Sometimes, the couple faced each other, improvising a few quick steps and moves in time to the music.

The round-cut skirts which we all wore, designed to flare out when we spun around, enhanced the sense of lively, energetic movement.

There were no suggestive pelvic movement - a la "Elvis". No bodies catapulted across the floor, performing somersaults. No one flew through the air in any direction or ever ended up perched on a partner's shoulders. While we moved vigorously and energetically in time to the music, our feet were always firmly fixed to the dance floor.

Always included at a party or dance would be a number of slow dances. For those more romantically inclined, this was the opportunity to dance closer, rest a head on a shoulder or dance cheek-to-cheek. Not so pleasant if you were stuck with someone who fancied you, but the feelings were not reciprocated.

There might be a subtle stiffness of movement if the girl resisted being drawn closer to her partner, trying to maintain a respectable distance between them. I was often called "stuck up" for employing such methods with unwanted admirers.

In the film, all the young males owned cars which they drove with wild abandon. Their main function appeared to be to attract the girls, any and all female friends and acquaintances, all of whom were duly impressed by their pretentious, ostentatious behaviour.

The few families I knew who had cars (we didn't) never allowed their sons to borrow them. No male teenage friends or acquaintances ever bought or borrowed a car, not even a very old one. They were all too young to take the driving test and had no money to spare for buying cars.

The wild parties depicted in the film were entirely run by wild teenagers. They were events at which anything could happen. One character even feared that she might be pregnant.

Any party to which my friends and I were invited was always attended by adults in the background. There was no thought or concern about anyone becoming pregnant.

In the 1950's, there was no sex before marriage, only marriage, and hopefully sex ensued after the marriage vows. These rules were obviously not always adhered to as we did hear of unwed mothers, but they were not among our friends.

From our judgemental conditioning, we had developed a very supercilious attitude towards individuals in these precarious situations. We viewed them as wildly promiscuous. They were to be pitied and avoided. The thought that any of us could be in such a situation was beyond our comprehension.

One year, neighbourhood gossip suggested that someone who lived only two streets away "had to" get married to her boyfriend. As she was not a close friend, I did not climb down completely from my superior perch, but as I did know her, I managed to feel some genuine sympathy for her predicament.

THE COTILLION

As they were excluded from any association with white groups, the black elite developed their own children's camps, clubs, schools, colleges, sororities and fraternities. These groups selected mainly well-off professional people and their children for membership in their organisations.

Their families may have been college educated for three generations, sent their children to private schools and summer camps and often spent summer holidays abroad. They not only owned their expansive houses but also owned houses in summer resorts on Cape Cod, MA.

Neither my family nor any of my friends' families actually belonged to this exclusive group. We were hard-working, respectable and aspiring but were families of sparse means compared to the professional class.

In large cities, many of these professional groups sponsored debutante cotillions for girls who were in their senior year in high school. My Aunt Rebecca who was a physiotherapist in a suburban hospital, was a member of one of the sororities that promoted the cotillion in Boston.

It was through her that I received an invitation to the 1950 Cotillion. Escorts had to be approved by the sponsoring committee. The grounds on which they were accepted or rejected were unfathomable to me. I suspect they revolved around future ambitions to attend college or university. (I knew of no young men with ordinary jobs who attended this event).

To attend the cotillion, we were required to attend many rehearsal weekends where we were all taught how to dance the waltz and how to bow properly. The last of the activities which we had to attend was a special tea to which all the participants brought their approved escorts.

Both families, mine and my proposed escort's, vetted their teenager's choice of partner. Was the individual presentable, from a respectable family, planning further education, college or university preferably. As my chosen partner, Ray, was planning to become a doctor, he was above reproach. I, too, had plans to go to a four-year college or university so also passed his family's approval.

The Cotillion was held in the main ballroom of one of Boston's grand hotels. Our first dance was a waltz. A large orchestra provided a variety of different kinds of dance music for the teenagers throughout the evening. When we had left the venue to attend our friends' parties, the orchestra played more sedate music for the parents and other adults for the rest of the evening. Parents and relatives were seated at small tables around the edge of the dance floor. The women were tastefully bejewelled, wearing long gown with elbow length gloves. The men were in tuxedos (i.e., dinner jackets) and black ties.

I wore a long white gown. The entire outer layer was decorated with fine silver thread, woven into delicate flowers and leaves which shone as I moved in the light. Underneath the many loose layers of tulle, was a flexible wooden hoop to ensure that the skirt maintained its buoyancy at all times.

I, also, had elbow-length gloves and a white fur jacket to complete the outfit. My father had rented the jacket for the weekend of the cotillion, as I certainly did not own one.

After an evening of dancing with our escorts, we attended one of many post-cotillion parties, at various friends' houses. For the first time, there were no restrictions on the time that I should return home. I could stay out until after midnight with no repercussions. It was a wonderful, a truly memorable occasion. I was delighted to have spent such a splendid evening, dancing well into the early hours of the morning with friends and my very attentive and attractive escort, Ray.

HIGH SCHOOL RELATIONS

SEPARATE GROUPS

At high school, black and white students continued to intermingle freely. Boys and girls were friendly. They joked together, discussed the joys and woes of whatever classes they shared and sometimes even shared the results of homework assignments.

But there was never any question of being more than just friends. No one ever looked across the colour line for a boyfriend or girlfriend. It was not a subject that was discussed at home or anywhere else. This fact indicates how effective the conditioning had been by both black and white parents against inter-racial mixing.

While remaining friendly, neither group had any desire to engage in more intimate social behaviour. The lines of demarcation were clearly drawn. Social avoidance at this level was the accepted norm.

Outside of high school, we all segregated ourselves into separated social groups, according to the colour of our skin. All the parties and dances I attended were for black people only.

The Girl Scouts and the Episcopalian Church to which I belonged were predominantly white as was the Baptist Church I had walked to when I was a child. All the schools to which I had gone and would go were populated predominantly by white students. These were more formal settings where everyone met as racial equals but not as close friends socially.

The only event where teenagers of both groups fraternised socially was the high school prom, but, of course, every individual came with a partner of his or her own colour.

An acquaintance at Boston University had a party to which two white male students, friends of hers, were invited. Everyone danced with them. It was unusual but no one appeared shocked. Despite that, we didn't hear of their desiring to date any of the attractive young girls present.

There was a huge state of shock and horror throughout the neighbourhood, when my friend, Jeri's sister, a student at Boston University Medical School dated a white medical student.

"What was the world coming to? She ought to know better. What did she think he wanted? Was she out of her mind? Nothing good would come of it."

I never knew the details of the situation, only the gossip and rumours that galloped around the houses, leaping from one street to the next.

Critical adjectives abounded: disgusting, disgraceful, shameful. The idea of interracial dating rendered everyone full of profound disapproval and especially suspicious of his intentions. I was as shocked as everyone else. I had learned that only women of low moral virtue would ever consider such an idea.

I had met Jeri's sister many times. She appeared to be a sensible, highly intelligent individual, more interested in her studies than in engaging in illicit relations with anyone. But, so great was the feeling of disapprobation, people in the neighbourhood felt that it was their moral duty to report and denigrate this nefarious dating incident to one and all.

OTHER ASPECTS OF HIGH SCHOOL

When I first went to high school, I had turned 13 only two months prior to my entry. It was a fact that I never mentioned unless asked. Everyone else was 14 and some were close to being 15 years old. Wanting to be accepted on an equal basis with the other students, I went out of my way never to mention the subject of age.

In high school, I met a new group of black girls. Most were taking business and secretarial courses and one or two were taking the general course which allowed students to decide later whether they wanted to pursue business studies or college subjects. There were usually a few black students taking the college course, but as there weren't many, I was often the only black student in most of my classes.

In my first year of high school., I was introduced to a "Slam Book". It was a book with the names of everyone we knew written in it. We were expected to write a comment in it about each person with whom we were acquainted. As I idly perused the contents, I could see that many insulting and derogatory comments were boldly written on everyone's pages.

What was the purpose of this book? I couldn't decide. As its aim seemed to be to denigrate everyone, I found reading it a seriously unpleasant experience and decided to write only true and positive comments about everyone. I reasoned that only negative comments hardly produced a balanced picture. No-one that I knew was composed of completely negative traits.

Of course, after looking at the book, the next deliberate act in which everyone engaged was to turn immediately to the page with one's own name on it. Given my initial rational response to the existence of the Slam Book, I was unexpectedly surprised at my response to what had been written about me.

The words I read were all critical. They were humiliating, shocking and soul-destroying. The gist of all these negative comments was that no-one approved of me. The most complimentary phrase written was: "She's OK", hardly an overwhelming endorsement of my character or personality.

I was conceited, a snob, thought I was better than everyone else.

Don't even try to be her friend, she'll always make you feel inferior.

I starched my bras so had stiff boobs.

I was ugly but thought myself beautiful.

I was frigid and hated men.

Thinks she's smarter that all of us.

I was devastated and overwhelmed by these revelations. How could I be seen in such a negative light with no redeeming qualities at all? As the day progressed, I began to feel physically ill. Is this what these people who were friendly during school and even at parties really thought of me?

I began to question what sort of relationships I really had with everyone. I couldn't believe or accept some of the opinions about my behaviour. I was the only one from my neighbourhood willing to be friends with the new black students who weren't from our area. Some of the people I knew refused to associate with these students as they were reputed to live in a less desirable neighbourhood. On my part, being friendly was not a particularly well thought out piece of behaviour. I just didn't see the point of being unfriendly to people for no specific reason. I asked myself "Who was actually displaying consistently snobbish behaviour?"

As for the starched bras, all the bras of the 1950's had circular stitching on each cup that ended in a stiff cone at the end. They were, apparently, meant to emulate the uplift that movie stars exhibited in sweaters. I was completely unaware of this selling ploy in relation to my underwear. Due to the way that the garment was designed, I'm fairly sure that everyone's bras must have felt extremely rigid as well.

My immediate reaction to the idea of stiff boobs was that the person who wrote this comment was no gentleman. He shouldn't have been grasping me so tightly that he was aware of what my upper body felt like.

The idea of hating men and being frigid, I knew exactly where that idea came from. When dancing slow dances, some young men always attempted to draw the girl in, very close to them. I always resisted this manoeuvre, feeling that this was impertinent and presumptuous behaviour, and that such dance movements should be reserved for those who were girlfriend and boyfriend.

Having no boyfriends, at that time, amongst my high school friends, no doubt, also contributed to the idea of my being a man-hating individual.

Thinking myself beautiful, I was no different from any other adolescent. I was racked with doubts about my appearance, what to wear and how to behave. It's true that I never thought that I was ugly but the word beautiful was not even a burgeoning possibility in my angst-ridden mind.

Could they really think me conceited because I was taking the college course? It was a topic that I never mentioned unless asked directly about what subjects I was taking.

Not long after the slam book incident, I was telephoned by one of my new "friends". She had rung to tell me that everyone had been invited to a party. They were all meeting up and would soon depart. "What was I doing for the weekend?" My heart sank. They had deliberately left me out. I consoled myself with the knowledge that I was not even acquainted with the person who was giving the party, but I was still aware of the fact that no-one had chosen to ask me to go to the party as they had with other friends.

I was learning, painfully, one of life's harsh lessons. Rejection may relate to nothing you have said or done. Some individuals and groups have developed their own private agenda which they choose to project onto others. Their unfounded preconceptions determine whether people are found acceptable or wanting in some way and unsatisfactory.

Sometimes I wondered where did I belong? Where did I fit in? Rejection by white society was a fact of life and as I was discovering, there was no guaranteed acceptance into black groups either. No group was extending a welcoming hand without absurd expectations.

I did have friends during high school, and they changed as I matured and the years progressed.

Recognising where to place the blame for rejection was a long slow process. Ultimately, it was a liberating endeavour but also a disappointing one. Whether conscious or unconscious, negative bias is responsible for the prejudice towards individuals and groups. Where it exists, it always functions to the detriment of harmonious relations and plants the seeds of discord and distrust amongst everyone.

Circumstances forced me to regard the world of human relationships far less idealistically and to view human interactions on a more realistic basis.

As a teenager, I was discovering that my world could be highly enjoyable and entertaining, but it was also permeated with prejudice, division and an aversion to anything different from the "norm".

WIDENER LIBRARY

WAR and PEACE, TOLSTOY

From the age of 15, I had been working one or two afternoons a week and all day on Saturdays at Widener Library, the largest of all Harvard University's many libraries.

A few of us, mostly high school students, went in search of any book requested, with the appropriate form, whether from students, professors, visiting lecturers or those with special privileges.

My weekly salary was deposited into a bank account as saving for my eventual college tuition. My parents, both fervent advocates of further education, assumed that both my brother and I would attend a four-year college or university and would save any money earned for that purpose. They were already putting aside any savings they could spare with this intention in mind.

Initially, I was overwhelmed by the profusion of books in the stalls but even more so, by the numerous subjects with which I was totally unacquainted. Fortunately, anyone who worked in the library was allowed to borrow at least 3 books a week for their own reading pleasure.

In an attempt to make a small dent in the magnitude of the abyss of my general knowledge, I determined to read a book a week on any subject I chose. The selection was haphazard, depending upon the section of the library to which I was sent.

Never one to be daunted by the size of a book, I chose as my first reading adventure, Tolstoy's "War and Peace", knowing that it would be a requisite on any 2educated" person's reading list. In the initial chapters, I eagerly anticipated some sort of human interaction between the main characters, something that would spark my interest in the unfolding story.

Instead, I was confronted with lengthy chapters of the French invasion of Russia and Napoleon's ultimate impact on Tsarist society. My interest slowly waned as I completely drowned in the huge mass of historical fact and endless battles. I could read no more and eventually, had to admit defeat, while simultaneously recognising that this was not a propitious start for ending my ignorance on matters unknown.

Someone suggested that I may have picked up one of the early copies of the book. They contained numerous essays and detailed descriptions of Russian history, all of which were deleted from later copies.

I rather doubt that that was the case, as later, when in college, I read "War and Peace" in its entirety. Once again, I found myself resenting the initial chapters, bogged down by the historical detail and facts, long before the narrative ensued. But, by this point in time, I had developed enough patience to view the initial chapters as the context required as background for the narrative which followed.

As time progressed, my fervent desire to learn about everything that I was exposed to, slowly mitigated. It became glaringly obvious that there were certain subjects which I had no desire, nor any intention of pursuing, a few examples: accidence-the study of inflection in grammar, thanatology - the study of death and its customs, semiotics-the study of signs and symbols.

WIDENER LIBRARY 2. THOMAS DE QUINCY

My random reading choices led me down some unexpected paths. Having seen the title, "Confessions of An Opium Eater" by Thomas deQuincy, published in1821. I was curious to discover what effects drugs had on human behaviour.

De Quincy purports to write the book as a source of instruction to warn against the negative effects of taking the drug. To relieve the pain of toothache, he first took laudanum (a tincture of opium) and always remembered it as a joyous and intensely delightful experience. He remained indignant with critics who suggested that the use of opium could lead to enervation, loss of vitality and depression.

He lamented the fact that the rich could afford to buy opium to relieve the pain of daily suffering while the poor had to tolerate mental and physical distress, without distraction or alleviation.

He described the qualities of the drug as exceeding the limits of human experience. While listening to opera, his senses are heightened and his reactions more responsive. De Quincy continued to use opium, but it was only when he became so debilitated that he could no longer focus on his writing that he seriously decreased its use, despite the mental and physical agony of withdrawal.

I found myself in agreement with De Quincy's critics. He had spent more time extolling the virtues of opium than in discussing its deleterious and harmful effects.

When I finished the book, I was left more with an uneasy and furtive desire to experience one of De Quincy's transcendent moments than a feeling of being repelled by drug-taking.

It was not until, years later, when I saw Eugene O'Neill's play, "Long Day's Journey into Night", that I gained a much more balanced view of the effects of opium. The play was based on O'Neill's mother's experience, her long and contracted battle with opium addiction with no hope of recovery.

She was first administered opium to relieve her labour pains during Eugene's childbirth. She spent the next 25 years attempting to relinquish its use and did eventually succeed in the last 8 years of her life. (O'Neill did not depict this fact in his play.)

While I remain to this day curious about ecstatic drug experiences, my desire to engage directly in such behaviour has, over a protracted period of time, contracted and diminished.

WIDENER LIBRARY 3. THE FOUNTAINHEAD, AYN RAND

The next title which aroused my interest was The Fountainhead by Ayn Rand. It was her first book, published in 1943, and instantly became a best-seller. It was later made into a feature film which I never saw. It was because the book was so popular that I thought it must be of some merit.

The protagonist is Howard Roark whose actions are propelled by his egocentric needs and interests, without any regard for the interests of others.

Ayn Rand strongly supports individual liberty and espouses the belief that individuals, not society, are the fountainheads of civilization. The interests of the individual take priority over any interests or demands of the state or any social group.

Reason can be the individual's only guide to action. Pursuit of one's own self-interest and happiness is the highest moral purpose in life and will create a society for everyone's mutual benefit. The ideal economic system is laissez-faire capitalism.

I view my reading of The Fountainhead as a significant step in my development as it was the first book which challenged my assumptions about how society should ideally function. I felt it important to think about each of her propositions and to counter everyone with a well-considered argument.

I could not accept the idea that feelings and emotions should play no part in any aspect of human relationships and should be considered an impediment to those pursuing their own goals.

Following one's own objectives, does not necessarily lead to happiness or inevitably contribute to human progress, as Rand suggests.

I concluded: that being a self-directed, self-indulgent individuals might be more likely to produce transactions directed to their own self-interest than to the benefit of others. I had always viewed people as biologically programmed from birth to be totally reliant on the care of others and therefore assumed they were inherently social beings.

Parents following primarily their own interests would be incapable of providing the nurturing which babies and young children require. The two demands are diametrically opposed.

Logically, it would seem that these adults would relinquish having children on two grounds:

(1) They would have to acknowledge the importance of emotional involvement in child-rearing.

(2) They could no longer allow their own interests to take precedence in their lives.

Rand's image of individuals forging through life without anyone's support, interest, or even taking notice was not appealing nor did it seem a realistic model for the development of any healthy society or any healthy individual.

It was not until years later when John Bowlby's theory of attachment (around 1985) appeared, that I felt my understanding of human behaviour was vindicated. Bowlby, a psychoanalyst, suggested that babies are pre-programmed to form attachments with others as others will help them to survive.

At the time, I did not consider the other areas to which her philosophy might be applied. In 2008, Alan Greenspan, was Chairman of the Federal Reserve (the central banking system which establishes the monetary policy of the USA). Since the 1950's. he had been a good friend of Ayn Rand's and an enthusiastic follower of her philosophy of Objectivism. Until her death in 1982, he maintained their friendship.

He believed very much in laissez-faire capitalism, no rules or regulations should be put into effect as they would inhibit the self-regulatory capacity of institutions.

Various congressmen had tried to persuade him that allowing banks to regulate themselves was a risky decision, but he rejected their counsel. He later admitted that he failed to predict the financial downturn of 2008 and that banks, when acting in their own self-interest, had not protected either their shareholders or their equity.

WIDENER LIBRARY 4. JH FABRE

My greatest discovery was the work of JH Fabre, (1823-1915), a 19th century entomologist. As was the custom of the time, entomologists derived their knowledge from their observations of dead insect specimens.

Jean-Henri Fabre chose to follow his own methods and remained innovative in his approach. He insisted on studying wasps, bees, grasshoppers, beetles, spiders, flies, caterpillars, glow-worms, and scorpions in their natural habitats. This was a completely new procedure for investigating insect behaviour.

A passionate pursuit of truth and exact, detailed observations were the distinguishing characteristics of his writing. In his books, facts were never presented as a series of isolated, unrelated remarks, but were always integrated into an understanding of how it helped or hindered the insect to function.

Initially, insect life was not a subject in which I was seriously interested, but from the moment I opened one of his books, I was mesmerised. It was as rewarding as reading any good novel and sometimes better--the descriptions and suspense could be compelling.

These were insect biographies written more as a narrative, detailing the actions, reactions, and interactions of these small, mysterious creatures, the hazards of birth, exposure to the outside world, the search for food, finding a partner, attacks by enemies. Some were working as individuals, others in groups, surviving or succumbing to the adverse effects of intruders and sometimes meeting an untimely death.

Due to his elegant and lively style of writing, Fabre popularised the subject of entomology in his own lifetime. His 10 volumes on insect behaviour were widely admired and appreciated. Fabre's precise and accurate insect studies drew the attention of Darwin who described him as an inimitable observer. Pasteur and John Stuart Mill visited him.

His marvellous text about truffles, written in 1878, was recognised as outstanding. My son-in-law, Brian Taylor, who sadly died in March 2012, shared my enthusiasm for Fabre. He was one of only two people I knew who had ever heard of him.

When Brian was ill, I was pleased to find publishers who would reprint some of the texts no longer available, and at a cost that was equal to the normal price of a book. As a result, I was able to supply him with reading material that still enthralled him.

I use the word still, because I discovered that, as a teenager, he had become so obsessed with Fabre that he had read all of the books that had been translated into English and that proved to be all ten volumes of his work.

WIDENER 5. BRENDA

Also working at Widener Library was my friend, Brenda. We were already acquainted as we were both taking the college course in high school, so were often members of the same after-school groups, French Club, Latin Club, and the Senior Book Club.

On Saturdays, Brenda often invited me home for lunch. Her parents were Orthodox Jews who had immigrated from Russia. There was always a table of her mother's beautifully prepared Kosher food. These lunches were my first introduction to Jewish cuisine, and I loved them. Most memorable was the taste of the slightly sweet and sour borscht, either cabbage or beetroot. It was a novel and delectable flavour for me.

From Brenda, I also learned about some of the religious practices of Orthodox Jews. I was particularly drawn to Shabbat, where every Saturday, over candles, blessings are recited, particularly for God's gifts but also for food, wine, and the family. I was very impressed because it seemed that Christianity provided no such comparable ceremony to celebrate the importance of the family.

She also taught me the catchy tune "Tzena, Tzena." in Hebrew. It is danced to the Hora and was later made famous in a more popular version by Pete Seeger.

When I recently attended a relative's Orthodox wedding, (one of my husband's nieces), to the surprise of those around me, I, the only Goy in view, burst into song in Hebrew as the orchestra played the familiar staccato sounds of "Tzenz,Tzena." I actually remembered most of the words.

Tzena, Tzena (Hebrew transliteration)
Tzena, tzena, tzena, tzena ha-banot u-rena
Hajalim ba-mosheva

Al na, al na, al na, al na, tithabena
Mi ben hayil, ish tzava

English translation
Go out (4x) girls to see the soldiers in the mosheva (farming community)

Do not (4x) hide yourself away, from a virtuous man (a pun on the word for soldier) An army man

We both went to Simmons College but because we were in different departments, she was taking subjects to become a librarian and I was initially, in the science department, our paths seldom crossed.

After I was married, she visited us (Roger, Kim and me) with her husband and her first child. We haven't kept in touch, but I understand that she lives with her husband and children in Massachusetts in the States. I still have fond memories of the times we were together.

After marrying Roger and visiting my English, Jewish father-in-law, I fully expected to have a replica of the wonderful Jewish food that I had eaten at Brenda's house. I was sadly disappointed to discover that they had become so anglicised that they ate a purely English diet. As they were no longer Orthodox Jews, they were not practising Shabbat, a ceremony that ensured the production of delicious Jewish food.

To indulge my love for Jewish food, I visit the restaurants in Golders Green to order chopped liver, cabbage salad, salt beef sandwiches on rye bread with dill pickles and if I can manage it, apple strudel to finish.

I will always be grateful to Brenda for introducing me to a warm Jewish family, Jewish customs and a novel, delicious cuisine.

A DIFFICULT TEACHER

In my last year of high school, I, like most students, was concentrating on achieving good enough marks to perform well in the SAT. The SAT is a standardised admission test taken by all prospective college students and is a prerequisite for entry to most colleges and universities. It tested verbal ability and mathematical reasoning.

For the first and only time, I was receiving very low grades in English. Our weekly essays comprised a large percentage of our assessment and they were ten to fifteen marks lower than those in my previous three years. I never failed but my marks were never as high as they ought to be for college entrance. As these would be the most recent grades on view when I applied to college, I was seriously distressed.

Week after week, I was in a state of despair when I saw yet another low mark for all of my sincere efforts. We were marked on class participation and mine could have been worthy of attention. My hand was frequently raised to respond to questions with the correct answer. But the teacher chose to ask for my answer, seldom and very rarely.

As this was our senior year, the teacher felt it appropriate to discuss our future plans. She went round the classroom asking each student to which colleges they had applied. When I stated that I had applied to Boston University, Simmons and Radcliffe, she looked amazed. Her only response was: "Oh, really!!" No positive comments or encouraging words as there were for the other students. I remember thinking that we'd both be surprised if I were accepted at any college with the grades you are giving me.

I had never experienced the dislike of any teacher and had always had an easy, untroubled relationship with them. I put this down to the fact that my grades were usually nearer to those at the top of the class rather than to those in the lower stream.

I did begin to question myself. I was perplexed about the teacher's motives. Was I becoming paranoid? I could not ignore the low marks nor was I mistaken about how infrequently she asked me to give a correct answer when she asked a question. As I had not said or done anything to upset her, I wondered whether she might be racially prejudiced. After all, I was the only black student in her entire classroom. I was reluctant to draw this conclusion as I had never experienced racial prejudice from any teacher.

I have been asked why didn't I protest about my situation. It was 1949-1950. The teacher's word and decisions were final and absolute. There was no committee or even a concerned group aware that students could have problems or suffer a grievance. And there could be no suggestion of any racial prejudice. Where was the proof? As any teacher or headmaster would inform you, "They were proud to live in a democratic society where everyone was treated equally. As for racial prejudice, it just didn't exist within the walls of the Cambridge High and Latin School."

All official figures within the school would have been outraged at such a suggestion. Challenging the authority and the reputation of a long-standing teacher was beyond my capacity and not worth the opprobrium that would inevitably follow. We all grew up pledging our belief in 'liberty and justice for all' but those who were the recipients of injustice knew that life wasn't always fair and didn't always operate on such high-minded moral principles.

My only hope was to perform well on the SAT and hope that good exam results would take precedence over any low grades received during the year and hopefully be considered more representative of a student's abilities.

SENIOR YEAR, PART 1, DRAMA CLUB

I was anxious to join the Drama Club. For two consecutive years, I had tried to become a member, but had been rejected each time. After my last attempt, the drama teacher had informed me that my voice was too high to play any part convincingly.

As my voice registers around the middle range, I found that comment disturbing. But I had to accept that in the circumstances, it may have been true, a nervous reaction in a very tense situation. I was persistent in trying out again as, when I was younger, I had experienced great joy and great success performing in a few plays.

I applied for the third and last time and tried to remain composed as I read the piece I had chosen. To my great delight time, this time I was accepted.

The customary procedure was that the teacher chose the plays, and everyone auditioned for the parts they wanted to perform. The teacher had the final choice about whose performance was the most convincing.

While I was queuing for an audition, the teacher told me that it was likely that I would have a part in the new play. I was overjoyed. It would be my first time to be on the stage in a high school play. She said she thought I'd be very good in a particular part she had in mind.

I assumed that she'd seen an acting role for which she thought I had some particular talent. "Which part is it?", I enquired. "The maid," she responded. "I'm giving you the part." I suppose I should have been honoured to have been officially chosen but I was stunned and brimming over with consternation and dismay. I had not even been asked to audition for any of the major parts for which I had been queuing.

Nor was I asked to audition for the role of the maid. Was it taken for granted that I'd know how to play the role without even trying out for the part?" And why would anyone think that? I was literally affronted and insulted.

The teacher's denying me an audition for any part in the play was a great injustice and merely assigning me to a minor, inferior role was an even greater insult.

No doubt, the teacher thought she was doing me a good turn by ensuring me a part in the play. But why was I the only one chosen to be the maid? Anyone would have to query the assumptions behind that noble gesture.

If the teacher considered her treatment of me acceptable (and she did), I wanted no part of the Drama Club and I left immediately, never to return.

INTERVIEW WITH THE DEAN

Further preparation and guidance for entry to college consisted of an interview with the Dean of Senior Girls. It was 1950, not long before we had to submit our college applications. At our meeting, the Dean enquired first about my plans for the future. I told her that I was applying to Boston University, Simmons, and Radcliffe College.

No shocked response or look of surprise. Good, I thought, but I soon realised that she had her own agenda for me. "Had I considered other options?" I replied that as I could only apply for three colleges, I didn't think there were any other options.

Totally ignoring the fact that I had already chosen the colleges which I wanted to attend, she said "No, no, you are mistaken, you do have other options." "Did I know that there were colleges established for black people in the southern part of the United States?" "Yes, I did. I knew of Howard University in Washington DC, and Fisk University in Nashville, Tennesse." "Had I considered going to one of these colleges?"

I knew that these institutions had very good reputations as their scholastic achievement was outstanding and equal to the best white colleges. What the Dean failed to mention, was that there was much less funding for at least some of the southern colleges for black students. As a result, their facilities and resources were sometimes inferior and their educational standards sometimes lower than those in the north.

But what was happening to my plans to attend a college or university in Boston or Cambridge? I was already concerned that low grades in English might prohibit even my acceptance for a college interview.

And now the Dean was telling me that I should be applying to different colleges, in the southern part of the US. A feeling of doom was descending on me. Maybe, none of my plans for the future were at all realistic.

I was jolted back to the present reality when the Dean stated that I might be happier in a college for black students, as I would be "associating with my own people". She highly recommended that I apply to at least one or two of these colleges and generously offered to help me in any way that she could.

I found her suggestion somewhat incomprehensible. Why should I be happier in exclusively black academic atmosphere? I had spent my entire life in integrated schools and had never found that problematic in any way. I attended an integrated high school and had never any problems with the students. For three years, I was elected the homeroom representative by the thirty odd students in the different classrooms. All classes were predominately white, so there was no question of being elected by a "black majority".

White students expressed no antipathy toward me, nor did "black" students display any particular propensity towards me.

The idea of attending a southern black college had little appeal for me. I couldn't see how "being with my own kind" would further my educational goals in any way.

Most of these colleges were in former slave states, all of whom had established what were defined as "Jim Crow" laws. They were specifically designed to maintain the separation of the black and white populations. Serious punishment could ensure for anyone not complying.

Jim Crow laws mandate "separate but equal" status for black Americans living mainly in the southern states. They were established by law in 1876, and enforced until 1965. Drinking fountains, buses, trains, schools, colleges, hotels, restaurants, toilets, all were segregated according to race. Most facilities for black people were inferior to those of the whites.

The public schools designated for black students were allocated fewer facilities and instruction was not of equal status to that of their white counterparts, forever condemning the black population to more menial jobs and opportunities of only humble rank.

I don't suppose it helped the Dean's case that I had recently borrowed from Widener Library, Richard Wright's 'A Native Son', which had been published in 1940. Richard Wright had grown up in Natchez, Mississippi, and was deeply affected his entire life by two lynchings of people he had known, his step-uncle and a friend's brother.

Though he did not witness their deaths, they left an indelible mark on him. He writes "The things that influenced my conduct as a Negro did not have to happen to me directly....Indeed, the white brutality that I had not seen was a more effective control of my behaviour than that which I knew".

Lynching was a cruel and vicious act of murder. Black men were brutally beaten and hung from trees by mobs of white men, indignant that they transgressed white expectations of black deference. It was also a powerful means of subordinating the black population through fear. It ensured that white supremacy was upheld in every influential area of life – political, economic, and social.

Wright describes the predicament of black people at the time very clearly and succinctly. "Our bodies will be swung from the limbs of trees, will be shot and mutilated. And we cannot fight back, we have nor arms, we cannot vote, and the law is white".

After reading 'A Native Son' my fate was sealed. Why would I subject myself to the whims of white people deluded by their own sense of superiority and with a desire to demean or even murder anyone not made in their own image?

There was the question of my complying with the Dean's wishes. I rejected the idea totally, and only much later realised that it was in no way feasible. I would have to work every summer to pay one half of my college fees and my parents would have to pay the other half. There was literally no spare money to pay for additional travel and boarding frees to any institution in either the northern of southern part of the US. It was a forgone conclusion. I could not have afforded to study at any institution that was not within commuting distance of my home.

AN ADDENDUM

From observing my experiences with teachers in high school, it is evident that racial prejudice in the north was not clearly delineated nor officially proscribed as it was in the southern part of the United States.

It was subtle and intangible and resided in the low expectations, the derisive assumptions, and the derogatory assessment of black people in general. Acts of kindness were often shrouded in patronising gestures of assistance and support. Covert discriminatory practices, which led to exclusion of minority groups, were imperceptible to public view.

Those who dared to suggest that racial prejudice was a phenomenon that actually existed, always met with a unified response to total denial on the part of the general public and those in power. Challenging a 'non-existent' problem proved well-nigh impossible, particularly if you were action on your own.

White people may have viewed racial prejudice as a paranoid projection, but black people found its effects demeaning and oppressive. And so the injustice remained unacknowledged on one side, while destroying and eroding lives on the other.

JERRY LEWIS

All of us who worked at Widener Library were on a casually friendly basis with the librarians, one of whom stood out as he was the only black librarian at the front desk. I worked there for nearly two years before he decided to ask me for a date. Flattered as I was, I remained surprised at his invitation because of the difference in our ages.

As he later confessed, his request was instigated by a dare and, I thought, probably had nothing to do with being attracted to me. His friend who had been teaching at a college some distance away, had returned home for the holidays. He challenged Jerry to ask the teenage girl at his workplace for a date.

Jerry complied. My father knew of his family which was a point in his favour. Not only did he have a degree from Colby college in Maine, he had also acquired his librarian's accreditation.

The fact that Jerry was eleven years my senior greatly appealed to my father. He immediately saw him as some sort of protector for his innocent, young daughter. But he still had to abide by the rigorous rules for dating, no drinking or smoking and home by 11:30 pm, later it was twelve.

Jerry became a constant companion for three years. While I was seeing Jerry, I was also dating other boys, closer to my own age. It was always with the seniors in high school or the younger college students that I went to parties and dances.

At parties, we proudly wore our tightly gathered skirts which formed a circle of bold, insistent waves and ripples as our partners twirled us round to the beats of the music. For dances, we were always attired in long gowns as these were more formal occasions.

Although there were always initially more slow dances, by the end of the evening, despite the length of the gowns, we were all energetically jitterbugging to the lively beats of the music.

With friends, I occasionally attended gatherings at the International Society. We found foreign students intriguing and challenging as they often espoused very different beliefs and ideas from ours. We engaged in many heated discussions about what was the best form of government and how best to decide the public affairs of any country.

With the students I dated, I was leading what would be considered a "typical" teen-age life: dances, parties, dating and learning about the unpredictable outcomes of adolescent relationships. I wasn't quite so prone to infatuations and crushes as some of my friends (were). They seemed to be madly in love or miserable and suffering continually when the latest boyfriend departed.

I never dated one person to the exclusion of all others. I preferred to have more casual relationships but have to admit, that I was, from to time, strongly attracted to someone I found handsome and charming.

It took at least, three disastrous experiences for me to recognise the wisdom of two familiar adages: the first - Looks do not make a man, and the second - Appearances can be very deceiving.

While truly enjoying the social outings with the teen-age boys, I was simultaneously dating Jerry who introduced me to myriad aspects of a wider world. We went to hear the trumpeter, Louis Armstrong, play his famous New Orleans' Jazz. Although I had half-heartedly listened to jazz on the radio, I had never before focused my entire concentration on the music.

The strong, rhythmic beats were appealing but what fixed my attention were the solo and ensemble improvisations. They were unpredictable and totally spontaneous. I found their performances electrifying and intensely compelling.

He took me to Josephine Baker's last US stage performance. I had acknowledged that I was barely aware of her existence. She was the American-born dancer and actress who, due to racial discrimination, decided to reside in France. She was a civil rights activist and a muse for Ernest Hemingway, F. Scott Fitzgerald and Langston Hughes. Internationally, she became famous for her sensational, erotic dancing.

Jerry also introduced me to my first night club. In Massachusetts, it was illegal to serve alcohol to anyone under 18. I was 17+, nearly 18, but not quite.

In my attempt to look older and more sophisticated, I asked Jerry for a cigarette. As I had never smoked, I asked him to light it for me. With the assurance of a cigarette delicately poised between my fingers, I proceeded to request a Pink Lady, my very first cocktail.

As the waitress left the table, I put the cigarette in my mouth, inhaled and immediately, noisily and uncontrollably erupted into an incessant fit of coughing. Jerry maintained his composure and constantly plied me with water throughout this embarrassing outburst.

When the Pink Lady arrived, I was pleased that I had successfully evaded the legal regulations, but took great care to sip it very, very slowly for fear of disgracing myself again by gulping it down too quickly and suddenly becoming ill.

So involved was I with my own convoluted emotions, I scarcely knew what was happening around me. Instead of enjoying the evening, I was overcome by an overwhelming fear of looking foolish and ridiculous.

It was only when Jerry and I started to dance that I began to relax and could hear the syncopated beats of the instruments being played. The evening then slowly transformed itself from one of all-encompassing self-consciousness into one of total absorption in the dance steps and the rhythm of the music. Despite my angst-ridden beginning, by the time we left, I was enthralled and fascinated by my first evening at a genuine night club.

NOT A FIASCO

The most handsome man that any of us had ever seen appeared in our midst when I was about 17 years old. It was not just us, frivolous teenagers who commented on Robert's attractive features. Our mothers, usually very reserved, to our surprise, also took note of his striking appearance.

Not long before he attended our parties, he had been dating a very beautiful girl from our neighbourhood, but she had recently ended the relationship. I was overjoyed when, at a party, he asked me to dance and then requested a date.

On our first date, Robert arrived in a very distressed state. He had forgotten that he had a prior appointment. We would drive to his friend's house and still have time to enjoy ourselves later. Most of the evening was spent in Robert's car, rushing to fulfill his obligation to visit his friend. It was a very brief visit and a very tedious drive home, as he had taken a wrong turn to my house. We never did have that promised time together.

On one of our last dates, he requested a double date. He would bring a friend and hoped that I could supply a girlfriend. All four of us would go to the well-advertised dance in the next town. It was coincidence that my mother was entertaining her cribbage group the same evening that we were to attend the dance.

She explained to her friends that my friend and I were waiting our dates to pick us up. And unlike my mother, who was always very restrained about making comments of a personal nature, she added that my date was a very attractive, handsome young man.

As the evening progressed, everyone could see that my friend and I were in an agitated state, waiting impatiently, for our dates to arrive. And time ticked on, 15 minutes, half an hour, an hour late. It was now one and a half hours after the agreed time for meeting, with no sign of our dates.

Not only were my mother's friends aware that the very handsome man had not arrived, but also that there was not even a phone call to explain his delay.

We had a moment of worry thinking that something disastrous had happened, but that was short-lived. Due to Robert's inability to organise his life in any reasonable manner, he was often late, so my overwhelming reaction was one of anger and fury. We concluded that these two young men were not going to appear. To our embarrassment, it was blatantly obvious for all to observe that we had been abandoned.

We left, telling my mother to inform Robert that we were at the dance, if he did manage to call. About 20 minutes after our arrival, (We were both, thank goodness, dancing with other partners) we saw Robert and his friend slowly approaching us.

Endless apologies, serious car problems, repairs took much longer that they had expected. Fine, but why, at some point along the way, couldn't he have rung to let us know what was happening. Any considerate person would have done that, at least.

I was less that pleased. "No, I didn't want to dance with him. He could find somebody else. I was here to enjoy myself." Was it really too much of an effort to phone us to explain his situation, rather than leaving us stranded? I ignored him for the rest of the evening.

He later rang me at home to apologise but I was reluctant to go out again with someone so consistently undependable.

As girls were so anxious to date him, I felt that he had no need to reform his lackadaisical ways. That, I decided was the downside of being so good-looking. There was no incentive to examine his behaviour or how it affected others. I was now happy to leave him to his own devices.

NOT A FIASCO, CONTINUED

A few weeks later, I was invited out by a young medical student, Martin, now the ex-boyfriend of the same beautiful girl who had first dated Robert.

Through the teen-age grapevine, I was informed that his ex-girlfriend didn't like the idea that he was dating me. I found her comments absolutely ridiculous. She no longer wanted to see him, so he was free to see whomever he liked.

I decided that her reaction was a result of the fickleness of teen-agers feelings and maybe due to jealousy. But why would anyone be jealous of another person having someone that you didn't want?

One summer evening, Martin accompanied me to a very popular party. Everyone we knew was there, including his beautiful ex-girlfriend. To this day, I do not know what actually happened. Martin and I really enjoyed the first dance together, but that was, quite literally, the only time I danced with him all evening. He simply vanished from sight.

Initially, I sat in a state of disbelief. How could anyone be so rude? Had he really asked me to the party, danced happily with me once and then just dumped me? I sat and waited, to no avail. I was forced to accept the truth of the situation. He had completely disappeared and never returned to dance with me.

I later spotted him with his ex-girlfriend. They were obviously and undeniably spending the evening together. I decided to make the best of a very bad situation. As a reasonable number of boys had requested dances with me, I did not feel particularly left out of the activities. That meant that I couldn't spend too much time feeling sorry for myself.

But I did remain hurt and angry. What insulting behaviour on Martin's part!!

A little later, when I was dancing very energetically with a very pleasant young man, I caught sight of a familiar face, the handsome, Robert, smiling and heading straight towards me. My initial reaction was to try to escape. I'd experienced enough of his unpredictable behaviour and endless excuses.

He stood there genuinely pleading and trying to make amends. I, honestly, felt sorry for him. He was sincerely trying to rectify his past misdemeanours. Expediency tipped the balance of my feelings. He wasn't a bad dancer, and I was, after all, in the position of dancing with just about anyone who asked me, just to prove that I wasn't a wallflower because Martin had rejected me.

After a brief hesitation I accepted Robert's invitation and we enjoyed two or three lively dances together. And then, suddenly the party ended. Had that much time really passed? How was I going home? I began to panic, certainly not with Martin, even if he asked me to do so.

In a state of desperation and disbelief, I heard Robert asking to take me home. What a lifesaver!! What a profound relief!! At least, I would have a partner to escort me to my front door, a fact I hoped that Martin would observe.

As Robert was standing in the queue, retrieving my coat, Martin suddenly appeared. He apologised, with no credible explanation for his behaviour and announced that he would take me home.

"Well, that is my decision, not yours", I responded. "Thank you, I already have a gentleman to escort me home."

Robert arrived and helped me on with coat. As we walked down the front steps together, Martin followed in hot pursuit, protesting, and proclaiming his regret, and apologising profusely. As Robert opened the door of his car, I threw Martin a victorious smile and a triumphant glance and sped off into the night with my saviour, Robert.

As recompense for his rescuing me, I agreed to date Robert again. But sadly, his unreliable behaviour had not altered, so we managed only one more date which I decided was to be the last.

As for Martin, I felt his behaviour had been outrageous!! I wanted him never to treat anyone as he had treated me. So, despite numerous phone calls, I refused adamantly, ever to see him again.

ROMEO and JULIET

Jerry continued to indulge my passion for the theatre and accompanied me to any play that I desired. As I was studying Romeo and Juliet for exam purposes, we went to see the stage performance in Boston.

The teacher always chose which sections of any play that we should read and which section we should memorise for homework. As a result, we never read every word of the written text.

The initial part of the play seemed familiar, but as it progressed, I became distinctly more uncomfortable. This was definitely not the play that we were reading daily at school. The themes of the play were the same, the Capulets and the Montagues were at loggerheads with each other. Due to their feuding families, Romeo and Juliet's love affair, was inevitably, destined for a disastrous end.

But I was unacquainted with the text that the characters spoke, laden, as it was, with numerous allusions to sex. The servants made rude references to how they would deal with maids (otherwise known as virgins).

Mercutio's speeches with Romeo and the Nurse were full of double-entendres. In fact, the Nurse and Mercutio engaged in dialogue peppered with sexual innuendo.

Juliet, the innocent young maiden, was more than impatient to leap into Romeo's arms and "lose a winning battle". Was she really asking to be a maid no longer?

Sitting next to Jerry, I was squirming in my seat with embarrassment. I dared not look in his direction.

I'm sure that I missed half of the suggestive connotations delivered, because I, often, required text notes to clarify Shakespeare's use of language. Just as well, my piecemeal comprehension of what I heard was disturbing enough.

It was a shocking revelation to realise that the teacher's deletion of text could so skew and bias everyone's understanding and interpretation of an entire play.

Hearing the words with unexpurgated, bawdy speeches, totally altered and enlarged my perception of the characters demeanour and gave me a new insight into what Shakespeare actually wrote.

Unfortunately, for fear of shocking the examiners, I dared not display or even flamboyantly insert my newly acquired knowledge into any of the answers for the English exam.

GEORGE BERNARD SHAW

I loved the theatre and with a girlfriend, occasionally, say plays at one of theatres in Boston. More frequently, I went to the Brattle Theatre near Harvard Square. It was only just over a mile from my house.

Thanks for Jerry Lewis's generosity, I saw almost an entire season of George Bernard Shaw's plays at the Brattle Theatre.

I admired his strong, feisty women and the wordy, principled speeches that his characters uttered. He investigated controversial topics: the class system, poverty, and prostitution. Due to his anti-war stance, his criticism of religion, and his ardent socialism, his ideas were unacceptable to many.

He often portrayed amusing clashes between the sexes and suggested that women could be the stronger sex. They were often victorious over men, frequently for their own purposes.

I was overjoyed to see Pygmalion for the first time, later to be recreated and made famous as 'My Fair Lady'. I saw 'Don Juan in Hell', the third act of 'Man and Superman'. Because it is part of a very long four act play, it is often performed separately.

Despite the lengthy speeches, I found Shaw's plays challenging and stimulating. I greatly appreciated his command of language and his scintillating wit.

It was the first time that I had heard such contemporary subjects openly discussed. Why is socialism preferable to capitalism? Are women really superior to men? Should we look at prostitutes in a more positive light? Do we need a superman, some sort of morally superior being, to shape the development of mankind? I was delighted that he raised such controversial subjects for scrutiny on the stage and forced me to ponder these topics in depth.

ADOLESCENCE

When I was about 16, I started to question everything about my existence. In no way was I attempting to become a rebellious teenager. Having acquired a set of beliefs from my parents, I simply wanted to delineate what differences existed between what I had been taught and what I really believed.

Sometimes it was new knowledge that unexpectedly punctured my firmly held beliefs, for example, thinking about the diagram of the food chain which the biology teacher had given us led to my ultimately questioning the basis of my religious beliefs.

THE FOOD CHAIN

The food chain is composed of a series of living organisms. Each member feeds on another in the chain and is in turn eaten.

Plants and algae compose the first level. They are the producers who, through photosynthesis, convert sunlight to make food for animals.

Herbivores (plant-eaters) are the primary consumers and use the producers (the plants) as their source of food, (examples are cows, deer, most birds, elephants, and mice).

Carnivores (meat-eaters) eat the primary consumers as their source of food, examples are: (cats, dogs, eagles, spiders, sharks, wolves, lions, and tigers).

The Omnivores, like man, are capable of eating both plants and animals. They function as primary and secondary consumers. As they cannot directly absorb the sun's energy to make food, they are dependent on eating other organisms (plants and animals) as a source of food.

Pain and suffering seemed an inherent and inseparable aspect of how the food chain functioned. Each creature was merely live fodder for the next in the chain.

In addition, in any food chain, more than one creature usually eats a particular species. Regard the life of the tiny field mouse. Its enemies include cats, dogs, wolves, owls, bears, hawks, and snakes. With such a numerous list of predators, the odds seem unfairly stacked against its likely survival.

To commemorate these offensive facts and in recognition of lines originally written by Jonathan Swift, I composed a short rhyming verse. But first let me introduce Swift's Satirical verse, The Siponaptera.

Big fleas have little fleas,
Upon their backs to bite 'em,
And little fleas have lesser fleas,
And so, ad infinitum.

Sometimes, a second verse appears, with lines such as:
And the great fleas, in turn,
Have greater fleas to go on;
While these again have greater still,
And greater still, and so on.

My verse is as follows:
The sun infuses plants with life,
And in this act, there is no strife.
The plants benign, give up themselves for grazers, all to eat them.
These herbivores, themselves in turn,
Have carnivores maltreat them.
While these again have greater still,
The omnivores defeat them.
And so the ghastly process
Proceeds ad infinitum.

I, somehow, had to come to terms with this hierarchical system designed very efficiently for the destruction of living creatures. If God had intentionally created life, how could he allow it to be annihilated at a moment's notice and in such a cruel manner?

How could I reconcile God's indifference to the daily termination of individual creatures with my concept of a just, fair, and caring God?

And, as for the over-population argument, it brings me back to the same conclusions. We can't allow human beings or animals to proliferate endlessly or there will be no room left on the planet. Fine!! But couldn't a merciful God have conceived of a more compassionate method for eliminating surpluses in both man and beast, a method that inflicts the minimum of pain?

HOME and RELIGION

I had decided that I would ask my parents about their religious beliefs. I was finding it more and more difficult to believe in the miracles of either the Old or New Testaments.

How was it that when Jesus blessed only five loaves and two fishes, they were instantly increased in number, enough to feed 5000 people? How could Jesus have turned water into wine as he did for the wedding guests at Cana?

Did my parents really believe that Jonah lived in the belly of a whale for three days and three nights and the whale, then politely, deposited him unharmed on dry land? When the Israelites were crossing the Red Sea, God provided food, allowing Manna (a kind of bread) to fall from heaven, providing enough for their journey. I won't go on, but I questioned all such incredulous stories.

My parents were Baptists and I had always felt that, for some reason, my father was more of a fundamentalist than my mother. He tended towards a strict, literal interpretation of the Bible (as he had been taught). But I never heard my mother make any comments about her faith. She was a quiet believer, not given to making overt statements about religion.

I was hoping for some kind of rational discussion and was oblivious of the fact that my father and I were situated in two opposing camps and headed for collision.

My father started from a position of faith, as a believer in Baptist religious doctrines. By asking questions, I was expecting him to supply some kind of proof to substantiate his beliefs. He, unfortunately, did not view my questions in such a dispassionate light. He felt that by querying the verity of the Bible stories, I was attacking his beliefs.

At one of our evening meals. I had managed to ask only two questions before he exploded and forbade me to speak at the dinner table. I was hurt, I was angry, I was silenced. So much for a reasonable discussion with my parents. My mother had said nothing. There was no point, even if she had wanted to-She could see how strongly my father felt about this issue.

There was also an air of incredulity about my father's response. How could I, raised as a good Christian, baptised as a baby in the Baptist Church, and at my own request, confirmed in the Episcopalian Church, be sitting at the family dinner table asking such outrageous questions?

Eventually, I was allowed to speak during dinner, but of course, never offered any opinions on religion. Despite our great affection for each other, the subject of religion had created a great gulf between my father and me. With such wide differences in opinion and outlook, it was, sadly, a rift never to be resolved.

THE CHURCH and THE KOREAN WAR

One Sunday morning, as I sat listening to the sermon, the tone of the minister's voice caught my attention. He was making a strongly felt statement about the horrors of war and expressed alarm at the amount of suffering and loss of human life, occurring every day.

The year was 1950. The United States was at war with the Communists in Korea.

I sat visualising their dreadful destruction and bloodshed, the ground everywhere strewn with injured and dead soldiers. I anticipated that the minister would request that the congregation should pray for the injured, the dead and dying, and for their distressed friends and families.

I was startled to hear the next words that he uttered: "Let us pray for our American soldiers and the UN troops that support them." I queried this request. Should our sympathy be directed specifically to those who uphold the same political beliefs?

As good Christians should we be taking sides at all? Surely all suffering human beings are worthy of empathic consideration.

This sermon was the first step in compelling me to realise that the church could be as secular as all the institutions surrounding it, the difference being that educational, social, and political institutions were especially designed to deal with the problems of the mundane world. The church was meant to be a beacon, set aside from the morass of worldly matters, to act as a spiritual guide and a moral compass for ordinary mortals. It was definitely not erected to function from a position determined by the latest headlines or the present political situation.

I had reached a point in my development where I was trying to define my own moral guidelines. While trying to establish the basis for my own beliefs, and examining the church's application of its beliefs, more chinks and doubts about my Christian faith were beginning to appear.

The minister's partisan, political approach to compassion for the dead and dying soldiers seriously disturbed me. I wondered whether the minister was adhering to the Christian doctrines that he espoused.

This incident created my first serious doubt about how the church actually functioned. How much did those in charge, Ministers, Bishops and Archbishops, attempt to apply their beliefs to the wider world in which we live, and how much was their outlook formed by the politics of the day?

THE CHURCH – THE SOCIAL SIDE

Aside from attending the Sunday church service, I was not engaged in any other church activities, nor had I established any social ties within the church community.

The teenagers there were superficially friendly, not antagonistic to the presence of black parishioners (there were very few), but they remained distant and aloof. We were never invited to join the singing groups, the dramatic society or any of the other numerous church activities.

We were always free to join ourselves, without invitation, but were not inclined to do so. The teenagers who were members of these groups were the children of the intellectual elites of Cambridge and Boston: lecturers, musicians, businessmen, politicians, teachers, doctors, all of whom were well aware of their privileged positions in society.

They quite ostensibly and politely chose to maintain the status quo, and we had no desire to make inroads into such well-established, exclusive cliques.

Occasionally, the minister attempted to apply Christian morals to everyday situations. During one Sunday sermon, he admonished those who prevent black people form moving tinot the more desirable housing areas in Cambridge.

I don't know if her was aware of the practices of real estate agents, who denied black people access to housing, except for specified areas in Cambridge. Or was her referring to the congregation in the totally exclusive, all white, leafy neighbourhoods, whose populace resided in massive, mostly white colonial houses surrounded by large, well-kept gardens, often within but also beyond the perimeter of Harvard Square.

It was a noble task to take a stance against this form of prejudice, but it was, at best, an inconvenient, uncomfortable observation, unlikely to be acted upon by anyone in the entire parish. It might have been a more effective stand if he had asked the congregation – who would be willing to live next door to a black family.

No white church member had ever extended the hand of friendship to any but their own white friends. But he may well have known just how far he could push his critique of the social habits of the good Christians assembled.

Three factors: my evolving doubts about which aspects of Christianity I was prepared to believe; criticism of what I saw as the church's erratic moral stance on important social issues; and the less than welcoming reception of my peer group at the church, were responsible for my decision to dissociate from the church.

But it was overwhelmingly the huge discrepancy between the church's Christian values, and how it overlooked the need for their implementation in everyday life, which I found most hypercritical. It was predominantly this realisation that finalised my resolve to sever my relations with the Episcopalian Church forever.

COLLEGE ENTRY

Before I started to fill in the applications forms for college, I was well aware that my chance of gaining admission to any college was very low. Every college and university had quotas aimed at limiting the number of black, and Jewish students. (1)

Out of 300 applicants, the yearly intake for most colleges was 2 black students. Boston University which had a higher yearly intake of students, allowed a slightly higher quota. The maximum allowance for Jewish applicants was about 10%. Historically, Catholics had been considered less desirable than Protestant applicants by college admissions departments.

To combat this type of discrimination, in 1863, the Catholics had founded Boston College. For the same reason, Jews had founded, in 1945, Brandeis University in Waltham, MA. There was no similar institution established for black students in Boston or in the northern US at all.

Amongst minority groups, the size and existence of quotas was common knowledge and evident from the very small number of these students accepted at colleges every year. White students were totally unaware of these admissions policies. If the subject were broached, they would argue vehemently, as loyal Americans, against their existence and never considered that quotas would ever be allowed.

We learned not to discuss such topics, even with our very good white friends. The consistent act of outright denial was too great a hurdle to overcome.

The college application forms were designed to detect ethnicity. Of the 3 references required, it was suggested that one should be submitted by the applicant's religious leader, possibly leading some to think that they wanted to take in only moral, upright, and honest citizens.

A recent photograph of the applicant was obligatory.

As my friend, Brenda and I had noted, there would be no question about her ethnicity once she supplied the name of her rabbi.

Nor would there be any questions about my origins, or more precisely, what I was not, once they had seen my photograph. I was most certainly not a White, Anglo-Saxon.

A SMALL DIGRESSION

I must mention here the Seven Sisters Colleges. They were the private, elite women's colleges in the north, renowned for their academic excellence. Radcliffe, to which I was applying, was one of this esteemed group.

In the late 19th century, it was not mandatory to include photographs with application forms. A few individuals who were very fair, but had some African ancestry, were unknowingly admitted to some of the Seven Sisters Colleges, to the consternation of trustees, faculty, and students. These events occurred at a time when there was strong opposition to black women attending white colleges, particularly the Seven Sister Colleges.

I have no doubt that photographs became an entry requirement to prevent further surreptitious admissions of undesirable students, though I can find no printed or written evidence to this effect.

Undoubtedly, the aforementioned women, with fair skin would never be detected by the submission of a photograph as they looked totally white, any African ancestry was in no way obvious or evident. But those whose colour was more conspicuous would be more easily recognised.

My church affiliation, Episcopal and Protestant, would be deemed highly acceptable for admissions procedures. Christ Church, in Harvard Square, Cambridge, MA., whose congregation included many families associated with worthy educational institutions, the most well-known being Harvard and Radcliffe College.

This group, Protestant, well-educated and often wealthy, was the one whose children were considered the most desirable, prospective, college students.

Despite the fact that I attended their church, I was not one of them. I was well aware that race would always predominate over religion in the hierarchy of rejection.

Most colleges openly acknowledged their preferences for legacy alumni, the children and descendants of the privileged graduates. Their parents, through generous contributions to college funds, wielded a disproportionate influence over who was acceptable for college entrance. As the trustees of these institutions readily admitted, the children of these already advantaged families were given precedence over other applicants, no matter how intelligent or deserving. (2)

These two policies, quotas, and legacy preferences, based on ethnicity, race and class prejudice, were the weighty obstacles we had to overcome before the merit of our academic qualifications could even be considered for college entry.

Increasing the numbers of black college and university students did not come without its problems. When more black students were admitted to universities, many were segregated and forced to live separately from the white students.

On the 5th of February 1952, I, along with other residents of Cambridge, MA, was alarmed to read that a cross was burned in front of Stoughton Hall where black students of the class of 1955 resided. (The burning cross is recognized as a very powerful hate image. The Ku Klux Klan in the southern US always used it as symbol to terrorise black people).

Two first year Harvard students had perpetrated this deed, but they received no serious penalties for their behaviour and the university did not reveal their names. Any black student who reported this incident to the media in Boston was threatened with suspension.

Because the two individuals working for the Harvard society for Minority Rights refused to censor the news, the incident was reported in two Boston newspapers. The Crimson (the Harvard news chronicle) and The New York Times and in other parts of the USA. and internationally. (3)

REFERENCES

1) The Long Ugly History of Racism at American Universities by Leslie M Harris printed in the New Republic—26 March 2015

"Following the Civil War, historically white colleges, North and South, diverged only slightly in their willingness to admit non-white students. These schools also limited or prevented the enrolment of other groups, such as non-Protestant Christians or Jews.

Quota systems were used by universities in the north.

In the south, legal segregation prevented black students from attending colleges and universities. In northern schools, quota systems limited the number of blacks who could attend.

In both the North and South, schools limited the enrolment of non-Protestant Christians, such as Catholics, and Jews, among other groups. These practices reinforced racial and religious hierarchies until the late twentieth century."

2) The History of University Admissions, Review by Laurence Veysey, Source: Reviews in American History, Mar., 1980, Vol.8. No. 1 (Mar., 1980), pp. 115-121

Published by: The Johns Hopkins University Press—p 116

"Racial preferences are only the most flagrant among a whole series of preferential categories which are endemic to admissions decisions, whether to the undergraduate college or to professional schools in such prestigious areas as law and medicine...

Among colleges, one immediately thinks of the long tradition of giving preferences to athletes, to prospective students from particular geographical areas, to sons of alumni, recommended by local alumni committees as being of unusually "good character."

"But the single largest point that emerges from the new evidence on university admissions... is the relative absence of meritocracy in admissions decisions made during this century and, instead, the existence of a mutual interplay among...admission factors, most of them extraneous from the point of view of the students' intellectual abilities...

Instead, the traditional aim of our most prominent universities was to place the renewal of a social elite ahead of all other considerations.,..."

3) This information was retrieved from The Crimson—Cross Burning in Harvard Yard by Chester Harris—September17, 2014

The Crimson is a Harvard University student run publication.

THE RADCLIFFE INTERVIEW, BOSTON COLLEGE AND SIMMONS

My first interview for college was at Radcliffe. As I crossed the threshold of the room, the interviewer was glancing from sheets of paper on her desk, towards me as if trying to make a connection about the information spread before her and the person entering the room.

She looked up, "Joan Allen"? "Yes", I responded. "Do take a seat." Her first question, "Why is your English mark so low?" I wanted to say that I thought that the English teacher had undervalued my essay writing. It was the only year that my English marks were so low.

Obviously, any such statement would have been perceived as the response of a very arrogant student, daring to question the teacher's competence. Common sense prohibited my answering this query honestly.

In the end, I stated that I didn't think the teacher always liked the topics I chose to write about. "What topics for example?" "Well, we were asked to write an amusing essay. I wrote about a case of mistaken identity". A long pause ensued. She didn't pursue the subject and conversation on this topic ended rather abruptly.

"Why was my French mark so high?"

"I see that your mother is Canadian. Do you speak French at home?"

"No, no, I don't"

I was surprised at the next question. "Did any of my grandparents come from a foreign country?"

"No, they hadn't." A question raised because, possibly, she was not 100% sure of my ethnicity.

Due to my mixed-race background, I have often been mistakenly identified as belonging to a variety of different groups, Italian, Jewish, Egyptian, South American, etc., but never an accurate guess about my true ancestry.

Well, that was it!! Two questions about my marks, one about what language I might speak at home and one about the origin of my grandparents. All further discussion was as follows:

"Do you know that there are many colleges in Boston to which you can apply. You only have to write to the college requesting the application forms. If you experience any difficulty, I'm sure your school can help."

She then began listing the many institutions in Boston and the subjects in which they excelled. Listing the colleges and repeating her statement that I must write to the colleges for application forms consumed my remaining interview time.

Never a question about why I had wanted to attend Radcliffe or what I might want to study.

It was blatantly clear that I had been rejected there and then. Those 4 perfunctory questions were hardly meant to assess my merits as a candidate. What I found most distressing was that no interview had even taken place. Most of the specified time was spent with the interviewer trying to dispose of me, trying to send me to any college in the vicinity to study, to any college other than Radcliffe.

Not a very promising start for college admissions.

I left the premises feeling downhearted, wondering if I had claimed foreign grandparents, would that have dismissed any doubts about my background?

Could I then have been considered a worthy candidate for a genuine college interview?

Or had she decided that I belonged to that class of students considered undesirable and accepted only by quotas? Given the dismissive, desultory manner in which she conducted the interview, I concluded that I had been assigned to this unwelcome, unsatisfactory category and was, therefore, considered unsuitable for admission.

After Radcliffe, I had two more interviews. Despite my low grades in English, I realised that this fact hadn't prevented me from being considered as a prospective student. I left both of the following interviews feeling more hopeful about the possibility of college entrance.

Both Simmons College and Boston University accepted me and in addition, Boston University offered me a scholarship.

In spite of the fact that I needed the money, I accepted the offer from Simmons College. Because the classes were smaller, I felt that fewer students would create a more intimate atmosphere and allow more space for a proper exchange of ideas through debate and discussion.

Without doubt, the fact that my friend, Jeri, was already a student there strongly influenced my decision to accept this offer.

MY DIFFICULT ENGLISH TEACHER and A NOTABLE EVENT

At the end of the year, my very difficult English teacher requested that each student should state which college had accepted them. When my turn arrived, I was truly gloating and with a wry smile of malicious delight, replied "Simmons College", while secretly thinking "No thanks to you."

I thought that maybe three years of Latin might have stood me in good stead. We were always told that colleges preferred students who studied Latin.

But above all, I was convinced that my SAT results had prevailed over her devious methods to discredit me. Since Boston University had offered me a scholarship, I must have performed well.

The teacher looked at me blankly and reiterated, "Simmons College" with what I assumed was a note of disbelief. After what may have appeared to her my inconceivable and incomprehensible response, no further words were uttered.

A NOTABLE EVENT

As I was delighting in my success at being accepted at two colleges with very good reputations, I was suddenly dismayed to read an article in the local paper. It stated that Margarita Ericson would be a student in the freshman class at Radcliffe College.

Up to the age of 13, Margarita Ericson had been a student in many of my classes. I recalled that she lived very near the school in the very desirable middle-class neighbourhood and that her father was an architect.

The reason that I remembered these two details was that I always found it an anomaly that someone from such a prestigious, academic background should perform so badly in all of her school subjects.

In our last year of high school, she suddenly appeared in my English class. Apparently, she had transferred from a private school where her marks had not been outstanding. The same assessment could be made of her performance in our English class.

I was astounded!! How could someone with no evident ability in any subject be accepted at Radcliffe? I who had a good academic record was never even considered as a prospective student and this young woman, slow to learn and slow to understand, was considered preferable and offered a college place.

Her acceptance only demonstrated what disastrous choices can be made when prejudiced opinions and family influence determine policy instead of academic ability.

My only satisfaction resided in the knowledge that their retribution would be that "they would deserve what they got." This particular individual had little chance of success in an institution which prided itself on having students who consistently performed to very high academic standards. It would be to her detriment and theirs when she failed to meet their lofty expectations.

THE QUAKERS

One weekend while sauntering through Harvard Square, Jeri and I saw an advertisement for a conference sponsored by the American Friends Service Committee (otherwise known as the Quakers). The speakers were discussing issues related to American Foreign Policy and Communism, highly relevant topics at the time.

Jeri and I arrived early, in hopes of finding out more about the AFSC, an organisation with which we were totally unacquainted and to attend the conference. Quite inadvertently, we met a well-informed middle-aged man who answered all our questions about Quakers and The American Friends Service Committee. He turned out to be Russell Johnson, the official organiser for all their conferences.

Because it had been a spontaneous decision to attend the conference, I had arrived, to my chagrin, with not quite enough money for the entrance fee. Russell, very graciously, overlooked this fact, but afterwards, with a smile on his face, always referred to me as: "the young lady in distress."

The meeting with Russell proved to be a truly serendipitous occasion. Over time, he and his wife, Irene, became very close friends. Irene and I attended art classes together. In the evening, she worked as a nurse, and I became the regular baby-sitter for their 3 children.

Irene was a Quaker and Russell (though not a Quaker) had been a conscientious objector during the Second World War, performing ambulance duties instead of fighting at the front. Both were about 15 years older than I was. They became political sounding boards against whom I could bounce my endless questions and slowly changing political opinions.

The young Quaker group and the AFSC conferences were the arenas where I was exposed to different ideas and different interpretations of the world of politics. I had generally accepted the government's interpretation of political events. But armed with new facts and new questions, my undisputed political stance slowly altered to one of challenging the conventional government perspective and ultimately led to a more considered, more radical approach to politics.

THE CONCEPT OF NON-VIOLENCE RESISTANCE

I had encountered the concept of non-violent protest when, during my second year at college, I read Thoreau's Essay on Civil Disobedience. He refused to pay taxes to a state which supported slavery and was engaged in a battle of which he disapproved, the Mexican-American War. As a consequence, he was sent to prison, a punishment which he was prepared to endure.

Later, when I joined a Quaker youth group, I began to explore the concept of non-violence in greater depth. For the first time, I actually saw an example of a non-violent protest enacted in real life. It was a film of the Salt March of 1930 which was an act of civil disobedience, or satyagraha, as the Indians described it. It was led by Mahatma Gandhi to publicly object to the tax on salt which the British had imposed on the entire population of India.

The Indians were prohibited from collecting and selling salt. Those jobs were confiscated by the British in order to create a sizeable revenue for the British Government.

Gandhi's few dozen followers slowly augmented in each village in which he spoke until the few dozens of protestors reached tens of thousands by the time they had reached the town of Dandi, on the Arabian Sea. From being a powerless, oppressed group of individuals, they were transformed into a confident, authoritarian group of people, demanding just treatment in the face of a firmly entrenched colonial power.

In the 1960's, I reached a deeper understanding of the power of non-violence when I supported the activities of the Civil Rights Movement. Viewing the fortitude and restraint of non-violent demonstrators, standing firm in the face of unrelenting violence, engenders both awe and admiration for such feats of heroic courage.

HISTORY OF THE LATE 1940'S

World War Two had ended in May, 1945. The US had dropped atomic bombs on Hiroshima and Nagasaki and thereby ended the war with Japan.

Britain, the United States, and Russia had together defeated the Germans. In July 1945, the three great allies met in Potsdam. The cohesion that had existed previously amongst them had disappeared, once the common enemy, Germany, had been defeated.

Their differences had become so wide, an irreparable gulf appeared which severed their former alliance forever. There were a few problems: 1) No free elections were taking place in Poland as had previously been agreed by the three of them. Britain and the US feared that this outcome was due to Russian intervention in the political process. They were concerned that the communists were definitely taking control of Eastern Europe.

As Franklin D. Roosevelt had died, Harry S. Truman was now president of the US. He had sanctioned the dropping of the two atomic bombs in Japan.

2) The second problem was that Stalin was an ally but he felt betrayed by the activities of the US. He had not been informed of the development of the atomic bomb nor had he been consulted about the bombing the two cities in Japan. Relations between the Allies continued to deteriorate.

In 1946, Churchill condemned Stalin for securing even greater control Eastern Europe. He designated Stalin's new lines of demarcation in Europe as the "Iron Curtain." The Cold War had truly begun.

The predicaments that had created the contentious political activities of the late 1940's and 1950's were determined by Stalin's distrust of the West and fear on the part of the West that, not only, was communism spreading around the world, but also, the fear that communists might attempt to take over the US.

Suspicion and fear augmented on all sides. Both Russia and the United States began to use more subtle and elusive methods to gain access to information about enemy activities. The era of espionage and spying had now begun.

In 1945, HUAC (the House Un-American Activities Committee) was established to investigate any real or likely communists that might be in any influential positions in the US.

In 1948, HUAC investigated the case of Alger Hiss, a US State Department official who was accused of spying for the Soviet Union. He adamantly denied the charges throughout his life. A first trial ended in a hung jury but in a second, he was convicted of perjury and served 44 months. It was such a controversial case that it left historians disputing his guilt or innocence for many years. It was this notorious trial that paved the way for Senator Joseph McCarthy to commence his relentless pursuit of communism.

HOW MY BELIEFS CHANGED

Most US citizens, including me, were firm in their stance against communism. The government informed us that the Communist were attempting to annihilate the United States and there was evidence that spies were operating within the country. Senator McCarthy set up HUAC (the House un-American Activities Committee) to investigate what he saw as the widespread influence of communism.

The McCarthy hearings relating to charges against the army were televised in 1954. It was the first congressional inquiry to appear on national television. The House Un-American Activities Committee (HUAC), McCarthy's questioning style and his examination techniques were visually presented to the entire nation.

Despite the presence of spies in the US, I was shocked by McCarthy's public performance. Once seen on TV, I decided that he was a raving maniac and couldn't believe that the US public had allowed him to gain such power.

The dictionary definition of a demagogue could not have described him more accurately, i.e., "a leader who wins support by appealing to people's prejudices, rather than by reason", prejudices, I must add, that he had helped to create.

It was meant to be a harmless joke that we all saw "Reds under the beds", but given the state of public paranoia that prevailed, such thoughts were not far from the true feelings of many.

Despite the fear that McCarthy had engendered, once his appalling investigative techniques were revealed, newspapers reported that the general public was alarmed by his rudeness. Any individual who came before him was publicly bullied and attacked remorselessly. He pressurised them to "name the names", to declare anyone who might be a suspect in his eyes. Any hesitation meant that they would be labelled "red", a communist. This label would ruin their reputation before a word could be uttered in their defense.

It eventually became evident that the man who purported to be defending America's democratic freedoms was quite literally destroying them, before our very eyes.

In March 1954, Edward R. Murrow, a journalist, who hosted a TV series, "See It Now", launched a bold attack on McCarthy and his trial by innuendo. Stating, "We must never confuse dissent with loyalty", "accusation is not proof...proof depends upon evidence and due process of law." Murrow was credited with helping to destroy McCarthy's reputation and reign of terror.

McCarthy's influence began to collapse and in 1964, the Senate condemned him on two counts, firstly, for failing to cooperate with an investigative committee by repeatedly abusing members trying to carry out their duties. Secondly, for bringing the Senate into dishonour and disrepute.

By this time, he was generally considered to be a man without honour, particularly by those who believed in freedom of speech.

TRUMAN and THE RUSSIANS

We were all aware that President Truman had not informed the Russians about the development of atomic weapons. If asked, I would have supported this policy, on the grounds that the Russians could not be trusted. Much later, I realised that there were serious consequences related to Truman's decision.

It provided Stalin with a genuine reason to suspect western intentions. After all, he was ostensibly in alliance with the west. With the US owning very superior weapons, he felt vulnerable and feared an American attack.

I now accepted that US refusal to share nuclear secrets with the Russians had directly contributed to the intensity of hostility during the Cold War. Slowly, I was widening my perspective on the causes for the entrenched enmity between the East and the West.

For the first time, I had to admit that serious reasons existed for mutual distrust. It was not always a simple case of "the good West versus the evil East", as had always been presented to us in the media and in government statements.

NEW PERSPECTIVES ON COMMUNISM

It was not until I read John Reed's book, "The Ten days That Shook The World" that I understood the historical context from which communism arose and ultimately, acknowledged that, in some instances, people might have a genuine desire to become communists.

John Reed was an American journalist who witnessed the events preceding and during the Russian October revolution of 1917. Though the rural peasants were no longer serfs, they endured dreadful economic and social conditions. I found myself strongly supporting the case for the beleaguered and downtrodden peasants within the society against the autocratic, oppressive Czar.

Reed describes how the peasants, with the help of the soldiers, led by Lenin and the Bolshevik Party, overtook the Russian state and forced the Czar to resign.

Although Reed acknowledged that he was partisan and supported the Bolsheviks, his description of actual events is objective enough for him to include criticism of some acts of the new revolutionary government.

While reading this book, to my utter surprise, I found myself advocating the rights of the peasants, workers, and soldiers to overthrow the corrupt regime of the Czar, in order to establish a new communist state.

According to Marxist, Leninist ideology, this state was meant to establish a socialist order. Through class conflict and revolutionary struggle, the community (the proletariat) would own the means of production. Private ownership would be abolished, and they would attempt to create a classless society.

A society where everyone has the same rights and status and where the means of production is owned in common were worthy aims with which many people were in accord. Many were attracted to the Communist Party because of its favourable stance toward equality and the labour unions and their opposition to fascisim and war. Even I who had been such a firm anti-communist, felt that I could support such a vision.

Unfortunately, observing the societies defined as Communist at the time, in particular, Russia and China, I saw states controlled by one authoritarian party which determined all the important aspects of how the society functioned, controlling the economic and political systems and by means of repressive treatment, forcing citizens to comply with their demands.

Considering these distressing facts, I concluded that a truly Marxist, Communist State had not yet been implemented anywhere in the world. Those states deemed "communist" were the antithesis of the kind of society that Marx had so idealistically proposed.

THE SPIES

During the trail of the alleged spies, Ethel and Julius Rosenberg, in some quarters, serious doubt arose as to whether Ethel had ever been involved with spying.

When considering just punishment for convicted spies, a general consensus maintained that execution was the appropriate treatment.

It was one of the reasons that, in 1953, I, along with thousands of others, signed a petition requesting a stay of execution for the Rosenbergs.

The danger of enforcing capital punishment includes the risk of implementing a sentence that cannot be rescinded. We do know of innocent people who have been executed in the past.

In the case of the Rosenbergs, David Greenglass's testimony sent his sister and brother-in-law to the electric chair. Many years later, David Greenglass confessed that his sister was innocent. She had not typed the notes for the Soviets as he had testified. Through other independent sources, it was verified that Julius Rosenberg was a spy.

David Greenglass's defense was that he had lied to save his wife and children. I do wonder what sense the Rosenberg's children ever made of their uncle's testimony.

Klaus Fuchs was undoubtedly guilty of passing US secrets to the Soviets. In 1957, Roger and I moved to Vermont where we became friendly with a Quaker family who lived not far away. The wife turned out to be the sister of Klaus Fuchs. We did discuss the reasons why her brother chose to share atomic secrets with the Russians.

He, as well as other scientists working on the atomic bomb, questioned the wisdom of only the West having possession of such a lethal weapon. There was a strong sentiment among some scientists that only when atomic information was shared internationally, could world peace be maintained, when some kind of equilibrium between the antagonistic nations could be established.

Up to this point in time, it had never occurred to me that it was possible to pass atomic secrets to the Russians for pacific and well-meaning objectives (i.e., to maintain world peace) and not primarily for hopes of establishing communist world domination.

THE SCIENTISTS

J. Robert Oppenheimer, who had helped to develop the atomic bomb, represented the dilemma in which scientists were placed after the war had ended. Seeing the consequences of their scientific endeavours, the dreadful destruction of cities and the long-lasting insidious injuries inflicted on human beings, led him and many of his colleagues to question the continued uses of such weapons.

After the war, Robert Oppenheimer opposed the development of the even more powerful Hydrogen Bomb. He was accused of being a communist and lost his influential position within the scientific community.

In 1945, after the two atomic bombs had been dropped on Japan and the Japanese had surrendered, I joined the entire nation in rejoicing because the war had ended. At that time, the American public had no realistic idea of the immensity of the destructive nature of atomic weapons.

Some of the scientists who developed the atomic weapons were the first to question their use. Though discredited by the government, it was difficult to ignore their genuine concern for the widespread loss of life and fear of the consequences if the weapons were used again.

With information gathered from many sources, I began to re-examine my attitudes and beliefs regarding the detonation of the atomic bombs. I attended lectures and conferences where these issues were discussed and read scientific and political articles delineating the pros and cons of the subject.

One has to remain in awe of anything that forces us to stare death in the face. The destructive power of the atomic weapons was of a totally different magnitude to the weapons used previously.

My initial reaction of joy that the war had ended with the dropping of the atomic bombs slowly changed into feelings of apprehension and fear, because now the two great superpowers were now in possession of these weapons.

If atomic bombs were ever to be used, Russia and the United States would be capable of committing genocide and the extinction of all life as we know it, from the face of the earth.

SUMMER JOB

Having worked for two years after school and during the summer holidays at Widener Library, I was finally forced to relinquish my job. An afternoon class at Simmons College, a 3-hour biology lab, meant that I could no longer work the hours required.

As I was enrolled in the pre-med course, I wanted to experience how I functioned in a hierarchical, medical environment. I found a summer job as a nurse's aide in the Boston-Lying-In Hospital, a maternity hospital in Boston which pioneered many advanced programs in the practice of obstetrics.

It was not considered a prestigious job-a step above that of the cleaners. The pay was low, but if I worked from the end of June to the first week in September, I could earn enough money to pay for half of my college tuition for the following year and my parents would pay the rest.

As the head nurse considered me too young to work the night shift. (I was 16, 17 in two weeks). I worked the 7am to 3pm shift every day. On the night shift (3 to 11 pm), I would not have arrived home until midnight. She assumed it was far too dangerous for me to travel alone on the subway at that time of night.

At 5:00 am, the alarm clock invariably shattered my sleep. After morning ablutions, I jumped into my pale, yellow uniform and walked briskly to the bus stop. After a ten-minute ride, I caught the subway train to Boston. I then switched from the train to a tram. After a short tram ride and another short walk to the hospital, my journey ended when I arrived at the hospital and punched in my 6:45 arrival time.

Initially, we had a short course of training to teach us our duties on the wards. We learned to make a hospital bed: i.e., each sheet must be absolutely flat, no wrinkles and totally squared corners. We then learned to change a bed with an immobile patient in it. We sorted and put away the hospital linen, cleaned the patient's basin, mirror and shelves, learned to give bed pans and bed baths and to take the patients pulse and temperature.

I found none of these jobs difficult and was occasionally reprimanded for talking too long with patients, only for the nurse to discover that I had already finished my tasks and was not shirking my duties.

I gained a reputation for being a fast worker, but it was not always to my advantage as everyone was always finding new jobs for me to do.

One of the perks of the job was that nurses' aides were allowed to see a live birth if they so desired. I was most definitely interested in taking up this offer. Having already bought an old copy of the nurses' handbook of obstetrics, I was trying to amass as much information as possible about the process of birth.

Finally, the day arrived when I was told to go to the appointed floor to view a delivery. As I was merely an observer and not expected to assist in any way, I had time to peruse the entire labour ward.

To my surprise, in every bed, there seemed to be a woman moaning or screaming. It was the year, 1950, and it was considered a great medical advantage that women were administered medication for childbirth.

As I glanced around, I concluded that this procedure must occur at a later of stage of labour because I saw no-one who was not suffering unbearably.

One woman had been given some form of medication, but before it could take effect, she jumped from the bed and ran towards a window.

Staff caught her and subdued her by strapping her to the bed until the medication could affect a more tranquil state.

I was perturbed, alarmed and in a state of shock, if this is what it was like to give birth to a baby, I would happily forgo this blessing.

One of the nurses eventually led me to the bed of a woman who was ready for delivery. She had been given pain relief and exhibited no dreadful signs of distress. With each contraction, she pushed as hard as possible to expedite the baby's birth.

It was unbelievable, watching the crowning of the baby's head, emerging inch by inch and slowly growing larger until suddenly, it seemed to pop out, guided by the doctor's hands, not a sound, only a beautiful head with a layer of dark, wet hair, two more pushes and the shoulders and the body gently slipped out. The doctor was holding a perfect, very, small human being.

After a minute or two, a loud cry emerged with everyone exclaiming what strong lungs he had. I was totally entranced and overcome with awe. I had actually witnessed the miracle of birth. When I left the hospital, I was still in a stunned and exuberant state. I arrived home full of enthusiasm, eager to tell my mother that I had actually seen a baby being born.

My mother's reaction was one of astonishment and disbelief. I was far too young to experience anything to do with the birth of a baby. How could the doctors have allowed this to happen?

I explained that it was part of my training as a nurse's aid, as we were working in a maternity hospital. As my revelation slowly sank in, my mother became progressively more and more pale. But in no way did her response diminish my pleasurable reaction to the situation. I felt somewhat unsettled by her shocked protestations and sad that we could not share this joyous experience together.

But she was still viewing me as her innocent little girl, while I was already feeling more of an adult than ever.

A week later, when I was given my list of patients, I was warned that one was unusual". She wanted to do everything for herself and refused the help of the staff. Every patient I had met was reclining in bed, exhausted, and was recovering from the medication they had been given for pain relief, so her behaviour was exceptional.

When I opened the door, the "unusual" patient greeted me warmly and was very communicative. She was not at all groggy and was walking around the room. In the corner of the room, was a bassinet and in it was her baby, sleeping peacefully and quietly.

All babies always remained in the nursery. "Best cared for there, until their mothers regained their strength and could look after them properly," the head nurse would inform the patients.

This patient told me her story. She had convinced her doctor to allow her to try natural childbirth, birth without any medication and had succeeded in this endeavour. Because she was not suffering from the after-effects of pain-relieving drugs, the doctor had convinced the head nurse that the patient was completely capable of looking after the baby and herself. It occurred to me that the title of the hospital, the Lying In Hospital, was a total anachronism in relation to how this patient was functioning.

The Boston Lying In Hospital was considered advanced in its approach to childbirth, but in 1950 and 1951, neither doctors or nurses were acquainted with the concept of "natural childbirth."

This patient was obviously a pioneer in the field and proved to be a great source of inspiration as a model for me in the future.

MY FIRST WHITE DATE

I had been attending political conferences, rallies and meetings organised mostly by the Quakers. I had met many interesting young men but as none of them were black, I had no intention of dating them.

The injunction never to cross the colour line had been strongly instilled in me, not just by my parents but was also doubly reinforced by the firm beliefs and immobile structures within the white society that I inhabited. Just the thought of committing such a forbidden act filled me with dread.

Who would willingly traverse the intransigent prohibitions of the colour bar? I, for one, had no intention of changing such well-established customs.

I was perfectly happy to have endless discussions and arguments about issues related to war and peace, the latest government policy, the most practical ways to effect change within society etc., with my white male acquaintances. These were entirely cerebral relationships based on intellectual exchange and I was content that they should remain so.

All was well, until one day, a young white doctor, a Quaker, asked me to go on a date with him. I was struck dumb. Had I heard correctly? What did he say? He couldn't have asked me to go out with him. He just couldn't do that!!

My mind ricocheted back and forth, between shock and incredulity to annoyance and irritation. He wasn't allowed to ask such a question. How dare he? Even if he had grown up in a foreign country, I knew he'd lived in the USA long enough to know the social rules.

He was attempting to transgress forbidden territory, with no discussion or any kind of argument. He was behaving as if there were no problem in interracial dating. His cavalier approach to the issue unnerved me. I was too unsettled by his question to even think of a reasonable answer. I thought that my perplexed, unbelieving expression and my inability to respond should have made him question the wisdom of his request.

But he persisted. I heard him asking me again, "Beverly, would you like to go to a concert on the Esplanade with me this weekend?"

I panicked. Maybe, I could put him off. I said I would have to check my appointment book when I returned home, (as if I might be inundated with numerous dates this weekend). I knew he would ring me at home, and I would be forced to give him an answer. I had only postponed the problem briefly and didn't know how to respond.

If I said "No, I was busy", he might ask me out again. I couldn't put him off forever. I was beginning to feel trapped into going out with him because I couldn't think of a convincing reason to say no.

It was impossible to tell him the true reason for my reluctance to go out with him. It would have sounded ridiculous and been embarrassing to relate that I wasn't allowed to date him because he was white. It was indeed a ludicrous, absurd idea when I repeated it to myself, and I knew he would find it so.

It seemed easier to go on the date than to face up to possible continual requests from Paul and continued rejections from me. That would move the problem to a different level. In the circumstances, I, very reluctantly, felt that accepting the date was my most expedient decision and it would certainly prevent me from having to concoct endless false reasons for not obliging his requests.

During the summer, the conductor, Arthur Fiedler, and the Boston Pops Orchestra performed free public concerts on the Esplanade, a park which meanders along the banks of the Charles River in Boston. What could be wrong with sitting on the grass, listening to some light classical music on a summer's evening with Paul?

Paul phoned and I agreed to the date. I was annoyed that he had pushed me into a state of unease and confusion, but also flattered that he had asked me out.

The next overwhelming problem was how to tell my parents of this disgraceful decision. For a few days, I walked around in a daze, rehearsing the most appropriate way of informing them. I finally concluded that there were no appropriate words to deal with the situation. They would, undoubtedly, be very upset.

I was terrified. I waited until half an hour before Paul was due to arrive to say anything at all. I, then told them that I had a date with a doctor who wanted to take me to a concert on the Esplanade. He was a Quaker, he worked in a hospital in Boston and (after a very long pause), he was white.

Suddenly, the world around me totally erupted. The words that burst forth from my parents' mouths were full of contemptuous questions and dire warnings. "What was I thinking? Had I lost my senses? Was I completely out of my mind?"

Wild rage and fury bombarded me from all sides. "White men don't date black girls. There is only one thing they want from you. and that is why you say no when they ask you out."

I tried to protest that he was religious, a Quaker, and a doctor. He wouldn't dream of harming me in any way. If they met him, they would see what kind of a person he was.

"Meet him, meet him, we'll do no such thing!"

The injustice of the situation genuinely upset me. They didn't even know him. All their fears would evaporate if they would only agree to meet him. Paul was so quiet and retiring, no-one could ever assume that he would inflict harm on anyone.

Slowly, anger overcame me. They wouldn't even give him a chance. I shouted," My choice of boyfriends is constricted to a very narrow range, not white, not black, only beige or preferably fawn to creamy-white. It's rather difficult to find boyfriends within such incredibly small margins."

The doorbell rang. My parents, overcome and spent with anger, retreated to another room, refusing to have anything to do with such an unspeakable, outrageous event. I rushed to the sitting room and down the stairs to greet Paul, firmly closing the front door behind me. I was frantically trying to shed any distressing, overwrought feelings that my parents' explosive reaction had engendered in me. I decided to be as light-hearted as possible, fearing that touching on any serious emotions would reveal how distraught I actually felt.

Paul and I spent a very relaxed evening on the banks of the river, quietly absorbing the orchestra's melodious tunes. When the concert ended, we strolled along the river's edge, watching the small boats waft by, creating gentle ripples and waves against the rocky banks. As dusk descended, we decided to depart for home.

Paul walked me to my front door and deposited a piece of paper into my hand-saying "I want you to have this." On it was the William Butler Yeats poem "Wishes for the Cloths of Heaven."

"Had I the heaven's embroidered cloths.
Enwrought with golden and silver light,
The blue and the dim and the dark cloths
Of night and light and the half-light,
I would spread the cloths under your feet:
But, I being poor, have only my dreams;
I have spread my dreams under your feet
Tread softly because you tread on my dreams

I was very touched and a bit overwhelmed and not quite sure how to react.

These deeply moving feelings were too powerful to relate to the situation we were in, we hardly knew each other. The words that had passed between us in no way merited the expression of such profound sentiments.

I needn't have worried. Paul never asked me out again. I wondered if my carefree attitude had conveyed the wrong message. Had I come across as someone who didn't take anything seriously? Through my friends, the Johnsons, I later learned that he had met the lovely, Claire, (She was one of my acquaintances) and was immediately smitten with desire.

Claire informed me that she thought that Paul might be serious about their relationship. He'd given her the most beautiful poem by William Butler Yeats.

I realised then that Paul's dropping this poem into the palm of whoever was his latest date must have become a habitual act.

Given the emotional turmoil I had experienced prior to dating Paul, I was not really upset. He was certainly not smitten with me. Although we had spent a pleasant evening together, I was greatly relieved to have no more worries about inter-racial dating.

I must add a note here about the role of colour in fraternising. Dating men of a light complexion was a matter of colour preference.

For most black people, this type of colour prejudice was commonly practiced. I strongly objected to rejecting men as unsuitable dates because they were of a darker complexion.

Dating a man whose skin was dark was considered something to be avoided but it was not a totally forbidden act as it was with dating white men.

Very much later, I reflected on my parents' reaction to my dating Paul and what I considered to be their irrational behaviour. It was, after all, the only time my father had not interviewed a man who had asked me out. If he had really believed that Paul would treat me without due respect or consideration, he would have prevented me from leaving the house.

During our highly charged disagreement, I had reacted as teenagers do, by defining the situation from only my own perspective.

Although there was some truth in my critical outburst, I was ultimately forced to acknowledge that their overly emotional response was not without any reason. In the United States, there has been a long history of sexual exploitation of black women, from the time of slavery.

Women slaves in the south were always regarded as the slave owner's property, labouring as either workers in the cotton fields or as nursemaids and maids in the slave-owner's house. Regardless of their position, the slave-owner presumed that they existed for his sexual pleasure. The result was that these conquests produced increasing numbers of mixed-race slaves at no extra cost to the owner.

Although slavery had been abolished in 1865, those black people who had migrated north to escape injustice and in hopes of building a better life, encountered the more subtle racial oppression of the north. Racial prejudice and racial stereotypes were less publicly avowed, but they definitely existed. The attitudes to black women retained similar prejudiced reactions to the ones they had experienced in the south.

My parents initial outrage derived from a deep desire to keep me from harm and to protect me from any emotional or physical damage that might ensue from such an encounter.

Why would they approve of a situation that could harbour the possibility of any kind of ignominious relationship?

DATE WITH A THEOLOGICAL STUDENT

A student from Boston University School of Theology asked if he could escort me to a dance one weekend and I agreed to accompany him. He was the first black person from the southern part of the United States that I had ever dated.

As he described his reaction to living in the north, I stood amazed and incredulous. In the south, there were signs everywhere prohibiting contact between the races, separate drinking fountains, toilets, schools, and churches. In those places where black and white people might mingle, for instance, in a shop or on a bus, there were always separate areas for sitting, eating, and drinking.

I had assumed that these restrictions were a great injustice and unbearable to endure. We had no separate public facilities in the north but, in some states, there were restaurants and hotels who chose not to serve black people at all.

He saw these signs of rejection as lines of demarcation in the south, clearly defining the limits regarding the association of black and white people. He stated vociferously that, in the north, the congeniality between the races was superficial and a deceptive façade.

"People feigned friendliness, enticed you in and then set up invisible barriers, ones in their heads that you can't see, to prevent the relationship from developing any further. He stated adamantly, "At least in the south, you know where you stand."

"Whites in the north support equality and rights for everyone but want to keep a measured distance from black people. No real closeness or intimacy is allowed. White people don't really mix on an equal basis, they only talk about it."

I couldn't disagree with him. It was a very well observed and accurate description of race relations in the north. I could understand the insecurity he experienced by not knowing where the boundaries lay, but I didn't think I'd ever prefer to live with the glaring discrimination which existed in the south.

This moment of understanding between us was to prove a brief interlude in our evening together. Jim thought that a woman's first duty in life was to marry and have children. He didn't disapprove of women being educated, but family life should take precedence over any thoughts of a career.

I don't know why I was so affronted. In the 1950's there was a general consensus that a woman's first duty was to marry and have children and to be in charge of house and home. I did wonder if his attitude reflected some sort of southern chauvinism or was he just deluded? In shock, I asked," What right did any man have to decide what women should do with their lives?"

He felt it was somehow decreed in the scriptures. The discussion which followed was heated, to put it mildly.

After he escorted me home, standing in my front hall, he asked whether I believed in God. I said that I wasn't sure that he existed. Disbelief and shock ensued. It was if he had never heard such an opinion expressed before.

It may well have been true. The southern United States is famous for being much more religious than the north. (Most southerners have a religious faith.)

He then retorted, "Everyone knows that God exists." I responded, "Prove it. There are no facts or physical evidence to prove that God exists. It is a matter of faith-which is a choice you make. If you choose to believe, you don't have to deal with facts or reason. You have to take a long leap into faith, which, by definition, means belief without proof."

He made no immediate response to my challenge, but his expression changed from one of astonishment to one of growing impatience and then anger which he was barely able to control.

He calmed down enough to lean over for a good-night kiss. After this brief and alarming encounter, I stated, "And that is all." There were many young men who had what my friends and I called "Roman hands and Russian fingers "(roamin' hands and rushin' fingers) and I was having none of it.

He suddenly exploded in fury, telling me that girls in the south never behaved like this. They went all the way. I didn't know whether or not to believe him, but was now becoming almost as angry as he was.

"What kind of a minister will you make, having sex with unmarried women? Is that a Christian act? Do you call that moral behaviour?" He swore at me, swung around and opened the front door. As he stepped outside, he slammed it as hard as was humanly possible.

My immediate reaction was one of relief. That was the last I'd ever see of him. But it was not the last I would ever hear of him. A few days later, I met an acquaintance-a white Boston University theology student-with whom I had conversed at many conferences.

He said that Jim was telling the entire school of theology what an evil person I was, sexually arousing men and then denying them any further pleasure. No-one should have anything to do with me.

This young man said that he had argued with Jim because he knew me and was convinced that I would never behave in the manner which Jim was suggesting. His reaction bolstered my faith in young, honourable, white men. They definitely existed.

As a result of Jim's remonstrations, Jim's room-mate-also black- decided that I was a woman beyond reproach. He placed me on a very elevated pedestal, one of total perfection and wrote me a love poem every day for 3 months. I named these poems, all written on postcards, my "one a day brand". It was a parody of a well-known vitamin ad, the one a day pill that cured everything.

It seemed as if I had somehow, suddenly become the object of multiple realities in the minds of different men which ranged from evil temptress to saint, only demonstrating how subjective the reality and the truth of any situation can sometimes be.

LILLIAN SMITH

To pursue an understanding of the complex racial attitudes in the southern USA, read Lillian Smith's, "Killers of the Dream", written in 1945.

She was a white southern writer who wrote honestly and openly about race relations in the southern United States and as a result, was ostracised by the society in which she lived.

She states that there are three ghost relationships that will linger forever in the southern US: "the white man and the colored woman"

"the white father and the colored child"

"the white child and his beloved nurse."

A note is required here to indicate that, in the 1940's and the 1950's. the term colored was used more as a descriptive term. It did not have such strong derogatory associations with disrespect and scorn as it does today.

The author states that the significance of these "ghost relationships" is never openly admitted or recognised by either the white or black populations. She describes the impact on both black and white cultures living in communities with deep racial, sexual and class prejudices and prohibitions.

MY MOTHER'S DEATH

It was a warm summer's evening. As we all rose early in the morning for work, we went to bed at a reasonable hour, about 10:00 pm. My father, who rarely left the house in the evening, was visiting a friend, so had not yet arrived home.

The house was very quiet, only the click of a ticking clock, the occasional beep of a distant car and the muffled sound of footsteps on paving stones could be heard. In the silence, I thought I heard an unusual, indistinct sound. As I arose, I realised that it was coming from my mother's bedroom.

I rushed into the room and was alarmed to see her looking pale and weak and struggling to speak. I asked if she wanted me to ring the doctor. She nodded yes and slowly sank into unconsciousness, her eyes rolling towards her upper eyelids.

I rushed to the phone and dialled 911 for an ambulance. My father appeared just before the ambulance arrived. When I told him what had happened, he couldn't speak. He stood transfixed on the spot where he stood. After a brief interchange, everything became a jumble and a confusion of words and feelings, none of which I can remember. In a state of overwhelming dread and fear, we entered the ambulance to accompany my mother to hospital.

When we arrived at the hospital, we were ushered to a row of empty seats. We sat quietly, in a state of silent anxiety, heads down, incapable of putting into words our worst fears.

Every sound of leather heels echoing down the corridor, lifted our spirits. We assumed that news of the state of my mother's health would be imminent. We waited impatiently for what seemed hours, but no news arrived. We were told that the doctors were doing everything they could to deal with my mother's situation and that was the only information we ever received.

Eventually, we were told to return home. The nurse would ring in the morning to explain how my mother was faring.

My mother did not survive the night. The year was 1950. She was only 49. We all felt that she should have had many years ahead of her. She had suffered a cerebral haemorrhage. If she had lived, she would have been paralysed and possibly unable to speak. That was an image that none of us could accept and one that my mother would have detested. It was inconceivable that someone who had been such an active person with a highly functioning brain could accept living in a dependent and totally incapacitated state.

Our mother was a lively, energetic woman, full of life and always busy. She was the one who organised our lives and our entire household. We had flourished under her unwavering rules, her approving smile, and her reassuring comments. How were we to survive without the supportive structure that she provided for everything?

At home, she created the guidelines to which we adhered and against which we sometimes balked, only to realise, much later, that those daily rules and admonishments had constructed the reliable, to be depended upon, environment which had shaped and moulded our entire lives.

Her death created an unfathomable void in our everyday existence. We shuffled around the house in stony silence. It might have been better if we could have embraced each other and acknowledged our grief, but that was never an option.

My father found the situation so unbearable that he forbad my brother and I to cry in front of him. It was obvious that he felt that our tears would instigate his and he feared drowning in a pit of unrelenting sorrow.

The next few weeks were a misty haze of endless visitors, relatives, and friends, everyone bringing food, cooking meals, and producing order out of confusion and chaos.

At her funeral, the minister's words resounded around the church. My mind was drifting, I caught wisps of "everlasting life", "eternal joy in heaven". I envisioned her in a state of calm repose, no more cares, no more worries, in a more peaceful and tranquil universe, in heaven.

Suddenly, I found myself urgently pleading with God to make it so, to make sure that she was there. But no matter how earnestly I entreated God to send her to heaven, I reluctantly accepted that I could not will her ascension into that more holy sphere. And how could I be appealing to God, someone whose existence I had so recently questioned?

I stood motionless, unhappily realising that my anguished plea had probably fallen on silent terrain. If my mother went to heaven, it would be as a result of her fervent faith and the unshakeable beliefs of the rest of the congregation. Despite my impulsive aspirations for divine intervention, I hesitantly conceded that my mother's final resting place would have to be on earth with us.

I don't know how long we remained at home, avoiding contact with the world. My father was forced to remind us that, "Life must go on".

With his encouragement, I returned to work at the hospital. I was, after all, still expected to earn half of my college tuition which was due in the autumn term. As a family, we were all left to deal with my mother's death in our own individual ways. None of us could compensate for that huge empty space that her absence had left in our lives.

DIFFICULTIES WITH FATHER

After my mother's death, it became obvious that a great empty space dominated the centre of our family life and that our existence would never be "normal" again.

A month before my mother died, I had just turned 18 years old and had completed my first year at college. My brother was only 16 and still in high school.

Our entire lives, all our comings and goings, had been arranged and regulated by my mother. Never having been involved in the organisation of the house or the events in our daily lives, I think my father somehow expected the details of life to carry on as usual.

I was now expected to cook dinner. Although I had always assisted my mother in the preparation of meals, my mother had done all the cooking. I barely knew the rudiments of how to boil an egg.

My father was a very good cook. (He always prepared and cooked Sunday breakfast for my brother and me) and it was only under his tutelage that I learned to cook anything.

In desperation, I would ask, "Why is the fish sticking to the pan?" Without looking, he would know that the oil wasn't hot enough.

He would remind me, "Cook the corn for only 3 minutes. It's fresh, it was just picked today." "If you want to remove the skins from the tomatoes, just sit them in boiling water for a few minutes."

It was only too evident that I had much to learn as a cook. I never attempted to make bread or bake a cake, or even cook a Sunday roast.

The meals were very simple, a chop, a steak or a piece of fish, anything that required quick cooking on two sides with a green vegetable and possibly some rice or potatoes, sometimes sweet potatoes. But as they grew in the south, they were a seasonal treat. For dessert, there was mainly fruit and occasionally we treated ourselves to my mother's preserved pears, peaches or cherries stored in the cellar.

My father was deeply unsettled by my mother's death and the responsibility of bringing up two teenaged children weighed heavily upon him.

As my brother was in no way questioning or challenging my father's beliefs, he posed no problem. I was, most certainly, the object of his concern. I was leading a very different life from what he had anticipated for me.

He hadn't met my friends, Russell and Irene Johnson, but he did have their address. As Irene had returned to nursing, I babysat frequently, and my father had to know where I was.

He had met my new college friend, Arlene Baker, and Betty Lou Goldman as they both had spent the night at our house. Arlene went on double dates with my boyfriend, Jerry, and me. She was unusual because she was the only white girl I'd ever met who agreed to go on a date with a black man. She joined us for parties and the theatre and sometimes dated, Jerry's friend, Richard.

I don't know if she ever would have developed a relationship with Richard but every time they met, Richard would offer her a glass of wine. She never drank more than two glasses and then would promptly fall asleep for the entire evening. This situation occurred at least three times. Richard was so annoyed that he never asked her out again. We'll never know what might have been.

Betty Lou often joined my friend, Jeri, and me for long walks or outings to the cinema or the theatre. Both Betty Lou and Arlene lived in the college dormitories and Betty Lou was especially delighted to spend a weekend away from the dorm, just to experience a bit of life off campus. Before my mother died, she met Betty Lou when she spent a weekend in Cambridge, sleeping one night at our house and one night at my friend, Jeri's.

My father never disapproved of my friendship with Arlene and Betty Lou. As all my new friends, including Russell and Irene, were white, I think he added them to the list of things that I did differently from his "normal" expectations. Due to quotas, there were no other black girls in my college classes. I was attending the youth group at the Quaker meeting House where everyone was white and due to my burgeoning interests in politics, I frequented conferences, where, aside from Jeri, I never met any other black women or men. It was inevitable that in such circumstances, all my friends would be white.

Recently, my father had begun to be critical of my association with my friend, Jeri. He felt that she was responsible for my changing attitudes and beliefs. Whenever he made such statements, it always rankled because he gave me no credit for being able to think for myself or to make my own decisions about what I believed.

One weekend, disagreements between us rose to new heights. With a few friends from the young Quaker group, I had volunteered to go to a weekend work camp, to clean and paint as much of the conference centre as we could.

My father insisted that I couldn't go unless he knew that girls and boys slept in separated buildings. As I had no idea where anyone slept, the matter only escalated in intensity.

He called in a neighbour whose judgement he trusted. To my annoyance, she sided with my father. When my friends came to pick me up, I was forced to tell them that my father wouldn't allow me to go with them.

I spent the day feeling very disconcerted and tried to explain why I wanted to attend the workcamp.

But he had made his decision and didn't want to discuss the matter further. He then lost his temper and said: "If I didn't like it at home, I could leave". That was all I needed to hear, I could leave home. I immediately, rushed to my bedroom and packed a small bag. I was just about to pack a towel when my father said: "You can leave that here." I, very dramatically, replaced the towel in the drawer, closed my bag and proceeded towards the sitting room, gaining speed as I went along. I hastily ran down the steps and opened the front door.

The colours outside appeared slightly indistinct. It was dusk. The cold air unexpectedly hit my cheeks and brought me to my senses. My urgent departure to where? What was I doing? I stood paralysed on the veranda.

Where was I going? I had not the faintest idea. My main focus was to escape this impossible household, with my father's endless rules and regulations. I felt no elation at the thought of leaving, only distress at the thought of not knowing my next destination. I could go to my friend Jeri's house but that would be the first place my father would look.

The only alternative was the American Friends Service Committee. I knew all of the staff there as I had been doing voluntary work one afternoon a week, repackaging the air mail edition of Peace News which was flown from England weekly to send to American subscribers. And, there was a room at the top floor that was rented to two girls with whom I was friendly.

I arrived felling very downcast, explained my predicament and was given a very warm welcome. Ann offered me a spare sleeping bag and the spare mattress became my bed for the night.

In the morning, George, the director of the AFSC discussed my situation and agreed that I could remain there. But he did ask if there were any hope that my father and I could reconcile our differences. I assured him that it was unlikely.

I lived at the AFSC for over two months. During the Christmas holidays, I took a job selling sweaters in a small department store to make sure that I could pay the rent.

My brother joined me in the men's department next door. (I'm sure they were sorry to see him go as he sold more sweaters than anyone in the entire department).

I was in constant contact with my brother. The morning after I had so hastily departed, I rang him to say where I was staying. Of course, he could relay the news to my father. I lived in constant fear, worried that my father might just turn up at the front door of the AFSC and insist that I return home.

About two weeks after my departure, my father developed a serious case of sciatica. He had experienced a similar attack a few years ago. I knew how painful and restricting it could be.

I went home, offering to do the shopping and any other jobs that he required. I even ssuggested that I would return if he would relax the rules about my going out on weekends. He found that suggestion outrageous. As long as I lived at home, I would remain under his jurisdiction and accept his rules.

I did some food shopping and left. The very next week, a committee of three from the AFSC talked to me again about sorting out the differences with my father. One of the characteristics that drew me towards the Quakers was their desire and willingness to try to resolve conflict situations, trying to be fair and have regard for both sides of any issue, particularly in difficult political situations.

I had never envisioned any attempt on their part to resolve personal problems between my father and me.

They visited my father and returned to inform me that he still expected me to accept his rules without argument or confrontation. It was probably only a week later that I did actually return home.

My brother had told me that my father was thinking of consulting a lawyer. He didn't think that I could leave home legally. I asked a friend whose uncle was a lawyer to find out when parental responsibilities ceased. As I never received a clear reply, I decided that I had better return home.

I didn't want staff and friends at the AFSC to endure any more inconvenience or upheaval on my behalf. I preferred to return home under my own volition rather than have any sort of scene or legal entanglement.

On my return, the situation between me and my father was cool and distant, but not impossible as long as I followed his dictates. Life carried on as normal. I attended my classes at college, worked a second summer as a nurses' aid, continued to see my friend Jeri at college, and my boyfriend, Jerry, at weekends and went to occasional parties and dances with new dates.

I continued to attend the Quaker youth group and their conferences. After two summers of working as a nurses' aid, I changed jobs and worked as a telephone operator at the AFSC to earn money for college.

CHANGE FROM PRE-MED STUDIES TO EDUCATION COURSES

In the US, by the third year, college students must definitively choose what will be their major focus of study. There are then two years to acquire the requisite credits in their chosen subject. To become properly qualified in any field, further study at institutions of higher education, often at master's degree level is required.

During my first two years at college, I had taken a pre-med course and had one more subject to take (inorganic chemistry), when I suddenly changed my mind about wanting to become a doctor.

There were two reasons for this abrupt alteration of my plans. I found myself seriously challenged and inspired by the English literature courses I was taking. I was more attracted to and engaged with the kind of prose the author used, the choice of words, the manner in which ideas were expressed and presented, the character development, than I was with the very precise and accurate procedures of scientific experiments with which I was already familiar.

I still found the idea of becoming a doctor appealing but realised that my imagination was more highly aroused and stimulated in the pursuit of literary and artistic subjects than in scientific ones.

In addition, as I had occasionally dated medical students, I had become aware of the huge amount of memorisation required to pass four years of examinations.

I had always found that with proper concentration and application, I could usually produce the desired results. Despite this, memorising numerous facts in various subjects did not seem an inspirational act, even though I could be accomplished at it.

I was eager to explore new areas of interest, to use my brain in different ways. Poetry, art, literature, and philosophy might lead me in more novel directions, raise different questions and different ways of observing people and the wider world.

When I changed my course of study, lingering in the background was a very practical consideration. Given our difficult relationship, I was not sure that my father would continue to support my educational studies. Paying for a further four years of a very expensive medical course for a daughter whom he found challenging and difficult, might not have been what he really desired to do. But, since I had already decided to alter my major subjects, I never had to discuss this matter with him.

For my future career, I chose to pursue courses in education and decided that I would teach young children. I had always believed that young children were receptive to learning everything, whatever the topic might be.

Some were critical of my desire to teach young children, stating that it was more prestigious to teach specific subjects to older students. I was simply not interested. I was intrigued by the intrinsic desire that young children possess to explore and learn new things.

As for adolescents, I had always projected my worst fears into the idea of teaching them. I could think of nothing worse that standing in front of a class of teenagers, rebellious and resistant to imbibing any of the information I wished to impart. I was pleased to settle for engaging with the more curious, open minds of younger students.

THE DEVELOPMENT OF MY IDEAS ABOUT EDUCATION

In the course of my studies, I was introduced to many impressive educational theorists. There were three individuals with whom I felt an immediate affinity: Maria Montessori, Jean Piaget, and John Dewey.

Maria Montessori (1870-1952) found that many children classified as subnormal could perform academically as well as children of normal intelligence.

Jean Piaget (1896-1980) discovered that maturation was a prerequisite to particular stages of learning.

John Dewey (1859-1954) emphasised the importance of two sides of the educational process, the psychological and the sociological.

While these contributions were significant milestones in the history of education, I was more impressed with the fact that, independently, they had all evolved a similar picture of how children learn.

All the children these educators worked with learned mainly through exercising self-motivation and through experimenting with objects that commanded their attention.

All three concluded that engaging the child's interest appeared to be the basic premise for learning. The child was no longer the passive recipient of the teacher's knowledge but the active agent in his own learning.

Why was I so attracted to the educational approach of these particular individuals?

The world in which I had grown up had a prescribed and precise image of how children learned and how they should behave. In the 1940's and 1950's, adults exercised an authoritarian influence over children's lives. The rules for education and upbringing were directly transmitted from adults to children. What interested children was not of prime concern to either educators or adults. Children were polite and obedient and expected to accept of the parents' rules without doubt or question. My parents, whom I felt were nearly Victorian in outlook, followed this model of child-rearing.

Teachers exerted strict discipline and demanded respect and hard work from all students. The subjects we studied required prescribed answers, usually only one. Neither questions, debate, or any kind of creative activity, was encouraged to explore and expand our understanding of any subject.

There was always an implied fear that without the presence of strict rules, children would become unruly and disobedient. There was a rebellious creature lurking, ready to leap out unless kept under constant restraint.

There were noteworthy influences that had created the strict rules requiring complete obedience and exact performance. Some condemned the child's inborn qualities and abilities.

We were all religious. Christianity taught us that we were all born in Original Sin. We entered the world tarnished by innate wickedness, forever damned by the disobedience of God's first creation, Adam.

The idea of a child being uncontrollable, demanding and self-centred was promoted by the promulgation and acceptance of Freud's psychoanalytic theory. He stated that the newborn infant arrived in the world with the most primitive part of his personality (the Id) fully functioning.

Its aim was to seek immediate gratification for its biological drives - eating, drinking, eliminating waste, gaining sexual pleasure, and avoiding pain -irrespective of whether or not it was appropriate in the situation.

It is no wonder that parents, religious leaders, teachers, and social reformers supported a repressive model of child-rearing. Education was meant to condition, train and civilise the unreasonable, irrational tendencies which the child possessed, whether inborn, inherited from parents or derived from Adam, it made no difference.

I had never believed that children were innately evil and in need of consistent restraint to control their unruly tendencies. How could anyone look at an infant and see only a creature imbued with wickedness?

Underlying the basic premise of all these new educators was a constructive, very positive image of the child—one that was curious, inquisitive, eager to investigate and one who took pleasure in learning. This representation of childhood seemed to match my own, incidental observations of how children functioned.

The teacher's task was to nurture the children's curiosity and desire to explore. Praise and approval were observed to be more influential in encouraging desired behaviour than criticism or finding fault.

I found this vision of education inspiring and was determined to acquire the skills that would promote this type of learning. I felt that my own educational background had not prepared me for this type of challenging learning.

AN UNEXPECTED REVELATION

While I was adjusting to the uneasy challenge of changing my career choice mid-way through my college studies, I was, one day, completely taken aback by the English teacher's sudden, astonishing disclosure to the entire class.

Instead of directing us to take out the book related to our latest assignment, he turned to the class with firm and determined deliberation and asked, "How many of you know that all the colleges you applied to practise discrimination against black students?"

The room was suddenly consumed with silence, total silence. There was a huge intake of breath all round. And then, quite suddenly, a classful of noisy voices was clamouring for attention. Everyone erupted with protestations of denial and disbelief.

Most students were incredulous. "That's impossible. We live a democracy. Colleges wouldn't be allowed to practise discrimination against black students. It would be unconstitutional."

"All the colleges in Cambridge and Boston have policies that limit their annual intake of black students. This information is about to be revealed publicly and all the colleges are indignantly denying it."

Some students sat stunned, looking as if they were trying to take in these shocking facts. One student expressed feelings of dismay and concern.

As I was the only black student in the class, I feared that all eyes would soon be focussed on me, and everyone would expect some kind of a response.

Fortunately, in the midst of the outburst of myriad emotions, I was a forgotten figure. Everyone was too preoccupied with their own unsettled feelings, too overwhelmed to think of anything or anyone else.

I sat in total silence, inwardly reassured, that someone who was in a position to know how colleges functioned behind the scenes had revealed the truth about their clandestine, discriminatory practices.

His revelation was confirmation of what black students already knew was a common practice. Our beliefs were not paranoid projections nor were we walking around with innumerable chips on our shoulders.

A white lecturer of high esteem and in a position of authority had transmitted this unwelcome information to everyone. Though, at first, it was greeted with total disbelief, he had punctured the cosy, insular world of some white students and had created a small crack where the unpleasant reality of the actual practices of college authorities might, at least, be questioned and acknowledged and possibly, one day, even believed.

BREAKING OLD PREJUDICES

I had decided that I would date any young man who seemed interesting, pleasant, and respectable. He might already be working; he needn't have particular educational qualifications or college ambitions. As long as he was black, it wouldn't matter what colour skin he possessed. Within the black community, those of lighter complexion were considered preferable as partners.

We did not regard this as prejudice. It was simply the norm, the accepted standard of belief and behaviour that we had imbibed since birth.

Any prejudice which exists advantages some individual or group within society and therefore inevitably disadvantages others. In choosing not to follow the community's practise of acceptable behaviour, particular in relation to the choice of skin colour, I knew I was deciding to break the barriers of prejudice that some considered unassailable. I expected that my behaviour might produce mild shock and possibly disapproval within my family but that was not aim.

I just didn't see the point in including or excluding people from acquaintance or friendship on the basis of skin colour or the presence or absence of a particular type of education.

Whenever my father interviewed any individual who was not a student and already working, he never failed to produce the same response, "That boy lives from day to day. He has no ambition because he's given no serious thought to his future prospects." Obviously not to be placed on my 'to be followed up list.'

The first man with a very dark complexion whom my father interviewed, produced a revealing reaction. "You don't have to go out with everyone who asks you for a date. He seems pleasant enough, but couldn't you find someone closer to your own colour?" I responded, "Is that so important? He is a student at Boston University-studying journalism. I thought you'd approve of him."

I had assumed that my choice of dates would engender some criticism because of his skin colour but the vehemence of his rejection was unexpected. My father was blatant and unashamed in his attitude. He was attempting to uphold the prejudiced assumptions about his daughter's correct choice of partner, in which he firmly believed.

Neither of my parents had ever demonstrated any overt dislike or prejudice towards people of a darker complexion. In fact, they were very good friends with a couple who had the darkest skin I had ever seen.

It was only in relation to their daughter's boyfriend or likely suitors that skin colour became an issue.

My relations with the opposite sex were definitely becoming problematic for them to deal with. Fortunately, it was only occasionally that I spent an evening with an "inappropriate" individual. The young men were generally within the prescribed range of acceptance, medium to light skin colour and respectable high school or college students.

A DISTANT WHITE BOYFRIEND

On Sunday mornings, I often attended a Quaker meeting with my friends, Russell and Irene Johnson. When the Sunday TV religious programme broadcast the Quaker service at which I was present and my face appeared on the screen, a few neighbours became aware of my association with the Quaker Meeting House.

Various reactions of surprise and curiosity and querying my reasons for leaving the Episcopalian Church ensued. As I felt it was not a matter for their concern, I chose to answer them politely but not engage in further discussion.

Our neighbourhood consisted of black and white families living next door and across the street from each other. Most individuals on both sides of the colour bar knew a great deal about how individual families functioned, who was working, who was studying what jobs they had and what holidays they took, which teenagers had boyfriends or girlfriends and even what time they might return home after dating.

All this information derived mainly from direct observation and sometimes from occasional conversations with the people involved. Most people, with the exception of one cantankerous Irish family, were on casual speaking terms with each other.

I would describe the relationship between the races as superficially friendly as all verbal exchanges occurred when they inadvertently happened to meet on the street. There were no invitations to have a chat or a cup of coffee or tea or to step inside anyone's private abode, from either side of the racial barrier.

The racial interaction was different for the children. they accompanied each other to school, attended the same classes and eagerly joined together in after school games and activities. No problem with children in the neighbourhood being reluctant to associate with each other.

But, as soon as puberty appeared, all the adolescents retreated to their own racial groups for social contact. From both groups there was a tacit agreement between the sexes, there was to be no crossing racial boundaries.

Despite the brief interlude before puberty, this exclusive but not unfriendly behaviour would be maintained and continue to define the nature of adult racial relationships, regardless of how often the individuals in the two groups might meet.

The subtleties of prejudice were such that I had imbibed these lessons without any overt statements from either parent. Well-defined forms of prejudice became deeply implanted parental and societal injunctions.

I was deeply shocked by the first white man who asked to date me because he was breaking a racial taboo which I had no desire to abandon.

As time progressed, in my process of questioning almost everything that I had ever been taught, I was beginning to alter my outlook even further.

I had already dated a few black men who had jobs and weren't studying for a college degree. This undesirable behaviour met with mild disapproval from my parents. I think they feared that I might end up with a man who had fewer chances for success than I might have with my prospective college degree.

After much consideration and numerous discussions with my girlfriend, Jeri, I was coming to the conclusion that there was no logical reason to uphold these firmly engrained racial injunctions. It was only the entrenched prejudice of both white and black people that prohibited racial mixing.

Although I was rejecting certain ideas and attitudes with which I had been imbued, I was in no way dissociating myself from the black community, and I was still dating black men.

I had to accept the fact that I had never hated white men. I had always had open and friendly relationships with the few that I knew fairly well. I only disliked the idea of dating them and that attitude, I reasoned, was the result of unjustified prejudice.

At a conference, one weekend, when I was discussing politics with a friend, a tall young man with blond hair joined our discussion to disagree with the point I was making. When heated discussion and passionate points of view were at an end, we all unwound and began to relate to each other in a more relaxed manner. It was only then that I noticed his particularly well-chiselled features.

As he did not live in Massachusetts, he had endured a long train ride to attend the conference. He had worked in a supermarket for two years to save money before going to college. He wasn't sure what he wanted to study and had taken time out to consider his prospects.

As he lived so far away, I seldom saw Ted, but we did become fond of each other. He was a reluctant letter writer so there was little correspondence between us.

One weekend, I received a letter stating that he was coming to Cambridge to attend an AFSC conference to which I was going. He would come to my house to pick me up so we could go together.

I stood immobile, in a state of shock, remembering my parents' reaction to my first white date. It was too late to write a letter to change his arrangements. He didn't have a phone so I would just have to deal with the situation as best as I could. I would definitely have to avoid the trauma of a repeat performance of my father's shock, horror and fury at such an undertaking.

I told my father that I was meeting a girlfriend and would be home at a reasonable hour. I then inveigled my brother to help me. I described Ted as accurately as possible and posted my brother at the sitting room window.

He was to tell me when Ted was approaching, when he saw him walking down the street and how close he was to the house.

I would run down the stairs, open the front door and greet Ted before he could startle my father with the sound of the doorbell ringing. We would then casually descend the front steps and stroll down the street without my father being any the wiser.

I spent about fifteen minutes feeling terribly ill with anxiety, concerned that my father would walk into the sitting room and somehow discover my subterfuge. Fortunately, that didn't happen. My secret endeavours went according to plan.

I always started these "secret dates" brim full of anxiety and overcome with fear that my clandestine objectives would be discovered. I can't imagine what anyone dating me must have thought. I was always too flustered and embarrassed to make any excuses and tried to appear as normal as possible, not wanting to discuss family problems or my father's attitude to interracial dating.

In order to avoid my father's anger and my own fluctuating fears, I usually arranged to meet a white date anywhere but at my home. There were never more than three or four white men that I ever agreed to date.

Although Ted and I had developed a close friendship, he was so distant and wrote so infrequently that it was impossible for the relationship to develop further. I convinced myself that it was wiser not to invest in false hopes and tried to put my feelings to rest, until I next saw him.

KENNETH PATTON and THE CHARLES ST. MEETING HOUSE

It was my friend, Russell Johnson, who first suggested that I might like to attend the Charles St. Meeting House, ostensibly a church of Universalist denomination in Boston.

Russell informed me that the services were considered radical and the minister, Kenneth Patton, eccentric. His approach to Universalism was not confined to the beliefs of Christianity nor to those of the Protestant faith. His desire was to create an inclusive community, a world fellowship which included humanists, atheists, theists, and naturalists.

As we entered the Meeting House, the painting on the wall facing us instantly dominated our line of vision. It was a large mural painted by Kenneth Patton, depicting The Great Nebulae in Andromeda, one of the largest constellations that can be observed.

Hanging on the opposite wall was the depiction of an atom.

The congregation sat between the "macrocosm", the all-enveloping universe to which we all belong and the "microcosm", the atom, the smallest unit of matter from which we all derive.

The strategic location of the pews was meant to emphasise humanity's connection to both worlds.

Believing that moral truths and enlightenment did not reside in any particular person or religious group, Kenneth Patton drew his inspiration from numerous religious sources.

On the lecterns, would be, not only, the Bible and the Torah but also other religious books: the Bhagavad Gita, Native American texts, and sacred books from diverse parts of the world.

The service was appealing with its emphasis on the idea that all humanity belongs to one world. I was in total agreement with the statement that we must recognise our connection to each other and to nature, in order to avoid alienation and the possibility of future destruction.

Quite unusually, Kenneth Patton believed that Universalism should also encompass all forms of creative expression. He felt that the arts represented profound reactions to life experience and were a fundamental part of our enduring religious heritage. Around the church, many religious symbols were on display. Many I had never seen before. As I was investigating these fascinating and curious objects, a young man with a head of dark, curly hair approached me. He explained that he attended the Charles Meeting House and was trying to recruit new members for the book club.

A brief conversation ensued. He told me his name, Roger Franklin, and stated that he was English and had come to the Us to study for his PhD at MIT. I agreed to attend the book club the following week but politely refused his offer to take me home after the service.

I informed him that I had been invited to visit the Meeting House with my friends, the Johnsons, and felt that I should return home with them.

FIRST MEETING WITH ROGER and (MY RELATIONSHIP WITH JERRY LEWIS)

The next week, as agreed, I arrived at the book club and received a warm welcome from a lively, congenial group of people. Roger greeted me and introduced me to some of the members. When the meeting ended, he leaned over to ask if he could take me out sometime. We arranged to meet the following week.

I was still dating Jerry Lewis, the one man who met with my father's approval. Over a period of three years, we had become very close friends. Late Friday afternoons, after college classes, we often met for a secret rendezvous in a secluded French restaurant in Harvard Square. My order was always the same, one glass of Chablis, camembert cheese and biscuits.

Jerry and felt completely comfortable in each other's company and could discuss just about anything that was on our minds, be it familial, political or social. When my mother died, he had been very supportive, but very little was ever explored regarding the emotional side of our relationship.

I looked forward to these casual, nonchalant meetings with Jerry and found it a lovely way to unwind at the end of a hectic week of study and lectures. If my father ever asked why I was later than usual returning home, I always responded with the same statement, I had been studying in the library.

I had come to the conclusion that it was better to fabricate my whereabouts than to upset him by telling the truth. (He would have been horrified to discover that I had drunk alcohol, drinking was totally forbidden). As I was now nineteen years old, I was beginning to take less heed of what I considered my father's unreasonable expectations.

SOCIAL LIFE WITH ROGER

My dates with Roger were always secret meetings. We sometimes did mundane things, like skipping stones over the surface of a lake for what seemed to be hours. At other times, Roger would take great delight in making origami birds, assemble them in size and then present them to me.

He gave me a lovely cowrie necklace of small pink and cream shells. In each shell, he had managed to drill holes for inserting a nylon thread. As he had tried many tools and shattered many shells, in determining the most efficient way to puncture holes in the shell, I was very impressed with his persistence and determination to complete the task, despite these obstacles.

Much later, I was informed that he had given a similar necklace to another girl. Remembering Paul and the Yeats poem, I thought that Fate had decreed that I should receive lovely presents from men who persisted in giving all girlfriends the same gift.

We sometimes attended drive-in movies. In the 1950's, they were a new phenomenon in Massachusetts. They were always situated in a huge car park at one end and at the other an enormous screen would be erected where the film was displayed.

The advertisers described the experience of seeing films in this environment in glowing, nearly romantic terms. Everyone could watch a film in the cosy comfort of their own car, sitting under the twinkling stars. These claims were somewhat exaggerated as not everyone owned a convertible. So for many, the presence of the car roof completely obstructed the sparkling, starry night.

Roger was particularly fond of country walks and as he owned a 1936 Ford, we could travel outside the city to more distant areas for rural excursions. The Berkshires were the mountains closest to us. We spent many a long day there on challenging but not unduly strenuous treks.

As I was a city girl, I was unaccustomed to climbing mountains of any description. I occasionally suggested that I would sit it out while Roger strove to the very top of the mountain. As these reactions to minor fatigue usually occurred within reasonable walking distance of the summit, Roger would accept none of my feeble reluctance. He would urge me on. "What was the point in making this long journey if we never reached the top to see the extensive views?" Despite my complaining, his protests drove me on with fervid determination until I reached our ultimate destination. And it was inevitably, as he had predicted. There would always be a marvellous view to behold.

One spring weekend, my college friend, Betty Lou, joined us for a mountain hike. Roger drove us to New Hampshire where we spent an exhilarating day climbing Mt. Monadnock, meandering along a winding trail, clambering over bare boulders and walking through densely spread red spruce forests.

Due to the fact that the original settlers had set fire to the forests to deter wolves from settling and to create new agricultural land, the summit was totally devoid of trees and appeared exposed and vulnerable. Recently forest rangers have reported that the red spruce are slowly invading the bare spaces and determinedly climbing toward the summit. Hopefully, a more prolific spread of trees will provide the present climbers with a more lush and dense view when they reach the highest point on the mountain.

TOPICS OF INTEREST BETWEEN US

HENRY DAVID THOREAU

During an English Literature Course, I was introduced to Henry David Thoreau (1815-1862). He was renowned for his book "Walden", published in 1854 and for his essays, particularly Resistance to Civil Government, more commonly referred to as Civil Disobedience, published in 1859.

Walden was a two- year experiment in self-sufficiency, carried out at Walden Pond in Concord MA. Thoreau felt that earning money to enjoy life was a pointless enterprise if you had no clear aims and no idea of how to accomplish them.

In an attempt to discover what principles would help him to live a more meaningful life, he made an effort to confront himself by living alone and providing for his own basic needs without outside help. It was a fascinating journey of spiritual discovery and an experiment in finding inner peace and contentment.

In 1894, as a protest against slavery and the Mexican War, he refused to pay his poll tax. He was willing to pay taxes for the good of the community, for schools and highways, but would not render that part which he felt supported unfair treatment of others. He stated, "If a law is of such a nature that it requires you to be the agent of injustice, I say break the law."

He was imprisoned for taking this stand but spent only one night in prison because one of his friends, against his wishes, paid the tax.

His theory of non-violent resistance against an unjust state exerted widespread influence, especially on Leo Tolstoy and his writings on non-violent action. Both Mahatma Gandhi and Dr. Martin Luther King stated that his essay on Civil Disobedience had inspired their marches of dissent: Gandhi's for Indian independence and Martin Luther King's for equality in civil rights.

In the 1950's, Joseph Mc Carthy believed Thoreau's essay on Civil Disobedience was so inflammatory that he banned all copies from the United States Information Service.

As Roger shared my admiration for Thoreau's moral stance against injustice, we continued to explore the significance of his stand on civil disobedience.

A.S. NEILL

Aware of my interest in education, Roger introduced me to the work of the Scottish educator, A.S. Neill, founder of the residential, co-educational school Summerhill.

He, like other progressive educators, believed that the child's interest was the fundamental basis for acquiring knowledge. Instructions from the teacher were viewed as an impediment to the child's spontaneous learning.

His aims were to prevent society's repressive habits from influencing the child and to maintain the child's happiness. Parents and children were to have equal rights, though Neill did acknowledge that parents had a duty to protect children from danger.

He believed in self-governance. The school's general meeting which included both teachers and students, was meant to be a substitute for the teacher's authority. All rules derived from decisions arrived at through the deliberations of the entire community.

Neill was more radical than other educators in his approach to authority. Most progressive teachers encouraged some kind of minimal guidance for children. Neill declared that all authority was unnecessary and destructive for learning.

As he was such a strong advocate for promoting the child's interests, I was enthusiastic about his teaching methods. But I did retain some reservation. He did not seem to recognise that lack of exposure or even prejudice within the child's environment might shape what seemed to be a child's interests.

It was at this level that I felt that a teacher might usefully intervene to expand the child' curiosity in new and different directions. It would have been an act of which Neill would firmly disapprove, as it would be deemed interference on the teacher's part.

Roger and I discussed A.S. Neill at length. When his parents divorced, Roger was nine. He was sent to boarding school where he felt he never fitted in and grew to dislike the Public School System.

Not only was he forced to leave his family and familiar surroundings, but he was also subjected to what he felt were interminable and inexplicable rules.

The idea that a child could pursue his own interests in pursuit of learning was a novel and very appealing concept to him.

He highly approved of teachers and students jointly creating rules for their own community. Not only would it encourage a more democratic approach to governing the school, but it would also banish irrelevant rules from the students' lives forever.

THE YEAR 1953

The year 1953 produced a series of issues about which Roger and I were seriously concerned.

The spread of communism dominated the US government's political agenda. McCarthyism was rampant. Once labelled a communist (whether true or not), individuals lost their status in the community and lost their job as well. McCarthy's consistent attacks on US citizens aroused unwarranted widespread responses of fear and unease throughout the general public.

In February 1953, President Eisenhower refused to sign the clemency appeal for Ethel and Julius Rosenberg who had been accused of spying. Despite the fact that there was a strong belief that some evidence required further investigation, in June 1953, they were both executed.

We were living at the height of the Cold War. Both the US and the Soviet Union escalated the development of nuclear weapons, each side determined to excel in this enterprise.

In January 1953, the US announced that it had developed a hydrogen bomb.

In October 1953, The Soviet Union announced that it too, had developed a hydrogen bomb. In late October 1953, President Eisenhower stated that the US had increased its store of nuclear weapons to counteract the threat of communism.

We tried to publicly exert our disapproval of government policies with which we strongly disagreed by signing the clemency appeal for the Rosenbergs and joining marches protesting the development and escalation of nuclear weapons.

There were other events which were already faits-accomplis on which we could have no impact. But the decisions made in 1953 would have long-term consequences, leading to endless, future conflict with these countries which we are still dealing with today.

After three years of battle, the Korean War had ended in 1953. The ceasefire, (not a peace treaty), left Korea a divided country. The North remained under communist control while the South remained a capitalist regime, under the supervision of the United States.

North Korea has developed nuclear weapons which has been a continuous concern for the US. Summits arranged between North Korea, South Korea have not produced either a peace treaty or denuclearisation of the North.

In 1953, the US Central Intelligence Agency helped to overthrow the democratically elected government of Mossadegh in Iran and replaced it with a monarchy run by the Shah.

Mossadegh wanted to limit the control over Iran's oil, particularly in relation to the Anglo-Iranian Oil Company. Both Britain and the US were displeased with Mossadegh's stance and feared a communist takeover. Hence, the necessity, they thought, for the change of government.

British and American relations with Iran have been consistently contentious and remain so today, especially since their more recent concern that Iran was developing nuclear weapons.

OUR RELATIONSHIP

I introduced Roger to my friends, Russell and Irene Johnson. We all shared a genuine concern about the state of national and international politics.

Roger joined me in attending conferences examining areas of social and political conflict, organised by the American Friends Service Committee.

Despite the innumerable problems everywhere, we were both filled with the optimism of youth and earnestly hoped that with the help of dedicated, like-minded people, we could all work towards more peaceful, economically just societies.

It became obvious that between us there was a general concurrence of opinion about religion, education and the general state of the world. This meeting of minds was proving to be a strong attraction on both sides.

We had known each other for only four months but had possibly become more attracted to each other than either one of us had initially, been prepared to recognise. I loved the fact that that there was a spark of intellectual stimulation when we were together.

I always liked the challenge of being presented with a new perspective or a different angle on a subject as it forced me to reconsider my stance and exposed me to new ways of examining issues.

For me, it was a great joy to find someone with whom I could discuss the topical problems with which I was so involved. I did so with my friends, the Johnsons, and with individuals in the young Quaker group, but not always with the young men that I dated. I liked to know that they shared an interest in such matters before I bared my soul.

ROGER'S PARENTS IN THE USA

Roger had a complicated family history. His parents, Cyril Franklin and Miriam Israels, had met and married in England, but after ten years had divorced. His American mother remarried the Russian constructivist sculptor, Naum Gabo and they had one child, Nina.

During the Second World War, Roger and his two brothers, Joe and Owen, had been shipped to Canada with a governess to continue their academic studies and to escape the war.

When they returned to England, Roger attended Stowe School for one year and then went to Trinity College, Cambridge from which he received his physics degree.

Due to the divorce and the years spent in Canada, there was a prolonged period of separation where neither he nor his brothers ever saw or visited their mother. Roger's decision to study for his PhD at MIT in Massachusetts allowed him to re-establish contact with his mother.

His mother, Miriam and stepfather, Naum Gabo, had lived in Cornwall during the war but decided to settle in the United States once the war had ended. They were living in Woodbury, Connecticut when Roger invited me to meet them.

I informed my father that I was spending the night with my friend, Arlene, and she was prepared to confirm this in case my father had any reason to ring her.

Having been told that Roger's last girlfriend had not met with total approval, I feared that I would be under close scrutiny for the entire two days of my visit.

I met his mother, Miriam, his stepfather, Gabo, his eleven year old half-sister, Nina, and Snieshka whose name Gabo informed me meant snowball in Russian. She was the white, fluffy, very friendly Samoyed dog who accompanied Gabo on his daily excursion for exercise.

Roger' mother ran the household very efficiently and though never described as such, was also Gabo's secretary.

Gabo spent most of his time in his studio but did appear at mealtimes where an animated discussion often ensued. He was repeatedly upset upon hearing the daily news, particularly if there were any reports of Russian wrongdoing or hostile behaviour reported.

As Miriam was a devoted gardener, the house was full of lovely flower arrangements, including the bedroom where I slept. Miriam was a very accomplished artist but had decided to stop painting in order to run the household for Gabo and their daughter, Nina.

From the moment I arrived, Miriam had made me feel very welcome. I helped her with a few household chores and helped to weed the garden. At no time did I feel that I was being assessed.

As Gabo was a much more strongly opinionated individual and we were in contact only at mealtimes, I had no idea what his impression of me might be.

MIRIAM'S RELATIVES

BELLE MOSKOWITZ (5-10-1877 to 02-01-1933)

In 1928, Miriam's Mother, Belle Moskowitz, was the most politically outstanding woman in the United States. She was working in New York, as Al Smith's political advisor when he ran for Governor and later, in 1928, when he became a presidential candidate.

She was born in Harlem, New York to immigrant parents, Isador Lindner, a watchmaker, and Esther Fryer. Both her parents were from East Prussia in Germany.

She was the sixth of seven children and attended Teacher's College but stayed for only a year. She became a social worker at the Educational Alliance in 1900.

In 1903, she married Charles Henry Israels, an architect and artist, with whom she had three children Carlos, Joe and Miriam.

After her husband died, in 1911, she worked for the Council of Jewish Women. She was involved in trying to rectify many social problems: protecting children who were working, funding for parks and playgrounds, and the prevention of tuberculosis.

She instituted legislation that reformed the widely attended dance halls which were seen as places of prostitution. The New York Times reported that, "These laws did more to improve the moral surroundings of young girls than any other single social reform of the period."

After a fire at the Triangle Shirtwaist Factory that killed forty-nine people, she promoted legislation which improved the working conditions of all the employees.

In 1913, she married Dr. Henry Moskowitz who was a leader in many community activities. He was a Romanian Jew who had moved to New York. In 1917, he was appointed Commissioner of Public Markets. He co-founded the Downtown Ethical Society and was the founding executive director of the League of New York Theatres. He was also a civil rights activist and one of the co-founders of the NAACP (The National Association of Coloured People).

From 1918 to 1932, Belle worked for Al Smith. She became his press agent in 1932, when he attempted renomination for the Democratic Party.

In 1933, Belle Moscowitz died at the age of 55. Al Smith found her contribution to his campaigns of immeasurable value. He came to rely on her advice in relation to making political decisions and creating new programmes of reform.

He claimed that "She had the greatest brain of anybody I ever knew."

JOSEF ISRAELS

Another of Miriam's well known relatives was the painter, Josef Israels (27-01-1824 to 12-08-1911). He was Dutch, born in Groningen, The Netherlands, to Jewish parents.

His great desire was to study art in spite of his parents' insistence that he become a rabbi. After prolonged objection to his parents' wishes, he was finally allowed to study art at the Minerva Academy at Groningen in 1835 and then studied at the Royal Academy of Fine Arts in Amsterdam.

From 1845 to 1847, he worked in Paris as an apprentice to the history painter, Francois-Edouard Picot at the Ecole des Beaus-Arts. After two years in Paris, he returned to Amsterdam and devoted himself to Dutch history paintings.

In 1855, for health reasons, he stayed at Zanderwoort, a seaside town. It was here that, instead of portraits and history paintings, he changed the subject matter of his paintings to local scenes with rural labourers. His work was compared to that of Jean-Francois Millet. In addition, he painted scenes of the Jewish ghettos in Holland.

In 1870, he moved from Amsterdam to the Hague and became nationally and internationally the most renowned painter of the Hague School of painters. He was awarded the Cross of the Legion d'Honneur in 1867 and won the Grand Prix in the 1889 and the 1900 Expositions Universelles in Paris.

In the nineteenth century, he was considered the most important Dutch painter of the time and was the most prominent member of the Hague School of landscape painters.

He settled permanently in the Hague from 1871 until he died in 1911.

Josef Israel's work can be found in museums worldwide, the Mesdag Collection in the Hague, in Amsterdam in the Rijksmuseum and the Van Gogh Museum and in South Holland at the Dordrecht Gallery, and at the Ashmolean, the Fitzwilliam Museum, the Aberdeen Art Gallery, the Glasgow Museum, Museums Sheffield and The National Gallery, London.

NAUM GABO – (1890-1977)

Roger's step-father, Naum Gabo, was born in Bryansk, Russia in 1890. He is considered one of the most influential sculptors of the twentieth century and was a leader of the Constructivist Movement.

In Russia, in 1920, he and his brother, Antoine Pevsner, produced the Realist Manifesto which marked a significant step away from representative art and promoted new forms of art concerned with space and time.

The Constructivist Movement was suppressed in Russia, forcing Naum Gabo and his brother to flee to Europe and introduce their revolutionary approach to art to the West.

In 1921, Naum Gabo produced the Kinetic Sculpture, Standing Waves, which is often considered to be the first kinetic work of art. From 1942 to 1971, relinquishing the conventional use of mass or volume in sculpture, he used nylon thread to make linear constructions, creating various forms of interior space in his work.

Both he and his brother were major influences on the world of modern sculpture.

MARRIAGE PROPOSAL

Roger had originally entered the United States to acquire his PhD at MIT but after a year had decided not to pursue this course of study. He was now working as a research assistant in meteorology for a professor at MIT. One day, he casually informed me that his US Visa was out of date.

When he finally visited the US Immigration Department, he found himself in great difficulty on two counts, the firs, that he had no right to remain in the US as his visa had expired, and the second, that he had changed his status from one of being a student to that of being an employee. Both actions were considered serious transgressions. If he wanted to work, he should have returned to his country of origin to change his status.

It was possible that he could be deported and not given a voluntary departure. If this were to happen, he could be prevented from ever entering the United States again. In the course of relaying this distressing news, he stated that he would like to marry me.

I was completely taken aback as marriage was certainly not on my present agenda. I had recently informed a friend that I might contemplate marriage about the age of twenty-five, after I had completed a master's degree, found a suitable job and saved enough money to go travelling. I had projected the idea of marriage into a very far away, distant consideration.

I responded to his statement with total incredulity, "You can't be serious. You don't expect me to sit here and wait for you, possibly forever. You don't even know if you'll receive a voluntary departure. We could be on opposite sides of the ocean. I wouldn't have the money to travel to England and you wouldn't be allowed to enter the USA."

I remained in a state of shock regarding his proposal of marriage at the very moment that he could be banished from my life and from my country for his entire lifetime. The impact of his news catapulted me down a pathway that I was in no way anticipating. There was no sensible train of thought that followed from his announcement. From an informal, relaxed state of enjoying each other's company, we were hurtled into a different realm altogether, one of urgency, action, and immediate decisions.

In due course, over the period of a week, we were quite unexpectedly and to my surprise, discussing marriage. I have no clear idea how we came to that decision. It all happened very quickly and in a state of heightened emotion and concern over his likely curtailed existence in the US.

As I write this. It occurs to me that he might have been able to remain in the US if he were married to a US citizen. I must assure you that this thought had not occurred to either one of us. I was in such a state of disarray, I could never have thought of anything so useful and practical.

We were discussing how various family members might react to our marriage when he received notice that he had to attend court to receive a decision about his leave to remain in the country.

Fortunately, Miriam's brother, Joseph Israels, was a lawyer and lived in New York where Roger's case was to be tried. He agreed to find a lawyer dealing with visa problems who could defend Roger in court. We were all delighted when thanks to the lawyer's diligent and conscientious presentation of the case, Roger was allowed a voluntary departure from the United States.

We decided to marry on the 27th of June 1953, a date halfway between Roger's birthday and mine.

RUMOURS

As I walked to the bus stop one morning, on my way to college, I saw Mrs. Johnson and slowed my pace a little to greet her. Unexpectedly, I met with a distinctly cold stare as she turned away. I was perplexed but didn't register the significance of the problem at the time.

As the weeks progressed, this situation repeated itself many times. It slowly dawned on me that every neighbour I had spoken to had quite deliberately chosen to ignore my greetings and had quite deliberately shunned me. Sometimes, if they saw me, they preferred to project a stony glare and as they walked by in total silence.

Although I had known that dating white men was breaking a serious racial taboo, I could not believe the extent to which people would go to uphold their prejudiced beliefs.

When out on a date with Jerry Lewis one weekend, he informed me that his aunt had been told that my girlfriend Jeri and I were lesbians. This was the early 1950's. Being labelled either a lesbian or a homosexual was considered one of the most derogatory taunts that could be directed towards another human being.

I was simply stunned. How could anyone come to such a conclusion? Everyone could see that I had dated Jerry Lewis for three years and if not Jerry, some other respectable man. The accusation made no obvious sense.

The following week, as reported by Jerry's aunt, I had become sexually promiscuous with the white men I had dated. Jerry's aunt had met me but still professed to believe the rumours. I do know that Jerry Lewis found these accusations preposterous and told his aunt so.

When news of our wedding reached the ears of the gossip mongers, the rumours went from bad to worse. The last and final bit of titillating neighbourhood news issued forth. I was pregnant. I must be or he wouldn't be marrying me.

How could an entire group of people who had known me from the age of four, believe any of these unjustified attacks on my character? How could they attempt to malign me in this manner?

Deep hurt turned into a feeling of anger and betrayal. Those daily friendly greetings that I had grown up with were merely a façade that existed only so long as one played by their rules.

What I was experiencing was the retribution of prejudice in the northern United States. There was no public rebuke. In fact, not a word was spoken. It was an overt form of disapproval, a silent attack to punish anyone who refused to maintain their impenetrable racial divide.

The direct rejection that I experienced emanated from the black families in my neighbourhood. There was no need to ask what the white neighbours thought of my crossing the colour line. It was a foregone conclusion that they also disapproved.

This profound expression of deep-seated prejudice against inter-racial dating was upheld by both the black and white communities, though, without doubt, for different reasons.

Roger and I naively believed in a better world, one where skin colour did not determine the nature of human relationships. Given the reaction of my neighbourhood, prospects for ever creating such a world appeared highly unlikely.

Within my community, the only glimmer of hope was a black couple for whom I used to babysit. They belonged to CORE (the Congress of Racial Equality), an organisation of which I had minimal knowledge.

CORE had been founded in 1942. It was created to fight racial segregation by a group of people who believed in non-violence. There had recently been a Supreme Court ruling stating that racial segregation in interstate travel was unconstitutional.

In 1947, CORE had sent eight white and eight black people into the deep South to test whether or not this ruling was being enforced. They gained a certain amount of notoriety when, in North Carolina, three of the black people were sentenced to work on a chain gang for thirty days while the white participants were imprisoned for three months. The discrepancy in punishment was due to the white judge's anger that white people were attempting to dismantle segregation in the south.

In the 1940's, these individuals were the first group of civil rights activists –the precursors to the 1960's Civil Rights Movement.

This couple, younger and more enlightened about racial issues than the rest of the neighbourhood, proved to be the only individuals who spoke to me during the malevolent campaign of malicious gossip.

JERRY LEWIS'S REACTION

I dreaded telling Jerry Lewis that I was planning to marry and how soon it was meant to be. We had become very close and were very fond of each other. But I had never invited him to a party or dance as he was so much older than I was, and I knew he would feel out of place with a group of teenagers.

He did occasionally invite me to parties with his friends, where I felt somewhat uneasy. His friends already had degrees and jobs and lived in a world that I hadn't yet experienced. They seemed so confident and sure of themselves whereas I was brimful of questions and still sorting out my beliefs.

I had prewarned him that I had something important to tell him. He said that he had tried to prepare himself for the fact that I was to be engaged but in no way was he expecting me to say that I was about to be married. He suddenly became anxious. I could hear the frantic tone in his voice.

He insisted that I come to a film with him, immediately. It was Lili. Leslie Caron and Mel Ferrer played the main characters. It was the story of a young girl who fell in love with a beguiling but unsuitable young man. For various reasons, she ignored the man who truly loved her.

Over time, she recognised the devious nature of the man she adored and eventually accepted the man whose intentions had always been sincere and genuine towards her.

We sat silently through the film. I knew that he wanted me to take the message of the film seriously. He had acknowledged that he had fallen in love with me on New Year's Eve. I had no desire to face him because I knew how distraught he was.

He asked if I knew what I was doing. How well did I know him? What was it that made him so attractive?

I felt that my answers only made the situation worse. Regardless of what I said, he knew that he was losing me forever. His anguish was clearly tangible. I had a strong desire to comfort him, but any sign of a physical embrace could have been so easily misinterpreted.

I tried to remain aloof despite my feelings. I didn't want to convey any message of hope or give him the idea that I might change my mind. I couldn't bear to see him so upset, knowing that I was the cause of his distress.

When we arrived home, he told me that it was a dreadful coincidence that the same day that I was to be married, his best friend's girlfriend was also marrying someone else. He and his best friend had decided to spend that dreadful day, the 27th of June, together to commiserate about how unlucky they were.

FAMILY REACTION TO OUR FORTHCOMING MARRIAGE

Roger was Jewish. How would his family feel if he married someone who wasn't of his faith? I had learned many years ago, from my friend, Brenda, that Orthodox Jews insisted that their offspring should marry someone with the same Orthodox beliefs. It was not acceptable to even marry another Jew if he or she were of a Reformed or Liberal persuasion.

Because his great-aunt Lily Montague had founded The first Liberal Synagogue in St. Johns Wood, London, and his immediate family in England were Liberal Jews, I thought that his family would , at least, expect him to marry a Jewish girl if not a Liberal Jewish girl.

Roger was not at all religious so matters of faith were of no concern to him. He seemed indifferent to what family members in England might think of our marriage, even his father and grandmother who appeared to be the most influential people in his life in England.

He wrote a letter to inform them of the date of our wedding, and stated that I was the colour of honey. I asked if there would be any objection to his marrying someone who was black and not Jewish. And would it matter if I were of very dark complexion? He had no definitive answer and indicated that none of these issues mattered in the least.

Miriam and Gabo, both being non-religious and not at all racist in their views, proffered approval for our proposed marriage. Gabo was mildly disgruntled at the thought that he might be required to wear a tuxedo. Once reassured that this was unnecessary, he was pleased to accompany Miriam and Nina to the wedding , attired in a very respectable suit. Miriam sent me a lovely letter, welcoming me into the family. I also received a surprising letter from a friend of Miriam and Gabo's, Bill Ivins, who was the curator of a museum in Connecticut.

Miriam's Letter :

Dear Beverly,

I have always known that somewhere the girl that Roger would marry was growing up and that, like the prince in the fairy tale, he would someday find her. And here you are and I welcome you into this family as I hope he will be welcomed into yours. I am so glad for the two of you-I think you will lead a good life together and so find happiness together, that by-product of life which cannot be pursued but always has to catch up with people, sometimes when they least expect it.

I hope we shall have much to say and tell each other and we are all three so glad you are coming this weekend so that we can really embrace you and make plans together. We should all three like to be at the wedding, and Aunt Grace, whom Roger will have told you about, is waiting to meet you too. I hope this letter is not too incoherent, one feels a little emotional about the first romance in the family and I shall be very new to the business of being an in-law. I hope I shall do a good job of it and in the meantime, I send you my love and my blessing and my heartfelt wishes for your happiness.

Affectionately,

Miriam Gabo.

BILL'S LETTER

Dear Beverly Allen,

It occurs to me that when young girls get married it may be pleasant for them to have in their pockets a few pennies with which to acquire some small foolish this-or-that for themselves without any asking or by your leave or consultation or accounting, and so instead of giving you and Roger a wedding present (which you probably would have no use for), I have taken the liberty of sending you the enclosure to be used by Beverly, on Beverly, for Beverly, and I pray, enjoyably, prettily, and not at all sensibly. Remember Montaigne's nos folies sont nos sugesses.

Sincerely,

Bill Ivins

When we went to Cape Cod, I had a pair of hand-made sandals fitted in a shop that was owned by Isadora Duncan's brother. He and his assistants produced shoes in original and unusual designs.

I now had the undesirable task of informing my father of our wedding plans. Roger had once accompanied me home after classes. As my father always returned home from work much later, I had ample time to prepare his dinner and leave before his arrival. Roger was standing beside me when I suddenly heard a key in the front door lock. I froze. It could only be my father. What was he doing here at this time? He was not due home for another two hours. How could this be happening? Too late to send Roger scuttling away. My father was already approaching the kitchen. I could see him.

I said, in a quaking voice, "This is a friend, Roger. Roger, this is my father." Roger said, "Hello" and I tried to gesture to him to leave but he did not understand what I was trying to do. As my father turned to remove his coat, I whispered, "Go, go. You have to go." I wanted him to run in haste but that was not how Roger moved. He did not do anything swiftly. His movements were always slower and more considered. I gave him an urgent push in the direction of the door to the back stairs and he finally complied.

I then had to face my furious father. He exploded, "I never want to see you with a white man in this house again."

You can imagine my angst at having to tell him that I was going to marry one and the very one that he had forced to leave so abruptly a few weeks ago.

I told him that Roger and I were to be married. It would be in a registry office on the 27th of June. We were paying for all the wedding expenses ourselves.

My father, in an outburst of violent anger, swore at me. I was trembling and more shocked at his swearing at me than by his overpowering anger. In all of my nineteen years, I had never heard my father swear. I accepted it for what it was, a sign of uncontrollable rage in reaction to my decision to marry a white man. In a fit of fury, he walked out of the room, refusing to discuss the matter further.

I was an utter social disgrace and he wanted nothing to do with me or the situation that I had created. Not only was he angry, I was a serious disappointment. How could all his effort and hard work have produced a daughter who had become so disobedient and reacted in total defiance of everything he believed?

Our life at home remained distinctly cool and distant. We spoke only when necessary.

Roger and I were content to carry on with our wedding plans, until my father's sister heard of what was happening. My Aunt Rebecca telephoned me to say that my father's ideas were sealed in the past. What more could he expect of any man? Roger had, after all, asked to marry me. He was just being ridiculous. Pay no attention to him.

My mother was no longer here to guide me, so she and my father's younger sister, Cecilia, would help me to arrange the wedding. I explained that we were to be married in a registry office with two witnesses. There was no need for a large wedding. She would have none of this approach to a wedding. If marriage was on our agenda, it would be done properly and she would convince my father that he had to prepare for a proper wedding when his only daughter was to be married.

"You have to decide how many bridesmaids you want and who is to be the maid of honour." I knew that I would be overjoyed if my aunt could alter my father's attitude and persuade him that our wedding was acceptable. Living daily under a cloud of anger and rejection was vey disturbing and very unsettling.

I felt that if she could remove my father's resistance to the wedding, I should accept the wedding plans that she proposed, just to keep the peace. If my father were to agree to the idea of the wedding, how could I suddenly become difficult and complain that these plans were not what we wanted.

I then had to convince Roger, who didn't liked anything formal, that, as he had brought his formal suit from England, he should wear that to the wedding. He very reluctantly agreed to do so.

So, my wedding party which had started life with the idea of only two witnesses, concluded with seven participants: the Best Man, John, a friend of Roger's; three bridesmaids, Nina, Roger's half-sister, Adele, my friend from college, and Barbara, a long-standing friend of many years. My Maid of Honour was Jeri, because she insisted that she was my closest friend, "We were soul-mates". Leda, Russel and Irene's daughter was five. Walking behind me, she strewed rose petals along the aisle. My cousin's adorable boy, who was about four, was the ring-bearer.

My Aunt Rebecca had performed a miracle as far as I was concerned. Not only did my father pay for all the wedding expenses and the reception that followed, he officially gave me away to Roger at the wedding ceremony. His compliance didn't mean that he approved of our marriage. My Aunt Rebecca had managed to convince him that it was his duty to support his only daughter when she married. Despite the fact that he was not pleased with my choice of partner, he behaved in exemplary fashion at the wedding.

It was a truly multicoloured, interracial wedding ,something unheard of at that time. I regret that I have no photo of the entire wedding party --only pictures of Roger and me and others with family members.

On the 27th of June, 1953, we were married at the Charles St, Meeting House in Boston by Kenneth Patton, the radical Universalist minister. It was, after all, where we had met 5 months previously. I was 19 , nearly 20 , and Roger was 26.

Roger's brother, Joe flew over from England to attend the ceremony and Roger's father rang from England to congratulate us.

We chose a quotation from the Lebanese poet ,Khalil Gibran's work, to be read at the wedding ceremony . We preferred it to the conventional Christian ceremony because there was an acceptance of total equality between the partners and of their working in harmony with each other to allow space for each to thrive.

"Love one another, but make not a bond of love:

Let it rather be a moving sea between the shores of your souls.

Fill each other's cup but drink not from one cup.

Give one another of your bread but eat not from the same loaf

Sing and dance together and be joyous, but let each one of you be alone,

Even as the strings of a lute are alone though they quiver with the same music.

Give your hearts but not into each other's keeping.

For only the hand of Life can contain your hearts.

And stand together yet not too near together:

For the pillars of the temple stand apart,

And the oak tree and the cypress grow not in each other's shadow.

When this basically humanist service ended, my grandmother, my father's mother, a devoted Christian, exclaimed in disapproval ,that she had not heard the name of God mentioned at any point in the service.

At the present moment, on the internet, you can find a wedding picture of Roger and me--not a wonderful picture. It was a discarded wedding photo. Type in : Joan Allen and Roger Franklin. It was put on the internet by someone who was interested in the history of interracial marriage.--without my knowledge or Roger's. My grandson, Gabriel, accidentally found it when he was "fooling around on the internet." It was originally printed in what was then, a fairly new magazine called JET.

As it was 1953 and such marriages were highly disapproved of, I would say the adjectives that could be applied to the picture were not flattering-- scandalous and shocking come to mind.

In 1953, interracial marriage was forbidden by law in 31 states in the USA.

It was not until 1967 that these laws were ruled unconstitutional.

THE WEDDING

It was a truly multi-coloured, interracial wedding, something unheard of in the early 1950's. I regret that I have no photo of the entire wedding party, only pictures of Roger and me and others with family members.

On the 27th of June 1953, we were married by Kenneth Patton, the radical Universalist minister, at the Charles St. Meeting House in Boston, MA. It was, after all, where we had met five months previously. I was nineteen, nearly twenty, and Roger was twenty-six. Roger's brother Joe flew from England to attend the ceremony and Roger's father rang from London to congratulate us.

We chose a quotation from the Lebanese writer, Khalil Gibran's poem 'The Prophet', to be read at the wedding ceremony. We preferred it to the conventional Christian ceremony because there was an acceptance of total equality between the partners and of their working in harmony with each other to allow space for each to thrive.

"Love one another, but make not a bond of love:

Let it rather be a moving sea between the shores of your souls.

Fill each other's cup but drink not from one cup.

Give one another of your bread but eat not from the same loaf

Sing and dance together and be joyous, but let each one of you be alone,

Even as the strings of a lute are alone though they quiver with the same music.

Give your hearts but not into each other's keeping.

For only the hand of Life can contain your hearts.

And stand together yet not too near together:

For the pillars of the temple stand apart,

And the oak tree and the cypress grow not in each other's shadow."

When this basically Humanist service ended, my grandmother, my father's mother, a devoted Christian, exclaimed, in disapproval, that she had not heard the name of God mentioned at any point in the service.

At the present moment, on the internet, you can find a wedding picture of Roger and me, not a wonderful picture. It was a discarded wedding photo. Type in: Joan Allen and Roger Franklin. It was put on the internet by someone who was interested in the history of interracial marriage, without my knowledge or Roger's. My grandson, Gabriel, accidentally found it when he was "fooling around on the internet." It was originally printed in what was then, a fairly new magazine, called JET.

As it was 1953, such marriages were highly disapproved of. I would say the adjectives that were applied to the picture were not generally flattering, scandalous and shocking come to mind.

Interracial marriage was forbidden by law in thirty-one states in the USA in 1953.

Laws permitting interracial marriage in every state in the USA, only occurred in 1967, when Virginia, the last state to forbid such liaisons, agreed to rescind the law forbidding it.

PUBLIC REACTION TO OUR MARRIAGE

I was taken aback by the number of people who felt it was their duty to declare their concern about our unconventional marriage and any children that we might have. As I was walking down the street one day, someone yelled at me in a hostile voice, "You were lucky he married you", implying that any relations we now had would be legal.

One of the few black students at college, someone I didn't know, stopped me in the hall to state that she had seen our picture in Jet magazine. "What kind of a marriage was it when the husband looked so unhappy?"

What skin colour our children possessed preoccupied a number of white people. "What would we do if we had a black baby? You could have a throwback." Throwbacks were babies showing characteristics of an ancestor that precedes its parents. Black people were composed of individuals with a wide spectrum of colour from very light to very dark and knew that they could have children of varying complexions.

The idea that we could produce a black baby appeared to white people, a very disastrous prospect. I could not believe how much residual prejudice existed around this issue. If we had a black baby, we would love it because it was ours. And what concern of theirs would it be?

I was asked this question so frequently that I determined to discover what the true facts were. I made an appointment with the Head of the Biology Department. I explained that many people seemed concerned that we could have a black baby. It was not a problem for me, but I wanted to know the facts. "Was it possible for Roger and me to have a black baby?"

I then received a short but illuminating lecture. "Skin colour is determined by a number of gene variations, probably more than 10 and possibly even twice that. The gene variants control the amount of melanin or pigment produced, some for lighter skin and others for darker.

The particular genes that a child inherits from their parents and ancestors is a completely chance process. These facts hold true for children whose parents are both 100% Caucasian and for those whose parents are of different colours.

He refused to use the word race as he pointed out that amongst human beings, it is of no significance. It refers to a group of people of common ancestry with distinguishing physical features, such as eye, hair, and skin colour. Some choose to define people with minor physical differences as belonging to a different race, but, in terms of classification, it has no taxonomical importance. All human beings belong to the same species, Homo Sapiens.

He then stated that if one parent is 100% white and the other is of darker complexion, any child produced could not be darker that the darker parent. It was biologically impossible.

Having acquired this information, I decided not to use it in response to any queries regarding our marriage and black babies. I was genetically excluded from their concept of a dire problem as their projected disaster related to a non-existent problem. I, had initially, laughed when presented with questions about a black baby. I always said that they were asking the wrong person. I didn't consider it a problem. They should be addressing that question to my husband.

I now felt that I should challenge them directly. "What was wrong with having a black baby? I'm very displeased that you so disapprove of the existence of black children." By the time I had arrived at this decision, most of those who were audacious enough to ask such questions had vanished, with the exception of my "good friend" Betty Lou. She was the one who had climbed MT. Monadnock with Roger and me.

After her first year at Simmons, she had transferred to a different college. I wrote to her to say that Roger and I were getting married. She sent a very concerned reply. After I had read her letter, I sincerely wished that I could have spoken to her face to face. She had always described herself as a very liberal-thinking Jewish girl. The best I could do was to respond to her letter.

Her mind was firmly set against the idea of our getting married. It was definitely a shocking act of which she could never approve. I'm sure that she felt that she was conveying a responsible attitude with her sincere anxiety about our predicament if we proceeded with the wedding.

"We would suffer. The children would suffer. Had we thought about how all of us would be treated?" And the last concern, "What colour would the children be? We might have a black baby."

I responded to my 'good friend', Betty Lou, stating that we had supportive friends who didn't believe that either skin colour, or one's religion, defined the essence of a human being. They had the courage to look beyond superficial differences to find the worthy person beneath.

We are not about to surrender our beliefs about equality for everyone and the right to choose whomever one desires for friendship or for marriage. We have no intention of succumbing to the petty prejudices of others, even if they are in the majority.

As for colour, whatever colour our children are, they will be loved, even if they arrived with pink spots and purple stripes. We did not expect to dole out love according to gradations of skin colour.

You have obviously felt it imperative to support and maintain the derogatory prejudices which you have absorbed from family, friends, and your community.

If we or our children have any problems, it will be as a result of people who refuse to relinquish their racial and religious prejudices and denigrate those whom they see as different from themselves.

For some strange reason, since 1953, Betty Lou has never again been in contact with me.

AFTER THE WEDDING, THE QUEEN MARY

After our wedding reception, we returned excited and exhausted to the co-operative house where Roger lived. There were four or five students and one older woman who already resided there. They had all concocted a wonderful, lightly intoxicating punch and some refreshments which contributed to a continued evening of festivity and merriment.

We had a month before we sailed to England on the Queen Mary. We considered our trip to England our official honeymoon, but as we had time to spare, we planned a "pre-honeymoon trip", departing in the 1936 Ford to go camping in the woods. As the sun shone most days, we really enjoyed being outside, away from city sounds and noises, surrounded by tranquility and the intoxicating aroma of pine trees.

I arrived home covered in bites and was very annoyed to discover that mosquitoes flew quickly over my husband, leaving him unscathed and unmarked but rushed to attack me on any area of exposed flesh that they could find. Sadly, the mosquitoes' discrimination in my husband's favour, was maintained throughout our marriage.

Roger's father had booked our tickets for the voyage. "Did we want first class? This was, of course, how Roger's family had always travelled on holidays. Roger refused to dress formally for dinner every night, so we opted for second-class. I concurred with this decision as I had no desire to wear gowns every evening and I was worried that I couldn't pack my own gowns without creating huge wrinkles in the lengthy skirts. (No one bothered to mention that it was likely that one of the maids or cleaners on board could iron these gowns for me). But as I would not be wearing them, it was information of no importance.

In addition, we were travelling with friends, who, because they were both still students and cash was sparse, were booked in steerage, third-class. The idea of our swanning around in formal outfits while walking on deck with our friends in very casual dress was truly ludicrous.

The night before our departure for England, we stayed with Aunt Ruth and Uncle Joe. He was the lawyer who had successfully arranged for Roger's voluntary departure from the USA. They had a large, tastefully furnished, apartment opposite Central Park in New York, one son and a young, black maid.

Our stay was without incident, with the exception of the maid who served us dinner. I seemed to be the only one sensitive to the situation that was occurring. That may have been because I was the only one who became the centre of her attention. Upon seeing me with Roger, she spent the entire evening in a state of mild alarm. Her eyes constantly darted in my direction, as if I, the object of her gaze, was some sort of apparition.

As she was so obviously disconcerted in our presence, I offered her a friendly smile. That only served to increase her unease. She stopped staring and determinedly turned her head away from me. As I was such a serious source of unpleasant distraction, I feared she might lose concentration and have some sort of unlucky accident. But she did manage to serve the various courses and remove the appropriate dishes, as required.

When we eventually left the table, to include us all in her last steadfast stare. She stared mildy, shaking her head from side to side, conveying her incredulity and her disapproval, 'What was the world coming to?'

THE QUEEN MARY

The following morning, Roger, Joe, Roger's brother, and I were boarding the Queen Mary. We were overwhelmed by the noise and the large crowds of people. There was an endless line of people queuing, children laughing, crying, screaming, unsettled by the loud sounds and constant disturbance, and anxious parents trying to distract and console them. More relatives, smiling, hugging, kissing, and crying, sending good wishes, and waving and gesticulating happy and sad good-byes.

Suddenly, a blast of tooting horns announced our departure. The three red funnels at the top of the liner started moving slowly out of the harbour. The cacophonous crowds, the confusion and disorder became more and more muted and slowly faded into the distance. We were surrounded by the rippling sound of the sea's waves washing against the ship's sides and the welcome warmth of brilliant sunshine. But its heat never penetrated beyond our outer layer of clothing as there as was a continuous breeze blowing in every direction that we ventured.

Apparently, the ship was full. On board, were just under 2000 passengers, about 711 in first-class, 707 in second-class, and 577 in third-class.

The ship, itself, was a floating city, composed of ballrooms, dining rooms, shops of every sort, mostly designer clothes and expensive jewellery, numerous bars, barbers, hairdressers and beauty salons, libraries, two swimming pools, dog kennels, a lecture hall, children's playrooms and areas for exercise and games to play on deck. There was also a garage for thirty-six cars and telephone availability to anywhere in the world.

It was the first liner to provide a Jewish Prayer Room which demonstrated Britain's stand against antisemitism during the time of Nazi propaganda.

The second-class swimming pool spanned over two decks in height. Cabin class, also described as second-class, provided a Verandah Grill on the Sun Deck at the upper aft of the ship, which was an exclusive, a la carte, restaurant for eighty people in the daytime. At night, it was transformed into the Starlight Club where passengers imbibed cocktails and alcoholic beverages.

We never saw the first-class cabins, but they were reported to be luxurious, especially for the standards of the 1950's. In second-class, we, at least, had our own, not very large, ensuite bathrooms. Third-class was located in the bow of the ship, where the ship's movement was most pronounced. Our friends' room was composed of bunk beds with ladders and a shared bathroom, outside in the hall. Their modest accomodation was adequate, but small and crowded.

Despite the cramped sleeping quarters in third-class accommodation, the rest of the facilities, though fewer, were of a very high standard. The dining room was tastefully furnished with brightly-coloured curtains on the large windows on both sides of the room. The red, orange, and cinnamon floor blended well with the room's colour scheme. The chairs were made of highly polished light mahogany.

There was no swimming pool, but a well-equipped nursery was available with a rocking horse and numerous toys and books.

The strangest and most unexpected objects in our room were the saltwater taps, used for washing only. There was some suggestion that saltwater baths were healthy and improved certain ailments. My amazement at their existence was not accompanied by a wildly welcoming acceptance of their use. As my skin lost its moisture and became more dried out every day, I decided to relinquish the thought that salt water was of any beneficial effect. It was a remedy for ailments for those with a far sturdier constitution than mine.

At our first dinner, we were faced with a queue of spoons, forks, and knives, lined up on either side of the plate. In amazement, I stared, not knowing where to begin. I had no idea which utensil was meant for what delectable item that was meant to arrive. I discovered that I was not the only one looking so perplexed. Someone at the table said, "Start from the outside and move inward." As we ordered what we desired from an endless array of possibilities on the menu, the utensils which were superfluous were very efficiently removed, and soon we were able to manage the meal with a significantly reduced amount of silverware.

We spent the days on board with our friends meandering around different decks of the liner. A walk around the promenade deck, apparently, was considered the same as walking the entire distance of Regent Street.

We amused ourselves by following the progress of the ship's journey as we crossed the Atlantic. In the second-class dining room, there was a large map which illustrated the two routes taken. The winter/spring route always ventured further south, to avoid icebergs. The summer/autumn route was more straightforward. During each crossing, a motorised model of the Queen Mary would track the ship's progress en-route.

We all often spent a very relaxing time in the Observation Bar, a lounge, decorated in Art Deco style, with large windows offering a wide vista of ocean views.

Once on board our super liner, I was determined, if possible, to observe the phosphorescence in the sea. I can't remember where I learned of this amazing phenomenon, but it sounded so miraculous that I had longed, for years, to view it.

Bioluminescence occurs in marine environments where the sea is disturbed, mainly in the wake of ships at sea. Microscopic organisms and a variety of bacteria that can react with oxygen in the water are the swarms most frequently seen and shine brightly as if electrified in the sea.

Bioluminescent algae and plankton multiply in dense layers at the surface of the water. These sea sparkle events are caused by warm water and calm sea conditions. Given the temperature of the sea, I wondered whether these blooms would ever be on display for me to view.

As bioluminescent organisms live throughout the water column, from the sea's surface to the sea floor, and from the sea's shores to the open ocean, I thought that, with luck, I might view this riveting event.

Wrapped fairly warmly, I spent 4 of the 5 nights available perched on the stern, searching the trails of the ship's waves in hopes of catching sight of a glowing, blue or green mass, riding on the crest of the waves.

Neither Roger nor his brother were so taken with my enterprise, and I returned each night cold, wind-swept and defeated. To this day, I have never seen phosphorescence at sea. As for many years, I have travelled by plane, my chances of viewing this event have become even more unlikely.

MEETING ROGER'S FATHER

After 5 days, our trip was over. It was time for us to set foot on dry land. As we were approaching the gangplank, there was a small commotion in front of us. Someone was walking in the wrong direction, up the gangplank, instead of down. As the queue for departure was already congested with children, crowds of people and numerous suitcases, a few people started to protest at this intrusion.

All I could see was a head, taller than most, slowly growing larger. As it approached the deck, the shoulders emerged from above the crowd and suddenly arms started flailing frantically. A loud voice was calling, "Roger, Roger." It was Cyril, Roger's father, who had come to pick us up. He had impatiently boarded the boat, not willing to wait until we alighted on shore.

Our brief introduction took place amidst the clutter of baggage and the clamour and confusion of all the departing passengers.

Cyril drove us home at great speed in his very comfortable, leather seated Rover. He was a very good driver but was also a very fast one. As I preferred not to see what I feared we were about to hit, I sat for most of the journey with my fists clenched and my eyes tightly shut.

As Roger's father had bought a new house while Roger had been studying in the US, Roger was as curious as I was to see the new residence. We drove up West Heath Road and suddenly took a sharp left turn, almost imperceptible from the road. On the right, there was a small dwelling, probably originally the gatekeeper's cottage to the large estate. On the left, hidden inside a further drive, was a large house where individuals belonging to some religious order lived. As we continued up the small hill, we drove under a brick archway and were immediately facing a large two-story house with a flat brick façade.

Cyril parked the car in the garage, next to the archway. There were three other cars already in situ, a Bentley, a Buick and a Daimler. Cyril pointed out that the flat next to the archway was the gardener's dwelling where he lived with his wife and three children.

We approached the house, Cyril rang the doorbell and the new maid ushered us into the vestibule. Dorothy greeted us warmly. She had been the children's nanny for many years and had later become Cyril's long-standing companion. A few years after my first visit to England, they were officially married.

We went up two steps to the hall and proceeded left towards the sitting room. As I drew closer to our destination, a large picture with extremely bold perspective leapt into my line of vision. It turned out to be an Utrillo. As I sat down, I looked up to see a head of Nefertiti sitting nobly on top of a huge loudspeaker in the far corner of the room.

The maid arrived with tea, and I sank into my chair to have a good look around the sitting room. Bookcases lined the lower walls, but as I was sitting too far away, I could not read their titles. When the maid had removed the tea dishes, Cyril rose and walked with us to the end of the sitting room. On the left, were large glass doors, leading to the patio.

On the right was the entrance to the music room. In it were two pianos. The grand piano sat open, as if ready to be played, the other, smaller upright, sat bathed in sunlight from the garden window. This room often provided a space for concerts, always of a high calibre, for well-known and some not so well-known musicians.

In front of the grand piano and a few feet away, looking out at the garden, was an imposing, bronze bust of a woman by Jacob Epstein. On the wall facing the bust, was a painting of a reclining, nude woman by Mark Gertler. My father-in-law was quick to inform me of the artists' names of all the paintings in the room. The walls of both this room and the sitting room were lined with other paintings which I did not recognise.

As it was a lovely day, Cyril opened the patio doors which revealed the view of the rear garden. On the left, as we strolled along the lawn was a firmly established rose garden. Some of these roses were of ancient origin which meant that not only were their colours enticing and distinctive, but they also produced a distinctly fragrant perfume.

Behind the rose garden was a much larger space filled with numerous azaleas. When in bloom, they exhibited a magnificent and greatly varied display of colour.

A few years hence, at the end of the rose garden, a new swimming pool would be ensconced for the pleasure of family and friends.

Beyond the rose garden, was another huge space which contained the tennis court. It was enclosed with an open-wire fence to prevent the balls from disappearing into the undergrowth. Turn right and the path to the tennis court eventually led to the kitchen garden and a greenhouse where fresh vegetables for the family were grown. There was always a surfeit of tomatoes, probably due to the fact that the gardener was Italian.

Turning left and walking along the path from the tennis court, there was a barely discernible path, buried amongst bushes, which led down to a well-hidden gate. It was a private entrance to Golders Hill Park. The secret gate allowed privileged access to the park but, I always felt, it could also be seen as an invitation to robbery as it was also so easily accessible to the rear garden.

My initial impressions of the Franklin household were slowly beginning to register. My first reaction was one of unexpected astonishment at the sight of four cars in my father-in-law's garage. Aside from the Buick, I was not yet familiar with the manufacturers' symbols on the bonnets of the cars. I did not know that these specimens were some of the most expensive and luxurious makes of car that existed at the time. When asked why he didn't own a Rolls Royce, my father-in-law stated that it was a car always bought by the nouveau riche and was, therefore, seen to be far too ostentatious.

Looking at the walls and bookcases, I assumed that this was a very artistic and learned family, full of information and knowledge with which I was unfamiliar. It was similar to my experience when I worked at Widener Library at Harvard University. At first, I was overwhelmed by the vastness of the knowledge which surrounded me, about which I knew absolutely nothing.

It took about two weeks for me to begin to relax. But as I began to know my new in-laws and relate to them as the individuals that they were, I gradually accepted that I could converse with them without being daunted by ideas of their being imbued with great realms of knowledge to which I could not relate.

Cyril loved classical music and was often, with the latest up-to-date equipment, playing something from his large collection of records, particularly opera. He was constantly asking Dorothy which pieces she recognised. I gently suggested that he was expecting rather a lot from Dorothy, as she hadn't grown up listening to classical music as he had.

When, one day, I told him the title and author of a piece he was playing, (It was Traumerei by Robert Schumann), we became immediate friends. I had played it sometime during those six years of piano lessons I had experienced from 10 to 16. My father-in-law was delighted. He thought he had found in me the kind of person he was so clearly looking for, someone who would sit and listen to music for as long as he desired. He had me in tow, a captive audience of one. Although I enjoyed these music sessions, they sometimes lasted much longer than I would have desired. At first, not wanting to appear rude, I found it extraordinarily difficult to extricate myself from the situation, which greatly pleased my father-in-law.

But I fear that I never totally complied with my father-in-law's expectations regarding how much time I should spend with him, listening to music. As we were invited by various relatives to lunches, teas and dinners and were also either sight-seeing or shopping, we were constantly otherwise occupied.

AN AMUSING POSTSCRIPT

The pictures that Cyril and his brother, Michael, displayed on their walls, I was later told, had been inherited from their father, Ernest, who was a great art collector. Only gradually did I come to realise that possession of paintings and sculpture does not necessarily entail great appreciation of the art displayed nor did it imply great knowledge of either the artist or of his techniques.

When my father-in-law died, I received a complete set of the books of Dickens, the very ones that I had viewed in the bookcase the first day of my arrival in England. Just the sight of these and so many other books on display led me to conclude that this must be a very well-read and learned family.

As I carefully opened each book, one after the other, to my surprise, I discovered that many pages remained uncut, indicating that none of these books had ever been read.

I had to laugh at myself, that young bride who couldn't believe her eyes. I was forced to accept that my initial reactions to my new relatives had been an excessive and exaggerated projection on my part. I was shocked to learn that the paintings displayed were valued more for their monetary worth than for their artistic merit and that many of the books that lined the bookshelves had never been read. It was slowly dawning on me that prestigious possessions should be valued for what they truly are, admirable works of art and genuinely amazing pieces of literary writing. No assumptions should be made about how the owner views such worthy, expensive, property.

My reaction was a reflection of my initial unease in the midst of such overwhelming displays of wealth. I immediately assumed that I had entered a world where others knew everything, and I knew nothing.

I was not so bereft as I had, at first, imagined. When I could acknowledge to myself that I had studied the lives and techniques of specific artists, and that I had actually read some of the books so boldly displayed on the bookcases, I began to relax. It was only then that I found this new world much less daunting, and I was able to enjoy and explore my new surroundings without restraint.

PART TWO

MONEY and SHOPPING

Roger had explained to me that in the USA, we would always have to live on his salary which was not enormous. As my family had always lived within the means of what my father's salary provided and that was not enormous, I was in no way dismayed at this prospect.

My brother and I were always aware that we had to earn a living to support ourselves to become financially independent.

Now that we were in England, Roger had access to English money which the government did not allow to be exported. Although the war had ended nearly eight years previously, the monetary restrictions established at that time, were still in operation. He was allowed to spend his English allowance, but not beyond English borders.

How incredible and unreal this situation appeared to me. The idea of people acquiring inherited wealth was something that happened, occasionally, but only in books. The fact that I could spend any amount of money beyond my normally meagre allowance was initially something which I found incredible. I was trained and constrained by my upbringing never to spend extravagantly. I had to accept that the reality of the present situation meant that we were allowed to spend money much more freely in England.

Being informed of the activities I was expected to attend in England, I realised that my American wardrobe was totally inadequate. Roger agreed to take me shopping and when I asked how much I could spend on clothes, he responded, "as much as you like."

My original idea was to buy the clothes I needed for the requisite occasions. The first purchase was for a play. I bought a long gown as my father-in-law insisted that everyone wore evening dress to the theatre. As it turned out, the only people attired in gowns and black ties were a few elderly individuals who, like my father-in-law, were unwilling to change their accustomed habits. The rest of the audience were dressed in respectable but more casual clothes.

For the more formal dinners, at Roger's grandmother's, some new dresses seemed appropriate and something for the garden party given by Roger's grandmother at Glenalla, their summer residence in Donegal. This event was attended by the whole community and provided money for the benefit of the nurses and the local community.

As everyone was expected to wear white on the tennis court, I felt I should comply by acquiring a white tennis outfit to play the game. I was not a great player but, in the summertime, my brother and I had sometimes played on the public courts not far from our house.

I also needed clothes for the English climate. I had not come prepared for the cool weather, mist, and drizzle. I was accustomed to hot summers, not the persistent inclement weather in England and what was even worse, the seemingly never-ending rain in Ireland. It became a custom, particularly later when we had children, to buy raincoats in England. And then, when we arrived in Donegal, to purchase the Wellington Boots and a new hand-made Aran sweater for each child to fortify them against the rain and cold.

In England, I purchased Pringle sweater sets and woollen trousers to stave off the cool weather.

Roger took me to Simpsons, Harrods, Lillywhites and many shops along Bond Street. I started my shopping spree in order to be suitably attired for the occasions I was encountering. I then began to think of the small amount of money we had available in the USA. It was only Roger's salary and as I was not working this summer, he would have to pay my entire tuition. It was no longer my father's responsibility to pay half.

We would have even less money to spend than I had anticipated.

I decided not to confine my shopping to the clothes I needed in England. I extended it to include garments I could use in the USA as well.

As an American, I could get a tax discount if the clothes were being exported. This fact spurred me on to buying more clothes as I focussed on the huge amount of money that I was saving. My behaviour altered. From being a very cautious, careful spender of money, I was transformed into what could only be described as an exuberant and extravagant purchaser of goods.

I also bought gifts for friends and family, gifts that I never could have otherwise afforded.

My father-in-law was alarmed at the number of purchases that we were making and complained loudly every time we entered the house. I took to leaving Roger to pay the taxi and enter the front door, hoping that his father would greet him in the hall and both would proceed to the sitting room.

I tip-toed around the side of the house and opened the kitchen door as quietly as possible. As I left the kitchen, I would check that the hall was empty and race upstairs, laden with bags, and hope to reach our bedroom before I was discovered. I scrambled to hide purchase under the bed and in the cupboards before my fathering-law entered the room, always asking the same question,"What have you bought now?"

I'm sure that Roger thought that he had completely misjudged me. Standing before him was not the impecunious girl he had married but the most wildly excessive and lavish individual he had ever met.

It was a unique opportunity, and it became a unique occasion. I never again allowed myself to engage in shopping with such wild abandon. Although I had spent a great deal of money, none of it was wasted. In the US, I wore the clothes I had bought, for many years. When we visited England in the summertime, I often repacked the English clothes that I had already purchased as part of my summer wardrobe. I was seen to be wearing them when I was teaching school over two years later and even four years later when I became pregnant with my first child. The coats I had bought provided many years of wear. The few articles that I didn't use (because our life in the US was less formal) were contributed to the American Friends Service Committee to raise money for their local charity work and projects overseas.

In the end, my mad extravagance proved to be a sound decision as I rarely had to buy anything new for many years. I don't believe my husband ever recognised this fact, as years later he was heard to complain that I was a very extravagant shopper. In my defense, it happened only once.

Apropos of saving money, one day, Cyril received a telephone call from his mother. On learning that we were using taxis for transportation to the shops, Ooma had rung Cyril to protest.

What was the point of having a chauffeur if no-one ever requested to use him. What a terrible waste of money. Would we please use the chauffeur. She would arrange everything with him.

Roger was always reluctant to use any servants as he did not want to live a lavish life style, so, sadly, we never took advantage of this wonderful offer. At the time, I would have considered the gift of a chauffeur an interesting venture without undue or disproportionate compunction.

SOME FACTS ABOUT JUDAISM and MARRIAGE IN THE FRANKLIN FAMILY

If one looks at the family history, opinions regarding Judaism and marriage have been challenged and altered over successive generations. In his will, Lord Swaythling stated that no inheritance would be passed on to any child who married a Gentile and the cause of Liberal Judaism was to receive no money from his financial resources.

As an Orthodox Jew, he was concerned that the beliefs and customs of this section of Judaism should be maintained.

When three of Lord Swaythling's daughters, Roger's grandmother, Henrietta, and her two sisters, Marian and Lily, chose to leave Orthodox Judaism and Lily established the Liberal Jewish Synagogue with their support, there was obviously a deep schism in the traditional religious beliefs within the Franklin family. None of Lord Swaythling's children ever married anyone outside of the Orthodox Faith but successive generations did marry people who diverged from Orthodox practices.

As mentioned previously, Olive, Roger's grandmother, Henrietta's daughter, had married a Gentile.

Ivor Montague, a grandson of Lord Swaythling, was a zoologist, well known table tennis player, and film maker, who claimed that reading religious texts had made him an infidel. The God of the Old Testament was not a just God. He was particularly distressed that He allowed suffering among the innocent.

His reasoning reminded me of my own reactions to The Bible when I was a teenager. I found unjust events, particularly in the Old Testament, and miraculous events in both the Old and New Testaments, which forced me to question the nature of God and the veracity of his reported deeds. Rational doubts and questions about the purpose of suffering in the world ultimately led me to relinquish my religious beliefs altogether.

In 1927, Ivor married someone who was a typist and stenographer. For nine days, he was pilloried and lampooned in the newspapers for marrying someone of a different class, a lower class. Blatant headlines were printed for all to see what a dreadful marriage he had made, stating: "Baron's Son Marries Secretary."

It was obviously a matter of some concern, so much so that Queen Mary, who was a close friend of Ivor's mother, wrote to her saying: "Dear Gladys, I feel for you." 'May.'

Herbert Samuel, The First Viscount Samuel, (Ivor's cousin), the very one who invited us to lunch had become a non-observant Jew. Having read Darwin when he was at Balliol College, he felt he could no longer accept Jewish beliefs as reasonable explanations for the origins of life. As a result, he came to relinquish all religious faith and belief.

In 1960, Monk Gibbon, an Irish writer and friend of the family, wrote a biography of Roger's Grandmother called "Netta". In it, he states that two of Ooma's grandchildren had married Gentiles and one has married a coloured American. I have to smile.

Am I not a Gentile? This important fact is dismissed as probably the more shocking one is that I am coloured. Does this count as two points against me?

My immediate reaction was one of amusement a la Lady Bracknell. To have one point against me might be considered a misfortune, but to have two, looks like a disaster.

It did make me wonder how much being a Gentile and coloured, in addition, might make my acceptance totally impossible to some. I had already experienced disapproval and rejection in the US. I did not really expect life to run a completely smooth course in England. (In the 1950's, coloured was a neutral, descriptive term without the negative, derogatory associations it has acquired today, except in the southern United States and South Africa.)

Those who were of Orthodox persuasion could not be expected to approve of my marriage to Roger.

I had married into a very upper-middle class English family which meant that, like many middle-class families, there would be no histrionics, no public protest, no unfavourable opinions ever expressed openly, even if there were general disapproval.

P.S.

While some of Ooma's great-grandchildren have been brought up to follow the Jewish faith, many have not, particularly those who married Gentiles. Lord Swaythling and all Orthodox Jews are right to be concerned about dilution of the faith when people "marry out". I can, in no way, feel responsible for this outcome of diluted Jewish beliefs, as when I married Roger, he was already an atheist.

He was aware of his Jewish heritage. Under the influence of his grandmother, he had participated in Liberal Jewish practices but later came to relinquish any association with religious beliefs.

MEETING ROGER'S GRANDMOTHER

Probably, the most influential member of Roger's family that I was to meet was his grandmother, The Honourable Henrietta Franklin. When I asked why the title, I was informed that her father was Baron Swaythling. She could not inherit her father's title as she was a female. But, in recognition of her father's rank, she was entitled to be addressed as, "The Honourable."

Her father, Baron Swaythling, was only the second Jewish man to have been appointed a peer in England. A Rothschild had been the first.

The Honourable" was also referred to as "Netta" by friends and as "Ooma" by her grandchildren and their companions. I always addressed her as "Ooma" which means Grandmother in Dutch. When she asked us to dinner at her residence, at 50 Porchester Terrace, very near Kensington Gardens, we, of course, accepted, saying that we'd be pleased to attend. Sadly, Roger's grandfather, Ernest, had died a few years prior to our marriage, so I never met him.

I was unsure as to how I would be received into this Liberal Jewish family. Roger told me that his aunt Olive, had married someone who was not Jewish and in addition, was a Communist. Some family members had vociferously expressed disapproval regarding both these acts. I felt that I should, at least, prepare myself for a cool reception from Roger's grandmother and possibly other family members.

When we reached Roger's grandmother's residence, Letty, the Irish maid, answered the door and led us to the sitting room, announcing our arrival. I was immediately struck by his grandmother's impressive and imposing presence. With her erect posture and her steadfast gaze, she radiated a regal confidence that left me totally in awe and quaking somewhat at the thought of having to approach her.

To my relief, she greeted me warmly, allaying my imminent fears about acceptance, and introduced me to other guests and family members. Of all the people that I met that evening, it was only Aunt Lily who absolutely refused to shake my hand.

As far as I was concerned, the dinner party was a reasonable success, meaning that although initially hesitant, I was able to converse with individuals with whom I was unacquainted, irrespective of their social position.

As the dinner party drew to a close, Roger's grandmother suddenly rose, smiled at the guests and as someone pulled out her chair, she started walking past the guests towards the dining room door. One by one, each woman guest rose and seemed to be guided by her example. As I was observing this procedure and slow to grasp what was happening, I was the last to rise and to follow suit. For one agonising moment, I realised that I was the only woman in the dining room. A little perplexed and terrified, I assumed that I should follow suit and make a dignified departure as soon as possible.

As I walked to the end of the room, I suddenly felt as if I had been thrust into a very remote and distant past. I was experiencing the time-honoured tradition of men and ladies withdrawing from each other's company after dinner, each to follow their own pursuits. Thank goodness, I had read a few novels where this practice had been described. Otherwise, I might have been at a total loss to comprehend what was happening.

The men were left to smoke cigars and to drink port. The ladies genteelly retired to the sitting room to chat informally amongst themselves. Maybe they indulged in a little sherry or maybe not. I don't really know. As I walked out of the dining room door, I heaved a great sigh of relief and decided not to join the ladies immediately.

I wandered in a leisurely way down a hall and quite incidentally, bumped into some of the servants. It seemed that they all remembered my mother-in-law, Miriam, who was also American and insisted that I sounded exactly like her, not really true but we did both have American accents.

As the servants were more spontaneous and said what they thought, the conversation flowed smoothly. I had absolutely no reservations about talking to them, totally unlike some of the titled people around the dining room table whose dialogue could be ponderous and sometimes tediously solemn, especially when talking about the serious decline in the number of servants available to work.

When I later entered the sitting room, Roger's grandmother, whom I thought might be annoyed at my disappearance, proffered me a welcoming smile. When the men eventually appeared to take their partners home, she asked me to stay behind to help her choose which dresses she should send to the Victoria and Albert Museum.

This house, 50 Porchester Terrace, had been bombed during the war and London County Council was taking it over, to build a new school in its place. I could not believe that this beautiful home of parquet floors and marble fireplaces was to be razed to the ground.

As her home of 50 years was to be demolished, Ooma was moving to another newer house, but it was smaller. In order to accommodate her new surroundings, she was reducing the size of her possessions, her furniture, her books and her wardrobe.

I had no idea which dresses the V&A might accept and she, no doubt, knew that. I accepted her request as a gesture of kindness and a way of making me feel accepted in the family.

She was 86 when I met her and at the age of 88, she moved to her new dwelling in Carlton Hill, St. John's Wood.

When I queried people about Aunt Lily's reaction to me, I was assured that it would have been due to serious distress that I was not Jewish and would have nothing to do with my colour.

On learning more about the family, it was evident that they had already established a reputation for being Liberal in politics and liberal and free-thinking in regard to people of different ethnicity.

In the 1920's, Geoffrey, Roger's uncle had brought the internationally renowned, black singer, actor and Communist, Paul Robeson, to sing at Porchester Terrace. A famous woman poet from India, Sarajni Naidu, had been invited to stay there as well. Many years previously, both Ooma and her sister Lily, had travelled to the East End to hear Mahatma Gandhi speak at a prayer meeting.

Ooma had very generously welcomed me into the family, and I was pleased that we could be friends. Over the years we corresponded often, transmitting the news via hand-written letters. When I became head of the board of the nursery school in Putney, Vermont, it was a small, rural enterprise and every mother was asked to take on this task for a year, she informed various members of the family of how well I was doing and praised my managerial skills, which, I may add, were barely, newly burgeoning at the time.

If Ooma had indicated that she had reason to disapprove of me, my entrée into the Franklin family would have been far more problematic. She was, without doubt, the matriarch of the family. Her opinion was always sought when important decisions were to be made.

Even after her death, some members of the family attempted to settle differences by stating: "Mother would have liked that" or "Mother would not approve."

I continued to correspond with her until her death at 96. In her will, she left me a long necklace made of Russian malachite and an even longer Victorian necklace of amber and onyx.

MEETING SOME OF THE RELATIVES

BARON SWAYTHLING

Upon investigating the Franklin family history, I became aware of what a distinguished family they actually were-not because of their titles but because of their many accomplishments. Roger's great-grandfather, Baron Swaythling, (1832-1911), an Orthodox Jew, was a prominent politician in the Liberal Party and a well-known philanthropist and art collector.

He had changed his name from Montagu Samuel to Samuel Montagu, most likely for business reasons. He had founded the large merchant bank in London, entitled Samuel Montague and Co. Ltd., which was still extant when I first arrived in England. For many years, all my English purchases were duly recorded in my English chequebook from Samuel Montague and Co. (SM and Co.) no longer exists as it merged with the Midland Bank sometime in the 1960's and underwent later transformations with other banks.

OOMA

Roger's grandmother, The Honourable Henrietta Franklin, (1867-1964), was Baron Swaythling's eldest daughter. Her accomplishments are almost too numerable to list.

Although never mentioned by anyone, she walked on a wooden leg for almost half of her life. In her early forties, she had developed a malignant tumour in her leg, and was forced to have an amputation at the hip. Despite walking with either one or two sticks, she was of such a stoic character that she never complained of the constant pain she experienced in her phantom limb.

She was a great defender of women's rights and women's education. A woman doctor delivered her six children. She employed the first woman surgeon in England, Dame Louisa Aldrich-Blake, to perform her amputation. In Tavistock Square, there is a double-faced monument erected to her memory.

She received a CBE for her work in education and with Charlotte Mason, promoted the work of the PNEU-the Parents National Education Union which offered a more liberal and individualised approach to learning than the prevailing customs generally allowed.

She believed in co-education, an unpopular concept at the time, and sent her four sons to Bedales, a school which was considered radical and progressive, giving the students more autonomy than public schools ever allowed.

She strongly promoted the idea of higher education for her daughters when girls were generally denied access to colleges and universities. Her daughter, Olive, had an Honours Degree from Girton College and a Diploma from the London School of Economics. Marjorie, the eldest, became a psychiatrist and a psychoanalyst. She helped to establish the Institute for the Scientific Study of Delinquency-which later became the Portman Clinic. In the 1930's, she founded the Q Camps for juvenile delinquents. She was a Fellow of the British Psychological Society and a founder of the Planned Environment Trust.

Not only was Ooma a member of the British Suffragette Movement, but she also assisted in the establishment of the Jewish League of Women Suffrage. When women were accorded the vote in 1929, she joined the National Council for Women which promoted social and welfare programmes for women and children. In 2018, Henrietta Franklin and fifty-nine fellow suffragists were commemorated on the Millicent Garret Fawcett statue in Parliament Square.

During the War, her home became a refuge and meeting place for many refugees, escaping the terrors of WW2. As so many refugees were cared for at 50 Porchester Terrace, her residence was nicknamed "The Henrietta Arms".

At my U3A (University of the Third Age) classes, I have met at least four people who have told me of the warm reception their relatives received in Ooma's house. Many credit her with sponsoring and saving many distressed and distraught individuals.

I have just been informed by one of the people in my U3A writing class, Lily, that she was refugee from Czechoslovakia and went to a boarding school in Wales. When she came to London, she went to 50 Porchester Terrace to obtain some clothing. She remembers taking two dresses, that were hers to keep. They were important, as she had few possessions of her own.

It is all the more surprising to realise that Ooma's overwhelming number and variety of accomplishments occurred at a time when women were seen as incapable and unsuitable for important educational pursuits and serious careers. All classes, including the rich, upper classes and the aristocracy were in total agreement with these beliefs.

Ooma was born in the Victorian Era (1837 to 1901) and lived through the Edwardian Era (1901-1910) and the pre-Suffragist era. These were times when men were most vociferous in expressing their prejudiced misconceptions about women.

Her own husband, Ernest, did not believe in votes for women, but always stated that the women he liked best were Suffragists. (How diplomatic!!)

When Louise Aldrich Blake performed Ooma's leg amputation, she received no credit from Ernest. He informed friends that, contrary to belief, a woman surgeon had not performed the operation.

Ooma wrote to the surgeon named, Sir Victor Horsley, to ask what was his contribution during the operation. When he replied that he was merely an observer, we trust that the matter ended there.

I was, at first, shocked at Ernest's attitude but he was, in no way, exceptional in his outlook. He was merely reflecting the opinions of most, if not all, men of the time.

EDWIN MONTAGUE

Roger's great-uncle, Edwin Montague, his grandmother's brother, was Secretary of State for India from 1917 to 1922 and was also a member of Parliament.

In 1917, the Balfour Declaration was instituted. It declared that the British supported the establishment of a Jewish homeland in Palestine. It also stated that the civil and religious rights of the existing non-Jewish citizens would not be prejudiced.

Edwin Montague felt passionately that this document was anti-semitic and announced that he would not support it. Of interest is the fact that Herbert Samuel, his cousin, and also a Liberal politician strongly opposed his stance.

Of course, it was too late for me to have met Baron Swaythling or The Rt. Honourable Edwin Montague, but one of the first people to invite us to lunch in England was Herbert-the first Viscount Samuel and his wife, Beatrice.

He had been very influential in promoting the Balfour Declaration which established the state of Israel. He was appointed the First High Commissioner of the British Mandate of Palestine from 1920 to 1925. It was a very difficult job as there was fluctuating dissension amongst both the Arab and Jewish nationalists.

He was the leader of the Liberal Party from 1931 to 1935. When I met him, he was the leader of the Liberals in the House of Lords from 1944 to 1955 and had remained president of the Institute of Philosophy (1931 to 1959). He had already published at least 2 books interpreting philosophy.

EWEN MONTAGUE

Ewen Montague (1901- 1985) whom I never met, was the second son of the second Baron Swaythling. He was a British judge, a writer, and a Naval Intelligence Officer. He played a leading role in "Operation Mincemeat", which misled the Germans into attacking Greece when the Allies whom they wanted to attack were situated in Sicily.

Ewen Montague wrote a book about it, entitled, "The Man Who Never Was." It was later made into a film.

Ben McIntyre made a BBC documentary about this deception, "Operation Mincemeat", stating that it was a true story which changed the course of WW2.

The plot was an original idea of Ian Fleming's, produced when he was working with two British Intelligence Officers, Charles Cholmondeley and Ewen Montague. Their clever plan was put into operation with the assistance of a very well-informed coroner. The British planted a dead body with evidence so convincing that the Germans were totally misdirected in their attempts to annihilate the enemy.

ROSALIND FRANKLIN (1920-1958)

Rosalind Franklin, Roger's second cousin, was another member of the Franklin family whom I never met. She was a chemist and an X-ray crystallographer. In her research at King's College, she produced the now famous photo no. 51 which revealed that the helical structure of DNA had two strands with phosphate bases attached in the middle.

Due to the dreadful prejudice expressed towards her by the men working at the institution, she felt obliged to leave King's College and began doing research at Birkbeck College on virus particles. She and the scientists working in this field from 1953 to 1958 made the significant discoveries which established the foundation of modern virology.

She was no longer allowed to continue any research on DNA. Maurice Wilkins who was working at King's College-removed photo no. 51 from Rosalind's Research, without informing her and passed it on to Crick and Watson. In 1962, Maurice Wilkins, Francis Crick and James Watson received a Nobel Prize in Medicine for discovering the Structure of DNA. At this time, no credit was then given to Rosalind Franklin's contribution.

Watson, in 1968, wrote" The Double Helix "and portrayed her as a difficult, uncooperative and incompetent individual, incapable of interpreting her own data.

Rosalind Franklin died in 1958 of cancer. It is only in more recent decades that the scientific community has paid tribute to her pivotal contribution to the understanding of how DNA is constructed. There are now important scientific institutions and research grants and scholarships for women established in her honour, rectifying the injustice of her previous position and publicly acknowledging her unique contributions to the discovery of DNA and to the developing of virology.

MADGE

Dr. Marjorie Franklin, or Madge, as we called her, was the well-known psychiatrist in the family. She was Cyril's elder sister and lived in Hampstead, not far from her brother's residence.

With the Quaker, David Willis, she was a co-founder of the Q Camps which provided a caring and controlled environment for seriously maladjusted boys. They proved to be a great success but sadly, at the end of WW2, the Q camps came to an end.

Madge had never married and when we arrived for tea, we were greeted by two very lively, affectionate dogs, excitedly barking at the new guests. Any attempts to calm them down lasted for no more than two minutes. The dogs were very likeable but clearly lacking in discipline. It seemed that their rambunctious behaviour could not be quelled.

I idly wondered if the rules Madge had so successfully applied to difficult human beings might not also be employed with difficult animals. It was a matter of enforcing consequences for undesirable behaviour.

When I later became acquainted with the famous dog trainer, Barbara Woodehouse's work, in the 1960's, my meandering thoughts were vindicated. Her motto was: "There were no bad dogs" and I hastened to add, "only untrained dog-owners".

A few years later, Madge came to visit us in Putney, Vermont-after the arrival of our four children. She had developed very bad arthritis. As she entered the door for the first time, she found me holding a baby in one arm and with the other, quickly attempting to remove all the scatter rugs from the floors so that she wouldn't slip as she hesitatingly manoeuvred through the rooms with her stalwart cane.

As I was busy ferrying children back and forth to Nursery School and Primary School and Roger was teaching all day, Madge was happy to sit ensconced in the Putney School library, reading.

Roger and I had both noted that she never went anywhere without a hat on her head, a fairly distinctive and unusual characteristic. One day, as Roger was on his way to pick Madge up from the library, one of his students rushed to him excitedly, to tell him that he had just seen the famous English cartoonist, Giles's grandmother. She must be his model and here she was reading in the Putney library. Roger and I laughed many times about this incident as it was a very accurate description of Madge's appearance. This student's powers of perception could not have been more acute.

OLIVE-THE PARSONS FAMILY

Next on the list of invitations was the one from the Parson's family, which consisted of Olive, Henry, and their three children. Olive was another of Cyril's older sisters. Nicholas and Diana were both at university and Damien was studying architecture.

Marrying a Gentile and a Communist, Olive had acquired the reputation of being a rebel. I had envisaged her as impulsive and likely to act without thought for the consequences. But, indeed, totally the opposite was true. Her opinions, political and otherwise, seemed to be arrived at through careful consideration and her demeanour was calm and measured. She and Henry appeared to be delighted to meet us.

When we lived in Putney, Vermont, Nicholas, the youngest son, and Owen, Roger's youngest brother came to visit, with their friend John Geidt. Later their daughter, Diana Holiday, her husband, Robin, and their children came to visit us in Vermont when Robin was either lecturing or doing research in genetics in the States. When we eventually moved to Radlett, Herts, in England, we re-established contact with Diana, Robin and their four children as they lived in the town next to us, Ellstree, Herts.

Many years later, my daughter, Michèle, and Damien became very good friends, attending classical music concerts and art exhibitions together. Damien bought a number of her husband, Brian Taylor's, sculptures.

ANGELA and GERALD LOEWI

We then accepted a very generous invitation from Angela and Gerald Loewi, who had been married only a few months prior to our wedding. Angela was Roger's first cousin, Michael's daughter. Gerald was a German, Jewish pathologist, who was educated in England and working at Oxford.

Angela was a marvellous cook, having been trained at a hoteliere school in Switzerland. They very graciously escorted us round the sights of Oxford and much later came to visit us in Vermont when Gerald had completed his Fellowship at Columbia University in NY.

When we first came to England, we re-established our friendship with the Loewis. Angela, who was teaching then, was particularly informative about the state school system which helped me to decide which school the children should attend in Great Missenden.

There were other invitations from other family members, but some of the people mentioned above were the first of the family that we met.

THE SAVILE CLUB

Michael, Cyril's younger brother, invited us to join him for afternoon tea at the Savile Club in Mayfair. It was established in 1848 by a group of well-known artists and writers at the time. Members included Charles Darwin, Lord Rutherford, Robert Louis Stevenson, H.G. Wells, Thomas Hardy and C.P. Snow. It still exists today in a large building on Brook Street in London.

It was a gentlemen's club to which many of the Franklin family belonged. Their members engaged in convivial conversation, food and drink and sleep, played bridge, poker, and snooker, and retreated occasionally to the seclusion of the club library. They were expensive, all male institutions created for the pleasure of their very wealthy clientele.

I was amused to think that the prospect of the two sexes being in each other's company for any prolonged period of time was such a strain for the males that they had constructed organisations and associations to escape the company of women.

Michael informed me that I should feel honoured to visit the Saville Club, as previously women were totally forbidden entry. This generous concession involved providing a special entrance for women which was definitely not through the main door. As I walked unsteadily on a path of large cobblestones, we reached an unobstructive, clandestine entrance somewhere to the rear or side of the main building.

Although women were allowed to enter their hallowed premises, but such a fact was obviously to be hidden from public view. I found this form of discrimination against women preposterous and was more affronted than honoured when I realised that women were still being treated as second-class citizens.

We all entered a room of burnished dark wood, leather couches and chairs with studded, leather backs. Michael ordered tea and I was suddenly faced with an array of gleaming silver containers, which the maid placed ever so carefully on the glass tabletop. The shiny, large teapot, an even larger container of hot water, a sugar bowl, a small jug with milk, china teacups and saucers, and silverware for the tea, scones and cake.

I had, by this time, learned that there was a ritual for serving tea in England. Most insisted that the milk to be poured in the cup first and the tea was to follow. To pour the ingredients into the cup in the wrong order could cause great consternation and, I was told, could produce an unpalatable beverage.

I was very grateful that I had acquired this knowledge before commencing to serve anyone. Common sense dictated that I confirm again the correct procedure for what I used to think was a simple task. With all eye upon me and specific instruction, I did manage to provide cups of tea for everyone, following the approved etiquette.

The concealed entrance to the Savile Club and the rituals of serving tea, were two more incidents that I added to my ever-growing list of learning about different aspects of English life.

As for making a cup of tea at home, Roger very clearly informed me that the teapot must be warmed first, i.e. rinsed first with boiling water, the tea leaves and boiling water to be added afterwards.

In his estimation, the use of tea leaves was sacrosanct. An infusion made from tea bags was not considered a proper brew. It was assumed that the presence of the bag inhibited the flow of the fresh flavour of the tea leaves.

ARRIVAL AT GLENALLA

As the days progressed at 110 West Heath Road in London, everyone seemed to be focussed on one subject, preparing for the summer holiday at Glenalla, in Ireland.

Ooma, my husband Roger's grandmother, had been brought up by strict nannies and strict German governesses. On her summer holidays, she was allowed a brief break from her daily lessons. This meant that she could walk for one or two hours to and fro along the sea-front, always accompanied by her governess and adorned in her elegant clothes and buttoned boots.

Determined that her children would never have to undergo such a constricted regime, she was inspired to buy (with her husband, Ernest), Glenalla, a large house in Donegal, Ireland. It was in southern Ireland known as Eire, though geographically it was in the northern part of the country. She was in hopes of providing a more wild and challenging environment in which the children could experience and explore the wonders of the natural world.

The original house was constructed in the early 18th century and has obviously been greatly altered since then. It was the place where Roger, his family, relations and numerous friends always spent their summer holidays. As it was composed of at least 15 bedrooms, there was ample space, but it was so popular that various family members took turns to visit in successive weeks.

We flew to Belfast, a short flight-just over an hour and a half. When we arrived at the airport, John, our driver, was already waiting to greet us in a car he had driven from Glenalla that very morning. After arranging our luggage in the boot of the car, he drove continuously until we reached Dungivven Pass where we suddenly stopped. Thermoses of hot tea and a variety of different sandwiches were provided for everyone. Family custom determined that a picnic tea for all travellers to Glenalla would always be offered at this junction.

The journey continued to Londonderry, Letterkenny and Ramelton. Eventually we reached the bridge at Ray and then Lough Swilly, after which we turned into the woods approaching Glenalla. On the left was the Gate Lodge, the only sign of any human presence to appear along this part of the journey.

As we proceeded, the dappled sunlight bounced off the clusters of trees. It seemed that we were surrounded by a forest, truly dark and deep, which emitted bold rays of light only intermittently and unpredictably. And then, there was an abrupt change. There were no trees, only a huge meadow on the left. Suddenly, the road was flooded with sunlight and as I turned my head, I caught sight of my first glimpse of Glenalla.

John, noisily and persistently tooted the car horn, announcing our arrival. As he did so, I looked out of the car window to see a number of servants running to the front of the house. John unexpectedly spoke and said they were lining up to meet the new bride, to meet me, a bride of barely two months. In nervous anticipation and surprise, I looked at Roger. "What should I do? "How should I greet them?"

Roger was the rebel in the family and did not really approve of his family having servants. He shook his head and shrugged his shoulders, indicating that he didn't know what the appropriate greeting would be. To my dismay, I accepted that there was to be no assistance with protocol in my novel predicament.

We had already been chastised by his father for being too friendly with their maid. This friendliness consisted of one, possibly two conversations that were not directly related to her line of work. We did not know how to comport ourselves properly with the servants. It was important that a certain distance, physical and psychological was maintained between the employer, his family, and the servants. In addition, no large tips were to be given to anyone working there.

Not adhering to these rules could alter the servants' expectations. They might assume that a friendship could develop between themselves and their employer. Or they might become discontent with their present salary which, up to this point, they had found perfectly adequate.

Remembering my father-in-law's words, I decided that shaking hands would probably be considered a gesture far too familiar in this situation. As we stepped out of the car, Ooma approached and led us to the front of the two queues of servants. At the head, standing a little apart, was Kay Daly, the manager of the house throughout the year. I was first introduced to her and as we exchanged greetings, she extended her hand, and I politely shook it.

I then stood staring at all the maids, adorned with stiff, white hats, decorated with a little ruff in front and a line of black uniforms, covered with starched, white aprons which fairly glistened in the sun.

Behind them was another queue which consisted of the head gardener and various workmen, all dutifully standing to attention.

Ooma, then introduced me to them as "Mrs. Roger" which was the correct form they were to use to address me. With three Franklin brothers, it would have been too confusing to have three Mrs. Franklins on the premises. The three wives, two of whom were wives-to-be, were to be distinguished, one from the other, by use of our husband's names.

As I was introduced, I uttered a quiet hello and tried to include each one in my glance. I wanted to appear friendly but wished I actually knew if what I was doing was the accepted behaviour for this occasion.

When this slightly unnerving ordeal was over, Ooma escorted us to the front door. Heaving a great sigh of relief, I walked over the threshold and stepped into the vestibule of Glenalla.

As I entered the house, I was thinking that the servants would have been surprised to realise that I was ill at ease, not knowing the appropriate way to greet them. Someone in my position was always meant to know the correct procedure. But in this instance, they had the advantage over me.

They had been trained in how to relate to their employers, with diffidence mostly and not ever putting their own ideas forward. Class differences were accepted and acknowledged at this time, maybe more so among the uneducated, poor in Ireland, as without training, they had few choices for work. Many had no option but to go "into service" and work for the rich.

They admired and respected their employers. It might have seemed almost self-evident that they were superior in every way. They were obviously more wealthy, more educated and more knowledgeable than anyone in their family or in the surrounding towns and villages would ever be.

GLENALLA

As I stepped over the threshold and into the house, facing me was a very large and very dignified portrait of Ooma when she was younger, commonly referred to as the Sargent portrait by the family. Roger's grandfather, Ernest, had commissioned John Singer Sargent to paint it many years ago.

On the small, round table beside her are her books. She is devoid of any jewellery with the exception of a watch or bracelet on one arm. Her hands are resting demurely, one on the other. Her quiet, slightly retiring glance combined with the presence of her books suggests a woman of learning and erudition, a woman of serious pursuits.

Some of her friends thought it was unlike her because she looked too relaxed, whereas they identified her as a woman constantly busy and full of energy. I always thought that the portrait made her appear more reticent and less dynamic than she actually was in reality.

The first room everyone enters is a very large reception room with shiny wooden floors. Near the centre is the table-tennis table and not far away is the large piano. On the wall facing it is a remarkably good portrait of Ernest painted by my mother-in-law, Miriam.

In one corner there is a fireplace with peat from the surrounding hills-stacked in front of it, some comfortable chairs and books and bookcases along the wall. This is the family room where children play cards and games, construct puzzles and play music or table tennis, if they are old enough.

Along the outside wall are window seats with pelmets and matching patterned cushions and curtains. Across the room is a folding bridge table with puzzles and photos in the drawers.

Behind the doors on the left, is the comfortably carpeted drawing room which is basically white with pelmets and rose-coloured curtains. Blue and white Dutch tiles surround the fireplace and bookshelves are extended on the walls around the room.

I have only become acquainted with pelmets since coming to England. They are the ornamental strips which hide the curtain rail. I realise that all Americans are devoid of this essential piece of curtaining as their curtain rails are often display in full public view.

In the middle of the three, huge drawing room windows, stands Ooma's Chippendale desk. Every morning, she sits here to deal with her correspondence and to consult with the manager about the accounts, the daily chores for the staff, and the shopping list for meals for all the guests.

On Saturday mornings, everyone was invited to attend a brief Liberal Jewish Service in the drawing room. Guests who were not always of the Jewish faith, often participated. I most certainly attended and along with others, read certain passages from printed pages that were given to me.

The doors from the drawing room led directly into the dining room. They were painted by Miriam, my mother-in-law. She had originally come to England to study painting before she had ever met her husband-to-be, Cyril.

On the dining room side of the doors, each of the eight panels was decorated with a different kind of vegetable, beautifully drawn, and a very accurately observed insect is incorporated into the composition.

The dining room furniture consisted of a very long table of dark wood with matching chairs and various sideboards. The main meal of the day was always served promptly at one o'clock and announced by the striking of a metal gong. The uniformed maids served all courses at this meal and were on duty in the kitchen to respond to any requests.

If anything was required but not available, Ooma rang the bell hidden beside her underneath the table and a maid appeared immediately.

Cold dishes were the generally accepted food for the evening meal, set out in silver, covered dishes on the sideboard. Often, a hot soup accompanied the meal. Guests were always arriving at different times from their various outings, so it was considered more practical to allow them to cater for themselves.

Behind the dining room were the back stairs which the maids used to reach their sleeping quarters and a very large kitchen with an Aga and scullery where the dishes were washed. Further along was the boot room and a room where the fishing rods were kept.

The steps at the front of the house led from the large reception room to the first floor. As we went up the stairs, I noted that the carpet was fixed with a thick brass rod at the bottom of each step, keeping each section sturdily in place.

I had never seen stairs carpeted in this manner before and thought how lovely the brass rods were, shining in the light. But no thoughts about incorporating them into my lifestyle as they would be yet another cleaning chore for the busy housewife.

The entire first floor of the house was devoted to bedrooms for the family and guests and two large bathrooms at either end of the floor. The servants' quarters, which were out of bounds, were on the second floor.

Flowers from the garden were on display in any nook or recess that could accommodate them. As we opened our bedroom door, there was a vase of purple, yellow and white flowers standing on a bureau, spreading a lovely scent throughout the room.

Bedrooms were appropriately but not extravagantly furnished. The furniture was practical, but no expensive antiques were on show. It was, after all, a summer house meant to survive the rain and mud and all the guests' out-of-doors excursions.

All guests were encouraged to appear for breakfast. Ooma was always there, probably before anyone else had arrived. She was an early riser. My father-in-law, Cyril, was the only person exempt from this arrangement. As he rose later, one of the maids brought his breakfast on a tray to his bedroom when he awoke.

Well, then and there the idea had been planted in my head. What would it be like to have breakfast in bed? As I always had to rise early for school, a job, or to perform chores in the house, I had never experienced the joy of having breakfast in bed.

Roger was very accommodating and the night before, ordered breakfast from one of the maids in the kitchen. The next morning, a knock on the door announced the arrival of our breakfast tray.

It was wonderful and I thoroughly enjoyed it, but my puritanical conscience wouldn't allow me to totally yield to such hedonistic pleasures. I had a niggling feeling that any pleasure derived from this self-indulgent act might not last. It was just too good to be true.

My foreboding proved to be justified when we sat down to lunch that same afternoon. Ooma, who was sitting near me, smiled sweetly and stated: "We did not see you at breakfast today. Have we offended you in some way?" The message was clear and succinct. We, like all other guests, were expected to attend breakfast. And so it was that all thoughts of self-indulgent pleasures came to an abrupt end.

The accepted regime of this household, as arranged by Ooma, did not tolerate indolence or any form of self-indulgence. I'm sure my dastardly deed could be described as exhibiting both characteristics.

During the afternoon, all guests were expected to engage in some sort of excursion in the open air, usually regardless of weather. Ooma would stand on the glass terrace outside of the drawing room, pondering the clouds in the sky and the rain pouring down. She would then say: "It's not very pleasant now but I can see that it is lightening." I constantly scoured the sky for that special bit that was lightening, and I have to confess that I never found it.

But I was in no position to question Ooma's meteorological assessment of atmospheric conditions. Her words signified that we were all to resume our plans for our out-of-doors expeditions.

There were many options. A walk around the grounds would include the two Mill Houses in the rear of the grounds with ducks and hissing geese who chased away all pedestrians. Nearer the front was Glenbeg, the octagonal house in which Michael, Roger's uncle, lived.

A short meander on the left, leading away from the house and one is drawn to the sound of falling water. In a small, dark recess in a high hill, a waterfall comes into view, not far from the well- trodden path where the cars approach the house. The tennis courts, within short walking distance from the house, were always available for those who were so inclined.

Anyone who could row was free to take people out in the boat on the imposing pond in front of the house. We could climb the Peat Hill, distant but not too far from the house. Further afield, we could climb Mt. Errigal which was higher and more of a challenge. Let it be known that we were usually climbing under an overcast sky in the mist and drizzle and not infrequently, in the rain.

On sunny days, there were beach excursions, always picnics and bathing, at Kinnegar or McCarmish, and also frantically searching the sand at Ballywhooriskey for cowries. I fear there are very few left, as Roger is reported to have collected a thousand at the age of seven or thereabouts.

I often found it an anomaly that the children, dressed in woollen sweaters, raincoats, and rain-hats were expected to divest themselves of their protective clothing and go jump into the freezing Atlantic at the slightest sign of sunshine. But, of course, being children, they did, and they thoroughly enjoyed themselves.

There were longer trips along the coast to watch gannets diving off the high craggy cliffs and caves to explore, one of which was so tight that one human body at a time could just about squeeze through the enclosure.

When salmon were at their most prolific, Cyril and his brother, Michael often went fishing in the local loughs with any guest who cared to accompany them. We were usually taken in a boat, not far from the coastal bays, to watch the seals bobbing, up and down in the surrounding, cold, dark waves.

To purchase new Aran sweaters, made with wool from the local sheep, there were trips to Carrigart, to be measured and choose a pattern that one liked. And there were many from which to choose. We bought yards of Donegal tweed; the original tweed was reputed to never wear out. As it was so stiff, by no means was that observation an exaggeration. The tweed was always brought back to England to be taken to an English tailor to be turned into jackets and suits.

THE MANAGEMENT OF GLENALLA

I used to jokingly say that that I'd married into the end of the feudal era when I first realised how many servants were working at Glenalla. Their number was a much reduced version of how life was lived there, even a decade before my arrival. Refer to the TV series, "Downton Abbey" to acquire an understanding of how previous generations of Roger's family had lived, though not on so grandiose a scale.

When I arrived in England, there was a consistent theme discussed at most of the households we visited, the paucity of servants. How difficult it was to find either English or Irish girls to work as maids. The last resort was to hire foreigners, insisting that they speak good enough English to perform the tasks required. My father-in-law had been forced to hire an Austrian maid.

The same problems did not apply to the situation in Ireland. An Irish family, situated near Glenalla, provided the main supply of three or four permanent maids and at least two of the men who worked on the property. Their service had been reliable, faithful, and long-standing.

There were occasional difficulties finding and keeping scullery maids to wash dishes and pots and pans, as well as someone to pare the vegetables for the cook.

The days of ladies' maids had disappeared, or I would have been forced to have one as my mother-in-law had. Miriam and Roger's Aunt, Olive, told me similar stories regarding their personal maids. They had both, unintentionally, reduce these close companions to tears.

Miriam had, innocently, put some stockings in a suitcase that was being packed for a journey. Olive, who was an adult, had tried to brush her own hair. As both these jobs were always performed by the maids, they were immediately distressed, thinking that their jobs were under threat.

For the first time, I realised how constricting the relationship between the lady and the maid actually was. They were mutually dependent on each other. But once the lady declared her autonomy, the maid's function was made instantly redundant and superfluous.

There was still a laundry maid to whom we were expected to take our "smalls". When I enquired about "smalls", I was told they referred to underwear. I found the idea of giving these items to anyone to be washed by hand, extremely objectionable. I told my father-in-law that I'd be using the washing machine. Being set in his ways, he refused to believe that any machine could ever wash as well human hands.

Behind the kitchen was a huge laundry house in a separate building. There was a washing machine and ample space for hanging clothes to dry. Ooma proudly told me that many years ago, she had sent some laundry maids to a Laundry School in London where they could be trained to care for clothes properly.

It was the days of copper vats of boiling hot water, where a dolly was used to clean the clothes. A dolly was a wooden appliance with arms, used to stir the clothes in the washtub. Washboards were also in use - a ribbed board for scrubbing clothes by hand.

One can see that with the advent of machines, large numbers of servants would inevitably be replaced. Now, even the need for ironing is much reduced with the manufacture of man-made fibres.

Later, when grandchildren had arrived, my sister-in-law, Francis, Joe's wife, insisted that we should buy a clothes dryer and I supported her in this request.

It was never very warm at Glenalla. The main source of heat derived from the peat fires and the hot water bottles that the maids placed at the foot of our freezing beds every night.

As it rained frequently, it was problematic to dry clothes completely. Hanging them outside was an infrequent occurrence. My father-in-law eventually relinquished, and we were overjoyed to have dry clothes for the children.

Larders were in constant use both at Glenalla and at my father-in-law's house in the 1950's. A larder was a a cool room , sometimes with a screened , open window with marble slabs used to keep food cold. Despite the fact that both residences had refrigerators which kept food colder longer than larders, both houses continued to use larders. Milk and cream were covered with fine nets to keep the flies out. There seemed no necessity to put cold meat in the refrigerator as it was cooked and kept perfectly well in the cool larder. I was informed that eggs changed their flavour once put into the fridge, so best to keep them in the larder.

As time passed, and servants dwindled, I did see these habits slowly change. and all food, even eggs, sometimes found a special place in the refrigerator.

John, the general handyman and fixer of anything broken, and his wife, Maureen, had moved into the Gate Lodge at the end of the drive, after living in one of the small Mill Houses for many years. They had five children, similar in age to ours whom, I thought, would make good playmates for our children.

The following incidents after Ooma's death. I'm not sure that she would have approved of the children of gentry playing with the servants' children. She did believe in education for all children and supported and educated her secretary's son after both his parents had died.

We made it a practice to take John's children to the beach when we were taking ours. So unaccustomed were they to going to the beach that they appeared in their Sunday outfits, velvet dresses (hand-me-downs from Maureen's sister's children) and white shirts and ties. They might have been thought appropriate because they were going out with Mr. Franklin, the owner's, grandchildren.

I had no choice but to let them run around barefoot in the sand and pray that they wouldn't get their church outfits wet in the salt water. It had not occurred to me that, of course, they had no bathing suits.

Despite the inappropriate clothes, the children, after initial hesitance, relaxed and soon they were all running around madly, chasing each other in the sand dunes and paddling in the water.

I was always amazed at how deserted the beautiful Irish beaches were. Only visitors ever played in the pristine, clear, white sand. All the Irish inhabitants were working, most too poor to have a car. There was no public transportation in the vicinity, so they had no access to the sea.

We took all of the children, John's and ours, to see the latest children's films that were on in the summertime. Sound of Music was, apparently, the one no-one ever forgot.

The incident of the tricycles, it seems, was also of long-standing significance. When we visited many years later, John remembered my standing up to my father-in-law about John's children playing with our children's new toys and tricycles.

He never forgot my father-in-law standing rigid in the large, first-floor window, agitated, and shouting at the top of his voice: "Why had John's children taken over the toys we just bought them for our children?

I tried to reassure him that everyone was taking a turn with the new toys. As he grew more destressed at the sight of the grandchildren, the gentry, playing with the servants' children, his protests only grew louder and increased.

As the real cause of his distress was far too delicate a subject to argue about in front of the parties concerned, I told the children to continue playing with the tricycles, without addressing the issue between my father-in-law and me. I quite surprisingly discovered that John's family, apparently, remember it fondly and expressed only approval and admiration.

At all times, Roger supported me in my protests with his father. He was our reliable and knowledgeable driver for all excursions, particularly as I was completely unfamiliar with the Irish terrain. He did not condone the class system and intensely disliked the idea of servants. So convinced was he that they were all underpaid, that, on our departure, he gave every worker at Glendale a huge tip.

When Roger's father discovered his generosity towards the servants, he was, of course, not pleased. As he explained, once again, Roger was raising expectations in a situation where everyone was already completely content.

Despite our somewhat disruptive influence, my father-in-law always insisted that we stay at Glendale and was never happy when we left to take further excursions on the Continent, as we often did when visiting for the summer.

I often felt that my father-in-law's conditioning in relation to the class system prevented him from befriending people who he really liked. But, in his favour, I have to admit that he often went fishing with a local Irish policeman, an act unheard of at the time as people from different classes never mixed socially. Someone suggested that Cyril's behaviour only indicated how desperate he was to have company during the prolonged, silent hours, that he spent fishing.

The same was true for Madge, Roger's aunt, who was psychiatrist. She had spent most of her life, devoted to helping difficult adolescents from all classes. I was shocked, when we were sitting on a beach one day and an unknown family arrived to swim in the sea. Madge's first question was: "Are they gentry?" My immediate thought was, "Does it matter?" Of course, it did. My next assumption was that if they were, she would have found it appropriate for us to associate with them.

The Glenalla of today has retained two or three of the original maids. A cook is not now a semi-permanent member of the household and can be hired as necessary. The most dramatic change at Glenalla has been the temperature. Upon entering, no-one is greeted by a cool, slightly damp atmosphere. An even warmth pervades every room and there is no waiting for the arrival of the morning sun to create heat as it moved from one room to the other.

For ecological reasons, everyone agrees that peat must be preserved. A central heating system has been installed, and as a result, the sight of men shovelling slabs of peat from the surrounding hills for fireplaces at home is no longer, a visible part of the Irish landscape.

But drinking water and bath water still come from two different sources. Everyone still draws bath water from the local area, surrounded by peat which turns the water a hue of golden yellow.

In a room adjacent to the kitchen, a freezer now stands, which means that fresh vegetables can be quickly frozen and some meals can be prepared ahead of time. A telephone was installed many years ago just off the large reception room. The former difficulties of contacting anyone in such a remote and isolated place have totally disappeared with the use of computers and mobile phones. The estate is still maintained today by a generous trust fund set up by Cyril's older brother, Sydney Franklin.

THE MAGIC OF DONEGAL

The strange atmospheric effects of dark, rain clouds and beams of pale, yellow sunlight, in proximity, create a profound glow on the surrounding terrain. Loughs, heather, the gorse and grass, even the dark brown ferns that proliferate everywhere are all flushed with a warmth and brightness.

Only once, did I see a painting which did justice to this unusual and fascinating phenomenon. It was one of my mother-in-law, Miriam's oil paintings. She absolutely captured the feelings of the strange weather conditions and the glowing radiance which pervaded all aspects of everything which lay beneath.

A LITTLE ASIDE

The subject of heat always produced a difference in outlook between my father-in-law and me. The main reason is that I had grown up with central heating and he had not.

Like many English people of his generation, he grudgingly admitted that sometimes a warm room was a pleasant experience. But if central heating supplied the warmth, such a statement was followed by a series of complaints. "It was too expensive". "It was unhealthy to inhale the heated air." In addition, " the change in temperature from a centrally heated house to the cold air outside was the cause of the common cold".

"People were healthier before central heating ever arrived."

The entire time my mother-in-law lived in England, she suffered from chilblains. Doctors diagnosed the cause as lack of calcium. She was distressed that no-one would even consider cold as a contributing factor. When she returned to the US, to centrally heated housing, to her relief, her chilblains completely disappeared.

I do now know of a number of older English people, including Roger, who proudly live in houses without central heating. The suggestion usually is: "That it is somehow better for you".

Being told of the benefits of cold showers and cold houses, and the detriments of warmth and central heating, I concluded that the English, with such courage in adversity, possessed more than a little streak of masochism.

END OF THE SUMMER OF 1953

Having met all the relatives who desired to make our acquaintance and having enjoyed a few weeks at Glenalla, we decided to take a trip to the Continent. Roger purchased a car, and we bought the requisite camping equipment. This was not meant to be a trip of extravagance, living in luxurious hotels and indulging in expensive meals. Roger was in charge of map-reading and all the driving as I had not yet passed my driving test.

I found the idea of exploring foreign countries very appealing as the only travelling I had done had been under the auspices of the Quakers, attending conferences in different States, mainly examining relevant political issues and their consequences, with not a lot of time to explore our natural surroundings.

Since he was a child, Roger had been taken on skiing holidays to Switzerland so was already familiar with various parts of the European landscape.

In 1953, camping in Europe was a fairly popular concept but all campsites were not always well-equipped for the needs of the traveller. Some were still being constructed. In those cases, basic supplies were available i.e., a cold water tap and a hole in the ground for toilet facilities. Some of the longer established sites provided more comfortable amenities, hot and cold water, showers, toilets with seats and occasionally, even the use of a washing machine, though stone sinks with running water were the normal provision for clothes washing.

We travelled for nearly a month, camping everywhere, and it rained every day but three. As we were mostly driving and visiting the local tourist attractions in each country, the rain proved not to be too taxing a feature of the holiday.

We experienced two unfortunate incidents related to the weather. Practically unheard of, a small hurricane in Belgium. When we returned to the campsite, all tents were either flattened or had blown away. Ours was the only one left standing. Unlike most people, we lost only a few articles that were left out to dry.

It was one of the newer tent models with crisscrossed ribs, filled with air and looked exactly like an igloo. To our surprise, it confirmed the blurb we had read in the advertisement about its extremely strong construction.

The second incident occurred in our campsite, just outside of Rome. Due to torrential rain, our entire line of washing had fallen into large puddles of mud. I was upset. I had no choice but to accept the dreadful circumstances. It was not a situation that could not be rectified. Rinsing and washing the clothes again by hand, unpleasant though it was, was not an impossible task, but I secretly vowed that future holidays would have to include the use of a washing machine.

We dined out during the day, testing out all the unfamiliar foods and varied cuisine in every country. I bought all the essentials for cleaning and washing and food for the evening meal. Roger was mostly in charge of setting up the tent and lighting the portable gas stove. Supper consisted of sliced meat or cheese, with fresh salad and fruit and warm drinks, sometimes consumed with a reconstituted dehydrated soup.

The fun and madness of this trip consisted not only of dealing with the consistently inclement weather but also the fact that Roger had decided to see how many countries we could visit in this one short trip. This decision could only be put down to the exuberance and high spirits of youth. Who on earth would attempt to take in the sights of 15 (it may have been 16) countries in one month?

Included in the list of countries visited were some that I never knew existed. San Marino, in north-eastern Italy, is considered a micro-state and is surrounded completely by Italy. I discovered that three constitutional monarchies existed. Luxembourg was headed by a grand duke and is the very last existing grand duchy.

The second was Lichtenstein whose main leader was a member of the royal family, and the third was Monaco who was ruled at the time by Prince Albert.

Also included in the list of countries visited was the Vatican City. It is defined as a city-state, surrounded by Rome, definitely a separate enclave.

List of countries visited: France, Belgium, The Netherlands, Switzerland, Austria, Germany, Lichtenstein, Luxembourg, Monaco, Italy, San Marino, Vatican City, Greece.

Part of my excitement at the idea of travelling to see many countries was the splendid opportunity to see the original artwork that I had been poring over in books for many years. In our travels, we did manage to include many museums. The Louvre in Paris, particularly to see the Mona Lisa, and the impressive eighteen-foot sculpture of the Winged Victory of Samothrace, elegantly draped in a clinging, wet and wind-blown rob. Despite the queues in Vatican City, we saw the Sistine Chapel and some of Michelangelo's sculptures, including the Pieta. In Florence, I was overwhelmed by the size of his statue of David.

When we reached the Uffizi, in Florence, a very knowledgeable man sitting behind the first desk we approached, offered to take us on a guided tour of the museum, gratis. It was one of the most informative and interesting art tours I have ever experienced. It was wonderful. As he explained the mythical significance of the stories relating to the paintings and sculptures and how the artists worked, the art displayed seemed to take on a new significance. I don't know what inspired his act of great generosity, but his vast knowledge encouraged me to alter the way I viewed art. I began to engage with the artist's technique as well as putting the work in its historical context.

I felt compelled to see the works of Giotto. I had discovered him in art history books and had become fascinated with his paintings. Compared to the painters who had preceded him, his work appeared more modern in approach. The bodies were less flat and iconical in form, and the faces began to express recognisable, human emotions. We went to Padua to see the Scrovegni Chapel where the walls are covered with what are often considered some of his masterpieces.

In whatever country we entered, we were accustomed to viewing any exhibition or work of art that we desired. It was at Pompeii and Herculaneum, both cities that had been buried in volcanic ash from the eruption of Vesuvius in 79 AD, that we encountered our only difficulty.

It was at Pompeii that, as we were about to enter a building, a guard rushed over, gesticulating wildly. He stood in front of me, both feet planted firmly on the ground, and put his hands up to indicate that I was not allowed to enter. Roger and I stood perplexed. We said that we were married and were travelling together. "What was the problem?"

Roger was taken to one side, and in sotto voce tones, he was told that only men could enter this site. I would have to wait outside. It was a brothel and was not considered a suitable place for women to view.

Roger explained the situation to me, and we agreed that he should enter the doorway that was forbidden to me. The very erotic frescoes adorning the walls depicted ancient Roman sexual practices in a very direct and detailed manner.

These frescoes and other artwork were thought so shocking that they were locked away for long periods of time. When they eventually re-appeared, they caused such outrage that they were, once again, removed from public view and hidden away. It was not until the year 2000 that these works could be seen again by the general public.

On a much later trip to Pompeii, women were allowed to enter the forbidden premises and I viewed the prohibited frescoes. There was no room now for shock or surprise as I had already seen many of them in art books, as illustrations of ancient Roman art.

I was overwhelmed by the wide range of scenery in Europe from the flat lands of tulips and dykes in the Netherlands to the towering snow-covered mountains in Switzerland and Austria, and the pink-hued Dolomites in Italy. We saw castles along the Rhine, swam in freezing mountain lakes and the luxuriously warm water of the Adriatic Sea. We were astonished to find an exotic cactus garden in Monaco and were mesmerised by the clear reflections in the water of the Blue Grotto. When we reached Venice, we chose to hire a small barge as we considered the fares charged by the conventional gondolas exorbitant.

It had been a momentous and exciting summer, meeting Roger's relatives, learning how the rich lived, and viewing the varied and spectacular scenery of Europe. One of the highlights was seeing some of the pictures that I loved turned into real life paintings and three-dimensional sculptures.

It was now time for us to return to England, pack and fly home to our respective jobs and studies. I did wonder how life would seem after all the unexpected and exciting adventures that we had experienced. I needn't have worried. As life proceeded in its own inevitably, busy way, it proved to be as exciting and challenging as was necessary to keep us seriously occupied.

RETURN TO THE US, (1953)

Our return home went without incident, except for the fact that our BOAC flight stopped at Reykjavik, Iceland for refuelling. The name was so distinct that I never forgot it, as it was the capital of a country that I had never had to learn in school.

During the flight, we filled out forms, item by item, indicating which clothes were completely new and which had been worn. This tedious process was required for American tax purposes. The English allowed Americans or any foreigners to buy clothes tax-free to encourage sales while the Americans placed a duty on imported goods as a means of increasing their revenue.

We arrived home to settle in the flat we had rented before our departure. It was conveniently situated not too far from MIT where Roger was working. The immediate neighbourhood was comprised of mainly Polish people with a Polish supermarket quite close by.

We took the flat because the rent was cheap, and it had 5 rooms of reasonable size. Some of the walls were badly in need of a fresh coat of paint and, to my surprise, the bathroom contained only a shower. I had never before seen a house or a flat without a bathtub or even knew that such types of bathrooms existed.

The area could be described as less than salubrious. We were the last house on the road. After our dwelling, only factories were to be seen continually emitting offensive-smelling chemicals.

Despite the cheap rent and the spacious flat, there were obviously disadvantages in living so close to so many factories. There were times when we felt that the air must have been seriously polluted, especially when unpleasant vapours were released into the atmosphere.

Only once, did I hang the wet clothes outside to dry, because, when I retrieved them, they were completely flecked with tiny, black particles of something. We never determined the composition of these undesirable substances.

I, very quickly, learned never to open our back door as cats (no-one knew how many), had set up residence near the rear entrance of the ground floor.

On the first floor, there was a manager for all the flats. A Polish family of six lived rent-free in exchange for the wife's dealing with any problems that arose. Broken lightbulbs in the hall were always replaced. The stairs were spotlessly clean. The rubbish bins were labelled and kept in their allotted places. The pavement in front of the house remained clear of stray paper and debris but the manager admitted that cleaning the back stairs was a task too far.

As the cats were feral, she feared being attacked if she tried to remove them. In collusion, the tenants locked their back doors. They never used the stairs in the rear of the house and the cats remained in situ. No doubt triumphant in their success and glowering at any human intruders.

We were on the third floor, (the second floor, in England). In the bedroom, a chest of drawers was wedged against the wall. It was now a permanent fixture as no one could budge it in any direction. It was useful, with the exception of one drawer. Only by banging on one end and aligning it with the other end, could it be opened at all.

On the kitchen ceiling, some of the paint was peeling off in small flakes, The evening that a piece of loose paint with a bit of plaster fell into the dinner I was cooking, I decided that I should, at least, remove any weak sections of paint and plaster from the ceiling, to prevent any more meals being ruined.

Roger and I disagreed about how much repair was necessary for us to endure living there. I thought that most of the flat needed painting. It did not take Roger very long to conclude that my standards were unrealistically high. After further discussion, I decided that he had no standards whatsoever. The situation seemed impossible to resolve, but despite our differences, we did manage to paint two rooms together, but it was never as many as I would have liked.

I had assumed that, given Roger's background, he would expect to live in pristine surroundings. My assumptions were totally mistaken. Our differences in standards of maintenance continued throughout our marriage.

I was shocked that I had not become aware of areas where our opinions differed. But, of course, these were early days in our marriage. I was always focussing on areas of agreement, the harmony between us and the similarity of our religious and political outlooks. Prior to our marriage, my rose-coloured spectacles had been too firmly fixed for me to even recognise any dissimilarities between us. Such differences could only be revealed after we started living together.

Despite our disagreements about decorating, we did agree about the kind of furniture that we would purchase. During our Saturday morning meanderings around Cambridge, we found second-hand shops and charity outlets where we eventually bought everything we needed. Both of us were very pleased that not one item had cost more than $1. But I did protest loudly when, one Saturday morning, Roger returned home with a second-hand mattress. "It didn't matter how clean it looked, you never knew what might have been on the surface or what might have soaked into the stuffing of the mattress." Poor man, he did look perplexed as what he considered my impossibly high standards had surfaced once again.

Useful would be the adjective to describe what we had bought, although the simple constructions made of unstained, pine wood were more aesthetically pleasing as sometimes, inadvertently, simple, classical lines prevailed.

I am referring to our bookcases made of slabs of pine boards upheld with two or three red bricks and a simple table constructed of a circular pine top mounted on two thick upright pine oblongs.

Due to the low price we were willing to pay, our furniture could only be described as a motley collection, a variety of old and new pieces, definitely more functional than beautiful.

AN UNEXPECTED EVENT

When we arrived home, Roger and I had some free time together. We were leading fairly busy lives, especially on weekends, before we returned to work and study. We went out with friends to films and the theatre and the occasional dinner party. We tended to eat out in reasonably priced restaurants rather than cook for friends.

At the Charles St. Meeting House, where we had been married, we were meeting friends at the Sunday service, attending a book club and a self-help group as well as going to all the Quaker political conferences, organised by my friend, Russell Johnson.

We visited my father who lived in a more respectable area of Cambridge and couldn't understand why we chose to "live in the slums." Once a month we drove to Connecticut to visit my mother-in-law, Miriam and Gabo and Nina, Roger's 11 year old half-sister and Snieshka , the totally white Samoyed.

We sometimes drove farther into the hills to climb a mountain. On our country walks, we took the caretaker's five children with us. As they had never travelled farther than the mile it took to walk from home to school, they found these excursions an exciting treat. They were delighted to have us as neighbours, particularly as we helped them with their homework and took them out on Saturdays.

When I gave the caretaker my superfluous wedding presents, she was overjoyed, stating "It was better than Christmas." The wedding list in the department store had not yet been invented, where everyone signed up for the presents the bride and groom had designated they would like.

As no-one knew what other wedding guests were giving, there were often duplicates of gifts. The caretaker received salt and pepper shakers, a sugar bowl, two damask tablecloths, two bedspreads, an iron and a toaster along with various dishes designed for condiments and hors-d'oeuvres.

It was the first autumn of our marriage and I had asked Roger to come to an International Dance with me. As it was a formal occasion which he disliked and dancing was not his forte, I was delighted that had acceded to my wishes.

It was the custom that men could approach a young woman to ask her to dance. If she were with a partner, the most polite approach would have been to ask at the end of the dance but it was also the custom to ask during a dance. Roger and I were chatting. The dance music had stopped very briefly. Everyone was waiting for the next dance to start. Suddenly a very tall, handsome, African appeared from nowhere to ask if he could dance with me. Roger agreed.

Three dances later, when he realised that I was still being entertained by this attractive gentleman and thoroughly enjoying it, Roger cut in briskly and whisked me off to the other end of the room to dance with him. I was giddy with excitement as it was one of those rare occasions when two people dance completely in tune with each other and are swept away with the sounds and the rhythm of the music.

I felt a slight pang of guilt that I should be enjoying myself so much with a man that was not my husband, but I later convinced myself that it was no crime to enjoy dancing, whoever I was with should be of no concern.

Roger and I were enjoying life or so I thought, until the day that Roger informed me, quite unexpectedly, that his spirits were low. He spoke of feelings of hopelessness and despair. I was alarmed and, at first, found it incomprehensible that he should feel hopeless in the face of our wholehearted happiness. If Roger had sunk into such a dejected state of mind, I was convinced that it couldn't be due to the state of our marriage.

In spite of not understanding how Roger's altered outlook on life had occurred or what had set these feeling into motion, my immediate response was to help. But what should I do? I had never known anyone who was depressed. If he were depressed, I was unsure of how to proceed. On one of the psychology courses I had taken, the symptoms of depression were discussed but there were no specific instructions on how to dispel them.

Roger could not have felt more low than he aleady was. I was shocked when he asked: "What is the point in living, feeling like this?" I was struck dumb. Did our being together mean nothing? Had our marriage and all the feelings we had attached to it, come to naught? I tried not to dwell on this aspect of the situation. It was too painful.

All I could see before me was someone who was truly in pain, a kind of distress with which I was totally unacquainted. The only thing I could do was talk to him. I had no cure or cures. It seemed to me that I was talking incessantly, trying to get responses, with little success or only one or two word answers.

We had only been married three months. How could this be happening to us? I thought I should try to help him discover what had instigated these dreadful feelings.

Roger did admit that he had felt like this before, more than once. It just came upon him, like a black cloud over everything. That revelation did put things into some kind of perspective. I was sure that nothing had happened between us to instigate such overwhelmingly, sad feelings. I could now accept that this bout of dreadful depression related to his past history and was not, in any way, related to us.

I don't ever remember talking so much in my entire life, constantly trying to help him to understand where these feelings derived from, but I was no therapist and had not acquired the techniques for dealing with such entrenched problems.

I do not know how long Roger continued to feel so low but, to me, it seemed endless. Thank goodness, this proved not to be the case. He did slowly recover and returned to work at MIT, and I returned to my college studies, but neither he or I ever knew the reasons why he fell into a black depression.

This traumatic experience definitely altered the way that I interacted with Roger. It is not that I never expressed disagreement or stated how my opinions differed from his. I did as often as was necessary. But I tried never to allow these differences to escalate into heated arguments. It was a precaution, an attempt to prevent thrusting him into another depressive state. For the rest of the marriage, even when it was very difficult to do so, I tried to keep everything on an even keel to maintain his equilibrium.

RETURN TO SIMMONS

It was my fourth and last year of study. I couldn't believe how much I was enjoying my courses since I had changed from pre-med studies to education. I needed only one more education course to fulfill the requirements to undertake teacher training. Over the last two years of study, I had chosen a variety of courses, Shakespeare, Poetry, Criticism and The American Mind, as well as two economics courses, two psychology courses, a history of art and a philosophy course.

The challenge of seeing the world through the artist's eyes, exploring how the brain works and why we behave as we do, examining how language is used in poetry, looking at how free will vs. socialisation and parental nurturing in determining who we are, I was finding all these new areas of study challenging and stimulating, so much so that I was devoting more time to background research and essay writing.

My marks were consistently high, especially in English. In the first two years of college, I had started socialising more, with the result that my grades were not outstanding. I was now determined to rectify this problem.

I had taken two advanced English courses and received an A in both. The head of the English Department who was the lecturer, invited me to visit him anytime to discuss any matters related to the course. Everyone knew that A's and even B's were not easily acquired from Mr. Stiler. Upon asking, I discovered that he had not extended this invitation to any other students in my classes.

I decided that he had not had many or any black students who had performed so well in his classes. There were only eight black students in the entire four year student intake of 1200. In any one year, had any of them taken his advanced English courses?

We had a number of meetings, discussing a wide variety of subjects, most of which were not related to English, Shakespeare or Poetry. We discussed politics, religion, holidays, my family background, my plans for further study and what sort of job I wanted.

I was so inspired by the questions raised and the subjects discussed on these English courses that I began to imagine different possibilities for the future. I let my mind wander and thought how interesting it would be to inspire students to read and examine English literature, to explore the subjects and characters the authors introduced, and the devices used to construct the storyline.

When Mr. Stiler asked about my future plans, I said that I might consider becoming a lecturer at a college or university. I knew that I would have to complete a Masters Degree in English and do further study for a PhD.

He responded enthusiastically, "You would be able to acquire a good Masters Degree and, no doubt, a good PhD as well. But you do know that you could not teach in any college or university (i.e. in northern colleges and universities, where the student body was predominately white, and the white lecturers were always white). Neither institution hires black lecturers. There is not one that I know of that has ever done so."

In my flight of fancy, I had not even considered this obstacle. The fact that I was not aware what teaching at university or college would actually mean for me, indicated that I was living in the realms of supposition and possibility, ignoring the reality of the world in which I actually lived. Any ambitions a black student had were always suffused with the barriers of prejudice.

At one level, I was pleased that Mr. Stiler's outspoken response had shocked me into realising what sort of future I faced if I continued with the idea of becoming an English lecturer. He was honestly informing me of what my prospects were as a black student.

But that day, I left his office, never to return, the main reason being that he never proffered any reaction at all to the prejudice that had created the impossibility of my ever becoming an English lecturer. I felt that anyone who believed in any sort of equality would have made some sort of statement or comment regarding the injustice of such prejudice. He was indifferent, accepting the status quo without criticism or judgement.

He had just stated what bright prospects I might have as an English student and without a qualm or a pang of conscience, proceeded to tell me that despite this, there was no place for me within the echelons of the academic world.

But Mr. Stiler's attitude was not unique. Most white individuals, unaware of their prejudiced conditioning, would espouse that everyone was equal, while simultaneously believing that Black people were inferior to Caucasians. Such unacknowledged beliefs, inevitably, led to a denial of equal chances in acquiring jobs.

Given the widespread, generally clandestine prejudiced practices of the north towards black people, opportunities to succeed in many spheres were very restricted.

The Quakers and the Universalist Church where we were married stood out as institutions upholding beliefs which were exceptions to the generally accepted prejudices of the time. But despite their good will, they held no public sway and had no particular influence to change attitudes in the powerful institutions which governed our lives.

As for the initial interest that Mr. Stiler had shown in me. He was not interested in my ideas or in exploring ideas related to his essay topics which was the sort of exchange I had anticipated.

He found a bright black student an anomaly and was perplexed as to how this aberration from the norm had been created. I concluded that his interest in me was merely a case of banal curiosity. He turned out to be just another prejudiced white person that I would encounter in the course of my life's aspirations.

GERALDINE (Jeri) and JUNE

My friend, Jeri had always had her heart set on becoming a veterinarian. In her fourth year at Simmons College, she applied to various veterinary schools in the United States.

In the 1950's, most veterinary schools and (maybe it was none) accepted women as prospective students and not one had ever accepted a black student. The outcome was as she expected, she was rejected by all the white veterinary schools to which she had applied.

At this point, she had but one option, to apply to the Veterinary School in Alabama, in the deep south. Tuskegee Veterinary School was first accredited in 1949 to teach and train young students to become veterinarians. It states in its brochure that: "It was established as a place where black Americans could study veterinary medicine".

After completing two years at Tuskegee, Geri was forced to leave as doctors had discovered the growth of a large tumour which required immediate treatment. She returned to Massachusetts to have an operation but when she recovered, she decided to continue her veterinary studies elsewhere. She worked for a long period of time to save money to go to Norway.

Once there, she worked as a laboratory assistant in order to save enough money to learn Norwegian and then to finance her studies at a Norwegian Veterinary College. She qualified as a veterinarian and lived a very contented life working as a vet in the countryside and was eventually happily married to a Norwegian broadcaster.

DR. JUNE JACKSON CHRISTMAS

Geri had an older sister, June, who by dint of a brilliant brain and an outstanding scholastic record, had been accepted at Vassar College, one of the elite Seven-Sister Colleges.

In 1941, she was one of the few black students to be accepted by this college. It was only in the previous year (1940) that they had agreed to take their first and only black student.

In June's request for accommodation, she specified that she would like a roommate, but was told that she would be happier in a single room. To explain the college's policy, she was informed that Vassar had accepted two black students that year but was not ready to "integrate the dormitories".

She met with a series of racist incidents relating to the prevailing prejudices of the time. When she arrived with her friends from Vassar at a

Poughkeepsie, New York skating rink, she was not allowed to enter on the grounds that she was not white.

As she had been unsuccessful in finding anyone who would rent her a room for her black date for the freshman prom, a white friend was required to rent a room for her.

Leading privileged and secluded middle-class lives and probably having no experience of intelligent, educated black people, the students insisted that she didn't talk like a black person, and one of her professor's stated that her very well-written essay didn't sound like a Negro's writing.

In her latter years at Vassar, some discriminatory policies changed. June lived in a cooperative house on campus, where the women lived communally and cooked and socialised together.

Vassar's record on integration was not remarkable in any way, except for its resistance to instituting practices of equal opportunity for everyone. It was the last of the seven-sister colleges to accept black students.

QUOTAS

Of the Seven-Sisters Colleges combined there were rarely more than one or two "black students" per class until the 1950's. There were only seven black students who graduated from Vassar in the entire 1940's.

Twenty-five years later, their entrance policy allowed at most three black students a year. Sometimes none were admitted.

The statements above were taken from the article which described June Jackson's experiences at Vassar, entitled: The African American Female Elite, The Early History of African-American Women in the Seven Sister Colleges (1880-1960) by Linda M. Perkins, Hunter College, City University, NY.

Up to this point, I had no success in finding articles which discuss colleges policies on quotas in the 1940's and particularly in the 1950's. People often ask: "How do I know there were quotas when I went to college?" My answer is always the same - you could count them, the same few minority numbers (two usually or even less), every year in classes of approximately three hundred students in every college in both Boston and Cambridge, MA.

Quite by chance, I found this article on the internet after browsing for nearly two years. The quotas of the Seven Sister Colleges are confirmed by the direct experience of the students who attended these colleges for a period of four years . Quotas were certainly in force.

As time has progressed, and the demands for equality emanating from the civil rights movement began to impact on private and state institutions, college policies have slowly altered in favour of more acceptance of minority groups.

JUNE'S CAREER - Dr. June Jackson Christmas

After Vassar, she received a medical degree from Boston University School of Medicine, one of only seven women in the class.

After a residency at Bellevue Hospital, NY, she received her certification in psychiatry.

She founded the Harlem Rehabilitation Centre at Harlem Hospital, a community-based, innovative, psychiatric programme. In addition, she co-founded the American Psychiatric Association of Black Psychiatrists.

From 1972-1980, she headed President Carter's transition team for the Department of Health, Education and Welfare.

She has served as Commissioner for Mental Health, Mental Retardation, and Alcoholism Services under three New York city mayors.

Her awards are too numerous to list here from: Vassar College ,Boston School of Medicine, The Phelps Stoke Fund, the National Association of Health Service Executives, the American Jewish Congress.

She is a Fellow of the NY Academy of Medicine, a Lifetime fellow of the American Psychiatric Association and of the American Orthopsychiatric Association.

She is married with three children.

TEACHER TRAINING

After obtaining my BSc. from Simmons College, my next educational goal was to acquire my Teacher Training Certificate. With a recognised college or university degree, only one further year of study was required to obtain certification.

I could have applied to Harvard University and, if accepted, would always have the prestigious name of Harvard associated with my qualifications. My father was genuinely distressed that I never even considered applying to Harvard to obtain a Master's Degree in Education.

Despite its renowned reputation, the programme which Harvard offered was based more on traditional teaching methods. I was looking for a course which promoted child-centred education and encouraged progressive teaching methods within the state school system. At the time, I found that no such course existed in any school or college in Cambridge or Boston, the two areas closest to me where it was purported that every kind of educational institution deemed necessary existed.

As I was later to discover, educators within the state school system generally espoused not only criticism but also a marked antipathy towards progressive teaching methods. Within the entire area, the only course available offering this training was a private institution. And so it was that I applied to the Shady Hill School to enter their apprenticeship program, undertaking a very good but not very well-known teacher training course.

Shady Hill School is an independent, progressive day school which was founded in 1915 for the education of children from pre-kindergarten through eighth grade. Their educational approach diverged from the customary attitudes and practices. Fundamental to their outlook, was the fact that they viewed the child as naturally inquisitive, curious, and creative. They were individuals whose interests deserved respect and support.

Most educators had traditionally conceived of young children as self-willed, obstreperous, and unruly. As a result, they concluded that children required harsh rules and strong discipline to train them and restrain them.

The basic tenet of Shady Hill's curriculum was that: "the process of learning is as important as the right answer." They encouraged students to be curious, take risks and make mistakes. The traditional methods of teaching which I had experienced were absolutely opposed to these guides to learning.

My state school education was renowned to be of a very high standard, preparing students well for college or university entry. But, and I had a big but about it, I felt that we were required to memorise and regurgitate too many facts, figures, and formulas in many subjects, without necessarily arousing our interest in the subject matter. The imperative aim of this approach was to produce the correct answer which was not always stated with the relevant understanding of the issues or factors involved. Self-development and self-expression were not skills particularly fostered with this approach to learning.

I had arrived at my appreciation of progressive education through my study of John Dewey, the American philosopher and educator and my reading about Summerhill, the radical, progressive school established in England in the 1920's by A.S. Neil. I had been introduced to Neil's concepts of education when Roger presented me with one of his books that had captured his interest.

Neil's ideas sounded quite idealistic and similar to those of Jean-Jacques Rousseau, the 18th century philosopher. They both emphasised the child's innocence and natural curiosity and a need to pursue their interests without adult interference or attempts to mould them in any way.

Although truly inspired by their positive concept of childhood, I did maintain a few reservations about how they viewed the role of adults in the educational process. Neil believed that children should follow their own interests completely and would never attend classes unless they desired to do so.

The impression I received was that, left to their own devices, without adult supervision, be it from parents or teachers, children would grow into happy, intelligent, creatures functioning without difficulty in society. I was somewhat uneasy with the suggestion that this is the only concept of how children learn.

I loved the emphasis on following a child's interests as an important key to inspire learning. But their interests, who they are and how they evolve, all these significant aspects of development, have not taken place in a vacuum.

Children are born social creatures and from birth, learn to interact with others. They are all surrounded by different social and cultural influences which affect their interests and how they function. They may be born innocent and curious but each one is born into a different kind of environment which impacts on every aspect of their physical, emotional, and intellectual development.

Difficult or ineffective parents could impede the child's progress in any or all of these areas. I viewed good, caring parents as providers and nurturers of the child's development and viewed good teachers as performing an extension of the parental role. They all could be facilitators in the child's education and development. I could not accept the idea that children left to function on their own, in the absence of caring and concerned adults, automatically turned into intelligent creatures of virtue who interacted well with others socially.

Although Shady Hill was a progressive school, it believed in classroom teaching and all students were expected to attend school every day. I thought it provided the facilities and necessary resources for effective and innovative learning.

SHADY HILL SCHOOL

In June 1954, I received my BSc. From Simmons College and began the teacher-training programme at The Shady Hill School in September 1954.

I wanted to work with young children only. I loved their lively curiosity about absolutely everything and believed that with such inquisitive minds, they were receptive to exploring all sorts of new and different ideas. I was appointed an apprentice in the First Grade with six- and seven-year-olds. Miss Rowan was the teacher in charge.

I helped with reading, writing and maths. Initially, in maths lessons, the children worked with Cuisenaire Rods, wooden blocks of different colours, used to visibly see how arithmetic calculations were created. More blocks are added as the calculations became more complicated. I was impressed that, with the use of the Cuisenaire rods, their understanding of the calculation always preceded their recitation of the correct answer. With this approach, there was no stating the right answer without comprehension.

I worked on various assignments: Preparation of the Classroom Before the Children's Arrival; The No Guns Policy in School; The Routine involved in Getting Children to Hang their Clothes in the Right Place. This was a job slightly more complicated than it might appear, particularly in winter-time, when each child arrived with a coat or jacket , leggings, boots, scarves, hats, and mittens.

How a House Was Built was the project I chose to work on with the entire class. There were discussions about what materials were used, how many rooms were needed, what utilities were installed and how their houses were the same or differences. This exchange of ideas led to led to a further project on why there were different kinds of houses all over the world.

I was pleased to be engaged in all these activities but was disappointed that Miss Rowan had allowed me to be in charge of the entire class only once and then, very briefly, when I presented my project on housing. I remained eager to gain more experience of teaching, entirely on my own.

BEING THE SOLE TEACHER

One morning, Miss Rowan informed me that she was having trouble with the vision in her left eye. That same evening, she rang to tell me that she had checked into hospital and had been diagnosed with a detached retina. She was awaiting an operation and would be there for an indefinite length of time with sandbags on each side of her head to ensure that she kept her head still.

The following morning, I was to take over the teaching of the entire class. I was upset to hear of Miss Rowan's diagnosis as there was a possibility that she could lose her sight in the affected eye. But, as I pondered the news that she had just relayed to me, a wave of anxiety swept over me.

I had not yet developed the skills nor experienced the training necessary to be in charge of the entire class. Becoming the primary teacher would, undoubtedly, prove to be a challenging and demanding task.

The next day, I arrived at school very early to make sure that all the necessary equipment was in place before school started. I carefully monitored the children putting their outside clothes in the correct places.

When they all sat down, I informed them that Miss Rowan was in hospital so would not be teaching for a for a few weeks. We then began the short session of "news." Any individual who wished could stand in front of the class to present his or her news to the class. Individual news reports consisted of no more than three or four sentences. As everyone was completely engrossed in the news reports, I could see that everything was going very well.

The schedule after this was to carry on with sounds and combination of letters, helping them to write short stories, and engage in short discussions of relevant topics, and sometimes reading poetry. The session which followed this was maths, then a short break for biscuits and juice and afterwards a music session, (often with a music teacher) or a special project.

There was a break for lunch and depending on the day, they engaged in working with clay, painting, drawing or carpentry. We were sometimes preparing parts for a play, they were writing or creating costumes for celebrations like Halloween or Christmas. We made collages and sometimes created pictures on a group theme to hang in the classroom.

As soon as we commenced work on the more serious subject of sounds and letters, I could detect that everyone was not as focussed as they should have been on what I was saying. Two people in the back of the room were whispering. I told them to stop, and they did. Someone else passed a pencil to the boy in the next seat. I asked, "What was the problem?" "If someone needed a pencil, they were to put their hand up to ask me for one." There was silence for a short period of time.

Someone opened a desk. I stated, "There was to be no opening of desks until the lesson was over." The desk immediately closed.

When I looked back on my first day of being in charge, I was not satisfied with my performance as a teacher. The class had never been totally out of order, but a few children had felt they could flout the rules until I corrected them. They would never have behaved in that manner in Miss Rowan's presence. What was I doing wrong?

The following day I made sure that I stuck to the timetable, not allowing too much time between one activity and another. A little extra time gave the livelier ones a space to be naughty, particularly William. William sat almost directly in front of me.

He would lean over to whisper to anyone sitting near him whenever he thought my eyes were averted. I always stopped him but any time he thought my attention was directed elsewhere, he reverted back to misbehaving again.

This was the second day of my teaching alone and the second day of William's deliberate misconduct. I decided to take the matter firmly in hand. "William, stand up and go to the craft room. Make sure you close the door behind you."

The craft room was at the end of the classroom. It was the place where we engaged in arts activities and became "the naughty room" to isolate students who were continually misbehaving.

William walked to the craft room and closed the door. Everything proceeded very well for about 5 minutes. But after this brief period of time, I slowly became aware of titters and brief giggles erupting in the classroom.

When I extended my gaze to the rear of the classroom, I spotted William's face glaring through the glass window of the craft room door. He was making grotesque faces, sticking out his tongue, twisting his ears and then noisily jumping up and down on a chair with great glee.

I rushed to the end of the room, opened the door and firmly told William to put the chair back in its place, come back to the classroom and remain in his seat in total silence.

The classroom was completely quiet again, no noise or snickering to be heard. I glared intermittently at William to keep him under control while I still attempted to teach. It was a strain, but I did manage to keep the class under control.

I was unnerved by William's unruly behaviour, and those few who felt they could misbehave. I was not sure what to do next. I decided to employ a new tactic, I would reason with them.

I had a short session the next day of trying to reason with the class, explaining that they were never going to learn anything until they put all their energy into listening to what I was saying. They would see the results by looking at the good work they were producing in reading, writing and maths. Some appeared to understand what I was saying but even I couldn't quite believe that this message was forceful enough to prevent the naughty ones from disturbing the others.

There was a school assembly that morning. Every teacher walked with their class to the main auditorium. As we started along the path outside, one boy, (Jock was his nickname), for no apparent reason, decided to have a temper tantrum and suddenly screamed that he wasn't coming with us.

I was alarmed. This sudden, unexpected outburst was occurring in view of the entire school faculty. A teacher whose class was ahead of mine, kindly asked if I needed some help. When I said yes, she took Jock by the hand and marched him into her queue of students. Not another sound was heard from him.

I had not even had time to try to calm him down but now felt something of a failure for not sorting out the situation myself. When thinking about this event later, I had to acknowledge that Jock had never had any temper tantrums when Miss Rowan was teaching.

I thought I had tried everything, sticking closely to the outlined schedule, leaving no gaps for misbehaviour to occur, stopping pupils when they behaved badly, trying to reason with them about the consequences of their behaviour. I did think that this last attempt was the weakest link in the strategies I was employing.

I was downhearted and discouraged. If I couldn't gain complete control of the classroom, I would have to accept that I was not a good enough teacher, and if I believed that was true, it would mean considering a different career.

My fear of failure was great but, in this instance, my determination to succeed became paramount. I had to conquer this problem. I felt that my entire future was at stake.

As I tried to analyse where the problems lay, I decided that it was of the utmost importance to be more diligent in preventing unruly behaviour. I concluded that I was allowing too much leeway before correcting pupils. My reprimands were appropriate but my reactions to each situation were far too slow. I had to stop incipient bad behaviour as soon as it was evident, "nip it in the bud". The next day, I would establish a stricter regime from the time they entered school to the time they departed.

Having arrived at this decision, I was finally forced to admit that I been reluctant to employ stricter methods of discipline in the classroom because of my own school experience. Accompanying the teacher's strict application of rules was always a harsh, often unjustified criticism Of a particular student of students.

In my mind, strict control of a classroom was always associated with unfairly denigrating the students. I had to somehow to dissociate stricter discipline from unjust disapproval of students behaviour.

Taking firm control of a classroom ensured that a viable space for learning could occur. In no way did it necessitate unprovoked outbursts of anger or treating students badly. Once I had acknowledged the real reasons for my reluctance to become a stricter teacher, I gave myself permission to enforce the classroom rules with greater conviction.

The next day, as soon as we started the first lesson, I could see that William had no intention of settling down. I spoke to the entire class, telling them that we were about to do some writing, but no-one was to pick up a pencil until I told them to do so.

William's hand immediately grasped the pencil in the groove on the top of his desk. I looked him straight in the eye and said: "William, put the pencil down". He complied. He then attempted to open his desk. I firmly repeated the procedure." William, close your desk, now". Again, he complied.

Someone whispered. I called her name, "Sarah, this is not a time for talking". She stopped. I felt that now was the time to put a stop to all these undesirable activities forever.

Whatever rules I tried to enforce, there were always a fer (very few) who felt they could test the rules. My aim was to gain control of the classroom and that included the naughty ones who did not comply.

Desperate to mange the classroom properly, I had borrowed a book from the library which described different teaching techniques. When difficulties arose, three specific methods appeared to put the teacher in charge and gain the attention of the entire classroom.

All of these approaches appealed to me because they relied on reason and the students' agreement to follow the rules and not the teacher's anger, which induced compliance through fear.

The first technique was putting heads down quietly for one minute, to reset the composure in the classroom. The second was a countdown by the teacher from ten to one. When one was reached, the whole classroom was to be silent. I decided to employ the third method, I informed the pupils that we could do no work until the entire classroom was totally silent.

I explained that we could not begin until everyone was listening. "There is to be no talking. No-one is to make any noise. I want everyone to put their hands in their lap. No questions are allowed until after the room is totally quiet." Slowly, slowly, one after the other, those who were talking finally stopped. Two looked around in total astonishment as all discussion finally ceased.

Eventually, not a sound was heard. The classroom became so quiet that we could all hear the birds singing outside in the trees. As everyone continued to remain tranquil, I instructed them to start work. No-one did anything unless I instructed them to do so. There was to be not talking without permission. If anyone wanted something, they were to raise their hand and ask me for whatever they needed.

"Pass the papers to the person behind you. Pick up your pencils and write your name on the top of the paper". As I continued this consistent vigilance throughout the entire day, I remained in charge of the entire classroom.

I had seen long-established teachers who could merely cast a glance or project an intense look which was convincing enough to control any difficult situation. I had not yet developed such admirable abilities. I felt obliged to correct each misdemeanour as it occurred until such time as my authority alone induced order in the classroom.

By the end of the week, the headmaster had sent a supply teacher to take over the teaching of the essential subjects. I was left to my own devices from 12 o'clock onwards every day.

After the initiation of persistent discipline, any kind of consistently unacceptable behaviour had virtually disappeared from the classroom, but I had to remain constantly vigilant. As time progressed, I slowly relinquished the role of the unremitting disciplinarian. Eventually, the quick resolution of difficult situations and the tone of my voice did become sufficient guidelines to establish order.

The experience of having difficulty in controlling the classroom sufficiently revealed to me yet another very important role for the teacher. Not only must she be capable of imparting knowledge to the students, but she must also be able to regulate the classroom in order to create an appropriate climate where learning can take place.

Miss Rowan returned to teaching after two months away from the classroom, fortunately, having experienced no loss of eyesight. During this time, through many attempts at trail and error, I had learned how to control a classroom and felt that I was finally justified in referring to myself as a bona fide teacher.

LOOKING FOR A TEACHING JOB

Having duly completed my year of work and study, I was a fully trained teacher. It was now my responsibility to find a teaching job. Initially, I had two interviews but failed to obtain either post. I never knew why.

Having grown up in Cambridge, I decided to apply for jobs on my home territory. One day, in Harvard Square, I, unexpectedly, bumped into my old boyfriend, Jerry Lewis. Upon hearing that I was applying for jobs, he offered to write a reference for me. I was more than pleased as I felt it meant that he bore me no ill will for not taking him as my marriage partner.

When I arrived at the next interview, I was surprised that all the questions directed at me related to my training at the Shady Hill School.

"Did I know that the classes there were smaller than those in the state schools?"

"Had I realised that the methods I had learned were unlikely to be appropriate for larger classes?"

"Public schools believed in classroom teaching, not in teaching individual children."

"Students didn't determine the subjects taught. The teacher determined the curriculum."

I took a deep breath and tried not to let their misconceptions and outright hostility to "child-centred" teacher training unnerve me.

I replied, trying to answer each criticism in turn.

"At the Shady Hill School, in every class, teachers always followed a set curriculum. Most teachers accepted that actively engaging children's attention in the subject they were teaching was the quickest way to encourage children's learning. This awareness of how children learn was considered one of the basic teaching tools in all classrooms."

"Children did not determine the curriculum. Assessing students' knowledge prior to teaching, might alter how a subject was taught. Less knowledge might suggest more input on the teacher's part, as a basis for future learning. More knowledge would suggest that less input is required."

"I saw no real difference in classroom discipline between the methods at Shady Hill and those in the Public Schools. Unruly pupils were never allowed to disrupt any teacher. They were always reprimanded and removed from the classroom."

"If a teacher had developed the skills to establish discipline in the classroom, the size of the class should make no difference. She would be able to command the class's attention and create order in any situation."

I was expecting one or two of the interviewers to question me at length about my responses. Not so. Although I didn't realise it, the interview had ended. No further discussion about teaching or my application for a job.

The mood of the interviewers changed abruptly from one of serious discussion to an atmosphere of light-hearted statements and questions.

"We see that Jerry Lewis has given you a recommendation. He went to very good college, Colby, in Maine and now he's a librarian at Harvard. He has done well for himself. "

"Did I know that he had run for the track team in high school? He had such a remarkable record. Everyone knew him. It was unfortunate that he couldn't continue running. He had to give up such a promising career."

I vaguely remembered Jerry telling me that he had loved running in high school but had given it up after a serious knee injury.

My naïve assumption had been that using Jerry Lewis's name as a reference would bear some weight, due to his being employed as a librarian at Harvard, one of the most famous colleges in the United States.

I hardly expected that all of my interviewers would know exactly who he was due to his famous track record. I was far too young to have known about his popularity. But I was secretly resentful that half of my interview time was spent discussing Jerry Lewis's past history. They were obviously not interested in elaborating on any statements that I had made or in querying how I would apply any teaching methods that I had learned in the classroom

It was evident that my teaching credentials were not to the interviewers' liking. They all disapproved of "progressive teaching methods." Whatever I said, no matter how rational or reasonable my responses to their criticisms were, their view would not alter. Given their preconceptions , it was unlikely that I would ever be teaching in a public school, certainly not in Cambridge.

A few weeks later, I received a letter stating that I had failed to obtain a teaching job in Cambridge, the reason being that I was a married woman and married women were not allowed to teach. I was furious!! Why did they bother to interview me when they knew from my application form that I was a married woman? The truth of the matter was that the statement was an outright lie. I had only applied for the job because the previous year, the state of Massachusetts had rescinded the law which stated that married women could not teach.

As a married woman, my chances of being hired should have been equal to everyone else's. It was obvious from my interview why I had not been offered a job. I felt it was pointless to pursue the matter further, but I was indignant at the excuse they had concocted to eliminate me.

I was beginning to wonder if I would ever find a job when I had my fourth interview. It was at the Meadowbrook School of Weston, Mass, a small private school within driving distance of Cambridge.

The headmistress could not offer me full-time work all day. She wanted me to work full-time only in the morning and continue with part-time work in the afternoon. This meant that I would have my own independent reading groups prior to lunchtime and assist the main teacher with all the classroom activities for the rest of the day. As I had no other interviews scheduled and this was the only offer to date, I accepted this post.

After about 8 weeks of my split teaching day, the Headmistress asked if I would like to become Head Teacher for the Nursery Class. The present teacher was leaving at Christmas time. At first, I was reluctant because I had never been trained to teach such young children. But she explained that I could spend every morning with the Nursery teacher, from 9 to 1, to learn the teaching methods and curriculum for four to five year olds.

Having liased with the Nursery school teacher for at least 6 weeks, I experienced no difficulty taking over the class and discovered that I thoroughly enjoyed working with this younger group of children. The headmistress informed me that she was very pleased with my teaching and very much approved of the projects that I had introduced.

I would have happily continued as a nursery schoolteacher for a very long period of time but, as events turned out, this was not to be the case. For other reasons, I eventually decided to leave this job.

ADDENDUM

Not long after I had been rejected for a teaching post in Cambridge, my good friend, Russell Johnson, from the American Friends Service Committee, told me of an organisation, run by acquaintances of his. They were interested in breaking down the quota system used for hiring teachers in Cambridge.

It was a quota system of which I was completely unaware. They informed me that only five black teachers had ever been allowed to teach simultaneously in the entire history of the Cambridge Public School System. They would be in contact with the Cambridge Public School Board in order to try to alter this discriminatory practice. They wanted to use me as their first test case. I agreed to this collaboration and was looking forward to helping them expose these unjust practices.

When I had agreed to work with this group, Roger and I felt we were permanently settled as Cambridge residents but sometime later, we altered our plans. I had to inform the group trying to eliminate discriminatory practices within the Cambridge educational system, that I would not be available for the period of time they would need to prepare a case against the Cambridge Public School Board, as my husband and I would soon be moving to a different state. So sadly, I was not available to assist in revealing and removing the discriminatory practices employed in hiring public school teachers in Cambridge.

It was the summer of 1956, and we were, as usual, in England for our holidays. This time we were alone. Previously, we had spent a summer in England with our friends, the Frosts, and the following summer with my brother, Bob, and Arlene, my college friend and bridesmaid.

To my surprise, I discovered that I was pregnant. We were both overjoyed at the prospect of bringing a new life into the world. We had been married for three years and I had already taught for a year at the Meadowbrook School of Weston.

Up to now, there had been no consideration of starting a family. I had a strong desire to prove that I could survive independently if ever the need arose. Having acquired my BSc. and Teaching Certificate and proven to myself and others that I could teach, I felt ready to change direction.

By the time we reached Glenalla, I had already started taking a daily dose of calcium pills. Because I never drank milk and rarely ate cheese, I felt that the baby might not be receiving enough calcium for its proper development.

When I returned to my teaching job, I informed the headmistress that I would not be working for the entire school year due to my pregnancy.

But when I finally decided to depart, the Headmistress convinced me to stay longer than I had originally planned, telling me what a wonderful teacher I had become. She even offered to hold the job open for me, to return after the birth of the baby.

Of course, there was no question of my relinquishing the care of my baby for a teaching job, even if I did enjoy the work. I was determined to have some free time to prepare a room and to buy some baby clothes before the impending birth.

I soon realised that the headmistress was very determined that I should stay at Meadowbrook. She was flagrantly resisting my plans for departure, thinking that she could cajole and convince me to remain for a longer period of time.

I knew that I would have to present a case that had no room for manoeuvre for her to accept the idea of my departure. In the end, I informed her that the doctor said that I had high blood pressure and that diagnosis meant that I was to leave work by the end of December. It worked!! There were no more discussions or attempts to manipulate me into carrying on teaching.

I now had approximately two and one-half months to make preparations for the birth of the baby. There was also enough time to make some furniture for our sparsely furnished flat.

One of the more interesting aspects of my teacher-training had included learning the basic aspects of carpentry in order to help the children with woodwork. By the end of the course, all the apprentices had made a kidney-shaped table. Mine was proudly displayed in front of the couch in the sitting room.

I drew up a list of the furniture that we needed: bookcases, a small cabinet, and a badly needed chest of drawers. I knew that constructing drawers was beyond my abilities so would not even consider making this last piece of furniture.

I first approached Ed Yeomans, the headmaster of the Shady Hill School, to investigate whether or not it was feasible to request some guidance from the carpentry teacher for my project. As they both approved my plans, I began to build a sliding-door cabinet. The sliding door was actually the carpentry teacher's idea.

I had drawn up all the correct measurements for the slabs of pine wood but needed help with the grooves in the sliding door. As I had only hand tools, the carpentry teacher cut the desired pieces with his electric saw. I went in daily to complete the task and began to consider making more pieces to furnish our residence. They would be an improvement on the practical but not so beautiful furniture that we had acquired so cheaply.

But my plans to build new furniture for our apartment did not last for long. One morning, Ed Yeomans arrived in the carpentry room to ask if I would take on the task of teaching a group of eight to nine year olds. Their teacher was ill, and he had not yet found a replacement. I agreed to become the supply teacher but realised when I took a look at their writing and maths notebooks, that this teacher must have been ill for longer than anyone had suspected.

The books were in a state of disarray and mistakes hadn't been corrected for some time. One child had totally illegible handwriting and there was another not far behind him. With the assistance of another teacher, we assessed what should have been covered.

The class had already experienced two or three different teachers, a situation which always leads to pupils acting up and testing out any new teacher who might arrive.

I walked into the room with my "control the classroom" skills firmly in place. As I was now a more assured teacher, I did not face any serious outbursts of misbehaviour, though there were occasional attempts at disruption.

Having established three reading groups of different levels of ability, I had to make sure that while I heard one group reading, the other two groups were quiet. There was one boy in each of the lower reading groups who had difficulty in waiting for help. James suddenly yelled out that he needed me. I was reading with another group. I responded, saying, "James, you're interrupting. I will help you when I read with your group. Wait until then and no more yelling."

As I said this, I looked up to see Ed Yeomans sitting in the back of the classroom. I had no idea how long he had been sitting there. Momentarily, I felt overwhelmed and wanted to freeze on the spot. Of course, I could do no such thing, I had three reading groups who required my attention.

As the class was orderly and even the naughty James was silenced briefly by my response, I could only hope that what he saw had met with his approval.

I did approach him later to say that March was approaching, the month my baby was due. Would he be prepared to call an ambulance in case of the baby's arrival?

I was still teaching on the baby's due date but gambled on the fact that first babies were usually one to two weeks late. I did eventually stop teaching before his birth and used the rest of the time to finish my sliding-door cabinet.

Roger transported my great creation home in the back seat of our 1936 Ford, that Ford, being the one that startled everyone in Harvard Square (Cambridge, MA). The car sometimes stalled at a red light. When this happened, I was forced to rev up the engine in the middle of traffic. I removed the long L-shaped crank and attached it to the knob on the front of the car, winding up the engine until it spluttered into starting.

Such antique cars and such antique methods for starting cars had long ago disappeared. It was inevitable that I became an object of comment and bizarre curiosity when these incidents occurred.

VISITING MIRIAM and GABO

When we lived in Cambridge, MA, we saw my father and stepmother fairly frequently as they lived not far from us. Five years after my mother's death, my father had remarried a local Cambridge resident. She was a well-respected, religious woman who attended a Baptist Church, as did my father. I think this affiliation was a strong bond between them.

As they lived farther away, in Middlebury, Conn, we saw Miriam and Gabo less frequently but stayed for weekends as the drive there was a long one. On one visit to Connecticut, Miriam invited me to go swimming with her at her local swimming club. It was situated not far away, on a small, freshwater lake.

After half an hour to forty-five minutes of leisurely swimming, Miriam and I prepared to depart. The only other person in the water was a middle aged woman who approached me as I was nearing the platform next to the clubhouse. Smiling sweetly, she asked if I were a member. I told her that I was not. I had come as a guest, of my mother-in-law, Mrs. Gabo.

We left, thinking no more of this particular encounter. We were preoccupied with finding some fresh corn on the cob at one of the roadside stands for dinner. As it was approaching late afternoon, many of the stallholders would have packed up and departed for home. We were fortunate to find one stall still open and purchased numerous freshly picked cobs for dinner.

As we approached the house, we could hear the telephone ringing. Miriam parked the car in the garage and as the ringing persisted, commented that the caller was very insistent. As she thought it might be something urgent, she rushed to the phone.

It was the manager of the swimming club. He sounded very hostile, not at all like the very friendly, charming man that she had come to know. "Is that Mrs. Gabo?" Not waiting for an answer, he stated: "You have transgressed the rules of our establishment. "

Miriam was astounded. "What ruled could I have broken. I have brought one guest to swim with me and the rules state that this is allowed."

"And that is precisely the problem. You brought one guest to swim in the lake but she was a black guest. We simply don't allow black people to visit to swim in the lake or to join our club. You have most definitely transgressed our rules."

"Well, where are these rules written? You never mentioned them when I joined the club, nor do I see any notices pertaining to this fact tacked on the walls of your office. Why don't you reveal your reveal your prejudiced attitudes publicly? Don't even bother to answer that question. Any club that supports such undemocratic, discriminatory practices is not a club to which I wish to belong. I hereby resign." And with that decision, she put the receiver down.

Miriam and Papa were truly shocked that such blatantly racist beliefs had been expressed by people they had met and that such an incident had occurred at a club to which they belonged. A discussion then ensued about the nature of prejudice in the north. There would never be any signs stating what the accepted discriminatory practices were, as there were in the south.

The absence of such signs and the observation that blacks and whites associated equally in public arenas, often gave the misleading impression that black people were treated as equals to those who were white. Prejudice in the north was invisible and insidious. Its existence was widespread and caused serious, unrecognised harm to those who were its recipients.

Clandestine prejudice and gentlemen's agreements, not codified rules, specified what were acceptable and permissible practices regarding black people. Most good white Christians refused to allow black people access to decent housing or to move to more affluent neighbourhoods. The job market was restricted to mainly the most menial jobs and access to education limited by the numbers allowed to enter higher educational institutions.

In the 1950's, such practices existed throughout the north but were rarely exposed and continued to blight the lives of the black people who encountered them.

A NEW BABY

In the summer of 1956, Roger and I were once again in England, visiting his family for the summer. We were pleasantly surprised to discover that I was pregnant.

I had planned to start a family after completing my teaching qualifications and gaining some teaching experience, but not before I could prove to myself that I could earn a living independently. I was determined to have a job that I could perform should life become financially precarious in the future.

I bought a book entitled, Childbirth Without Fear by Dr. Grantly Dick-Read, an English obstetrician. At the time, medical intervention and the extensive use of anaesthetics were routine events during labour. He felt that such practices interfered with the normal process of delivery and advocated natural childbirth-birth without the use of drugs.

I had already met one woman who had experienced this type of birth, when I had worked at the Boston Lying-In Hospital. She was the only person on the ward standing upright, looking well and able to look after her own baby within 24 hours of delivery.

The combination of seeing this woman's remarkable recovery and reading Dr.Grantly Dick-Read's book confirmed my desire to try natural childbirth.

As Roger and I had not registered with a doctor, we went to my family's doctor to monitor my health and that of the baby. My family favoured Jewish doctors as they felt they were clever, performed their job well and actually listened to their patients.

I explained to the doctor that I wanted to try natural childbirth, if possible. Having seen a ward of women in labour, each one screaming louder than the next, I was left with a question of whether I could or would survive the process of birth at all.

Dr. Grantly Dick-Read emphasized the normality of childbirth without undue emphasis on the duration of the pain involved. The secret, I was told by friends, was to relax and breathe deeply during the contractions to facilitate the birth.

In the 1950s, natural childbirth was considered a new phenomenon and was generally disapproved of by the medical profession. Despite this fact, our doctor did not reject my wish to try this approach.

But when I arrived at the hospital in labour, I was met with a different set of beliefs and attitudes. I could hear the nurses outside the door to my room complaining and puzzled as to why I was refusing injections for pain. They were constantly 'popping in' to administer them and I was consistently saying "No".

I was becoming exhausted with painful contractions and the need to also find the strength to reject the nurses' proposals to intervene. I became so tired, and my labour was so painful that, at the second stage of labour, I relented and allowed them to give me an injection. As it was a first baby, the labour was not at all fast. As a result, the effects of the medication eventually wore off and I found myself still experiencing agonising contractions.

When I finally told the nurse that I was pushing, she screamed that the head was crowning and ran to fetch the doctor who confirmed this. I was delighted. Crowning meant that they could see the baby's head, so I knew the birth was imminent. Fortunately, up to this point, there had been no problems or complications.

I was asked to lift my head and thinking that they were about to put a pillow under it, I raised myself, only to see a mask approaching my face. I was horrified. As it was applied over my nose, I desperately tried not to breathe, impossible!! What was I inhaling? I had no idea. I lost consciousness and that was all that I remembered of what I was hoping would be a wonderful, ecstatic birth.

I awoke in a haze. The room was spinning. I had been unconscious and was weak and completely light-headed. Where was my baby? The nurses said that they couldn't bring him to me for 24 hours. Why? There must be something the matter. Roger was at my side, telling me that the baby was fine. I didn't believe him. Had he seen the baby undressed? Did he look normal? Did he have 10 fingers and toes? He hadn't seen the baby undressed, but the baby was fine, he was definitely normal and had 10 fingers and toes. There was nothing wrong. I had nothing to worry about.

When they finally brought him to me, despite his strange complexion (he was grey), he was, as everyone had said, perfectly normal. The reason they had refused to remove him from the nursery was that they were waiting for the effects of the Ether that was administered to me to wear off. The drugs given to the mother do affect the baby, regardless of the reassurance given to the parents that this did not usually happen.

As for Ether, we were given to understand that anaesthetic doctors had stopped using it 50 years previously. I later discovered, from a doctor working in hospitals in Boston, that it was common practice for doctors to administer drugs and to remove the baby with forceps during normal births, not just the ones involved in complications where such measures would be necessary.

These were the procedures that had been employed on me without my knowledge and without my consent. There was no point in protesting as, I was told, doctors had the right to decide what anaesthetics were to be used and how the baby was to be delivered. Theses were not my decisions to make.

As I was surfacing that evening, the nurse approached me with the offer of a pill. Given the hospital treatment that I had received, I was obviously wary of their intentions. "What is it?", I asked abruptly, remembering that women were often given pills to prevent the production of their milk.

I had told the doctor that I wanted to breastfeed. He appeared astonished and stated that only animals feed their young. When I spoke to the nurses, they informed me that no one engaged in that activity anymore. Reluctantly, I had to accept that I was on my own and would receive no help from health professionals with this matter. Breastfeeding had definitely gone out of fashion in the mid-1950s.

What the nurses had said proved to be correct. I was the only person breastfeeding in the entire ward and all the women on the ward were requesting to view this aberrant behaviour. One after the other, they all asked the same question, "Do you feel like a cow?"

I did wonder if they had acquired some special knowledge about nursing cows that I was not privy to. My experience of bovine creatures was limited to observation. I had never questioned them about their feelings.

When I had a problem breastfeeding, the doctor advised petroleum jelly to soothe the affected area. I knew that petroleum jelly was only an emollient. My friend, Jeri, came to my rescue. She was now studying veterinary medicine and knew that petroleum jelly was of no use. She brought me a sulphur salve used on cows with similar problems. I could hardly believe my good fortune. It was a miraculous cure which remedied the problem within days. Perhaps, after this experience, I could genuinely say that I felt like a cow.

As I never drank milk, Roger obligingly carried a quart of powdered milk, flavoured with coffee, to the hospital for me very day. I had hated the taste of milk ever since I was a child. But, as I was feeding the baby, I knew that my diet now required extra calcium, so I drank this concoction every day.

As the days progressed, my son Kim's complexion improved, and I began to feel more 'normal'. Seven days in hospital was the usual length of stay after childbirth, but I convinced the doctor that I was well enough to go home after 5 (days). Roger drove us home and carried the baby upstairs to his new home.

When he left to return to work, I became aware of the front door closing once again. It was the sound of a distinct line of demarcation in my life. Five days ago, when the front door closed, I left home as Roger's wife. But I had returned not only as a wife, but as a mother. When the door clicked shut, I looked at my beautiful baby and froze. I felt suddenly alarmed and alone and was instantly overcome by the prospect of the task ahead of me.

For a few minutes, I was thrown into a state of panic. I knew absolutely nothing about new-born babies or looking after them and now I had our baby, a real human life in my hands. Was I really capable of taking on this responsibility? As I stood immobilised and feeling helpless, the baby began to cry. It was such a sudden shock that I was brought back into an inescapable state of reality.

As I fed him, I very slowly calmed down and tried to dispel my fears, and an intense feeling of deep love washed over me. I murmured a whisper of reassurance in his ear, "Don't worry. We are fine. We will have a wonderful and exciting time together."

And thank goodness for my very generous friend, Arlene. She had bought complete outfits for him, all the clothes he needed for the first three months of his life, including diapers. Thanks to all the gifts we received and Arlene's generous layette, our son was beautifully attired for the first 8 months of his life, entirely by friends and family.

For no apparent reason, I suddenly remembered the last disapproving comments that were circulating just before Roger and I were married. "The only reason he's marrying her is that she's pregnant. Wait and see."

As I cradled our son in my arms, I thought, what a prolonged wait they've had, those gossipmongers, three months short of four years. They might encounter some difficulty in trying to account for a 42 month pregnancy.

DIAPERS

A year or two before Kim was born, a new and wonderful service had arrived in the United States, a diaper service that dispensed fresh, clean diapers, as needed, to exhausted parents.

I literally jumped for joy at the thought of eliminating all the chores involved in producing continual piles of clean, laundered diapers. As I spent ages perusing our weekly budget, I was forced to draw the much resented conclusion that there was no way that we could ever afford such a delightful timesaving but ludicrously expensive service.

For the next few years, life would be a matter of flushing soiled diapers in the toilet and soaking all diapers in bucket of water and rinsing them individually before placing them in the washing machine. When we first had Kim, we had no washing machine. We found the closest laundromat or occasionally used a friend's washing machine. The inconvenience of carrying bags of soiled diapers down two flights of stairs to the laundromat was recompensed by the fact that I did, at least, have the use of a drier for the diapers.

In our first flat, I couldn't hang the clothes out to dry as there were so many factories in the area, they constantly belched forth pollution of various sizes and shapes in the form of black spots, specks and little flecks which descended on any damp laundry blowing in the breeze.

It was only when we moved to the country that I first made use of a washing line to dry the clothes.

In winter, to avoid the problem of diapers freezing on the line, the drying procedure involved draping them over the lukewarm radiators and, replacing the dry ones with wet ones until the entire pile eventually disappeared with, of course, new stacks of soiled diapers constantly accumulating.

CYRIL and DOROTHY'S VISIT

Roger's father, Cyril, rang from London to say that he and Dorothy were planning to visit the United States. They stayed first in New Rochelle, New York with Roger's brother, Joe, his wife, Francis, and his first grandchild, Rodney.

He then planned to stay with us for the following weeks. (He didn't say how many). They wanted to meet the latest grandchild in the family, Kim, who was now about four months old.

I was horrified. We had rented a second-floor student flat close to where Roger was working at MIT. Everything needed a new coat of paint. The plaster was loose in the kitchen ceiling and the bathroom was composed of only a toilet, a washbasin, and a shower in which there was barely standing space.

To my surprise, there was no bathtub. In my unsophisticated state, I had never seen a bathroom with only a shower and never knew that flats could be built without the essential washing requirement of a bathtub.

I was adamant that we couldn't allow Cyril and Dorothy to stay with us in such dilapidated accommodation. Joe and Francis had an expensive, beautifully furnished flat, complete with a cleaner and baby-sitter.

In our flat, the rugs were threadbare, the furniture was all second-hand and some of it in need of repair. Cyril was accustomed to servants, a hot bath daily and having meals on time. I couldn't provide that kind of service, particularly with a four month old baby whose erratic sleeping patterns made setting up any kind of schedule impossible.

In addition, we had only one double bed and another double second-hand mattress on the floor in another room in case anyone wanted to spend the night. There was no second bed to accommodate Cyril and Dorothy.

There was only one solution, book them into the closest hotel in Cambridge where they could reside in comfort and more luxurious surroundings and have meals served as and when they so desired.

When Roger explained the situation to his father, he was not a happy man. Nevertheless, Roger picked them up from the airport and drove them to their hotel where they proceeded to check in.

They were delighted to meet Kim who greeted them with a piercing stare which always alarmed anyone trying to produce a smile. For a baby present, they gave us an English pram with a detachable top. Despite its weight, it was a practical way of transporting Kim in a car without ever having to disturb his sleep. We were delighted as, on Roger's salary, we could never have afforded such an expensive present.

To entertain his father and Dorothy, Roger drove us all to various sightseeing spots in Cambridge and Boston, including trips to the countryside and the Berkshire Hills in the western part of Massachusetts.

Throughout our time together, Cyril constantly complained about their staying in a hotel. It was too far away. It was really only thirty minutes away in driving time. Everyone in the hotel was a stranger. Hotel staff were indifferent to them. He wanted to be with the family. He had only Dorothy to talk to.

It became obvious that without the continuous sound of classical music in the background as he had at home, he was suffering from ennui, literally, a profound dissatisfaction that arises from boredom. With nothing to do and nothing to distract him, he was becoming more irritable and even more demanding.

While I sympathised with his predicament, I explained that we had no bath, meals were never served on time and that we had only one double bed, the one that Roger and I were sleeping in. Despite my opposition, he persisted in enunciating a list of complaints to me daily.

His unrelenting expression of discontent eroded my resistance to his recurring pleas. It was an act of attrition. Already exhausted by sleepless nights with Kim, I simply didn't have the strength to argue with my father-in-law every day.

I finally relinquished my resistance to his dogged determination to stay with us. As Cyril was a tall, overweight man, I didn't think that he could manoeuvre himself onto a mattress on the floor without great difficulty, so Roger and I moved to the double mattress on the floor across the narrow hall, taking Kim and all his belongings with us.

Once Cyril was settled, we were both relieved to hear no more of his grievances. I was continually busy with Kim's needs and cleaning the flat. I spent the rest of the time planning meals for everyone. All dinners were cooked following instructions from a United Nations Cookbook, we had been given as a wedding present.

One evening, to entertain Cyril and Dorothy, we decided to take them to the cinema. The caretaker of the flats' eldest daughter came to babysit Kim. We had barely settled in our seats before Dorothy started moaning with pains in her stomach. As the pains became progressively worse, we all became seriously concerned about her condition.

In a state of alarm, we all hastily left the cinema. Cyril was escorting Dorothy, wracked with pain, to our car. Roger drove to the A&E department of the local hospital where she was seen rather quickly by a doctor on duty.

He diagnosed diverticulitis. She was given antibiotics, told to eat more fibre and to avoid spicy foods. She was suffering from inflammation of the diverticula, the small sacs that protrude from the colon. For the rest of her stay, Dorothy did as instructed and experienced no more attacks of this nature.

VISITS TO MY FAMILY

To welcome Cyril and Dorothy to the United States, two of my father's relatives felt it was their duty to invite my father-in-law to dinner. The first engagement was at my Aunt Winnie and Uncle Tom's flat. As everyone desired to speak to Cyril and all attention was centred on him, Cyril loved being there. He even commented on the wonderful reception that my family had produced for him and Dorothy, making them both feel that they were very special guests.

In a more affluent area of Boston, my Aunt Rebecca provided a similar reception for them at her home. As her house was much larger, she invited more members of the family to dinner to celebrate their arrival.

The rooms were spacious with high ceilings, fitted with glistening, crystal chandeliers in the hall, dining room and sitting room. Just as in Cyril's house, adjacent to the sitting room, there was a music room with a large, grand piano standing upright in the centre of the room. The dining table was covered with a handmade linen tablecloth, embroidered with delicate brightly coloured flowers and matching napkins, and set with fine crystal glasses and silver cutlery laid at each place. The numerous silver objects in the house, including the cutlery, were all made of solid silver. My aunt considered silver plate to be of no merit whatsoever.

A splendid, delectable feast was prepared by Aunt Rebecca and Aunt Cecilia who were both excellent cooks. Aunt Cecilia ran her own catering business so one course after another appeared to arrive effortlessly at the table.

When the meal ended, Cyril strode through to the sitting room, and on his way, noted the very expensive decoration and furnishings he encountered. He turned to me and said: "Mother would have like it here. She would have approved."

Even as adults, for anyone in the Franklin family, the greatest accolade for any act, deed or accomplishment was their mother's endorsement.

My Aunt Rebecca would have been pleased to hear those words as, not only did she want to welcome my father-in-law, but she also desired to demonstrate that we were also a black family with respectable material standards. It has to be noted that her standards were far higher than my family's as we never owned a house of such magnitude replete with furnishings of such great expense.

Absolutely overwhelmed with my family's enthusiastic reception, Cyril compared their geniality and generous hospitality to that of Jewish people, commenting that they both always made strangers feel welcome.

Unfortunately, none of that warm Jewish hospitality was forthcoming when later, my father and stepmother made visits to England. As no invitations were proffered, I had to insist that he, at least, invite them for afternoon tea.

The reticence to receive and entertain guests was a pronounced characteristic that Cyril displayed towards everyone. My family was, in no way, a specific target.

When Cyril and Dorothy were planning their return trip to England, they pronounced their trip to us a great success.

They both expressed delight and surprise that the doctors had diagnosed Dorothy's condition so quickly, perhaps revealing their distrust of American doctors. Cyril was not only overjoyed at the reception he had received from my family but also secretly pleased that his unrelenting campaign to leave the hotel and stay with us had actually worked and of course, they were both very pleased to have become acquainted with Kim, the most recent, grandson.

ROGER LEAVES MIT

When we first met, Roger was engaged in research in meteorology at MIT. When that job ended, he took another research job at MIT, this time in metallurgy. His salary was important as it was the only money that sustained us while I was still studying. But I often wondered whether these jobs were insubstantial in maintaining his initial curiosity and interest in science.

Neither seemed to provide an incentive or an overwhelming desire to pursue further study or research in these areas or in any other scientific subject.

An uncertainty about where to focus his future scientific interests, combined with a genuine concern about the devastating effects of recent scientific developments i.e., the development of nuclear weapons, led him to question whether or not he desired to continue a career in science.

His overriding concern related to the fact that many available positions were directly or indirectly connected to the production of weapons. As this was his belief, he was reluctant to apply for many types of scientific jobs.

We engaged in many intense, earnest discussions, trying to determine the most appropriate course for him to follow. I protested vociferously that not all scientific jobs were associated with the war effort. I feared that he was on the verge of throwing the baby out with the bath water. I argued that he was a scientist. He had devoted considerable time and effort to acquire his qualifications.

Using the scientific method in the pursuit of knowledge was an entirely neutral activity. Discovering and examining the laws of the physical world does not engender taking sides or in making moral decisions.

Only when individuals decide to what ends their scientific discoveries will be put does the question of morality arise.

The scientific method still remained the most useful discipline for acquiring knowledge, particularly in its stance of objectivity which aims to avoid bias and prejudice in its results.

Given his background, a BSc degree in physics from Cambridge University, teaching science seemed a reasonable and possibly interesting path for him to pursue. I felt that he might prove especially good in this field as he had the ability to explain scientific questions and problems very clearly and succinctly, an obvious advantage for any good teacher.

I cannot remember the sequence of events which led Roger to take up teaching science as a new career. Was it before or after we attended the lecture by the charismatic American educator, Morris Mitchell, who was the director of a radically different type of teacher training for college graduates?

I do remember that after hearing the aims and goals of the Graduate School curriculum, we were both so inspired that we decided to become students at this unusual institution.

And so it was that in September 1957, we packed our belongings and those of our son, Kim, who was now 6 months old. Despite his very brief existence with us, he had acquired many more possessions than either one of his parents.

We left family and friends in Cambridge and ventured forth to start a new life in the setting of what seemed the very remote, rural town of Putney, Vermont.

THE GRADUATE SCHOOL

The Graduate School of Teacher Training, often referred to as Glen Maples, was situated in a large house in Putney, Vermont, surrounded by extensive woodlands. Morris Mitchell, the director, presented the idea of a radically different form of education based on John Dewey's principles of experiential learning.

Dewey's belief that experience is the basis for knowledge and growth was never an idea meant to be narrowly confined to classroom situations. His educational methods expanded to a wider vision of society and were the basis of what he described as "education for democracy."

Experience within communities leads individuals to become observant and critical citizens. As they acquire collective knowledge, they become aware of the problems facing their communities. By working together, they can improve and rectify these difficult situations and in doing so, they create a democratic society for social change.

While the Graduate School was directly involved in promoting teacher training in classrooms, Morris Mitchell always hoped that the students would not limit their efforts at dealing with problems exclusively to the classroom. His aim was to foster their vision further so that they would become agents for social change within the wider community.

Students were introduced to problematic issues within communities and within society at large, in an effort to inspire them to explore ways and means of finding practical and reasonable solutions for the problems they encountered.

The first steps taken in gaining knowledge of oneself and others resulted from our experiences of communal living at the Graduate School and later on, our six weeks study trip together.

The classes were small but diverse. They were always composed of both sexes, some foreign students and were never totally Caucasian. In our year (1957-1958), there were 10 students. After the first term, a couple from the deep south of the US and a foreign student departed as the programme was far too unconventional for their purposes, so our final numbers were smaller than our initial intake.

In our group, there were three international students, Roger, from England, a female Swedish student, and Labhu a male student from India. The rest were all Americans, male and female. They included another married couple and their three children. Lhabu and I were the only two people of colour on the course. One of our teachers was from Scotland.

THE CURRICULUM

Students were expected to keep what was described as a "Cumulative File". It was a study plan for the year, consisting of the student's goals and practical steps on how to achieve them. The file was a document for assessing one's own learning and specified areas for growth, improvement, and reflection. It was also one of the main documents required by the Vermont State Board of Education, as well as the thesis, for assessing the student's educational achievement.

The autumn term was composed of a variety of activities, lectures, speakers, and seminars of many topical problems.

The winter term always included a study trip to various educational institutions in the eastern part of the USA, Mexico and sometimes Puerto Rico and Guatemala. Other visits, sometimes to troubled spots, usually took place in the more distant southern parts of the USA.

The final part of the curriculum involved The Apprenticeship Program, where students were directly engaged on teacher-training courses at different schools.

Although Morris Mitchell, with his dreams of a better future for everyone, desired students to find more challenging jobs that would aim at solutions for specific social problems. To my knowledge, only a few ever became involved in such endeavours.

Students usually had to find occupations that would support them and, in some cases their families as well. For practical reasons, taking teaching jobs became a matter of expediency.

The final piece of work required was the Thesis. It was often an examination of the work completed during the apprenticeship or in some cases, an account and assessment of the more challenging and adventurous jobs undertaken.

OUR YEAR AT THE GRADUATE SCHOOL, 1957-1958

THE AUTUMN TERM

There were trips to progressive schools and visits to local institutions, the history society, The Putney Food Cooperative, and the Putney Credit Union. There was also a visit to a managed woodland to understand the significance of a self-sustaining enterprise. The owner, while proud of his self-sufficiency, was also aware of the economic and ecological   impact of his endeavours.

We gained valuable experience in learning how to organise the local Putney High school students to help in the mundane activities required to keep any institution going. We raked leaves, gardened, gathered fresh fruit and vegetables, erected and mended fences, and took on any practical jobs that were required. The students were willing assistants, as helping us was part of their stipulated outdoor work programme.

A local visit to the wife of the well-known filmmaker, Robert Flaherty, proved stimulating. As he had died, his wife Francis Flaherty, was now in charge of his estate. Robert Flaherty is often described as the first documentary filmmaker. "Nanook of the North", made in 1922, was a huge success, revealing the difficult existence of the life of the Inuit people. "Moana" was set in Samoa and "Man of Aran", located on the Aran Island off the coast of Ireland. Both studies revealed struggles for existence in a very challenging environment.

I am sure that the purpose of these visits was to expose us to Robert Flaherty's philosophy of non-preconception. It was an approach that he accidentally found after he had arrived on Samoa.

He was so disappointed that there were no sea monsters to engage in horrendous battles as he had anticipated, it took him some time to deal with his distress. As he relinquished his deluded expectations, he slowly recognised that his own preconceptions were a barrier that nearly blinded him to seeing what existed before his very eyes, the uniquely fascinating world in which the Samoans resided.

By the time that Francis Flaherty spoke to us, she was relating his theory of non-preconception to that of Zen Buddhism, emphasising the importance of maintaining an attitude of openness and eagerness to the examination of any subject that one approached.

When we studied further afield, we visited officials at the United Nations in New York, to hear of the problems they were attempting to solve. In New Jersey, we visited a hospital for the mentally ill and were taken around various wards while those in charge discussed the various treatments they were employing to alleviate the patients' conditions.

Our constant exposure to myriad problems meant that we were experiencing directly a wide variety of difficult situations as they actually existed in society. The aim was to gain an understanding of how individuals and various institutions were attempting to produce relevant solutions and to examine the efficacy of these approaches.

THE WINTER TERM and THE STUDY TRIP

During the winter term, Morris Mitchell and all the students departed from the snowy, icy climate of Vermont and ventured forth on a study tour, always heading towards a warmer environment in the southern United States. No two trips were the same and they always varied in length. Our trip lasted six weeks, from the 1st of December 1957 to the 10th of January 1958.

The study trip was really the central focus of the educational experience at the Graduate School. Travelling together in a Volkswagen van, the students were constantly exposed to new and different social situations, some in the heat of serious turmoil. I could see that this trip would be the most exciting and challenging aspect of this educational year. I certainly did not want to miss out on this experience, under any circumstances, but I did have an eight-month-old baby to consider.

In the past, some families had taken their children on the trip. I would never have considered this as a reasonable possibility as Kim slept so badly at night, I knew that I would be constantly worrying that he would be disturbing everyone.

Once a week, my friend, Connie Fischer, looked after Kim and her two children, one only three months older than Kim. This arrangement meant that I had some free time to catch up on some reading for the course. It was she who insisted that I should not forgo the most important part of the Graduate School experience. She would happily look after Kim. What a wonderful and generous offer!!!!

There was only one problem, my very strong resistance to leaving my son. Could I survive that length of time without even seeing my baby? After many prolonged discussions, I was finally convinced to join the others on the study tour. Leaving Kim proved to be a most challenging and agonising decision. Throughout the trip I was plagued with an intense desire to see my baby every day.

THE STUDY TRIP 1957-1958

The trip always drew attention to environmental and community problems and examined areas of positive improvement as well. We visited two experimental groups, entitled Macedonia and Koininia. They were described as intentional communities, where groups of people had decided to live together, sharing possessions and responsibilities.

The agenda always included cooperatives and credit unions, but, as important, were the many dams that had been built, in particular, the ones under the control of the TVA (the Tennessee Valley Authority). They had not only controlled flooding but had also transformed the lives of the local inhabitants. What had once been derelict and unproductive land was now a thriving landscape of farming produce.

When we arrived in Mexico, we investigated agricultural experiments, regional developments, and new power stations. In Patzcuaro, we met with leaders of CREFAL, the cooperative supported by UNESCO which promoted adult education in Latin America and the Caribbean.

These visits were part of the unusual and varied experiences to which we were exposed. There were others but I shall focus on some that I considered the most memorable, most thought-provoking, and sometimes even disturbing.

In 1954, the US Supreme Court had ruled that "separate but equal facilities" had no place in the field of public education. On our travels, we stopped at a high school in the south where the teachers proudly showed us the new facilities that had only been recently installed. These renovations were meant to be evidence of their attempt to follow the mandate of the Supreme Court.

In an effort to demonstrate that everything was equally balanced between the races, they showed us the new equipment the school had purchased, particularly for the black students. For the girls, they had built rows of cubicles with hair-dressing equipment and for the boys, there were endless numbers of waiter's uniforms. The tables, laden with dishes and silverware, were awaiting the boys' arrival so that they could learn how to set the tables properly.

I could hardly believe my eyes. In the north, no one would have considered these facilities appropriate for high school courses. They would be practical skills pursued on training courses, outside of the learning acquired in secondary school.

Such ideas were indicative of what were considered enlightened and liberal southern attitudes at the time. When we asked, "Where were the science laboratories?" we were told that, as the black students were not interested in science, there was no need to provide them.

It was our first encounter with the deplorably unreasonable and prejudiced assumptions of white southern educators.

As we drove through the countryside, the landscape became more rural and less inhabited. There were vast tracts of farmland growing different kinds of produce, planted in straight, parallel rows. As I peered through the Volkswagen window, I was shocked to see a scene that I experienced as deja-vue, though I had never been here before. Rows of people were bent over, half-crouched with long, white bags slung over their shoulders, dragging behind them.

So intent were they in pulling the white fibres from the cotton plants, that they rarely looked up. But when they did so, black faces revealed themselves as the only workers in the fields. It was scene that I had seen before, and it came straight from a page in the geography book that we all had in the fifth grade.

It was a large, oblong, black and white picture of slaves, bent over with long, white bags attached to their bodies picking cotton, an exact replica of what I had just viewed. But that was history or so I thought. Had nothing changed? That picture was taken in the 1860's or even earlier. This was 1957.

It slowly registered in my unbelieving brain that for some black people, little had changed in nearly 100 years. Slavery had been abolished but the conditions in which they lived and the manner in which they earned their livelihood had changed not at all.

We saw the dilapidated shacks built along meandering streams with no toilet facilities, only basic bedding and maybe a table. There were chairs, possibly, but we could only catch a glimpse of the interiors if an occasional door had been left open so couldn't properly estimate the extent of the poverty.

Gunilla, the Swedish student, upon seeing this kind of deprivation, was also in a state of shock, but for very different reasons. She couldn't understand how the United States, the richest country in the world, could tolerate having such appalling poverty and misery in their midst. Why didn't they do something to alleviate these conditions?

I was as shocked as Gunilla. I never knew that such abject poverty existed, particularly in the United States. Some part of me wanted to believe what I had been taught my entire life about the American dream, if you worked hard enough, to the extent of your ability, you could conquer all obstacles and make a success of your life.

But my own experience of living in a prejudiced society had already taught me that as a member of a minority group, sometimes the obstacles produced prevented you from moving forward and blighted your chances of success at every turn.

I still was not prepared for the scene that had assaulted my vision. The lives of those descendants of slaves were frozen in time. They were free of their slave masters but not of the incessant labour they had demanded. These cotton-pickers were still performing the same back-breaking work as their ancestors had. Disillusionment set in. As I watched them, toiling under the searing, white heat of the sun, I felt that the American Dream was evaporating before my eyes. The scene exemplified a blatant rejection of any ambition for the future and had become what could only be described as an "Annihilator of Hope."

LITTLE ROCK, ARKANSAS

Prior to our voyage to the Southern United States, Morris Mitchell and the students discussed and agreed on a modus operandi for the study trip. As we were a racially integrated group, we would eat and sleep only in places that accepted everyone as guests.

Facilities in the south were completely segregated. Black and white people were never allowed to associate in any public places. There were separate water fountains, toilets, motels, hotels, restaurants and even hospitals, each labelled with signs indicating "White or Coloureds Only".

We all agreed that if we were to unexpectedly face any racial attacks, we would respond non-violently. Many discussions followed on whether and how it was possible to think clearly and remain calm in the face of a deliberately provocative attack.

Wherever we went, Morris who was from Georgia and had retained his strong southern accent, always preceded us, and introduced us a group of international students. The southern accent and the international aspect of the group paved the way for our entry into restaurants and motels which would not normally have been available to our inter-racial group. When we were travelling, Morris suggested that Lhabu, the Indian student, should wear his native Indian clothes. White Southerners were more accepting of foreigners of colour than they were of their black compatriots. They didn't view them as menacing or troublesome but tended to see them as unusual curiosities.

We were sometimes denied entry to what appeared to be a respectable restaurant. The thought of a mixed-race group entering their premises proved far too threatening a proposition. Morris always operated on the assumption that most people in restaurants with a middle-class clientele were less likely to become overtly violent upon seeing a racially mixed group of individuals than the less well-off clientele who might attend cheaper diners or cafes, some of whom might possibly be more accustomed to settling disputes violently.

When we entered the southern part of the US, we were entering a territory with which I was unacquainted and soon realised that I viewed as alien. Ever since they had lost the Civil War in 1865, the southern states had regarded this defeat as a grievous injustice imposed on them by cantankerous northerners. These enduring attitudes had led them to resist implementation of Constitutional Laws, particularly those related to race issues. They felt very strongly that the latest Supreme Court ruling threatened to alter their "way of life" and the structure of the entire south.

To oppose the Supreme Court's 1954 ruling, Brown vs. the Board of Education, which stated that segregation of the races in public schools was unconstitutional, many southern states issued the Southern Manifesto. It was a document written in 1956 to prevent racial integration in public places. It was signed by 11 southern states, one of which was Arkansas, a state we had been scheduled to visit on our study trip.

The Southern Manifesto saw the Supreme Court ruling as an "unwarranted exercise of judicial power" and accused it of being unconstitutional. Its effects were catastrophic, destroying the friendly relations that had been built up between Whites and Negroes over many years and supported by the "good people" of both races. Where previously amicable relations had existed, now only strong distrust and hatred flourished.

It was in the midst of this climate of hostility to the concept of integrated schools that we viewed the crisis at the Little Rock High School in Arkansas. President Eisenhower had never publicly approved the 1954 Supreme Court ruling, believing that you couldn't change the hearts of men by changing the law.

Eisenhower had not attempted to implement the 1954 ruling until 1957 when Governor Faubus refused to accept the Supreme Court's decision. Governor Faubus rejected President Eisenhower's verbal entreaty to integrate the schools. It was an act of outright defiance. President Eisenhower called out the National Guard to assure entry to the High School of the nine black students who had won a court order which mandated their attendance at an integrated school.

The television pictures of angry, white mobs ridiculing and intimidating the nine black children attempting to attend the school, were broadcast worldwide. President Eisenhower stated that mob rule could not be allowed to override the decisions of the courts. He finally deployed troops from the 101st Airborne Division to Little Rock to facilitate the children's entry to the school. The famous photos of Little Rock pictures the historical moment when the troops escorted the nine children up the steps of the school. The High School would become notorious in the south for being the first school to experience integration in Arkansas.

Not only did we see the troops staunchly standing in front of the school, but we also had an interview with Governor Faubus, arranged for us by Morris Mitchell as part of our study trip. Governor Faubus proved to be very affable and amiable and welcomed us warmly into his office. However, he proffered absolutely predictable explanations for the crisis at Little Rock and proceeded to clarify the situation.

Despite the presence of troops on the high school steps, the orders from my office to prevent the children from entering the school, were well-intentioned. Everyone was aware that the presence of those students would cause mayhem. Violent disorder might erupt. I called out the National Guard to protect the lives of those little children, to prevent any harm that might ensue from angry individuals.

We are not resisting integration. You all should know that my grandson attends an integrated nursery school. I, so badly, wanted to interrupt to say; "I expect his nursery school is not in Arkansas, is it?" It took great control to resist asking what could have been interpreted as a deliberately sarcastic question.

Governor Faubus was definitely in friendly, defensive mode, masking any negative racial attitudes behind the façade of concern for the welfare of the nine children. He expressed distress at the deliberate misinterpretation of his noble intentions by the press. When asked when the schools in Arkansas would be integrated, he had absolutely no idea when that would be feasible.

THE LEGACY OF LITTLE ROCK

Eisenhower's decision to send troops to Little Rock was of great significance historically. The Federal Government, for the first time since Reconstruction (1865-1877), the period just after the Civil War ended, had demanded equality for Black people in the South. Eisenhower expected southerners and the citizens of Arkansas to "preserve and respect the law even when they disagreed with it."

The government's overt action at Little Rock was considered a major event in the fight to end segregation and advance the cause of civil rights in the USA. But the story of Little Rock did not end there.

On their way to their classes, the nine students had to negotiate rioting, pro-segregationist crowds who taunted them, provoked them and spat at them. The authorities were so concerned about the unruly mobs, on the first day of school, that after only three hours on the premises, the nine students were escorted home.

They were harassed daily by jeering crowds on their way to school and when there were no soldiers to protect them, inside the school, the white students bullied and tormented them. Only if these incidents occurred in front of a teacher, were these students ever reprimanded for their behaviour.

Due to these continued attacks, both verbally and physically, only one of the nine students graduated from Central High School. The rest left to attend school in less hostile environments.

After a year of enforced integration, Governor Faubus insisted that the citizens of Little Rock had the right to protest about the federal decision to integrate the schools. Rather than support school integration another year, he closed the four public schools in Little Rock. In 1958, this decision resulted in a "lost year" of education for both the black and white students.

White citizens blamed the black community for the school's closures. Random black people, as well as the parents of the nine students, became victims of serious criminal attacks.

On the 18th of June 1959, the Federal Government declared the closure of the schools and the withholding of school funds, a breach of the law. With the installation of more moderate board members, the schools reopened in August 1959. However, once again, the black students became targets of hate crimes and mob intimidation.

While desegregation was very slowly implemented in Little Rock, it was not until busing was introduced in 1971, that racial integration began to be a serious physical reality. But, as soon as busing was established, those with more adequate means fled to the suburbs to attend the white, segregated private schools at their disposal.

MORE RECENT REPORTS OF LITTLE ROCK

It is a fact that today the schools are integrated but possibly in a manner which was unpredictable at the time of the 1954 Supreme Court ruling.

Central High School is composed of 56% black, 30% white and the rest a mixture of Hispanic, Asian and international students. The school has attempted to attract more middle class white students by introducing enhanced courses and international studies.

Some of the racial situations reported are familiar to me although our high school was predominantly white with a very small percentage of black students. One of the Little Rock students observed that the high school was desegregated but not integrated because integration comes from the heart of the people who go there.

In the dining room, white students sat on one side of the table and black students on the other. At my northern, integrated high school, black students sat at one table and white students at another or even at the same table in separate groups.

One black pupil took advanced studies so is in classes with only white students. He had friends in that group but was sometimes singled out by them as being very different. He felt no-one really liked him. He didn't really belong anywhere as the black students were critical of his having white friends. They called him an Oreo, black on the outside and white on the inside.

I was usually the only black student in most of my classes and had the distinction of being called not only an Oreo but also a Coconut by some of the other black students.

Some students do admit that staying with the familiar and the kinds of people you already know acts as an impediment to furthering better race relations. That they can concede this fact is evidence of some, though maybe not substantial, progress in racial attitudes since 1957.

In 2014, Little Rock had reached the same level in race relations as we had in the 1950's, integrated but separated, with no intention of moving beyond this situation.

THE STUDY TRIP (CONTINUED)

We drove to Clayton, Georgia, where we had an interview arranged with Lillian Smith, a white southern writer who espoused liberal racial attitudes. At the time, she was fighting a long battle with breast cancer and sent her apologies for not being well enough to receive us. We were all very disappointed, especially those who had read at least one of her books and I was one of them.

In 1944, she published Strange Fruit, probably her most well-known book. It was banned in Massachusetts and the American Postal Service refused to deliver it. Some said that this decision was due to lewd language, but it was generally agreed that it was unacceptable, provoking anger and ire in many, due to the fact that it depicted an interracial relationship.

She viewed white southerners as having a damaged psychological identity based on an unwarranted sense of superiority and an unquestioned justification of their right to degrade others.

We did manage to visit another outspoken, liberal, white southerner in Petal, Mississippi. In 1953, P.D.East established The Petal Paper, whose articles attempted to change racial injustice in the south. His editorials claiming that black people should be treated equally at all levels of society and his positive review of John Howard Griffiths book, "Black Like Me", led him to lose all of his local supporters.

Despite this disaster, the Petal Paper survived until 1971 when P.D.East died. In 1959. The P.D.East Committee was formed in New York. With their support and that of the 50 states in the US and 6 European countries, more sympathetic customers were found. At the Graduate School, many of us were avid readers of this small but controversial publication.

Due to criticism of racism in all its forms, both Lillian Smith and P.D. East met with unduly hostile reactions of rejection and hatred by many in their own communities. In 1963, P.D.East was forced to move to Alabama after continual harassment and menacing threats to his wife and child.

He so enraged his mother that she wrote to him, proclaiming that he was a disgrace to his state and his family and was nothing but an SOB.

In her lifetime, Lillian Smith was either criticised or ignored by local literary groups and felt totally rejected by the literary world in the USA.

I considered these two people beacons of hope in the midst of a world of oppression, degradation and violence. It took boldness and courage to critically analyse the southern human experience and its impact on both black and white individuals. Though they may now be remembered for their moral stance against southern injustice, it should also be noted that they both suffered unrelenting hostility and rejection for their unpopular views.

P.S. Black Like Me was written by John Howard Griffiths. The author came from a privileged white southern background. He deliberately darkened his skin in order to experience directly the way in which southern, black men were treated in the Deep South in 1969.

MONTGOMERY, ALABAMA

The famous bus boycott in Montgomery, Alabama had lasted from the 1st of December 1955 to the 20th of December 1956. When we arrived there in the first week of January 1958, the bus boycott had ended but its ramifications continued to be felt everywhere.

Our study group met with leaders of the Negro Labor Movement and some of the local residents. The success of the bus boycott and the legal battle which followed had created a new consciousness in the minds of the local population. Theirs had been a protest of moral indignation against a situation of human injustice. For the first time in their lives, they recognised their potential power to effect change in their community both socially and politically.

We were aware of their feeling of pride in the unity of the community and a sense of achievement in what they had accomplished. They were cautiously optimistic about future changes for the better for black people. Due to their boycott, the buses had been desegregated in Montgomery. But in every other sphere of life, segregation remained an impenetrable barrier that they were forbidden to cross. They had won only one battle of many that had to be pursued if true equality were ever to exist.

In March 1957, three months after the boycott had ended, the city officials passed a law to ensure that enforced segregation was to remain firmly entrenched in everyday life. In addition to the existing segregation laws, white and black people were never to be allowed to eat together or to play games with each other, either outdoors or indoors. Such behaviour would constitute a punishable offence.

As Morris had taken the Volkswagen to a near-by garage for a check-up, The Study Group had a free afternoon. We decided to go to the local cinema. Although we knew that cinemas were segregated, everyone did not understand how the southern rules of segregation were enforced.

Sometimes, it involved black and white people going to different institutions i.e., schools and hospitals or using different facilities, i.e., toilets and water fountains.

It might also mean that everyone was allowed to enter the same building or institution but be forced to sit in different places, as in cinemas and lunch counters. I explained that if the ticket-seller decided that Lhabu and I were black, we would be relegated to the top of the cinema, to be seated in the gallery. The others would be automatically seated on the ground floor.

We followed our agreed procedure, not to separate as a group under any circumstances. Someone took over Morris's role, explaining that we were a group of international students and would like to buy some tickets to the cinema.

Until entering the cinema in Montgomery, I had not felt singled out or different from other members of the Study Group in any way. But upon entering the premises of the segregated cinema, I identified completely with the prospect of what life would be like if you were a black person living in the south.

It was the first time on the trip I feared that my identity as a black individual could have been directly challenged and could possibly have put the entire study group in jeopardy.

My reaction was not one of outrage but one of total fear. Many white southerners felt it was their right to preserve their separate, segregated way of life and did not hesitate to express their anger both verbally and violently. All the ticket-seller had to do was to publicly point us out as a mixed-race group or yell and point a finger in my direction or Lhabu's and we could all become the victims of public hatred and vicious abuse.

I could feel my heart racing. It was pounding in my chest. For a few minutes I was overcome by the fear of what might occur in the face of a brutal attack. My breathing became laboured and I began to feel very light-headed. I leaned against a wall and taking a few very deep breaths, tried to calm my anxiety. Rationally, I tried to come to terms with the situation we were in. What was I reacting to? Someone was asking for cinema tickets in a totally segregated Southern city. My extreme distress related to hearing those words spoken to the ticket-seller.

I continued to lean against the wall and decided to walk slowly away from the situation. I listened intently. I heard no objections expressed, no raised voices. Then, there was a long period of silence. What was happening? Even in the midst of the great silence, there had been no commotion, no angry reaction. I was forced to admit to myself that nothing, nothing had actually happened. The cinema tickets had been purchased without incident. I was over-reacting, simply projecting my own fears into our being in a totally segregated building. As I walked on, I began to relax and could physically feel my adrenaline levels diminishing.

I began to take stock of my surroundings. I looked down and saw that someone in our group was passing me a cinema ticket, in fact, each one of us had been given a cinema ticket. Without fuss, without comment, and without any attack, we were all walking to our seats, and we were all together on the ground floor.

I have no idea what film we saw. I was far too busy processing why I had reacted the way I did. I had caught a glimpse of the kind of distress that can be induced in individuals, particularly, through worry and fear. I realised, for the first time, what could be some of the emotional consequences of having to live continually under a regime of unremitting segregation. There would always be enormous risks, both psychological and physical, that individuals took when trying to defend their legitimate rights to protest about racial injustice.

Southern black people were often labelled as subservient and acquiescent. No great insight was involved in comprehending why some individuals would comply with the unfair, degrading system imposed upon them. Anyone could easily succumb to the pressure of fear and violence in defence of their own survival.

It took a whole community coming together with the common purpose of fighting injustice to deprive the segregationists of their power. Viewing themselves as a coherent unit, they found the will and energy to mobilise themselves into a group of peaceful protesters. With their new-found strength and finally, the support of the law, the citizens of Montgomery had become an inspiring example for other dissident groups to follow.

A MEMORABLE MEAL

As we travelled through the south, Morris continued to introduce us as an international group of students. When we gained entry to an eating establishment, I always felt that Morris's lilting, Georgian accent must have been a reassuring factor in our success. God forbid that a northerner should bring an interracial group of students to southern territory.

We did not always accomplish our purpose and were sometimes turned away by those individuals who found just the sight of our group so distressing that the thought of our entering their premises could never be contemplated.

Despite the fact that a manager or a hotel official might make a quick decision, permitting us to enter the dining room, customers did not always receive us with pleasure. I will recount an experience in one memorable restaurant.

We were pleased that the manager had allowed us to enter, and a waitress very politely ushered us to our table. We all began to read the menu and one by one, ordered a variety of different dishes. No-one looked up or took any notice of us. It seemed that everyone was too preoccupied with their own gastronomic requirements.

The dining room had only a few empty places. The walls adjacent to us were full of tables with people eating or waiting to be served. Directly in front of us was a wall covered with huge squares of tinted glass. It was an enormous mirror, reflecting the images of the individuals seated behind us.

Is there a name for that sensation when you know and can really feel that someone is staring at you? We became aware that that a person at a side table was looking at us. Slowly, two more people at her table lifted their heads and joined in her unrelenting gaze.

Suddenly, it was as if a secret message were being passed round, as if this steady, intent look were a contagious thing. As we looked round, there was no doubt that our table was becoming the object of everyone's attention. The mirror revealed even more concentrated stares and a few gaping mouths on the faces of the people behind us.

Our presence had cast a pall of unmitigated tension around the entire dining room. People had stopped eating. A few sat almost immobilised as if in a state of shock, barely able to replace their silverware on the table.

None of us could quite understand how what appeared to be a room full of relaxed, indifferent diners had silently transformed itself into what felt like an angry, hostile crowd. Not a word had been spoken but the antagonistic feelings that they projected were definitely tangible.

It was difficult to eat and maintain a state of calm composure in the midst of the unexpressed fury surrounding us, but we felt that it was imperative to do so.

With the eyes of all the diners pointed in our direction, we were becoming somewhat disturbed and alarmed. In our corner of the room an unnerving feeling of blatant fear swept over everyone. Those silent gazes of pure hatred had penetrated all of us. Our fear was a more than justified reaction to an awareness of possible danger. We did not know what sort of situation might occur.

Jumbled, unconnected thoughts, ran through my mind. I told myself not to look frightened or they'll think they've won.

What about the necessity for Lhabu to wear his outfit from India? It had obviously done nothing to make him impervious to racial prejudice.

That wretched mirror!! Was it really necessary to see the reactions of the people behind us as well as those in front? Being surrounded on all sides by anger only promoted feelings of claustrophobia and made it more difficult for us to remain calm, cool and collected.

As we left our tables, the stares persisted. It was as if they had to see that we were not just leaving but were willing us to be gone forever. The manager said nothing to us except to mention that we should pay at the desk on the way out. We were greatly relieved to have retrieved our coats and were nearly ready to depart.

Lhabu was in charge of our finances. Seeing that the bill was about to be paid, we all heaved a huge sigh of relief. Some of us were discussing the fact that we felt that the eyes of hatred in the dining room had pierced the walls and had followed us to the till, but thank goodness, no individual or group had actually pursued us.

Lhabu was meticulous, checking out each item and the price recorded. Someone whispered, "Just pay the bill and let's get out of here". I don't know who was more nervous or fearful, the individual dealing with the bill or the individuals in our group. We couldn't wait to leave, the tension in that dining room had been ready to ignite into we didn't know what kind of conflagration.

We had escaped any dreadful consequences for just being there and now Lhabu, instead of settling the bill, was examining every order, only prolonging our agony. As anxious as we were to leave, we knew that we couldn't. It might appear as if we were trying not to pay the bill. So, we all stood round feeling anxious and uneasy, ready to scream at Lhabu.

In his own good time, Lhabu sorted out the bill and indeed a mistake had been made in calculating the total on the receipt. We were even more worried when Lhabu pointed this out as it might be construed as an insult or possibly an accusation. The words were uttered by the only brown male in the group, and he was stating in a very direct and clear voice that the cashier, a white person, had made a mistake in his calculations. In the deep South, brown and black people would never dare to question the word of a white person.

Everyone's heart skipped a beat. Someone quietly gasped-We heard a sharp intake of breath. Anxious faces and wrinkled brows appeared. Lhabu was ever busy being the efficient accountant, totally unaware of our concerns or the possible danger of his position. To our great relief, Lhabu eventually paid the corrected bill, and we could all escape!!

By great good luck, nothing untoward had actually occurred but we left feeling that we were truly fortunate to have escaped the wrath of the angry diners. This experience, having run the gamut of all our emotions, had left us completely exhausted and drained of energy. Although we met with more incidents of serious intolerance, none had ever felt so much on the verge of explosion as this particular event.

THE STOCKBRIDGE SCHOOL

After nearly 6 weeks of travel, we started our return trip home to the Putney Graduate School. As we left the warm, sunny climate of the south, we tried to brace ourselves for the ice and snow of the Vermont winter.

I was very anxious to reach Putney as quickly as possible and was very upset when we did reach our destination that it was too late to pick up Kim. He would have already been sound asleep for many hours. I was, of course, anticipating a joyful reunion, one full of chuckles and smiles, but instead, I was greeted with a long, contemplative stare.

Kim often reacted like this when perusing the faces of strangers, but I was his mother. Did he really not know me at all? Had he really forgotten me? My friend, Connie, placed him in my arms. He came to me without protest, but no sign of familiarity even penetrated his intent gaze.

As I embraced him, he made no sound, but he did quietly snuggle into my neck. I was now completely reassured by this deliberate act of physical contact that he did recognise me.

Reflecting on Kim's experience, I realised that it must have been a totally unexpected surprise to see both his absent parents standing before him, talking in rather loud, excited tones, completely overjoyed to see him. But, for him suddenly seeing us was, no doubt, a very shocking event. His reaction of stunned silence would seem a very appropriate response. We carried him back to the Graduate School and life carried on as before.

We had attended the Graduate School so that Roger could acquire his teaching qualifications. An apprenticeship was arranged for him at the Stockbridge School in Interlaken, Massachusetts. Hans Maeder, the director, had established a private, co-educational, progressive boarding school. From its inception, he had insisted that the school be international, interracial, and non-denominational.

In the 1950's, the intake of most private boarding schools was composed of white, Protestant students, mostly of only the male sex. The Stockbridge School was notable for standing in opposition to the insular prejudices of these institutions.

We assumed that Roger's apprenticeship would include monitored supervision in relation to his teaching practice. As the school needed a science teacher, they had hired Roger, but not to teach either physics or maths. We didn't know until after we had arrived that he was to teach biology, a subject which he had never studied. And, as it happened, no teacher training programme was ever put into practice. So, he was left on his own with no teaching experience to teach a subject with which he was totally unacquainted.

Although we both admired the ideals and aims of this institution, it was obvious that, in practice, it sometimes failed to realise to its own proclaimed aims. Aside from providing no suitable teacher training, there was a certain laxity in providing guidance for some of the more difficult students. The teachers did manage to teach most of the students but there seemed to be few established procedures for dealing with those who seriously transgressed the school's rules.

The school assemblies were, we both agreed, a more impressive example of the school's attempt at achieving its ideal intentions. Attempts at running the school on democratic principles meant that school meetings were conducted with both staff and students attending. Together, they discussed any problems or matters effecting the school and voted on what the outcome should be, although, the headmaster, as in many progressive schools, could enforce a veto.

While we were at the school, I was primarily engaged in the full-time care of my son, Kim. I was offered the not too taxing job of tutoring two foreign students in English. But that was my only teaching experience during our residence at the Stockbridge School.

When Roger finished his six months of teaching, we returned to the Putney Graduate School for the last few days of the course. Most of the time was spent in evaluation of all aspects of the year's events and subsequently, planning sessions for the projected curriculum for the following year, 1958-1959.

Not long after we had arrived home, Roger had an interview at the Putney School, the private, progressive, co-educational boarding school which had been established in 1935. It had a wonderful reputation for excellence in the arts as well as in academic subjects.

Everyone was expected to be physically active, and the relevance of physical work was emphasised. Students performed various jobs on the farm and work crews. They took turns milking the cows and shovelling out the dung.

If anyone wanted chicken for Sunday lunch, he or she was required to first kill the chicken, all performed under expert supervision, so the chicken didn't suffer.

As the school was situated in the midst of the local mountains, school hikes and mountain walks were considered normal outdoor activities. During the winter months, with enormous snowfall arriving between November through February, skiing became the most popular sport for the entire school. They erected their own special rope ski lift to mount the highest hill near the school. Even young children managed to hang onto the rope to reach the summit, which meant that skiing became an enjoyable family sport as well.

We had heard so many wonderful reports about the school, we were delighted when Roger was accepted as a teacher of maths and physics to commence in September 1958. We rented the cottage opposite the Graduate School and began a new and very different kind of life in the countryside, surrounded by the pine-covered landscape of Putney, Vermont.

OUR YEAR AT THE COTTAGE

The cottage was rather picturesque, perched on a hill with wooden steps leading to the front entrance. Directly behind it, was a sparkling stream which followed the rugged terrain adjacent to the road and found its way to the bottom of the hill.

As we had decided to have another baby, I was 3 months pregnant when we moved into the cottage.

Morris had already informed us that the rent would not be extravagant because all the rooms were desperately in need of a coat of paint. As the ceiling in the open -plan kitchen -dining room area was too high to reach with a paint brush, Roger constructed a scaffold and proceeded to apply a few coats of white emulsion paint which immediately altered its grubby appearance.

I confined my painting to the walls of the two bedrooms, the bathroom, and the kitchen area. The entire painting of the cottage was completed in good time, before Roger started teaching.

The Putney School faculty were friendly and welcoming. I was introduced to other wives with small children. The fact that there were other mothers with children of similar ages to mine would prove to be a godsend during my time in Putney.

Roger liked the school and found he was particularly good at teaching those who were curious about his subjects (maths and physics). He admitted to having less success in inspiring those students who evinced no interest at all.

Our first daughter, Michèle was born on the 26th of December. I thought that all those pleas and prayers that she shouldn't be born on Christmas Day, uttered to I don't know who, had definitely been miraculously answered.

My doctor had agreed to the idea of natural childbirth but I thought I had sensed a little reservation. All doctors, at this time, were unaccustomed to delivering babies without medicating the mother.

I always waited probably, far too long, to decide that I was really in labour. It took about 40 minutes to reach the hospital. By the time I arrived at the reception desk, the baby would definitely be on its way. There was not much time left in which to consider whether or not to administer any sort of medication. So, this time, the birth was as I had hoped, without drugs.

The real bonus was that I saw my baby at birth. Times had not yet progressed to placing the baby on the mother's chest for her to embrace it.

The cord was cut, the baby was held up for all to see and quickly whisked away to the nursery.

Once again, I was the only mother breast-feeding and was told by everyone that I must feel like a cow. This continued to be my experience throughout all four births as the popularity for bottle feeding remained paramount. At least, this time the doctor had no objections to my not following the most popular feeding practices.

Not long after I arrived home with the new baby, the roof in our bedroom started to leak. We placed two buckets at the bottom of the bed to catch the slow but continuous drops of water. When Michèle awoke for her middle of the night feeds, I was obliged to empty the buckets before I even attempted to feed her as they were always nearly full to overflowing.

Feeding her at two or three in the morning, I would resentfully think that this quaint, picturesque, little cottage is not so idyllic after all. Such thoughts proved to ring true, particularly during one of Roger's mother's visits.

I had been complaining that some creature was secretly visiting one of the cupboards and had eaten a hole in a tea towel. Roger suggested that it might be a squirrel. I was worried that it might be a rat. We were, after all, living in the country. I felt that I should steel myself to deal with any problem that might occur, whatever that involved, even rats.

Miriam was alarmed and said that the noises she heard in the night were so loud that she couldn't sleep. She and I suggested that we set a trap immediately. Roger was concerned that we might kill a live animal in a cruel manner. The matter was resolved when Miriam sent us a trap that caught but did not kill animals.

The trap was set and placed in the designated cupboard. When taken out, the following morning, the trap revealed a large, grey rat. beady-eyed and boldly staring at us. I was shocked. It was the first time that I had ever laid eyes on a rat. I looked in horror and froze, thinking that if he were loose, he could harm one of the children.

Roger took him to some remote part of the Putney woods to release him and thank goodness, we didn't see or hear of him again. I was now frantic for Roger to repair any holes through which he may have entered the house. Roger did obligingly, set to work repairing any apertures, especially ones with nibbled edges while I was slowly trying to come to terms with the unfamiliar joys of country living.

THE PUTNEY NURSERY SCHOOL

The Putney community had informed everyone that they were looking for a new nursery schoolteacher. As caring for two young children had truly become a full-time occupation, I had no intention of engaging in any type of work outside of the home.

Once they learned that I was a qualified teacher and had taught nursery school, the entreaties began. With the offer of full-time help from another mother, I was finally persuaded to take on the job for five mornings a week.

Mornings were hectic. Roger would leave for work. Schools in the States usually start earlier than British ones. I always tried to have a quiet few moments feeding Michèle on my own before the chaotic time-table took over. Changing nappies, feeding Kim, dressing the children in their winter gear, hats, snowsuits, mittens, boots for Kim and we were ready to depart.

In the 1950's, seatbelts hadn't yet been invented so Kim sat on the back seat with Michèle's carry cot next to him. As snowploughs came out at all hours of the night and early morning to clear the roads, we could usually reach any desired destination without too much difficulty. I drove down our hill and up another (much steeper) to my friend's house where the babysitter was awaiting her brood of young children for the morning.

After depositing Michèle, I drove down the hill again with Kim to the Little Red Schoolhouse. It was a somewhat dilapidated structure, in need of some renovation, but just about adequate for our purposes. There was enough space for the activities of 10 or 12 lively, young children. Running water was available in the cold tap but we had to make do with a chemical toilet.

We teachers provided the weekly materials required for specific projects, for which we were later reimbursed. Despite the need for new paint and the absence of enough equipment, we had many amusing and enjoyable educational sessions with all the children who attended.

The following year, when more suitable facilities were found, the Nursery School moved to a building on the Putney School campus, a renovated chicken coop, and a full-time teacher was found to replace the two of us.

THE FARMHOUSE and CHILDREN'S MISHAPS

As Roger was hired to teach a second year, we decided to move closer to the Putney School. Staff usually lived in the dormitories but as there were no family spaces available, we rented a house in the community. We found an old farmhouse not too far from the school.

The end of the drive was near the intersection of two roads but the house, itself, was situated at the very top of the driveway. Fortunately, this meant that the children were prevented from running rashly and suddenly into a dangerous road.

The house was furnished with well-worn furniture which was highly suitable for our family. With two lively young children to care for, I did not want the burden of having to worry about the state of someone else's precious belongings.

In the cellar was a very old boiler-not very efficient, but it did produce enough heat in the middle of winter to keep us from freezing.

The main attraction was a huge, brick fireplace with unusable Dutch ovens for baking bread at one end, situated in the front wall of the sitting room. On bitterly cold winter evenings, we all loved sitting in front of the blazing fire toasting our bitterly cold fingers and toes.

The well which supplied the water for our house was only 15 feet deep. In the summer, as the water table fell, we, inevitably, became more cautious in our use of this precious commodity as it could run out completely and did so during the summer months every year.

The house was composed of two bedrooms upstairs and two downstairs, one of which doubled as a playroom. The idea of a playroom was practical, but its title was far from accurate. A more appropriate name would have been a storage room for toys.

When their friends visited, the children carried their toys from the playroom into the next-door sitting room to play. When they were on their own, they hauled them through the sitting room into the kitchen where I was always very busy, washing the dishes, cooking, cleaning, or doing the laundry. The playroom was, as the children said, where the toys went to sleep at night and that was the only time that they could be found there.

With the help of our friend, Michael Rieber, (my college friend Arlene's husband), Roger insulated the roof upstairs. Without this extra layer of warmth, that floor was too cold for anyone to inhabit for a good night's sleep. Once I had painted the rooms, the children couldn't wait to move to their new bedrooms at the top of the stairs, under the roof.

As the entire place was badly in need of brightening up, I later busied myself painting the floor, walls, and ceilings of the rest of the house.

I loved little babies and really enjoyed being a mother. I found the development of each child a unique and fascinating affair. There was no question that, from birth, they were very distinct little creatures who revealed very different types of personality.

Kim and Michèle proved to be such good companions that we decided to have two more children. Two years and 5 months after Michèle's birth, Natasha was born and twenty three months later, Leda arrived. After Leda joined her siblings, I was ready to accept that our family was complete.

There is no question that a fourth baby meant more work and more physical exertion on my part. But I hadn't counted on the assistance I would receive from the children. All three found the new addition an object of interest and curiosity. They were constantly dropping toys in her bassinet for her to play with. I was forced to ban these generous gestures as their fluffy toys were nearly as big as Leda and sometimes rested on her face which, I feared would not allow enough room for her to breathe. After much discussion, it was agreed that smaller soft toys laid halfway down the bassinet would be acceptable.

They were all very good baby-sitters. When Leda cried, each one was quite happy to bounce her up and down in her metal spring-back chair. If she cried and her dummy was nowhere in sight, I was shocked to discover that, to pacify her, Kim willingly offered her his own thumbs to suck. She was surrounded by three caring siblings and was very much the centre of their attention.

When the children were small, I always allowed time for us to do something special together. I wanted an interval between all the endless chores to enjoy being with them.

Due to my teaching experience, I had acquired the habit of saving any items that might prove useful for future use, discarded cardboard boxes, toilet rolls, plastic cups, bits of wallpaper, straws, pipe cleaners, buttons, old clothes etc. We made constructions out of anything that was lying about. Sometimes one of the children chose to live in a large, cardboard box for the morning. We made collages from a variety of bits and pieces, puppets out of old socks and necklaces with buttons and macaroni. We painted, read, and created little stories for the puppets to act out. We sprouted beans and even planted a little garden outside.

Initially, I allotted a special play time with Kim and Michèle. Later when Kim went to school and Michèle was in nursery school, I engaged in similar creative activities with Natasha and Leda.

I don't wish to idealise the difficulties faced in rearing four children. It was a rewarding but exhausting venture, especially in winter, a time when everyone became ill. When Kim had croup, Roger had the brilliant idea of using the electric frying pan to moisturise the room. It did work. The room was filled with moist air, but the rapidly boiling water evaporated so quickly that we were both forced to take turns all night continually refilling the parched frying pan.

There were sleepless times for all of us, when everyone caught the latest virus simultaneously, there were nights of hacking coughs, high temperatures, endless crying, one child waking another, everyone needing attention. It was only at times like these, when I was almost too tired to stand that I wondered what had possessed me to plan to have four children, but there wasn't one that I could ever have dreamt of relinquishing.

As was to be expected, each child suffered his or her fair share of mishaps growing up. I shall relate only a few. Starting with Kim.

KIM

Kim was outside playing barefoot on the newly cut grass. As he opened the screen door to come in, I yelled at him to stop. I was in the process of sweeping the kitchen floor for the second time as I had just broken a glass. "Stay where you are and don't walk any further." He obligingly stopped and put his foot down where he was standing, only to let out the most ear-deafening scream.

It couldn't be!! I had just swept the floor twice to prevent this from happening. How could he have managed to find the only splinter of glass left and how could it have landed completely across the other side of the room? When I peered at his foot, I couldn't see anything. But every time I approached a particular spot, he. screamed even louder.

It was Michèle's nap time. There was no hope of postponing her sleep. She could sleep in the car. I quickly changed her nappy and put her in her car seat. I carried Kim to the car and put him on the back seat. As I drove the thirty to forty minutes it took to reach Brattleboro, the cries of the two children resounded around the entire inside of the car.

Michèle might have dozed off, but Kim's intermittent shrieks continually woke her every time her eyes closed. By the time we arrived at the doctor's office, we had spent a harried hour together, surrounded by unrelenting screams and cries.

With Michèle almost asleep in my lap, the doctor took Kim. Amidst his screams, with the aid of a magnifying glass, and the aid of a nurse, he removed a very minute speck of glass.

Neither losing sleep nor having a piece of glass removed was a seriously disturbing event for either child. When we arrived home, Kim, unconcerned, was walking on his lightly bandaged, foot and Michèle was sound asleep.

It was I who appeared to be in a state of shock. Being bombarded with the children's incessant cries for such a long period of time and having no means of alleviating them, had taken its toll. I was a shattered wreck. Unfortunately, Kim, no longer, had an afternoon nap. My only solace was to have a cup of Lapsang Souchong tea, hoping that it would give me the strength to carry on.

It is for prospective mothers that I relate this tale as an example of a lesson to be learned. Remember that children will usually be left unscathed and evince no serious suffering, or even serious signs of pain, by the events they have caused, which leave you totally traumatised.

MICHÈLE

Because Roger was studying further maths courses at a college in Connecticut for the summer months, we had rented a small house in the area for June and July. For a special treat, we decided to take the children to the local swimming pool. With Kim and Michèle standing beside us, Roger and I were exchanging a few words. I glanced down to see that that Michèle had somehow vanished from sight.

We looked around to see that she was running, headed for the highest ladder in the swimming pool. She was fast and without fear as a child. I knew it was a question of Roger climbing the ladder to rescue her as quickly as possible, before she could reach the top.

If he didn't catch her before she set foot on the highest step, she would definitely take a leaping jump like the very experienced divers she had been watching when she was standing beside me. She was only 18 months old. As Roger was the expert swimmer, I sent him to capture her before disaster struck.

With not a second to spare, he did rescue her. She was reaching for the top step when he grabbed her. We never figured out how she had disappeared so quickly. In the blink of an eye, she had escaped.

Needless to say, for the rest of the summer, I was on diligent watch near any water, especially ponds and swimming pools.

AN INCIDENT WITH KIM AND MICHÈLE

I was standing near the top of the drive and could hear Kim and Michèle playing cheerfully not far away. I was about to check their exact whereabouts when I suddenly glimpsed our very old, second car rolling down the hill behind me.

I didn't have time to think. I turned around and darted after it, running as fast as I could. With each step, it just evaded me. As I looked into the car, I saw Kim in the driver's seat and Michèle sitting beside him on the passenger's side. I wanted to keep the car from running down the driveway and into the road, but I couldn't reach it. Luckily, the steering wheel was turned at an angle so the car swerved and rolled into the side of the house. As it had been rolling slowly down the hill, no-one was injured or even disturbed by the experience. In fact, both Kim and Michèle were laughing loudly. They obviously considered this experiment a great adventure.

I was the perfect picture of a parent full of contradictory emotions, so greatly relieved that nothing dreadful had happened to the children and simultaneously, very angry that their lives could have been unnecessarily endangered.

As I screamed furiously at both of them, Michèle said that Kim was only showing her how to drive. He had managed to unlock the hand brake which, of course, had caused the car to start moving. I stood stunned, in a state of incredulity. I couldn't believe that a child of eight not only knew how to unlock the hand brake but also had the strength to do so.

I immediately made a new, firm, and unyielding rule. No children were ever to enter a car unless accompanied by an adult. I then vowed to remember to lock all the car doors every time I left the car.

NATASHA

In the evening, Roger always read the children their bedtime story. As he read, he loved creating a number of interesting characters using different inflections and voices and the children loved hearing them. After this blissful time, it was kisses all round and good night to everyone.

One evening as Roger leaned over Natasha to say goodnight, she whispered in his ear that she had something special to tell him. He leaned in closer, and she quietly stated that she had put a bead in her nose. Roger brought her downstairs and we both examined her. Neither one of us knew how to retrieve the bead without pushing it farther into her nasal passage.

Another hurried trip to Brattleboro, this time with Natasha in the back seat of the Volkswagen. My fear was that the bead might be inhaled and end up in one of her lungs. I encouraged her to blow her nose, but to no avail, no bead had appeared.

The doctor put a long tube in her nose which was attached to a suction machine. Once it was turned on, there was a great whirring sound and the bead suddenly appeared to leap out of the tube. Natasha smiled sweetly and looked very pleased, as if she had expelled the bead herself, obviously relieved and totally unaware of the trauma she had caused.

A SECOND INCIDENT

One summer, when our well had run dry, Roger had started digging a hole in the ground, not too far from our house. It was an area where three streams met, and he was sure that water would soon fill the hollow cavity. We could fill our buckets, use it for flushing the toilet and for watering the garden, (we always grew our own fresh vegetables in the summertime.)

For drinking and cooking purposes, we were filling large cider bottles and numerous other containers with water from the Putney School taps and trying not to outwear our welcome by using friends for baths.

I was preparing some nibbles for the children one morning when Kim's six year old friend arrived breathless at the kitchen door screaming that Natasha had fallen into the water. I rushed down to the water hole to see Natasha, face down, arms and legs outstretched with her purple parka billowing up with air, looking as if it were keeping her afloat.

I instinctively jumped into the water, not knowing how deep it was and pulled as hard as I possibly could to lift her from the surface of the water. She was, of course, very heavy as all her clothes were soaking wet. As I pulled her out, I shook her and started hitting her on her back. If she had swallowed any water, I thought she might regurgitate it, but she expelled nothing.

She looked pale and bleary-eyed. Friends advised me not to let her sleep. I thought that advice was meant for concussion. I didn't think it was appropriate, but I wasn't sure and as it was her naptime, it was impossible to keep her awake.

Another trip to the doctor, this time with all the children. He examined Natasha and declared that she was fine. There was nothing to worry about. For some reason, both lungs remained clear. It didn't appear that she had inhaled any water. We concluded that she must have been holding her breath. Thanks to Kim's friend, she seemed totally unscathed.

LEDA

Until she was about six, Leda had survived without any major, traumatic events in her childhood. One day as we were all sitting round the dining room table having tea, Leda reached out to pick up a sandwich and as she did so, her arm knocked over the pot of hot water. As it soaked into her sweater and tee shirt, she screamed in pain.

I snatched her from her seat and rushed to the kitchen to put her scalded arm under the cold water tap and very carefully removed her wet clothing. The skin was bright red. I wasn't sure how deep the burn was.

Thank goodness, when we had moved, we found ourselves closer to the doctor's surgery. I rushed Leda into the car and within a few minutes, we saw the nurse who said it was important to keep the wound clean and expose it to the air. I went home with that advice feeling very uneasy. How could I keep her from bumping into things and irritating her unprotected skin even more?

Fortunately, a nurse who was visiting a friend across the road saw Leda's burn and was shocked at the advice we had been given. She suggested that we go to hospital immediately to get it properly treated. For the next few weeks, we went to the doctor for a series of dressing changes. Luckily, there was no deep skin damage, so she recovered without any scars as soon as the skin was totally healed.

LEDA AND THE HOLIDAY THAT NEVER WAS.

We were in Austria on a skiing holiday. It was the 1960's, so long ago that we had calculated that, aside from the cost of using the ski slopes, it was cheaper to stay in Austria than to remain in England. We stayed in the cheapest accommodation available, a small house at the top of a mountain, offering beds, breakfast, and dinner at very reasonable rates. We went farther down the mountain to buy food in the supermarket for our afternoon meal.

Often the sun was so hot that we removed our ski jackets and applied sun cream to all exposed areas before we could even consider sitting on our waterproof ground sheet to eat our picnic lunch.

Roger always drove from England to Austria, negotiating all the daunting Alpine, hairpin curves until we finally arrived in Solden, and then drove to the top of a very high hill where Haus Pauli was situated. Occasionally, if it had snowed recently, Roger had to apply chains to the snow tires in order to create enough grip on the road for us to proceed up steep terrain.

Haus Pauli was populated by a family with five children, mostly teenagers or older. When guests arrived, some slept two to a bed, in order to free enough beds for the paying clientele. I am sure it was the children who had cleaned the rooms because a variety of shoes and articles of clothing could be found tucked under all the beds.

As the Austrians, like the Swiss, were famous for their cleanliness and tidiness, I always claimed that we had found the only unkempt house in all of Austria. But relations between us and the family were so warm and friendly, I thought it best to overlook the unexpected presence of an odd pair of shoes or a misplaced jumper. I feared that the very busy Frau Klausner would feel that she had to reprimand one of the children, and I certainly didn't want to be responsible for that.

The only disadvantage of this skiing holiday was that there was no washing machine in the entire town of Solden. Part of my holiday time was spent washing all the dirty clothes by hand and hanging them out to dry in the freezing, cold air. When I retrieved the stiffly frozen objects, they were dispersed on the radiators in the children's rooms to dry. A scene reminiscent of my childhood when I helped my mother to bring in the frozen laundry.

Roger had gone on skiing holidays in Switzerland since he was a young child. The children had grown up skiing, the first attempts were starting on the hill in our back garden and sliding down the driveway. I, who had not grown up skiing, had decided that on this holiday, I would join a skiing class to improve my very basic skills.

At breakfast the next morning, Leda said that she felt unwell. She ate no breakfast and seemed rather listless. She had a slight temperature, but it wasn't very high. Soon a very light rash appeared on her chest and arms. With the aid of my German dictionary, and my very literal translation from English to German, I consulted Frau Klausner, I knew that the German was probably outrageously incorrect as I'd never studied it, but we did somehow manage to communicate. The outcome was that neither one of us recognised the rash.

Two days later, the blisters appeared. Immediately, we both knew that it was chicken pox. With the exception of the first day or two when she had a slight temperature, Leda remained very bouncy and appeared to be quite well. I kept her inside for a few days but when the blisters crusted over, I knew that she was no longer contagious.

To her surprise, I did allow her play outside and I was delighted that she was able to return to her beloved skiing.

I think the moral of the tale (if there is one) is that mothers do not always have choices, nor do they always have holidays even when they are purported to be on one. They just have to learn to adjust to each unexpected situation as it occurs.

A MOTHER'S TIME – OTHER ACTIVITIES

Although I loved being with the children, there were definitely times when I thought that my brain must have atrophied. I didn't want to accept the fact that I no longer did any serious reading and never engaged in any new or challenging activities.

It was a matter of energy. I was mainly preoccupied with all the activities engaged in looking after children. They were constant and continuous, leaving no time for rest, contemplation, or anything else. I wanted to feel that I was still capable of involving myself in pursuits that required thoughtful consideration. As a consequence, every so often, I was compelled to challenge myself to learn something new.

I started by learning to make bread. Having been given the Betty Crocker cookbook as a wedding present, I was pleased to find a substantial section devoted to making different kinds of bread.

My friends and I contacted a farm in Pennsylvania which supplied a variety of whole-grain flours, soya, rice, whole wheat and rye etc. It was cheaper to buy them wholesale. When the large bags arrived, we weighed them and dispensed equal amounts to everyone. We all went home, pleased to realise how much money we had saved and were ready to test out making a different kind of bread loaf every week.

In the end, the children wanted to be involved. They loved punching down the dough after the yeast had forced it to rise and couldn't wait for it to rise again so they could spoon it into the loaf tin to bake.

When they were older, we made flowerpot bread every Saturday. Each child had his or her flowerpot to make their very own special loaf of bread.

I extended my own experiments to puff pastry, coffee cakes, Danish pastries, cheesecake, apple tarts, blueberry muffins and other types of desserts.

We all loved Roger's mother's marmalade. When we visited Miriam and Gabo in Connecticut, we always enjoyed the bitter marmalade happily residing in a beautiful Bernard Leach pot on the lazy-susan. When the Seville oranges arrived from Spain, Miriam was always preparing a new batch of marmalade for the next year.

As she very generously had given us the recipe, Roger and I made the same marmalade, to be given as Christmas presents every year along with my homemade Christmas cake, full of crystallised fruit and nuts. The cake was always very popular as it was so moist. The secret was to pour a bottle of very good brandy over it, immediately after I had removed it from the oven. The alcohol did not evaporate but soaked into the cake and remained there to keep it from drying out. Over the period of a month or two, I continually added a bit more brandy to keep it moist in its tin.

My next project was to read a book, one that had been on my reading list for many years, Proust's, The Remembrance of Lost Time or Things Past as it is sometimes called. It was usually after the children were in bed that I decided to claim my reading time. As I was often just too tired to focus on anything that required concentrated attention, I would have to change my mind and succumb to tiredness.

Given its inordinate length, The Remembrance of Things Past was a very demanding book to finish. There are many themes presented throughout the book's entirety: the unintentional recall of past experiences, the many sides of personality which he suggested everyone possesses and the vagaries of love ,to name but a few.

Each section introduces the reader to different aspects of French life during the late 19th and early 20th century. Some of the most memorable revelations relate to the behaviour of wealthy, educated, exotic individuals in Parisian society, some of whom were totally eccentric and unconventional in pursuit of their hedonistic interests.

Proust aspired to become a part of this society. He began his social life as a participant of the salons and their unorthodox habits and later became an observer and writer about this very world to which he had belonged.

He remained in poor health throughout his life, publishing only intermittently until he was 30. He lived with his mother who cared for him until she died.

After her death, his health slowly declined, and he withdrew from salon life. It was only then that he started to devote himself to his writing seriously and began to write A La Recherche du Temps Perdu. He spent the last three years of his life in bed attempting to bring this huge tome to an end but when he died at age 52, it was still unfinished.

It took me months to complete it, but I did finally succeed. I was left feeling pleased that I had made some new revelations about human existence and left hopeful that maybe a few cognitive cobwebs might have been dispersed.

My last attempt to prove to myself that my brain had not wasted away through serious neglect, was to try to learn to play the flute. As I had studied piano as a child, I could read music, though, I hasten to add, my ability to read music had slowed down considerably through disuse over the years.

We were fortunate to have residing in, Brattleboro, internationally, well-known musicians, Blanch Honegger Moyse, a violinist, Louis Moyse, her husband a flautist, and Marcel Moyse, Louis' father, also a famous flautist.

I felt I did not have the courage to ring such a revered musician as Louis Moyse to request music lessons. He was accustomed to working with musicians of the highest calibre and I was a complete beginner who, at this time, didn't even own a flute.

Various friends encouraged me to pursue my desire so I did eventually ring and Louis Moyse agreed to take me on as a student. I was delighted and petrified. Although I practised as much as time would allow, I remained nervous and full of trepidation at every lesson.

After Natasha was born, I took a few months off but did return. I managed to learn the three octaves and produced a reasonably pleasant sound, though there was definitely room for improvement.

On the days that I had flute lessons, I left my children with a friend for two hours. It meant that she was looking after her own four children and, in addition, my four children as well. The number of children now sounds more than a bit overwhelming, but all of my friends were accustomed to looking after groups of children of different ages.

It was due to the fact that most already had at least four children and one had five, (the last was an unexpected surprise). Most of the time, we exchanged children of similar ages, which didn't add to the numbers.

When we left Putney, I, sadly, gave up studying the flute and have not, for a variety of reasons, seriously pursued it since.

THE TOWN MEETING AND THE SCHOOL SITUATION

Every year Putney designates the first Tuesday of March as Town Meeting Day. Residents meet to discuss their local concerns as well as business issues and town officials are elected to office.

Over time, many towns had done away with such meetings. I was elated to think that I would be seeing democracy in action, as it had been practised historically in many states. Citizens met face-to-face to discuss, converse and argue about any issue they felt was of public concern.

While I was interested in how the democratic process would actually work, in the course of the meeting, problems arose which proved to complicate the smooth running of all decision-making at the town meeting.

While Putney, on the surface, appeared to be an idyllic, tranquil rural community, the meeting revealed long-standing divisions within the community. The town consisted of local residents, mostly farmers, people who ran the three local shops or others engaged in small businesses, trying to remain self-sustaining. Over the years, a few educational institutions had established themselves here. They were all private organisations, one college, an institution for international students, a primary school, and the Putney School. Despite the Putney School's attempts to bridge the gap between the town residents and the school, there remained a schism between the local residents and those involved directly in private education.

Educational institutions were always exempt from local taxes. They always donated money to the town. But annually, at town meeting the question always arose as to whether these institutions should be free from the obligation to pay taxes. There would be heated discussions on both sides. Some townspeople even supported the exemption of taxes on the grounds that the private institutions provided jobs for some in the local community. Having looked at the 2016 Town Meeting Reports, I note that the same controversial subject continues to produce the same conflicting opinions amongst the same two factions, as it has done from time immemorial.

Because town meetings are run democratically, it sometimes means that decisions made by the majority may not always be in agreement with one's own desires. Having found that there was little or possibly no fluoride in the local drinking water, a group of citizens had campaigned against adding any to the water. They were Christian Scientists and believed that if God hadn't put fluoride in the water, it would be a sin or at least a serious misdemeanour for local citizens to do so.

Having read studies which indicated that fluoride could prevent tooth decay in children as well as adults, I was very unhappy about this situation. After discussing the problem with our dentist, I asked if he could prescribe fluoride for the children. He was happy to do so, for each child, a drop a day.

When I became pregnant with Leda, knowing that her teeth were being formed, I asked if I could take a daily dose of fluoride for the baby. As he hadn't read any studies about the efficacy of fluoride in pregnancy, he was, at first, reluctant, but I persisted. It was, after all, only what most babies were receiving in areas where the water was already fluoridated. As he found no medial reason not to do so, he did prescribe fluoride for me. As he said, "One drop a day for the baby."

My efforts were vindicated when, for many years, my children had no tooth decay. Our dentist was amazed and stated that if all families had such good teeth, he would soon be put out of business.

THE SCHOOL SITUATION

Some of these parents were unhappy about the size of the classes in the state primary school and in addition, were critical of their teaching methods, i.e., there was too much rote learning.

Prior to our arrival in Putney, they had established a small fee-paying school, The Grammar School, in an old building, accessible from the nearest road. A devoted, young couple was in charge of almost everything from all the classroom teaching to sports and music. They were assisted by one or two more teachers.

I had visited the state school to make my own assessment of the teaching situation and concluded that I more-or-less agreed with their criticisms. There was little space for discussion. Individual thinking, curiosity and drawing one' own conclusions were not encouraged. Producing the right answer, without query or any time to examine why such answers might be right or wrong, seemed to be the ultimate aim in all subjects.

I noted that the teachers were competent and were dealing with large classes which they handled well. The children were learning the required curriculum, albeit without much or any emphasis on promoting questioning, curiosity, or individual development.

I always felt that education in many states in the USA posed a problematic situation for those who believed in democracy and in sending their children to state schools. Parents might fervently believe in sending their children to state schools, and want them to associate with all nationalities and all classes of children, but be seriously challenged by the old-fashioned teaching methods employed in the classrooms.

Why were most, if not all, the state schools following conventional, old-fashioned teaching methods? Why were none promoting more child-centred approaches to classroom learning? I had faced the same dilemma when I trained as a teacher. If I wanted to learn progressive teaching methods, I was forced to do so in the private sector, as the state schools in Massachusetts did not offer this type of training and adamantly took a strong stance against it

I had not made a decision about what to do about Kim's education when, due to unexpected circumstances, I felt that I had no choice.

It was the year that I was the Head of the Board of the Nursery School. Roger's grandmother, Ooma, felt that my position demonstrated that I had great organisational skills. I never convinced her that it was a job that just rotated around the mothers of the nursery school, and did not rely primarily on anyone's specific skills. Most of us took turns to undertake the responsibilities involved. We were never elected, only asked to take on the task. It was a co-operative enterprise. Parents helped. They checked on the condition of the nursery school equipment and were consulted about the state of the school accounts and the hiring of new teachers. I arranged meetings with the parents to discuss practical and financial matters and discussed the proposed programme for the nursery school with the new teacher.

I attended a meeting with the nursery schoolteacher one day to discuss school matters and on the very next day, I was summoned by her to a meeting about my son. It felt odd to have been in charge one day and then to be the recipient of her bad news the next. I knew it had to be bad news from the inflection in her voice when she rang me.

She informed that Kim had started the year being a very polite child full of imagination and a delight to have in the classroom but had now become an obstreperous individual determined to commit as many bad deeds as he possibly could. He erased things she had written on the blackboard, he refused to return the crayons, he had turned over the wastebasket, etc.

I was mortified and couldn't understand why he was engaging in this confrontational behaviour. When I asked Kim, he responded without guile or deception, rationally and without concern, stating that every time he was naughty, the teacher gave him a sweet. The more naughty he was, the more sweets he received.

I then began to get complaining phone calls from other mothers that their children were being given sweets at school. Their children were naughty as well but, but it appeared that Kim was the worst. In the circumstances, I couldn't take any pride in realising that he was quick to learn, as he was learning all the wrong things far too quickly.

I discussed the situation with the teacher, but matters were not just left in my hands. The parents and other board members had to decide whether to look for another teacher or try to get this one to change her ways. We were having serious difficulty finding a new recruit. Nursery schoolteachers seemed to be non-existent in our vicinity at the time, so it was agreed to keep the one we had.

I was now desperate to undo the lessons that Kim had learned at nursery school. I felt that he couldn't continue at the nursery school repeating his newly learned bad behaviour. But he would only be five when the next school year began. State schools only accepted children when they were six years old. This was the law in every state.

In desperation, I approached the director of the Grammar School and asked if he would accept Kim as a pupil, despite his being a year underage, explaining that he didn't have to learn anything academically. It was for social reasons that I wanted him to enter school. It was very important for him to learn how to behave with a teacher in a classroom and how to behave with other children. Fortunately, he was accepted. And as he was never rewarded for bad behaviour, I was pleased that the teachers never reported that he had a problem with learning acceptable social behaviour.

I didn't realise it initially, but I had created a little problem for myself. While Kim's behaviour miraculously improved, he had been exposed to a new and exciting activity, that of reading. He returned home every day, fiercely determined to acquire the skills that the other children possessed in order to read himself.

Every afternoon, when he returned home from school, he was very tired but always announced that he wanted to learn to read. He was so exhausted that I tried to get him to take a nap, no success there. I then tried distraction, any games that he liked to play. A snack only momentarily stopped him from insisting that I teach him to read. His persistence eventually wore me out. I finally relinquished and agreed to help him learn to read. At school, he had learned most of the sounds of the letters so that was a step in the right direction.

But I was simultaneously trying to look after the other three children while trying to teach him. I tried to engage the others in some activity that they liked to do so that I could concentrate on reading with Kim. It worked sometimes, but not always. It was a real struggle to give him the undivided attention that he needed. After many turbulent and frequently interrupted sessions, he was eventually able to start reading completely on his own. But I would say that it was his firm resolve and perseverance, more than my efforts at teaching in such unfavourable circumstances, which made him attain his goal in the end.

SPUTNIK – ALICE – MARLBORO

In 1957, the Soviet Union launched Sputnik, the first satellite ever to enter space. The United States was caught completely unawares. Totally stunned, it was forced to accept the fact that they were no longer the leaders in space exploration.

The satellite moved in a low orbit which was visible from earth. To the chagrin of the US government, their citizens became engaged in a new preoccupation. Evenings were spent spotting the satellite and then tracking its movement across the sky at night.

Programmes were immediately set into motion to improve the standards of maths, science, and language teaching. The federal government willingly paid to send secondary school teachers on crash courses to raise the level of their knowledge and their skills. The Physical Science Studies Committee, (The PSSC), was established to renovate textbooks in order to include the most recent research and knowledge in the fields of maths and science.

Roger and his colleagues were very involved in learning the new science programmes and what was defined as "the new maths". During the 1950's, the Cold War between Russia and the USA stimulated competition and the race to be first in scientific discovery. As long as this situation lasted, the US continued to pour money into the reform of scientific education.

But when Neil Armstrong walked on the moon in 1969, the US felt it had reclaimed its supremacy in the field of science. Federal support for renovating the curriculum and the retraining of science, maths and language teachers seemed to end quite abruptly. The ten-year era of extravagant funding for science and languages was definitely over, never to return again.

Roger became a part of this retraining programme. The first summer he attended a college in Connecticut. Families who applied very early were allotted rooms in the dormitories. Other families who were not so fortunate, rented houses or rooms off campus. We were in the latter category.

Where one lived dictated where one could go. It was a simple fact that, I'm sure, no-one had thought through until they were in the midst of the situation. The mothers who lived on campus had the use of the family car when their husbands were attending classes.

There was no public transportation in the beautiful New England countryside, but those who lived off campus relinquished the car for their husband's use. It was the only way he could reach the college to attend his classes. These mothers were stuck at home with no transportation to the town. They could not do the shopping or access other facilities like the library or the swimming pool or even contact other mothers and children.

It was not a disaster. We all survived. When we did meet up at a college party, there was general agreement amongst the off-campus mothers that they wouldn't be repeating the experience. We all had similar expectations. We would be meeting new people. The children would have new playmates. We would be living an ordinary life, taking the children for outings in a new environment. Shopping for the week's food supplies was taken for granted. Instead, most of us felt immobilized and isolated, stranded in the countryside and during the day, never able to speak with another adult.

Roger departed for a second summer to further his studies in "new maths" but this time, we did not accompany him. When he returned home on the weekends, he always received a very boisterous welcome from all the children. Though we all missed each other, and despite Roger having to drive home on weekends, it was a more satisfactory arrangement. Roger was pleased to have more space during the week for his studies and he did not to have to squeeze in the food shopping and countless other activities into his hard-earned free time.

I took the children on many swimming outings either at the Putney Pond or at my friend's home-made swimming pool. My friends and I could have a chat and a cup of coffee or tea while all the children played noisily not too far away. There were lots of sleepovers and exchanging children for more than a day or two.

This familiar, social interaction maintained my buoyant feelings for the entire summer. A second, very inspiring, source of pleasure was my attendance at the Marlboro Music Festival classical concerts.

For seven weeks every summer, the Marlboro Musical Festival was held in Marlboro, Vermont, fortunately, within driving distance of Putney. It is a retreat where classical musicians of advanced standing can take further training. Many famous musicians arrived in Marlboro every summer to participate in the concerts but also to teach, which helped to maintain consistently high teaching standards for the students.

It was founded by two reputable musicians, Adolph Busch, a violinist, and Rudolf Serkin, a pianist. They recruited Blanche, Louis and Marcel Moyse, two famous flautists and Blanche, a renowned violinist. With the exception of Adolf Busch, they were all refugees from the Third Reich.

The concerts were always of the highest calibre and the musicians often played pieces from their chamber music repertoire. Many string quartets and solo performers who studied here have later become internationally famous musicians.

In order to go to these concerts, I booked Alice, the main baby-sitter for the entire community.

ALICE

Alice was an older woman, probably in her fifties, when we met her. She was living with and looking after her father who was totally compos mentis but not very active physically. Alice informed us that he had attended Harvard for two years but had to leave due to a heart condition. It was obvious that money was not abundant, and the house was in need of a good coat of paint and some repairs.

Alice's baby-sitting was her main source of income. As she was the only adult in Putney performing this service, she was in constant demand. I used to wonder how she coped every day with so many children of different ages. Crying children sat on her father's knee. He could be seen cajoling and coaxing two children at a time, one on each knee, into a more jovial state. He told them stories and fed them as the need arose.

Despite what the parents saw as mayhem, the children loved going there. They received their fair amount of cuddles and consolation when things went wrong and there were always other children for companionship.

My children adored her molasses sandwiches. I was horrified!! In terms of nutrition, I saw them as unhealthy lunches, merely sugary syrup on starch. When I think of it now, it was really no worse that the strawberry jam sandwiches that my English friends fed their children for tea. When I discussed the matter with Alice, she reassured me, it wasn't as dreadful as I had thought, because she used dark molasses, the kind known to have more iron in it.

The children's greatest joy was feeding Alice's pigs. The children adored the pigs, and it seems, the pigs adored the children. When the children appeared, they always ran expectantly to the gate of the pen to eat the scraps of food the children threw in. Pigs are very intelligent, social animals. I always believed the children who said they'd been talking to the pigs and the pigs answered back. I was sure they would have had an intelligible conversation of some kind.

Alice's house was full of baby equipment. We all gave her cots, prams, baby tables, bouncy chairs, and every kind of toy imaginable. It was sometimes a struggle to get children to leave a new, coveted toy behind, knowing that they didn't have the same one at home.

When Alice babysat for us, we always had prolonged conversations about the latest book she was reading. She read profusely and had become interested in Chinese history and its present-day politics, as had Roger. As she read continually in her free time, she eventually became even better-informed than he was.

Since she had become such an expert on the history and the current situation in China, she was asked to lecture at a local college about everything Chinese, its culture, music, the arts, history and politics. Alice had never had the opportunity to engage in further education, so we all acclaimed her success, describing her as the college lecturer with no credentials.

But, to our dismay, our relationship with her as a daytime baby-sitter ceased, when our paediatrician in Brattleboro closed down Alice's premises. We were all devastated and in a state of disbelief. But, on a rational basis, we couldn't argue with him.

As she was the only available daytime baby-sitter, everyone in Putney left their children with her. As a doctor, he was experiencing the consequences of this situation. If one child at Alice's were ill, it was likely that all the children visiting that day also became ill. They then carried whatever bacteria or virus they'd acquired, home to the rest of the family where it could be spread further.

I'm sure he saw her premises as a health hazard where any illness or disease could be easily acquired and quickly spread throughout the community.

He was justified but we worried about how Alice would survive. She felt less secure but could survive because she owned a fairly successful plant nursery and was now receiving money for lecturing, and she still had the pigs and grew and preserved her own vegetables and fruit.

When it was cold, she buried her parsnips in the ground to make them sweeter. She assured us that we had no need to worry because she "wouldn't go without". The parsnips and the pigs would always provide food throughout the long winter.

VERMONT – PROTESTS – NUCLEAR WEAPONS

Although, after the arrival of our four children, I had less time to devote to my political interests, my serious concerns regarding nuclear weapons, the civil rights movement, and injustice in various parts of the world, particularly the apartheid system in South Africa, had not diminished.

For many years, Roger and I attempted to keep abreast of national and international problems by attending The Family Institute, a summer conference run by our friend, Russell Johnson for the American Friends Service Committee. Well-informed lecturers spoke about the social, economic, and political problems of the day and later participated in small, animated discussion groups.

As many families were in attendance, further discussion groups were offered, relating to the role of parents, child-rearing, and the difficulties that many families might encounter.

Carers were provided for the different age groups of children. This meant that mothers might be free to take part in examining relevant topical events and meet with other like-minded individuals.

As most of my time was spent with the children and their pursuits, I really looked forward to this conference every summer. It was a brief time when my life was not engulfed predominantly with domestic concerns. I sometimes, actually had the space to focus on and discuss with others significant contemporary issues, and I relished the opportunity to do so.

We continued to attend nuclear protest marches, but not as frequently as previously had been the case. During one of our many trips to Connecticut to visit to my mother-in-law, Miriam, and Gabo, we joined a small anti-nuclear march. As I was seven months pregnant with my third baby, (Natasha), I became so tired when walking up a steep slope that I was forced to asked Roger to push me to the top of the hill.

When Papa overheard us nonchalantly laughing about the matter, he became alarmed immediately, exclaiming that despite the good cause, there was no need for me to join the protest, especially, in my condition.

I think he found pregnant women something of an enigma and thought that any physical exertion would lead to overwhelming exhaustion and ultimate collapse. I never convinced him that my being tired for a few minutes was not a serious concern for either myself or for the baby.

I put his reaction down to his being only vaguely aware of the lives that women actually lead. (I'm sure he would agree as he was always commenting on the fact that when he lived in Russia, young children were the responsibility of women and men were not allowed to help in any way.) At home, I was constantly on my feet, running around after two very lively and sometimes mischievous children. As they no longer had naps, there was no allotted time to sit down and put my feet up. My everyday regime was really far more exhausting than my one-time attempt to walk up a steep incline. But I was truly touched by what I considered his misplaced anxiety.

In Vermont, I joined the Women's League for Peace and Freedom and when possible, attended meetings. Our group, along with many others, went on an anti-nuclear march to Burlington, the capitol of Vermont. While there, we visited our elected representative to convey our concerns about the cold war and the frightening possibility that nuclear weapons could once again be detonated.

The United States presented the Soviet Union as a continual threat, ready to attack the US with nuclear weapons at any moment. Given that assumption, it was important to stay ahead in the nuclear arms race which meant constantly producing increasingly potent nuclear weapons.

The Russians were behaving in similar fashion, accusing the US of preparing to launch a nuclear attack on Russia. The result was that both nations were engaged in an escalation of producing more and more nuclear bombs, creating stockpiles of weapons, which could obliterate the world and its inhabitants many times over.

In 1961, I joined the demonstration sponsored by The Women's Strike for Peace. In sixty cities in the US, approximately 50,000 women gathered to protest against nuclear testing and the ensuing atmospheric effects, carrying risks to children's health. Strontium 90 had been found not only in cows' milk sold over the counter but also in mothers' milk. It was the result of fallout from nuclear testing in the deserts of the US.

Our small group was part of the 1500 women from Vermont who, carrying our symbolic doves of peace, marched in Washington, D.C. to the foot of the Washington Monument, to make our concerns more publicly known.

It was the largest national women's peace protest of the 20th century. The actions of the Women's Strike for Peace were considered to have been influential in encouraging the signing of the 1965 Nuclear Test Ban Treaty.

THE CIVIL RIGHTS MOVEMENT – IN PERSPECTIVE

Looking at the literature, the history of the civil rights movement and the use of non-violent action started only in the 1950's. But significant protests, prior to this time, have often been overlooked.

In 1944, Irene Morgan, a 27-year-old woman, refused to move to the segregated area on an interstate bus. Interstate travel was supposed to be desegregated but southern states enforced segregation within their own state borders.

She was arrested and jailed in the state of Virginia. Her case eventually went to the Supreme Court. In 1946, they ruled that no segregation was allowed on interstate buses.

In 1947, The FOR, the Fellowship of Reconciliation, the AFSC, the American Friends Service Committee, and CORE, the Congress of Racial Equality, sponsored a Journey of Reconciliation. Sixteen men, eight white and eight black, travelled on buses through states in the upper south to test the implementation of this 1946 ruling. They were, as a group, committed to the use non-violent tactics, in the face of any attacks that might occur.

They met with intimidating mob violence in many places and were arrested twelve times. The judge in North Carolina was so incensed, particularly, by the white participants that he told the white members of the group: "It's about time you Jews from New York learned that you can't come down here bringing your niggers with you....Just to teach you a lesson, I gave your black boys thirty days on a chain gang and I gave you ninety."

The 1947 Journey of Reconciliation, often considered the first non-violent action group, set the precedent for later protests i.e., the Freedom Rides of 1961.

Through our friend, Russell Johnson, at the Cambridge, AFSC, we met Bayard Rustin and Wally Nelson, both participants in the 1947 bus rides. Bayard Rustin, a well-known Quaker and pacifist, was an elegant speaker at many conferences we attended. He was later responsible for organising with Martin Luther King, the 1963 March to Washington.

Wally Nelson and his wife Juanita stayed with us twice in Vermont. Juanita wanted to join the men on the 1947 journey on the buses. The officials of the three organisations feared for her safety. It was the very early days of non-violent action, and no-one knew what the outcome of those who opposed their tactics would be. She reluctantly acquiesced and did not participate in the 1947 attempts to desegregate the buses.

They loved our simple, rural setting in Vermont and seemed to survive a house full of boisterous children of varying ages, constantly running about. Most impressive was their firm commitment to work non-violently to challenge injustice despite the inevitable hostility and likely violence which they might incur.

BACKGROUND TO THE CIVIL RIGHTS MOVEMENT.

From 1875 to 1954, the southern states in the US all under the aegis of the Democratic Party had established the region's racial order. It was exemplified by legalised segregation in every aspect of daily life. There were social, education, political and legal systems in which only whites were in positions of power and authority. The black population was expected to be submissive and accepting of white dominance without disapproval or protest.

Belief the inherent inferiority of black people led many white people to believe that black Americans were not only content with their status, but actually enjoyed it. The idea of their opposing or resisting white authority was completely incomprehensible.

The NAACP (The National Association for the Advancement of Coloured People) had been established in1901 and had, particularly since the 1930's, legally attacked various forms of discrimination against black people.

In 1954, the NAACP had brought a legal case against segregated education in the USA. It was the now famous 1954 Brown vs. the Board of Education Case of Topeka, Kansas.

The Supreme Court ruled that: "in the field of public education, the doctrine of 'separate but equal' has no place. Separate educational facilities are inherently unequal."

Throughout the southern part of the United States separate educational institutions were firmly entrenched. White students attended the better-funded all white schools, while the black students were relegated to the inferior, insufficiently funded ones. White southern officials always claimed that all educational facilities were "separate but equal".

Eisenhower was the president and strongly disapproved of the Supreme Court's decision stating: "I don't believe that you can change the hearts of men with law".

In 1955, the courts issued what came to be known as the Brown Two Legislation to deal with the 1954 Brown decision.

States had been asked to desegregate their schools "with all deliberate speed". But as no specific deadlines were specified, southern school authorities and judges used delaying tactics in order to perpetuate segregation.

The border states and The District of Colombia began to desegregate their schools without compulsion, but various southern legislatures, resisting and rebelling against implementing these new laws, allowed white parents to use public funds to send their children to private schools.

To further prevent school integration, these legislatures also passed laws imposing economic reprisal on anyone who dared to advocate desegregation.

State legislatures in Alabama, Mississippi, Virginia, Georgia, and South Carolina produced resolutions which declared the court's decision was null and void and had no effect.

1955 was a significant year full of incidents which helped to galvanise the Civil Rights Movement. In Mississippi, it was an election year.

Those who attempted to voter were met with harsh resistance and violence. In Mississippi, three black Americans were murdered that summer, two for trying to vote and a 14 year old boy, for whistling at a white woman. Deaths of black males, particularly in the South, often went unpunished even when the murderers were known to the authorities.

The notorious case of Emmett Till, the 14 year old who was beaten, shot, and dumped in the Tallahatchie River, was broadcast to the entire nation. An all-white jury declared the men involved innocent of the murder. The exposure of the brutal racism of the south resulted in condemnation and public outrage.

Within a few months of this incident, in Montgomery, Alabama, Rosa Parks refused to give her seat on the bus to a white woman, thereby, rejecting the segregated bus policy which stated that because she was black she could sit only in the rear of the bus.

Her actions ultimately led to the Montgomery Bus Boycott of 1955-1956. Due to loss of fares the boycott damaged the economy of the city's bus system. People were seen to be walking, cycling, and even riding their mules to their desired destinations. Some white women drove their own cars to pick up their servants for work. Carpools were organised as a substitute means of transportation. A lift cost the price of a bus fare. City officials tried to fine drivers who didn't charge more.

In support of their resistance to bus segregation, the churches sent money and shoes in good condition.

Those in the boycott were often physically provoked and threatened with violence. In opposition to any sort of desegregation, White Citizen Councils had emerged everywhere in the south. In Montgomery, Alabama, their members consistently increased in response to the boycott.

Violence was used as means of intimidation. Four Baptist Churches were bombed. The houses of the two ministers, visibly supporting the boycott, Ralph Abernathy and Martin Luther King were bombed as well. Martin Luther was fined $500-00 and sent to prison for "hindering" a bus.

The boycott lasted for just over a year (381 days), until the 4th of June, when the Federal District Court ruled that segregation on Alabama's buses was unconstitutional.

Its ultimate success in the face of massive white opposition inspired civil resistance in other areas of segregation and helped to establish Martin Luther King as an important leader in the Civil Rights Movement.

THE THREE PRESIDENTS

Three presidents, Eisenhower, Kennedy, and Johnson are generally credited as being enablers or promoters of civil rights issues. While all three did ultimately become involved in civil rights legislation, this simplistic view of history ignores the uncertainty and resistance, the opposition and sometimes outright rejection that these same individuals initially expressed towards civil rights demonstrations and the implementation of specific civil rights rulings.

Eisenhower never believed that federal legislation would change the prejudiced beliefs of the white southerners. As a result, he never publicly endorsed the civil rights movement.

The 1957 the Civil Rights Bill had originally contained a very strong section to protect voters rights. Eisenhower produced the alterations which resulted in a much weaker bill.

Although he passed the 1957 Civil Rights Bill enabling Black people to vote, there were those who believed that he did so for his own self-aggrandisement. The passage of the bill ensured that he would receive the black vote and would hopefully remain in office. Whether this is true or not cannot be verified.

Lyndon Johnson, a Texan, was the Democratic Majority Leader at the time (not yet President). The Democratic Party was composed of liberally minded northerners and the very conservative, right-wing southerners. Because he feared a split in the party, he stood in opposition to part three of the 1957 Civil Rights Bill which stated that a suit would be filed against anyone who obstructed voter registration. To placate the southern wing of the party, Johnson also made sure that part three of the bill was totally eliminated.

For this decision, Johnson hoped to receive kudos from both the northern and the southern Democrats simultaneously. He expected support from southerners for directly restricting the power of the bill. And, as it was the first civil rights bill to be passed in eighty-two years, he was awaiting praise and congratulations from the northern section of the party.

Initially, neither John Kennedy nor his brother, Robert, were involved in the civil rights struggle. Many Democrats, including the Kennedy brothers had voted against President Eisenhower's 1957 Civil Rights Bill. John Kennedy was anxious to become the 1960 presidential candidate and did not want to alienate southern Democrats and lose their votes.

Later, when Martin Luther King had been imprisoned in the deep south, fearing violence and possibly a lynching, John F. Kennedy intervened to have Martin Luther King removed from jail. After this intervention, Kennedy won the black vote, and many assumed that he would support civil rights issues during his time in office.

But, believing that the only way to promote the cause of civil rights was through implementing executive orders, the Kennedy administration did not support the idea of the marches and demonstrations which were the mainstay of the civil rights protests.

A MORE DETAILED DISCUSSION OF THE DECISIONS OF EISENHOWER, JOHNSON, AND KENNEDY DURING THE CIVIL RIGHTS MOVEMENT

PRESIDENT EISENHOWER

Eisenhower made no attempt to enforce the 1954 Supreme Court legislation prohibiting segregated schools until the year 1957. He received an insistent message from the Mayor of Little Rock, Arkansas indicating that he needed help in the face of serious unrest and likely violence as white mobs were attempting to prevent black children from attending a white school.

Eisenhower had done nothing to alleviate the situation. It was only after he received the governor's urgent request that he decided to send troops to escort the nine black students to Little Rock High School.

Martin Luther King sent a telegram to President Eisenhower, asking him to publicly condemn the white racist southerners for the violent attacks they were perpetrating against black people. Eisenhower responded stating that he couldn't see what good another speech would do. When Martin Luther King expressed his dismay at receiving no support from the president, Eisenhower rewarded him with an interview with Vice-president Nixon.

Under Eisenhower's time in office, no statement ever emanated from the federal government condemning the violent behaviour of its southern white citizens.

THE SIT-INS and FREEDOM RIDES

PRESIDENT KENNEDY and ATTORNEY GENERAL, ROBERT KENNEDY

Both Sit-ins and Freedom Rides were forms of non-violent action used by students and activists to combat segregation. During sit-ins, an inter-racial group would sit at a segregated lunch counter, refusing to leave until they were served.

They were usually forcibly removed from the premises, sometimes with brute force and with the police turning a blind eye to any violent attackers. There was strong public resistance to the sit-ins. The lunch counters often closed rather than serve inter-racial groups. After prolonged discussions between the business owners and the leaders of the protest movement, the gradual desegregation of the lunch counters did actually occur. I always suspected that the change in opinion might have been propelled by a strong element of self-interest. After all, the closed lunch counters produced no income at all for their proprietors.

In 1961, the Freedom Rides began. A group of black and white individuals, including northerners, attempted to desegregate buses, water fountains, restrooms, and bus terminals. The Supreme Court had ruled that racial segregation was prohibited in waiting-rooms, restaurants, and bus terminals where buses crossed the state lines.

In the states closer to the upper southern border like Virginia and North Carolina, the Freedom Riders were confronted with racial problems, but none were so serious as those they encountered when travelling through the deep south.

On the 4th of May 1961, the first Freedom Rides began. Their plan was to travel through Alabama and Mississippi, ending up in New Orleans where a civil rights rally was planned.

The Freedom Riders had arranged to travel on two different buses. Unbeknown to the Freedom Riders, the KKK had planned two assaults, the first in Aniston and the second in Birmingham, Alabama.

On the 14th of May 1961, the first bus arrived in Aniston. The KKK immediately attacked, slashing the bus tires, and firebombing the bus. They held the bus doors closed, hoping that the passengers would die in the flames.

Something so startled the KKK that they momentarily disbanded. Some thought it was due to the fact that the fuel tank had burst into flames or possibly someone outside had fired a gunshot. As the Riders fled the bus, they were met by the KKK who again viciously attacked them. Fortunately, highway patrolmen, brandishing guns arrived at the scene to rescue them and prevent further injury.

Many of the Riders were hospitalised but did not remain in safety. A frenzied mob had surrounded the hospital, so they were prevented from leaving. At two am in the morning, Reverend Shuttlesworth and local citizens who were armed arrived at the hospital to rescue them. Despite the threatening presence of the angry white mob, their defiance was successful in preventing even further violent attacks.

When the second bus arrived at the bus terminal in Aniston, the KKK again attacked the Riders, leaving them in a state of shock, badly injured and barely conscious in the back of the bus. When the bus arrived in Birmingham, the riders were then assaulted with baseball bats, iron pipes and bicycle chains.

The Police Commissioner, "Bull Connor", had colluded with the KKK, allowing the KKK fifteen minutes access to the Freedom Riders without fear of any ensuing arrests.

James Peck, a white participant, was so severely beaten that he required more than fifty stitches to his head. Amidst the horror of so many vicious attacks, US Attorney General, Robert Kennedy, dispatched his assistant, John Siegenthaler, to try to do something to improve the situation. Much to the dismay of the Freedom Riders, Robert Kennedy suggested that the Freedom Riders should use more restraint, making no comment at all regarding the instigators of the violence.

The Riders had originally planned to continue their trip from Birmingham to Montgomery and then carry on to their ultimate destination in New Orleans. There were new reports of even more mobs amassing on the way to their next stop in Montgomery. The Greyhound Company then informed the Riders that their drivers refused to drive them anywhere.

Those protesting felt that the media had broadcast the plight of the Freedom Riders, thus publicising their stand against racial injustice in the USA. Accepting that no public transportation was available, some decided to halt the Freedom Rides and fly to New Orleans where the rally for the Freedom Riders had been planned.

Students in Nashville, Tennessee and the SNCC (the Student Non-Violent Coordinating committee) refused to relinquish the Freedom Rides and would not accept the idea that southern violence should determine the course of human justice. They rode the bus to Birmingham where they were immediately arrested and imprisoned.

Bull Connor, The Police Commissioner, was so incensed at their unrelenting singing of freedom songs that he released them from prison and insisted that they be dropped off at the border of Tennessee. But they refused to be thwarted in their aims and returned once again to Birmingham.

The SNCC encouraged other people to continue the Freedom Rides and on the nineteenth of May, a committed group of individuals attempted to resume the Rides. It proved impossible as the bus drivers were intimidated by the angry crowds assembled and refused to drive the buses.

Fearing more violence, the Kennedy administration felt pressurised to act. They compelled the Greyhound Company to provide a bus driver. Governor Patterson who had declared that "Integration would come to Alabama, only over my dead body" was ordered to provide protection from the KKK and the angry mobs. Initially, he resisted but by late evening, he had agreed to comply with the orders issued.

The Highway Patrol escorted the Riders from Birmingham to Montgomery but abandoned them as they arrived at the border of Montgomery. Once again, an angry crowd attacked them with baseball bats, iron pipes and clubs while the local police did nothing to intervene.

John Siegenthaler, Robert Kennedy's assistant, attempted to assist someone who was being attacked but was hit on the head with an iron pipe and left unconscious on the road for half an hour.

Ambulances refused to help or take the injured to hospital. The local black citizens of Montgomery rescued them and found hospitals that would accept them. At this time, white hospitals in the south never accepted black patients.

On the 21st of May, Martin Luther King and various civil rights leaders held a service to welcome the Freedom Riders at Reverend Ralph Abernathy's First Baptist Church. Fifteen hundred local citizens were in attendance to honour them.

A mob of three thousand individuals had gathered around the church, placing it under siege. There were a few US Marshals protecting the church, but the local police turned a blind eye to what was happening. Rocks were thrown through the windows and tear gas soon followed. The mob threatened to burn the church and to beat or kill anyone who tried to leave. The terrified inhabitants were forced to remain in the church until the next day.

In desperation, Martin Luther King phoned Robert Kennedy to ask for assistance to protect the lives of the fifteen hundred hostages. Kennedy really wanted the situation resolved at a local level. He put Governor Patterson under intense pressure, informing him that he would send federal troops if the governor refused to provide protection. Very early, the next morning, Governor Patterson finally sent the National Guard to control the mob and to escort the fifteen hundred hostages to freedom.

The next day, the 22nd of May, more Freedom Riders agreed to continue the bus rides into Mississippi. The Kennedy administration made a secret deal with the governors of Alabama and Mississippi. If the governors provided police and the National Guard to prevent mob violence, the government would allow the local police to arrest the Freedom Riders when they challenged segregated facilities at the bus depots.

On the 24ᵗʰ of May, Freedom Riders were arrested when they tried to use the segregated facilities at the bus depot in Jackson. The arrest of subsequent Freedom Riders to Jackson continued. As they were continually stopped in Jackson, Mississippi, the Freedom Riders decided to fill the jails there.

When the jails were filled to overflowing, the prisoners were transferred to the disreputable, Parchman Farm which was the local State Penitentiary. There they were denied all ordinary privileges.

More than three hundred people were jailed in Parchman Farm. Those in jail remained there for thirty-nine days. They could then appeal for bail and post bond. In the one hundred degree heat, some were hung outside from their wrists. Others were compelled to engage in forced labour.

The Kennedys felt that the civil rights demonstrations undermined the reputation of the United States, creating a very negative picture of the country, particularly at the height of the Cold War. President Kennedy saw the Rides as disloyal to US international interests and the Riders were told to have a "cooling off period". Those who supported civil rights were aggrieved at this statement. They believed that the government had a duty to support the Constitution of the US and to protect citizens who were attacked when exerting their Constitutional rights.

The Core leader, James Farmer, responded by saying: "We have been cooling off for three-hundred and fifty years. If we cooled off anymore, we'd be in a deep freeze".

In the face of huge public outcry concerning the treatment of the Freedom Riders and the shameful exposure of US race relations in the media in November 1961, Kennedy ordered the ICC (the Interstate Commerce Commission) to desegregate all public facilities and to remove all signs designating coloured and white, thus making these facilities available to everyone.

The legacy of the Freedom Riders was long-lasting, inspiring many successive civil rights campaigns. In the south, particularly, they encouraged the establishment of black autonomy. White students taught black citizens reading comprehension to pass the complicated literacy tests required for voter registration. Black History was taught for the first time in the Freedom Schools which were established.

A series of out of control outbursts occurred continually in the south during the Kennedy administration which meant that President Kennedy had to take control to end the violence and uphold the law.

In 1962, James Meredith, a black student had won a lawsuit allowing him to attend the University of Mississippi. When he attempted to enter the premises, the Governor blocked his path, proclaiming that as long as he was governor, no school in Mississippi would ever be integrated.

Robert Kennedy, the Attorney General, sent in US Marshals to enforce the ruling of the court. Riots followed. Dozens were injured and two people were killed. But James Meredith, flanked by two marshals, was finally admitted to the university.

On the 3rd of May 1963, in Birmingham, a group of students from college, high school and elementary school went on a peaceful march to protest the discriminatory practices in this very segregated city. Birmingham police, dressed in full riot gear, used police dogs and fire hoses to intimidate and attack the students.

The threatening police presence and their violent attacks on the protesters contrasted sharply with the non-violent protesters who had no weapons and no means of self-defence. Pictures of children being knocked to the ground by the force of water from the hoses were broadcast around the world. One particular picture of a police dog attacking a terrified young marcher may have damaged the reputation of the USA far more than any other.

It was a revelation and a shock to the world that such heinous behaviour could occur in the USA. It was reported that the Kennedys were so horrified at the violence in Birmingham that they were galvanised into action. These pictures refuted the claim that the USA was the home of freedom and democracy. In fact, Kennedy was aware that scenes such as these were a gift to Russian propaganda.

Once again, there was a great public outcry objecting to the scenes of children being viciously attacked. President Kennedy intervened and issued orders that discrimination in all public venues musts be eliminated.

Because the government had enforced the law in Birmingham, white southerners gave vent to their feeling of fury and anger. There were serious repercussions within the black community. Martin Luther King's brother's church and a motel were bombed. Four months later, four young girls were killed when the Ku Klux Klan bombed a Baptist Church in Birmingham.

Kennedy was now convinced that new legislation for equal public accommodation would be the only way to encourage the demonstrators "into the courts and out of the streets". On the eleventh of June 1963, he first sent the military to the University of Alabama to ensure the enrolment of two black students. At the time, Governor George Wallace was publicly preventing their entry to the university.

Later that evening, President Kennedy addressed the nation, seeking approval for his new Civil Rights Bill. He claimed that the civil rights issue was a moral one and should accommodate equal rights and equal opportunities for all Americans. This was his first televised speech on the subject.

Many who believed in civil rights felt that he had finally embraced and fully supported the position of the civil rights movement.

The KU Klux Klan found Kennedy's speech insufferable and unbearable. They retaliated by murdering Medgar Evers, the field secretary of the Mississippi NAACP.

On the 19th of June, President Kennedy submitted his Civil Rights Bill to Congress.

The next big event that Kennedy had to deal with was the March on Washington, scheduled for the 28th of August 1963. He was not in favour of the march going ahead. He felt that its very existence demonstrated disapproval of his approach to civil rights. In addition to this concern, he was also anxious that congress might perceive the march as some kind of excessive force to compel them into action.

Fearing that violence might erupt during the march, Kennedy very much wanted the federal government to help with the planning. When Matin Luther King agreed to this proposal, Kennedy finally gave his approval for the organisation of the march to proceed.

The March was a great success with over 200,000 people attending. Crowds gathered in front of the Lincoln Memorial to hear Martin Luther King's famous "I Have A Dream" speech. While some praised the Kennedys efforts to produce more powerful civil rights legislation, others criticised him for not doing more to protect protestors and southern black citizens from vicious, violent attacks.

While the Cold War and issues like Cuba and Vietnam were prominent in the news, many in the Democratic Party begrudged the amount of time spent on civil rights. But due to national and international coverage, Kennedy could not ignore the problem of southern segregation and feared criticism from both the northern and southern states as well as the rest of the world.

THE KENNEDY LEGACY for THE PROTESTORS

The Kennedy administration had never really approved of the civil rights protests. They were predominantly worried about their providing propaganda for the Soviet Union which their leaders could legitimately use against the USA.

As a result, they were constantly suggesting different methods for civil rights activists to achieve their aims. They wanted all public demonstrations to cease. Robert Kennedy told the Freedom riders to concentrate on voter registration, saying that they had all made their point on segregation.

When Kennedy told the Freedom Riders to have a "cooling off period", the Riders felt that they were being blamed for the white violence that occurred when they were attempting to defend their Constitutional rights.

The government's collusion with state governors to allow the Freedom riders to be arrested demonstrated the Kennedys strong determination to put an end to all their protests and demonstrations.

After Martin Luther King appealed to the Kennedys for government support, he was told that Negroes should negotiate with state officials to settle their issues, again ignoring the fact that state officials rejected the idea of discussion and desired only violent solutions for any black person's desire for civil rights.

PRESIDENT JOHNSON

I have already mentioned Vice-President Lyndon Baines Johnson's collusion with the Southern Democrats to exclude the strongest section of the 1957 Civil Rights Bill. The consequence was that black people had no protection against the violence and intimidation perpetrated against those who tried to vote.

On the 22nd of November 1963, President Kennedy was assassinated. The nation was in shock. Following accustomed procedure, Vice-President, Lyndon Johnson, became the new President of the United States.

During 1964, civil rights workers and local citizens, using non-violent techniques, attempted to desegregate the Mississippi political system. This act was usually referred to as the 1964 Freedom Summer Project. Black citizens had never been allowed to vote in the state of Mississippi. They decided that the all-white Democratic Party was not representative of the state.

They stated clearly that the Mississippi delegates to the Washington convention represented the views of only the white population and excluded those of black citizens. To challenge the position of the white delegates, they held a parallel election and appeared at the Washington Convention as the Mississippi Freedom Democratic Party.

Once again, President Johnson feared losing southern Democratic votes. He had no intention of seating the entire Mississippi Freedom Democratic Party but he did allow the white Mississippi delegation to be seated.

During this controversy, the bodies of three civil rights workers had been discovered in a dam in Philadelphia, Mississippi. Media attention was suddenly concentrated on events in Mississippi. The proceedings of the Convention were being televised to the nation which meant that the statement of the MFD Party would be on public view.

Fannie Lou Hamer, a poor sharecropper, stood before the delegation and described the beatings and threats that she and the people she knew received when attempting to register to vote. She delivered a moving speech in favour of voting rights. "If the Freedom Party is not seated now, I question America. Is this America, the land of the free and the home of the brave, where we have to sleep with our telephones off the hook—because our lives be threatened daily?"

Hoping to prevent this impassioned speech from being broadcast, President Johnson instantly called a press conference, hoping to obliterate Fanny Lou Hamer's message from the TV screens forever. But it was too late. Neither her image or her message had disappeared from public view.

Later that evening, the TV news broadcasted her statement to everyone in the country. Many supported her position and admired her staunch stand against Mississippi's Democratic Party.

To allay the concerns of the Mississippi Democratic party, Vice-President Hubert Humphrey and Walter Mondale, the Party Leader, crafted what they described as a genuine compromise. The MFDP were allotted two seats but they could not participate in the proceedings and could only watch from the floor.

Because the undemocratically elected delegates continued in power and the MDFP delegates were prevented from voting, the MDFP rejected this unfair "compromise offer".

At this time, the disappearance and discovery of the bodies of the three civil rights workers had created a national outcry. President Johnson was forced to deal with the public outrage. The two white activists had been shot. The black activist had been savagely beaten and shot three times.

It was generally accepted that President Johnson passed the Civil rights bill of 1954 as a way to honour President Kennedy and to deal with the uproar about the three civil rights activists. It proved to be an important piece of legislation as it provided full legal equality to black citizens and nullified the state laws which required discrimination.

In early 1965, there was continuous police violence in Selma, Alabama when local citizens marched to exercise their voting rights. The peaceful demonstrators were beaten with bull whips, billy clubs, rubber tubes wrapped in barbed wire and tear gas. Due to the brutal violence, this campaign was labelled Bloody Sunday.

The TV footage showed the state troopers savagely and violently attacking unresistant marchers, evoking responses of revulsion and disgust. Martin Luther King led a second march. They were attacked again, and the Reverend James Reeb was killed. His death created another outburst of public anger from the general public and many prominent organisations.

In the midst of overwhelming public disapproval of unprovoked violence, President Johnson appeared on TV to announce that a new voting rights bill was now required. He stated: "Even when we pass this bill, the battle will not be over. What happened in Selma is part of a far larger movement which reaches into every section and state of America. It is the effort of American Negroes to secure for themselves the full blessings of American life."

"Their cause must be our cause too. Because it is not just Negroes, but really it is all of us who must overcome the crippling legacy of bigotry and injustice. And we shall overcome."

Dr. King led a third march trying to secure voting rights for black citizens. This time, President Johnson sent soldiers, the federalised National Guard, FBI agents and Federal Marshals to protect the marchers. Twenty-five thousand individuals marched to Montgomery in support of voting rights. Unfortunately, the KKK ensured that this march also ended in pointless violence. Many were seriously injured and Viola Liuzzo, a white civil rights volunteer was shot and killed.

President Johnson signed the Voting Rights Act of 1965 on the 6th of August. It removed all barriers from registering to vote and authorised federal examiners to replace local ones if any discrimination in voting occurred.

Some felt that President Johnson, in later life, did want to change the south. He passed two important civil rights bills in 1964 and 1965 and in 1968, passed the Housing Bill which prevented discrimination amongst those dealing with the buying and selling of property. It was felt that passing these Acts demonstrated that, in the end, he really desired a better life for black people, that he wanted to establish the "Great Society" with great improvements and equality for everyone.

Others felt that President Johnson's legacy was far more controversial. His acceptance of the idea of equality came too late for some black people.

His attempt to annihilate the voice of the MFD Party was a totally autocratic act. Democracy bestows no right on any one individual to determine who has the constitutional right to vote. Some members of the MFD Party, seeing Lyndon Johnson's autocratic behaviour decided that democracy would not support their rights as US citizens. In desperation, some fled to the Black Panthers, a more radical and sometimes violent group. In doing so, they relinquished their non-violent stance in an effort to acquire their constitutional voting rights by any means possible.

Perusing the history and actions of all three Presidents, it is evident that they did not always endorse or support the civil rights movement or their public demonstrations to gain equality, even though they did ultimately pass important civil rights legislation.

I shall leave the last word to Martin Luther King who stated that legislation for civil rights was passed only when what was morally right also became politically desirable, when those in power could no longer ignore public outrage and the deluge of international criticism regarding race relations in the USA.

THE BLACK PANTHER MOVEMENT

There was frustration that the rate of change in implementing civil rights legislation had been far too slow. Little had changed in the everyday lives of ordinary black people. Others were distressed at the way their story was being told. The surge of violence against black people was never accurately reported.

It was certainly true that the media gave an inordinate amount of coverage to the deaths of white civil rights workers while often focussing less attention on the much higher death rates amongst black civil rights workers and ordinary black citizens.

The Black Power Movement arose in response to what they saw as the slow rate of change for the better in the lives of black people who were using non-violent methods to achieve their aims.

While the Black Panther Movement did a great deal to promote black pride and encouraged black independence, they strongly believed in armed self-defence and non-integration with the white community. Their stated purpose was to attain civil rights for black people but that meant condoning the use of violence against anyone who interfered with their aims.

Armed combat did achieve some success. The KKK ceased their activity in communities where they were confronted with violence in return.

Their platform legitimised violence as a means of protest and encouraged people to vent their violent anger. The outcome of their beliefs led to anti-social behaviour, the destruction of property and the deaths of white people. In some cities, serious outbreaks of violence led to riots and urban devastation in the black community.

I speak only of those protestors who followed this path. Not everyone did so. At this point, schism in the civil rights movement was very pronounced between those who advocated non-violent techniques and those who believed that the use of arms was a legitimate means of attaining civil rights.

The Black Panthers have been described as the most influential movement of the late 1960's as well as being accused of being criminals, communists, and drug dealers. It cannot be denied that their influence was widespread. They directly challenged police brutality and established many community projects for the poor. From the1970's, dissolution of the leadership and infiltration by the FBI meant that the activities of the Black Panther Party dwindled and had all but ceased during the 1980's.

CIVIL RIGHTS ISSUES – THE MARCH ON WASHINGTON

The most renowned gathering of the Civil Rights Movement was the March on Washington, the 28[th of] August 1963. From all parts of the USA, 250,000 to 300,000 people, including 60,000 white participants, met in front of the Washington Monument to demonstrate for Jobs and Freedom.

1963 was a significant year as it was also the 100th anniversary of the signing of the Emancipation Proclamation by Abraham Lincoln.

Various liberal organisations, both white and black, were involved in the planning. They included unions, religious groups, the labour movement, and a number of civil rights organisations.

Thousands travelled by chartered and unchartered buses, trains aeroplanes, and cars. No one knew what to expect. There were preliminary warnings of possible riots, on the grounds that so many opinionated black people were meeting in one place that there were bound to be violent eruptions. Just the fact that the march would be composed of predominantly black Americans produced dread and fear in the hearts of some.

In case of rioting, the Pentagon had 19,000 troops prepared for mass arrests. The government had supplied agents who were instructed to turn off the microphones if the speeches overexcited the crowds and they became uncontrollable.

On the day, when the march was due to begin, the leaders of the march were at a meeting with members of Congress. The marchers had assembled and noted that it was past the time that the march was meant to start. Tired of waiting, they initiated the march themselves. They started walking from the Washington Monument to the Lincoln Memorial. On Constitution Avenue, the main officials finally arrived and rushed forward to link arms in front of the marchers so they could be properly represented as the leaders of the march.

A number of famous singers performed: Mahalia Jackson, Odette, Dylan, Peter, Paul and Maryand Marian Anderson. (Marian Anderson was a black contralto who was denied permission to sing at Constitutions Hall by the right-wing racist group, the Daughters of the American Revolution. President Roosevelt and his wife, Eleanor, were so shocked at her treatment, that they arranged a later concert. She performed to wide and deserving applause at an open-air concert at the Lincoln Memorial on Easter Sunday,1939.) We were all delighted when Joan Baez led the entire congregation in a very uplifting rendition of "We Shall Overcome."

There were several official speeches delivered by significant speakers from all sections of the community. Amongst all the considerations, declarations and demands being made, Martin Luther King's "I Have a Dream" speech was definitely a pivotal point in the day's listening.

Due to the success of the march, President Kennedy now felt that his Civil Rights Bill would be passed. He met with the 10 march leaders, including A. Philip Randolph and Bayard Rustin who were the main organisers. During the meeting, it was proclaimed that the march was a "triumph of managed protest."

I don't know if President Kennedy ever considered that the predominant feature of the march was not that of "managed protest." The triumph might have been due to the attitude and demeanour of the thousands of marchers who had all come in peaceful protest and never had any intention of provoking unrest. The ubiquitous friendship and the firm commitment that justice should reign over evil produced a climate of harmony and goodwill which prevailed throughout the day.

Roger and I had driven to the march with our friends Maris Corbin and Jean from Haiti. As we approached the outskirts of Washington, a sudden and unexpected camaraderie seemed to burst forth. Car horns tooted; passengers leaned out of their windows to wave. Excited greetings were exchanged with total strangers. This feeling of friendship and kindly intentions permeated the spirit of everyone we encountered.

There were many emotive moments during the events of the day but none so overwhelming as Martin Luther King's speech. His sonorous voice combined with the rhythmic pacing of his words instantly captured our attention. Under the spell of his passionate zeal, we were all transfixed. He transmitted to us a feeling of hope and a firm belief that his vision of a world without hatred and injustice could actually exist. His expectation of peace and friendship between the races sounded like more than a plausible likelihood.

We were all there, black, and white together demonstrating peacefully on behalf of our common humanity. Our very presence was testimony to the fact that his dream was not a fictitious hope but could become a genuine reality.

A SPECIAL ACKNOWLEDGEMENT

In the public history of the Civil Rights Movement, the contributions of two great activists have not been widely recognized. They have been mentioned and alluded to, but unjustifiably remain somewhat inconspicuous, the reason being that they were both homosexuals.

Despite their continual loyalty, devotion, and commitment to overcoming racial injustice in American society, those of a more conservative outlook viewed them with scepticism and their hard work and accomplishments have come to be marginalised.

James Baldwin, the eminent black writer, worked unflinchingly for civil rights, consistently writing, speaking, and bringing the issues involved to the attention of the public and the American Government. Some were expecting him to speak at the 1963 Washington March, but he was not encouraged to do so. His absence was a conspicuous omission.

Bayard Rustin was known to my friends, Russell and Irene Johnson as a Quaker and civil rights activist. Russell invited him to speak at a number of the Quaker conferences which I attended.

He was influential in encouraging Martin Luther King to accept non-violence as a weapon to overcome injustice. That he was one of the main organisers of the March on Washington is a quietly recognised fact but not a widely advertised one.

A QUAKER CONFERENCE

We had been attending Quaker conferences over the years, but this one stood out as being different.

The Quakers were seriously concerned about violent racial disorder constantly covered in the daily newspapers. They decided to make a special effort to encourage more black people to attend their conferences. Civil rights was a problem which could not be ignored.

In the mid 1960s, Roger and I participated in one of these conferences. I was expecting much heated discussion and possibly admissions of ignorance on the part of the white participants who had not realised the extent of racial prejudice and how it had affected black individuals.

I envisioned a meeting where both groups revealed conflicting feelings, attitudes and opinions as a basis for exploring the gulf between their differing outlooks.

On the first day of the conference, the speakers for the morning session were introduced and the newcomers were warmly welcomed. Someone made a brief statement declaring that throughout history Quakers had always been involved in efforts to create peace.

"There was no need to look beyond the boundaries of the US to find areas of conflict. The United States had its own serious struggle for justice going on every day, resulting in deaths and injuries of Americans, mostly black. But it also included the deaths and injuries of their white supporters. We would like to open a discussion on the issue of civil rights and offer our services in any way that might help to resolve these problems."

Suddenly, a black man two rows in front of me shot up out of his seat. "We don't want your help or your services. We don't want your discussions. We will be in charge. We're tired of words and promises. You .... you white people can't do anything for us."

"All we want is your money. The money will go where it's needed in the struggle. But we will be in charge. White people won't be telling us what to do."

There was a stunned silence in the auditorium and on the stage. I sat squirming in my seat and shocked at his outburst. The Quakers were the one group who stood by their word and suffered for their beliefs. They were pacifists and went to prison rather that kill people.

They had hidden run-away slaves when they were trying to reach the north to escape their masters, a deed for which when discovered they would be punished. They were offering assistance, freely given and without restraints or restrictions. This man had just completely rejected the help of the Quakers. He had also written off all white people as useless.

A new voice in the civil rights movement was expressing its concerns and its stance was rigid and unyielding. There were people and groups who felt that the progress of the civil rights movement was exceedingly slow. They were resigned to the fact that non-violence hadn't yet achieved what they wanted.

The Black Power Movement had been created to restore justice to the victims of inequality. They had a powerful impact in terms of creating greater self-esteem and developing racial pride amongst its members. They were responsible for the appearance of the natural Afro style of hair, untouched by anything except African combs. It was the first time that the use of the word black was considered a complimentary description of racial characteristics possessed by the descendants of Africans. Prior to this time, the term black had always been considered derogatory. Pride in one's background and African racial origins were promoted amongst many disenfranchised black people.

But believing in neither non-violence nor in establishing relations with white people, the stance of the Black Power Movement was difficult to align with a Quaker approach to the issues of racial prejudice. Many members of the Black Power Movement supported the use of violent methods to demand their rights. They wanted complete separation and total independence from everyone in white society. They believed that it was a case of outcasts casting out their oppressors by taking power and control.

Given these attitudes, the suggestion of talking and exchanging ideas with the enemy, whom you really wanted to annihilate, was anathema to those in the Black Power Movement. No plate was passed around to gather money for them. The organisers used all their persuasive powers to try to convince the new black participants, mostly couples and a few individuals, to remain at the conference. They really wanted to hear what the black people had to say.

To complicate matters, a few husbands had told their wives that they were taking them on an unusual holiday. When their wives realised that they were expected to sit and talk to white people all day, instead of lying on the beach or exploring new sights and surroundings, they were none too pleased with their situation.

I overheard two wives complaining that this was no holiday. There was no alcohol. You couldn't even have a glass of wine. It was, after all a Quaker conference where alcohol was an unavailable beverage, a fact of which their husbands might not have been aware. The reasons for the black newcomers refusal to participate in the discussions would seem not quite so straightforward as it had at first seemed.

The organisers had convinced the black participants to stay but the women in the groups I attended did not really enter into any discussions and remained a separate group. They did not appear to be hostile to the presence of white people, but they were not communicating with them at all. I was not privy to what occurred in other groups, but I understood that the men, on the whole, spoke only to express their anger and didn't relate to any but those in their own racial group.

I attempted to talk to the women but when they discovered that I was in an inter-racial marriage, I became the enemy and all communication ceased. The Black Power Movement could not be blamed for their reaction, because rejection of inter-racial marriage had been a long-standing conviction of black people long before the existence of that organisation.

The Black Power Movement's attitude precluded any means of interacting between black and white people and prevented any hope of working together on anything. I knew that the Quakers would not relinquish trying to resolve what appeared, at the time, to be the insoluble problems of the day.

Many of us left the conference feeling more dejected than ever. Expectations of any improvement in race relations were definitely at a standstill. Could we ever cross the insurmountable barrier which the Black Power Movement had erected around the issue of race relations.

Our only hope was to seek out those individuals and groups who were not totally overcome by despair and the futility of the situation, people who could envision a future where racial problems could be considered a topic open for discussion by everyone, regardless of colour.

I left the conference with the marked realisation that neither our marriage nor our family could have survived the unashamed, hostile reactions of either white or black extremist attitudes towards interracial relationships.

FIRST PART – ASPECTS OF THE 1950'S and 1960'S

During the decades of the 1950's and 1960's some very significant historical and scientific developments occurred. I mention only a few.

DNA

In 1953, the complex structure of DNA was discovered. Rosalind Franklin, Roger's second cousin, a research scientist at King's College had produced a photograph which revealed the double-helix structure of DNA. Crick and Watson used her photograph in their research and won the Nobel Prize for their contribution to the discovery of DNA. But they never acknowledged that her work was pivotal to their research. Sadly, her scientific contribution remained, at the time, wholly unrecognised. She never received any credit for her great achievements.

POLIO VACCINE

Dr. Jonas Salk developed the first polio vaccine. We had experienced the tragic consequences of two people who acquired the virus, my brother and the boy next door. Tragically, the boy next door died and my brother survived.

When the vaccine became available to the public in 1955, I was relieved to know that my children would not have to suffer the debilitating effects of this terrifying disease.

CONTRACEPTIVES

In the 1950's, only two states in the USA, Massachusetts and Connecticut, prohibited the sale of any medicine, implement or article designed for the purpose of preventing contraception. Failure to comply meant that guilty individuals could be imprisoned for 60 days or a fine of $50 could be imposed. Although the law was rarely, if ever, enforced, such legislation made acquiring any sort of contraceptive not only difficult but impossible for most people.

Massachusetts and Connecticut were composed of mainly Catholic populations who followed the dictates of the Pope. As he had publicly pronounced the use of all birth control devices an immoral act, it was inevitable that the sale of contraceptives within their borders was totally forbidden.

I could say that I was unfortunate, as the only states to which we were connected were Massachusetts and Connecticut, the latter because we frequently visited Roger's parents, Miriam and Gabo there, and Massachusetts because both my father and stepmother, and Roger and I, resided there.

When I married in Massachusetts, in 1953, procuring a contraceptive was a secret, under the counter affair. Someone had to know a doctor or have a friend who knew a doctor who would be willing to sell you one, illegally. When Roger and I visited England and I met his grandmother, I was pleased to discover that she held very progressive views about women. She was a strong feminist and engaged mainly professional women to look after her medical needs. She sent me to her gynaecologist where, for the first time, I could openly discuss the issue of contraception without feeling that I was guilty of a crime or committing an offence by transgressing state laws.

In 1965, the US Supreme Court ruled that it was unconstitutional for the government to prevent married couples from using contraceptives. But, unmarried women, even in 1965, were denied access to any kind of birth control. By 1972, birth control finally became legally available for everyone, regardless of marital status.

THE VIETNAM WAR (1954-1975)

In North Vietnam, in 1954, the Communist regime of Ho Chi Minh defeated the French colonialists at the battle of Dien Bien Phu. The country was then divided into the Communist North Vietnamese Government and the South Vietnamese Government which aligned itself with the West.

The United States decided to increase its military and financial aid to South Vietnam in order to mitigate the possible spread of communism throughout south-east Asia. Both the Soviet Union and China then increased their military aid to North Vietnam.

As more money and more men were poured into north and south Vietnam, the pace and nature of the conflict between them intensified. More and more civilians and soldiers were being killed.

It was not until 1963 when President Kennedy sent combat troops to South Vietnam that US military involvement in Southeast Asia gained the attention of the media. As the number of casualties increased dramatically on both sides, the number of public demonstrations against the war increased in the United States and in many other countries in the world. From 1965 onwards, there were large demonstrations, silent vigils, and massive marches protesting about the futility of the war and the pointless deaths of so many young men.

In 1973, US withdrew its combat troops from Vietnam. And in 1975, the war finally ended when the North Vietnamese advanced rapidly on the South Vietnamese army and defeated them.

In the 1950's, the Quakers were one of the first groups to oppose US military involvement in Vietnam. They feared that the actions of the United States would lead to a war in the area. In the late 1950's, I joined them in their stance against sending more money and troops to South Vietnam.

At this time, the media was not reporting anything about US activities in Vietnam so the US public was hardly aware of its activities. As the war intensified, I maintained my anti-war stance.

When I was unable to attend public demonstrations against the war, I made financial contribution to the organisations who sponsored and supported these demonstrations, SANE-the Committee for a Sane Nuclear Policy, the WRI-the War Resisiters League, and the Women's Strike for Peace. They were three of the groups who organised some of the largest protests against the war.

In 1966, we moved our family to England. As the Vietnam War lasted until 1975, the international demonstrations continued until the war officially ended. During this time, Roger and I continued to support the groups who organised these demonstrations.

THE SUEZ CANAL

In 1956, Nasser, the head of the Egyptian government, nationalized the Suez Canal. It had been designed by a French developer and it was agreed that the British should control it to keep it open for all countries.

The US and the British had promised to loan Nasser money to build the Aswan Dam which would have been a great asset for the Egyptian economy. Due to Egypt's ties with the Soviet Union, both countries refused to provide the money needed for the dam, so Nasser decided to take control of the Canal.

Britain, Israel and France then invaded the canal. When the Soviet Union sided with the Egyptians, the US became worried that they might be drawn into a war with the Soviet Union. As a result of this consideration, they forced the Israelis, the French and the British to withdraw.

The outcome of this incident demonstrated where the real balance of power now resided. Britain's prestigious role in the world had suffered a serious setback. After Suez, its reign as a great colonial power was very much diminished.

CUBA

In 1959, Fulgencio Batista, the military leader of Cuba, was overthrown by Fidel Castro and Che Guevara, establishing the first and only communist government in the west. The fact that the Soviet Union later supported the Cuban revolution led to dissension between the Soviet Union and the United States. The fact that a Communist government had been established so close to the borders of the United States had totally enraged officials in the US government.

In 1962, President Kennedy discovered that Russia had sent Cuba operational missiles. The incidents that followed were designated the title "The Cuban Missile Crisis". To forestall the possibility of conflict, the US made a proposal. If the Russians withdrew their missiles, the US would agree not to invade Cuba.

For 13 days in 1962, many citizens, including Roger and I, and many of our friends became acutely aware that the US and the Soviet Union were teetering on the brink of armed conflict. The prospect of war was a dire consideration. It raised the likelihood of a struggle using nuclear weapons and the dreadful destruction and devastation of territory and possible annihilation of people that could ensue. I actually met some people who were considering going to Australia to avoid the consequences of nuclear fallout if war occurred.

Not all US citizens responded to the ominous threat that enveloped the nation. Everyone had lived with the Cold War for so long that tense relations between the two great super-powers seemed an ongoing certainty. It was difficult for them to grasp the seriousness of the situation, so they remained aloof and passive.

While some saw nuclear weapons as a protection against war, others began to question their commitment to some US scientific advances and observed that US policy and its concomitant technology could pose a danger to the world.

For those who perceived a threat, there were 13 days of speculation and conjecture and unrelenting worry and fear. Not only was the question of Cuban missiles a paramount concern, but Soviet freighters supplied with military goods were travelling to Cuba and constantly being stopped by the US military. People feared that officials on either side could incite serious conflict at any time.

Fortunately, the Soviet Union accepted Kennedy's proposal. A huge weight had been lifted from those who had feared a colossal war between the two strongest and most powerful nations in the world and the universe as everyone knew it remained intact.

HEART TRANSPLANTATION

In 1967, Dr. Christiaan Barnard performed the first human heart transplant in Capetown, South Africa. The drugs used to suppress the patient's immune system had left him susceptible to infection. Despite the fact that he died of pneumonia 18 days later, his heart had functioned completely normally after the operation. This result was considered a great advance in the very experimental field of heart transplantation.

In order to indicate some of the topics of interest during the decades of the 50's and 60's, I shall include a list of the books that I read at the time. It is by no means a totally inclusive one.

To the delight of the American public, in 1953, the Kinsey Reports on male and female sexuality were published. A wide variety of sexual practices were studied. Many activities considered unusual by the general public were found to be more widespread than expected. Genuine interest, morbid curiosity as well as endless controversy encompassed the wide range of reactions to these publications.

The books remained popular, despite criticism of their scientific validity. They were translated into 13 languages and were credited with having broadened the public's understanding of different sexual practices. But they were also accused of providing the information which instigated the era of "free love" in the 1960's.

The 1950's was a time renowned for being conformist and socially conservative, vehemently anti-communist and highly materialistic. A combination of factors had appeared to encourage everyone to buy to excess. Advertising had grown rapidly, augmenting the public's desire for new and more modern merchandise.

The government had provided low-interest loans to WW2 veterans to buy new homes and for the first time, credit cards became available as a new means of borrowing. money. The flow of easily accessible money with payments deferred until later, led to a long period of overindulgent consumerism.

THE BEATNIKS

In the midst of this excessive glut of goods, a new movement arose, attempting to counteract the often flagrantly displayed goods for "conspicuous consumption". The Beatnik Movement, dubbed so by Jack Kerouac, one of their well-known authors, lasted about 10 years and was most popular during the 1950's. The Beatniks were composed of young adults and teenagers who protested against the beliefs and mores which had produced the prevailing, materialistic culture.

Jack Kerouac's book, On the Road, full of spontaneous writing, was declared a life-changing experience by some and was considered inspirational by many others. Travelling across the USA, Jack and his friend were hoping to escape the pressures and conventions of their overindulgent societies.

In their search for self-understanding and self-fulfillment, they were fuelled by drink, drugs, sex, and jazz. They welcomed new adventures and challenging situations as long as they were removed from the aims of the existing society.

Some writers in the Beat Movement, one of whom was Alan Watts, turned to Eastern religions as a source of inspiration because they believed that eastern practices could elevate the consciousness of American society to a higher plane.

The Beatniks were the first large movement to vociferously criticise mainstream culture and society. They wanted to substitute the groping for success in society with the "freedom of the road". Their outlook was defined by feelings of dissatisfaction and marginality in relation to the dominant beliefs in society and included a strong desire for self-betterment. Though vociferous in their complaints, they produced no plan or programme for specifying how to attain their aims.

THE HIPPIES

Adhering to similar beliefs, another protest movement arose in the 1960's, the Hippies. They felt that conventional society whose main purpose was to produce mainly material goods and ostentatious wealth was so corrupt that it was incapable of producing any meaning in life.

They went further than the Beatniks in trying to create a different, more idealistic model in its place. Many attempted to live in communes with people of similar beliefs, often sharing possessions and even partners. In their quest for self-understanding, they were also attracted to Eastern philosophy and began exploring Eastern cultures and beliefs. Many went to ashrams in India in order to experience a genuine spiritual awakening.

They were often vegetarian and tried to establish organic farms and eco-friendly environmental practices. Often critical of government policy, they were strongly opposed to the Vietnam War and nuclear weapons.

Because they believed that psychedelic drugs could expand human consciousness and heighten awareness of their immediate environment, the Hippies advocated the use of LSD and other hallucinogenic drugs.

Timothy Leary, the Harvard professor who became a leader of the Hippie movement, stated that Hippies are: "tuned into their inner consciousness and tuned out of the comedy of American life". "For every visible Hippy, barefoot, beflowered, bearded, there are thousands of invisible members of the turned on underground, following the goals of peace, love and freedom."

While I was in agreement with much of the Beatniks and Hippies critical analysis of society's failings, I remained reserved about their proposed solutions to the problems. Because I was a married woman with 4 young children, I realised that I was not in a position to view the world from the position of those who were young, unattached and had no particular responsibilities for anyone except themselves.

In my opinion, free love was the prerogative of individuals who were not engaged in serious relationships, were not married and had not established a family. If engaged in another relationship, neither individual would have sufficient time to fulfil their obligations as a parent or as a partner and would find it difficult to carry out their duties to whatever job or jobs that sustained them.

This opinion derived from my everyday experience of the kind of labour and emotional energy it took to try to maintain the physical and psychological well-being of the family. I found that caring for everyone was too time-consuming an operation to contemplate engaging in any other type of activity.

There were, of course, those who not only disagreed with these beliefs but also managed to find the time for extra-marital relationships, so marriage was definitely not an inevitable barrier to free love.

I was intensely curious about effects of drugs on the human brain. Many had read Aldous Huxley's book, The Doors of Perception, relating his experiences, particularly with mescalin. I had read some excerpts but acquired most of my knowledge from the biochemist, Robert S De Roop's book, Drugs and The Mind. His was a very comprehensive study, and included the effects of coffee, tea, cocoa, Benzedrine, marihuana, mescaline and LSD.

As I had always feared the idea of not being in control of my conscious mind, I had no serious desire to take drugs of any kind. The idea of relinquishing the world I knew, to enter unknown and possibly terrifying territory, even for the remote hope of experiencing an impressive ecstatic state, was not an appealing thought.

Because Hippy ideas were totally antithetical to the mores held in conventional society, many objected to their way of life, their appearance and most definitely their beliefs.

Some Beatniks declared that they could exist on the excessive waste that society produced. Some refused to work and lived using food thrown away by shops but still in a good enough state to eat. They took the clothes and furniture that people were discarding to create the semblance of a reasonably comfortable life for themselves. I felt that their behaviour was a justified criticism of our extravagantly wasteful society.

New communes were being established all the time. The fact that so many failed I put down to the idealism and naivety of those who established them. There was a definite lack of experience and little informed judgement about the vagaries of the human mind and human behaviour. Few, if any, knew how to deal with the difficult or even disturbed individuals who joined the communes.

Inevitable conflicts arose between those who were 'free spirits' and believed that no rules or restrictions should be placed on human behaviour and those who viewed rules as essential, a means of avoiding chaos and being considerate of others.

Those who tried to be self-sufficient found it was a struggle to provide adequate shelter and enough produce for survival. Many were defeated by the problems of trying to organise a disparate group of individuals, problems similar to the difficulties that the communes were experiencing.

Despite the difficulties, some organic farms and communes did survive mainly due to their hardworking clientele and their determination to find a co-operative, mutually agreed way to accomplish what they desired. Many of these successful groups established order by adhering to communally accepted rules.

Like all idealistic movements, misfits, runaways, and those who interpreted the Hippie dream in their own distorted way also flourished. I did sometimes meet people who could be described as "freeloaders". They reasoned as follows: We don't believe in privilege. We want everyone in society to be equal. Those who were living in comfort should share with those who were less privileged. The assumption behind this attitude was that any material goods attained were probably acquired at the expense of some hard-working labourer who was taken advantage of and totally underpaid. To redress this injustice, the more advantaged should feel obliged to share their goods with the less fortunate.

A young woman I knew went to one of the largest department stores in London, placed her baby in the most expensive pram she saw and walked out of the store without paying and without being questioned by any store officials.

She felt that she had every right to steal the pram. The store was a capitalist enterprise and had, thereby, taken advantage of its workers. By stealing from the store, she reasoned that she was somehow rectifying this unfair treatment.

I have also experienced individuals who stayed as guests initially and were mortally wounded when, after weeks of free food and lodging, were asked to leave. They never offered to contribute financially to any expenses and thought that occasionally offering to dry the dishes would suffice as a generous gift. Fortunately, such individuals did not predominate in the Hippie Movement.

The Hippies were unashamed and flagrant in their rejection of what were assumed to be the correct and proper sexual customs. Within mainstream society, there was a great public outcry against the Hippies irreverent and disrespectful attitudes. It was at best, a very hypocritical stance.

While publicly criticising the Hippies sexual behaviour, many were behaving in a very similar fashion. Having obtained the pill, they felt free to experiment with more than one sexual relationship. But there was no public rejection of prevailing sexual mores which specified that there was to be no sex before marriage and there was no public discussion of their altered sexual behaviour.

The Hippies had established a community in the Haight Ashbury area of San Francisco, California, which attracted world-wide attention from the media. In the summer of 1967, which they called the 'Summer of Love', there was an influx of approximately 100, 000 people, all attempting to survive in Haight Ashbury. They were hoping to experience a summer of adopting alternative social values and to experiment with sex and drugs.

Haight Ashbury could, in no way, accommodate so many people. The area began to deteriorate under the strain of overcrowding, teenage runaways, problems with crime, the homeless, drug dealers and those with mental problems. As a result, the Hippies staged a mock funeral entitled 'The Death of the Hippie'. Its aim was to warn people to stay at home, to establish the revolution from wherever they lived. It was in the midst of this amassed conglomeration of disparate groups that quite suddenly, the Hippie dream came to an unexpected and abrupt end.

ADDENDUM

I have been informed that a more well-rounded portrayal of Beat culture and lifestyles is portrayed in the following 2 books by Jack Kerouac: The Dharma Bums and The Desolate Angels.

THE BEATLES

The arrival of the music of the Beatles in the 1950s is a phenomenon that cannot be ignored. In Liverpool, the four young men who created the Beatles became the most widely acclaimed rock band of the era.

Experimenting with different styles, they moved from rock and roll to pop ballards, Indian music, hard rock and music related to psychedelic experiences. Those with alternative lifestyles often identified strongly with their ideals.

Their stupendous popularity was labelled "Beatlemania" and led to their becoming the best-selling band in musical history.

The Rolling Stones, the other outstanding rock and roll band of the era, were not formed until 1962. In 2012, they celebrated their 50th anniversary and in 2016, played a free open -air concert in Cuba. Still going strong, they have announced that they are scheduled in 2017 for a concert at the Stade de France in Paris and possibly a concert tour of France will follow.

SECOND PART OF ASPECTS OF THE 1950's and 1960's

A continuation of books read regarding issues of the day,

FARENHEIT 451

For the first time, science fiction became a widely popular genre. Ray Bradbury's Farenheit 451 was published during the McCarthy era when people were concerned about the possible censoring of publications, particularly, if they were deemed to be a threat to national security.

The book's most dramatic scene portrays a book-burning whose aim was to destroy completely any published material which contained controversial or dissenting opinions, those considered to be in opposition to the officially accepted views of those in power.

It was received with enthusiastic public acclaim and won three literary prizes. In 1966, Francois Truffaut made a film adaptation of the novel and in 1982, the BBC dramatised it on radio.

SCIENCE FICTION

Arthur C. Clark and Isaac Asimov were also some of the best-selling science fiction writers of the time.

It was a casual reading of one of Isaac Asimov's short stories that introduced me to a different style of science-fiction writing. I can't remember which one it was as I read numerous short stories at the same time.

He focused not only on the impact of scientific technology on human beings, but more importantly, he explored the questions and speculations that its existence raised in the minds of human beings.

The sociological influence of scientific ideas on human society became his particular genre and his work was classified as social science fiction. In the nearly 500 books that he wrote, he examined almost every imaginable subject, religion, science, history and literature and their ramifications on social groups.

John Jenkins, who reviewed most of his work, stated that Asimov greatly influenced most science-fiction writers of the 1950s. They either refrained from writing in his style or they deliberately tried to emulate him.

THE CRUCIBLE

Arthur Miller's, the Crucible, also written during the McCarthy era,

demonstrates the way a witch hunt in the 17th century destroyed the lives of innocent citizens, through undeserved suspicious hints, insidious comments and malevolent suggestions.

THE DEATH OF A SALESMAN

In The Death of a Salesman, Arthur Miller focussed on another feature of American life, the American Dream which glorifies material success. It was viewed as the prerogative and privilege of those who worked hard and was considered the ultimate aim to which everyone should aspire. Evident acquisition of expensive material goods often proved to be the basis for social approval and acceptance.

As Arthur Miller demonstrates, following the dream is not always a fulfilling enterprise and can be pursued unsuccessfully, especially when it is at the expense of developing interpersonal and family relationships. It then becomes evident that the acquisition of mainly material prosperity neglects the development of deeply held emotional ties and distances any attempt to create a moral vision or purpose.

A CATCHER IN THE RYE

In J.D.Salinger's, A Catcher in the Rye, the protagonist, Holden Caulfield, is immersed in his own adolescent world, a complex world of confusion and uncertainty, often devoid of logic, right or reason.

The story is a convincing portrayal of adolescent insecurity, plagued by a lack of confidence and dealing with issues of exclusion and acceptance. Because it is such a credible revelation of teen-age angst, it remains a very popular book even today.

THE LORD OF THE FLIES

In The Lord Of The Flies by William Golding, a group of schoolboys struggle to survive in a world with no established rules. In their efforts to exist, the boys display many aspects of human behaviour, some not always complimentary to the human condition. The desire to belong and the desire to be in charge and take control tend to be in the forefront.

Sadly, the determination to dominate predominates. No veneer of civilisation remains as the boys' behaviour descends into confusion, cruelty, violence, and savagery.

While some feel the book is a pessimistic statement regarding aspects of adolescent behaviour, I believe it may be a more extensive, critical statement about human behaviour, in general.

The boys originally landed on a deserted island because the plane that was evacuating them from a brutal war at home, had been shot down. They are rescued by a warship which will return them to their homeland which remains in the midst of a violent war.

Their escape from the island is not a successful attempt to relinquish chaos and disorder. They leave behind the savagery on the island only to be plunged into the continual mayhem and violence perpetrated by the adults in their own country. Where had they learned the cruelty and violence that they perpetrated on others?

EXODUS

In EXODUS, Leon Uris describes how the new state of Israel valiantly emerges and survives despite being completely surrounded by enemies. I was overjoyed when Israeli independence was announced on the 14th of May 1948, particularly after the centuries of persecution which the Jewish people had experienced.

I didn't quite understand why the mother of my friend, Brenda, whose mother was a Russian, Jewish refugee was a bit more reticent about the wisdom of this decision. She, no doubt, recognised that the establishment of Israel was a far more complex matter than at first appeared.

The founding of Israel was always a controversial subject even when the provisions for its establishment were set up under the British Mandate of 1922. The topics and issues relating to Palestine and the controversies relating to the occupation of Palestinian land were not and are not resolved.

When I read the book, I was so much in favour of the Israelis having a permanent home, that I never realised how biased the narrative was in support of only the Israeli position. The issue of Arab rights was never considered on an equal basis. Over the years, the Arab perspective has been continually marginalised.

Not recognising the concerns of the Arabs vis-a vis the establishment of the state of Israel has had serious, recurring consequences. It has been a continuous source of dissension, leading to the present plight of incessant Arab Israeli conflict and strife.

A RAISIN IN THE SUN

A RAISIN IN THE SUN by Lorraine Hansberry was a play about a black, poor working-class family performed on the New York stage.

New York, rarely, if ever, staged serious plays about black people. It was the 1950's and issues relating to the positive contribution of Africans to art. the belief that women could pursue careers, the difficulties and prejudice faced by poor blacks and pride in black ancestry were issues unfamiliar to the public. Viewing Africa in a positive light and black pride were topics considered new to black consciousness as well.

My father-in-law, Cyril, and Dorothy, Roger's stepmother, had flown from England to visit Cyril's children in the USA. Roger's brother Joe and his wife Francis lived in New Rochelle, NY. Roger and I met them in New York for a bout of sightseeing and to see the play, as it was so well reviewed.

GO TELL IT ON THE MOUNTAIN

James Baldwin's, GO TELL IT ON THE MOUNTAIN, revealed the facts of his background, growing up in Harlem, New York with a mother and stepfather who was a Pentecostal preacher. At a young age, Baldwin also became a preacher but he was forced to leave the church when he realised that neither the church elders nor the congregation would ever accept the fact that he was a homosexual.

He was living in a state of profound social hatred, trying to survive the everyday prejudice of white people towards black individuals and the social rejection he experienced towards his homosexuality. When he left the USA, he emigrated to France, to live on the left bank in Paris where he was more favourably received.

In France, he was liberated from the social ostracism and rejection he experienced at home. Once there, he found the absence of conventional constraints provided the kind of support he required for his writing career to progress. In his poetry, plays, novels, and essays, he dealt with the issues of class, sex and race and established an international reputation.

In the 1960's, he toured the American south, speaking in many public venues to support the cause of the Civil Rights Movement. He wrote of his tragic experiences, describing the loss of three of his friends, Medgar Evers, Malcolm X, and Martin Luther King, all of whom were assassinated.

Due to conservative attitudes and prejudice towards his homosexuality within the Civil Rights Movement, he never received the public acclaim and recognition that he justifiably deserved.

THE INVISIBLE MAN

One of the books with which I most identified was THE INVISIBLE MAN by Ralph Ellison. Living in a world of racial prejudice, as a black man, his life is constrained by the beliefs, and demands of others which are continually projected upon him. His actions and reactions are completely limited by the narrow-minded, constricted expectations of both the black and white communities.

Examining his position, he concludes that he is invisible to those around him. The world is constructed by people who are so immersed in their own prejudices, their distorted vision obscures and misconstrues the image of the genuine, unorthodox person that he truly is.

Due to various prejudices that I had experienced, I reacted in a similar fashion to the assumptions and expectations placed upon me. My head was often full often full of internal dialogues taking note of the misconceptions of me in the minds of strangers, acquaintances and even friends. I often declared that people saw what they wanted to see. Their vision of me was a distinct distortion of the person who stood before them. Sometimes included were thoughts about injustice and racism, that I dare not express because it would have been to my detriment to do so.

After being chased by the police, the protagonist accidentally falls into a manhole and finds that he has landed in a cellar. He decides to remain there to pursue his own private existence. Not having to deal with the unrealistic demands of others, he becomes free to examine the totality of who he has been and who he is.

The concept of invisibility seems to have somewhat ambiguous meanings in the book. Invisibility initially engenders a feeling of loss of identity and loss of power in the protagonist. But when he retreats underground, his invisibility becomes an aspect of his character to be examined, explored and understood. Thus transformed, it becomes a means of liberating him from its original negative impact.

In this underground environment, he begins to write his own life story. Though feeling more psychologically visible to himself, he has to acknowledge that this act of separation means that he has become physically invisible to the outside world and has removed him from communication with other human beings. Feeling safe but completely ineffective, he finds this existence much too confining.

In writing his own narrative, he starts to accept his troubled past and resolves to establish his own identity. Emboldened by his burgeoning strength and embracing his authenticity, he decides to emerge from his seclusion.

Maintaining the veracity of this stance, he is now determined to re-enter society and confront the challenges presented by his community and the wider world.

THE FEMININE MYSTIQUE

In 1963, Betty Friedan published the Feminine Mystique, a book which unexpectedly created great interest in the publishing world. The subjects of her research were middle-class housewives of the 1950's and 1960's. They lived in the suburbs, were married, had children, and lived in beautiful, well-furnished homes.

The outcome of her research revealed that, despite appearing to have everything that women were meant to deem desirable, they were all united in their general unhappiness and dissatisfaction with the lives they were leading. Betty Friedan labelled women's lack of contentment in their allotted role, "the problem that has no name".

During the 1950's. women were marrying at younger ages and the number of children they produced was definitely increasing. It would appear, from quick observation, that the role of wife and mother was increasing in popularity during this decade. Betty Friedan's results, while incontrovertible, appeared to contradict these facts.

Her findings revealed the attitudes that prevailed in society at the time. Women's nurturing and home-making attributes predominantly defined her role in society. There was no public awareness or acknowledgement of the fact that women also possessed mental faculties that generally remained in suspension while they were performing their caring roles in the household. Dissatisfaction lay in the recognition of their unacknowledged and forgotten mental capacities that remained unstimulated and unfulfilled.

Her critics found her attitude to women's problems too narrow and ignored issues that were relevant to their daily lives such as, abortion, inequality in jobs, domestic abuse, and the experiences of gays, lesbians, and black women.

Despite these negative responses, the book's message resulted in publicizing the cause of feminism in the USA and in founding groups which promoted concerns important to women.

The Feminine Mystique was eventually translated into many languages and has sold millions of copies worldwide.

THE SECOND SEX

In 1949, Simone de Beauvoir published The Second Sex. It was not initially published in English, so I read it a few years after reading The Feminine Mystique. Hers was an in-depth study of the historical and sometimes psychological reasons why women throughout the centuries had always remained in inferior positions in relation to men.

Despite writing a book whose text strongly supported the cause for feminism, she never defined herself as a feminist and it was not until 1972 that she aligned herself officially with the Feminist Movement.

She was initially a very strong Marxist which led her to believe that it would be through class struggle and the establishment of a socialist state that women's equality would be established. But after the proclaimed Socialist revolutions in the USSR and China, she became very disillusioned when she realized that women were educated and had jobs outside the home but were still expected to do the housework and care for the children.

When my mother-in-law, Miriam and Gabo went to visit Papa's relatives in Russia in the late 1960's, Miriam made exactly the same observation, saying that women's workload had only increased under socialism. Not only did they have the children and the home to look after, they were now also expected to support the family by having a job as well. The men were also working but did not consider it their responsibility to help their wives with any work in the home.

Simone de Beauvoir felt that men had always regarded women as the object, the "other", as deviant, and abnormal in relation to men. They were never seen as autonomous individuals. Such stereotyping had created the oppression of women. Males maintained their elevated position in society by classifying women as unequal to men and thereby justified relegating them to an inferior position in their hierarchy.

One of her more well-known and generally accepted tenets stated that: "One is not born a woman but learns to become one. At each level of a girl's development, society's mores, customs, and rules engender in her, an acceptance of passivity and a denial of her subjectivity.

Gender is a social construct, gradually acquired. Imbalanced gender roles exist because women are denied the possibility of developing their capabilities in either work that leads to independence and self-sufficiency or jobs that lead to creative fulfilment. Within the confines and prejudices of their society, women have learned that they are consigned to the roles of wife and mother with no hope of accomplishment elsewhere.

She felt that women had to strive for their own liberation. Obtaining a job was viewed as a first step towards acquiring independence but did not resolve all problems. She hoped that in a well-organised society, child-rearing would be a shared responsibility and not left only to mothers.

When her book was first published, it caused no great sensation in the conservative French society of 1949. It was not until nearly 2 or 3 decades later when feminism had become more accepted that she was widely recognized and acclaimed for her analysis of women's position in society. In the 1990s, she was given credit for the fact that due to her ideology, women were now equal members in the French legislature and that special, supportive programmes were eventually developed for women and children.

Many famous feminists have acknowledged their debt of gratitude to her substantial study of women and have used it as a basis to instigate and lend strength to their own feminist writing.

THE SILENT SPRING

In 1959, Rachel Carson noted two distressing facts. The first observation related to the cranberry crops in the USA. They could not be sent to market because they contained such high levels of pesticides.

The second concerned the title of the book. The Silent Spring had occurred due to a decrease in the bird population which she designated "the silencing of the birds." Her scientific assessment led her to conclude that both problems were caused by excessive spraying of chemical insecticides.

At the time, to combat malaria, DDT was the chemical most popularly used. Many people, including me, believed that spraying large amounts of DDT was the most effective way to annihilate the mosquito population. This principle was based on the assumption that the more you spray, the more mosquitos you kill and as a result, it is more likely that malaria will decrease.

When Rachel Carson advocated spraying as little as possible rather than abundant spraying to kill the mosquitoes, the policy seemed incomprehensible. But the general public were uneducated in the life cycle of the mosquito and the consequences of massive spraying. She had noted that mosquitos reproduce often and not all of their offspring are annihilated by DDT. Those that remain alive can transfer their resistance to the next generation. It was in this way, through excessive spraying, that DDT had gradually lost its power to fight malarial infection.

The fact that seven to ten years after spraying, there is widespread insect resistance to the chemical used, is now an accepted scientific truth. The companies which produced these chemicals attacked Rachel Carson's views and accused her of trying to ban the use of chemicals altogether. She never was in favour of an outright ban. She wanted the judicious use and carefully regulated control of insecticides.

Eventually, her observations and conclusions led officials to create a complete ban on DDT, particularly in the field of agriculture.

As a result of her scientific research, many environmental groups were formed including the US Environmental Agency. David Attenborough has stated that the most influential book after Darwin's origin of the Species was Rachel Carson's The Silent Spring.

THE YEARS 1965 –1966

It was the summer of 1965. The sun's rays illuminated and intensified the red, orange, and yellow hues of the trees. Teeming with wild birdsong and scampering squirrels, the forest emitted a profusion of sounds, shimmering light and startling colours that enveloped me in their radiant warmth. How fortunate we were to be living in such a remarkably beautiful part of the country and in such an unusual and generally hospitable community.

As an inter-racial couple, we met with no problems and were treated no differently from any other married couple. It was a situation that we should have encountered wherever we went. But, given the prevailing prejudices of the 1950's and 1960's, I was more accustomed to accusing stares, disapproving glances and derogatory comments behind my back when not with liberal-minded friends.

Of the couples with whom we had become acquainted, all the husbands and some of the wives were teaching at the Putney School. Because everyone was enlarging their family at the same time, none of our children lacked friends and often had playmates of varying ages.

We had been renting our quaint and somewhat-in-need of repair farmhouse for many years. When we first arrived, it was prudent to pay rent. Roger was a new teacher at the Putney School and, like all new teachers, was obviously on trial. Because he had been teaching for seven years, I felt that his job was secure, and that paying rent was now a waste of money. We could be using the rent money to pay a mortgage. Why didn't we buy this house into which we had invested so much time and effort?

Although Roger did not immediately agree to the proposition of buying the house, he did eventually agree to do so. When he set about buying our residence, I was overjoyed to know that we would be permanently settled in Vermont. Having made that decision, in my mind, everything seemed to augur well for us and particularly for the children.

One of the great advantages of teaching at the Putney School was the fact that the children of faculty members could attend the school free of charge. This arrangement was, possibly, an unavoidable concession as none of the teachers, given the salary they received, could ever have afforded to send their children to the Putney School.

I was delighted at the thought that the children would be receiving a really well-balanced education on an academic, practical and artistic level. If they developed any interest in crafts, art, music, carpentry, gardening, sport (particularly skiing), drama or academic subjects, their interests would be acknowledged and encouraged by a supportive staff. I felt that they couldn't have a better chance to investigate and explore their own interests and develop their own individual characters. To attend a school of such merit could only provide them with the basis for a really promising educational future.

THE WATER

Despite my general feeling of contentment about our family having permanently settled in Vermont, my joy was somewhat overshadowed by the immediate problems that beset us. We were dealing with our recurring difficulties related to the water running out every summer. Everyone agreed that the water table was dropping. The fact that more people had moved into the area and the advent of holiday visitors who stayed for weeks to enjoy the views had only exacerbated the situation. Every summer, the water ran out at about the same time, near the end of spring, but always seemed to return even later than the year before.

I had always thought that the solution to the annually disappearing water was to deepen our fifteen foot well. But I never convinced Roger that it was worth investing the money to undertake this task. Neither one of us had any indication of what the price might be. Roger was adamant about not pursuing this course of action, so I never asked anyone to assess the likely cost of such a project. Roger was dealing with the lack of water in his own way.

He was, as usual, filling all our empty cider bottles and empty containers at the school to provide us with our basic water supply. Due to the construction of Artesian Wells on the grounds, there was no shortage of water on the school premises. I also took the children to the school where we availed ourselves of the water, filling numerous empty vessels and bottles.

To further alleviate the problem, Roger had decided to dig a hole halfway down the hill in our back garden. He hoped it would interrupt the flow of the underground stream which terminated along the path at the bottom of the hill. As a result of his laboured efforts to improve the situation, he was indeed successful. The deeper he dug, the more the stream water seeped in and began to fill the hole.

We all took turns to carry buckets laden with water up the hill, onto the porch and into the house. We could, at least, flush the toilet more easily and water the vegetable garden. Every summer, we always grew a variety of fresh vegetables, just about enough for our own use.

I was relieved that everyone was toilet trained. There were no longer any trips to Brattleboro, over fifteen miles away, with bags of dirty diapers to wash and dry in the laundromat. That fact was almost the only positive thought that ran through my mind that summer.

Baths were impossible so I evolved what I called my stand-up washes with soap and a clean flannel. Each child was allowed a specific amount of water for washing and rinsing and then a rubdown with a towel. For those who were in charge of washing themselves, I noted that the amount of mud on the towels greatly exceeded the amount in the dirty water. The children were only two, four, six and eight so spotless cleanliness was not to be expected.

My stringent rule for water was that it had to be used twice. No water could be just thrown away or poured down the sink. We all scooped up the dirty dishwater, collected the water from cooking and the stand-up washes to pour into a bucket to be used to flush the toilet.

Our little town of Putney had only three shops: a Coop which sold a small variety of merchandise and very little fresh food, a butcher's shop, and a General Store which was well-stocked with a bit of everything and usually sold the specific item which you desired. No-one had yet found the need to install a laundromat, so it was off to Brattleboro for all our food shopping and the laundry when the water ran out.

Roger's new water hole was definitely an asset, but I had to admit that it was also a great liability. Natasha, after all, had fallen into it and could have drowned. I wanted Roger to build a fence around the water hole, but he was very busy and very reluctant to carry out this task. So, the water hole, despite its usefulness, remained a danger to the children.

As it was halfway down the hill in the back garden, it couldn't be seen at all from the kitchen window. Doing any housework or preparing any meals in the house necessitated my worrying about the dangers lurking around this unprotected area. I always asked the children to stay alert and be vigilant while in that vicinity. But, given children's short attention spans, I knew that they could not be relied upon to continually monitor the situation. So, I was constantly running out of the house to check up on what was happening.

Aside from the worry, if the children went anywhere near the hole, they arrived at the kitchen door either completely speckled or covered with layers of sticky, gooey mud. Of course, no-one would admit to enjoying walking or sliding in the lovely, squishy mess.

The presence of so much mud everywhere only added to the endless cleaning problems. Clothes were left to dry in the sun to hopefully harden and loosen the layers of wet, soft blobs or, if the kitchen stove were on, clothes were hung on the oven door and spread on chairs around the heat. Inevitably, the stand-up washes and the dirty laundry increased considerably at a time when the water was most scarce.

I cannot ever remember being more tired in my life. I had thought that the worst experience I could undergo occurred when all four children were ill, nearly simultaneously. Endless crying and trying to comfort distressed children who appeared inconsolable, despite all my concern and well-intentioned efforts, usually ended in many sleepless nights. But, as the illness receded, such enervating and exhausting activities eventually came to an end, and I could slowly return to a more normal existence.

The water problem had continued for five, maybe six months, and I felt at my wit's end. Not only was I exhausted beyond belief, but part of my drained energy could also be put down to anxiety because I saw no solution to the problem. Other people, that year, were dealing with the problems of living with little or no water, but not for the inordinate length of time that we had.

I was told that someone in the village was buying water. I rushed to the village to find out who this person was and to ask about the price of buying water. After knocking on a few doors, I found her and she explained that, after the water was delivered, she stored it in a very large tank. I did enquire about the price of water but realised that this information was now irrelevant. As we didn't have any means of storing water, I could see that this solution would not immediately answer our water problems. I would have to look elsewhere.

OUR RELATIONSHIP

As I became more and more exhausted, I began to ask Roger to help more at home. He was teaching during the week and had two classes of evening activities. All teachers were required to devote two evenings a week to teaching extra-curricular activities. When Roger taught astronomy as an evening activity, the students came to our house to peer through his telescope to examine the constellations in the night sky. I provided hot cocoa or apple cider and home-made biscuits. But this was a one-off event. Most evening activities took place at the school, so it was unusual for the students to visit teachers in their homes.

Roger was often away on weekends, taking students if they desired, to conferences in other towns. Two teachers always went on these expeditions. If no-one had offered to do the driving, I was sure that the school would have had some kind of rota. But Roger was away weekend after weekend. I, concluded that he obviously, chose to go away rather than listen to his frazzled wife telling him that she needed more help.

On the weekends that he was at home, particularly on Sundays, we often planned a family walk in the woods, an activity which Roger always loved. But due to two unexpected interruptions, our plans were sometimes thwarted.

On Sundays, the few students who wanted to attend church required a driver to take them to their respective destinations. Roger was often asked to take on this task and I knew that he found it impossible to refuse. I suggested that he tell them that he had other plans. Other teachers could volunteer. It was a responsibility that should be shared. As I was not successful in convincing him to relinquish the driving, we frequently waited for his return home before we could commence our Sunday excursions.

The second reason for interference with our Sunday plans was the arrival of Jehovah's Witnesses. I would have told them that we were going out, but Roger felt that he could convince them to listen to his point of view on world matters. I tried to tell him that they were only interested in converting people to their way of thinking. They weren't open to listening to any other point of view, but to no avail.

I was beginning to feel that my opinions didn't matter or were of no consequence to him. If his opinions were different from mine, there seemed no way to talk to him about our distinct but separate points of view.

I thought that if we could both express our feelings, or even momentarily lose our tempers, it would clear the air and we could get on with discussing the issues that were problematic. At first, I asked him to help more but, as I received no more help, my entreaties became more urgent. Daily, I was feeling that I was more and more on the verge of total exhaustion and complained that even on Sundays and weekends when he could have been at home with the family, he left early to drive students to church or to go away to conferences.

We were at loggerheads, but it wasn't we, it was me. I was the one who always vocalised what I thought was a problem between us. My complaints began at a very rational level, but my words never received any response. They seemed to fall on deaf ears. Feeling dismissed and unheard, my annoyance escalated. The more distressed I became, the more quickly Roger retreated. He, eventually, departed from the house any time I wanted to talk to him, going somewhere where my words could no longer reach him.

When my frustration turned to anger, there was no hope of any sort of communication between us. Anger was a difficult area for both of us to deal with. I had been brought up never to express anger towards my parents, any close relations, or any other adults. Children did as they were told, never daring to question a parents' authority. Parents were allowed to be angry but, as they were always right, it followed that we had no basis for protest. The fact that I could actually express my anger towards Roger, indicated to me how immoderate and intense my feelings had become.

Up to this point in my life, I had never exploded in anger towards any other individual. I had been accustomed to talking about my anger with my friends but never expressing it. Roger was always more reserved in his approach to life and far more adverse to expressing anger than I was. He appeared more even-tempered and calmer in most situations. I had never seen him bust forth with strong emotions of any sort. So, we never engaged in that heated discussion which was meant to clarify our differences of opinion.

There could be no resolution to any problem with the tactics we were both using. I was constantly confronting, and he was constantly retreating, all to no purpose whatsoever. It was truly a case of and never the twain shall meet.

One evening, I went to bed for my usual few hours of fretful sleep. When I finally fell into a deep slumber, I saw that I was in a room that was completely grey. No light penetrated the opaque gloom which surrounded me. As I glanced round, trying to establish my bearings, I realised that I was mistaken. It wasn't a room at all. I was standing alone inside a lift which was slowly descending to its ultimate destination. I began to experience that sinking feeling in my stomach that often precedes an old lift coming to a sudden and abrupt stop. Despite feeling queasy and ill, my journey continued.

I suddenly looked up to discover that I was not standing alone in a lift. I was alone, not standing, but lying directly underneath it. I was staring up at the underside of the lift, wide-eyed and petrified, paralysed with fear and unable to move as the lift proceeded on its downward trajectory. Holding my breath, as the solid steel mass with no definable shape drew closer to compress me, I awoke with a sudden start, unable to recognise my surroundings, persistently coughing and battling for breath.

I was stunned and relieved to find that I was still alive but completely drained of all energy. I remained on the bed limp and lifeless, fearful of falling asleep again, in case I was forced to survive another disorientating dream. The nightmare which I had experienced seemed to symbolise my own predicament. I felt I was submerged in a hopeless situation which was about to annihilate me. If I continued to feel helpless, envisioning only a bleak future there was no doubt that I wouldn't be able to carry on and could stop functioning completely. Despite awakening terrified and breathless, the implications of this nightmare so frightened me that I felt compelled to try to look at my very difficult situation differently. My negative thinking was slowly debilitating my energy and my effectiveness.

No circumstances had changed. There was no water to be seen on the horizon. Roger wasn't going to offer any more help. Accept it, accept it, I told myself. I tried to reason my way into a more neutral position. Try to be less upset, less angry. My strong feelings were helping neither the situation I was in nor our relationship.

The only thing that could possibly change was my attitude to this dreadful situation. If I carried on in such a state of negativity, I wouldn't be able to look after the children and if I collapsed, who would look after the children? That question so disturbed me that I refused to contemplate what the outcome might be.

I told myself to be more hopeful. The water would surely return. It always had. But, if I'm honest, I was fighting my depressing feelings every day. I was not feeling very confident. How could I? there were no signs of water appearing in the well and it was now past Christmas. Never before had the water taken so long to return. I was finding it almost impossible to be positive in what felt like a desperate situation.

The children, thank goodness, seemed to have adapted to the situation without any ominous signs of stress. Things could have been much worse. They, never once, complained of any inconvenience regarding the scarcity of water. I was forced to acknowledge my blessings in that respect and that recognition did lift my spirits momentarily.

We examined the well every day but, to my dismay, the drought continued and persisted throughout December. New Year arrived and there was still no sign of water. It was not until the second week of January, when we peered, once again, over the edge of the rim of the well that we were shocked to discover that water was trickling into the murky darkness. We could glimpse its glistening, moving surface. Water. water, we had water!!! I could have danced for joy.

We could hardly believe our good fortune. It didn't rush in with great force but the fact that it was there at all meant that, in time, the problem would eventually be solved. Nothing could compare with the feelings of relief and happiness I experienced at the sight of running water when it eventually emerged from the kitchen tap. It was the most miraculous event that I had ever hoped to see in the year of 1966.

ROGER'S JOB

As the water rose in the well, my depressed mood was definitely lifting. I had hoped that normal communication would, at long last, be resumed between us. Roger no longer had to deal with either my pleas for help or my anger when nothing happened. But we continued to lead what appeared to be separate lives. I could see no difficulties in openly discussing our situation but was well aware that Roger was avoiding talking to me. Except, for sorting out practical matters, we were engaged in only inconsequential conversations.

I thought he might have been harbouring anger and resentment toward me for, as he saw it, creating dissension between us. So, I didn't even attempt to approach the subject of our inability to communicate as I felt it would make matters worse.

This situation continued for some time, until one day, Roger said that he had something important to tell me. As his demeanour appeared to be so serious and his eyes turned away from my glance, I remained a little wary and in a state of suspension. He spoke his words without inflection, in a low monotone. I sensed that whatever he wanted to tell me, it wouldn't be good news. There was a very long pause and then, he said, "I've lost my job."

I was stunned into silence for a few seconds and then the questions erupted one after the other. "What happened? Why did you lose your job? What did you do?" I knew that he wouldn't have broken any school rules, there was some other reason for his dismissal.

The headmaster had decided that he needed more information about how each department within the school was functioning. Various teachers were asked to assess their departments and discuss the results with the headmaster. Observations within the science department revealed that Roger had no problems with teaching the physics and maths curriculum, but he did have a problem with classroom discipline. We had spent a year at the Stockbridge School where he was meant to have received teacher training, but, in fact, he received no assistance or assessment of any sort. He was left completely on his own to get on with classroom teaching. In addition, he was assigned to teach biology, a subject about which he knew nothing. He was merely used as a substitute teacher and never had the opportunity to learn about how to control a classroom.

His teaching could not have been that disastrous or he would have been removed years earlier. I'm sure it helped that most of the students who attended the Putney School were actually interested in learning so had no intention of disrupting the classroom. But, of course, students who wanted to test the rules sometimes appeared to challenge authority and it was these students who could cause havoc and that he had difficulty controlling.

Although shocked, my first reaction was surprisingly calm and practical. I would try to help him. After all, I had struggled to learn how to control a classroom myself. I thought that the only way to observe what was happening in Roger's classroom was, to be there when he was teaching. I could point out where he could have intervened or when he allowed a difficult situation to carry on for too long. But as soon as I visualised myself in the classroom, I, immediately, rejected the idea.

I would have been a great distraction. Not only that, what teacher had his partner sitting in the rear of the classroom while he taught every day? My presence would raise too many questions and be more problematic than it was worth, even for a few sound observations on discipline. It became obvious that there was nothing that I could do practically to help. I had to accept that I couldn't save his job.

It was only then that my initial shock transformed itself into serious distress. My mind wanted to reject what I had heard, to deny the reality of Roger's having lost his job. My body was reacting in its own way. The impact of this dreadful news made me overwrought and agitated.

My world had been turned upside down. In one fell swoop, our entire existence was shattered into a million unhappy, unfixable pieces. This life which we had built over eight years, was now in tatters. Our friends, the children's friends, the house we had just started buying, this accepting community to which we were so attached, we would have to leave it all behind. And what of the children's wonderful progressive education? When would they have access to such wonderful opportunities again?

I thought that maybe I should return to work, to start teaching again, but the younger two children were not yet of school age. If I worked, I would have required a baby-sitter. Most of the money I earned would go to paying her salary with not enough remaining to support the entire family.

In desperation I, at first, thought Roger could mind the children but soon rejected that idea, the first reason being that he would not have wanted that role and the second reason being that we completely disagreed about the practical side of child-rearing. Theoretically, we agreed that the methods employed in bringing up children and educating them should be child-centred and not revolve around the needs of adults. But there was no agreement about how to implement this ideal approach. As it turned out, our ideas were diametrically opposed. His laissez-faire attitude which allowed children to do whatever they wanted, with no rules whatsoever was in contradiction to my beliefs that children required some boundaries and limitations on their behaviour.

He wanted no adult intervention of any kind while I advocated adult guidance and teaching children there are consequences for transgressing rules, particularly if their behaviour harmed or hurt another individual.

To Roger, rules always seemed a form of oppression which repressed children's natural needs. Looking at Roger's upbringing, I concluded that this way of thinking might have evolved from his very strong reaction to his own background.

He had grown up in a household with nannies who had enforced their own restrictions and regulations in child-rearing. He was then sent to boarding school at the age of nine. There he encountered a regime of rules and expected obedience with not a lot of room for indulgence or leniency. As with many young children who had been sent to boarding school, their resentment at being sent away could sometimes be reflected in a desire to reject the school rules and sometimes a desire to reject rules altogether. I suspected, though I couldn't confirm it, that such experiences may have contributed to Roger's present attitude.

It was not difficult to see why he was drawn to the educational proposals of AS Neil who believed that children should follow their own natural inclinations without encouragement from adults to follow their rules. Although I admired Neil's respect for children's feelings and their intelligence, I could never fully accept that young children were always the best determinants of their fate. There was always an important role for adults to play in their development. Therein lay the insurmountable gulf between our approaches to child-rearing and education.

Though the children might have an interesting time with Roger, I did not feel that they would be safe in his care. I concluded that I could not start teaching again until everyone was old enough to attend school all day.

I was secretly hoping that we could stay in Putney. If Roger had a different job, not too far away, we could stay put and the upheaval of us all starting again somewhere else could be avoided. I started looking for jobs in the area for which Roger could apply. I found one or two which might have been promising but Roger wasn't interested in pursuing them and was even less interested in being interviewed. He finally informed me that he wasn't going to be looking for any jobs, he was, no longer, going to work.

Not work! What did he mean? Not work. Everyone worked. Everyone had to work. How were we going to survive if he didn't work. Having already concluded that it was impractical for me to work, the situation seemed dire. He was adamant. There was no room for discussion. He was simply refusing to work. What about his family?

Any idea of a future for us in Putney was looking very bleak, particularly when Roger refused to look for work anywhere in the vicinity. We would, inevitably, be forced to leave our life and our friends in this community.

Having just survived the ordeal of the water crisis, I now had to face the challenge of Roger being unemployed. I could see that Roger was in low spirits and refusing to deal with the situation, but we had to make some serious decisions. We had a family of four children which meant that if we moved, we would have to find a house or a flat to live in and sort out a new school for the children. And Roger would have to find a new job. To me, these issues were of the utmost importance and Roger was avoiding talking about them.

I could feel the tension rising within me but vowed to sit on my feelings, lest I drive him further away. I was still hoping that we could, together, make a practical decision about where we were planning to go, once we left Putney, but Roger was making no decisions and appeared to be headed in no direction whatsoever.

I was becoming frantic. We couldn't stay here. We would have no income. In desperation, I thought, maybe, if he returned to England, he would feel more at home and come to his senses. I approached him with this suggestion. He didn't object which encouraged me to think that he found it a reasonable idea. I was greatly relieved. At least, I now knew to which country the family would be going. There was no discussion as to which part of England would be most desirable or if it mattered at all where, in England, we went.

Because Roger had actually agreed to one important decision, I didn't want him to feel pressurised, so I didn't immediately explore any other aspects of our move. When, about a month later, I suggested that we should start thinking about where we wanted to live, Roger wasn't forthcoming with any ideas. So, I finally asked: "Where are we going to live when we move to England?" His response was direct and immediate. "We'll live with my father." I was crestfallen. We had stayed with his father every summer that we had visited England. It was always a mixed blessing. We had comfortable accommodation and a beautiful garden, but his father's irascible nature meant that life was fraught with unpleasant emotional outbursts. Roger found them as unpleasant as I did. I had no desire to stay in that volatile atmosphere with the children, nor did I think that Roger's father would be overjoyed to have us staying there for any protracted length of time.

Living with my father-in-law was no solution to our problems. As it so happened, that very same evening, Miriam, Roger's mother, rang from Connecticut to see how everyone was faring. When I answered the phone, she asked how we were, and I burst into tears. All my pent-up emotions could no longer be constrained. I explained that Roger had lost his job and that we were moving to England. But I was very distressed because Roger thought that we could live with his father. We needed to live on our own, in a separate dwelling.

Miriam completely understood my feelings. She had, after all, lived with Cyril for ten years and found it impossible to maintain a relationship with him. I felt relieved when she said she wanted to talk to Roger because she was the one person who might be able to convince him that we needed a residence of our own.

Just knowing that Roger was talking to his mother buoyed my spirits enormously. He always listened to her suggestions. I felt somehow reassured that, once in England, we would have a house of our own to live in.

A STRANGE HAPPENING

I hadn't been sleeping well, and dreaded going to bed, knowing that I would engage in another night of restless sleep. I feared that I would endure another terrifying nightmare and was beginning to wonder how many calamities and stress one individual could endure.

One morning, I awoke to realise that I was in a state of complete relaxation. My mind and body were so calm and free from tension that I experienced no strong urge to get up. But I did and as I slowly rose to dress myself, I felt that I was living on a different plane, a completely different level of existence. The world which I beheld was exactly the same as it always was. Its physicality had, in no way, altered but my experience of this very normal world had changed completely.

Two aspects of my existence had shifted significantly. The first related to my totally distorted sensation of time. Every action that I undertook seemed to take forever. It was as if everything that was happening around me was occurring in slow motion. My rational mind was functioning, but it had lost its power to convince me to rush to get things done. I could reason with myself to perform certain activities, but I could not conduct any activity in haste. I was living in a state of euphoria and felt no urge or compulsion to remove myself from it.

This state of bliss was the second feature of the new state of consciousness that I was experiencing. It would have been lovely to remain there, relaxed and doing nothing, but my rational mind informed me that I had to get dressed, prepare breakfast, and get the children ready for school. So, I carried out these activities in a time span that felt like days.

Being in such a delightful state of happiness and contentment, I found it impossible to get annoyed or, in fact, to experience any negative emotions at all. The children's bickering or even arguing over a toy, I handled with a totally calm demeanour and never once felt the need to raise my voice. Regardless of what Roger said or did or did not do, I could, in no way, become critical or irritated and related to him with the utmost equanimity.

The person I was, the I and the me of my everyday life had disappeared completely. There was no line of demarcation between me and the outside world. In this undifferentiated universe where there were no boundaries between the subjective and objective world, I merged with the surrounding objects, other people, nature, the space around me and the entire universe. This extreme state of consciousness was suffused with joy, serenity, calmness and an all-encompassing love. I can only describe it as transcendental because it went beyond the range of any normal, human experience.

Fearing that he might think I was mad or about to become so, I tried to explain my altered state to Roger. Although he listened, I didn't think that he comprehended in any way what had happened to me. I did not blame him. It was a state that was almost impossible to describe and was certainly not a familiar part of anyone's everyday existence.

Being thrust overnight into such a strange, unknown world, I might have decided myself that I was going mad. The only reason that I didn't draw this conclusion can be accounted for by my past reading. When I was about 15 or 16 years old, I had first read about such odd states of mind in Thomas de Quincey's Confessions of an Opium Eater. Many times, he very clearly described being in a euphoric condition with intense feelings of excitement and delight after imbibing opium. I was enticed and very much attracted to the idea of experiencing the buoyancy of spirits that often overwhelmed him but much less drawn to those frightening and disturbing incidents that he described.

William James, the American psychologist and philosopher, (1842-1910) described similar states of being when he explored ecstatic, mystical and religious experiences. Personality disappeared in the contemplation of objects and individuals became immersed in the world, feeling that they were a part of everything.

Aldous Huxley, in The Doors of Perception, (1954), reported warped time experiences after taking mescaline and LSD. Changes in temporal perception have frequently been reported by drug users. Some overestimated the amount of time that had actually passed while others, less frequently, reported a shrinking or compression of time.

Just knowing that such unusual and unutterable states of mind existed and had been experienced by ordinary human beings reassured me. I am not sure how long I remained feeling immersed in my surroundings. It seemed an eternity, but I know that it occurred in the early morning and did not last for the entire day. My altered sense of time seemed to last longer.

I told myself that I must try to return to my previous reality as that is where I truly belonged. Each and every day, I felt that I was somehow, bit by bit, achieving this aim. The time taken to perform any action seemed less stretched and to more closely approximate the actual time that the action lasted. I had no means of forcing myself back into my prior way of relating but, for the sake of the children, I felt it was important to do so.

Many studies have reported that periods of prolonged exercise or even just fasting can produce euphoric states of consciousness. The consumption of drugs and alcohol has long been known to alter perceptions of time and can produce substance-induced states of ecstasy and intense feelings of well-being.

The results of living with high levels of stress usually suggest that exposure over extended periods of time will eventually develop into serious depression with the concomitant side effects of poor organisation and inability to focus and concentrate.

I had not been involved in any form of exercise or fasting. Nor had I been taking drugs or drinking any alcohol. But I had been living for a prolonged duration of time under high levels of stress but was not now suffering from its usually debilitating side effects, totally the opposite. I was elated, undertaking all tasks with calm composure and quiet efficiency.

I mention these studies because, as you can imagine, I was quite determined to try to discover how and why I had been thrust into such a strange state of being. Unfortunately, none of the literature I read provided the entire answer.

I extended my reading to include those events which some describe as spiritual or mystical. A small number of mystical experiences can occur unexpectedly when a person is alone and quite relaxed. Jane Goodall, the internationally famous primate expert, reported one such occasion when she was in the jungle. "Lost in the awe of the beauty around me, I must have slipped into a state of heightened awareness. It is hard, it is impossible really, to put into words the moment of truth that suddenly came upon me then. Even the mystics are unable to describe their brief flashes of spiritual ecstasy. It seemed to me, as I struggled afterward to recall the experience, that self was utterly absent. I and the chimpanzees, the earth and trees and air, seemed to merge, to become one with the spirit power of life itself."

She seems to describe an experience similar to mine, but, unlike Jane Goodall, I was not alone nor was I in a state of mental relaxation.

Many different cultures, sects and religions have evolved a variety of methods to attain mystical experiences, aiming to acquire similar states of bliss which they describe as enlightenment. Such techniques can be used for diverse aims and purposes. Chanting, meditation, breath control, hypnosis, sensory deprivation, sleep deprivation and yoga are some of the more familiar procedures used to promote such ecstatic experiences.

After days of prolonged periods of stress and continuous nights of agitated sleep, I awoke one morning in a state of supreme serenity in a bed with my husband beside me. Why the unrelenting weeks of unsettling experiences didn't propel me into a chaotic state of depression, I do not know. I might have guessed that I was suffering from high levels of the stress hormone, cortisol, which can produce adrenal fatigue and lead to insomnia, anxiety, and depression. After all, those were the symptoms that I was living with on a daily basis.

But it was as if my brain were flooded with serotonin, the neurotransmitter which propels the signals between nerves and is known to elevate mood.

Possibly, there was some disturbance in my brain's right temporal-parietal lobe. In 2007, Henrik Ehrrhson, at the Institute of Neurology, London demonstrated that something very similar to an OBE (out of body) experience could be produced under laboratory conditions. When the researchers scrambled visual and tactile sensations in the subjects in their study, a sense of disembodiment was created in the individuals involved.

People do not have to be mad, as is sometimes thought, to experience out of body experiences. As the researchers demonstrated, disembodiment or feeling you have left your body may be all in the mind. It is a question of how the brain interprets the sensory information that it is receiving.

As I am not religious, I have not attempted to attribute this experience to a superior power or a divine being. Having explored various other paths, I have no definitive answer as to why I experienced this ecstatic event. There is no question that it defied description and was beyond the realms of ordinary consciousness.

I found an article on mystical experiences which stated that they are a common event and can occur unbidden to a person perhaps once or twice in a lifetime, if at all. This article was a reaffirmation of the fact that ordinary human beings from various and sundry parts of the world undergo these experiences. I think I was attracted by the word, unbidden, because it was such an accurate description of how this event occurred to me at the time. But it provides no explanation for the causes or the reasons why it happened. I may just have to accept the fact that I have experienced a most unusual event which I have found no specific or evident explanation.

Once this miraculous state of being had disappeared completely, I was left with a sense of well-being and a feeling of great optimism. Both these qualities would prove essential to buoy my spirits for our next venture, that of leaving Putney and moving to England. Our first task would be to sell the house that we had so recently decided to buy.

The year was 1966. In 1954, the Supreme Court in Brown vs. the Board of Education, had ruled that separate schools for black children was unconstitutional. It was now 12 years later, and equal educational facilities were still not available for black children, particularly in the south. Many were still living in economically and educationally deprived communities.

Through the Quakers, we had been sending money and books to southern organisations who dispatched all useful gifts and materials to areas where they were needed. As Roger had informed me that the Post Office was charging exorbitant prices to post books to England, I mailed all of my books, mostly literature and some college and teaching textbooks, to be dispersed to southern colleges and libraries.

The children chose which books and toys to give away and which they wanted to keep. I included new books, paper, notebooks, pencils, pens, crayons, and coloured pencils in the parcels which they donated. The largest parcel also contained a complete set of the Children's Encyclopedia Brittanica.

The next task was to organise the sale of our furniture. We owned nothing of great value. We had bought most of our furniture from the landlord who had rented us the house, so nothing was new. We were not seriously concerned to earn money from these old articles, so everything was sold very cheaply. I was sad to part with the sliding door cabinet that I had made when we were first married. Gabo's wedding present to us, one of his sculptures, always sat on its surface, taking pride of place in our sitting room.

The very last task was to mail to England the possessions that we wanted to keep. These consisted mainly of the Gabo sculpture, some lovely pottery, a set of dishes and cutlery that we had bought in England and were now sending back. Roger had found a firm that packed all our belongings in barrels to ship them to England.

Not long before we departed, Roger told me that we would be renting a house in Great Missenden, in Buckinghamshire, for a year. I was very impressed that he had sorted out a place for the family to live in England.

Our friends in Putney gave us a royal send-off, taking us out to one of the best restaurants in the area for a truly memorable evening.

With everything sorted and completed, we said our final goodbyes to the USA and flew to England to start a new chapter in the Franklin family saga.

92 Chilton - family home

*1880 Wedding Photo Annie (Bessie)
Jenkins James Fowler*

*Annie (Bessie) Fowler, Juanita
Pearl Fowler's mother*

Berverly on Peace Protest, Vermont

Beverly and Roger Wedding, Carlos Israels,
Bob Allen, Nina Gabo, Miriam Gabo, John Allen,
Beverly Allen, Roger Franklin, Joe Franklin

Beverly aged 16

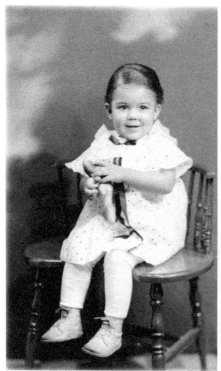

Beverly aged 17 months 2

Beverly and Kim, Vermont

Bob and Beverly   *Beverly with her mother, Pearl. Cotillon 1950*

Beverly on Anti Bomb Protest Vermont

Misha, Leda, Roger, Kim, Michèle,   *Beverly, Michèle, Leda, Kim, Natasha*
Dash, Natasha, Gabe. Pat, Beverly,
Nadia, Lillis, Ruby

Cyril, Roger, Joe, Glennalla Ireland

Gabo, Miriam, Nina, Owen, Roger, Beverly, Joe, Snieshka 1955

Grandma Susan, Father John, Aunt Winnie, Beverly

Beverly and Jess

Henrietta Franklin, Roger's paternal grandmother

Juanita Pearl Fowler (Beverly's mother)

Kim, Leda, Roger, Michèle, Beverly, Natasha

*Leda with Grandpa Allen
(Beverly's father)*

*Michèle and Brian's wedding, 1988.
Beverly, Roger, Michèle, Brian.*

Michèle, Kim, Leda, Natasha, Beverly

Susan Allen (Beverly's paternal grandmother)

*USA family 2011
Back row: Natasha, Roland, Brent,
Brandon, Betsy
Front row: Jason, Liza, Jacqueline,
Beverly, Jack*

PART THREE

ARRIVAL IN GREAT MISSENDEN, BUCKINGHAMSHIRE

Roger was driving in leisurely fashion along the highway until one of the children spotted the sign indicating the turn off to Great Missenden. He quickly veered left and eventually reached the road he was looking for. It was not long afterwards that he turned again. Suddenly, the car climbed a short steep hill, and stopped abruptly in front of a small, nondescript, wooden garage.

Turning down the window, I leaned out and glanced cautiously down what was the driveway to our newly rented house. I became instantly apprehensive, realising that I would soon be manoeuvring down this sharply sloping incline which led directly into the main road.

Fearing that such a task was far too dangerous an undertaking, I felt I had to convince myself that I could manage it. No one else was going to buy the children's clothes and shoes, do the food shopping, doctor's appointments, the school drives, and the afterschool activities. It was a case of needs must. Necessity, rather quickly, would propel me to control my fear and to undertake whatever driving was essential.

We all clambered out of the car, each laden in one arm with sundry, precious belongings and lugging a suitcase with the other. As roger unlocked the front door, we pushed it open and entered a not very large hall with a door on the right, leading to a small, very tidy sitting room.

As I was busy assessing the size of the new family room, shrieks of delight erupted from the children. They had spied in the far corner of the sitting room, a small TV.

In Vermont, there had been no TV in any corner of our sitting room. We lived in a valley where reception was poor and had no access to the one decent, educational channel.

It was the early days of television. The programmes on the few channels available were unenlightening and unexceptional. For these reasons, we decided not to purchase a television.

The children were hardly deprived. During the day, they were often to be found at their friend's houses, all of whom had television. They saw the best and no doubt, the worst of the cartoons and children's films and could be heard discussing them loudly and in animated fashion with everyone.

We climbed the stairs to the bedrooms, one master bedroom with a double bed and two smaller bedrooms with two single beds in each. The rooms were not so large as the ones they had in Vermont, but the space was adequate for everyone. The children were not complaining. In fact, they did not even notice the size of the rooms. Nothing could suppress their overwhelming joy at having access to their very own TV. Unfortunately, there are moments when you realise that your own very high educational and creative standards have not been imbided by your children.

The name designated to our house was "The Spinney". No doubt, a spinney (a small wood) had flourished in the area where our house now stood. Behind the house, lay a rectangular garden with green grass growing above the sticky, clay soil. Along the back border, were a few trees and bushes, attesting to whatever thicket may have originally prospered there. Despite the nature of the soil, I could see that there was ample room for the children's outdoor activities, so try to put any critical thoughts about clay to one side.

They were delighted be here and so was Roger, though for different reasons. The idea of living in the Chiltern hills really pleased him. I knew he would enjoy these surroundings but, I always felt there was another aspect to his love of the countryside. He had also absorbed his grandmother's critical attitude towards living in cities and towns.

By the 1890's, many middle-class English people, including Roger's Grandmother, had adopted the image of the countryside as a rural idyll. Their vision was of a land, encircled by clean, fresh air which would be inhaled from the natural environment of meadows and woods. All creatures, humans, plants and animals, would grow and thrive in these areas, untrammelled and untroubled by the noise, pollution, and crowding of the industrialised, manufacturing cities and towns.

I, who had grown up in a reasonably large city, Cambridge MA, in a residential area, far from pollution had never created in my mind such a strong dichotomy between city and country living.

My countryside experiences were associated with a prolonged period of outdoor exercise (usually walking, sometimes hill climbing), intriguing and unusual unaccustomed sights, sounds and aromas and sometimes unexpected panoramic views. When in the countryside, I always had the opportunity to indulge myself in physical and sensory pleasures.

City living offered choices of a different kind. With access to the numerous art galleries, museums, concert halls and theatres, the city also provided opportunities to indulge one's senses. To satisfy my intellectual curiosity, there were lectures I could attend or colleges and universities for more serious study.

I had lived quite happily in both city and country and could still do so.

Here we were in Great Missenden, and I was truly pleased that Roger had chosen a place where we could all enjoy the countryside and settle into our new home in England.

SCHOOLS IN GREAT MISSENDEN

About a month after our arrival in Great Missenden, the local schools were due to open for the autumn term. My first concern was to decide which school the children should attend. Various schools were available, but which was the most appropriate?

We were fortunate because Roger's first cousin, Angela Loewi and her husband, Gerald, lived not far away, in Gerard's Cross. I can't remember whether Gerard was still doing scientific research or was now working as a doctor. Angela was already working as a teacher in the area. She spent many long hours on the phone and over many delicious dinners that she had prepared, explaining the English primary school situation to me.

It became apparent that there was no separation of church and state as there had been in the United States. The children would be saying prayers every day or listening to readings from the Bible. As there was a choice for children to opt out of prayers if the parents weren't religious, Roger wanted us to state that the children wouldn't participate.

I disapproved of his decision because I felt that the children would already be viewed as very different from everyone else, first, due to their strange American accents. And second, there was the possibility that they could be of a lower educational standard because schools in the USA start at six years of age, not five. The third reason was a large question mark. Would they be classed as different because they were seen as "mixed race"?

As it turned out, there could have been a fourth reason, they were all taller than their classmates, but this physical trait proved not to be a problem.

There was another reason, I believed it was important for the children to know the significance of the basic tenets of Christianity if they were to understand the art, history, and literature of Western civilisation. How would they ever comprehend Milton's Paradise Lost, Dante's Inferno, Blake's paintings, the Crusades or even Christmas itself which we celebrated every year. Roger finally agreed with my decision so our children, like all the others, would be hearing parts of the Bible read to them every morning.

With Angela's assistance, we chose the Church of England School. The headmaster suggested that we bring the children to school prior to its opening to familiarise them with their new surroundings.

Trying to be efficient, I carefully laid out all the children's clothing the night before their first school trip, really to avoid those dreadful mornings when someone has misplaced a sock or can't find a shoe and makes everyone late for whatever appointment we had to attend.

When we arrived, the headmaster greeted everyone warmly, asked the children a few questions and then proposed that they might like to go outside.

Already tired of politely answering the headmaster's questions, the children excitedly rushed out of his office to find the playground. As we plied the headmaster with further questions, the three of us slowly followed the children's footsteps into the playground.

They were all scampering wildly over different parts of the climbing frame. The headmaster, turning to Roger, stated that it was a pleasure to see how much they enjoyed physical activity. As he had addressed his comment to Roger, I turned my head and looked upwards to a startling sight. Natasha's bare bottom was merrily hopping from one bar to another. My immediate thought was, "Please, please, don't try a somersault."

In a state of alarm, I tried to coax her down. I feared that the headmaster would also gasp in disbelief if he encountered the same shocking sight. The headmaster, overhearing my entreaties and, no doubt, thinking that I was an overanxious mother, yelled to me that she was obviously enjoying herself. I responded with a feeble yes, edged further away from him and continued to quietly encourage Natasha to descend from the climbing frame. It was a gentle battle between the headmaster and me which I urgently felt that I had to win.

Natasha eventually climbed down and stood before me looking perplexed. Before she could say anything, I produced a Kleenex, covered her nose and said "Blow" in a very loud voice. As she was protesting, "Mummy, Mummy", I tried to stifle her questions by reassuring her that everything was alright. We were all just getting ready to go home.

As we walked slowly towards Roger and the headmaster, the other three children were tumbling from the climbing frame to greet us. The headmaster assured us that the school would welcome them, and he was sure that they would have no problems.

As we departed, over the headmaster's goodbyes, the disgruntled voice of five year old, Natasha could be heard, justifiably complaining that she didn't have a cold and why couldn't she have as much fun in the playground as the others.

Once the reasons for her hasty departure were explained to her, Natasha stopped and stood, looking bewildered and shocked. In a tone of deep contemplation, she asked, "How could that happen?"

Her query about the situation suggested an acceptance of what had occurred and seemed to erase any feelings of injustice or resentment that she had previously felt.

So, we proceeded home in a more relaxed and contented state of mind.

ENGLISH PRIMARY SCHOOL

My next job was to find the shop which sold the school uniforms the children needed to attend their local primary school.

My initial aversion to the idea of the children wearing school uniforms, centred around the idea of regimentation. Why was everyone required to look the same?

It was explained to me that when everyone wore the same uniform, children from poorer backgrounds could not be distinguished from those who lived in more favourable economic circumstances. Understanding the reasoning behind this practise, I became less critical and tried to view the matter from the point of view of the English. I saw it as an attempt to produce a kind of equality in attire for all students.

In the United States, children always wore their everyday casual clothes to school. While there may have been differences between the middle class children and those from poorer backgrounds, they appeared minimal. No school ever assumed that the kind of clothes you wore defined your economic status.

During the first two or three months the children attended school, I began to realise that the similarity in dress, though worthy in its intentions, did not eradicate the differences in accent and grammar which were blatantly evident amongst the students.

Such distinct differences indicated to me just how pervasive the class structure was in English society, and especially in the schools.

Always having lived in the country and accustomed to wearing only trousers, the girls were overjoyed at the idea of wearing dresses all day. What a treat! Dresses were worn only for birthday parties so they couldn't wait for school to begin.

Kim, on the other hand, faced for the first time with ties and shirts that buttoned, was none too pleased. He objected so much to wearing a tie, he declared that he couldn't learn how to tie the knot in the front. So, initially, every morning, over his very loud protests, I became his official knot-tier, in order to send him to school in a presentable state.

The children remember my telling them that they might be a year behind academically as children in England started school at five, not six, a year earlier than American schools. I also told them that English schools were stricter than the ones they were accustomed to, so they were to pay particular attention to what the teacher told them to do. The children were surprised and delighted to find no differences at all in teaching methods and found that the teachers were certainly not stricter than the ones they had experienced.

When I had time to think about it, I realised that most of my knowledge about English schools had derived from novels, probably relating to customs in the 19th century and when I thought further, the schools under discussion would never have been about state schools.

Leda was only three, too young to enter the local primary school. Most nursery school places were already full when we started trying to find a place for her. Fortunately, we managed to enrol her in one of the last places available in a Montessori Nursery School which she always loved attending.

Natasha was five and in reception. Michèle was seven and in second form, Kim was nine and in year five. The children's assessment of their first day of school was a unanimous declaration, "They fitted in". They had no problems. They had all made new friends.

All my fears about how they might be received were totally unfounded. Their American accents were a subject of interest and curiosity and not pointed out as a sign of difference. Their academic performance seemed to be on a par with their English classmates. There was no subject in which they appeared to lag behind.

In fact, Kim, after only two months in year five, was promoted to the top junior form with the ten and eleven year olds. He was still only nine but started to really enjoy school once again because lessons were challenging enough to capture his interest and gain his attention.

No comments were ever made about the children being "mixed race. In Great Missenden, in 1966, with only white, English families in the community, racial issues were not considered a problem.

As one of my children pointed out: "We didn't think of ourselves as different from anyone else because we weren't." I was overjoyed to hear that simple but true statement. I felt as long as the children maintained their self-esteem, they would possess a very strong asset to deal with any future problems and prejudice that they would encounter.

FISH and CHIPS

After four days of school, the children arrived home very excited, bursting to tell me their news. On Fridays, none of their friends ate dinner at home. The children were in three different classrooms, and I found it hard to believe that not even one of their parents was preparing dinner for them on Friday evenings. "It's true it's true," they all insisted. "They all said so."

"That's very odd. It must be a new English custom that I have never heard of. If they don't eat dinner at home, tell me where they do eat dinner. "They eat dinner outside, on the street with their friends."

"On the street" suggested to me that they were buying food to eat from the local shops. I was quickly corrected about that misinterpretation of the facts. "Oh no—They buy their dinner from a van. It comes round every Friday night and always sells them fish and chips wrapped in newspaper."

"Wrapped in newspaper?" I was horrified "Whoever heard of eating dinner from a newspaper? What about the ink? Wouldn't that rub off on all the food?". The children continued to badger me to join their friends in this new venture. They obviously relished the idea of eating food from newspapers.

The thought of anyone eating a meal from papers covered with ink and handled by numerous, unknown individuals seemed totally unhygienic and distasteful to me. So, amidst protests and grumbles, the children continued to have dinner at home, as usual, on very ordinary but clean dinner plates.

Many months later, a friend enticed me to try fish and chips, wrapped in the daily paper. Although very hesitant and wary, I indulged and found, to my surprise, that the fish, coated in batter, was very tender and tasty. The chips were also delicious but less to my liking only because they weren't as crispy as I desired. As I saw no signs of stained ink on any particle of food, and was reassured by everyone that the food was never contaminated by ink, I was forced to relinquish my opposition to the forbidden meal.

The children were, of course, overjoyed and to this day consider fish and chips, wrapped in newspaper, a most delicious, delectable meal.

OUR YEAR IN GREAT MISSENDEN

I had always told the children to inform me if they wanted to have a friend visit after school. I would ask the child's mother if they could spend the afternoon and have a meal with us and I would drive the child home.

I was pleased to note that the children, unlike their some of their English relatives, made no distinction between the "working class" and the "middle class" children. Never having been brought up to allocate superiority or inferiority to anyone, they mixed freely with everyone.

Directly after school, I served the children nibbles, cheddar and some other kind of cheese cut up in cubes, some biscuits to go with them, carrot and celery sticks or raw peppers and cucumber, and a piece of fruit. Drinks could be a glass of milk or fruit juice.

Before they went home, the children always had a light supper composed of sliced ham and sometimes salami or some other kind of sliced meat, brown bread and butter, and a green salad with tomatoes and maybe some pickles or olives. Fruit for dessert and fruit juice to drink.

As this fare was not what they ate at home, we often had many discussions, short and long, about food. They loved the salami. Many of them had never eaten it before, not the kind we bought. They ate the brown bread but found it strange as they were only used to white, sliced loaves. Fruit was obviously eaten but only occasionally. I could easily understand that situation as I complained all the time about the outrageously expensive price of fruit in England.

Most of the children said that they ate bread and jam and tea when they returned home from school, so coming to us was considered a real treat, despite some rather odd and unusual food.

After many enjoyable afternoons spent with their friends, the children began to complain. "They always come to our house, but we never go to theirs." It was true, the mothers were always happy to have their children taken off for an afternoon but the invitations to visit were not usually reciprocal.

Very slowly, I began to realise that exchanging children after school for playtime and a meal was not an English custom, at least not with most of the children we invited home. Michèle had become friendly with a little girl who lived not far from us and was invited there for afternoon visits. She was one of the few middle-class friends who appeared on our visiting list.

There was one family who proved to be an exception to the dearth of invitations that the children received. The result was that Kim and Michèle became very good friends with two children who lived in one of the council houses quite near the school. All four children really played happily together and spent many lively, noisy afternoons in each other's company.

When taking or picking up children, either Roger or I would always stop to chat with one of the parents. They were keen on out-of-doors activities and had a prodigious knowledge of English birds. If we hadn't moved after our first year in Great Missenden, I always felt that we might have developed a deeper, more long-lasting friendship with them.

✳ ✳ ✳

During the year of 1966, I was feeling very pleased. The children had been at school for a few months, even the winter months, without succumbing to any of the infections to which all children are prone. In Vermont, I had become accustomed to what felt like endless winters of childhood illness, sometimes one child after another feeling unwell.

As it turned out, my joy was short-lived. But it was not the children who were ill, it was Roger. He awoke one morning with a fever and an ache in both jaws. As the day progressed, the glands under his jaw began to swell.

There was no doubt about it, Roger had developed a serious case of the mumps.

I checked all the children who were merrily sprinting up and down the stairs, no signs of swelling or temperature. But none of them had ever been diagnosed with the mumps. They couldn't have been vaccinated against the infection because the mumps vaccine was not available in the USA until 1967. We had left in 1966.

I didn't know what to think. With all the illnesses they had acquired every winter, maybe a light case of the mumps went undiagnosed or was masked by the more prominent symptoms of another disease. There were so many times that the doctor couldn't put a name to whatever illness the children had developed, I felt that this interpretation of events might be a feasible explanation.

I rang the doctor and told Roger when he was due to arrive. It was then that I suddenly remembered that Roger had given up wearing pyjamas. He went to bed totally naked. I immediately felt an urgent desire to buy him a pair just to preserve his dignity in front of the doctor.

I rushed out to the next village and returned with an appropriately conservative pair of pyjamas. I unlocked the front door and started running up the stairs to Roger's room. I quickly stopped in my tracks as I overheard two voices conversing. It was too late. The doctor had already arrived. I consoled myself with the fact that, after all, as a doctor, he had seen it all before. As I introduced myself to the doctor, he informed me that Roger had a rather severe case of the mumps. Childhood diseases are always worse when acquired as an adult. There was nothing to do but let the illness take its course. There was no treatment available.

Roger's main concern during his illness seemed to be that he could become impotent. There was a general belief at the time that if a man caught mumps as an adult he might not be able to contribute towards the production of any more children.

I never knew if that assumption was a genuine fact or just a frightening fear but Roger's main concern was most certainly not at the top of my "things-to-be-worried-about" list. We had planned each one of our four children. They had all arrived happy and healthy. I had no intentions of adding to the numbers we had finally chosen. My feeling was that, if it arose, we could both survive the problem of impotence without too much difficulty.

Negative thoughts around the idea of another pregnancy did not encourage me to extend my sympathy to what I thought was Roger's misplaced anxiety.

Roger was busy meeting new people and making new associations through the people he met at Housman's, the bookshop on Caledonian Road in London which sold books on sociology and radical politics. Peace News, the pacifist newspaper which I spent a summer mailing to subscribers in the USA when I worked as a volunteer for the American Friends Service Committee. was available to read and to buy here, While Roger was making contacts further afield, I was busy re-establishing family contacts. On weeks-ends, I invited Angela Loewi and her husband Gerald for a family meal. Angela had been of great assistance when we were trying to decide which school the children should attend in Great Missenden. I also prepared Sunday lunches for my sister-in-law Frances and her husband, Joe, as well as Sonja, my other sister-in-law and her husband, Owen. Although I was cooking even more than I usually did for the family, I was always trying out new recipes so cooking became a challenging enterprise rather than a chore.

Roger's father, Cyril, always wanted to visit us. Going anywhere was an adventure for him. He spent most of his time in his sitting room listening to classical music. I was never sure how much he was actually taking in and how much was a diversion for boredom. In his chair by his record player was the place where he resided most days of the week. He did play tennis on his tennis court at the bottom of the rose garden, but he had developed chronic bronchitis, so could only play in doubles matches infrequently. I never saw him use his swimming pool which some of the family had encouraged him to build. If anyone went on a walk around the garden, he would always join them with his secateurs and his wooden basket for the clippings he produced after pruning the roses.

Cyril had worked as a director in his family's bank, Samuel Montague and Co. for many years. But managing the bank and any concomitant business attached to it did not seem to interest him greatly. Miriam, Roger's mother felt that he might have been less irritable if he had been allowed to follow his own interests and become an engineer. Visitors discovered that he was more than reluctant to allow anyone to leave. He would insist that you had to listen a lovely aria from Mozart or some other moving piece of classical music. If you did so and rose to go when it had finished, you were then plied with a liqueur or offered an alcoholic beverage. Most guests, by this time, became more vociferous about their need to leave immediately. Suddenly everything they had planned to do, became urgent. They grabbed their coats and tried to politely extricate themselves from the situation, all the while listing the reasons that forced them to make a hasty departure.

I was told that he had always been a difficult and demanding person whose behaviour had somewhat improved over time. I could become as annoyed as anyone else at some of the scenes he created, but when I was in the guise of my most mature self, I saw a very intelligent, lonely old man who was very bored with the life he was leading. When I first met him, he went to the bank a few hours every day. But after he retired, he was at home all day. We all used to say that we were grateful for Dorothy who had been the children's nanny and whom he eventually married many years after he and Miriam had divorced. She was his constant companion who sat on the couch in the sitting room every day while he sat in his armchair in the corner facing her, endlessly playing her different classical records which, he hoped she would eventually recognise. We all thought she was a saint. She put up with his difficult behaviour and even tried to control it without too much success, but he did sometimes listen to her protestations.

I decided to invite Cyril and Dorothy to visit us on Sundays. We could all take a pleasant walk in the countryside with the children and have an interesting lunch in a pub or not too expensive restaurant. Everyone was talking about a marvellous book on eating out in England. It was The Good Food Guide which was very helpfully divided into the various regions of England, so it was very easy to find the most suitable eating places in or near our vicinity. Since WW2, England had suffered from a variety of complaints about English food. The quantities served were too small, often not well prepared and the waiters were rude. I felt it was my great good fortune to have The Good Food Guide available with its enthusiastic reviews of so many good places to eat out in England.

These Sunday outings were very popular with Cyril. Dorothy was her usual, amiable self, often cracking a few jokes. Cyril's delight at being asked out for the day meant that his irritability often totally disappeared, until it came time to pay the tip. To Roger's dismay and mine, he always argued about how much money Roger left for the waiter. "It's' too much. They don't expect it. You're raising the standards, they'll come to expect this all the time."

It was at times like this that the great political divide between Roger and his father became all too evident. Roger's father was a conservative Conservative and still displayed the snobbish attitudes of the upper middle class held towards workers and servants that he had imbibed in his childhood. Roger didn't believe in the idea of monarchy, nor did he support the English class system.

Cyril often replaced Roger's money with what he considered an adequate amount. Roger would object and attempt to rectify the situation. There could be many exchanges of Roger's tip and then Cyril's. If Roger managed to be the last to leave his money on the table, as we walked to the car, Cyril would suddenly turn around and go back to the restaurant to replace it. So, our jovial Sunday afternoons with Cyril and Dorothy always ended on the same disconcerting note, leaving some of us feeling that the lovely day had not ended well.

When we weren't inviting Franklin relatives to visit us, we were driving to London to visit them, especially on weekends. Great Missenden wasn't that far away from London, but Roger wasn't a particularly fast driver. It took us approximately, two hours each way. Trying to keep four children amused with games, songs and stories was my job.

Roger preferred to drive. I started to feel that all this driving was totally unnecessary. There was no particular reason that we were in Great Missenden, except that Roger had chosen it as a suitable pace to live in the countryside. I was really very pleased that he had chosen a place for the family to live, particularly as, when we were in Vermont, I had been very angry with him for spending no time with the family and leaving everything to me. The fact that he had taken the time to find a house in England for us indicated to me that the family did really matter to him.

Roger didn't need convincing. He was quite pleased to relinquish four hours of driving on most weekends. But he would only move closer to London if he could live in The Green Belt, the area of open land around a city in which building is restricted. Although we viewed many properties farther out in Buckinghamshire, we eventually decided to buy a house in Radlett in Hertfordshire, a part of the Green Belt which was closest to London. Therein began the next saga of our life.

OUR MOVE TO LOOM LANE, RADLETT, HERTFORDSHIRE

As soon as we started to look at houses, I started to worry about money again. Roger wanted a larger dwelling and I agreed with him. In our present house, the rooms were very small, and the children's bedrooms were just about large enough for the beds. I also thought that it was about time for Kim and Michèle to have separate bedrooms. In addition, Roger had decided that he needed a separate study where he could carry on with his writing.

These new requirements meant that we were now looking for a 5 bedroom house where one bedroom was suitable for a study. Suddenly, the price of houses soared and in my opinion, became astronomical. As an American, I was still adjusting to the great discrepancy in prices between England and the United States. All cars, any kind of machine, clothes, food, rent and houses were definitely more expensive on this side of the Atlantic.

At these exorbitant prices, I wondered whether we could afford to buy any kind of house with five bedrooms. I asked Roger, once again, about our financial situation. How much money did we have to spend? Roger would never answer this question directly and was very reluctant to discuss finances. His sidestepping such issues and his absolute refusal to disclose his financial position was one of the more frustrating and nerve-racking areas of our marriage.

He did inform me that we could afford to buy a house with five bedrooms. For a moment that fact was reassuring but it didn't clarify what his real financial position was and what kind of limit there was to what I could expect to spend. We did eventually move to a new house in Radlett, Herts. With a study, two single and two double bedrooms, there was adequate space for everyone. Natasha and Leda shared a double bedroom. On the ground floor there was even a playroom for the children.

I had a Nat West Bank account and a Samuel Montague and Co. chequebook for food shopping and buying the children's clothes and mine. I spent what I needed and was not at all extravagant.

Roger had always been generous with his money, particularly towards friends and worthy causes. Now that we were in England and he was no longer working, he still maintained his philanthropy towards friends, CND and also towards those I deemed as less-deserving individuals who found him an easy source of money with which to sustain themselves.

Whenever I tried to pursue money matters any further, his response was always the same; "You can go to the bank. Go to Samuel Montague and Co. They'll explain the situation to you."

The idea of going to the bank was complete anathema to me. My understanding of how the bank functioned was probably different from Roger's. He saw the bank directors simply as managers of money. I saw these same directors as a bevy of older men whose ideas about women and banking remained ossified in the beliefs and prejudices of the early 20th century.

Men had always been in charge of money and husbands had even more of an obligation to be so as they were the sole support of their wives and children. Middle class women had no need to be educated or to work as their husbands were meant to provide for them. As their husbands were in charge of the finances there was no need for women to know anything at all about matters relating to money. I had the impression that bank officials at Samuel Montague and Co, found it a great inconvenience and very unconventional to discuss financial matters with women.

Attitudes towards women had changed and some areas of life had become more inclusive for females. But not everyone's outlook had altered towards a more progressive one of more equality for women.

Whenever I imagined a meeting at the family bank, I envisioned a long, dark shiny, mahogany table with two or three bank officials who had deigned to meet me sitting at one end of the table and me, sitting alone at the other end, with that endless expanse of shiny wood glistening between us.

I feared a hostile or at least a dismissive response to my request to reveal the state of Roger's finances to me. In addition, I was almost sure that there was no provision in law that required husbands to clearly state their financial situation to their wives. I didn't really believe that the bank would give me the information I wanted. As a result, I never made an appointment with anyone at Samuel Montague and Co. I felt it was pointless.

Having accepted that attempting to discover anything about our financial situation was a futile endeavour, I began to concentrate my efforts on registering the children at the local schools and buying them their new school uniforms

AN ADDENDUM

A few years later, I found that some of my wary feelings about visiting the bank proved to be justified. Roger's brother, joe, took me to an arranged meeting at the bank to discuss my financial situation. Joe made many helpful suggestions about what might be practical to do with the funds that I had. We left waiting to hear which ideas they had approved. We waited and waited but sadly, never heard from any of them again. Joe was completely perplexed and thought it might be due to the fact that I didn't have enough money for them to consider investing in anything. It was true. There weren't any large bundles of anything in my account.

Joe, who was my spokesman, had made it clear that I wanted no money invested in armaments, Coca Cola or Tobacco. There was a longer list of companies not-to-be-invested-in which I now do not recall. They were also informed that I wanted investments in companies that would benefit the third world.

These proposals must have seemed ludicrous to men who only dealt in business transactions involving huge amounts of money in wealthy countries and the idea that whatever small amount of money I possessed would be struggling to see a profit in some much poorer country must have seemed even more ridiculous.

Joe and I were shocked at their rudeness in not even bothering to respond to the questions raised at the meeting they had attended. Maybe they had found my proposals too unrealistic, by their standards to even consider.

I'm not sure why they agreed to a meeting in the first place. Maybe, they felt it was rude to refuse a request which was made by the great-grandson of Lord Swaythling, the founder of the bank. These are all conjectures and I have no way of knowing why they chose to needlessly waste their time and that of the bank's one fine morning in the 1970's but they did, and the matter will just have to rest where it is, in a state of bewilderment and confusion.

SNOW IN ENGLAND

We had been living in England only two or three years when the pleasures of what I had called the "mild English winter" became a misleading description of the weather we were enduring in the year 1968.

To everyone's surprise, Radlett in Hertfordshire had experienced light snowfall for a few days, a truly rare occurrence, to be expected very occasionally this far south.

Most individuals were delighted as the snow had sprinkled a feathery light white covering on all the houses and trees. Due to the high level of traffic, all the main roads were completely clear. But the one day that I had decided to go to London, a dense snowstorm had descended on this part of the countryside.

When I left the station in Radlett, I realised that I was walking on three or four, maybe five or six inches of very sticky snow. As I started climbing the hill to reach Loom Lane, I was shocked to see that the road was choc-a-block with cars, facing in every direction, from the very bottom of the hill to the very top.

In desperation, one or two had been abandoned, blocking that particular part of the road permanently, but most had drivers who were desperately struggling to steer themselves out of impossible spins. Swerving backwards and forwards, they were barely missing each other's cars as they did so.

I had never seen such reckless, dangerous driving. There was bound to be an accident. Looking at this scene of complete mayhem, I was so frightened about what might happen that I lost all inhibition and yelled at the top of my lungs: "Drive into the spin. Don't slam on your brakes." I yelled these instructions several times, all to no avail. No-one responded in any way at all.

Under the rigid strain of concentration that these dangerous driving circumstances had imposed upon them, I doubt that anyone had even heard me.

I did not hear of any serious injuries but later, did experience several outbursts of fury and anger about the dreadful conditions of the snowy, icy roads, mainly driven by everyone's fear in unfamiliar, frightening circumstances, I felt.

One fine, sunny morning, my front doorbell rang. When I answered it, a very petite lady, very politely asked, if I could tell her why the path around my house was so clear when everyone else's was covered with snow. "Well," I responded, "not long after it snowed, I shovelled the paths and pavements and sprinkled some table salt on them. As salt lowers the freezing point of water, I was hoping to prevent the next layer of snow from settling on the ground and turning into ice."

Instantly, I was treated as if I were a genius for knowing that bit of scientific information. In countries where snowfall is a more frequent occurrence, facts of this kind are considered common knowledge and are also immediately put to practical use when snowstorms occur.

In many countries with high snowfall, rock salt (calcium chloride) which has crystallised into larger, coarser pieces of salt is commonly used to de-ice roads. It is a much cheaper product than table salt and it does melt the ice, though, possibly, at a slightly slower rate than table salt.

Those countries, tucked in between the high mountains of the Alps, where snow falls annually and frequently and where snowstorms abound, are the ones who are propelled into action immediately at the first sight of a blinding snowstorm. Local people are to be seen clearing the snow from around their houses and making an accessible path to their cars.

Snowploughs appear at all hours of the night to ensure that cars can use the roads the very next morning. Not even those in very remote areas are cut off from human communication or the products they require. Tracks are cleared so the trains can manoeuvre up the sharply, sloping mountainsides, bringing fresh food to the restaurants perched on their summits.

The trains are running. The roads are clear. Everyone goes to work. The children attend school and leisure activities are open for the tourists.

It has taken a community effort to accomplish the smooth running of these towns again, but the same local effort is exerted every time snowstorms occur during the winter.

I have observed that the arrival of snow in England does not produce reactions similar to those who live in constantly snowy climates. To be fair, snow falls occasionally and not even annually along the south-eastern coast of England. The knowledge of how to cope with snow, acquired through myriad years of dealing with heavy snowstorms is not to be expected here. Snowfall, snow flurries, snowstorms, they are all events that occur too infrequently to be occasions for either teaching or learning.

Initially, the English find the sight of snow falling something to be admired and a great pleasure to watch. But this state of wonder slowly transforms into one of awe, suffused with distant respect and fear as soon as the white flakes touch the ground. In the face of a few inches of snow on the roads and on the pavements, they become immobilised and come to a complete standstill.

When I am seen shovelling the pavement in front of my house, everyone who passes by proffers a warning of caution or likely catastrophe. "Remember, you're not as young as you used to be." "You've taken on rather a lot there, haven't you?"

"Be careful, you might have a heart attack."

"Take it slowly. Have you checked with your doctor, it's ok to be shovelling?

One or two suggested that I'd give myself a back injury.

As I look up, I can see that no pavement has been cleared along the entire length of my road, well, as far as I can see in either direction, and I am the only mad individual engaged in this activity.

I conclude from their comments to me, their fear of potential disaster stops them from even thinking about what they might do to prevent the worst from happening.

English people are not renowned for giving up before they even attempt to start a new activity. Most, I'm sure, would be upset to think that I could suggest that anything like this could ever happen.

I have a theory that the quirky, fearful English attitude towards snow could be altered if they were given the proper information and a few practical suggestions.

Before snowstorms are forecast, the local citizens should lobby their councils to provide rock salt and sand. Before the snow accumulates to any great height, the rock salt should be spread on the roads and the sand should follow.

If the council is not co-operative, each individual can carry a shovel, rock salt and sand in the boot of their car. Wherever snow needs to be melted. spread some rock salt. To provide traction for your tires, sprinkle sand under the wheels.

I am informed that kitty litter also provides very good traction for tires.

For your own safety and that of any visitors, clear the path to your front door. (The person who brings the mail will sing your praises forever).

It is to be hoped that armed with new knowledge and some very useful suggestions, English people may relinquish some of their anxiety and worry in the face of snow and the ensuing lethargy that follows. Just recognising the fact that the ravages that snow can thrust upon the environment can be mitigated or even overcome can induce a feeling of hope. This more positive outlook might provide the resolve and determination required to become more proactive when the next great snowfall descends.

MAKING FRIENDS IN RADLETT

On the first day of moving into our new house, we were emptying our suitcases of their contents, when there was a loud, persistent ring on the front door bell. It was our next door neighbour whose house we could barely see through the very thick hedges at the side of our garden. He was a pleasant, old man about eighty years old who felt it was his duty to introduce himself to the new neighbours.

As the door opened, he must have been nearly overcome by the shrieks and howls of laughter that emanated from the long staircase in the hall. The children, still in their pyjamas, were tumbling down the stairs on the boxes we had flattened to make a slide for them.

He stood staring in shocked surprise for a moment until I told the children to stop as the noise was too overwhelming for visitors, I did ask him in for a cup of tea or coffee, but, no doubt, still recovering from the chaotic scene which first greeted him, he made he made his excuses as to why he couldn't stay.

Before he left, I asked about the state school system. I was always asking about people's impressions of the state school system but began to realise that it was a pointless query. The people who lived in houses with five bedrooms or more had all sent their children to private schools so had no knowledge of the state school system.

Our new neighbour was quick to admit that he wasn't acquainted with the state school sector. He thought that the education might be alright but there was always the question of the accent. "You never knew what sort of accent the children would pick up at the state schools." I was astounded at this blatant display of class prejudice revealed in such a benign, matter-of-fact manner.

Our neighbour smiled sweetly and appeared quite pleased that he had proffered such a useful piece of information. He then very, politely departed.

After this encounter, I was left wondering what kind of neighbourhood we had moved into and worrying about what kind of neighbours we would have.

In the post, one morning my first letter had arrived, addressed only to me. It was a beautifully embossed invitation inviting me to a coffee morning with a neighbour who lived two streets away from me. When I arrived, my neighbour and her friend greeted me warmly and ushered me into the very spacious sitting room.

They passed on much useful information, where the library and the churches were situated, the best hairdresser in the main shopping centre and what type of shops there were in the area.

I asked again about the state schools and received the expected response. No, they didn't have any knowledge of them and told me of the wonderful private schools the children could attend not far away.

They invited me to join various groups, but it soon became obvious that they were all religiously orientated. As I had relinquished my conventional religious beliefs and no longer attended church, I had to accept that I did not really belong in this milieu.

I thanked them both politely for a lovely morning and for making me aware of the amenities and activities available in the community and very discreetly departed.

Since we had come to England, we had made two major moves with the children. It was our good fortune to discover both times thar Roger had relatives living nearby.

Roger's first cousin, Diana, who was married to Robin Holliday, and their family lived in Borehamwood, just a few miles away from Radlett. Robin was the head of the Genetics Department at the National Institute of Medical Research. They had chosen to live in Borehamwood as it was in a beautiful, rural setting from which Robin could commute to work.

They had four children, younger but very close in age to ours. They had stayed with us in Vermont one summer when Robin had just finished a year of lecturing in California. It was a hectic but happy visit. Sometimes the children would be scrambling madly between the tall grass at the side of the garden and others would be trying to play in the sand pit without interruption (a hopeless task with so many little ones). Despite moments of upheaval and disorder, they all seemed to get on well and survived whatever calamities occurred.

When we moved to Radlett, Diana graciously initiated the first exchange of children's visits to each other's houses. Thereafter a series of visits continued so the children became acquainted with their second cousins almost as soon as we moved into our new home.

Diana and Robin continued to invite us to dinner parties and certainly made us feel as if we were commencing a happy new life after our year in Great Missenden.

It was Diana who introduced me to the music teacher in Radlett. After a gap of twenty-four years, I started taking piano lessons again. I took the children to the teacher's group sessions where they learned to listen, play instruments, and create their own music.

At a much later date, she invited Roger and me to a dinner party where we met a group of local people with whom we were completely unacquainted. The time at which we met was a very busy one for me so I never pursued any of the new acquaintances, I do not know what reason they would give for never trying to contact us. Despite the music teacher's good intentions, no new friendships evolved from our lovely evening together.

The couple who had sold us our house explained that our garden had been twice its present size. They had removed their tennis court and some rose gardens to produce the plot on which they had built their new house with very extensive gardens adjoining ours. In fact, both houses had large gardens though theirs was most definitely more spacious than ours. The Farrells introduced us to our neighbours who lived on the corner, directly opposite our house.

Diane and Peter Charles also had four children, from the oldest to the youngest, they were a year or two younger than ours. Though the children visited each other's house fairly frequently, it was Lindsay the only girl in the Charles family and our youngest, Leda, who became very good companions.

When we met him, Peter was a management consultant and later helped to run the Novotel chain of hotels. Diane had been an athlete of great competence a few years before we met but I was unaware of her history when I met her.

As Diane Leather (her unmarried name), in 1954 and 1958, at the European Championships, she won two silver medals at 800 metres.

At the International Cross Country championships, she had won the women's race in 1954 and 1955.

Between 1954 and 1959, she ran five world bests for the mile. She was ratified as a world record holder three times.

In the 1960 Rome Olympics, she was, unfortunately, past her best and was eliminated in the heats of the 800 metres.

As one reporter proclaimed, she was the best British athlete you may never have heard of.

Looking at her athletic record, there was one outstanding race that was never acclaimed and for which she never received the credit she deserved.

In 1954, Diane Leather was the first woman to run a mile in less than five minutes. In Birmingham, she broke the five minute barrier at 4:59.6.

Three weeks earlier, Roger Bannister had broken the four mile record at 3:59.4.

Roger Bannister's achievement was applauded throughout England while Diane Leather's achievement was never recognised and never mentioned in the public media, not on the radio, tv. or in the major newspapers. Diane's important run was never recognised as a world record, only as a world's best. The reason for this omission as that the Athletic Board, the IAAF, only recorded records for women up to 800 metres. It took until 1967 for the IAAF to recognise women's world records for the mile.

As has been noted, while Roger Bannister became a lauded legend, Diane, his equivalent, became known 'as the one who also ran'.

By the time I met Diane, she was completely engaged in child-rearing. She was very modest about her athletic achievements and never mentioned them unless someone asked her a question directly. There was a very brief period when she encouraged me to go running with her early in the morning before our children woke up. We started running in all kinds of weather. What can I say, I could only describe my performance as slow and pathetic, never having run in my life. How was I to keep up with a world record holder?

When I ran races at school, I remember being good at sprinting short distances. I don't think I was cut out for running longer distances.

Diane must have been desperate to exercise to take me on as her companion. She was very encouraging but our little early morning outings did not last long. One by one, her children and mine discovered our secret escapade and started to join us. Our roles suddenly changed completely. We found ourselves encouraging our children to climb to the top of the hills, instead of coaxing ourselves to finish the course we had planned. As we slowly accepted that with numerous small companions, we could no longer focus on improving our running skills, we decided to end our early morning outings.

Diane and I continued to be good friends for the six years that we were in Radlett. She introduced me to the other good friend that I made there, Jeanne who lived about two streets away. Quite unexpectedly, the lives of all three of us were to become more entwined as time went on.

CANING IN BRITAIN and IN ENGLISH SCHOOLS

One morning, as I was listening to the radio rather inattentively, my attention was drawn to a discussion about caning in Britain. I stood in amazement and astonishment to think that such a subject could still be a matter for discussion in the present day. Surely, such incredibly, cruel practices had died out by the end of the Victorian era.

To be fair, the use of the cane as penalties for punishment had, over time, greatly decreased in use but this practice had not completely disappeared, and this was the year of 1967. In 1948, prisons had disallowed the use of caning for juveniles and adults, but in 1962, the islands of Guernsey and Jersey continued to use the cane on teenage boys who had committed crimes.

On the Isle of Man, most people were in favour of caning, believing it to deter criminal behaviour and maintain the residents' safety. They did eventually consent to abolish it, but not until 1976.

What totally shocked me was the fact that caning was still prevalent particularly, in the English Public School system.

In the USA, we were all brought up to revere the English school system for the breadth of knowledge it inculcated in the students and the high academic standards that it maintained.

It was only after arriving in England that I realised that it was only the English Public Schools that we had held in such high esteem. We were given no knowledge of the State School System, how it was run or how it performed.

Everyone knew of Eton and Harrow. When I learned that entry to both schools was available to mainly wealthy individuals and that caning was still the approved method of punishment, my very high estimate of both these institutions plummeted rather rapidly.

Apparently, caning was common practice in most English public schools, heartily endorsed by headmasters and approved by the faculty. I found if appalling to think that such a superior education was attained through the implementation of such barbaric instruments of pain and suffering. Both Harrow and Eton officially maintained this type of punishment until the 1980's but, in my searches, I found less information about when this practice ended in Harrow. At Eton, it was mandatory for all parents to pay a guinea for the school's supply of new canes, irrespective of whether or not the family's child ever required caning.

State schools were not exempt from corporal punishment. They tended to use the rattan cane to strike the student's hands and for teenage boys, as in public schools, they were struck across the buttocks.

In 1986, in England and Wales, corporal punishment was abolished in private schools and in 1998, it was banned in state schools and in those private schools to which the government made monetary contributions.

It was difficult to believe that physical punishment continued for 20 years in private schools and 32 years in state schools after our arrival in England in 1966. I had assumed that none of the state schools in England which my children attended had practised corporal punishment. But, only recently, they have informed me that was not the case. At their first primary school in Great Missenden, the boys were constantly caned for misbehaviour. I was truly shocked but greatly relieved to realise that this was the only school which my children attended where caning was still in existence.

After moving, my first task had been to decide which schools the children should attend. It was unfortunate that all the nursery school places were taken by the time we arrived in Radlett. The consequence was that Leda, age four, went to a local Playschool, open only in the morning.

Natasha, age six, was old enough to go to the Cobden Hill Infant School, not too far from one end of Loom Lane, where we lived. Michèle, age eight, and Kim, age ten, went to the Fairfield School at the other end of Loom Lane.

Everyone seemed to adjust to their new schools without much difficulty. There was only one problem. Kim had skipped a class in Great Missenden and had proved himself academically very capable. He had no difficulty with any of the subjects he had studied and had completed form four a year early.

Regrettably, the headmaster at the Fairfield School was not interested in the fact that Kim had already passed the subjects to be studied in form four. He seemed very pedantic and insisted that, because of his age, he would have to repeat the year. No amount of reasoning or protesting on his behalf would change his mind. It was, as to be expected, a year of sheer drudgery and boredom for a very frustrated Kim.

I always feared that he would start seriously misbehaving just for something different and more interesting to do. He didn't present a problem in the classroom, but one teacher announced that the boy from the United States was not allowed to answer any more questions. He couldn't even raise his hand to answer them.

She clearly found him a problem because he knew the answer to everything, and she didn't know what to do with him. As Kim said, her only solution was to shut him up forever.

As the year progressed, he became more and more bored with the work that he was repeating. His attention began to meander, and I don't think he was paying any attention to any subject matter in any class, especially with teachers who were not allowing him to participate at any level. One report stated that Kim should not rest on his laurels. But what other options did he have?

With the exception of meeting Edward Hawkins, his lifelong friend, from the council flats near the school, 1967 was a completely wasted school year for Kim.

SCHOOLS IN RADLETT

Leda enjoyed attending the local Playgroup but missed the type of learning that she had been exposed to at the Montessori Nursery School, in Great Missenden.

Michèle was doing well academically and making new friends at the Fairfield School.

Natasha's school report was more complicated. She was pleasant and polite in the classroom. Her performance in maths was of a very high standard but she was having difficulty with reading.

When I asked her to read aloud at home, I was shocked to discover that she could read nothing at all. I started testing her to see if I could discover the reason for the problem. It soon became evident that she could not match the correct sounds to the correct letters in the alphabet. I was disappointed that neither the teachers in Great Missenden nor the teachers in Radlett seemed to be aware of this specific problem.

When I was a teacher and dealing with a student who was struggling, I always tried to pinpoint at least one of the problems causing the difficulties. It is not always easy to determine the reasons for a child's problems. They could be numerous. Tackling one problem and, hopefully improving it, might help to develop the self-confidence they would need to deal with future challenges.

I made cards with the letter of the alphabet written on them and later combinations of letters to teach her the phonetics she hadn't yet learned. After a bit of free time and an after-school snack, we would start work. It was not an easy task as she had already spent a full day in school and her mind was focussed on playing for the rest of the afternoon.

Looking back on the situation, both Natasha and Leda, I later discovered, would now be assessed as dyslexic, though Leda certainly had a much less severe case of it, especially in relation to reading. But this was 1967 and dyslexia was completely unknown as far as teachers were concerned. I had definitely not heard of it during my teacher training in 1955. Consequently, no professional help was available. Students were on their own and struggled on as best as they could.

With a concerted effort on both Natasha's part and mine, Natasha did learn to read before she left Cobden Hill Infants School. By the time that Natasha and Leda reached the Fairfield School, they could read independently and fairly fluently. Leda had needed no assistance with phonics but they both continued to have difficulties related to spelling.

Spelling homework was a nightmare, especially those assignments where the teacher dictated a list of words and expected the child to look up the meaning in a dictionary and write it down beside the word. Leda was always complaining that it was ridiculous to expect her to look up a word if she didn't know how to spell it. As English is not a completely phonetic language, they would be forced to make endless attempts before finding the correct word and putting it into a sentence.

Each one recognised her own difficulties and worked very hard to improve her spelling ability. Neither one became a proficient speller but when much later, spell check arrived with the computer, I think they both heaved a great sigh of relief. Their worries were over. Putting letters in their correct sequence for any word was no longer a problem. The computer corrected all spelling mistakes, without your even asking it to do so. I soon realised how useful new technology could be, at times, in removing situations of great angst and distress.

The three girls all became very proficient recorder players at the Fairfield School. For school events and celebratory occasions, they were always asked to perform. Leda played the descant. Natasha played the descant and the treble, and Michèle played the descant, the treble, and the sopranino. Kim was mainly unhappy in form four at Fairfield and took no interest in music at all.

At the end of his school year, we were given a list of ten or eleven schools to which Kim could apply. I was completely perplexed and went to Roger for help. But he was as unfamiliar with how to choose the best school for your child as I was. We decided to discuss the matter with the headmaster. He told us that the custom was to send your child to the school nearest home. Following his advice, we chose the Bushey Grammar School on the basis that the commuting would be reasonable.

I was feeling pleased that we had made a sensible decision for Kim's schooling until I started talking to a group of mothers who informed me that I should have applied to the Watford Grammar School as it was the best grammar school in the area. The headmaster had certainly not mentioned that there might be different standards amongst the Grammar Schools. I hastily applied to the Watford Grammar School, hoping to cancel my application to the Bushey Grammar School. But it was to no avail. I received a rejection letter, saying they couldn't take any more pupils. I was disappointed but had to leave matters as they originally were.

The very next day, the pupils in the fourth form were very animated abut the fact that the daughter of a teacher at Fairfield School was rejected by Watford Grammar School. But her mother was contesting it and contacting people to support her. When, a few weeks later, she announced that her daughter had been accepted by Watford Grammar School, I felt I had been at a great disadvantage, not knowing who to contact under the same circumstances of rejection. To make matters worse, the pupils complained that she wasn't very bright. I could only observe that sometimes who you know can be a great advantage, but not knowing any significant people to contact or how the school system actually worked, I was not in a position to alter the situation in any way. So, in the autumn, Kim went off to the Bushey Grammar School as had been originally arranged.

COMPREHENSIVE SCHOOLS

There had been continuous controversy and heated discussions about the English School System for a number of years. Grammar Schools were seen as too exclusive. The majority of students who passed the 11+ exam and then entered a grammar school were predominantly from the middle class. A few students from what was defined as the 'working class' also passed but the majority failed and went to a Secondary Modern School.

The idea of two different types of school for different types of education might have been an acceptable concept but there was a huge stigma attached to failing the 11+ exam. Those who failed it were considered less able and less intelligent than those who had passed it.

An education at a Secondary Modern School was always considered of inferior value even when students went on to gain further qualifications and acquitted themselves well in the working world.

But now there was to be a great, innovative change that was meant to alter these divisive attitudes and their emphasis on class distinctions. New Comprehensive Schools which amalgamated both the Grammar Schools and the Secondary Modern Schools were to be created throughout England. All children would go to the same school which would eliminate some of the artificial barriers that separated them and fostered the idea of great differences between them.

Coming from the United States, such an idea was hardly considered a novel way of organising education as High Schools throughout the country, had been established, composed of all classes and all types of people. I did not anticipate any serious difficulties amongst the pupils arising from combining the two types of school. The students had already mixed together in the same schools at younger ages.

While waiting to pick up their young children from school, the mothers who gathered would inevitably start chatting with each other. It was evident that the controversial topic for discussion nearly every day revolved around the establishment of Comprehensive Schools.

Due to my not so conventional opinions, I am convinced that that they found me a bit odd and a serious misfit in their world. It is true that I stood alone, arguing the case in favour of establishing Comprehensive Schools. They informed me very politely that I didn't really understand what was at stake. I fear that the problem was that I understood only too well what was at stake.

I was truly shocked when I heard what they considered arguments in defence of maintaining the present educational arrangements. "You never know what kind of children they'll meet." "You can't mix all types of children together and expect everything to go well." "Not all children are intelligent, the slow ones will be pushed too hard. You will be instilling false hope, telling them that they can get much better grades."

These parents obviously desired to uphold the status quo. No-one mentioned the teachers' lower expectations of students in the Secondary Modern School or the fact that the classes were larger, and some facilities often had to be shared. Money for education was often lavished on the Grammar Schools at the expense of the Secondary Modern Schools.

I was arguing in favour of making the education system more equal for everyone but the people to whom I was talking had a different agenda. They were not concerned about injustice or inequality but only interested in clinging onto their exclusive and privileged position. The structure of Comprehensive Schools undermined their advantageous status and consequently, they were viewed as threatening institutions.

There was no rationale for the position they espoused as almost all of them had sent their children to state schools at the infant and primary level. They implied that children who were not middle class would possibly be undesirable associates for their children. Their children seemed to have survived in the classrooms with these children until the age of 11 without undue harm or detrimental influence. Had these children who had become undesirable, suddenly deteriorated in character, morality, or intelligence because they didn't pass a particular exam?

I should have carried on these conversations with the mothers at the other end of Loom Lane, the ones who lived in the council houses. They were in a position to recognise the advantages that such a school might offer. If everyone went to the same school, the mark of inferiority associated with attending a Secondary Modern School would be eliminated immediately and I assumed a broader curriculum would be offered to students whose choices had hitherto, been restricted.

QUEENS COMPREHENSIVE SCHOOL

Kim spent a very successful year at Bushey Grammar School. Once again, he was engaged in learning and loved the demanding tasks that new and difficult material presented. He was anticipating a second year of challenging learning at Bushey but the year of 1968-1969 was destined to be Kim's only year there.

In September of 1969, Bushey Grammar School, and the local Secondary Modern School combined to become Queens Comprehensive School.

I firmly believed that Comprehensive Schools would help to eliminate the class barriers that were so evident in English society and in their education system. I hoped that they would provide more educational opportunities for those students who had previously been unable to gain access to specific language, science, and maths courses. If children from all backgrounds and from different cultures worked and studied together in the same classroom, there might also be some hope of modifying and even maybe eradicating some of the long-held prejudices towards people who appeared different from the ones they were accustomed to meeting.

I had no idea of how this massive, new school amalgamation would take place. Bringing two such different types of school together with two very different kinds of curriculum was a very demanding task. I assumed that there would be problems initially, as the changes they were undertaking were of a groundbreaking nature, Kim, at first, found the physical setup of the new school very daunting. There were many buildings scattered over a large area and an underground pass to cross from one side of the road to the other to reach some of his classes. Many students were often lost and bewildered, asking each other for directions to the building they were hoping to find.

Kim's very first complaints, inevitably, revolved around the difficulties of learning to navigate his way to the correct classroom. But he was even more upset that all his classes were so noisy. He dutifully went to school every day, but I could see that he wasn't spending much time doing his homework, as he had at the Grammar School. He seemed to be doing a minimal amount of work or none at all. He didn't dislike any of his teachers but continually complained that his classrooms were chaotic.

Kim met up again with his friend, Edward Hawkins, who had gone to the Secondary Modern School. They had never lost touch with each other but now that they were attending the same school, they saw each other more frequently. Their main topic of conversation was how dreadful Queens Comprehensive School was and how none of the students were learning anything.

On the first Parents Report Evening, I set off for the school determined to discuss Kim's grievances and to ask the teachers what they were prepared to do to rectify the situation that he and, no doubt, many others were in.

As I went from one classroom to the next, I soon realised that all the teachers were relating a similar narrative. They were not used to dealing with such large classes. Nor were they accustomed to having so many unruly students in the classroom who continually disturbed everyone. They appeared to be doing their best but were totally overwhelmed and exhausted just trying to keep order.

Each one, in turn, had commented on how bright Kim was and expressed regret at not having time to work with the very bright students, due to the time taken up with the unruly ones. I had arrived feeling distressed that Kim was merely vegetating in school and left feeling no better, having had my worst fears confirmed by the teachers.

My anxiety about Kim did not dissipate but my rising annoyance with the teachers did begin to subside. They had been put in an impossible position, there should never have been such a large contingent of students in any class who obviously weren't interested in what was being taught. It takes only a very few disinterested students to spoil the class for everyone. I left feeling disheartened, not knowing what should be done but knowing that the classes had to be organised differently if any learning was to occur.

Kim remained at Queens Comprehensive School for the first year of its existence and it was another tumultuous, totally wasted year for him. He had once again tuned out of learning and found that going to school was a waste of time. I feared that he would one day state that he wasn't going to school ever again as he so rarely learned anything.

My hope had been that Queens would alter the composition of its classes once they discovered how disastrous the teaching had become. Sadly, no such change ever took place during that first year. Queens Comprehensive School had proved an enormous educational disappointment. For Kim's sake, I felt I had no choice but to remove him from the school.

Roger and I had arrived in England, determined to educate our children in the state school system. The girls were functioning very well despite two of them having had some initial problems with reading and ongoing problems with spelling. Kim's was a different story. Two of his four years at school had been totally useless and had nearly annihilated his enthusiasm for learning.

He had gone to the only state school available for someone of his age in the area in which we lived, and it had failed him. I was reluctant to consider leaving the state system for private education and was so resistant that a friend visiting us from the States, accused me of clinging to my principles about education without even considering Kim's education to be of at least equal importance.

The only reason I could consider private education was that money had been put into trust for the grandchildren so funds for education were available. I realised how fortunate I was to have this money available to pay for Kim's education.

Roger's cousins had told us of a very unusual school in Golder Green, the King Alfred School. When it was founded in 1898, it was considered very radical as it educated boys and girls together, in the same classrooms. They are an egalitarian and child-centered institution. Their purpose is to maximise the potential of every child and personal development is considered as important as academic success.

Understanding of the children's social responsibility towards others is considered an important aspect of their growth and maturity. The school's aim is to run its programme without excessive external discipline but to rely on the community's development of social justice and a sense of concern for the welfare of everyone.

These types of schools used to be called "progressive", but I note that this description is now no longer used. It is run on very similar principles to those of the Shady Hill School in Cambridge, Massachusetts where I completed my teacher training.

Roger and I made an appointment to view the school and meet the headmaster. As it so happened, this headmaster who had sustained the marvelous reputation of the school was retiring. We were introduced to the new headmistress, Nikki Archer, who was replacing him in September,1970. All our queries and points for further discussion were pursued and adequately answered.

Michèle had just finished junior school, so was ready to enter the Kind Alfred School also. They were required to take a test for entry into the school. It was an assessment of their abilities, to decide at what level to place them in the school. It was not an entrance exam which determined whether they were accepted or rejected by the school, according to their results.

The one main difficulty with their attending the King Alfred School was where it was situated. Golders Green was not easily accessible from Radlett. After studying the public transportation system in great detail, we decided that school travel would take them an inordinate amount of time. Roger drove them to Edgeware underground station, from where they could take a train to

Golders Green, and then walk up the hill to the school. Leda and Natasha also became pupils of King Alfred's when we move to Hampstead.

PS. It was unfortunate that Kim attended Queens Comprehensive School in the first year of its establishment before they had recognised the need for streaming the classes. Once they had commenced streaming, where pupils of the same ability are taught in the same group, discipline problems greatly diminished and both teaching and learning of a higher standard began to flourish.

SWEETS

As soon as the children had started school, they immediately developed a new and urgent demand, thinking that they needed sweets every day after school. At first, I could not understand the cause for this unprecedented behaviour, but I soon discovered that it was common practice for the other mothers to give their children a packet of sweets every day after school.

Up to this point in time, visits to the dentist and discussions about tooth decay had seemed effective measures for preventing the children from overindulging in sweets. But, faced with their friends and classmates rapturous joy and positive delight in consuming every kind of tempting sweet imaginable, it seemed a lost cause to implement any kind of rationale or reason into the situation.

Not only did I have to deal with the children imploring me to give in, I also had a few mothers who were not reluctant in expostulating their views on the subject. Why is it that when someone is not following common custom, it is so often perceived as a threat or a criticism? I did not and had not expressed any disapproval of the children who were eating sweets. I merely told my children that they would have a snack at home.

A few voices were heard above the chatter: "A few sweets after school won't hurt them." "Their teeth aren't about to drop out." "Are they ever allowed any treats?" The children were allowed sweets, but just not every day. I was surprised that my very neutral statement had produced such a defensive response.

The children returned home to a glass of juice and a bowl of fruit. As they were hungry, they enjoyed consuming a piece of fruit but still bitterly complained that they didn't have sweets like their friends.

I did not relinquish fruit as the children's afternoon snack, but the children continued to harass me for sweets. The mothers who disapproved of my stance became less vociferous but possibly more critical of my behaviour.

We paid our annual visit to the dentist who always said that he would be put out of business if there were any more families like us. No-one ever required any dental work to be done. Remember that I requested the dentist in Vermont to prescribe my children fluoride as there was no fluoride at all in the local water supply. I put the absence of fillings down to their taking one daily drop of fluoride while their teeth were still forming.

But fluoride cannot prevent all damage. On one annual check-up, the dentist called me to one side to inform me that he had detected eight miniscule dark dots on Natasha's teeth. It could be the beginning of tooth decay. He was convinced that she had been eating sweets. I was sure that they had all been eating more sweets than was good for them. Their friends were very generous and shared their treats with their very deprived schoolmates. The others had probably cleaned their teeth more thoroughly. Natasha's less energetic cleaning had most likely proved her downfall.

Children may not take note of our concerns and remonstrations on their behalf, even when it is best for them to do so. I always found this aspect of parenting very difficult because reason doesn't always work. They have to test some things for themselves. One can only hope that they don't land themselves in too many difficulties, and work on oneself not to become the over-critical parent.

RADLETT CONTINUED

Now that the three older children were in school and Leda was in a play group, for five days a week, I had three free hours available with no constraints of any sort. Unencumbered space and time had slowly disappeared as the unrelenting demands of child-rearing had overtaken my entire existence.

I had given no thought to the possibility of having time for myself and was hoping not to fritter it away performing household chores. Hadn't we just purchased a huge house which would require an inordinate amount of cleaning? My overwhelming fear was that I would resort to my mother's very high standards of cleanliness which, given the size of our house, would consume all of my free time.

I organised weekly jobs for the children, and they were required to clean their bedrooms and change their beds on the weekends. But no amount of organisation could keep up with the amount of work the house required to maintain it in reasonable order.

We were all delighted with our new house which provided us with our very first dishwasher. It was ancient, sealed into a corner of the kitchen and could not be moved. Its presence meant that arguments about whose turn it was to wash or dry the dishes ceased to exist, except, of course, for the dreaded dirty pots and pans.

Roger was always adamant that we should never hire anyone to do the housework or gardening. The strength of his feelings, undoubtedly, related to his childhood memories, always surrounded by numerous servants, nannies, several levels of maids, cleaners, cooks, washerwomen, gardeners, odd-job men and chauffeurs. I don't know if his father ever had a butler or a valet, but it was the custom at the time to do so. He had seen servants treated without due respect and felt that their position was inevitably, considered an inferior one, especially by the people who hired them. For him, hiring anyone was tantamount to continuing a very degrading form of class exploitation.

As he considered the whole idea of cleanliness irrelevant to anyone's existence and an unnecessary occupation that no-one need undertake, he could not take on board my concern for some order and a reasonable level of hygiene. I had expressed my desire to hire a cleaner, but he was so opposed to the idea that there was no room for discussion.

The situation remained at a standstill until one Monday morning. the kitchen doorbell rang unexpectedly. (No-one ever rang the kitchen doorbell. It was the bell that had been used for the servants' entrance.) As I opened the kitchen door, I saw a small, white-haired woman whose face was composed of myriad wrinkles and very prominent cheekbones.

Despite her worn, somewhat exhausted appearance, her blue eyes sparkled as she spoke. As she introduced herself, her demeanour reflected a person of some self-assurance and even pride.

She explained that she was looking for a cleaning job and that her name was Mrs. Arthur. I could hardly believe my good luck! I ushered her into the kitchen. She stopped and looked round. "Nothing's changed here except the colour of the paint." I was perplexed. Waiting for an explanation, I led her to the hall. She then stated that she was very fond of this house. She was fifteen when she came to work here. It was her first cleaning job. If I desired to see a picture of her working here in her hat and apron which she was required to wear, she could bring it to me at any time.

She glanced down quickly at the hall floor, saying that it could do with a good waxing. That was a job she really enjoyed doing. I have to admit that it was a job that I never, ever considered doing.

She and her husband often worked together. She did the cleaning and he worked as a gardener. Would I be interested in hiring them? They hadn't found any suitable jobs recently so were worried about piling up debts.

The grass badly needed mowing and the roses that our neighbour had planted had been very seriously neglected. I suddenly thought that Mr. Arthur might rectify this situation, particularly as the neighbour who had planted the roses loved them and liked to visit to see how well they were faring.

After discussing their fees, the National Insurance required and which day they wanted to work, I hired them on the spot. My next duty was to convince Roger that hiring two people to work for us was not an act which furthered oppression and injustice.

I explained that Mrs. Arthur had actually come to our house asking for a job. She and her husband were in debt and badly needed work to sustain themselves. As they had not acquired a high level of education, their choice of work was obviously very limited.

As it turned out, Mr. Arthur had grown up in a remote village in Wales and had rarely attended school. He could neither read nor write. I emphasised the fact that we would be paying them a reasonable salary and would certainly not be maltreating them.

His stance was very reserved about the idea of hired help but he made no remonstrations about their working on the premises.

With the advent of the Arthurs, all my worries about drowning in household and gardening chores completely disappeared.

Just as I was beginning to bask in the idea of having five free mornings a week, I received a phone call from the children's school. It was Mr. Reeves, the headmaster, saying that he'd like to see me urgently. My heart sank. Which one of the children had done something really dreadful?

I pleaded with him to tell me what the problem was. He finally reassured me that there was nothing to worry about, but he would like to speak to me in his office.

Walking to the school, I slowly unwound but remained curious as to what was the purpose of my visit. When I arrived, he explained that one of the teacher's had been ill for two months and he had found no suitable permanent substitute. He required someone who could take the post immediately.

I enquired about why he had rung me. He was so desperate that he'd asked in all the classrooms if any of the students knew anyone who was a teacher. Apparently, one hand was raised in three different classrooms and the three children all named the same person as a teacher, their mother, "You, Mrs. Franklin." Would you consider working as a teacher in your children's school? This unexpected offer to teach completely shocked me.

I was delighted but also surprised that he hadn't asked me about my credentials, and he didn't know whether or not I was a competent teacher. I was convinced that these omissions were a sign of his desperation to fill the post and that he would enquire about these matters at a later date.

The idea of teaching again was very appealing but, as I told Mr. Reeves, I had one major problem, my youngest child was in a play group which lasted for only three hours every morning.

I would have to find someone to pick her up and stay with her until I arrived home from teaching. I told him that I would consider taking up the post, but only if I found a suitable carer for Leda.

My first port of call was Roger. As he wasn't working outside of the home but remained in his study writing every day, I thought he might agree to look after Leda from 12 to 3:30 for five afternoons a week. Sadly, I received a definite no for an answer. He didn't feel that he could spare the time from his writing to start baby-sitting. With the help of my neighbour, Diane Charles, I tried ringing various likely people to take on this task, but all to no avail.

I realised that I had been looking forward to working again. I had thought that I would enjoy the challenge of returning to teaching. But I was finally forced to inform Mr. Reeves that I couldn't accept his very generous offer. We were both very disappointed.

Instead, at Mr. Reeves's request, every morning I tutored a six year old Chinese boy who could speak no English. It was a demanding task, requiring imagination and a bit of ingenuity on my part. There were no textbooks available to assist me. Despite what, at first, appeared to be insurmountable difficulties, Yeu Fat continued to make considerable progress in communication throughout the year.

This brief excursion into teaching and working as a volunteer for the Girl Guides as White Owl were the only two jobs that I undertook while we lived in Radlett.

Given my family circumstances, I was forced to accept that permanent work would have to be deferred to a later date.

RADLETT – RELATIVES

Once in Radlett, we continued to visit Roger's father, Cyril, and Dorothy in Hampstead but it was a much briefer drive to reach them. Moving to Radlett had definitely proved advantageous as far as seeing relatives was concerned.

We were now in contact with Roger's cousin Diana Holliday, her husband, Robin, and their family. Our four children had an opportunity to become acquainted with their four second cousins.

My sister-in-law, Frances, who was married to Roger's younger brother, Joe, introduced me to her excellent hairdresser on Cork Street. Although my visits were infrequent, I always received very good advice on haircuts and styling.

Frances also accompanied me to Liberty's Department Store where there was an American designer, Bonnie Cashin, whose clothes were on display in the women's department. Unaccustomed as I was to buying anything out of the ordinary, I had always thought that designer clothes were not for me, especially, as the prices were so exorbitant.

I tried on various articles of clothing. They all fitted well, the dresses hung loosely over my curves and even flattered my figure. As I realised how attractive these clothes were and how well they suited me, my inhibitions about buying designer clothes were found to be ever so slowly diminishing. I, finally, succumbed and purchased two very simple, classically designed dresses. I justified the cost on the grounds that they would last for many years, and I was not mistaken in this assumption. Not knowing London at all, I was very grateful to Frances for acquainting me with what were new aspects of this yet to be explored city.

Frances was also a superb cook. The very first family parties that I attended were arranged by her with delectable food and drinks and often a cake or dessert that she had made herself.

It just so happened that both my sisters-in law were excellent cooks and party organisers. Sonja, who was married to Owen, Roger's youngest brother, came from Yugoslavia. Through Sonja, we learned about Balkan cuisine: zakuska, an hors d'oeuvre made of apple , onions and herring; gibanica, a spinach and cheese flaky pastry pie; and pasulj, a white bean soup made with ham hock; many other tasty dishes and of course, Turkish coffee.

Frances and Sonja always arranged all large family parties. As I had no live-in help at home, I didn't feel that I could cope with taking on such grand occasions.

My contribution to caring for Franklin relatives consisted of taking Cyril and Dorothy on weekend outings with our family and providing an annual Christmas dinner for them and their relatives.

✳ ✳ ✳

The first year that we lived in Radlett, Sonja, Owen and their two children visited us often on Sunday afternoons. After lunch, the children would entertain us with lively, unrehearsed puppet shows.

I had made a standing structure with three pieces of plywood and some hinges. It had an open window in the middle panel that served as the puppets stage. The children also used it as a house, a shop, a garage, a space for conversations with very unusual creatures who came to visit or were just passing by: lions, tigers, bears, hens, chickens, cats, mice, giants and very small people. But it was most of all, a refuge, a place to hide from all adults, especially when it was time to depart for home.

Sonja and I discussed at length how we felt as foreigners in a new country. It was the difference in temperament between the Yugoslavs and the English that she found so surprising. She was accustomed to gregarious, extroverted people who state their opinions openly and generally welcomed strangers. She found English reticence and their resistance to making contact with persons unknown, perplexing and somewhat incomprehensible.

My reactions were similar to hers, but I felt that I had a slight advantage as I had grown up in New England, a part of the States which is known to be more reserved in behaviour than in other parts of the country, particularly the South or the Midwest.

New Englanders, especially middle class people, have been accused of being cold and aloof as they tend to keep their distance and do not rush into establishing new relationships. As a bona fide New Englander from Cambridge, Massachusetts, I was not assuming that I would make new friends right away.

In addition, having grown up with racial prejudice, I had learned that not everyone desired to be your friend. So, through conditioning and experience, I suspect that my expectations about what social contacts might ensue were somewhat lower than Sonja's.

We need not have worried. In time, we both established very rewarding relationships with English people.

And without doubt, my adjustment to England was facilitated by the consideration and useful information extended to me by Roger's relatives.

AN ADDENDUM TO THE LAST CHAPTER ON RELATIVES—CHRISTMAS DINNER

Every year, I found the month of December a frantically busy time, trying to prepare everything for the coming Christmas season.

We three sisters-in-law did not exchange Christmas presents. We were all too busy arranging Christmas celebrations for our families, Sonja's family from Yugoslavia and Frances's from the English countryside.

There was also a Christmas party for the children. Initially, I found the idea appealing as there was no family occasion when all the children could meet and become acquainted.

My Christmas preparations always began by making the Christmas fruit cake a month before it was ready to be consumed. My second task was to remember to pour spoonfuls of brandy over it to keep it moist throughout the entire month.

Christmas shopping was an unrelenting chore, buying presents for Roger and the four children, Roger's family, my family in the States and the numerous cousins who attended the family Christmas party.

Roger always bought the Christmas tree as he was the only one who could manoeuvre it into the car or tie it on the car roof properly. Roger preferred to abstain from the preparations for the holiday season and could be heard continually repeating his mantra for this time of year, "Christmas is humbug", "Christmas is humbug."

For the festive season, the children and I baked a variety of special biscuits. Their favourite was the one to hang on the Christmas tree, made into different Christmas shapes and decorated with hundreds and thousands. They helped to make pies, crystallised orange peel, nut balls and many other Christmas nibbles. My first attempt at making Christmas pudding turned out to be such a disaster that I never tried again. From the time of that highly unsuccessful experience, I resolved that I would always buy the Christmas pudding.

As soon as Roger had set up the Christmas tree, we all began adding the shiny glass balls, the string of tiny lights that flickered on and off, the tiny bells, balls, stars, reindeer, sugar canes, tinsel, the home-made biscuits, and chocolates to hang on the branches and last of all, the angel for the very top.

For Christmas dinner, the children helped to prepare the vegetable and set the table. Having stayed up late on Christmas eve to put the presents under the tree, I wanted a lie-in on Christmas morning, but that never happened.

The large turkey I had bought always had to be put into the oven early in order to be ready for Christmas dinner.

While we were still asleep, the children opened their stockings. We could hear the shrieks of surprise and delight upstairs.

After breakfast, everyone rushed to the sitting room to open their presents. Once all the excitement of finding and unwrapping their new gifts had subsided, I began the preparations for the Christmas meal. It was usually about this time that the mayhem around the family's arrival began. It was always the same.

There would be a desperate phone call from Cyril who wanted to speak to me urgently. "I can't bring Madge (his older sister). You know she has arthritis and can't move very well. Her walking is difficult, and she can't lift her leg high enough to get into the Bentley"

I responded: "Cyril, I saw Madge a few days ago. She was moving quite well. I'm sure she can manage the Bentley if you give her a hand get in."

An adamant reply followed, "No, No. she just won't be able to come."

It was a well-known fact that Cyril and his sister, Marjorie, had maintained an ongoing antipathy towards each other for many years. I never knew the origins of this animosity but had the impression that it had persisted since childhood.

I knew that Madge was capable of getting into his car. Cyril just didn't want to bring her. Trying to appeal to his sympathetic side, I said, "She never gets out to meet people. She sits alone in her house all day, only speaking to the housekeeper occasionally. This would be an opportunity for her to, at least, speak with some members of the family"

Nothing would budge him. He absolutely refused to pick her up.

"Alright Cyril," I said. "If you won't bring her, then I will. I'll stop cooking the Christmas dinner, drive to Hampstead to pick up Madge and return to Radlett to start the Christmas dinner again. The dinner will be delayed by two hours so don't bring anyone until 3-3:30 is probably better.

"No, no, Roger cannot pick her up and if he does, we will still have to wait for him to return to start the dinner. That won't save any time."

"She is only a ten-minute drive from your house"

A long pause ensued. After many sighs and deep breaths, he spoke. "Alright, alright, I'll pick her up but if she has an accident, I am not responsible".

"Thank you, Cyril. Now I can continue cooking the Christmas dinner."

In due course, Cyril arrived with Dorothy, Connie, and Madge. All the children rushed out to greet them. It was a bitterly cold winter's day. Cyril had brought Madge, but he was sitting in the driver's seat waiting for someone else to help her out of the car.

Roger approached to help Madge. As he moved closer to her door, she started protesting in a very loud voice that she could get out of the car by herself. She didn't need any help.

After readjusting her legs and picking up her cane, she emerged from the car and stepped onto the frozen, slippery ice. She stood momentarily with both hands leaning on her cane. I looked down and was shocked to see that she was wearing no shoes.

Madge had a reputation for being eccentric in her behaviour and I feared this time that she had gone too far this time. But she insisted that that she had good reason for arriving nearly barefoot. Her feet had swollen, and she could wear neither her shoes nor her slippers. I suggested that the housekeeper could buy her both slippers and shoes in a larger size. She would have none of it. She wasn't considering buying anything. She was perfectly fine at home, walking in her bare feet. I enquired as to whether or not she'd visited the doctor to tell him that her feet were swollen. "I'm on the pills he gave a few months ago." That response meant no and I'm not planning to visit my doctor. Another Franklin, I thought, very reluctant to see the doctor about anything. Roger was the same. Maybe it was a family trait. The only time Roger had seen a doctor was a year ago, when we lived in Great Missenden. I had called him because Roger had gone to bed, so ill with mumps, that, for once, he didn't resist the idea of a doctor's visit.

Madge was a tall, overweight woman who was totally reliant on her cane for walking. She was fiercely independent and wanted no assistance from anyone. With each faltering step that she took, my anxiety level rose and then increased as I watched her cane slip from side to side on the uneven surface of the ice.

It was best not to try to help Madge, as offers of support only enraged and distracted her. Once upset, she could lose all concentration on her walking and I feared, might fall. I could be seen walking cautiously behind her, trying to prepare for a possible, sudden tumble, in which direction I couldn't tell. Not wanting to divert her attention, we all said nothing and stood in total silence, our eyes glued to Madge's walking stick and her unstable steps. When she stopped quite near the house, we all started to breathe normally again and uttered great sighs of relief.

It was a miraculous, perilous journey that she had made from the car to our kitchen door, but she did succeed, despite wobbly legs and an unsteady cane. She did allow Roger to help her over the threshold of our kitchen as the step actually was too high for her to reach.

Due to Madge's trepidatious entry, the meal had been delayed so everyone was more than ready to commence the Christmas meal.

Connie, Dorothy's half-sister, was now living with Cyril and Dorothy. She had always been of a nervous disposition and had never been able to work full-time. She was always very quiet and rarely spoke unless asked a question directly.

As soon as Connie had raised her wine glass and started to have a sip, Cyril would dramatically interrupt, telling her that she was drinking too quickly and then, proclaim loudly, "Be careful not to spill the wine". When she started to eat, there would be another outburst from Cyril. "You shouldn't gulp down your food and remember that you should have only one glass of wine."

At this point, I would often interrupt to tell Cyril that Connie was fine. "Just let her eat her meal." My intervention made little difference as he would always find something else to criticise. I often thought that Cyril's continuous diatribes were more than enough to turn anyone into a nervous wreck.

Madge would often tell us about amusing incidents that had occurred during her childhood and, inevitably, Cyril would correct her, saying, she was wrong. "It wasn't like that." This would incense Madge who would then screech that he was too young to remember. Cyril would then shake his head and yell that she was losing her memory. Madge, in a furious temper, would turn her head away from Cyril and say no more as if to indicate that this argument had ended.

I was always left in a state of shock and surprise that adults could behave in such an outrageous manner. I worried about what kind of example they were setting for the children.

Unbelievably, the children informed me that they don't remember any of these incidents that I found so disturbing. Being so engrossed in their own fun and games at the other end of the table, they paid no attention to what was happening with the adults. It is probably true that I was the only adult in the room to be so distressed by all the criticism and the angry exchanges.

All the other adults present had experienced this kind of behaviour before. I had never seen any adults conduct themselves in such an infantile manner and I did find it truly unnerving. It was as if the normal parameters of human behaviour had disappeared, and I didn't know what to expect next.

Roger, who had grown up hearing these unpleasant family interactions had long ago learned to blank himself off from the turmoil and seemed to become totally deaf to the ongoing situation exploding right next to him. I, suddenly, had a clue as to why it was impossible to engage him in any kind of discussion when things weren't going well between us.

It took me a long time to realise that, due to his background, he had learned how to avoid and escape problems but, sadly, not how to solve them.

We ended the meal with Christmas pudding, and then retreated to the sitting room for chocolate, nibbles, and further drinks while Roger's family opened their Christmas presents.

After having a sufficiency of food and drink, and packing away their new gifts, everyone would prepare to go home. There was always a jolly round of thank yous for Roger and me.

As everyone entered the Bentley and took their seats, to my surprise, not a word was spoken. There was an uneasy pall of rancour that hung over them all. Dorothy was angry with Cyril for upsetting Connie who, having endured Cyril's criticism, might now be in an anxious state. Connie sat quietly in one corner of the car, feeling distressed but had no desire to speak. Madge and Cyril were seething, determinedly clinging onto their anger, refusing to relinquish their fury towards each other.

Our wonderful family Christmas had ended with four angry people, sitting side by side, unwilling and unable to communicate with each other, driving home to leafy Hampstead in sullen silence.

PARTIES

When we lived in Radlett, everyone seemed to remember that we had three very memorable parties.

THE FIRST PARTY

Our first large party was planned for Natasha and Leda. While we were living in Great Missenden, Roger and I had started house-hunting rather intensively, hoping to move closer to Roger's relatives in London. As a result, I had no time to plan birthday parties for my two youngest children, hence the arrangement for a shared birthday celebration a year later.

As so many children were invited (at least 25), the party preparations took many days to complete. The children helped with everything, making the birthday cake, the sandwiches, and the jellies, blowing up balloons, wrapping presents and setting the table.

As each child arrived, he or she had to guess how many smarties there were in a jar. After everyone had assembled, they went on a lollipop hunt around the garden.

Everyone then made a huge circle to play 'A Ticket a tasket', and 'Here we go round the mulberry bush'.

We then moved to musical chairs and pin the tail on the donkey. The activities which followed were more energetic, the egg and spoon race, the one-legged race and the last, a tug of war.

Upon hearing that the refreshments were ready, they rushed into the dining room to find a seat. Sandwiches, juice, and crisps seemed to vanish before our eyes. I was very grateful to the children for having helped to prepare enough food to provide a reserve supply. After the dramatic moment when Natasha and Leda blew out the candles on their cake together, we ended the refreshments with slices of cake, jellies, and ice-cream.

It was now time to go outside again, this time, to break the pinata. Ours was not the typical Mexican pinata, made of brightly decorated ceramic material.

It was constructed of two very thick, large, brown paper bags acquired from the super-market, one carefully placed inside the other. On the outside, Michèle had painted a variety of beautiful animals in many different colours.

The children and I had spent ages wrapping up small packets of sweets to place inside the pinata. When it was full, we tied a string securely around the end to close it. We then tied a rope around the securely tied end to hang it on the branch of a tree in the garden.

An adult would be responsible for slowly moving the pinata up and down on the branch of the tree. Each child had been given a stick with which to hit the pinata as it moved close to where they were standing. There would be deafening shrieks and yells as the distance grew shorter and shorter between the pinata and the children. Sometimes they were able to bash it with great ferocity, creating a small tear in its side and at other times, the adult would move it tantalisingly close and then pull it sharply away.

The torment and teasing continued until the pinata was so damaged by heavy blows that it discharged all of its contents, in every direction imaginable, on the ground below. Turmoil, chaos, confusion, mayhem, all of these words could have described the scene that ensued. Everyone made a sudden, frantic dash to pick up as many sweet packets as possible.

With great determination, one boy literally threw himself on the ground, claiming that everything underneath him was his and his alone. I re-explained the rules of the game, discussed the meaning of sharing and what was fair for everyone. I was pleading to deaf ears. It was his booty and far too precious to relinquish under the influence of either persuasion or reason.

Faced with this wall of rigid resistance, I panicked. I was supposed to be supervising a party for 30 children (counting my family and one of the children's friends). Spending all of my time with one, uncooperative, recalcitrant child was an irresponsible act. "What should I do?" I bribed him. If he would get up, he could have two fistfuls of sweet packets, as much as he could carry in his two hands. The vision of having so many sweets in his possession in a few seconds, slowly overcame his obstinacy. He turned over and grabbed everything in close proximity. His two fistfuls were brimming over but, at least, others now had a chance to gather some of the great haul that he had claimed.

Everyone else, thank goodness, was behaving as expected, running around and joining in the mad scramble to scoop up as many sweet packets as possible.

In the midst of the tumult and confusion, the parents began to arrive to pick up their children. They stood perplexed, not knowing what to make of the wild scene being enacted in front of them. While they waited, they were offered juices or even a beer, if they so desired, while I explained the rules related to breaking the pinata.

Order was restored, but only when all of the sweets had completely disappeared, and I lined them up to receive their party bags before going home.

Later, parents occasionally stopped me in the street to tell me what a lovely party it had been and how much the children had enjoyed it. Others thought the party bags were wonderful as they contained so many useful items: super-bouncy balls, notebooks, crayons, coloured pencils , whistles and rubbers. From these unexpected reactions, I concluded that, for most of the participants, the joint party celebration must have been a reasonable success.

THE SECOND PARTY

The second gathering that we arranged was a party for teenagers. The children's cousin, Rodney, wanted to have a party but his parents, Joe and Francis, didn't think their house was suitable for this purpose.

Between their dining room and sitting room, stood a beautiful glass cabinet, filled with precious objects that I'm sure was of great concern. It housed Joe's grandfather's collection of Chinese porcelain which included some pieces reputed to have come from the Ming dynasty.

Francis asked if we would consider having a party at our house. I thought that the idea of a party might appeal to my teenage children. If the teenage cousins invited their friends, there would be more than enough people to have a really enjoyable evening.

I agreed that our house was more suitable as it did not contain many objects of great value. We owned only one very expensive piece of art. Papa's sculpture, (Naum Gabo's) wedding present to us. We could easily pack that away as we did whenever we went on holiday.

The day for the party arrived. We were all busy buying all sorts of nibbles, crisps, nuts, potato sticks etc., soft drinks and beer. My children always complained that there was no real food at the parties they had attended, only snacks. The boys quickly drank the beer and became inebriated, so the rest of the evening wasn't much fun. In an attempt to avoid this situation, we prepared some more substantial snacks for them to eat.

To make room for dancing, we cleared the sitting room of unnecessary furniture and left the refectory table free for refreshments. Rugs were removed from the large entry hall to make sure there was enough space for everyone.

I, naively, thought that that we were now almost prepared for the party. In the afternoon, I received a phone call from Rodney. He and his friends would be arriving with the equipment.

A number of miscellaneous items appeared and were carried into the hall. I use the word miscellaneous as I could not then and cannot now, attach a name or a purpose to most of the items that were on display. I am informed that there was a synthesizer and other pieces of electrical equipment which mimicked the sounds of various musical instruments. I recognised only the loudspeakers. When spread out, the musical paraphernalia seemed to occupy a huge amount of space in the area that I had just cleared for dancing. I was obviously totally unaware of what the real priorities for parties were.

For some time, there was much testing of sound and volume, reporting back and further testing until some agreed level of sound and quality of sound was found acceptable to everyone.

And then, there was an unexpected period of relief and silence before the guests began to arrive. When the music started to play, Joe and Frances, and Roger and I seated ourselves behind closed doors in the kitchen, not far from the hall and sitting room.

Having read in the news and seen on the TV, the disastrous outcomes of recent teenage parties where the much of the property was demolished and houses were left in total disarray, we were determined to behave like responsible parents. We remained at our posts, to make sure that nothing untoward happened, to prevent the party from becoming too wild, out of order or completely uncontrollable.

When the party was in full swing, food and drink were fast disappearing. There were urgent requests for more of both. Lots of noise, loud conversations, occasional singing, and lots of dancing, everyone seemed to be having a good time. But in the kitchen, we, literally, shuddered as the base beat from the sitting room was so consistent and so loud that we couldn't hear ourselves speak.

Requests were made to lower the sound and brief. intermittent attempts to comply were made, but within seconds, the volume always returned to its excruciatingly loud level. They all appeared unnerved and unable to function unless the decibels were at a deafening level.

I went outside to get a breath of fresh air only to discover that both sides of the road were lined with policemen. The neighbours must have complained about the unexpected and unwanted level of noise that had been thrust upon them. I didn't blame them. If I had known what teenage parties were like, I would have warned them myself. But my frames of reference were seriously out of date. As teenagers, we danced to records on record players. Who, in this generation, had even heard of such ancient and quaint contraptions?

As I explained to the policemen, we were hosting a teenage party that would not be going on throughout the night. Their faces remained unresponsive, and they only nodded as if they had understood what I had said. I had expected, at least, a complaint about the noise, but nothing at all was said about this matter.

Eventually, during the wee hours of the morning, the teenagers began to slowly depart in various cars and taxis that were hastily called. We were all greatly relieved when the music suddenly stopped. The teenagers disappeared completely and just as quickly, the policemen relinquished their posts.

For the next few days, I waited, warily, for the neighbours' complaints to arrive but, being English, they remained reticent and never expressed any irritation or annoyance to me directly. So, I was never in a position to explain or apologise for that evening's disruption to their lives.

I leave it to your imagination to consider what diatribes had actually attacked the perpetrators of the heinous act which had so disturbed the accustomed calm and tranquillity of their neighbourhood.

I assumed that our reputation was now in tatters but there was no way of rectifying it, so we would just have to live with the consequences of our unintended misdemeanours.

THE THIRD PARTY

The last party was inspired by a friend who was visiting us from Tonga.

Tonga is one of the Polynesian Islands in the Pacific Ocean. In 1900, the King of Tonga established a treaty to control foreign affairs with the British. The British, in return, were to protect the island from predators.

In 1970, its role as a British Protectorate ended under arrangements made by Queen Salote. It had always maintained its monarchy and its sovereignty and was never a British Colony.

In the early 1960's. Langy, from Tonga, had arrived as a new student at the Putney School in Vermont where Roger was teaching. He now had many qualifications and was soon to hold an official post in the Tongan government. We were pleased that, in his very busy travels, he had taken the time to visit us.

Langy met Sonja, Owen, and their children at one of our very lively Sunday lunches. While casually discussing local customs, Langy and Sonja discovered that, in their respective countries, pigs were cooked in exactly the same way, out of doors over an open fire.

In great excitement, we all decided to have a party the following Sunday, cooking a freshly roasted pig. In preparation, Sonja ordered a suckling pig from her Greek butcher. Langy's preparations were slightly more energetic and took place on the day of the party. He pruned some of the larger branches from trees in our garden and whittled them into shape, creating a stand with Y-shaped legs. He then pushed the spit, made from another tree branch, through the pig and rested it on the stand. The children helped to gather kindling to start the fire and keep it going while an adult was always available to check that the fire was large enough for roasting.

To the surprise of our guests, Langy was performing all of these tasks in his bare feet. When he was a teenager, he became a student in the USA and felt obliged to wear shoes for the first time in his life. He always complained that his feet felt permanently constrained in them. Given the opportunity to relax and revert to his more traditional ways, he was relieved to be walking without the restraint of shoes.

My children remember that he had, what seemed to them, large feet. It was a fact that Langy's feet were not small. He had experienced great difficulty in finding his size 14 shoes. But now that my children have a cousin who wears size 15 shoes, Langy no longer appears to be so unique.

For the party, Sonja and I invited numerous friends and relatives to celebrate this unusual event, with specific instructions not to come too early as it took nearly half a day to roast the pig.

I provided a large variety of hors d'oeuvres and drinks of all sorts while the pig was being roasted. Everyone shared the job of turning the spit and we left it to Langy and Sonja to tell us when the pig was finally cooked.

I provided a table full of salads, breads, vegetables, sauces for the roasted pig, drinks, and desserts.

Everyone, almost without exception, remarked on how tender the meat was and requested more. As the sun shone brightly all day with a very light breeze to cool the air, everyone relaxed and seemed to have no desire to leave.

Eventually, when darkness fell, the party slowly moved to our sitting room where everyone began spontaneously dancing. Langy then proceeded to teach us a song in his native tongue. In the wee hours of the morning, those of us who remained could be heard loudly singing in a language we'd never heard and with words not understood, but how delighted and happy we all were to do so.

A VISIT TO THE ZOO

Michèle had a particularly good friend who lived at the other end of Loom Lane, in one of the council houses. Lynette was a delightful little girl who enjoyed engaging in lively conversation with everyone in contrast to her five brothers who spoke only a few words briefly and infrequently.

Her mother was also talkative and very outgoing while her father was more aloof, although he did engage in conversation occasionally. Despite the fact that he was totally blind, he supported his entire family by making recordings for radio programmes.

Lynette came to play with Michèle sometimes after school, but mainly on weekends.

Whenever children from the council houses visited us, comments were always made about what a large house we had. My children, if they were invited for a return visit, would also remark on the fact that some of their friends lived in small houses.

I noted that the children's comments were appropriate observations and not value-laden in any way, though I did have to tell my children not to make comments to their friend's families about how small their houses were as it might be interpreted as judgemental.

Lynette's father did not fall into this non value-laden assessment of either houses or people. He was very impressed that I had invited Lynette to our house and informed me that the people at our end of the road didn't associate with the people in council houses.

I was aware that a class system existed in England but was shocked to have its consequences so clearly articulated before me. I was pleased that Michèle and Lynette's friendship was based on the magnetism of two lively personalities and interest in common and was, in no way, related to any kind of assessment of social hierarchy.

Having heard our family in lively conversation many times, Lynette's father asked if he could take the children to visit Graham Dangerfield's zoo. He wanted to record their spontaneous reactions when they first saw his impressive collection of wild animals.

In the 1960's Graham Dangerfield was a naturalist, an author, and a BBC broadcaster. He had established a private zoo for rescued animals in Wheathampstead, Hertfordshire.

When the day came for them to visit the zoo, Lynette's father and her brother arrived with Lynette and a small, white van full of recording equipment. They did somehow manage to find places for four more children inside and with great aplomb. They all set off for the journey.

It was nearly five hours later that everyone returned to Loom Lane. As soon as the van stopped, the children leapt out, each in quick succession, everyone eager to relate their wonderful experiences. In their urgency to convey what they had seen, they all began talking at once.

Lynette's father stepped out of the van and stood silently for a few moments, saying not a word. "Just listening, just listening," he said. I couldn't understand what had so captured his attention. He finally attempted to speak but his voice was drowned out by the sound of children's voices, all trying to describe the scenes at the zoo. In despair, he turned in my direction, saying, "That was my programme. That was what I wanted to record at the zoo."

I did wonder why he hadn't recorded what he had wanted at the zoo, particularly when his son would have set up all the proper equipment for him to do so.

He continued to focus intently on what the children were saying, almost as if bemoaning his fate. He could hear the children talking only a few feet from where he was standing but he was no longer in a position to record them.

He then explained that when the children first saw the animals, they became very excited and ran as fast as they could to greet them. But, as they drew closer to the cages and enclosures, their responses altered from loud and noisy anticipation to sounds that were nearly inaudible to the human ear.

They stopped and stared. It was as if they were mesmerised. They began whispering to each other, commenting on the unusual qualities of one creature and the inexplicable behaviour of another. So constrained were their responses that no sounds that were uttered would register on his instruments. It was pointless to try recording under these circumstances.

I could only imagine why the children had reacted as they did. They had already seen wild animals at London's Regent Park Zoo but were always surrounded by crowds of noisy children and adults. At this small zoo, they could observe the animals at much closer proximity without undue noise and distraction. On display were a motley collection of wildlife: stags, deer, otters, an orphaned seal, foxes, a lynx, cats, different kinds of birds, a gull, a macaw, and barn owls.

Watching the behaviour and antics of the animals in front of them must have been a fascinating experience. They were probably in awe of a situation with which they were completely unacquainted. Their initial boisterous clamour was reduced to feelings of sincere admiration and quiet wonder at the scenes being enacted before them. Without deliberation, the children had quietly and inconspicuously relinquished the excited and noisy reactions of their own everyday life to immerse themselves in the mysterious world of the animals.

When their allotted time with the animals had ended, the children started their short walk back to the white van. Now was the moment to capture their responses to what they had just experienced. Each child was asked to speak into the hand-held microphone to describe what they had seen. Still engrossed in the impressions of their very recent experiences, they were startled by the request and disturbed at the sight of a long black object being thrust in their faces. In a state of bewilderment, they froze, stared blankly at the microphone, took a deep breath, and said absolutely nothing. The more they were cajoled to speak, the more resistant they became.

More accustomed to the use of the microphone, Lynette spoke at length about her reactions to seeing wild animals. Michèle remembered feeling very relieved because now her father would have the recording he wanted so much and would stop insisting that she had to speak.

Lynette's father had taken the time and trouble to organise himself, his son, Lynette and all his equipment to drive four more children all the way to Wheathampstead in Hertfordshire. As the town is north of Watford, it was a lengthy ride and very noisy, surrounded by five incessantly chattering children.

I could commiserate with him, considering the time and effort involved in trying to create this unusual, unrehearsed project. But what he hadn't taken into account was the fact that children cannot be commissioned to perform spontaneously.

If only he had listened, just listened and waited for the moment when the children were bursting to relate their experiences to anyone who would listen, without exerting any strain or effort, he would have captured the programme he desired so much to record.

TRANSITION TO LIVING IN ENGLAND

When we decided to move to England, I had no worries or fears about settling down in a different country. After all, Roger and I had often visited England during the summer holidays. Due to our many visits to the Franklin family, I thought I had become familiar with the customs and traditions of English society.

But I hadn't realised that differences which seemed unusual or inconsequential became requisite observations on more prolonged visits. What I believed would be an easy transition to English life, proved, upon analysis, to be a more complex and time-consuming endeavour than I had, at first, anticipated.

DIFFERENT SIZES

All clothing and shoe sizes for adults were smaller than in the United States. Children's shoe sizes no longer came in widths. Girls' shoes were not made in larger sizes. One of Michèle's friends wore boys' shoes. She was only 12 but complained that English shops did not recognise the length or width of her feet as either normal or feminine.

ENGLISH NAMES

Common names of things had changed. Sneakers were now plimsolls. Girls' underpants were knickers. Men's pants were trousers. All candies were sweets. Cookies became biscuits.

SPELLING

Spelling changed. Aluminum became aluminium. Many words ending in or now had a u inserted before the r. (i.e.) behavior and demeanor. became behaviour and demeanour

THE GROUND FLOOR

The first floor of any building was labelled the ground floor. It took many bewildered minutes of wandering in shops on the first floor to realise that I had pressed the wrong button and could not exit the shop at this level.

WRITING CHEQUES

Dates were written with the day of the month first. The month and the year followed. In the USA, the month preceded the day and the year, a very minor point. But consider the consequences of writing a cheque for

3-11-1968 when it was really due on 11-3-1968. Many angry demands would be made for a payment eight months late and your credit rating would be ruined.

MEASUREMENTS AND TEMPERATURE

In the USA, degrees Fahrenheit were used to measure temperature for climate and for cooking. With the help of conversion tables, I changed English gas mark numbers to degrees Fahrenheit in order to bake cakes and to cook casseroles.

The approach to cooking measurements was different in both countries. In England, metric measures, by weight, were customary whereas, in the USA, quantities were measured by volume. Liquids were and are measured by volume, worldwide.

Dry ingredients (i.e., sugar and flour) are measured by weight in England but not in the USA. To use English recipes. I had to buy a scale and English measuring spoons to accurately produce the quantities required for any dish.

MONEY

English money was, of course, very different There were 12 pence to the shilling and 20 shillings to the pound. Initially, it took me some time to calculate how much change I should receive from any purchase I had made.

When the English first announced that they were changing to a decimal system, I should have been pleased. After all, that was the system that I had been accustomed to in the United States.

In February 1971, when the new system was introduced, I was probably the only person in England to be displeased. I had become so proficient in calculating in English money that I resented the loss of my newly honed skills.

Despite my irrational resistance to the introduction of the decimal system, I was forced to acknowledge that it was probably faster for everyone to calculate in a 10 point system rather than a 12 point one.

SEPARATE SHOPS

I was surprised to find that, in England, Individual shops still existed for different kinds of produce. Fruit and vegetable shops were separate from the butchers and the fishmongers.

I had frequented American supermarkets (far too large), but they did offer every kind of produce available under only one roof.

In their favour, I found the proprietors in the small, specialised shops were very willing to fulfil customers' requests, even when they required more time and effort to do so.

EARLY CLOSING

In 1966, when we left the United States, Sunday shopping was a phenomenon unheard of in the rugged hills of rural Vermont. I was not surprised to find that the same situation was true in England. But, when I tried to shop during the week, I was unexpectedly confronted with a new difficulty, that of early closing.

Apparently, English shops were required to close for half a day each week. The Shops Act of 1912 stated that all staff were entitled to one half-day off work, the day to be decided by each individual shop.

I was such a creature of habit that it took me two or three attempts to shop on early closing day before I altered my spontaneous and unthinking habits.

I have been known to leave one town, in dismay, because the shops were closed and drive to the next, only to discover that early closing was in force in that town also. Even when the Shops Act was repealed in 1994, many smaller shops continued this practice.

Early closing has been the bane of my existence in every place that I have lived, from Great Missenden to Radlett, some parts of Hampstead and even in Belsize Square. It is only since moving to Queens Park that I have been relieved of having to take early closing days into consideration on a weekly basis.

DRIVING

As all cars drove on the left-hand side of the road and I was familiar with traffic only on the right, I quickly learned that even crossing the road was a hazardous experience, if looking first in the wrong direction.

The real challenge of driving on the left would be the moment when I sat behind the steering wheel and attempted to change my automatic driving habits of many years. I decided to practise switching to the left when we were visiting Glenalla, in County Donegal. The roads there were almost devoid of traffic, compared to any English town

Roger had left Glenalla. He and his brother, Joe, had gone to England to check out the house we would be renting in Great Missenden. The children and I had a few free days before we left Glenalla to join Roger in our new dwelling.

For many years, the Franklin family had engaged in excursions to explore the local countryside. We had taken walks in the woods in every direction possible, explored caves, climbed the local hills and mountains. picnicked at various beaches, swum in the Atlantic Ocean, studied rock pools, collected cowrie shells, fished in the local lochs, meandered along the Atlantic Drive, stopping to take in the stunning views, driven to small towns to visit the weavers of Donegal tweed and the knitters of Aran sweaters, but no-one had ever found the small set of standing stones, reported to be only a few miles from Glenalla.

Not everyone had heard of them but those who had believed that they were difficult to find. I decided that it might be a challenging adventure to try to locate these relics from the distant past.

I ordered a picnic from "the kitchen". How I hated that term. It sounded as if there were a group of automatons who produced food without effort. Not so, it was a large room run by a cook and various assistants who worked extremely hard to produce the orders given every day.

I consulted John, the fixer and caretaker of everything, about which car to take on our excursion. There were cars meant to be available for family outings but the sight of one leaving the drive always instigated a very loud, emotional protest from my father-in-law. He was always complaining about the price of petrol, so I assumed that was the basis of his disapproval.

To avoid an angry outburst, I made sure that the children and I left before he detected my plans for the day. We left at 10. After breakfast in bed and a bath, he usually appeared downstairs about 11am, so I was sure we would escape without any intervention from Cyril.

Armed with a guidebook and our picnic basket, I set out with the children to find the standing stones. It was a bright, sunny morning and I was excited about the possibility of finding a genuine archaeological site.

As the roads were clear of traffic, I decided to practise driving on the left. I told the children to chant: "Keep left, Keep left" as I drove along and particularly when I stopped at corners. I understood that it was at junctions that switching driving from one side to the other was most confusing.

All went well. The children were shouting my instructions in unison, and I was, very competently, driving on the left.

Unfortunately, the guidebook provided only a minimal description of the area where the standing stones might be found. I stopped at several houses to ask for instructions but always to no avail.

Eventually, we found a farmer who pointed us in what he thought was the right general direction. He had been told that they were only "a few fields away."

After at least two excursions in the wrong direction, we managed to climb yet another fence and scramble again through overgrown, prickly, yellow gorse bushes to finally claim our reward.

In the distance, we could all see a small stone erection, small because it was so far away, surrounded by massive, stony fields filled with wild, uncultivated clumps of shrubs and bushes.

As we approached, we could see that it was a five-stone dolmen. As it grew physically larger, it seemed to take on a dignity of its own, standing in total isolation, immovable and magnificent, part of an ancient, mysterious civilisation.

It was composed of four large stones set vertically in the ground, supporting a large capstone or table. In Britain, Europe and other parts of the world, most stone structures of this type date from the Neolithic period (4000 to 3000 BC). The children could hardly believe that the structure they were looking at had remained standing for thousands of years.

We were all curious about who might have erected these stones and for what reasons. But almost nothing is known about the people, the social organisation or the religious beliefs, of the groups who created them. We stood in awe and admiration before these simple, elegant structures but with no history to help us interpret their purpose or their original significance.

After the children had nearly finished everything in our picnic basket and had spent time running about energetically in the fields for a while, we returned to the car and were homeward bound.

I was feeling especially pleased that I had found the elusive standing stones, particularly as a few people had intimated that I was highly unlikely to succeed. No-one else had ever found them.

Pleased with what a success the day had been for everyone, I was in blissful mood, driving slowly along the country lanes. After our wonderful discovery, we were all in good spirits. In the back seat of the car, the children had started singing loudly and joyfully as I drove through the countryside.

When I turned into the main road, I was basking in the pleasure of cruising along for a few miles with no traffic in sight. Everyone was still happily singing, when I glanced upwards to see an enormous lorry heading straight for me, at great speed and on my side of the road. It was definitely facing me and driving far too quickly to make a sudden stop.

Appalled and trying not to scream and fearful of frightening the children, I took a deep breath, squeezed the steering wheel, and swerved frantically into the opposite lane.

My heart was beating so loudly in my chest that I felt I had to pull over to the side of the road to gain my composure. I waited there until my rapid breathing and thumping heart beats had dissipated. I could not allow myself to think of what might have just happened to all of us.

The children were alarmed but by no means as shocked as I was. They were so involved in their own activities; they had not really seen the lorry but were startled and very upset at my sudden lunge to the left side of the road.

We discussed the fact that we all had forgotten to keep chanting "Keep left, Keep left". The children began the refrain again and dutifully repeated these words all the way home, until we reached the drive to Glenalla whereupon they started singing silly ditties they had learned at school.

I have never believed in shock treatment as a desirable method for learning anything and am still horrified at parents who throw their children who cannot swim into the ocean or swimming pool, saying now that they have no choice, they will definitely learn to swim, believing that the threat of drowning or dying was the quickest way to learn.

Despite my disapproval of shock tactics for learning, after this terrifying incident with the lorry, I have never again made such a dreadful mistake and have always remained driving diligently on the left side of all English and Irish roads.

OUR NEW HOUSE GUEST

Since arriving in England, Roger had, once again, become occupied with political issues. He had joined up with people working on a newly established magazine. Resurgence was first produced in 1966 by John Papworth. Satish Kumar, an ex-Jain monk, originally from India, had joined John in this enterprise.

Within its covers, were critiques of numerous topics: ecological, economic, environmental, social, and political. Not only was Roger writing the occasional article discussing problems relating to nuclear weapons, but he was also financially supporting the magazine.

As he was no longer working, I was pleased that he had found a niche for himself, working with people who had similar concerns and interests.

He and many others helped John to organise conferences to examine important and controversial political and social issues. As I was usually coping with the children's week-end activities, I rarely had the opportunity to attend these conferences.

One weekend, Roger asked if I could put up someone who had attended the conference but had no accommodation. I agreed but insisted that he should inform them that the facilities were very basic, a mattress on our hall floor. We had no guest room to offer for overnight stays.

As the proposed guest was young, these sleeping arrangements were totally acceptable.

As the conference was very well attended, Roger asked for more people to stay. We ended up with four people sleeping in the hall and one on the leather couch in the sitting room. In the morning everyone helped to tidy up and brought their sheets and pillowcases to the washing machine, with the exception of the man who had slept on the couch in the sitting room.

Roger explained that this "guest", in his forties, was a white Rhodesian who had been working with other Africans for an anti-apartheid magazine. Because they had not earned enough from magazine sales to pay for lodgings, they were all sleeping in the office where the magazine was produced.

All was going well until the landlord, unannounced, locked the office because they had not kept up with the rent payments. Unfortunately, our guest's suitcase was now locked away in the office, so he had no access to either his money or his clothes. He possessed only the garments that he was wearing.

I met the new guest for only a fleeting moment, as he was departing for the day. He was, as far as I could tell, a fairly intelligent, middle-class man, working for a worthy cause, who had fallen on difficult times. As a child, he had acquired polio which resulted in one leg being shorter than the other. The image of him walking across a room with a very pronounced limp drew immediate sympathy from me.

To help him out, I encouraged Roger to give him some of his clothes, everything he needed, and some money. Despite my concern for his well-being, I was appalled when I opened the door to the sitting room where he slept. I was immediately overwhelmed with the rank smell of stale perspiration. Our guest had already left the house, but his repellent body odour still pervaded the room.

I instantly rushed around to open all the windows to remove all traces of the offensive air.

I asked Roger to tell him that I insisted that he have a bath and put all his dirty clothes in the washing machine.

But the sight of his soiled underwear in the spotlessly clean washing machine was so disgusting, that I was forced to remove each piece with a pair of metal tongs and dispose of everything in the rubbish.

I wanted to know more about this enigmatic man who was staying with us. I asked Roger to enlighten me. To my surprise, Roger admitted that he really didn't know him or anything about him. I had assumed that he was at least an acquaintance of Roger's, though possibly a distant one.

When Roger was offering accommodation to people who had none, he had joined the queue and told Roger of his desperate predicament.

As the week progressed, there was no further mention of our new visitor's circumstances or any discussion of any future plans. A second week passed, and the situation remained the same.

He left every day for London to contact his friends and returned every evening.

My concern for his difficult situation was slowly diminishing as I began to suspect that our new guest thought that he had found a very comfortable place to live, gratis, and with two idiots who were quite willing to aid and abet him in this belief. Roger agreed with me.

I was annoyed with Roger for not doing anything to facilitate the departure of our "permanent guest" in any way, so I left the problem of dealing with him in Roger's hands.

Roger usually saw him in the morning before he departed. I sent him a message through Roger. He was to find himself a place to live. He couldn't live here indefinitely. He should try to sort out accommodation with his friends.

As a further week went by and then nearly another, he had a list of excuses as to why he couldn't find a place to live. Every evening, I began greeting him coldly at the door, asking him if he had found a new abode.

My initial annoyance turned to resentment and outright indignation at his resistance to leaving. I was not perturbed that we had helped him but was outraged that he was in no way motivated to help himself and seemed to have no conscience about living off the Franklin family.

Soon we would be preparing to take the children on a summer holiday. I had no intention of turning our empty house over to our unwanted guest. I informed him that he had better find somewhere to live as soon as possible as we were going on holiday.

I emphasized the fact that we always informed the police of our departure so they could survey the property when we were away in order to prevent any burglaries or break-ins.

I felt if he had any kind of murky past, the idea of being in contact the police would compel him to leave. Within only a few days of my conveying this information, he announced that he had found someone to help him.

I asked no further details as I was not interested. I was just happy to be rid of his continually irritating presence.

When he left, to my utter annoyance, he insisted on taking the same morning train that I took to London for my French class.

I sat uncomfortably beside him as he tried to converse. I protested that I couldn't hear him. The train was too noisy to talk. When we arrived at St. Pancras, I was greatly relieved as I was now departing on another train in a completely different direction.

I was horrified when I saw him following me off the train. As I turned towards him to say a quick goodbye, he clenched me in his arms tightly, giving me a large hug and a kiss on the cheek and thanking me for my generous hospitality.

He must have sensed my unresponsiveness as I once again said goodbye and hastened towards my train to central London.

Imagine my surprise when, a few weeks later, I chanced to tune in to a TV programme and saw the camera zooming in on the face of our "guest". He was part of a panel of people who were discussing their political views.

From the comments that he made, it was evident that he was not really supporter of the anti-apartheid movement. Totally the opposite. He believed that those who supported their tactics were in danger of creating more violence and unrest in South Africa. His assumptions led him to conclude that, for the sake of the stability of the society, anti-apartheid protests should cease.

I did note that there was no discussion of justice or freedom on behalf of the dispossessed black people. In total shock, I concluded that he was probably an informer and could even have been working for the South African government.

How could we have offered succour and support to such a deceptive individual?

It would be convenient to say that I had learned a lesson from this unexpected and unwelcome experience. But I am still left with my eternal dilemma.

How do you know who is genuine when you are face to face with the needy person in distress?

And, how do you decide whether or not to offer help?

PREJUDICE IN RADLETT?

PART ONE

I am writing this chapter in response to a number of people who have asked whether or not we had experienced any racial prejudice while living in Radlett.

My short and honest response to this question is no. As a couple, we were not aware of any unseemly or prejudiced behaviour directed towards us.

The children, however, did experience minor incidents of racial abuse. At the Fairfield School, the three girls were occasionally called names, but verbal insults were never hurled at Kim. He said it was probably due to his size, but, despite being tall, he was not excessively taller than his classmates. So, I'm not sure if his explanation is a valid interpretation of events.

There were no gangs of children who besieged the children, only a few culprits, most of whom belonged to the same family. No-one could utter the name of the Wilson family without immediately adding the family with fifteen children. Everyone knew that they were the cause of most of the problems in the school. The children remember them as being poor, smelly and almost never in a school uniform.

The Wilson family lived in two council houses which the children always passed on their way home from school. A group of little boys, most, smaller than the three girls, would rush out, yelling: "Go back to the jungle. Go back to the jungle." "Our big brother is coming to get you."

The first time it happened, the girls were really frightened because they did not know what their big brother might do to them.

Despite the same little boys screaming the same words and threatening the same attacks every day, their terrifying big brother never appeared.

The children slowly began to assess their daily confrontation differently. They took a good, long look at this group of pale, thin, scrawny little boys, and decided that they were pathetic. They were so small and weak; they were obviously trying to make themselves feel big and important.

They decided that they need take no further notice of these scruffy waifs or their meaningless verbal attacks.

As far as going back to the jungle, the girls had no idea of its implications, so the intended insult fell on deaf ears.

Natasha remembers being called a "Paki" and thinking that's ridiculous. She knew it was an insult and she knew it didn't relate to her, but she didn't know why.

When, occasionally, racist remarks were hurled in her direction, she did repeat the poem that I had taught her (the one that my mother had taught to me).

"Sticks and stones will hurt my bones,

But names will never harm me."

I, later, had second thoughts about saying these lines as a retort to verbal attacks. I was worried that some clever, little bully might decide to pick up the sticks and stones and use them to cause serious bodily harm.

Leda definitely remembered three little girls calling her "bad names" at school. She arrived home very upset and very perplexed. She didn't understand why they were picking on her. She hadn't done anything to upset them.

I said they were bullies who usually had other people with them. They never went around on their own but liked to pick on people who were on their own.

As she was so puzzled about why they were attacking her, I said: "Why don't you ask them why they are calling you names?"

The next day, when she turned round to ask them why they were behaving like that, they were so taken aback by the question that they just stopped in their tracks. They stood still, just staring at her and then at each other.

She was shocked and surprised that they said nothing at all. After this incident, instead of screaming insults and chasing her, they tried to avoid her presence altogether. From that day onwards, all harassment totally ceased.

PART TWO

In relation to the subject of prejudice, I must relate an amusing incident which occurred during our time in Radlett.

My neighbours, Diane and Peter Charles, decided to foster African twins. As their mother had died in childbirth, their father had left them in social care and had not visited them since their mother's death.

If everything went well, Diane and Peter, hoped to adopt the twins when they were legally allowed to do so. I was amazed as they already had four children. The youngest was the same age as the twins, two and a half years old.

There was no end to the mischief that the gang of three, very active, highly intelligent little ones could create. They emptied clean baskets of laundry on the kitchen floor, ran the water in the sink until it nearly overflowed, pulled up the newly planted bulbs in the garden and put new toilet rolls in the toilet basin, etc.

One day, when I was picking up my order for a leg of lamb, the butcher exclaimed that he hadn't seen my twins before, not until Mrs. Charles had brought them into his shop last week.

I was astounded. The twins in no way resembled my children, Roger, or me. It seemed a far-fetched idea that anyone could think that they were mine.

Of course, it was the fact that they had brown skin which inspired this deduction. I was the only non-white person in Radlett, therefore, the children must be mine.

When I informed the butcher that Mrs, Charles was fostering the twins and hoping to adopt them, the butcher stood dumbfounded with his mouth agape.

"Adopt them, adopt them", he repeated incredulously, shaking his head in shock. "Who would want..."

He looked up and suddenly remembered to whom he was speaking.

How could he say to me what he was really thinking? "Who would want to adopt black twins? "

I had lived in Radlett for five years, in full view of all its inhabitants and had never been pregnant. How could they assume that, overnight, I had produced two-and-a-half-year-old twins?

Absurd as it seemed, that the butcher thought I was the mother of the twins, there was a small neighbourhood consensus that concurred with this belief.

I can only conclude that irrational assumptions may sometimes be more powerful forces in making decisions than simple reasoning and direct observation which require proof and evidence to support their validity.

PS. THE TWINS

Diane and Peter Charles were never allowed to adopt their very much adored twins. Only a week before the adoption was legal, the father suddenly appeared with his new partner and said he wanted them to live with him.

Diane and Peter were devastated but they had to comply with the law, despite their strong family attachment to the twins.

PART THREE

Diane Charles's mother-in-law had come to visit Diane, Peter, and the grandchildren. One day, as Diane had an important dentist appointment, she asked if I would take her mother-in-law out to lunch.

I agreed to do so. I knew very little about Peter's mother except what Diane had mentioned in casual conversation. She was a working-class woman who was very proud of her son's success.

Peter didn't sound at all like his mother because somewhere along his path of further education, he had acquired a very middle-class accent and had married a very middle -class woman, Diane Leather.

The day arrived. I picked up Diane's mother-in-law.

I had proposed a trip to London, thinking that she might like to see the city and possibly eat at a foreign restaurant, as she rarely had a chance to engage in such activities. Diane informed me that she was definitely not interested in sight-seeing and preferred only English food.

On the appointed day, I drove to the centre of Radlett to a restaurant with an exclusively English menu. We spent a long time over lunch, discussing how much the children had grown, how nice it was that Diane and Peter were buying a large house with a large garden for the children to play in and what a lovely place Radlett seemed to be.

Time had passed more quickly that I realised. It was nearly tea-time before we decided to go home. As I escorted Peter's mother to her door, she thanked me for a lovely lunch and as I turned to go, she suddenly said, "Beverly, did you know that black people are related to monkeys?"

I was stunned. Did she really say what I thought I had heard? I turned round and said, "No, no. How do you know that?" What intrigued me was the matter-of-fact way in which she said it. This was obviously a firmly held belief.

"You can tell", she said. "You can tell by their hands. They are dark on one side and light on the other side, just like the monkeys." As she was talking, she turned the palm of her hand over to demonstrate the light side.

What could I say? I felt that my initial response was feeble but the impact of what she had said left me truly astonished.

I was amazed that the person I had just lunched with for nearly three hours and who had appeared to be reasonably intelligent, could draw such conclusions from a colour contrast on two side of someone's hands. I wondered if lighter black people were less related to monkeys as the colour contrast was not so outstanding.

The breadth of my shock consumed me. No rational, logical explanations emerged to counteract her absurd, simplistic assumptions. But part of this reaction was due to cynicism I didn't believe that any reasonable statement that I produced would alter her beliefs in any way. They were too firmly entrenched.

I did wonder how she felt about just having had lunch with someone related to a monkey. I should have asked her but didn't think of the appropriate question until much later.

Someone asked if I had been insulted. How could anyone be insulted at such a preposterous proposal? You would first have to believe it was true for it to have any effect.

My very simple message to my grandchildren is: "Never allow the irrational assumptions of others to determine how you perceive yourself."

PART FOUR

We lived in Radlett for over seven years. During that time, we were invited to dinner by only two families: once by the children's music teacher and more frequently, by our neighbours directly opposite us, the Charles family. Someone suggested that the fact that more people weren't making friends with us may have been due to disapproval of our marriage.

I know that adults in polite, middle-class societies do not generally verbally or physically attack those of whom they disapprove. When meeting undesirable individuals, they smile courteously and then, without undue fuss, protest or complaint, resolutely exclude them from all their social gatherings.

There will be no overt, visible sign that you are rejected or condemned. But if you are not included does that mean that you are disapproved of? Maybe yes, maybe no. If being a mixed-race couple led to a hesitancy in others establishing relationships with us, I will never know.

We were, no doubt, seen as an unconventional couple, with left-wing views, inclined to approve the aims of the Labour Party rather than the Conservatives, supporting comprehensive education and the CND movement. In 1972, we had even taken the children on the Easter CND march from London to Aldermaston. These were not the actions or commonly held beliefs of those who lived in this conservative, stockbroker community.

In addition, I had, inadvertently, irritated some of the mothers in our neighbourhood by not following the local custom of giving my children a packet of sweets after school every day.

I further annoyed them and even my friend, Diane Charles, by refusing to buy squashes for after school drinks because of the added sugar. I never criticised them in any way, but they viewed my refusal to behave as they did, as a criticism of them, which was never my intention.

I was only upholding my mother's strongly held belief that white sugar was not nutritious. It contained no vitamins or minerals and ruined your teeth.

So, the issue of not being invited to dinner or desiring to become better acquainted may have been for practical reasons. None of us had very much in common as a basis for instigating a friendship or any kind of relationship.

Our controversial social and political beliefs may have been a sufficient deterrent to immediate acceptance by others, without ever having to consider whether racial prejudice had any part to play in it.

I had no time to worry about such matters as I was too preoccupied with the children's needs and trying to decide what course I should follow in the future. Should I take a teaching job, or should I return to further education?

NEW STUDIES

It was suddenly 1973 and I was forty years old. Somehow, this critical event of decisive importance had arrived sooner than expected.

I was not experiencing a mid-life crisis. That had happened ten years earlier at the age of thirty. When I realised that the decade of my twenties had gone forever and that my truly youthful, vibrant years were behind me, I was devastated.

Forty was a significant point in my life's journey but I was not unsettled and accepted it unemotionally and with a degree of equanimity. I felt full of vitality and decided to focus my energy on making some important decisions about my future.

All the children were in school for a full day. I felt like a liberated woman. After years of child-rearing, I could reclaim my freedom, at least, from nine to three on Monday to Friday.

I was considering returning to teaching. I had already sent off my teaching credentials and my BSc degree to enquire if they were valid for teaching in England. To my delight, they were accepted, and I was given a specific number to put on all teaching application forms.

But, having passed this first hurdle, I began having second thoughts about becoming a teacher again. I yearned to do something new, something different that would challenge my intellect.

As an undergraduate, I had taken two psychology courses which, I remembered, had stimulated my interest in many topics. After a long period of consideration, I decided to try to obtain another BSc degree, this time, in Psychology, and as a mature student.

When I first thought about studying again, I did wonder about the feasibility of attempting such a daunting task. My academic study had stopped with the acquisition of my teaching certificate in 1955, after acquiring my BSc in 1954.

This was 1973. I had already experienced eighteen years of not using my brain for educational purposes. By the time I started study, it would probably be twenty years. Was I still capable of the academic rigour required?

I had a second concern. All my qualifications had been acquired in the United States. I thought that I should take an academic course in England to prove that I could pass an English exam.

The English were always so critical of college education in the USA, believing that English degrees were always superior. They are, but only, if you consider specialisation in specific subjects. But that is a topic to be considered at another time.

I decided to take a London University extension course in Social Psychology.

Diane's friend, Jane, had also decided to study the same subject. We drove once a week to the local college, were very attentive at lectures, and thoroughly enjoyed stimulating our quiescent, grey cells again.

Diane had already started studying for the first year of her social work course. Before the children returned home from school, Diane, Jane, and I sometimes met informally to chat over a cup of strong tea.

Each of us had produced four children, had juggled the housekeeping and the needs of husbands and children for many years. We were now overjoyed to be spreading our wings in different, unexplored directions.

The events of the summer of 1973 were a mixed blessing. Our academic ventures had proved successful. We had all passed our respective exams, but Jane and I found that our personal lives were in a state of disarray and confusion. Our relations with our husbands had become impossibly fractious.

I must add that our studies, had in no way, contributed to the development of these difficult relationships.

For many years, Jane's husband had maintained an important position in a publishing firm. The demands of the job meant that he was often travelling abroad to assignments overseas.

When Jane discovered that he was having an affair with a Scandinavian poet, she was overwhelmed with shock and feelings of betrayal, especially as their   marriage had seemed a reasonably contented one.

It was only Diane and Peter's marriage that seemed to remain intact and to be surviving without undue stress or strain.

OUR MARRIAGE

My position was very dissimilar to Jane's. Because Roger had decided not to pursue a paid occupation, he was working at home, writing, most of the time. But since he had become involved with the new magazine, Resurgence, we had hardly seen him at home at all.

I was not pleased and complained that he had no time for the family. He was not engaged in being either a father or a husband. If he graced us with his presence, it was only to eat and depart again. It felt as if he had quietly and unobtrusively disengaged from all familial relations, absenting himself from us most days and evenings.

Since Roger was only fleetingly at home, we had definitely become an estranged couple, rarely communicating and each of us becoming more critical of the other's behaviour. But he consistently refused to engage in any kind of discussion or conversation about our relationship.

For me, there was a second issue of serious concern. When Roger chose to dine with us, he had become even more disapproving than usual of my efforts to teach the children manners.

I had always felt that Roger, in his attempts to divest himself of the impediments of his background and upbringing, had concluded that the rules and regulations of the middle class, implemented by nannies, public school and elite, polite society were to be banished forever.

Rules, for Roger, were always construed in a negative context, as a prohibition which prevented everyone from carrying out whatever plans they wished to pursue.

I, on the other hand, conceived the function of rules in a more positive light, thinking that they had two purposes: 1) to protect the children from harm and, 2) to develop acceptable social behaviour.

There were, in society, some well-established customs that already existed which promoted the inculcation of these rules. They were, unfortunately, the ones that Roger was trying to dispense with altogether whenever I tried to enforce them, always thinking that I was just trying to control the children.

I could never consider that waiting for one's turn, saying sorry, please or thank you were options for them. Not saying these words at the appropriate time would have been too offensive and inconsiderate of others. The children would be social outcasts if they didn't learn how to interact politely with both children and adults.

I have explained, probably, in too much detail, the reasons for our unresolved conflict about manners.

I found myself constantly reassessing the state of our marriage. When we had moved from the States to England, our relationship was under strain. But the fact that Roger had taken the effort to find us a house in England, proved to me that he really did have the best interests of the family at heart.

But, only recently, I had learned that Roger's brother, Joe, had made all the arrangements for our move. It was complicated.

When Roger had first lost his job, my mother-in-law, Miriam, happened to ring to ask how we were. I had burst into tears saying that we were moving to England and Roger said that we were to live with his father.

It was Miriam who had asked Joe to find us a house in England, knowing how difficult her ex-husband could be. I was very disappointed to discover that Roger had not really organised anything on our behalf. If it were not for Joe's efforts, we might well have been living with my irascible father-in-law.

Despite feeling disappointed, alienated, and having serious differences of opinion with Roger, I was determined, particularly, for the sake of the children, to try to sort out our difficulties. Otherwise, I feared we would both remain in this situation of anger and hostility towards each other forever. But, whenever Roger saw me approaching to discuss our the state of our marriage, he avoided confrontation by heading for the nearest exit.

The more frustrated I was, about being prevented from finding a solution to our problems, the more agitated and angry I became. Initially, my requests to discuss problems were reasonable and low-keyed, but, as I slowly recognised how impenetrable Roger's barriers were, my approaches to him were increasingly demanding and more assertive. But neither method dented his defences. I made no impact whatsoever.

Since he absolutely refused to communicate, there seemed no way out of our predicament, and I felt quite hopeless.

CYRIL and MICHAEL and SUMMER HOLIDAYS

Like most of the Franklin family, we spent the summer holidays at Glenalla with the children and other family members and their friends.

Unfortunately, the beauty and tranquillity of the surrounding countryside did not always extend to the interior walls of Glenalla. Due to the behaviour of some of the residents, the atmosphere could be perfused with tumult and turmoil.

Michael, Cyril's youngest brother, who was living in Glenbeg, the octagon-shaped house on the path to the left of the front drive of Glenalla, would often arrive there just as the family was finishing lunch. Just the sight of these two brothers together induced disconcerted responses and despondent sighs in nearly everyone who knew them. The mood around the dining table shifted from relaxed discussion to one of wary and unsettled anticipation of what was yet to come.

Their proximity always presaged a shattering scene of disturbance and dissension. Michael had come to make arrangements to use the tennis court. "We want to play about 11am tomorrow. Is the court free then?"

"No, no, absolutely not", Cyril answered abruptly. "It's not free then." "Well, what about 12?" "We'll still be playing", was the immediate response.

"We can't book at one, that's lunchtime." "What about three or four? You should be finished by then."

"I'm sure some of the young have already reserved that time. You'll have to choose another day or come at nine or ten in the morning." Knowing that Michael never finished breakfast until after ten am, Cyril felt free to make this very generous offer.

Michael, exasperated by this time, exploded: "Why are you being so difficult?"

"I'm nothing of the sort. There's no need to be abusive." Cyril, trying to sound extremely reasonable, stated: "You can't use the tennis court when other people are already playing there. You'll have to book it for the following day."

"Tell me who is playing at three or four. Maybe, we can rearrange times."

"I don't know who is playing at that time. You'll have to ask the young people to find out who is playing. We don't keep records of who is next on court."

"That's ridiculous. Why don't you just tell me. I've got better things to do with my time than chase down every teenager at Glenalla all afternoon.

"I told you, I don't know", Cyril exploded.

We all sat in strained and uncomfortable silence, trying to eat the cook's delicious dessert of gooseberry fool.

Glances, stares, and querulous looks were being exchanged across the table.

Quiet whispering followed. Who had booked the tennis court for tomorrow afternoon? Everyone was inquiring. Eventually, there were no other people to ask. The culprit or culprits did not appear to be sitting around the dining -room table. It became apparent that no-one, absolutely no-one had reserved the tennis court for tomorrow afternoon.

As usual, Cyril was being intentionally cantankerous because it was Michael who was asking for something.

After his birth, Michael had become the favoured child in the Franklin family, much to the consternation of his elder brother, Cyril. Inevitably, jealousy set in. Both brothers became overly protective of their rights and possessions, argued incessantly, and remained forever resentful and suspicious of each other. There was no restraining the enormity of their anger towards each other, so all the guests were subjected to the harangues and aggressive, critical exchanges that continually flew back and forth between them.

Some suggested that Cyril, being the elder brother, should have overcome his infantile jealousy. But what would anyone do, when his younger brother's behaviour was equally as provocative as Cyril's.

One morning at Glenalla, Cyril was sitting on his bed, basking in the sunlight streaming through his bedroom window. But as he sat, enjoying the delectable warmth and peacefulness of the moment, he was suddenly disturbed by a strange noise in the garden outside, the sound of metal blades at work somewhere. The gardener didn't usually tend to the plants and flowers around the house until late afternoon, after checking the vegetables in the kitchen garden and the fruit trees and berry bushes even farther away. Cyril leaned out of the window to investigate the source of the sound.

A trellis of clusters of sweet-smelling pink and red roses adorned the entire wall and climbed from the earth below to reach as high as the windowsill just under Cyril's bedroom window. Some flowers were in full bloom and others were incipient buds, ready to burst forth in all their bold glory.

He poked his head out of the window and what he saw set his nerves on edge. A cream-coloured straw hat, a dark green gardening apron and a blue shirt with rolled-up sleeves, exposing untanned white arms, consistently clipping and cutting all of Cyril's roses, the ones in bud and the ones in bloom. It was Michael quite happily and efficiently stripping the trellis bare of its most prized display.

"What do you think you are doing? Stop this instant," Cyril bellowed out of the window.

Michael looked up as if he didn't know what the commotion was all about. "Mother said that I could take any flowers in the garden that I wanted."

"But my flowers are not in the garden. They are growing on my wall, next to my window and for my pleasure. That's why they were planted there."

"She never said anything about your owning the roses on this wall." "This is her garden. I can take what I like." As Michael talked, he continued to remove more clusters of flowers from their stems.

The paltry number of roses remaining were the ones too high to reach and hardly created a beautiful spectacle for anyone to linger and marvel at.

Cyril screamed at Michael, "You're a parasite. Never set foot at Glenalla again. Why don't you produce your own roses to clip and remove instead of demolishing perfectly lovely flowers that Mother planted for the pleasure of everyone."

The exchange of insults and offensive comments continued for another half hour before both men retreated into their respective houses where they could no longer see each other.

Argumentative scenes between Michael and Cyril were a common occurrence at Glenalla. I mused that such incidents would certainly set the servants chattering about the madness of their masters. But what the servants saw or heard seemed to be of no concern to anyone.

While the behaviour of some middle-class people could be unpleasant and irrepressible, from a servant's point of view, it was irreproachable and couldn't be criticized, at least, not in public and would only be commented on amongst the other servants.

From a middle-class perspective, the servants were of such a low order that their opinions did not merit consideration of any sort, so everyone was free to behave as they wished, whether commendably or otherwise.

It was a jarring revelation to accept that expectations of a restful holiday in the peaceful, Glenalla countryside was totally impossible, a dream beyond reach. There were daily arguments between the brothers, outbursts from Cyril about the impossibly high cost of petrol in the cars everyone borrowed for outings and outbursts about who might be stealing the alcohol in the drinks cupboard (no-one) and who dared to take a spoonful of the huge Stilton cheese sitting on the sideboard which we all thought had been bought to eat.

Everyone knew that Cyril did not have to worry about the cost of running Glenalla as his brother, Sydney had left a huge trust fund for the family for this purpose. We all considered these outbursts unjustified, unpleasant, and totally unnecessary.

There were special attacks, aimed at me because I had invited John, the handyman's children to play with our children on the terrace of Glenalla. They were the servants' children and therefore not allowed into the inner sanctum of the big house as equals. I had transgressed a serious boundary. These children would never know their proper place in society if I continued to ignore the rules relating to servants.

In addition, I allowed them to play with our children's brand-new toys. As I explained to my father-in-law, it was very important for children to learn to be cooperative with others, to share what they have. Or they could retain their possessions for their own use and remain lonely, isolated, unhappy individuals. Learning to participate with others was a significant step in their social development.

I ignored my father-in-law's remonstrations. As long as we were at Glenalla, John's children continued to play with our children and to join us in trips to the cinema and the beach.

We began to curtail our visits to Glenalla hoping to find a more convivial social atmosphere, and a less cold and rainy climate. We started to visit my sister-in-law, Sonja's summer home, on the island of Hvar, in Yugoslavia. With the children we spent many pleasant summers in friendly, cheerful company, enjoying the higher temperatures and the warmer waters of the Adriatic Sea.

SUMMER HOLIDAY (1973)

One Sunday, one of my sisters-in-law saw me in such a state of distress, she insisted that I ring her psychiatrist. In the end, once a week, both Roger and I had started seeing two different psychiatrists. With both of us in therapy, I had expected that our relationship might start to improve. But circumstances were difficult.

Roger was already leading a totally separate existence which seldom included either time at home or time for the family. Our lives were so separate that neither one of us knew what the other was doing.

I had expected my appointments with the psychiatrist to continue for some time, but it felt as though I had barely started therapy when it was time to stop. The school year had ended, and the children were at home all day.

We were, once again, going on holiday to Yugoslavia, to visit Hvar, the small island where my sister-in-law, Sonja's, father had a small restaurant and reasonable accommodation to let for the summer.

As we were preparing to pack, Roger informed me that he was not joining us for the family holiday. He had work to do. I had thought that he might want to spend some time with the children, but he had obviously made other plans.

Although I complained that Roger never helped with anything at home, he had always bought our tickets and the foreign currency for travelling.

When I finally remembered that this task was now my responsibility, I became very anxious. It was only five days before we were to depart, and I hadn't ordered any money from the bank. Foreign money was not readily available. After ordering it, there was usually a two to three days wait before it arrived in the bank. I immediately rushed to Nat West to rectify the situation.

The money, fortunately, arrived the afternoon of the day before our early morning flight. So, by only a few hours, disaster had been averted.

After a quick trip to the bank the next morning, we were all on our way to what turned out to be one of our last summer holidays in Yugoslavia.

The children loved swimming in the Adriatic Sea. The water was always so clear and warm, But the older ones had started complaining that there wasn't much for them to do. The thought of sunbathing every afternoon, as most of the adults were inclined to do, bored them to tears.

When they were younger, under Kim's tutelage, the children and their cousins had produced a new play every summer for the local community and the guests at the restaurant. Drinks, cakes, and biscuits were served after the performance to raise money for the local church. But now, they all seemed to have outgrown this very enjoyable and completely engrossing activity.

We did sometimes take long walks, slowly climbing the local hills which, at the top, emitted the pungent smelling scent of the purple lavender bushes. Gathering lavender flowers was the main occupation of the local residents and provided them with their main source of income. In the local market, lavender oil, perfume, and soaps were very popular, especially with the tourists.

At least, once during the summer, my brother-in-law and his wife would organize an outing for the day to another small island. The various sized motorboats would line up to collect the families, the food and drink and we would set off for deserted beaches with fine sand and crystal-clear water.

The older children helped with the fish barbecue, but their main joy was being part of a larger social scene with their cousins and friends.

It was true that there were not many activities available there to dissipate their adolescent energy.

In the evenings, after dinner, everyone played card games of one sort or another. It was the place to learn games that one hadn't ever played. I was always eager to learn but discovered that after two glasses of wine, my concentration wandered aimlessly, to everyone's annoyance.

The previous summer, there had been dancing in the evening. The music was generated by records, constantly changed by devoted staff. But, for some reason, this year, the local authorities were not in favour of promoting dancing after dinner. Even the very popular entertainment hall on the mainland, where everyone gathered for dancing, was closed. The children were fed up as they really had looked forward to spending the evening dancing with people of their own age.

To complicate matters further, one evening, I tripped down a small flight of steps and twisted my ankle. Owen, my brother-in-law, who was a doctor, assured me that it was only strained, not broken.

But two days later, attempting to sit down in his motorboat, I was suddenly thrown forward when a large wave hit the boat's side with great force. My right foot slammed onto the deck and when I raised it, my foot fell to one side. Owen took one look and said, "I can assure you, your ankle is definitely broken this time."

With no first aid on board, he was forced to use whatever was available on deck to stabilise my ankle. He wrapped it in a very thin sheet of malleable plastic, a bit like a sponge, and a piece of chicken wire, moulded into shape to keep my bones in place. Owen tried to get a splint in Hvar, but the local doctor was unavailable, and unlikely to return until the following week, the disadvantage of going to beautiful but very remote places on holiday.

The rest of the time I was given morphine and to my annoyance, Owen regulated it so well that I never had any wonderful hallucinations or exciting dreams. It was just enough to block out the pain.

Owen refused to send me to the local hospital as he said I would get the best treatment in England, and we were all flying there in three days. As Stanmore was the closest orthopaedic hospital to Radlett, I was to go there as soon as I arrived in England.

He arranged for a wheelchair to take me to the plane back to Heathrow and for one to pick me up at Heathrow to take us through the customs and baggage gates. The children were all in attendance and being very helpful.

I hopped up the steps to the aeroplane with a crutch Owen had borrowed from someone in Hvar, with the children following close behind. For very different reasons, we were all very pleased to be on our way home, going back to England once again.

LEGAL SEPARATION

When we passed through the customs and luggage gates at Heathrow, my first thought was that I must send the children home with a trusted black cab driver. As I somehow had to get myself to hospital, I would have to pay him and tip him to take the children to Radlett.

As I was explaining my plans to the children, they looked up and quite unexpectedly, saw Roger coming through the glass doors, headed in our direction. They were very surprised but very pleased to see him. I was in a state of shock but delighted that I didn't have to implement my complicated travel arrangements for the hospital or for sending the children home.

Roger drove me to Stanmore Hospital where I was admitted as a patient and prepared to have an operation the next day. I was greatly relieved that he could drive the children home. I had been worried that he might be away, and I would have to arrange for Diane Charles to check up on the children if they were home alone. Kim was going to stay in France with his cousins, Donald, and Rodney for a week so the girls would have been on their own in the house.

The next morning, I was prepared to have my ankle operation. I was taken to the operating theatre and that was the last thing that I remembered.

I woke up with my ankle resting on a cubicle and sighed with great relief because I knew the operation was over. Almost as soon as I opened my eyes, a nurse rushed in to say that I shouldn't eat or drink anything. "But, I've had the operation", I protested. "Surely, I can eat something now." "No, no, you can't. It was not a straightforward break, as the doctors had thought. Your ankle is broken in two places. It needs to be pinned. There was no time for such a complicated procedure today. Your operation is scheduled for tomorrow morning."

Roger brought the children to visit once before the operation and once after the operation, when I was still in a very groggy state. The children were amused because I never answered any of their questions or even finished a sentence with anyone who spoke to me. I just kept falling asleep.

On his second trip to the hospital, Roger informed me that he couldn't bring the children to visit any more. He was going on a trip that he had planned when we were in Yugoslavia, no explanation as to where he was going or with whom.

I was shocked. He was leaving the children on their own with no adult in the house. As he registered my startled reaction, he put the receiver down, not waiting to hear my protest about his irresponsible decision.

I tried to contact my friend, Diane Charles, but she was on holiday with her family. Initially, I couldn't reach Jane either, so the children were forced to fend for themselves. Roger had left them some money on the counter for shopping. They were not daunted by walking to the village to purchase groceries but found carrying the heavy shopping bags up the long hill to our house a very tedious undertaking.

When I did manage to contact Jane, she graciously checked up on the children and invited them to dinner when I was in hospital.

When I arrived home with my crutches and my cast which remained on for ten weeks, I was not alone. The children had fallen in love with a very friendly cat who consistently sneaked into the patients' beds. The nurses had convinced them that it was only young and needed a good home. After much pleading, I conceded to their urgent requests that we take it home. And that is how we acquired Rasputin, who the vet said, was the oldest kitten that he had ever seen, particularly, as his teeth were falling out.

As I was using crutches, I couldn't drive. I resorted to taxis to drive to the High Street to do the shopping and asked the drivers to help me carry the groceries into the kitchen. Shopping became a very prolonged activity as I had to hold my crutch with one hand for balance and try to use the other to put food into the trolley. In short bursts, I would push the trolley ahead of me and then hobble along on my crutches to catch up with it. I manoeuvred myself around the store in this fashion until the shopping was completed.

I was surprised at the number of taxi drivers who gave me their telephone numbers and asked if they could see me again. I always stated that I was a married woman with four children, but that piece of information didn't seem to faze most of them.

Before I went on holiday, I remember complaining to Diane and Jane that Roger left the house every morning and disappeared for the entire day. No-one knew where he was or what his intended destination might be.

When I met Jane again, she, very calmly. said, "You may not know where your husband goes every day but I do. He is visiting the woman across the road and her three young children. Every morning, I can see him arrive from my sitting room window."

I was not completely surprised. The thought had crossed my mind that he might be having an affair with someone. And now, I suspected that the reason he had refused to go on holiday with his family was that had planned to spend some time with this new woman and her children.

Whenever Roger returned home, our relationship remained as cool and frosty as ever. I accused him of having an affair which catapulted him into total flight mode. He escape all recrimination by removing himself from the house every day and when he was at home, he remained aloof in his study and refused to discuss the matter. We spoke to each other only when necessary and about practical matters.

I remained very angry because, despite the fact that I was using crutches and could not drive, I was expected to do the family shopping on my own.

We were both still seeing our psychiatrists but against my will and what I desired, I was beginning to accept that it was unlikely that we would resolve our problems, particularly when we couldn't even sit down together to define what they were. I remained very hurt and angry, especially as I felt that Roger was not even interested in trying to improve matters between us. There were four innocent children involved in this disastrous situation. I thought that we both had a duty, painful though it might be, to try to find a solution to our problems.

Because he was so determined not to talk to me, I felt totally rejected. We had clearly reached a deadly impasse where no progress seemed possible.

For over a year, when I saw him, I had continually stated that I couldn't carry on with our situation as it was. We had no relationship. I was planning to leave. Given my hesitation to act on this threat, he could hardly have believed that I would ever carry it out.

Nor could I. It was the last thing that I wanted to do. Leaving would be an act of utter failure and a stark acknowledgement that our marriage had ended forever. Why couldn't we attempt a reconciliation? I knew that such wishful thinking was pointless. But I found it's very difficult to accept that it was such a futile hope.

The unrelenting anger and anguish I was experiencing meant that I constantly felt weak, fragile, and exhausted. My public demeanour remained only a façade, a deceptive appearance, which barely disguised my inner turmoil.

I couldn't believe that my accustomed emotional stability was wavering and beginning to falter. I couldn't allow myself to collapse. I had to maintain enough strength for the children to have, at least, one parent they could rely on.

Fearing for my inevitable decline if I continued to remain within the marriage, I began to feel compelled to leave. Self-preservation to support the children seemed the only choice available.

As I was the one who finally decided to leave the marriage, I am often accused of being the person who really ended it. I feel that such a statement is a moot point. For over two years, prior to my departure, Roger was already leading a completely separate existence, away from all of us. As far as I was concerned, he had already left the marriage and the family.

It was only when Roger accepted that the fact that I was leaving that he deigned to converse with me. He was then prepared to talk, but only about practical matters relating to our separation, which only confirmed to me that he had already been thinking about plans for ending the relationship. We never, ever discussed our problems or what had caused them.

By this time, I was so distraught I didn't know in which direction to turn. Roger suggested that we go to his family's solicitor to sort out legally where we both stood. As I knew no solicitors, I agreed. I had met James previously and he seemed a reasonable person. I cannot believe how naïve I was but, I do know that, at the time, I was in no state to think anything through with a clear mind.

I trusted James to give a fair and unbiased opinion about all the issues we raised but, by the third session, I began to question whether he was capable of being totally objective, particularly, when it came to money matters. He had been working for the Franklin family for nearly twenty years, always defending the family's interests. He would have to follow the law, but his main concern might be to conserve money for the Franklin side of the family as he had always done.

In the last session with James, Roger and I agreed to have a legal separation. Why not a divorce? I was, rather unrealistically, thinking that we still might resolve our differences, so the children didn't have to suffer because of our problems.

Divorce sounded, to me, very final. I consented to a legal separation as it seemed to offer more leeway. It created a space for possible mediation and hope that our problems could be resolved.

THE FINAL SETTLEMENT

When I saw Jane again nothing definite had been decided about her marriage but, at least, she and her husband were examining their situation together. She was appalled that I had agreed to use the Franklin family solicitor. The first question that she asked was: "How do you expect him to solve your financial situation impartially? Do you really think that he will act with your best interests in mind?" She immediately gave me the name of a reliable solicitor who dealt with separation and divorce proceedings.

Mr. Richards was a very amiable person as well as a very good solicitor. He explained that we should focus on what my financial position would be once we had separated.

He asked what I had brought to the marriage, meaning goods or money. My response was: "My good name and no more as I had no money. I had not come from a wealthy family and from the age of fifteen had worked every summer to save money for my college tuition."

Mr. Richards continues, "And what is your husband's income?" I was truly embarrassed to admit that I didn't know. "Well, approximately, how much?", he asked. Again, I had to admit that I had no idea and didn't even dare to hazard a guess. I explained that I had asked many times about our financial situation, but Roger refused to discuss anything to do with money or his income. He always said that I should contact Samuel Montague and Co., the family bank, if I wanted to learn about his finances.

I had been told that the bankers who ran Samuel Montague and Co. were of the generation who believed that banking affairs and financial concerns of any kind were the prerogative of men only. Consequently, I was very reluctant to visit the bank as I was sure that I would be a most unwelcome client and probably unlikely to obtain the information that I wanted.

Mr. Richards, obviously astonished at my total ignorance about Roger's income, exclaimed that my situation was an unprecedented and incredulous one, particularly as we had been married for twenty years.

Not knowing anything about Roger's financial situation had most certainly proved problematic over the years. When we left Vermont, Roger had no job and had stated that he was not going to work anymore.

He did not seem at all worried about our predicament. I secretly waited for him to find a job, not really believing that anyone had enough money to support a family of six without a fixed salary of any kind. It may have been true that I was married to a very wealthy man but, not knowing anything about our financial status, meant that I endured bouts of unrelenting worry about whether we had enough money to survive. It was ludicrous!!

Mr. Richards said that he would try to gather details of Roger's financial situation, but his solicitors were under no obligation to tell him. He was correct. His solicitors refused to reveal anything about the amount of money that Roger received annually or about the trust money that the Franklin family had bestowed on him and other family members from time to time.

In separation and divorce proceedings, the law states that the wife and family should be kept in the manner to which they are accustomed. Hearing those words, I panicked. I had a sudden flashback and prayed that they would never discover anything at all about our droughts in Vermont, when our shallow well dried up every summer. Roger collected drinking water in old cider bottles from the school where he was teaching, and I carried endless buckets of water to flush the toilet from a water hole in the back garden which Roger had dug, an ordeal that might last anywhere from three to six months.

Fortunately, this era of our life remained a clandestine experience, unbeknown to the solicitors who knew only of our house in Radlett.

The final outcome was that the solicitors stated that the children would be supported from trust funds that had been set up for all the grandchildren by Roger's father many years ago, and money from other sources would be provided for my upkeep. Roger was obliged to provide a house for us 'in the manner to which we were accustomed'.

THE HOUSE

As Kim's first year at Queen's Comprehensive School had been such a disaster, he had moved to the King Alfred School in Hampstead. As we all had to move house, I thought it only sensible to have the four children at the same school. So, I arranged for the other three to be enrolled at the King Alfred School also.

I wanted a house near the children's school, hopefully, within walking distance of the school. With four children on my own, I knew that it would be impossible to keep up with their social gatherings, after-school activities and visits to friends. I could easily have become their permanent chauffeur to all of these outings. But I was determined that they would become more independent, walk to and from school and to most of their out-of-school arrangements.

The problem would be to find a house that met our requirements. I didn't know the first thing about looking for a house on my own. I approached one real-estate agent and told him that I required a five-bedroom house near the King Alfred School on North End Road, in north-west London.

When I realised that I had heard nothing from him in over a month, I decided that I should register with two agents simultaneously. Having more than one agent might be a more productive approach. At the time, I didn't know that it was common practise in house-hunting to have two or even three agents working on your behalf.

After a prolonged period of searching, I did find a house in the perfect spot on Wildwood Road, NW11. It was near the bottom of the road with a fence in the back garden which opened onto the Hampstead Heath Extension. Its most attractive feature was that it was most definitely within walking distance of the school, but a major drawback was that it was in great need of repair.

When I first viewed the house, a very sweet old lady (probably younger than I am now) ushered me into the sitting room which was in very good decorative order. She explained that she and her sister had never earned enough money to keep up with the house repairs or deal with the amount of decoration needed. As she showed me through the rest of the house, I was quite disheartened. In every room, old, crinkly wallpaper was literally rolling down the wall or had completed its downward trajectory and remained resting in a long tube against a wall of the room. And, none of the rooms in the house had been painted for many years. But worse was yet to come.

The surveyor's report was devastating. The house appeared to be slowly sinking into the ground and tilting slightly to one side. As a result, not one floor in the house remained in a level position. The report concluded that the foundations were very insecure. The house would have to be underpinned.

I knew that Roger would have to provide us with a house, but would he agree, in addition, to a very expensive bill for the house's structural support?

I informed him that buying this house meant that he would incur a very expensive bill for underpinning, but I had found no other residence so suitable for our needs. The house was being auctioned so all interested parties had to make whatever seemed a sensible bid. At the very last minute, I convinced Roger to make a slightly higher bid, higher than what we thought the others might offer, and a reasonable amount above the reserve price.

The next day, the real-estate agent rang to say that the house was ours. Our bid had been the highest, but only by a very small amount. So, the last minute monetary addition had worked in our favour. I was overjoyed. Now the many months of major renovation could commence.

I employed an architect and a quantity surveyor to start work on the house immediately. The underpinning started in the latter part of 1973 and was not completed until the end of October 1974. We were all relieved to relinquish the commuting from Hertfordshire to Hampstead five days a week for the children to attend the King Alfred School. Two days after the work had been completed, we moved into our new house in Hampstead. We were off to a good start as everyone was delighted to have their own bedroom and they all seemed to have made friends in their new school.

THOUGHTS ON SEPARATION and DIVORCE

Roger and I had separated in 1974. My mother-in-law had divorced her husband, Cyril, in 1936. Looking at the circumstances relating to divorce in the latter part of the 1930's, she faced many more difficulties than I had ever had to experience.

Before the First World War, divorce was a rare occurrence and was generally considered a scandal. Only men could request divorce on the grounds of their wife's adultery.

During the First World War, the number of divorces increased which resulted in many couples "living in sin" as the cost of obtaining divorce proved to be prohibitive for many.

Pressure for change and reform in divorce law was instigated particularly by dedicated groups of women committed to eliminating the injustices they experienced in law.

In divorce cases, fathers always were always given custody of the children because they were the only ones in a position to support them.

This decision was inevitable because, historically, women could own no property. When married, the wife's property was surrendered to her husband and any money she earned or property she acquired during the marriage, was allotted to him.

The laws were slowly changing and in 1923, the Matrimonial Causes Act allowed women to petition for divorce on the grounds of adultery without the need for additional reasons to be given.

In 1926, women were allowed to own and deal with their property on the same terms as men.

Laws relating to parental responsibility for children were also being transformed.

In cases where a husband assaulted a wife, a woman could petition for custody of the children under the age of sixteen and a legal separation was allowed.

But, in general practise, if a couple separated, the husband was awarded the children unless he had been convicted of a violent attack.

My mother-in-law, Miriam, and my father-in-law, Cyril, were married in 1925 and divorced in 1936. When they separated, their children, Roger, Joe, and Owen were nine, seven and three years old.

Miriam had found the strain of living with Cyril's unpredictable and volatile behaviour had pushed her to the margins of sanity. In order to maintain some kind of mental stability, she felt that she had no choice but to escape.

It was imperative that she remove herself from her husband, Cyril's, premises altogether. She found a lawyer and started divorce proceedings. In order to finance the legal cost, she was forced to sell her only valuable possession, her jewellery collection.

She was accused of deserting her children but given the way the law functioned in 1936, fathers still had the right to claim the children in divorce cases. She was unlikely to obtain custody of the children because she had no income to support them. But even more significant was the fact that the judge remained firmly opposed to her asking to divorce her husband. He still believed that only men had the right to divorce their partners.

He informed her that she was an evil woman for leaving her husband and breaking up the family home. She was reprimanded and denigrated before all those in court for behaving outrageously. The judge refused to consider that there could be any just cause for a woman's desire to leave the family home.

In 1936, women could divorce men, but in middle-class society, it was still considered a scandal and a heinous act and was not a common occurrence.

The judge continued to impress this fact upon her. She was a terrible wife, a bad mother, and a social disgrace. Given the judge's outright disapproval of her, there were no obviously constructive reasons for giving her custody of the children.

When I thought of my mother-in-law's separation from her husband as I sat in my new home in Wildwood Road, feeling isolated, detached, and friendless, I had to admit that she had suffered a far worse fate than mine.

The children and I were living together in a house that was ours. There had been no problems about financing the separation or the custody of the children.

Although separation and divorce were never considered desirable outcomes for any marriage, there was, now, at least, a wider understanding of the many factors which lead to marital breakdown and no labelling of those involved as pariahs or social outcasts.

MOVE TO WILDWOOD ROAD

WILDWOOD ROAD - PART ONE

Before we moved to Wildwood Road, Roger and I continued our estranged relationship in Radlett.

Roger continued to live his distinctly separate existence, often appearing with different individuals or with small groups of people, mostly young and unknown to me.

Although Roger was not talking to me, he did sometimes communicate with the children. They informed me that he was setting up a commune. The new faces that I saw were the people who were planning to live there.

To establish the commune, Roger had bought another house in Radlett. Where it was situated, I do not know, as I never saw it. To mark the first night that everyone moved into the premises, the new residents celebrated with a party which all the children attended.

With Roger's approval, I had approached a real-estate agent about selling our house in Loom Lane. Roger had said that he was moving but had not yet put the house on the market. I was, once again, concerned that if the house in Radlett weren't sold, Roger might not have enough money to pay for the house in Wildwood Road.

When we left Radlett, the commune was still in existence, but the children said that there had been problems and that it would soon be closing down. They then informed me that Daddy had told them they could visit him soon at his new house in Gloucestershire with his new partner and her two children.

As our relationship had definitely ended, I was no longer concerned about any liaisons that Roger had established but I did note that he had acquired a different partner who had only two children.

What really shocked me was the realisation that Roger had bought four houses: our house in Radlett, the commune, his new house in Gloucestershire, and, in addition, he had purchased our family house in Hampstead and was financing the underpinning. I was stunned by the thought that he must have access to truly enormous amounts of money.

I was not concerned that we had lived a frugal existence for eight years in Vermont and that I had counted every penny that I had ever spent. I was more concerned that, in every crisis in our marriage, I had been seriously worried about money. When Roger lost his job, I wracked my brain, worrying about how the family would survive and trying to figure out how to bring in some sort of income as Roger was refusing to work. For the same reason, I was reticent to look for a larger house for the family because I was concerned that we might not be able to afford one.

In retrospect, I'm now sure (though I wasn't then) that he had the money to dig our well deeper. We were not digging a new Artesian Well whose price could be exorbitant if water was found only at a very deep level in the ground. During the winter months, the well usually filled with water, which meant that the water table, despite dropping, was still accessible.

It was slowly dawning on me that I had spent my entire marriage living with Roger's immense guilt about having inherited money. He spent money on himself and his family with great difficulty but was delighted to give away large amounts to numerous strangers, sometimes to friends and to numerous charities. His attitude to money related to his desire never to use inherited money for anything but charitable purposes.

But why was he so adamant about not deepening the well? There was another, more incomprehensible response that coloured his outlook. Like his father, he refused to spend money on any domestic problem that required fixing. There was no rational or sensible reason that I could find for this implacable stance. But it was a firmly implanted attitude that he was unwilling to change.

It was too late to waste time being angry about this belated recognition that he had access to money that he refused to spend even when badly needed if it related to family needs. But we relied on it every summer when we went to England and Ireland to visit his beloved Glenalla. And from the time we settled in England in 1966, when he decided not to work anymore, he relied on it for an income.

I did regret the angst and anguish spent on worrying about the possible lack of money during our marriage and the privations we suffered when the well dried up.

But I had little energy left to spend dwelling on these matters as moving house was proving to be a more unnerving experience than I had anticipated.

When we moved to Wildwood Road, I experienced a great sense of relief as I was no longer engulfed in an atmosphere of anger and rejection almost every day. But the act of moving had produced its own tension and pressures so I cannot say that my first days and nights in Wildwood Road were without emotional strain.

Once the children were settled in their own bedrooms, I was suddenly plagued with all sorts of doubts and fears. I felt totally justified in my reasons for leaving the marriage but was very anxious about living in this new, completely alien environment.

I felt unsettled and uprooted and precariously plonked down in a community of strangers. Everything was unfamiliar, the houses, the landscape, the people. I knew no-one. There was no sympathetic relative to ring or contact.

The one person I might have rung was dealing with a very difficult situation, so I didn't attempt to contact her.

The main relatives available were the Franklins and I was not tempted to find out how they felt about our separation. Families can become very loyal and protective if they think an injustice has been done to one of them.

Since Papa (Naum Gabo) had died, Miriam, my mother-in-law had moved to England and was living in Tufnell Park. When Roger and I separated, I had not contacted my father-in-law, Cyril, or my mother-in-law as I was unsure of how they felt about our marriage ending.

I need not have worried. Both Miriam and Cyril eventually rang to enquire about how I was faring and to say that they had not heard from me in a very long time. Once contact had been re-established, my outings with my in-laws resumed and relations between us continued very amicably. I found myself in the unusual position of driving my mother-in-law to a classical concert one weekend and the following week-end, driving my father-in-law to another classical concert.

I continued to worry about the children. Had I done them a great injustice by removing Roger from their lives? We were now a one-parent family. Would I be able to cope on my own?

Jane rang and listened to my unrelenting questions about all the decisions I had made. She couldn't understand why I was so filled with self-doubt. "Of course, you can cope. You have always brought up the children on your own. Roger was never involved in raising the children, nor was he at home every day to help. Your situation hasn't changed just because you have separated."

Everything she said was true. My general level of anxiety was skewing my judgement and creating a warped, distorted state of mind about things that might happen in the present and in the future. Jane's response jolted me into a more realistic appraisal of my situation.

I promised myself that I would try to focus on creating a more relaxed atmosphere at home to provide a more balanced environment for the children.

WILDWOOD ROAD – PART TWO

When the house in Wildwood Road was put into my name, the architect explained that I would be living in Hampstead Garden Suburb, which was a well-known conservation area.

Residing there meant that I would require planning permission to alter the appearance of the house and possibly other parts of the property. I was shocked to discover that even the decrepit, decaying apple trees in my back garden couldn't be removed as they had a preservation order attached to them.

I had no idea of any of the wider implications associated with my having moved to this part of Hampstead. My primary aim had been to buy a house close to the children's school and I had succeeded in that objective. I was unprepared for the implicit assumptions and social reactions to my decision.

Every time I mentioned the words Hampstead Garden Suburb, eyebrows raised, oohs and aahs were uttered, and comments were always made suggesting that I had chosen to move into a very expensive and very snobby neighbourhood.

It is true that Hampstead Garden suburb was comprised of mainly well-to-do middle-class people but that had not been the aim of its founder, Dame Henrietta Barnet.

She wanted to establish a community with a mixture of classes, a community which would provide affordable, well-built housing and green spaces for the working-classes and houses for the more affluent. A place of worship and a community centre were constructed to create places where everyone could meet and establish relationships.

Dwindling attendance at both these institutions has obliterated the founder's dream of creating a mixture of classes in the Suburb and the rising cost of property has eliminated any possibility of high quality housing for the poorer members of society. As a result, Hampstead Garden Suburb has become a truly middle-class enclave.

But, at the end of Wildwood Road, about only six or seven houses away from me, there was a building of flats, predominantly occupied by people who did not originate from the middle class. It must have been one of the last vestiges of Dame Henrietta Barnet's vision still in existence.

WILDWOOD ROAD - PART THREE

When I had settled in my new residence, I was shocked to discover that, in my immediate vicinity, I was surrounded by Conservatives with a capital C. The only family that voted Labour lived across the road, next-door to their Conservative cousins. During elections, the antics of both families became an amusing spectacle.

A Vote Labour poster would suddenly appear in the front window of the house almost directly opposite us. Upon viewing this blatant notice, the adjacent house would immediately place their Vote Conservative poster in one of their front windows.

This antagonistic interaction continued until front windows in both houses were covered with posters. The battle then proceeded to their front lawns where posters on sticks were planted resolutely and firmly in the clammy, clay soil. At this point, the relentless opponents always ended their struggle abruptly.

I never understood why. Maybe, it was due to a consideration of matters of good taste, not wanting to clutter their properties with untidy displays of advertisements. I knew of no regulations that prohibited such behaviour.

To the amusement of the children and the nearby residents, during every election, whether for council or country, this demonstration of neighbourly antagonism was on permanent view for all to observe.

The neighbours were not unfriendly though we tended to be more casual acquaintances than very good friends.

My next-door neighbours on the right invited people in the vicinity to a party to meet me. Everyone I met was amiable and welcoming. Most of the men were established in business careers but I did meet one lecturer and one author. One of the wives held a full-time job in her husband's office but most retained positions in various clubs and institutions.

I was one of the youngest people there. Everyone else's children were adults or nearly so. Those children who were closer to the ages of mine were already attending more conventional, private schools so it was unlikely that any of them would ever meet or become friends.

The one other party that I attended was at the house of the people who voted Labour. They were actually acquainted with members of the Franklin family. It was a party scheduled for 11am in the morning. At that hour of the day, I didn't really expect people to be imbibing alcohol, though I'm sure the invitation stated somewhere that, that was the purpose of the party.

In Donegal, I had attended one or two similar gatherings but had not registered the fact that such parties also occurred in England.

Everyone seemed friendly and engaging and upon seeing my reluctance to drink any alcohol, vociferously encourage me to do so. I obliged and after two alcoholic drinks, I decided to depart for home. I still had to prepare Sunday dinner for the children.

Standing in the kitchen, chopping vegetables, I felt slightly light-headed and unable to concentrate on what I was doing. I could not believe that only two small alcoholic drinks could produce such a disruptive, distracted effect on my mind.

Drinking copious cups of coffee to clear my head, I vowed there would be no more morning cocktail parties for me, unless I ate one canape for every sip of whatever concoction I was drinking.

During the summer of 1975, while the children and I were on holiday, once again, in Yugoslavia, a dramatic catastrophe occurred in Hampstead, in the area in which we lived. It proved to be one of the most unusual English weather events of the twentieth century.

In less than three hours, a massive outpouring, (an amount estimated to be about three months' worth of rain), descended on Hampstead Heath. Surrounding areas were affected but none registered such disastrously high meteorological readings as those in Hampstead.

Many believed that the rain gauge underestimated the exact amount of precipitation as many of the hailstones accompanying the downpour, hit the gauge but were then bounced out of its funnel.

Statistics demonstrate that such a catastrophic event would probably occur only once in every 20,000 years. (Only one other incident in the British Isles has registered a higher level of rain. On the 19th of May 1989, 193mm of rain fell in two hours at Walshaw Dean Reservoir, West Yorkshire), though there still seems to be some dispute about the accuracy of these figures.

As a result of the storm, in parts of London, severe flooding occurred, gutters were blocked, ground floor flats were inundated, hundreds were left homeless. Most of the underground ceased to function as the electricity supply failed. Four of the main stations were flooded.

While this dreadful event took its toll, we remained in sunny Yugoslavia, blissfully unaware of what was happening. It was not until we returned home at the end of August that we were informed of the terrible news.

In Wildwood Road, particularly the end at which we lived, the deluge had been severe. Wildwood Road started at the top of a hill where it intersected with North End Road. It meandered around the Heath Extension until, at its lowest point, it merged into flat ground and levelled out along the playing fields.

As the water cascaded down the road, it struck the houses nearer the bottom of the hill with great force. Many houses, including mine, were badly affected. Fortunately, all of these houses had been built above cellars, so the water did not generally affect the ground floor, but the contents of the cellars were destroyed as were many boilers.

The neighbours had engaged the fire department to drain all the cellars, but it was the neighbours who pitched in to clear the soaked clothes and articles of every description which had been stored there. They had generously included me in their cleaning-up process.

As we entered the kitchen of our house, there was a distinct smell of stale dampness. Once the cellar door was opened, we could trace its source. From the four corners of the cellar and uneven parts of the concrete floor, where dampness remained, mould had started to grow. The boiler, though seriously damaged, remained standing. The completely defunct freezer lay on its side with the door open, devoid of all its contents.

Those who cleared up had the most objectionable job of collecting the unpleasant smelling food that had been floating in the water for, I don't know how many days.

Outside, the only indications of this disastrous event were several huge plastic bags stuffed full of the decaying remains of food and one disgusting bag full of food and maggots.

I rang the council, requesting that they collect the rubbish immediately but, of course, they were inundated with such calls and said they would come when they could.

I was very grateful to the neighbours who had taken the trouble to save my house along with theirs and set about trying to discover who these remarkable individuals were. Unable to think of an appropriate way to thank them, I settled for giving each of them a case of wine for their considerate endeavours.

I remained truly overwhelmed by their generous efforts on my behalf, particularly, as these were people I hardly knew.

After this neighbourly expression of kindness, any lingering feelings of alienation on my part, vanished completely though I never made close friends with anyone living nearby.

The children were pleased to be living closer to their school and I found myself slowly adjusting to my new environment. I wanted to pursue a new career and decided to begin a course of study in psychology somewhere in London by the first term of September 1975. That gave me a year to finish unwinding and to decide which colleges I would like to attend. For the first time in many years, I was looking forward to a future with a positive outlook and hopes of fulfilling some of my own desires.

PART FOUR

COLLEGE ENTRY IN ENGLAND

Having decided to apply for a BSc degree in psychology, I spent some time perusing the subjects I would be required to study. To my dismay, every course I looked up required statistics.

The idea of studying statistics so terrified me that I spent an inordinate amount of time trying to find a college or university that did not require this subject for a BSc. psychology degree. I never succeeded in finding one so reluctantly accepted that I would have to endure the ordeal of studying statistics.

My first interview was at Goldsmiths College. My name was called. My interviewer asked me to enter her room and sit down.

As I did so, she continued to flip over the pages of what turned out to be my CV. She, eventually, looked up and said, "You seem to have spent a great deal of time studying." I was startled. "Was she reading the correct CV?" It certainly couldn't have been mine. I had received my BSC in the States in 1954 and my Teaching Certificate in 1955. The year was now 1975 which meant that I had received my last qualifications at least 20 years ago.

In 1974, I had taken a London University Extension Course in Social Psychology—to prove to any English examiners that I was capable of passing academic courses in England. One course of study in almost 20 years hardly justified the phrase "a great deal of time studying".

"No, no", I responded. "I have been at home for many years, bringing up a family. I haven't had much time to study. But now that nearly all the children are teenagers, the youngest will be thirteen next year—I thought that I could return to studying again."

She quickly examined my CV again and made no further comments about the amount of time I'd spent studying.

"I see that you have four children. You do realise that you will be undertaking a difficult course requiring time to prepare work outside of the college timetable. With four teenagers to take into account, I should think that finding time for college work could be rather difficult. "

"Are you sure that you can manage writing essays, studying and preparing for exams?

"Yes, Yes, I can", I responded. "During the week, the children are at school all day. I'm free to attend classes or study, whatever the course requires."

She then asked, "Do you have any help with the children?"

"No, that's not necessary as they are in school all day."

She, once again, proceeded to comment on the subject of the children. "Teenage children can be very difficult. They can be very time-consuming as they develop into adulthood. I only mention these problems as, when and if they occur, they could interfere with your ability to complete the required course of study."

I said that I couldn't foresee any particular problems at this point. "We have always managed to deal with their worries and concerns as they arise, and I assume we will continue to do. It is not such a time-consuming operation that I have no space left to do anything else."

With that response, for the first time, she smiled, a very broad, deliberate smile, wished me well and said good-bye.

When I left, I felt the experience I had undergone could in no way be described as an interview with a prospective applicant to Goldmiths College. I had been listening to an interviewer express her prejudices and biases, albeit in the interrogative form, about why a mother was incapable of studying for a degree in psychology.

I was very disappointed. She never once asked me anything about psychology. Did I have any particular reason for wanting to study psychology? Did I have any particular field of interest? With no evidence to support her theoretical assumptions, she was convinced that, with four children to look after, I could not possibly do the work necessary to complete the course.

What really infuriated me was that a man with four children would never have been asked the same questions. Without any proof, it would have been assumed that he could cope.

I thought that I had prepared myself for these college interviews but I hadn't expected to encounter prejudice against women as part of the process.

I tried very hard not to be too disheartened. After all, I still had two more interviews in my appointment book. They all couldn't be as hopeless as this one.

MY SECOND INTERVIEW

My second interview was at Birkbeck College, well-known for offering evening courses in higher education. This particular provision meant that people who worked during the day had the opportunity to obtain education up to degree level.

I was interviewed by Michael Eysenck, son of the famous psychologist, Hans Eysenck. His first words were, "I am not at all sure that I should be interviewing you. You do know that this college is set up for people who work. Glancing at my CV, he stated, "I cannot see that you are working or have any sort of job."

These statements astounded me. Initially, I thought that he didn't really mean what he had said. But when I protested saying that I was a mother of four children and that was definitely a full-time job, he merely stared at me intently, as if in total disbelief.

With that response, I had no doubt that he really did mean what he had said. His contemptuous response only angered me but I couldn't allow heated emotions to destroy my chances for college entry.

I took a deep breath, composed myself and said, "If I were a nanny, looking after four children, you would say that I had a full-time job. I am a mother, looking after four children. We are both doing the same job. The only difference is that the nanny is paid and I am not. I have a job but work for nothing. There is no remuneration for my endeavours."

After my statement, there was a rather prolonged silence. Secretly, I was pleased as I thought I had defended my position rather well but was surprised when he made no attempt to respond.

Not another word was spoken about jobs or work of any kind. In the midst of the silence, he suddenly said, "Tell me what you know about Sigmund Freud."

I was startled by this sudden change of subject and started to speak nervously. I was half-way through a sentence before I began to regain my composure. I, then, stated that I wanted to start again as I could frame the answer better if I altered my approach.

I said Freud believed that the unconscious mind influences human behaviour. By bringing unconscious thoughts into awareness, people could gain insight into their behaviour. I was prepared to continue but he stopped me and said, "That was fine—Thank you."

The interview had ended, rather abruptly, I thought. Departing, I was pleased with what I had said about Freud. I knew that it was an accurate response. But I was left wondering if he should have asked me the question at all. I was applying to study psychology-- to learn about Freud. Shouldn't it have been asked of a student after studying a course in psychology—not prior to such an undertaking?

"No matter", I told myself. My answer indicated that I had some knowledge of Freud, if that is what he wanted.

As for the first part of the interview, I did not expect to receive any accolades for having so clearly revealed his bias against mothers and the subject of work.

I left feeling that his view on this matter had not altered but he remained in the situation of being unable to counter my statements with any reasonable argument.

Leaving the interviewer in an awkward and indefensible position, though unintentional, would hardly encourage him to be amenable towards me or my application.

It was, without doubt, another failed interview. Leaving the college, I was overcome with the feeling that, during our encounter, I had truly won a battle but had most definitely lost the war.

THE THIRD INTERVIEW

My last interview took place at Bedford College in Regents Park. Feeling that the first two interviews had been unsuccessful, I knew that this was my last chance to be accepted on a psychology course. What could I do to better prepare myself for an interview?

Quite incidentally, I saw a paperback in my local bookshop, entitled Psychology Today. It described the various branches of psychology and included a brief discussion of some of their most recent areas of research.

Developmental, clinical and educational psychology especially appealed to me but, trying to be practical, I decided that I should focus on educational psychology.

To become qualified in this field, I needed not only a psychology degree but also a teaching qualification and some experience as a teacher. As I had already acquired the teaching certificate (which was recognised in England) and had worked as a teacher, I could eliminate two years of further study.

The chapter I read on educational psychology mentioned a new and unusual method for the teaching of reading—The ITA System—The Initial Teaching Alphabet. It was meant to teach children to read more easily than can be done with the traditional spelling system of English. After learning the ITA system, children would then move on to learn standard English spelling.

This new method had proved successful, but not in all cases. Critics complained that, for some children, learning two different alphabets had proved difficult. Nevertheless, the system was already being used in some primary schools in England.

I was interviewed by Professor Brian Foss, the head of the Psychology department. When he asked me why I wanted to study psychology, I explained that I thought I might want to pursue a career in educational psychology.

I mentioned that I was particularly interested in problems related to the teaching and learning of reading. What was his opinion of the ITA teaching alphabet?

He said that he was not familiar with the ITA teaching alphabet. Educational psychology was not the branch of psychology which he had studied. (My heart sank. I saw, immediately, that all my clever preparations to impress him were completely useless).

When I asked him what branch of psychology he had pursued, he said that it was evolutionary psychology. I told him that I knew nothing of this field and, in fact, was unaware of its existence.

Whereupon he launched into a most fascinating lecture on the nature of evolutionary psychology. It focuses on how evolution has shaped the human mind and human behaviour. Due to natural selection, adaptive behaviours which are successful are maintained and transmitted from one generation to the next.

I was riveted. What he was saying was creating a new way of looking at human beings. He captured my attention completely.

At the end of his lecture, (I'm not sure that he recognised it as such), he smiled and straightened his tie. He must have known that his captive audience had been truly mesmerised by his performance.

Further discussion revolved around the curriculum at Bedford College and my opportunity, over time, to examine many different areas in psychology. I explained that I was anxious to start a course of study this year, if possible. He said he would make a note about how enthusiastic I was to start studying.

For a change, the interview had ended on a positive note, partly due, I thought, to the interviewer feeling that he had delivered a very good lecture. I had demonstrated a keen desire to study psychology and even specified a field of study. But I felt that our discussion about these matters seemed to take up much less time than his spontaneous discourse on evolutionary psychology.

I had a second interview at Bedford College with the Social Psychology lecturer. So far, no-one had mentioned anything about my being a mother. "This time, I had arrived, fully prepared, to justify my case for becoming a student.

As my interviewer looked at my CV, she noted that I had four children. At the first mention of the word, children, I sat up in my chair, erect, alert and ready to defend myself.

As I was preparing to respond, she commented, "Four children, that shouldn't be a problem. I have five and will soon have a sixth. People always think that you can't cope." There I sat, ready to hurl myself into defence of my application.

I was stunned into silence, almost inhaling the sentences I was ready to spout. Her words had, suddenly and quite unexpectedly, left me completely astonished and totally deflated.

I realised that I could relax. What a relief! We then engaged in a discussion of how mothers were never usually recognised as having the capacity to do anything but nurture children and certainly should not harbour any desire to do anything else.

We discussed some of the experiments I had studied on the London University social psychology course I had undertaken and whether or not it was a good idea for me to think of starting a career in this subject. I was so intrigued by the kind of studies that were carried out and what they revealed about social conformity that I was tempted to consider this field of study.

I did explain why I also might want to work as an educational psychologist. We came to no conclusion about what I should do in the future, but she did understand that I had a strong interest in psychology and desired to pursue some sort of career in the subject.

That was my last interview—It was the first time that I felt that I had undergone a genuine interview process. Both interviewers had focussed on the subject of psychology and were aware of my particular fields of interest. And they had listened to what I had said and had taken notes on my responses.

I thought that I just might have a chance of being accepted, but the competition to get into Bedford College was so high that I could, in no way, take it for granted.

In due course, I received my rejections from Goldsmiths and Birkbeck College. When the white envelope with the Bedford College stamp arrived, I stood motionless for a few seconds, not daring to open it.

I was so wary that after I had read the enclosed letter, I passed it over to my son to read to me again. "What does it say, Kim?" "Read it aloud. Don't make any mistakes." "It says you've been accepted as a student at Bedford College. The term starts in September."

What I had read was true, but I couldn't believe it. It had to be confirmed by someone else. Hearing Kim's words, I screamed with joy and walked around in a daze for the rest of the day.

I was overjoyed beyond belief. I was opening a new chapter in my life. I felt I could put all the upheaval and trauma of the last few years behind me. For the first time in many years, I allowed myself to contemplate a challenging but truly positive future existence.

REFLECTIONS ON COLLEGE ENTRY IN THE USA AND ENGLAND

When I attempted college entry in the USA in 1950, I had to contend with specific barriers which made acceptance at any institution of higher education very difficult.

The first was the favoured legacy preferences for children of alumni. The second was the publicly unacknowledged very low quotas for all applicants with black ancestry in all colleges and universities in Boston and Cambridge, Massachusetts.

In 1975, I, once again, applied for entry to college, but this time, in England. I, initially, thought that my racial background would not prove a hindrance to being accepted. But evidence was being produced which demonstrated how difficult it was for black students to be admitted to colleges and universities, especially to the Russel Group Universities. Apparently, selection procedures were not totally unbiased.

I based my hopes of acceptance on the fact that the barriers in England seemed less stringent than those in the United States. At least, I didn't have to cope with a very unfair quota system.

But what I did have to contend with in my first two interviews totally shocked me. I was completely unprepared for the fact that I would face discrimination of a different kind, that of gender.

I had, previously, dealt with overt gender discrimination only once in my life—when I applied to teach in Cambridge, Massachusetts. My application was rejected on the grounds that I was a married woman, despite the fact that the law preventing married women from teaching had been revoked a year prior to my application.

Until recently, outright denial on the part of the perpetrators of racial and sexual discrimination combined with the fact that they were often in powerful positions meant that these injustices existed untrammelled and unrestricted throughout society.

But, in both the United States and England, there is now public acceptance of the fact that both racial and sexual discrimination are prevalent within many organisations and institutions in society. Discrimination is now an open topic for discussion and hopefully some recently implemented laws do exist to prevent further dissemination of these unjust practices.

Although there is enormous room for improvement in both these areas, I am pleased that I have survived long enough to see that these hitherto clandestine and disavowed subjects are, at least, under critical examination and now on the public agenda.

MY TIME AT BEDFORD COLLEGE – PART ONE

Most of my time at Bedford College, I experienced as a pleasurable challenge and a jubilant success. But there were moments of unexpected worry and serious disquiet.

My first shock was having to attend a mandatory three hour lab, every Friday afternoon. Fine! But why from two to five pm? I was meant to be at home preparing dinner for the children by five pm.

My instantaneous reaction was one of guilt, dreadful guilt. It was the first time that the consequences of undertaking a full-time degree became evident. I would have to relinquish my accustomed role as provider of dinner every Friday evening in order to attend the lab.

There was only one conclusion. The children would just have to learn to cook dinner. We had cooked many things, made our own bread, different kinds of biscuits, cakes and desserts, prepared picnic lunches but never ventured so far as cooking an entire meal.

I, immediately, became engaged in teaching them how not to overcook the vegetables and how to cook fish and simple cuts of meat (mostly chops).

As I stood explaining to the children that they would have to cook their own dinner on Friday evenings, it became obvious that they were not in any way distressed or perturbed. They appeared completely indifferent to the fact that I would not be at home to prepare a meal.

I should have been overjoyed at their response. Wasn't it the desire of all parents to produce children who could be independent of them? Sadly, I thought, I must have remained in some sort of unrecognised time warp.

If it's a mother's prerogative to worry, I should have received first prize for taking that special privilege to extremes. Subsequent thoughts led me to be concerned that I had indulged them too much. They obviously relished the idea of cooking independently.

For practical reasons, I did manage somehow to curtail my self-criticism. I needed every free minute to read, write essays, produce lab reports and to conduct an original experiment in my first year at Bedford. Undue worry obviously served no useful purpose.

My next preoccupation related to writing essays. Twenty years ago, was the last time that I had composed fortnightly essays. My ability in this sphere had completely vanished. Initially, I found myself spending an entire weekend trying to complete only one essay.

In addition, to produce an acceptable essay, organising one's thoughts in logical fashion was only the first step in the process. We quickly learned what else was required, when my friend's essay was returned with critical comments and underlining. A paragraph at the end stated that the psychology department was not interested in the student's ideas, unless corroborated by supporting evidence which included the name of the researcher, the date the research was carried out and the conclusions that were drawn.

I suddenly remembered that when I had studied for my first BSc, I had written a paper using this format. In microbiology, I had completed a study of brucellosis, a disease which humans can acquire from drinking unpasteurised milk or infected, undercooked meat. Once again, my past learning seemed a long time ago and all methods of approaching scientific writing were but vague memories.

Despite my early concerns about the practicalities of essay-writing, I did not find the subjects we were required to study difficult to tackle, with the exception of statistics. As it dealt with numbers, I was immediately thrown into a troubled state of mind. Mathematics was never my favourite subject. I always passed the exams but never felt that I understood what I was doing.

To make matters worse, the statistics lecturer possessed what I called a "tangential mind." He never once explained how to complete any statistical test. He started off in good faith, probably thinking that he would complete the task at hand but seemed incapable of doing so.

His stream of consciousness would overtake him in mid flow, and he would start discoursing on a completely different subject which he felt was somehow related. The lecture would always end with some point being made about the new topic; with no further mention of the statistical test he was meant to complete.

Amongst the mature students who had never studied statistics, there was an increasing state of apprehension about the subject. We began to feel completely overwhelmed. The eighteen and nineteen year olds, who had already studied statistics, seemed in no way affected by the lecturer's "tangential mind."

The psychology department hired another lecturer who, on Wednesday afternoons, helped to clarify our problems. Although he mitigated our state of nervous tension, he was never capable of totally eradicating it.

I was always well-prepared for the annual statistics exam. But every year, I approached the exam in such a state of high anxiety that I always ruined my chances of acquiring very good grades in this subject.

In our third year, we had to undergo a six hour statistics exam. University students were paid to be subjects we could use to test whatever hypothesis we had chosen to prove. The technicians in the psychology department set up the equipment we requested to test the hypothesis. We then applied the proper statistical tests to the results to discover whether or not the hypothesis had been supported.

It proved to be a truly exhausting and very tedious day. After the exam, I asked Professor Foss why we had to carry out a six hour exam. After all, we had three hour labs with statistical analysis of the results every week over a period of three years. He stated quite firmly that it was important to prove that we could carry out a scientific experiment independently. And why were scientific studies so important?

One of the important roots of contemporary psychology derived from philosophy. Initial psychological studies relied on introspection as a method of studying mental processes, a method that had been inherited from philosophy.

It was in 1879 that Wilhelm Wundt set up the first psychological laboratory in Leipzig, supplementing introspection with scientific experiments.

Due to its philosophical origins, psychology has been left with a legacy of trying to prove that it is a science as robust as any other, which accounts for the necessity of a six hour statistics exam.

MY TIME AT BEDFORD COLLEGE –
PART TWO

As time progressed, I was adjusting to the somewhat intensive schedule that I had arranged for myself. I was overjoyed that I was coping so well, with the exception of sleep. My head was so full of thoughts at night that I was not finding it easy to unwind when I went to bed. Fearing that my concentration would be badly affected, I decided to make an appointment with my doctor.

I didn't want any medication but hoped she would offer some useful suggestions and perhaps some relaxation exercises. My doctor, who was female, was unavailable so I agreed to see a male doctor.

His first question was straight to the point; "Is there any reason why you aren't sleeping well, Mrs Franklin?"

I explained that I was revising for my second year exams. "And what are you studying?" "Psychology, I am in the second year of my BSc. Degree." "I see, and how are things at home. Do you have any help at home?" "No, I don't", I replied.

Glancing up from my file, he stated, "You have four teenage children, and you are separated from your husband. Is that correct?" "Yes, yes. That is correct."

"Looking at your circumstances, all four children are living at home. You have no help with either the children or with cleaning the house and you are studying for a psychology degree. I would suggest that you are living in a very stressful situation. Let me just take your blood pressure." Upon looking at the reading, the doctor's eyebrows suddenly raised. Seeing his taut expression, I felt my adrenalin steadily rising. His demeanour changed from casual concern to one of alarmed attention.

My blood pressure was unbelievably high. I could be in danger of having a heart attack or a stroke. "Was there any history of high blood pressure in my family?" "Yes, my mother had died at the age of 49 from cerebral haemorrhage and my father had survived an operation for an aneurysm on his aorta caused by high blood pressure.

As he listened, he was writing my prescription for high blood pressure medication. He insisted on prescribing diazepam as he was sure it would help me to relax. I protested vigorously as I was sure it would affect my concentration. He assured me that it was too a low dose to have such a dramatic effect.

"Do you have any further questions?" "I sometimes feel very hot. Could I be having hot flushes? Maybe I'm having an early menopause." Upon hearing the last statement, he laughed out loud. I was insulted as I thought he wasn't taking my symptoms seriously enough. "Some women do have an early menopause", I insisted. "Mrs Franklin, I do want to assure that all these symptoms will disappear, once you have finished your exams." I didn't believe him, but I was in a state of shock about my high blood pressure. I had no choice but to take the prescriptions he was writing to be filled.

Without hesitation, I duly took the prescribed medication for high blood pressure but managed to take the diazepam only once. My fear of experiencing blurred concentration during exams prevented me from complying with the doctor's wishes.

"As soon as your exams are over, your blood pressure will fall. I want you to make another appointment, after exams, to have your blood pressure tested again." I expect any hot flushes you've experienced will disappear too." I wasn't convinced that my blood pressure would fall into the normal range after exams, nor that my sleeplessness and periods of overheating would disappear. But the doctor's prognosis proved to be correct. As soon as exams had ended, my blood pressure returned to normal. My other disturbing symptoms vanished completely, and my sleep pattern improved. I returned to my normal level of worry which revolved mainly around my teenage children, but without the additional worry of exams.

Given my family history, I am a high risk patient, so I maintained my high blood pressure medication but at much lower doses and have continued to deal with the vicissitudes of life without any marked deleterious effects.

JESS VAL BAKER – PART ONE

At Bedford College, Jess Val Baker, one of the mature students, and I had become very good friends. I had attained the ripe, old age of forty-two. She always maintained that, given the fact that she was ten and a half years my senior, at fifty-two and a half, she was, inevitably, more mature, and wiser than I was.

As, during the last (academic) term, Jess and I had been seriously engaged in revising for exams together, I thought that, through the travails of study, we had come to know each other very well. As it turned out, I was seriously mistaken.

She and her husband, Denys invited me to join them on their boat which they sailed every summer to different countries around the Mediterranean.

Denys had written a very popular series of books describing adventures both on and off the boat with their family of six children. Now that their children were adults, not all of them joined their parents on their summer excursions so Jess and Denys invited various friends to accompany them.

Guests were expected to pay a reasonable fee towards expenses, contribute to the weekly food and wine bill and agree to perform certain tasks on the boat.

Their boat, Sanu, a converted motor-fishing vessel, could be propelled by both a motor and sails. During the winter, it was always moored in the last country they had visited. As Denys was bringing the boat to Barcelona, I agreed to meet them there. at the harbour. I flew to Barcelona, armed with my Spanish phrase book and dictionary as I spoke no Spanish.

As the boat was not due to arrive until about six pm, I decided to spend my free time taking a sight-seeing tour of Barcelona. Without too much difficulty, I found a taxi driver and, in broken Spanish, asked him what it would cost to take me round the most outstanding sights of Barcelona. To my dismay, he reminded me that it was siesta time. A sight-seeing tour was impossible as no museums, art galleries or any public buildings were open until much later in the afternoon.

Reluctantly, I asked him to take me to the harbour where I had resigned myself to reading my book until the boat arrived.

The trip to the harbour was uneventful as we did not attempt to engage in conversation but, as soon as we arrived at our destination, the taxi driver removed my suitcase from the boot and began speaking to me in fluent Spanish.

He continually gestured towards a piece of land not far away. I thought he was attempting to describe the landscape adjacent to where we were. As I stood looking perplexed and constantly consulting my dictionary, I finally comprehended what he was saying.

He wanted me to spend the afternoon with him on the not- too-far-away local beach. I was shocked and completely taken aback. Without thinking, I yelled in my very best Italian, "Sono una mamma, una mamma con quattro bambini. NO-NO-NO!!! I was sure that this statement would so shock him that all ideas of any liaison with me would be unthinkable. Not at all!! My outburst seemed to have produced the opposite effect. Smiling broadly, he totally ignored my protestations and unremittingly repeated the name of the beach that we could see in the distance.

His persistence alarmed me and reduced me to screaming even more loudly. "No, No, Assolutamente, No!!!! Assolutamente NO!!!" When he finally decided that my objections were to be taken seriously, he stood absolutely still, stared at me angrily and immediately doubled the fare.

I was furious!! I wanted to argue with him but looking around, I saw no-one within walking distance and only one vague figure very far away. I was standing in a very open space but was entirely alone with this strange man. I could be in a very perilous situation.

I was still angry that he was taking advantage of my situation and charging me an exorbitant fare but I was forced to suppress my rage in hopes of remaining safe and sound. I scrambled through my bag to find the impossible amount of money that he demanded, praying that this bribe would get rid of him.

As he accepted the money, a very slight smile appeared at one corner of his mouth. He looked triumphant and no doubt, thought that I was an idiot, another stupid tourist who should have understood the true value of the money I had given him.

I didn't care what he thought. I just wanted him to leave, to depart as quickly as possible. He took the money, turned towards the taxi and never looking back, sped off down the empty harbour road towards Barcelona.

I sat down on a low cement wall, greatly relieved but wondering if I had done anything to cause this incident. I knew that I hadn't. When I was travelling alone or looked as if I were, men sometimes approached me. Some spoke little English, and some were English. They asked to take me to dinner or to come dancing or to go off with them now, never indicating for what purpose. I was always standing in a taxi queue or waiting at a train station---in more crowded, less vulnerable surroundings.

There was no way that I could have known that the harbour that afternoon would be completely devoid of human beings. There was no need for self-incrimination. All I need do was to add it to my list of unpleasant events that I had managed to survive somehow.

LIFE ON SANU

Much later, in the afternoon, when Sanu had properly moored in the harbour, I boarded her and spent a very pleasant evening eating and drinking the local wine with the Val-Baker family and their friends.

Everyone took turns, two at a time to cook the evening meal. When we moored near any town, the cooks left the boat with shopping bags and the weekly monetary allowance and to buy all the food and alcohol required for the next week.

Everyone was allotted a daily job. Mine was given the ridiculous name of Incentives Officer. It was the job that everyone was hoping to avoid—cleaning the bathroom, the toilet, and the washbasin every day. Everyone knew that some of the younger members of the group could indulge in drinking too much alcohol late at night and as a result, the bathroom would always be the worse for wear. Though at times, it seemed an incessant struggle, I did try to keep the room in some kind of sanitary order.

In the evenings, the younger members usually, went into town to hopefully meet up with other musicians and spend the night improvising music with them until the early hours of the morning.

They always climbed back on the boat, happy and hung over. But, whatever state anyone was in, Denys expected everyone to appear at breakfast to sort out what was on the agenda for that day. There was often a bleary-eyed, nearly comatose group of young people sitting at the breakfast table, swallowing large cups of black coffee, trying to recover from the riotous antics of the previous night.

If we were in harbour, the boat always departed after breakfast for our next destination.

Denys was a marvellous captain and always remained steadfast at the stern whenever stormy weather overtook us, even when we once encountered force nine gales far out in the open sea. While he handled the boat with great skill during violent disturbances, he manoeuvred the boat into narrow mooring spaces with great difficulty. It was not an easy task. After several aborted attempts, he would ultimately succeed. I always admired his perseverance and insistence on overcoming all the obstacles which beset him.

My first morning on board, I noticed that when we were a few miles away from the harbour, everyone had suddenly disappeared. I had been told that Denys and the two men would be working in the engine room, so I assumed that they were engaged in their assigned duties there. But where were the women?

A few minutes later, I heard faint voices growing louder and louder as they climbed the ladder from the kitchen below to the upper deck. Imagine my astonishment when four young women, all in their twenties, emerged, one by one and stood casually on the deck stark naked. Two were Jess and Denys's children and two were their friends.

I was sitting, fully clothed, bedecked with my sunhat, sunglasses, and old leather sandals. While they all laughed uncontrollably at my startled reaction, I could only sit and stare in disbelief.

Jess's youngest daughter tried to explain the situation. "Didn't Jess tell you, no-one wears any clothes on the boat. We are free, free to enjoy the feeling of warm sun on our bodies, free to swim without any suits, free to be as nature intended!"

As she was engaged in explanation, Jess and her friend climbed on deck, also stark naked, but adorned with very large, floppy sunhats.

As they all stood proudly naked before me and stared resolutely at my clothed body, they were attempting by force of will and sheer social pressure to make me disrobe.

It was then that the gentle teasing began. "I was square. I didn't know how to relax. I was too inhibited, too conventional, to throw off the restrictions of socially acceptable behaviour. Had I ever tried to get in touch with my natural self?"

"All this analysis," I thought, "and for free. Soon they'll be telling me that my restrictive ego has suppressed my free inner child." I was resistant, very determined to withstand the constant pressure of their trying to embarrass me into joining them.

I resented the fact that any disagreement with the majority outlook labelled one as somehow an oppressed or repressed individual. There was no room for a different opinion.

One of the men suddenly rushed on deck to pick up something he had forgotten, and he was wearing shorts!

"I thought you said that everyone wore no clothes on the boat. Bob is wearing shorts," I pointed out. "Oh, the men don't strip because they are working in the engine room. They might get their willies caught in the engine," everyone rushed to explain.

"Alright," I said, "When the men take their clothes off, I will. From its inception, this insistence on stripping has been completely biased against anyone who doesn't agree and it's totally selective in its application. It's only relevant to the females on board." I sat on my deck chair fully dressed and defiantly refusing to comply with their wishes.

EVENINGS ON THE BOAT

In one other respect, I proved to be a strange and unusual guest for the Val Baker family. After dinner, everyone was to be found sitting on the deck, relaxing, and sipping another glass of the local wine.

The twenty and thirty year olds did not depart for town until much later. When inclined, they would take out their musical instruments and entertain us with a series of unexpected lively and spontaneous creations.

One of Jess's children was always asking to borrow one of my very mild cigarettes. As I only smoked occasionally, I was happy to comply with her request. But I couldn't understand why she would want my cigarettes as I knew that she preferred only the stronger variety.

As I saw her continually split the cigarette open and put something inside it, I finally asked Jess and Denys what she was doing. Why was she putting a black bean inside the cigarette?

The younger individuals overheard my question to Jess and Denys and initially, stared at me incredulously. After a few moments of quiet snickering, they all burst into riotous laughter. "A bean, a bean, a black bean", they chanted. Someone even started to play, improvising on the drum, creating a rhythm for "a bean, a bean, a black bean."

I did note that the cigarette was passed round to everyone to take a puff. But it wasn't held in the normal fashion, between the index and third finger. It was always poised between the thumb and the index finger, and each person took what appeared to be one very considered, very long puff.

No-one could believe that I had never seen or engaged in this very common ritual prior to tonight. "Where had I been all my life? What had I been doing? I hadn't lived."

They explained that it was cannabis or "pot" as it was commonly known then. "How could I have reached the age of forty-three and have never smoked pot?" Let alone, never even seen it?" They were the teenagers of the sixties and could never imagine a life without the presence of mind-altering substances.

I explained that I was otherwise engaged, in studying and working and producing babies. According to them, none of these activities should have prevented me from discovering the exhilarating effects of smoking pot. As they encouraged me, I became more curious. What effects would I experience if I tried it?

Very carefully holding the cigarette in the proscribed manner (I thought that might affect the outcome), I took my first puff of their cigarette, instantly started coughing and expelled the smoke.

With everyone cheering me on, I tried again. Everyone complained. "I wasn't taking a deep enough breath. I'd never feel the benefit. You have to inhale deeply."

They were right. I wasn't inhaling the smoke deeply. When I smoked cigarettes, I had trained myself not to inhale or to inhale as little smoke as possible. I seemed unable to break the habit. Under their tutelage, I tried several times but exhaling the smoke was such an ingrained habit, I never experienced that trance-like state of deep relaxation into which others seemed to disappear.

As I was wasting their precious store of cannabis, I insisted that they stop offering me puffs of their special cigarettes.

For the younger individuals on the boat, I was a quaint anomaly from another era, incapable of enjoying the pleasures of cannabis and obdurate in not following the group norm for nudity.

As we sailed round the Balearic Isles, the Val Baker family learned to live with their obstinate guest, and I learned to live with their mildly critical remarks. As a result, I spent my month happily on the boat, constantly teased, but cannabis-free and consistently clothed.

JESS VAL BAKER – PART TWO

Due to an incident which occurred in our third year, Jess and I were to become even closer friends.

We were attending the Friday afternoon lab, attempting to carry out an assignment for the Animal Psychology course. The task was to plan an original psychology experiment. Three of us had decided to work together to see if we could condition snails to cross a scratchy surface to obtain food.

We left the lab to explore the surrounding gardens. It was a cold spring day, overcast with patches of dark, grey clouds, a fact which hindered our ability to find snails easily. In our attempts to find these elusive creatures, we had all gone in different directions.

In the midst of our totally silent surroundings, we were all gingerly picking our way across the slippery ground and examining the shiny, moist bushes for any signs of snails. Two of us heard a sudden shriek and rushed from afar to eventually find Jess lying prostrate on the ground. She had fallen on her right hand and was in great pain.

At the college infirmary, the nurse put her arm in a sling. Our lecturer, Dr. Lawlor, insisted that I drive her to hospital immediately. The orthopaedic department confirmed that she had broken two bones in her right hand. After treatment, I insisted that she should come home to stay with me. As she could use only her left hand. Normal activities which required two hands would be impossible.

All my entreaties were in vain. Her daughter, Jill, had just produced a new baby and that evening the whole family was celebrating the occasion.

The following morning, she had another hospital appointment. It was a relatively short distance for her to get to the hospital from where she lived, so we agreed that she should go home for the night.

But, the next morning, due to her imbibing too much alcohol the previous night, she had overslept. When she realised that would be very late for her appointment, she dressed in great haste and called a taxi.

The nurses absolutely refused to allow her to see anyone when she arrived at the hospital. She was over half an hour late.

Jess was outraged but also a very good actress. She burst into tears, explaining that she had spent a dreadful night in pain and must have taken too many painkillers. That was why she had overslept. She couldn't bear another night in such agony. Someone had to help her.

Upon hearing this woeful plea, the good doctors were very sympathetic and rushed round in great haste to treat her painful hand. When she left, they admonished her to take only the dose stated on the prescriptions that she had been given.

That same afternoon, my kitchen doorbell rang. As I opened it, Jess, literally, fell into my arms. She had taken a taxi straight to my house after her treatment in hospital. She looked very pale and said that she was in pain and felt as if she were going to faint. Her X-ray had revealed that the two broken bones in her hand had slid over each other. The doctors had pulled them apart and put her hand in a cast. I gave her the prescribed amount of medication and put her to bed.

As I dressed and undressed her every day and cut her meat and vegetables into edible portions, I declared her my fifth child.

To the delight of my children, she stayed with us for approximately six weeks. Being teenagers, they loved her rebellious streak. Any shocking apparel or outrageous behaviour on their part always met with her approval.

Jess and I maintained strongly differing opinions about what teenagers needed. I set up certain rules that I expected the children to abide by. Jess said that I was boringly conventional and was restricting their freedom. This subject remained, forever, an unresolved disagreement between us.

During World War Two, she had learned a long list of bawdy poems which she proudly repeated for my children and always performed at parties.

After one or two glasses of wine, she would spontaneously start to recite some of the following ditties:

"Here's to the girl that lives on the hill,
If she won't, her sister will.
Here's to her sister.

✳ ✳ ✳

"One drink is good,
Two at the most,
Three I'm under the table,
Four I'm under the host."

✳ ✳ ✳

"Here's to the man I love, he is rich
And he adds so much to my life
He buys me everything I want
But please don't tell his wife."
"I want to be naughty and still be nice
I want the fun without the price
I want the thrill of a long-drawn kiss
I want the things that good girls miss

✳ ✳ ✳

I want the lights that brightly shine
I want the men, I want the wine
I want the arms and the heart of a man
And still stay single if I can
Now what I want is a little advice
On how to be naughty and still be nice."

✳ ✳ ✳

"Here's to the girl in blue
Who dresses neat from head to shoe
She always looks wise and is never surprised
No matter what you do."

✳ ✳ ✳

"Here's to the land we love!
And here's to the love we land."

✳ ✳ ✳

During our final year at Bedford College, Jess and I also decided to undertake a one year, one afternoon a week, introductory counselling course. We thought it might be an interesting and challenging career to pursue. But we needed specific training, training which a BSC psychology degree did not provide. We hadn't really decided what path to follow- after acquiring our degree.

In 1978, when we did officially receive our BSC Hons Degrees, Jess returned home to live at the Mill House in St Buryan near Penzance, Cornwall. Denys, her very patient and long-suffering husband awaited her.

When she was studying, they had lived together in a flat in London. But she had always banished him to Cornwall during exam time. He was a writer, and the incessant noise of his typewriter so irritated her that she couldn't concentrate on her studies.

This arrangement had never pleased Denys, so he was overjoyed to have her permanently at home once again.

THE CHILDREN'S EDUCATION

Throughout my time at Bedford College, I had been seriously concerned about the children's education. When Kim entered The King Alfred School in 1970, a new headmistress had been appointed.

Up to this time, the school had a marvellous reputation and I wondered if anything would alter under a new regime.

To my great relief, all the children liked their new school and were even enthusiastic about attending classes. They seemed to have made new friends without any undue difficulties. The school council, where pupils and teachers meet to air problems and make decisions about how the school was run, was particularly popular with them. It was their first experience of direct democracy. They found it a revelation that teachers and pupils' opinions were considered of equal importance.

I was delighted that they were gaining self-confidence and learning the true meaning of equality through exchanging ideas with both their peers and the adults at school.

My first main objection to public school education was that it promoted the development of hierarchical structures with clearly defined roles for domination and submission amongst the students and the second was that it blatantly fostered the idea of elitism. The students emerged feeling that they were somehow born to rule and that they were superior to those who were not from their class and had not had access to their privileges.

As the years progressed, my initial elation and admiration for King Alfred's began to waiver as the ethos of the school slowly began to change. Some teachers were not controlling their classrooms properly. Their students were becoming unruly and disruptive. The children were not receiving enough guidance about how to prepare for exams or about how to organise their time. There was a general laxness in implementing school rules. Despite the fact that parents were complaining about all of these problems, no practical steps were ever taken to improve matters.

Kim and two of his friends, all good students, had become very rebellious. "What is the point of going to school? We all just end up taking exams. We don't believe in exams. All that hard work for nothing. Who needs to have a series of letters after their name?"

Regardless of whether or not they believed in exams, school attendance was mandatory, and employers, colleges and universities demanded that everyone pass certain exams, either for work or further study. I tried to impress these facts upon Kim, to make him aware of the situation he was facing outside of and beyond the school environs. But I could see that my words fell on deaf ears. He was not about to take heed of anything that I was saying.

Feeling desperate about Kim' situation, I approached Roger, hoping that he might help. He had acquired a degree in physics from Cambridge University which had stood him in good stead when he had worked as a research assistant at MIT and later as a teacher in a progressive secondary school. I explained that Kim was refusing to study or to take any exams. His response astounded me.

Education had never helped him to decide what career he really wanted to pursue so he didn't see the point in Kim studying if he didn't want to. For the first time, I understood why he had always refused to attend any of the children's Parents Evenings. He really believed that education was utterly useless.

My heart sank. I felt that his answer was too egocentric and was mistaken in its premise. It revolved around his interpretation of the worth of his own education.

What really upset me was the fact that his son's future did not seem of paramount importance to him and that his point of view supported Kim in his most infantile behaviour.

The mothers of Kim's two friends were fighting precisely the same battle as I was. But with the help of their husbands, the two of them began to resolve their problems. One of Kim's friends eventually applied himself to his studies and went on to study music at university.

The second one left the school. Because his son was so recalcitrant, his father felt that he was wasting his money paying school fees. He joined his father in his photography business and for many decades, ran a very successful business on Oxford Street, taking passport photos.

I thought seriously about moving the children to a different school, one that offered more structure and support, particularly at the time when they were preparing to take their first exams.

But I began to have second thoughts about planning yet another change in their lives. They had lived through their parents' separation, a move to a new house and a new school and were obliged to make new friends, all, more or less at the same time.

They were adamant. They didn't want to move. They liked their new school and their new friends. Some of the teachers were excellent and really helpful with exam preparation.

I also suspected that drugs were circulating in the school. Some parents claimed that the school was very quietly dealing with a serious drug problem.

Whenever I asked the children if this were so, they always claimed not to know. Their response might have been a direct reaction to my very strong disapproval of drug use and drug culture.

There was no point in removing them from the school to avoid drugs. Most of the secondary schools, whether state or public, in and around Hampstead admitted to the existence of a drug problem. I finally decided that changing schools was not an option. It would only create distress and further problems for everyone.

So, in spite of my misgivings about King Alfred's, the children remained where they were. As the girls continued to study without any signs of protest, I remained hopeful that they would acquire the grades required for university or college.

Only after leaving King Alfred's did they discuss the drug problem at school. They informed me that the children who were involved with drugs did no work at school, constantly disrupted their classrooms and spoiled all the parties they attended. The rest of the students were so annoyed with their inconsiderate behaviour that they had no desire to follow in their footsteps.

Natasha and her best friend stopped going to parties because they complained that the boys were always drunk and bleary-eyed on beer not long after the party had started. They never commented on whether or not they suspected that drugs might have contributed to their non-communicative, lethargic state.

None of these statements assumes that my children have never taken drugs at any stage in their life. The time was the early seventies. Drugs were available at some of the parties that I was invited to then and for many years, were, undoubtedly, more prolific at the parties that the children attended.

Apparently, when my children attended King Alfred's, the school was rife with drugs. I am pleased but also surprised that none of them became seriously involved with any kind of drug-taking.

THE YEARS 1979 – 1980

The years after leaving Bedford College, proved not to be very productive ones. I had applied to study for a Master's Degree in Educational Psychology and had been rejected. I had been warned that the competition was very high but had clung onto a slim hope that I would be accepted.

But I never reapplied for a Master's Degree Educational Psychology. Professor Foss, the head of the Psychology Department, and I met one day to discuss my future prospects in that field.

He said that I was too easily discouraged. The last student who had applied for a master's in educational psychology had applied five times before being accepted. I mustn't give up so quickly.

I, somehow, did not find his words very reassuring. Applying for the same qualification for that length of time was not a very appealing prospect.

I was not a young twenty year old but a middle-aged woman with less time to spare. I preferred to try my luck elsewhere.

Because I had not made other plans, I was now at a loss to know which way to turn. Having teaching qualifications and teaching experience, I thought that working with children who had difficulties with reading or were dyslexic might prove an interesting and challenging area to pursue.

I found no courses for teaching dyslexics so I applied for what I thought would be the most appropriate course for teaching students with reading problems. I enrolled on a University of London Diploma in Education Course with special reference to the learning and teaching of reading.

The classes were composed entirely of teachers who were unhappy to learn that in the course of acquiring more professional qualifications, they were required to take a statistics course. After our first statistics lecture, several individuals sat glued to their seats in a state of heightened tension, declaring that they hadn't understood a word that the lecturer had said.

I regarded their plight with great sympathy. It was certainly a case of deja vu. The main difference between their experience and mine was that their statistics lecturer had explained each step of every test very clearly. If only our lecturer at Bedford had possessed this kind of teaching expertise, I might have approached statistics in a more relaxed state of mind instead of one with overwhelming high anxiety.

Seeing their distress, I offered to show them the steps required to set up their first statistics test. Everyone immediately exclaimed that I was a genius. There was obviously, no justification for that conclusion.

I explained that I had studied statistics for three years and after that, it was inevitable that some residual knowledge remained. When necessary, I continued to help students with further statistics tests. I was surprised and delighted that, despite my strong resistance to the learning the subject, I understood it well enough to teach others.

After receiving my Diploma in Education, I started applying for suitable teaching jobs. I filled in many applications but was almost never invited to attend an interview. For the two interviews that I did obtain, I was never informed about my position. Initially, I would wonder if I had been successful but after many weeks of no correspondence of any sort, I would conclude that I had been rejected. Being left in limbo about the outcome of interviews most definitely increased my anxiety about ever finding a job.

Friends tried to reassure me. Teaching jobs were always oversubscribed. I would find one sooner or later. I was beginning to feel desperate. To allay my fears, I decided to try a different path to find a job.

During the 1980's, various councils were promoting literacy programmes for adults who had difficulty reading.

Notes were posted on most library doors, encouraging non-literate adults to apply for courses. I rang one of the numbers listed on a library door in Temple Fortune, asking if someone could tell me who organised these courses. I was given the name of a woman whose office was in the suburbs, some distance from London.

When we met, she felt it was somehow fortuitous that I had rung. She was just about to advertise for someone to fill the post for teaching adult literacy. When she enquired about my qualifications, she remarked that I more than fulfilled the requirements for the job.

We discussed what particular skills might be required and the details of the programme that they employed. She could see that I was enthusiastic and said that if I were hired, I would be working with her. She wanted to hire me on the spot, but a second interview was required with the Director of the Literacy Programme. She would inform her that she thought I was the perfect candidate for the job. I left that interview feeling very elated and with very high hopes.

A week later, I was duly interviewed by the Director of the Literacy Programme. Technically, the interview appeared to go well. I answered all her questions adequately and asked her a few of my own. But when I left, I knew that I hadn't been accepted, though I could not specify why.

The interviewer had remained reserved and distant throughout the interview and had given me no indication that she thought that I would be the appropriate individual for the post. Knowing that I would be rejected left me feeling quite discouraged. I had glimpsed the possibility of doing something very challenging and very useful and was seriously disappointed not to have been successful in my quest.

A few months later, I went to a party with a friend. Chatting with some of the teachers, both male and female, I recounted the details of my last interview. They all seemed to know the name of the Director of the Literacy Programme.

Immediately, there was a general consensus amongst them. She would never have hired me. I had already acquired the proper credentials for the job while she was still studying and was in the process of obtaining the requisite qualifications. Given these facts, I felt that there was no doubt that she could have seen me as a threat to her position.

That explanation could account for the reason that I was rejected. Though it didn't make me feel any better, it did teach me a lesson.

Incidental factors might play an important part in the process of rejection. I, who was so prone to self-criticism and self-blame, in response to failure, might be denigrating myself in situations where I was in no way responsible for the negative outcome. At a time when I was not attaining interviews for jobs or was being rejected for them, I felt I would have to work hard to keep this lesson in the forefront of my thoughts.

THE CHILDREN'S TEENAGE YEARS and MY FATHER'S FUNERAL

While I was busy studying and trying to establish a career for myself, the children were growing rapidly and constantly changing.

Maintaining the balance between allowing them to make their own choices and setting down rules to keep them safe was an unsteady path on which I teetered all the time. As teenagers, desiring to make their own decisions, they were quick to perceive any rule as an injustice, something that crushed their independence, and I was told that my rules were always much harsher and more stringent than those that any other mother imposed.

I seemed to be either firmly supporting my rules and in constant argument and prolonged discussion with one teenager, or with another, watching the firm ground where I stood slowly receding as I felt I should gingerly relinquish control.

There are no rules to indicate when the magic moment of maturity arrives or that specify when a teenager is ready to become more independent and behave more responsibly.

When all four of them were pushing the boundaries and testing their limits and mine simultaneously, I remained in an exhausted and worried state of mind, concerned about whether or not I was making the right decisions.

When they began to leave home, I really missed them. But I can honestly say that I never missed this testing time in their development when my patience and endurance were so severely tried.

In 1977, Michèle was enrolled as an art student at Camberwell College. During her time there, she lived away from home in shared rented accommodation. Natasha left home soon after, in 1979, to study for a recently-established degree in Liberal Studies in Science (genetics and politics of science) at Manchester University.

Leda took a year out after she finished King Alfred's to study dance at the Floral Street Studios. Although she had never had any dance lessons as a child, she went to New York and was accepted as a ballet student at the Dance Theatre of Harlem. She eventually received a BA degree in philosophy and choreography from New York University.

Kim left home in 1980 but felt under no obligation to study as he had inherited some money. Many years later, he did study again at a college in

California, but he never completed his course as, in his final year, he returned to England to live.

By 1981, all the children had departed. I was now living alone and feeling very frustrated that I had not yet found a teaching position.

As I was having no success in acquiring work, I opted to return to study. While still looking for jobs, I had started another counselling course at the Westminster Pastoral foundation to follow on from the introductory course that Jess and I had taken during our final year at Bedford College.

During the second year of my course, my brother rang to tell me that my father was very ill. The four children and I flew to the States to visit him in the Mount Auburn Hospital in Cambridge, Mass. where he was a patient. After an exploratory operation, we were given the news that he had stomach cancer and it had spread. There was no point in operating as it was terminal.

The situation was very depressing as we all knew that he had only a short time to live, and there was nothing that anyone could do to help him. To control the pain, he was highly sedated with morphine, so he remained in a permanently drowsy state. Conversation was minimal and intermittent. We, sadly, watched him grow weaker every day until on the 29th of January 1982, he died peacefully in his sleep.

MY FATHER'S FUNERAL

My father's funeral took place at his church in Boston. In recent years, he had attended it infrequently, because he didn't find the sermons of the newly appointed minister very inspiring.

My brother and I prepared ourselves for a more emotive church service than we were accustomed to.

For many years, my brother and I were members of Christ Church, the Episcopalian Church in Harvard Square, Cambridge, Mass., where the minister was white, and the congregation was white. It was really the Church of England, the C of E, transplanted to the States. We followed the same order of service and used the same prayer book, but the Episcopalian church was no longer under the jurisdiction of the monarchy. In all other respects, they were exactly the same.

Sermons related to a religious or moral subject and were always a low-keyed affair. The minister's presentation was not without feeling but spoken as an orator might deliver a well-intentioned speech, with strong emphasis in significant places to create a convincing point of view.

We had attended a church with a predominantly black congregation only once before, at a celebration of Easter. We knew that black ministers were more enthusiastic and demonstrative in the delivery of their sermons and tried to make an emotional impact on their congregation, their voices ascending and descending in a measured flow of words.

At the funeral service, I listened intently. The rhythmic cadences of the choir singing combined with the lyricism of the minister's words unwittingly captured my attention and drew me in.

But as my focus shifted from the music to the spoken words, my rapture was bought to an abrupt standstill. A stark realisation struck me. Regardless of how hard I tried, I could not accept the content of what was being said.

I made an attempt, as I had at my mother's funeral, to believe that my father would reside in heaven with God and have everlasting life. But my strong desire and good intentions did not produce or create any new evidence that would force me to accept these beliefs as true.

My father believed that he would be reunited with my mother in heaven. True faith can bring great comfort in times of despair and disaster. Throughout his life, his faith and strong religious beliefs were his support through many a distressing misfortune.

Despite my fervent desire to believe, I had to accept that I had failed to achieve either strong religious convictions or a strong faith. Both had eluded me. I could only observe the power of these beliefs and never partake of their advantages or benefits.

LEAVING THE FUNERAL

As the funeral service ended, the family stood up and turned round to walk down the aisle to exit the church. I was shocked. The church looked almost completely full. Plangent organ music accompanied every step of our very slow departure.

I could clearly see the faces of the people in the aisles. Some I recognised immediately. Some were vaguely familiar from childhood and others were total strangers. I did not recognise them at all.

My father had a few good workmates, and a few close friends and relatives. They would never have been enough to nearly fill this entire church.

Everyone knows that the people who attend funerals are not drawn from a selective list. A notice usually appears in the local paper or papers announcing the date, time, and place of an individual's funeral. Anyone who desires to do so can attend.

I should have been pleased at the number of people there, given the generally accepted dictum that the more people that show up for the funeral, the more supported the family will be.

But many of these people were unfamiliar and unknown to us. It seemed unlikely that they had come to the church to offer support to a family they had never met and about whom they knew very little.

Many people we knew had rung to send their condolences to the family at this distressing time. But why had the people who had never seen or even encountered my father made the effort to be present at his funeral?

After prolonged perusal over the probable reasons for their attendance, I concluded that it may have been predominantly inspired by curiosity, curiosity about the offspring of a mixed-race marriage.

Lest you think that this response is indicative of my cynical expectations of human behaviour, consider the recent widespread speculation about the predicted appearance of Harry and Meghan's new baby.

The children of mixed-race marriages are often the objects of extreme curiosity, subject to numerous theoretical assumptions about their facial features, the texture of their hair and their complexion.

Have there been any other married royals where various artists and genetic scientists have presented prospective images of the unborn baby's appearance in the daily newspapers? No, none that we can remember. Certainly, William and Kate received no such attention in relation to the birth of any of their three children.

The very fact that such selective, supposedly scientific studies are undertaken only underlines my point.

In the congregation were also most, if not all, of the neighbours I had known since childhood. People had come to the funeral to pay respect to my father. But it was inevitable that they would see me.

My mind began to wander. My attention shifted from the funeral to the last open encounters I had experienced with my neighbours. Because I had the temerity to date a few white men, I had transgressed a serious social taboo. My behaviour was considered so reprehensible that I was socially ostracised. No-one had deigned to speak to me.

These were the people who had so blatantly disapproved of my marriage and spread such outrageous and devastating rumours about me around the community. For a moment, I wondered why they would even want to be in the same room as someone so disgraceful as I was purported to be.

Shifting my focus again to the funeral and the people assembled, I was forced to put all such thoughts to one side. People were in attendance for my father's benefit. I hoped that those who had come to mourn my father's death had no time to focus on me or my presence -but were consumed with sadness and sorrow for our great loss.

After we had moved to England, we visited my family in the States less frequently. Attending my father's funeral, was the first prolonged visit home that I had made since my wedding. Since I had returned, I had experienced some unexpected and unusual incidents. A woman whom I did not know, ran down the path in front of her house to greet me as I was passing by. She explained that she was the aunt of a teenage friend. I was perplexed as she acted as if it were important to make some kind of contact with me.

An ex-boyfriend's aunt asked why hadn't I invited her to my wedding many years ago. As I walked down a street, people who were strangers waved to me. The neighbours whom I met incidentally, greeted me pleasantly and seemed eager to speak to me.

I was stunned and baffled. Somehow a new, more positive outlook must have been caste on my previously unacceptable, despicable behaviour. From 1953, when I was married until 1982, nearly thirty years later, the world in which I had grown up had been ever so slowly changing.

Openly hostile feelings towards me and the idea of a mixed-race marriage had been transformed into what appeared to be a very polite welcome these many years later. I was surprised and pleased to take note of these changes.

In the 1950's, a mixed-race marriage was a rare phenomenon and a highly contentious act. Since then, so many more mixed-race marriages had occurred, the idea itself had become more commonplace and somewhat more acceptable, even if still not approved of by everyone.

I bore no grudges against the neighbours in my community although I was, initially deeply hurt when, in 1953, the entire neighbourhood had stopped speaking to me. I had survived their rejections and unjustified allegations against me.

As their prejudices had proved to be unfounded, over time, their attitudes had altered. I was pleased that their opinions had moved in the direction of a more accepting outlook on a situation which they had previously condemned.

But I was upset when I learned that due to the false rumours that were circulating about me, my parents had become very concerned and remained in a very distressed state of mind for a very long period of time. I deeply regretted any unnecessary worry and concern that they had suffered on my behalf.

Had they been alive, they would have been surprised to learn that, with the passage of time, my scandalous marriage so beset with deleterious rumours, had undergone a marked change. No longer notorious, it had become something of noteworthy significance, approved of now by the same neighbours who had so determinedly despised it.

FATHER'S AWARD

While sorting out my father's papers after his funeral, my brother came across an unusual, large white embossed envelope. When he opened it, carefully unfolding the neatly wrapped tissue paper inside, he discovered an award that had been presented to my father.

My brother and I both commented on the fact that he had never mentioned receiving any award. We were surprised that he hadn't wanted to share his good news with us. We were even more surprised when we saw that it was issued by the US Treasury Department.

As a port patrol officer, he had worked for the US Customs Department for as long as we could remember. We never recalled his having any other position or any other type of work.

He had devoted most of his mature life to this particular job: dayshifts and nightshifts, never missing a day's work, even when he felt unwell. Only once when he was in hospital with a seriously infected finger, did he feel that he had a legitimate excuse not to go to work.

Civil Service jobs were not that easy to acquire. A specific pass mark on a civil service exam was required before anyone could be considered for any type of work in this service.

Though never acknowledged, the civil service probably operated a secret quota system on the jobs available to black people. In over twenty years, only three black people had ever been hired as port patrol officers. My father considered himself fortunate to have acquired a stable civil service job with a secure pension.

Every so often, employees could take exams that would offer them promotion on their job. Year after year, my father took these exams and year after year, he was never promoted. The same situation existed in relation to the other two black employees. No matter how many times they took the exams for promotion, they remained static, in the same position which they had held for at least two decades.

They all felt that there was a barrier erected by the civil service which prevented them from ever achieving a position of higher rank.

These were the days when racial discrimination was unrestrained in most institutions. There would have been no organisation set up to challenge the discriminatory decisions of the employers and managers within the civil service.

But, despite constant and consistent defeat, my father never stopped trying to attain a promotion, He was always disappointed when he was, once again, told that he had not been successful.

My brother and I could remember that after such disappointing news, my father would arrive home in such a state of anguish and distress that he would sit downcast with his head in his hands.

To soothe him, my mother would bring him endless cups of hot tea with a slice of lemon as that was his favourite beverage. At some point in their conversation they usually commented on the fact that prejudice had ruined the chances of many hard-working black people who had good prospects. She commiserated with him and his relentless attempts to attain promotion to create a better future for the family.

Despite his loss of hope and his state of distress, my father would allow himself only one evening to indulge in these feelings. The next morning, it was if he told himself-Life must go on! He rose, put on his port patrol officer's uniform, never mentioning the previous night and went to work as if nothing untoward had happened.

He and his two friends were overjoyed to have acquired civil service jobs because the pensions were assured and more reasonable than those in some other occupations.

They all had nearly perfect work records, with no unjustified absences of any sort. Their aim was to work to the best of their ability and retire when they were allowed to do so, with a reasonable pension which would support them and their families in their old age. That had been my father's aim from the very first day that he had joined the civil service.

Imagine his state of shock and bewilderment when his manager informed him two years before his retirement, that he would have to be moved to a different state to work. He would keep the same position but would have to spend his last two years of work in Alabama or Mississippi. His other choice was to remain in Massachusetts--to continue working in the civil service but, at the post office, taking a job of much lower rank and at much lower pay.

Alabama and Mississippi were in the deep South, notorious for being two of the most prejudiced states against black people in the USA. With the support of the local population, the Ku Klux Klan had always flourished in these areas. They prided themselves on having established Jim Crow laws which enforced the practice of segregating black people at all levels of society.

In 1954, the famous case of Brown vs. the Board of Education of Topeka Kansas declared that segregation was outlawed in the public schools. This ruling had so angered the white supremacists that episodes of racial hatred and aggression had intensified and escalated in the deep south in the years following the decision. Legalised segregation lasted up to the mid-sixties in most of these areas.

The time was the early nineteen sixties. My father's superiors were insisting that he could keep his job and his pension only on condition that he walk into the hotbed of hatred that existed in both Alabama and Mississippi. No sensible black person would willingly choose to live in a state where white control and black subjugation were considered the norms of everyday existence.

My father very reluctantly took the job in the post office at much lower pay and in a position of low status. Under the pressure of their continually changing his hours of work and the tedious quality of unrewarding work, he decided to retire after working there for only one year. As a result, he, of course, received a much reduced pension.

My brother and I read the words of this distinguished award.

The US Treasury Department officially bestowed the Albert Gallatin Award to John Robert Allen on December the 30th 1964.

"This award is presented as an evidence of the esteem in which you are held by the Treasury Department which has been the principal beneficiary of your labors for so many years.

The fine contribution you have made to the public service well merits this commendation of your Government."

These worthless and insincere words clearly exude the hypocrisy of the Treasury Department's position. The Albert Gallatin Award must remain as a symbol of the Government's deceit and its refusal to fulfil its promise to recognise my father's years of loyal, hard work with a well-earned substantial annual pension.

MOVING FROM WILDOOD ROAD TO BELSIZE SQUARE

When all the children had left home, I had no need to live in a five-bedroom house. In 1982, I decided to look for a smaller residence.

When I put the house on the market, all of the real-estate agents that I contacted, assured me that my house would fetch a very good price and there would be no problem selling it as it was situated in a very appealing area adjacent to the Heath Extension.

It now seemed reasonable and sensible to move from a house to a flat as the requisite living space was so much less than I had previously required.

Having looked for about a month at unsuitable flats, I was overjoyed when I found what appeared to be the ideal accommodation, a basement flat in Belsize Square with an adjoining garden. The three bedrooms were absolutely necessary, two for Jess and me and one available for a guest or one of the children when they decided to visit.

I was disappointed that after five weeks on the market, I hadn't sold my house and I was desperate to acquire the Belsize Square flat. As I didn't have the money to buy the flat, there was only one solution, I would have to take out a bridging loan from the bank. I was reassured by the estate agents that I need not worry, my house was sure to be sold. They had been selling houses in Hampstead Garden Suburb for many years and had never experienced any problems. They certainly made me feel that I was worrying unnecessarily about how long a sale would take.

My mother-in-law encouraged me to ask Roger for a loan rather than pay the unreasonably high interest rates the banks were charging for loans. I was very reluctant to do so but was eventually convinced to ring him. He adamantly refused to loan me the money so I was forced to turn to the bank for help.

Having taken out the bridging loan and observing week after week that my house had not been sold, I queried the estate agents once again. What was the difficulty in selling the house? They had assured me a quick sale. I could see that they were avoiding my glance and in no hurry to respond to my question.

One of them finally mustered the courage to speak to me. Almost two months after engaging them, he informed of their fears concerning the housing market. Quite unexpectedly and for no apparent reason, house prices had begun to fall.

In order to sell my house, I would have to reduce the price. That the economic climate had become so unfavourable for selling houses seriously upset me. I had only taken out the bridging loan because they had guaranteed me a quick sale and a very good price for my house.

I became entwined in an infinite chain of domino reactions. At least four different offers were made to buy the house but because none of the prospective buyers could sell their houses, they were obliged to withdraw their offers.

With good reason, I had completely lost faith in the advice of real estate agents. I lost thousands of pounds because I believed that they understood the housing market and I could trust what they told me.

It was not until I moved into the flat in Belsize Square that I discovered that the third bedroom was too small for any bed to fit in. The builder who was renovating the kitchen measured it for the smallest beds and in desperation, one which could fold against the wall. It was all to no avail. No beds of even the smallest proportions could ever have fitted into that restricted space.

I did eventually sell the house in Wildwood Road but at a much reduced price and I, then, paid off the exorbitant bridging loan.

ADVICE TO ALL CHILDREN and GRANDCHIDREN

Don't ever believe that the real estate agent's advice is infallible. Remember that your house is not sold when the prospective buyer says he's definitely buying it. It's not until he signs the contract that the sale is completed.

Don't take out a bridging loan unless you know that the funds are available to pay it off. The interest rates are prohibitive.

If there is a small bedroom in any house you wish to buy, measure it, to assure that it will at least accommodate a bed.

The SURGERY

Every time I met my brother-in-law, Owen, who was a GP in London, he was perturbed by the number of problems patients wanted to discuss during their 6 to10 minute consultation, unhappy marriages, bereavement, children who were misbehaving, problem neighbours etc.

He always explained that doctors were trained to deal with physical problems, not emotional ones. He and his colleagues never had enough time to listen and were at a loss to know how to help them.

A friend of mine who happened to be present when he was speaking, proposed that he should consider hiring me. She suggested that, as a psychologist, I might be able to help with the patients' problems and possibly save the doctors some time.

As Owen felt that he and his colleagues were completely perplexed about how to proceed, he said he would ask them to consider her suggestion.

Many people assumed that it was due to nepotism that I was hired at the surgery. But this was most definitely not the case. I was treated as any prospective applicant for a job would have been.

I was invited to have an interview with Owen's seven partners and to discuss the qualifications I had which might be relevant for working with the patients. Initially, I was hired only temporarily to see how the patients felt about being offered someone to talk to and for the doctors to decide how much time such a service would save for them.

After a successful trial period, I was offered a job in the surgery. As far as I was concerned, it was the ideal working situation. I had the opportunity to deal with a wide variety of patients problems and an even wider variety of people. At the surgery, over one hundred and ten different nationalities were registered.

This apparently ideal situation was marred by only one setback. There was no job description in the National Health Service for a psychologist or a therapist to work with patients and their problems. The job they were hiring me for just didn't exist.

They looked through the list of jobs available for the surgery. Only a new receptionist's job could be offered. Wonderful, on the books, I was listed as a new receptionist. But there was one big disadvantage associated with my new position, I would also be paid the salary of a new receptionist. There was no other money available to pay me.

Although I was disappointed about the amount of money I would receive, I was so excited at being offered such a highly desirable and challenging job, I accepted the undesirable pay situation without protest.

I had no office but moved from room to room, using the empty room any doctor had vacated on his day off. In the beginning, there were some minor misunderstandings about the kinds of patients I should see. I ruled out psychotic patients as their perception of reality was so distorted that one could not easily establish any kind of relationship, something that was essential if we were to work together. Patients who required long term help from the NHS mental health services were not suitable either as the number of sessions I could offer was limited. The service was available for most patients at the surgery and for those with mental health problems who were stabilised on their medication.

When I first started working, I thought that there was a problem with how the doctors were describing the service I offered. Patients would arrive in my office, asking; "Why has he sent me to you? I'm not mad." "She must think I'm crazy." "I don't need a shrink."

The doctors were not actually misleading them. They just never explained clearly to the patients why they thought they should see me. The outcome was that the patients filled in the questions they had about me with their own assumptions and fears.

In the beginning, the patient's anxiety about me was so high that I was forced to spend many sessions explaining what I wasn't able to do, I didn't know what they were thinking, I couldn't predict their future prospects, I couldn't promise that I would resolve their problems nor guarantee that they would feel better at the end of our session. Broken relationships could be mended but not by me. Whatever happened depended on the decisions of the individuals involved.

I reassured them that my powers were only the ones that normal human beings possessed and that I only knew what they chose to tell me about themselves. I had no psychic powers nor was I able to read their minds. When we got to this point, I suggested that if they desired to do so, we might be able to look at whatever problems they wished to discuss. We would be involved in a collaborative process. With the information they disclosed to me, I could help them to look at how they were functioning. It would be their decision to either to leave things as they were or try to change the situation.

Everything looks so reasonable as I type out the words of what is involved in the therapeutic process, but the emotions involved can be unpredictable and sometimes volatile. I was often the brunt of a patient's anger when I refused to tell them what to do. This was the case many times over as I tried to explain that I was there to help individuals make their own decisions, a difficult situation when the individual involved is resisting this very process. Accusations could be hurled at me angrily: "The one time I really need someone to lean on, and you won't do anything." "Just tell me what to do so I can get on with my life." "I thought you were supposed to help me."

Fortunately, to carry on this type of work, everyone is required to have personal therapy and supervision. The former is particularly useful in clarifying what your own problems or difficult areas are and how they might interfere with the therapeutic process. The second really focuses on what happens in each session, what is going well or what might be altered or improved.

I was hired as a psychologist to work in the surgery but using this job title could prove problematic as people often thought that psychologists possessed special abilities to control or influence others.

The doctors thought that the patients would find the title of counsellor far less threatening than that of psychologist and suggested that I should be called a counsellor.

To illustrate what could happen when using a title that patients found suspicious: After our fifty minute session, the young woman I was seeing rushed to reception to enquire whether or not I was a psychologist. She had seen a book with the word psychology in the title standing between the many books on my desk. As the receptionist couldn't answer her question (she didn't know), she did return to see me. As we had already established a relationship, we were able to discuss her fears around seeing a psychologist and did continue our sessions. Had she known I was a psychologist before we started our sessions, she informed me that she never would have contemplated seeing me.

To my surprise, even the title, counsellor, did not initially prevent me from incurring the clients' worst worries and fears. It must be remembered that the time was the early 1980's. Prior to this time, counselling and therapy had never been offered in GP surgeries. The idea of dealing with emotional problems was a foreign concept and frightening to most individuals who were accustomed to having only their physical problems dealt with at the surgery.

THE COMPUTER.

One day, the head receptionist asked to speak to me privately. She informed me that a computer was due to arrive in my consulting room. She didn't know when, but it was definitely happening soon. "I assume that I'll be expected to use it," I stated. She responded that everyone assumed that would be the case.

I was furious that this decision was made without the consideration of even consulting me. After all, I was the person directly affected by this new transaction.

When, a few weeks later, the practice manager casually told me that a computer had been placed on my desk for my use, I exploded. I, who had never raised my voice at anyone in the surgery suddenly yelled at the practice manager, "You could, at least, have had the common courtesy to consult me about this" and turned briskly to exit the room.

The two nurses in the room and the receptionist at the photocopier turned in shock and surprise as I hastily slammed the door and climbed the stairs to my room. Suddenly, one of the nurses appeared outside of my door. "Beverly, you're upset. Maybe, you need a brandy or a cup of tea with a brandy in it." "No, no" I protested. "I don't need anything."

The second nurse then appeared, wanting to know if she could do anything to help. A minute later, the receptionist arrived to support me in my moment of distress. I was very touched by their concern and explained why I was so angry.

"The doctors often make decisions without consulting the staff. But when the staff is directly affected by their decisions, I think they have a duty to inform the people involved. I feel that my opinion is considered irrelevant, even in matters that relate to me. If they had consulted me, I could have told them that I was not computer literate.

Very generously, the receptionist immediately offered to teach me how to use the computer. One morning, before work, I learned how to set up the patient list for the day, how to check the patients out and contact reception for my next patient. It was not as difficult as I had anticipated.

As a result of my vociferous outburst towards having the computer installed, a meeting was arranged with the practice manager, one of the doctors and me. Although I had been paid as a receptionist for a long period of time, the doctors had recently decided that I was to become a permanent member of staff.

At the meeting, I explained that I was insulted that they would make a decision about placing a computer in my room without even discussing the matter with me.

I then proceeded to discuss my salary. The doctor immediately proposed a rise of £5.00 a month. Even the practice manager objected to this suggestion as it was so ridiculously low. I was even more insulted about her insignificant offer of a rise. "The cleaning lady is, no doubt, earning more money that I am and will continue to do so," I stated calmly. "I was hired as psychologist and should be on the psychologists table of pay."

Once all the doctors had agreed to this pay settlement, my salary increased, but not by any huge amount. I was paid more but started at the lowest level on the psychologist's pay scale. My salary was now set to increase at a higher set rate on a yearly basis.

But after two years of an automatic salary increase, the doctors announced that the surgery was having financial difficulties. There was to be a pay freeze for everyone working in the surgery. No-one was to have a salary rise this year nor as it turned out, the following one. Except, as the head receptionist whispered, the doctors.

Amongst the receptionists, there was some resentment as they felt that the doctors never charged the patients for any of the extra services for which they were meant to pay. They were referring to special reports for health clubs, accident and sickness reports for insurance companies, special travel vaccines etc. As our patient list was so high, they figured that the doctors (the surgery) would have been legitimately owed a great deal of money which the doctors never bothered to claim.

After two years, our salaries were reinstated. I started again on the psychologists pay scale. Although my salary rose steadily, for all the reasons I have mentioned, my salary remained consistently low throughout the time I worked at the surgery. The salary I received could never make up for the fact that it was very low to start with, when I received the pay of a receptionist and, in addition, there were two years that it had remained completely static.

In the early 1980's, there were no therapists or counsellors working in surgeries, and most certainly not in the council of Brent. When I started work there, I was told that ours was the first surgery to hire a counsellor. The doctors were considered very progressive in their attitude to the patients as they were focussing on them as human beings with emotions and were not just taking note of their physical ailments alone.

Because the doctors were so skilled at listening to their patients, our surgery gained the reputation for being one of the most popular in Brent. Whether we were the first to offer help for emotional problems, I do not know, as there have been no official studies to corroborate this fact.

THE ANGER ROOM

For many years, I had longed to have a special place which I could designate as the "anger room." No-one seemed to be aware of the level of uncontrolled anger with which many patients were burdened. Effusions of unrestrained fury were often unleashed during our counselling sessions.

It was almost inevitable that these bouts of extreme emotion would impact badly on their everyday lives and many of their social relationships.

An "anger room "would be a space where, without restraint, strong feelings could be released. I envisioned a padded room where patients could scream at the top of their lungs, stamp on or throw any objects they wished to, punch walls, jump up and down and generally expostulate, remonstrate, or denigrate anything or anyone they loathed or hated. The consistent expression of overwhelming outrage, justified or not, impeded investigation into the causes of such feelings and how they were maintained.

Shedding some of the tension might permit access to a more reasonable approach to their problems. As sensible as this proposition seemed to me, I knew that my desire was a futile cause.

No doctor would ever consider that an "anger room" served any good purpose, the reason being that most people, even when upset, often presented their more reasonable, rational side to their doctors, (though not always). Due to the nature of my job, I was, initially, more frequently exposed to the most vulnerable and most volatile side of individuals.

Given these parameters, I, reluctantly accepted that my secret desire would never be realised but I still maintain that an "anger room" would benefit the well-being of many individuals, would facilitate better relationships with friends and family and improve communication with all those with whom they come into contact.

DR PIETRONI – DEALING WITH ANXIETY AT THE SURGERY

Over a prolonged period of time, I noted that the doctors were referring a large number of patients to me who were very stressed, constantly worried and suffering from various levels of anxiety.

Some maintained permanently anxious personalities which meant that they were in a constant state of unease which became problematic when life became difficult. With others the causes were often family or work related.

Their symptoms were numerous, both psychological and physical, ranging from difficulty in concentration, heightened tension and lack of confidence, to headaches, indigestion and a large variety of aches and pains. The combination of unpleasant bodily sensations as well as anxious thoughts and feelings meant that interacting with people every day became a source of constant concern and sometimes intense alarm.

The wonderful talking cure that therapy provided might ease some of their tension, but it did not appear to be very effective in removing their anxiety altogether. I was concerned that the tools with which I was working were inadequate to deal with their problems.

It was obvious that it was important to reduce their high levels of anxiety, but I was not sure how to approach the problem. I determined that I would explore ways of diminishing tension to enable them to lead more tolerable and possibly more enjoyable lives.

My first port of call was a bookshop, to buy a book about Yoga. I had been told of the beneficial effects of practising this discipline which involved low impact physical exercise, controlled breathing, and relaxation.

I discovered that there were many different types of yoga, but all involved these three elements, despite having different formats and practices. All of them emphasized the restorative ability of controlled deep breathing and physical exercise to reduce stress and induce deep relaxation.

As effective as yoga was purported to be, I soon realised that it would be impractical to carry out any type of physical exercise within the confined space of my office. I concluded that I couldn't realistically practice yoga in the manner in which it was intended.

But having read the literature quite carefully, I accepted that there was a strong connection between the controlled breathing and relaxation, something which I thought might prove useful with the patients.

TRANSCENDENTAL MEDITATION

Returning home after work one evening, I saw new posters on the local buildings announcing that Swiss Cottage Library was offering a free course of lectures on Transcendental Meditation, one evening a week for eight weeks.

As TM was widely promoted as a technique for relaxation, "promoting harmony by meditation and the repetition of a mantra", I felt obliged to attend to learn what useful methods had been transmitted to the West from some of the earliest Hindu sacred texts.

The weekly lecture explaining how and why TM works was always followed by ample time to practise breathing and relaxation exercises.

But the explanations of how the body works and why TM was so effective appeared mysterious and incomprehensible to me. Every week I sat listening in a state of doubt and disbelief.

All that I had learned in physiology lead me to question the explanations that the lecturer offered.

The clash between the eastern, almost mystical, explanations and western scientific ones seemed very disorientating. The only way I could sit through the weekly lectures was to disengage from my attempts to believe what the lecturer said and to observe her descriptions in a more objective manner.

TM had, no doubt, originated at a time when Western Scientific thought had not even evolved. The progenitors of TM would have created their own very novel and very different reasons for how the body works according to the cultural traditions of the time.

There was no compunction for me to accept the reasons offered for why TM worked. Far more important was the fact that it was a useful method for helping to reduce tension.

After our eight lectures and eight sessions of practising breathing and relaxation, we were each given a mantra, a word which one repeats during relaxation to let the mind settle and ultimately uses to transcend thought.

Sitting in a comfortable position with eyes closed, silently repeating the mantra, the mediator should, with practise, be able to achieve a state of perfect stillness, rest, and stability.

I found that repeating the mantra in conjunction with the controlled breathing was useful in reducing my own stress levels, but I never succeeded in using the mantra to eliminate all my extraneous thoughts. I expect that I needed more concentration and more practice. For those who did succeed in using the mantra appropriately, they found it a very useful device for promoting relaxation.

DR. PATRICK PIETRONI

Quite unexpectedly, a leaflet, composed by Dr. Patrick Pietroni was mailed to our surgery, inviting NHS employees to engage in a new experimental programme. He was looking for participants to help him determine whether relaxation exercises could lower hypertension and reduce the need for hypertensive drugs.

Dr. Pietroniui was the founder of the Marylebone Centre Trust which provided alternative therapies as well as traditional ones for the relief of pain and stress. He firmly believed that healing does not necessarily require the use of drugs or surgery.

I decided to enlist on the programme as it would be another opportunity for me to investigate methods for reducing anxiety.

We met at the Marylebone Parish Church for approximately eight weeks. Each session consisted of a lecture explaining the causes of anxiety, how the nervous system works, its reactions when dealing with stress and how relaxation can overcome anxiety. After each lecture, we all lay on mats to practice learning Dr. Pietroni's method of progressive relaxation, releasing tension from the top of the head to the tips of the toes. It was similar to the type of relaxation that TM promoted.

My investigation into these different methods of relaxation had proved useful. Fast breathing, increased heart rate and high blood pressure, all symptoms of a stressed body, are decreased by breathing deeply to reduce tension. All three methods of reducing anxiety had confirmed this fact.

For my purposes, the procedures advocated by Dr. Pietroni were the most practical. The client had only to sit in a chair in a comfortable position to perform the breathing exercises. No space for physical exercise was required, nor was there any need to bestow special mantra on anyone.

For all stressed individuals, we practised deep breathing at all of our sessions in the surgery and I dispensed Dr. Pietroni's relaxation tape for them to practise at home.

For those individuals whose symptoms were severe and sometimes unrelenting, we discussed again the production of adrenaline as a response to exciting or worrying situations. Since it is the overproduction of adrenaline that causes disturbing symptoms of palpitations, high blood pressure and excessive sweating, it is important to reduce its presence in the body. I recommended cardiovascular exercise or going for a quick run to burn off the excess adrenaline they had accumulated as a result of becoming overanxious. There were two or three people who engaged in physical exercise and felt they were miraculously cured.

For the converts to deep breathing and relaxation, many found varying levels of relief from their worst symptoms.

For those individuals who refused to try these new techniques, often the most stressed, almost all insisted that they were already far too busy to find time to practise deep breathing and relaxation.

I had naively expected that most stressed individuals would rejoice at finding something that would overcome their problems. But some individuals preferred to remain with what was familiar, regardless of how disturbing and distressing their situation might be.

Learning something different requires change, leaving what is well known and trying something new. From their vantage point, clinging to their debilitating symptoms protected them from taking risks of any kind. The thought of taking a step into unknown territory produced a magnitude of fear that seemed to paralyse them both physically and psychologically and inevitably, condemned them to remain in the same unhappy, stressful situation forever.

I was seriously disappointed in the amount of resistance to change that I encountered. Thank goodness, most individuals affected did not fall into this category.

It was another huge learning experience for me. People may request help and even demand it, but when offered what they want, find it too daunting a prospect to undertake. Unfortunately, in certain circumstances, human emotion may predominate over reason, to the detriment of the individual involved.

I was forced to accept that I could help only those individuals who were brave enough to try to help themselves.

FURTHER STUDIES WITH JESS

When my father was ill, I visited the States three times before he died. These intermittent visits during the second year of my counselling course at the Westminster Pastoral Foundation meant that I was unable to complete the last year of the course.

I had started work at the surgery but knew that I still wanted to continue my studies. Quite fortuitously, I saw a notice in the British Psychological Society Bulletin announcing that a new two-year part-time Master's Degree to become a counselling psychologist was available. The course had been in existence for only one year. It was under the aegis of the University of Surrey but took place at Roehampton Institute. As study time was allowed under my contract at the surgery, I knew that I could attend this course.

In the midst of my contemplations about further study, I received a phone call from Jess. We had been in constant contact since she had returned to Cornwall. Her husband, Denys, who had been very ill for a long period of time, had died during the summer. Jess was now left distraught, feeling that her life was seriously disrupted.

I encouraged her to have a break and come to London to stay with me. I explained that I was applying for an MSc course and suggested that, when she felt up to it, she might consider joining me.

When we did apply for the course, we were informed that they had completed their intake for 1985. We would be accepted on the course the following year.

In desperation, I looked for another course for us to take in our year now completely free of study. We were delighted to be accepted on a three year counselling course at the Southwest London College.

To our surprise, I then received a letter from Roehampton Institute, stating that they could accept us as students this year on the MSc course as two students were unable to attend.

As both courses were part time, we attended each course one day a week. Quite unexpectedly, we discovered that they tended to balance each other out. The Master's Degree was mainly academic in its emphasis, following the usual format of lectures, essay writing and exams. It did have a practical aspect as well, as all students were required to be working as therapists or counsellors in order to be accepted on the course. We brought the problems that we encountered with clients we were seeing to our supervision group at Roehampton.

The Diploma Course in Counselling Skills was far more practical in its approach. Each week students practised their counselling skills, using different models of counselling and received constructive criticism from the students and the teachers about their performance. There were no essays to write or exams to undertake. Learning took place through direct participation in the activities and subjects that the students decided to investigate.

Contrary to our expectations, the Counselling Course proved to be more challenging than the MSc. Course. The concept of the course appeared quite revolutionary in its approach to learning. Continual self-assessment and peer assessment replaced evaluation by marked exams.

Every student kept a journal to record their progress throughout the year. It usually consisted of students stating a set of goals which they hoped to achieve in specific areas, i.e. personal development, interpersonal skills, particularly in relation to how one functioned in the weekly large group meetings and how well they were implementing the counselling model which they had chosen to follow.

Our peer group was in charge of our final assessment, deciding whether or not we had complied with the goals which we had set for ourselves. Tutors provided resource material when requested, monitored our activities throughout the year and were the final arbiters if controversial questions arose during the evaluation of any student.

Prior to the course beginning, the prospective students and the course tutors met for a weekend. The meeting was not as some imagined, a social gathering where we could befriend each other. Its main purpose was to ensure that the students were to plan their programme for the following year.

My immediate reaction was one of annoyance. Hadn't we come on the course to discover what we needed to learn to improve our professional work? Wasn't that the lecturers' job?

I was accustomed to only the conventional model of learning where the curriculum is already set out and the students' duty was to comply with the expectations of the specified programme.

This new model assumed that learning took place through direct participation in horizontal structures that we created and openly sourced information, rather than through instruction and resource material being imposed and implemented from above. The students take responsibility for their own learning and ultimately for assessing their own competence.

The function of the staff was to provide instruction, consultation, and the resources which the students might find useful.

There were forty-two of us enrolled on the 1985 to 1988 Diploma course. When we tried to establish a timetable, I felt that the size of the group most definitely contributed to the group's difficulties in making decisions. With each proposal of a particular subject for study, there were numerous arguments, both pro and con. Every position was upheld with great conviction.

We were learning about the powers of persuasion, the sway of the confident speaker and the impact of the well-reasoned argument. From Friday evening to Saturday evening, we had come to no conclusions at all about what should be included in our timetable. It seemed as if there were too many disparate opinions to make a firm decision about anything.

By the end of Saturday evening, I was so frustrated by the entire process that I was longing for the tutors to step in and make decisions for us. I was concerned that a group of forty-two was too unwieldy to sensibly implement planning our curriculum for even one year. It just didn't seem feasible.

Feelings of frustration emanated from everyone. An atmosphere of defeat permeated the room. I firmly decided that I would leave the course if we couldn't create a curriculum by Sunday. I couldn't survive a year of constant discussions and heated arguments that left us all dangling in mid-air.

Sunday morning, the tutors reminded us that the last time we would have to decide on our curriculum was today, this morning, in fact. We would all be leaving for our respective homes sometime in the afternoon.

Someone pointed out that postponing a course to a different term didn't mean relinquishing the course one wanted. The person who had volunteered to write the timetable stood at the front of the group, waiting patiently for suggestions. One or two people with very strong convictions immediately took their immutable stands.

Someone mentioned the pressure of time and that, possibly, we ought to consider how we could compromise to reach a decision about something. Just taking strong individual stands about what we wanted had produced one impasse after the other. We had to consider how we were to proceed as a group.

The idea that the schedule could be rearranged, subjects could be included at a later date and didn't have to be compressed into the first or second term, seemed to have an impact. I watched as this rigid, unyielding, uncompromising group of forty two individuals slowly transformed into people who were more pliable and understanding, and eventually, willing to make concessions in order to achieve the group's goal.

I felt as if a great weight had been removed from my entire being. Since waking up on Sunday morning, I had been feeling very dispirited and dreaded the thought of leaving the course.

The group that I had so ardently rejected on Saturday night had become a group that I was now proud to join. Great efforts had been made by everyone. Adamant and obstinate positions were deliberately put to one side. To everyone's delight, by Sunday lunchtime, without rancour or resentment, we had produced a timetable that suited everyone. We were all relieved and overjoyed to realise that the course would commence in September with our finally approved and officially accepted curriculum.

THE MOVE TO QUEEN'S PARK

Having lived in a flat in Belsize Square from 1982 to 1988, I decided that I wanted to live in a house again. The flat had proved too small for visits from friends and family, and I wanted to move closer to the surgery.

Having to sit in traffic in Swiss Cottage twice day, continually inhaling the unpleasant fumes from running cars, I realised that I was wasting at least forty minutes a day commuting to and from work.

To escape this daily ordeal, in 1988, I decided to move once again, this time to a house in Queen's Park. The house was beautifully situated facing the park and within only a few minutes' walk from the surgery on Brondesbury Road.

For many years, the surgery was located there on the first two floors of a private house. When money became available to build a new surgery, a new medical centre was erected on Lonsdale Road, just three streets away from its original location, where it still resides today. We were all delighted to make the move to the newly designed premises.

THE GRANDCHILDREN!!

When the children established long-term relationships. I began to hope that they might contemplate having children. As time progressed, it became apparent that the aims of the younger generation were very different from those that I had imbibed at their age.

People married young, in the 1950's, often in their early twenties and were expected to settle down and start a family. My children's generation established relationships, often choosing not to marry, and busied themselves improving their job prospects and establishing higher status positions at work. There was a reason for the differences in expectations between our generations.

In the 1950's, one of the most important advances of the twentieth century, the contraceptive pill, was invented. In the USA, the pill first became available in 1954, but only for women with serious menstrual disorders. It was not until 1960 that the first oral contraceptive was approved for use by women generally.

In England, the pill was introduced in 1961 but could only be prescribed for married women. Family planning clinics were permitted to give contraceptive advice to unmarried women on both social and medical grounds in 1967. Finally, in 1974, family planning services were formally provided in the National Health Service.

The arrival of the pill dramatically changed the mores in society, challenging long established social traditions in both countries. In the 1950's, ultra-conservative attitudes to sexual behaviour prevailed in both the USA and England.

Unmarried women who became pregnant were frequently ostracised and due to the unbearable social pressure were forced to give up their babies for adoption. Fear of pregnancy was the predominant concern for most young people. As no contraceptive devices were generally available for women, they were forced to rely on men to provide contraception. Concomitant with early expectations of marriage, at the time, was the obligation for women to stay at home to rear the children while their husbands went to work to support the family.

The pill eliminated the fear of becoming pregnant and producing unwanted babies. As a result, the pressure to get married diminished and many couples started to cohabit.

With the advent of the pill, both sexes were liberated. Men no longer had the burden of providing contraception and women, for the first time in history, were in control of when they became pregnant.

Becoming a mother and housewife was now, not necessarily, the most important and revered role available to women. They could choose whether or not to marry, when to have children, could pursue further education and even establish a career, at their own convenience, so long as the prevailing institutions and prejudices allowed them to enter the job market and engage in more advanced study.

I decided that I should leave the prospect of having grandchildren in abeyance. My children might not want to become parents until their late thirties and I, reluctantly acknowledged, that they might decide to have no children at all.

A very good friend in the States informed me that all of her friends' children were suddenly producing babies and she felt left out as she had no grandchildren. As we were both in the same position, I was the only person left to whom she could even mention this fact.

She had five children and not one was interested in becoming a parent. Eventually, she was overjoyed to have one grandson but as she said, "That was her lot." Her other four children chose to remain childless. I did not dwell unduly on having grandchildren as I was rather preoccupied with acquiring further qualifications to bolster my desire to find a permanent job.

My children grew up in the 1960's, accepting that living together was the norm and that marriage was an option, if they so desired.

We were not a religious family and neither Roger or I believed that the significance of a relationship was enhanced or increased by being sanctioned by either the church or state. But when my eldest daughter, Michèle, started living with Brian, I felt very protective and secretly wished that they would marry to establish a stable relationship.

Logically, my reaction was completely incomprehensible. I had only to look at my own marriage to confirm that thought. My marriage was stable for many years, but that fact did not preclude instability and permanent separation at a later date.

When reason finally prevailed, I accepted their living together without any qualms. My initial reticence to their cohabitation indicates how deeply entrenched are the beliefs that we acquire in childhood and that it is important to recognise that the emotions attached to these beliefs might linger longer than reason would allow.

A few years later, when Michèle announced that she and Brian were planning to marry, I was again shocked at my reaction. As they had been living together for ten years, I couldn't imagine why they had suddenly decided to marry. In disbelief, I asked was there a reason for them to change their minds about just living together.

It was Brian's wish that they marry. Both had decided that they wanted children and Brian thought it best that the children grow up with married parents. Michèle was indifferent but accepted Brian's desire to make the relationship an officially legal one. They married in 1988 and my first grandchild, Belle, was born in 1989.

Six months later, in 1990, Natasha produced a grandson, my second grandchild, Misha, and in 1992, another grand-daughter, Nadia, whom she co-parented with her partner Pat. Michèle and Brian decided to have two more children. In 1993, Dashiell arrived, in 1995, Gabriel was born. Leda and Simon did not marry until 2000 and then produced two girls, Ruby in 2001 and Lillis in 2002. I became the proud grandmother of seven lovely, lively grandchildren, four girls and three boys.

In my grandchildren's generation, the concern about producing unwanted babies has not disappeared but has, noticeably, receded to the background. The contraceptive pill can take full credit for this change in attitude in comparison to its predominant importance just two generations ago.

Some of my children's concerns about their children were similar to mine. They could sometimes choose inappropriate friends and their parents worried about whether they would become involved in drugs or imbibe too much alcohol.

The latter was particularly troubling as many girls had developed a new, competitive attitude to drinking. To enjoy the relaxing effects of alcohol, allowing them to overcome shyness or awkwardness in communicating, was never their aim. Instead, they set out to drink as much as was humanly possible.

As it was such an expensive proposition, they all started drinking at home where they could indulge themselves at a much cheaper price than in the pub.

Arriving half-inebriated to meet their friends, the convention was to engage in the excessive consumption of alcohol until everyone became totally drunk. They were reduced to a dazed state of grogginess and either became comatose or violent. Many ended up in police custody.

While concerns about drinking and drugs happened occasionally and mostly at weekends, problems related to technology seemed to be the major issue dominating everyone's lives.

Parents and children often disagreed about the right to download music without the consent of the musicians involved in the recording. Children downloaded music without any guilt or concern that the musicians should be paid anything. As they had free access to the music, they felt that it was free for everyone.

Parents had grown up in an age when musicians had fought very hard to obtain royalties each time a piece of music was performed. They were shocked to watch their children downloading music with absolutely no interest in the musician's welfare.

An unrelenting source of conflict has been the constant use of mobile phones. As children were permanently interacting with their most recently acquired mechanical device, little or no time remained to even think of relating to those closest to them, their family members. As a result. familial social relations have gradually dwindled in the face of the almost obsessive use of modern technology.

But it is not only children who are contributing to the widening gulf between parents and their offspring. Parents are often guilty of giving undue attention to their mobile phones or to be found persistently checking their emails, thus severely limiting the time available to relate to their children.

With the use of social networking and instant messaging on mobile phones, children now have the ability to control their communication with others without interference or involvement from their parents. What children see as a sense of independence and freedom from parental intrusion appears to the parents as a loss of family contact and results in a serious lack of communication between them.

As children's total absorption in technology has increased, parents' traditional roles have been undermined. Children now have access to information and individuals about whom the parents know nothing. The impact of these unidentifiable sources may prove rewarding but could also have deleterious effects upon the individual contacting them. Parents are left troubled by their children's engagement with these activities but are unable to control them completely.

I have commented on how my children's beliefs differed from mine. When Natasha and Pat decided to become a couple, I had already accepted their relationship. Two women living together posed no problem for me.

When I regarded how my children lived, my acceptance of their different modes of living indicated just how far removed I was from the beliefs with which I was raised.

The society of the 1950's reviled same sex relationships and saw them as worthy of only scorn and contempt. Sex before marriage was forbidden. The institution of marriage was sacrosanct which meant that it could never be questioned or changed. Therefore, the question of couples cohabiting or possibly never marrying could never arise as serious subjects of concern. It was assumed that all couples were heterosexual and that they would marry.

It is with pride that I recognise how the beliefs I acquired in my conventional, traditionally conservative upbringing have radically changed. I have relinquished many of the social conventions and beliefs that everyone once held dear. (Please remember there are those individuals who still uphold these very conventional standards of behaviour. Not everyone has changed.)

As the technological divide between generations has increased, parents have been overwhelmed by a sense of unintentional failure to supervise their children's social life, health, and well-being and remain unsure of how to curtail their children's excessive dependence on new technology.

JESS' RETIREMENT

After receiving our Diploma in Counselling Skills and our MSc in Counselling Psychology, Jess and I decided that we had no need to acquire any more qualifications. We were accredited by the British Association of Counselling and also accredited as Chartered Psychologists by the British Psychological Society. To work as authorised Chartered Psychologists, we were required to apply annually for a practising certificate.

When I was working full-time at the surgery, I proposed that Jess and I create a job-share. After Jess' probationary period, the doctors accepted my proposal which meant that Jess and I worked two and one half days a week. To increase our income, we both saw private clients two days a week.

Through friends, we heard of a new model of therapy, CAT (Cognitive Analytic Therapy), which was being developed by Dr. Anthony Ryle who was working as a psychotherapist at both Guys and St. Thomas' Hospital. He recognised the need for a treatment which was shorter and cheaper than what was then available within the NHS. He was constantly testing the efficacy of his evolving model of CAT.

CAT looks at the patterns that clients have developed when young as a means of coping. Changing behaviour centres on two areas: 1) recognition of how these patterns now create problems in their daily life and 2) learning how to make different and more rewarding choices.

CAT is a time-limited therapy lasting from sixteen to twenty-four sessions weekly and is recommended for a wide variety of psychological ailments. Feeling it would be useful to augment our knowledge and skills, Jess and I enrolled on a course of CAT therapy. Along with many others, we were trained in its methods and techniques but when we finished the course, qualifications were not yet available. The year after we completed our studies- the requirements for the CAT Course were formalised and for the first time. qualifications were issued. Within the NHS, there were numerous practitioners of CAT who found the methods useful but had no qualifications because they had studied before CAT's qualifications were officially recognised.

It was about two years after completing the Cat course that Jess turned seventy. As the doctors suddenly informed us, there was now a problem with Jess continuing to work at the surgery. The NHS contract firmly states that no-one is allowed to work after seventy.

As the doctors were reluctant to lose her, they proposed that the contract be changed. The new contract would state that I was working full-time but, informally, each pay day, I was to give Jess half my salary. This arrangement worked very well for about two years until one day Jess suddenly decided that it was time for her to retire.

We were all taken aback as it was so unexpected. We had no choice in the matter and were forced to accept her decision. The surgery was as sad to see her depart as I was. We had lived together for ten years. I would undoubtedly, miss her bright, lively spirit and her ability to provoke controversial discussions at any large gathering of people.

Although we had serious differences of opinion about child-rearing, we did share deeply held beliefs about the causes of social injustice both nationally and internationally.

We had both been on CND marches, supported the miners' strike and the Greenham Common Peace Camp protests against nuclear weapons being placed at Greenham Common, marched with the Gay Pride Movement, and marched against British and US involvement in the first Gulf War when Iraq was invaded by the US, Britain and a huge coalition to protect US oil interests in Saudi Arabia.

We condemned apartheid in South Africa and joined the boycott never to buy South African fruit of any kind. We protested against Arms Trade Fairs where the use of weapons is promoted as a means of resolving conflict and were often sold to countries who didn't uphold human rights.

When Jess retired, we no longer went on exciting trips during our summer holidays. We had planned trips every summer to visit friends and family but mostly to explore countries, distant and foreign.

In Europe, we travelled to Italy, France, Greece, Portugal, Turkey, Switzerland, and Prague in the Czech Republic. We visited the USA, seeing my relatives on the east coast and then travelling to New Orleans and California. We saw the Rockies in Canada and joined a five day cruise to Alaska.

When Jess' sister, Brenda was ill, we flew to Australia for three weeks where Jess visited with Brenda and her son and his family.

Our visits to the East included trips to China, Bali, Thailand and Vietnam. We did manage to visit Goa but have never been to India.

We took short, cheaper trips, for a week or ten days, to Morocco, Algeria, and Tunisia.

We made three very memorable trips, the first when we went on safari to observe numerous wild animals very closely in Zimbabwe and Zambia. The second was to the Galapagos Islands to view a variety of animals in their natural habitats, many surviving in conditions very similar the ones in which Darwin had discovered them. The third was to Cuba. As an American citizen, I was banned from travelling there. To overcome this difficulty, I became a British citizen. Due to the American embargo, the standard of living was not high but, with state subsidies, everyone ate a basic, healthy diet. Their literacy rate was 96%, one of the highest in the world and everyone had free access to medical care.

We did sometimes include friends on our trips or went on journeys with larger groups but mostly, they were undertaken by the two of us, travelling together as adventurous, intrepid companions.

PS   Unbeknown to us, we were secretly known as the Queens of Queens Park. Many people assumed that we were lesbians.

We were greatly amused as neither one of us had ever considered such an arrangement.

MY BROTHER'S DEATH

In January 1995, my sister-in-law, Carrie, rang to tell me that my brother was in hospital. Bob and his family lived in Hanson, MA, a suburb of Boston, the city to which he commuted to work every day.

He had, apparently, been slowly declining for the last few months. The doctors could find no specific reason for the weakness down his left side. While suggesting that a weak heart and pulmonary problems might be contributing to his breathing difficulties, they didn't feel that either one accounted for the severity of his symptoms.

On my flight to Boston to see him, I was consumed with thoughts about our life together when we were growing up. When he was young, my parents couldn't understand why he never wanted to read any books, not even the ones he seemed to like.

As both of my parents revered education, it was a foregone conclusion that their two children would excel at school and, later, attain a degree at college or university.

To me, he appeared very bright, always asking intelligent questions, was very good at maths, had a fantastic memory and could put together things like clocks and radios which he had dismantled, a skill which I had never possessed. He never failed any subjects at school but because he had difficulty reading, he never excelled at any subject he studied.

This was the era of the 1940's when children who were unable to read without difficulty were labelled dumb or stupid. Dyslexia was a condition unheard of and it remained totally unrecognised as a possible cause for children's reading problems until many decades later. At high school, he passed all the requisite subjects for college entry, but with only average grades.

To improve his performance, my father enrolled him in a private institution, The Manter Hall School, in Cambridge, MA. Overnight, his life appeared to be transformed. Not only did he receive high grades in all his subjects, he received exceptionally high ones in maths and science. In 1955, he attained his BSc degree from Suffolk University in Boston, where he was one of only seven black students accepted for study.

He then moved to New York to continue his studies. He attended City College, an institution which specialised in degree programs for working adults. To support himself while studying, he taught mathematics. He became a formulation chemist and worked many years for the Gillette Company in

Boston, until he became ill. Formulation chemists develop the chemical analysis that will produce the required properties for a variety of substances used in food, drugs, fertilisers, cosmetics, pesticides etc.

When we were growing up, we experienced the usual tiffs and disagreements, not often and not serious but as we grew older and our perspectives began to merge, we grew much closer. What I remembered fondly, was our having a very strong relationship when we were adolescents.

He approved of my stance against my parents when I protested about their unjustified objections to my dating a respectable, white acquaintance of long standing.

I wanted to discuss the question of dating across the mutually agreed colour barrier between white and black people. But the intensity of my parents' feelings precluded any discourse on the matter. Crossing the colour barrier was not a topic open for discussion. It was forbidden which meant that it would never be an issue worthy of their consideration. Full of disdain and anger, they refused to make any further comment.

An acrimonious atmosphere permeated the entire house. I felt stifled and restrained from saying anything at all to my parents. But I could always turn to my brother for many a heated discussion on the rights and wrongs of wanting to date people of any race or colour. He was a great support in my time of despair.

When, about three years later, Bob and my father had a serious disagreement and they were not speaking, (I never knew the cause of the problem), I supported him by offering him a place to live in the flat Roger and I were renting and to help him financially, if he needed it, to continue his studies.

He never came to live with us and only accepted a little financial help when his funds were seriously depleted. He spent many years trying to return the money. As I considered the financial help a small gift and not a loan, I always refused his offers of repayment.

When, in the midst of my recollections, there was a loud announcement that we would be landing at the airport in a matter of minutes, my concentration suddenly shifted. I was back in the present, once again feeling worried and distressed that my brother was ill, and no-one seemed to know why.

By the time I arrived at his bedside, the doctors had finally made a diagnosis. It was short and succinct. He was suffering from post-polio syndrome.

I could hardly believe what they had said. Post-polio syndrome. Who had ever heard of that diagnosis? At first, I was incredulous. No-one that I knew had ever experienced a return of polio thirty or forty years after their initial attack. For Bob, since he was about eight years old when he acquired polio, it would have been about fifty plus years since his first prolonged illness.

I was impelled to look up this new diagnosis. "Post-Polio Syndrome refers to a cluster of potentially disabling signs and symptoms that appear decades, an average of thirty or forty years, after the initial polio illness.

The greater your recovery after acute polio, the more likely it seems that post-polio syndrome will develop, perhaps because greater recovery places additional stress on motor neurons.

Throughout the United States, people who had developed polio as long as four decades ago, were slowly succumbing to the problems of weakening muscles and growing incapacity to cope with simple-taken-for-granted functions like walking and standing, eventually ending up in a wheelchair and were sometimes bedridden."

Bob was suffering from serious muscle atrophy in his chest muscles and on the entire left side of his body. These were the same areas weakened by polio when he was eight.

The doctors then, informed the family that this young boy couldn't possibly survive. In a state of sustained gloom, we tried to brace ourselves for his untimely death but to our shock and amazement, after a very long time, his condition began to improve.

His miraculous recovery was due to what was called the Sister Kenney Treatment. It included the consistent application of heat, intensive massage, and physiotherapy to the afflicted limbs.

The family was eternally grateful that he had survived this dreadful ordeal. We celebrated his unexpected gift of life every day. But, for the doctors, his outstanding achievement was that he had, after being paralysed, learned with great difficulty, to walk again.

This horrendous disease had not, as predicted, left him completely paralysed down his left side. For over fifty years, he functioned normally, with no sign of weakness anywhere but it did appear that he was now experiencing a second bout of the same illness. It was hard to take in, difficult to believe that this is what was really happening.

If I examined the facts, I was forced to believe the diagnosis. His condition had been slowly deteriorating for many months. Before he went into hospital, he had travelled everywhere in a wheelchair with an extra supply of oxygen.

Throughout his stay in hospital, his wife, Carrie, and his two sons, Roland and Jack, visited constantly. He remained very weak, and it slowly became obvious that he was not going to recover. As Carrie, forlornly, said: "I'm just biding my time, waiting for him to die."

It was a truth that none of us wished to hear. I was living from day to day in a state of limbo, not acknowledging, not wanting to acknowledge, that he would not, could not, survive.

On the 25th of February 1995, he died peacefully and, thanks to his medication, without pain. He was only 61 years old.

His death certificate lists chronic obstructive lung disease and cardiomyopathy as the causes of death. Post-polio syndrome most certainly exacerbated the symptoms of his chronic respiratory failure.

It is rarely life-threatening but in cases where someone's health is already compromised, it can cause a serious deterioration in health and should be listed as a contributing factor in the patient's demise.

P.S. After my brother's death, Carrie returned to her original home in the south to North Carolina. Sadly, she died suddenly not long after Bob had passed away, leaving Jack and Roland without both their parents. They were now my only relatives in the United States.

I have always suspected that I have some relatives on my father's side who reside in Virginia where he was born. But I have absolutely no information, not even names, to assist me in a search for them. I would like to make a genealogical search in Virginia for my paternal ancestors, grandparents, and great-grandparents as I did for my mother's relatives in Canada.

Recent trips to the United States have always included a family reunion with Roland and Liza and their children, Brent and Jacqueline and my other nephew, Jack, and his wife, Betsy, and their children Jason and Brandon. Natasha, Pat, and I always stayed with Jack and Betsy who treated us as very special guests, providing very comfortable accommodation, sumptuous meals and numerous trips to all the places of interest.

BARON SWAYTHLING'S FAMILY REUNION

It was probably in 1997 that members of our family received an invitation from David Montagu, the 4th Baron Swaythling, to attend a family gathering that would be attended by all his relatives, including close family members and those from his extended family. This invitation included everyone connected to this peerage whether by blood or marriage. Roger received an invitation at his house in Gloucestershire but probably due to his disapproval of royalty and titles of any sort, he chose not to attend.

The rest of the family considered this request an invitation to an unusual event. It was possibly the only time that so many members of the extended family would be assembled in one place. We were very curious to know who these individuals might be.

We were less concerned about any connection with the peerage. After all, it was only an inherited title, not something earned for exceptional contributions to society.

The great event was to take place in the ballroom of the Grosvenor House Hotel on Park Lane in Mayfair. As our family entered the lobby of the hotel, we were directed to an area not far from the ballroom where Baron Swaythling and his wife stood waiting to greet their guests.

After introducing themselves to us, we informed them to which branch of the family we belonged. My father-in-law, Cyril Franklin, was the son of the Honorable Henrietta Franklin, who was the daughter of Samuel Montagu, the first Baron Swaythling.

As we stood talking, we noticed that cameras were placed in strategic places around us. The entire family was asked to pose for a photograph with Baron Swaythling and his wife. For each branch of the family, similar photographs were taken. We were informed that when processed, the photos would be mailed to the appropriate family members.

Michèle, Brian, Natasha, Pat, the five grandchildren and I then proceeded to the ballroom. As we entered the great room, for a moment, we all stood in astonishment, gazing at this enormous space completely filled with people all sitting round carefully laid out tables.

Staring unbelievably at the number of unfamiliar individuals assembled, we found it difficult to contemplate that they were all actually somehow related to us.

We were acquainted with only a tiny fraction of these people. The rest, we had most certainly, never seen or even heard of before.

The writer, Stephen Poliakoff, was in attendance as his maternal great grandfather was Samuel Montagu, the first Baron Swaythling. His reaction and, I suspect, that of many others, was similar to our family's. He stated that he went to a huge family reunion in a posh hotel. When he entered the great ballroom, he noted that although all the people seated before him were relatives, he knew hardly anyone.

He later wrote a play, "Perfect Strangers" where a huge family reunion occurred in a different posh hotel. The play was one of intrigue, family secrets and crimes of concealment that bore no resemblance to our very relaxed and enjoyable gathering.

Although everyone acknowledged that we had all spent an enjoyable afternoon, eating heartily and drinking well, it was with a very small, select group of people.

Everyone behaved as people often do when confronted by a room full of strangers. We avoided contact with those we didn't know and walked around the room, greeting only recognisable faces. Once some kind of identity had been established, we immediately headed in their direction to establish contact and proceeded to sit near or beside them at one of the tables.

An imaginative organiser might have suggested that we all sit with people we didn't know in order to become acquainted with new relations. But that suggestion was never made. Nor did most of the guests involved have the temerity to even consider such a proposition.

The consequence was that we all remained with familiar friends and relatives, casting long, curious glances at those near and far, desiring to know what might be the connection that linked us all together.

The children were more fortunate. After eating whatever they desired from the children's menu, they were invited to go to a special room provided with games and videos for their entertainment.

Incidentally and quite vociferously, they could be heard happily interacting with the other children in the room. They made brief acquaintances and related amiably to their new friends but none of them was interested in family genealogy or DNA. So, despite being in close proximity to their relatives and having the opportunity to discover how they were related, they had no desire to investigate these issues.

Our family was delighted to have become better acquainted with one of their second cousins, his Asian wife and their two daughters who sat at our table.

Baron Swaythling sent all the guests a family tree, illustrating the relationships between people in several generations. The diagram did, at least, allow us to identify specific ancestors and lines of descent.

Reflecting on this splendid occasion, I felt it provided Baron Swaythling and his wife an opportunity to meet many of the numerous relatives in their extended family, but it will be remembered by many of us as an opportunity missed to meet those in the large room full of perfect strangers to whom we were directly related.

ISSUES I EXPERIENCED AROUND RACE IN LONDON IN THE 1980'S and 1990'S

During the 1980's and 1990's, topics relating to minority groups and women became prominent subjects of concern and open to examination. The fact that these issues were on the public agenda was mainly due to the effort of one individual, Ken Livingstone.

As leader of the Greater London Council from 1981 until it was abolished in 1986 and as Mayor of London from 2000 to 2008, his policies were pivotal in helping to implement a change in social attitudes towards these specific groups.

Under his administration, rules and laws also changed to support minority groups.

THE SURGERY

At the surgery, a white mother was referred to me who already had one child of her own and a mixed-race child that she and her husband had adopted. They were now fostering a second mixed race child in hopes of adopting her.

But a new law had just been introduced which stated that adoptive parents and children should be of the same race. It was based on the belief that parents of the same ethnic background as the children would deal most effectively with the racist attitudes and prejudice that the children would encounter as they were growing up.

My client was outraged. The council had already attested to the fact that these parents were capable of bringing up a mixed-race child by giving them a second one to foster. Of interest is the fact that the council left the second child in their care, despite the fact that the parents were not of the same ethnicity as the child. It was probably a legal loophole because the parents were only fostering her. But logically, one would think that the same principles would apply in fostering as well as adoption. My client was in great distress and cried incessantly. "How could they be denied any hope of adopting their second mixed-race child because of the colour of their skin?"

The West Indian family next door provided all the information they needed about black culture and customs. But now the prospects of providing a companion for their first mixed-race child were shattered forever.

Through many tearful, angry sessions, we considered the injustice of this ruling. Many objections could be reasonably raised. Colour-coordinating families did not automatically provide permanent and stable homes for these children. For the future well-being of children, love and affection had always been recognised as the major factors in promoting their healthy development rather than the racial composition of the parents. The ruling completely overlooked the very practical fact that there had always been a dearth of ethnic parents who wanted to adopt children which left children, particularly black children, languishing in institutions for many years. For some, this meant remaining in an institution until they were eighteen when they were finally legally dismissed from care.

The Children and Families Act of 2014 tried to rectify the disturbing consequences of the original ruling and advised against the over-emphasis on "ethnicity" which could lead to delays in adoption. Adoption into stable, caring homes has always provided better outcomes for children than those in residential or institutionalised care.

SOUTH WEST LONDON COLLEGE

The topic of race-matching and adoption also arose at the South West London College where I was attending a counselling course one day a week. One of the students, a white woman, who had adopted four black children was viciously, verbally attacked by another white student. She totally maligned her for having the audacity to think that she could raise black children without ever having experienced race prejudice herself.

The mother of these children had introduced each child to his own background by reading stories written by authors from their country of origin. She took them to museums to view the art, the artefacts and even the architecture produced by their respective countries. When they were older, they borrowed books from the library to read the history of their own country. She had instilled in each one of them a sense of pride about their background and about being black.

The dreadful attack on this white mother seemed unwarranted and misplaced, a case of political correctness carried to extremes. She and her family were providing the care and love which the children needed and were dealing with racial prejudice as the children presented these problems at home.

The founder of the college insisted that we could not ignore this provocative situation. The two individuals involved, confronted each other to discuss what they believed and how they felt. It was finally agreed that both parties were free to have different opinions about recent adoption policies, but differences of opinion should be openly aired and discussed and never take the form of an attack in which a person is demeaned or made to feel they are an object of contempt.

Racial matching in adoption, though implemented with the best of intentions, was never suitable for its purpose. I felt that rather than alleviating problems, it served to increase them. Many people approved the policies. Its failings were not advertised so it took many years (too many years) to change this policy, sadly, to the detriment of the children.

✳ ✳ ✳

STUDENT PROBLEMS at SOUTH WEST LONDON COLLEGE

When I was at South West London College, the five black students in our year found it difficult to get the issues of ethnicity put on the agenda of important topics to be discussed. Someone suggested that as no-one seemed interested in multi-ethnic issues, maybe the black students should set up as a separate group. I was horrified.

Precisely this situation had occurred on another course at the college. My friend, Jess, was a student on this course so I heard weekly reports of what was happening. The black students felt that the white students were not listening to them when week after week, they excluded discussions of multicultural problems from the group's agenda. Feeling that their actions reflected exactly the same kind of rejection that they experienced daily in society, they chose to sever relations with all white people on the course. They set up a black only group to run their own separate counselling course.

Brigid Proctor, the founder, tried to intervene to open the lines of communication but it was impossible. The black students were too angry to retreat from their stand. They dissociated themselves from any meaningful contact with white people and so it continued until the end of the course. The white students were distressed and some even felt guilty while the black students remained adamant in their stance.

It seemed an anomaly that on a course for counselling skills, no means could be found to reach a solution. But with one party refusing to resolve the problem, absolutely no progress could be made.

I was fearful of a repeat performance in our group. I felt it was important to keep the lines of communication open so grievances and injustices on both sides could, at least, be discussed. Most of the other black students were in disagreement with my suggestion. I could see that their patience was nearing its end. We were teetering on the edge of severing all communication with white students. Fortunately, for our group, after many months of anger and resentment on the part of the black students, the subject of multiculturalism was eventually included on the large group's agenda so the issue of black students creating a separate study group from the white students finally dissipated.

While I thought it important to remain inclusive to sort out issues regarding ethnicity and multicultural problems at the South West London College, I found myself taking a completely different stand some months later.

THE BRITISH ASSOCIATION OF COUNSELLING - THE (BAC)

I was already a member of the BAC (the British Association of Counsellors) but found that their constitution did not include any awareness of the cultural differences that exist in the multicultural world or prejudices that might exist in the counselling world. How these differences and prejudices could impact the therapy relationship should have been issues of the utmost importance.

I discovered that there was already a group in existence, the Association of Black Counsellors, which was promoting the inclusion of a clause or a statement by the BAC, acknowledging the importance of multi-cultural differences in relation to counselling. I immediately joined this group and attended the numerous meetings held, carefully following the proper procedures and wording to ensure the inclusion of such a statement in their aims and purposes.

The Association of Black Counsellors was an accredited and informed group of individuals, formed because their concerns about the lack of recognition given to the diversity and distinctness of different groups was continually ignored.

Being excluded, whether through indifference, apathy or ignorance, forces one to become an outsider. After more than two years of hard work, a clause relating to diversity and ethnicity was finally included in the BAC constitution.

The BAC, now called the BAPC, the British Association of Psychotherapy and Counselling, includes in its statement of ethics that it ensures appreciation of the variety of human experience and culture. It also accredits BAME, Black, Asian and Minority Ethnic counselling and is now wholeheartedly supporting awareness of the diversity of multicultural and minority groups in therapy and counselling.

Within the therapy and counselling field, other questions about racial issues also arose. For the first time, consideration about whether it was a good idea to match the race of the client to that of the counsellor was being explored.

On a practical level, in a surgery, the proposition was just not feasible. Most surgeries would not have had the luxury of offering such a service as most, if not almost all, the counsellors were white.

The staff at our surgery were from a wide variety of backgrounds: Asian, Irish, Afro-Caribbean, Indian, English, and African. No discrimination was allowed at the surgery in the patients' choice of doctors or nurses. Patient choice was adhered to in those instances where a patient requested a female doctor.

Jess, my colleague, who was white, and I agreed that she would ask black clients if they preferred a black counsellor. In all the years that she worked there, not one black client ever asked for a black counsellor.

MY CLIENT

Only once, in my experience there did I encounter a request for a black counsellor. The situation that occurred raised wider questions about the policy of racial matching client and counsellor.

The client, who was very persuasive, convinced one of the receptionists to give my telephone number to her, saying that she could not decide if I should be her counsellor unless she could have a long discussion with me.

When she rang, she had many questions. Was I really a black counsellor? What were my qualifications? Did I have supervision? With what organisation was I accredited? Did I have a practising certificate?

Interjected between questions, she would continually insist that she needed a black counsellor. I would assure her that I was the only black counsellor that the surgery had hired. At the end of this interrogation, she said that she would make an appointment to see me.

The day arrived when we should meet. There was a loud knock at the door. The door opened and standing there was a tall black woman. Holding the handle of the door and staring at me intently, she appeared unwilling to enter the room. She maintained a stern countenance and remained rigidly erect, never moving a muscle.

After a prolonged glare, she screamed at the top of her lungs, "You're not black. You're not black." Full of anger and rage, she screamed one last time, "You're not black" and with all the force she could muster, slammed the door in my face. She stamped down the stairs, deliberately and determinedly, banging each foot loudly on every step, making sure as she left, to slam the door at the bottom of the stairs as loudly as possible.

Throughout this ordeal, I remained seated at my desk, completely shocked and shattered by her reaction. Although I was completely taken aback by her response, I did understand what was involved in her violent reaction towards me.

A short history of race discrimination is required to explain what had just happened. Issues around the importance of the different shades and colours of black people have existed since the times of slavery. White colonialists created division amongst the slaves by giving preferential treatment to lighter-skinned slaves, promoting the idea that the closer to white you were, the more acceptable you became. These practices inevitably produced anger and resentment amongst those who were of a darker complexion.

Although colonialism no longer exists, its legacy remains today in the colour hierarchies that still exist in their ex-colonies everywhere.

Sadly, black people complain that these colour hierarchies also exist in England and the United States as well as in many other parts of the world. I've learned two new words, shadeism and colourism to describe discrimination based on complexion and perpetrated against black people of a darker skin colour. It is demonstrated by those white and black people who prefer light-skinned black people when hiring for almost any kind of job. These practices have induced not only resentment in people of darker complexions towards lighter-skinned individuals but, sometimes, also envy.

Understanding that no-one views dark skin as an asset in society, some dark-skinned people desire a fairer complexion to be more acceptable and to attain the privileges involved in possessing a lighter skin.

When my prospective client, a brown-skinned West Indian woman, saw me for the first time, she saw a light coffee-coloured individual, not even a decent chocolate brown, whose features were not demonstrably black and whose hair was, without doubt, not curly enough. She viewed me as advantaged, privileged and probably prejudiced towards her. Why would she want to establish any kind of relationship with someone like me? I represented people she had, for good reasons, hated and resented her entire life.

The counselling and therapy world were, generally unaware of the prejudices of black people towards other black people which is why they could naively assume that racial matching between counsellor and client was always beneficial. The policy could work in many cases, but, certainly, not in all. Clients should always be given a choice in order to overcome such pitfalls.

To my surprise, many months later, my door-slamming client appeared on the list of clients I was scheduled to see on a Monday morning. I began the session by saying that I wanted to say something before we started. We could discuss the matter later if she wished to do so.

I stated that I made no excused for my heredity. It was something that had been passed on to me from my ancestors. But she and I both knew that in this society, it didn't matter how much white ancestry I possessed, I would always be defined as black.

Surprisingly, she didn't react immediately. I felt that she must have re-examined her reactions to me, or she wouldn't have returned for another session. She explained that she hadn't given me a chance and that she thought that she should try again to see if we could work together.

Never once did she mention her furious, outrageous reaction towards me, but I think we were both aware of the reason for that. I knew that we could always discuss this situation at a later time.

"Seeing if we could work together" meant that we were both very wary of each other in our initial sessions. Eventually, as trust slowly developed, we did establish a long-lasting relationship that was very rewarding in many respects, but not without its problems.

TEACHING AT THE CITY LITERARY INSTITUTE – EARLY 1990'S

It was in the early 1990's that Val and I taught an Introduction to Counselling Course at the City Literary Institute in London.

We took turns weekly to introduce the topic to be discussed for the morning while both of us helped to implement the practical exercises which followed.

The class consisted mainly of teachers and social workers whose councils were paying for their attendance on the course.

As it was an introductory course, we started by focussing on some of the core counselling skills active listening, reflecting back, questioning and paraphrasing. As everyone felt they were practising the skills they wanted to use in their workplace, the exercises we provided were very popular.

On the day that we introduced our exercises on self-assertion, there were some unexpected outcomes. The exercises focussed on how to state a problem in a self-assertive manner. The important elements were to state clearly what their grievance was and to explain why they were upset. We discussed why it was important not to attack the other person. That approach usually led to the attacked person taking a defensive stance which closed down open communication and rarely led to a resolution. As many individuals felt that they had found a way to discuss differences of opinion without being angry all the time and knowing that unresolvable arguments would inevitably ensue, they found this exercise very rewarding.

At the next class, to my surprise, I was approached by two women, one a teacher and the other a social worker, who informed me that they had decided to test this exercise at home.

We had only introduced the topic of self-assertion. It was an academic exercise, meant to be further discussed and better understood before putting it into practise. I was shocked that they had so quickly applied the exercise in a real life situation.

One had confronted a very controlling mother who always knew what was best for her and never listened to what she wanted. The other stood up to a very powerful husband who constantly criticised and demeaned her in front of others.

I needn't have worried. The fact that they had stated their own priorities and verbalised their distress, for the first time in their lives, was so empowering, they felt they could deal with any untoward or inappropriate behaviour from the other party. Both of them were ecstatic about their newly acquired self-confidence which required them to trust in their own judgement.

The students were generally enthusiastic about the course, and many attended a planning day where, everyone attending, planned the curriculum for the following year. The overwhelming demand for the course to continue was very reassuring for both Val and me.

But, regrettably, not long after our planning day, we received a letter from City Lit stating that they were unable to continue the second year of the Counselling Course.

All the councils who had so generously paid for their employees to attend the course had, in an attempt to save money, withdrawn their financial support so the Counselling Course sadly, came to an abrupt end.

All of us, students, and teachers alike, lamented the cessation of what had proved to be a very successful educational enterprise which everyone had found beneficial in their relationships with colleagues, students and clients and some, unexpectedly, with their families as well.

GP FUNDHOLDING

When the Conservatives won the election in 1983, Mrs. Thatcher became prime minister for a second period. She initiated a series of major changes in the NHS which altered the functioning of the NHS for over a decade.

In 1983, The Griffith's Report introduced the idea of management to the NHS with an increase in manager's pay. When a manager was appointed to work in our surgery, an atmosphere of resentment permeated the air. The manager's post had been set up to save money for the NHS but, at the Brondesbury Road surgery, a general consensus existed that his job would be superfluous.

In 1987, A White Paper proposed the basis for the new GP Contract in 1980. It was a plan to improve how care was delivered, offering doctors extra pay for screening, health promotions and other preventative services.

On the 1st of April 1991, A radical reorganisation of the NHS was initiated. The major reform was that those who provided health services would be separate from those who purchased them.

The main purchaser organisations consisted of the GP fundholders and the district health authorities. The provider organisations were the NHS Trusts.

The ensuing alterations meant that both health authorities and doctors were trying to adapt to a series of varied changes which they sometimes found problematic. Attempts were made to assess the efficacy of the new reforms but the research yielded inconclusive results.

The purchasers, the district health authorities, and the GP fundholders, found that the new policies led to unforeseen difficulties. The resources available to the district health authorities were insufficient to meet the needs of all the patients under their care.

Due to inadequate funding, the need for priority setting or rationing of services arose. It was noted that there was a huge discrepancy between the health authorities' intentions about what they planned to do and their levels of funding for priority services. As a result, proposals were made to remove control of priority concerns from a local to a national level.

The government had assumed that competition between the national health trusts for service contracts from the purchasers would create an improved quality of care, greater patient choice and a greater level of efficiency.

In fact, many doctors were finding the results of this competition were contrary to the government's expectations. The new policies proved to be less efficient and had produced an unfair and unequal system of healthcare which did not provide for the needs of all patients—

Under the new scheme, it was optional whether or not GPs became fundholders. The doctors in our surgery had refused to become fundholders. It soon became obvious that those who were not fundholders were receiving differential and some said, discriminatory treatment. When the doctors tried to gain access to hospital care for their patients, they were experiencing great difficulties.

Studies demonstrated that when GP fundholders paid for their patient's treatment, the waiting lists were much shorter for their patients than those of the non-fundholders who did not pay for their patients.

The doctors in our surgery strongly believed that treatment should be freely available to all patients.

The fact that the government had created a two-tier system of healthcare, favouring the fundholding doctors and surgeries, aroused serious concern. At Brondesbury Road, all the doctors, with one exception, (a new doctor and a member of the Conservative party), found the new reforms insupportable. They made a decision to publicly demonstrate their disapproval.

One afternoon, during their lunch break, they all gathered to protest in front of our surgery on Brondesbury Road. They held placards clearly stating their objections to the new inequalities that the government reforms had created. In Brent, most surgeries had become fundholders and I was informed that we stood out as being the only non-conforming surgery in the borough.

I cannot affirm whether or not this statement was correct but there were rumours that some individuals at Brent Council were not pleased with the decision of our surgery. As Brent Council was overwhelmingly in favour of the government's position to promote GP fundholding, the decision not to become fundholders would have been problematic in their eyes. Their disapproval of our surgery's position might explain some of the antipathy Brent Council expressed towards our surgery at a later date.

The criticisms regarding the new contracts were many and too detailed to mention in great detail. The new contracts were prescriptive, specifying the health problems to be treated. Doctors were not allowed to prioritise the needs of their local communities. There was no provision for a much needed, more flexible approach, targeting specific problems in particular areas.

GPs lacked experience and expertise in contracting health services, a skill which was required to obtain the requisite care for their patients.

Though the new reforms were set up to save money, substantial costs were incurred for executing and monitoring the numerous contracts which ensued.

The new inequalities in health care for patients were, undeniably, in conflict with the values and aims of the National Health Service.

In 1999, a Labour Government was elected which abolished GP fundholding. New primary care groups were established who could commission care on behalf of their local communities.

Our surgery was greatly relieved as the doctors no longer felt they were living under siege. They could once again offer a service of equal health care to all their patients which is what they were all committed to originally under their NHS contract.

MY WORK AT THE SURGERY

My work at the surgery was far more demanding than I had anticipated. The knowledge required to do a satisfactory job expanded beyond a formal knowledge of therapeutic approaches to a vast array of emotional problems.

Patients referred to me were usually upset about distressing incidents which had occurred or the state of their lives in general. We always considered ways to alleviate their emotional problems but, it was important to recognise that the causes of their difficulties were widespread and numerous.

I shall list here some of the very wide range of problems with which I was dealing: depression, obsessive compulsive disorder, anorexia and bulimia, post-traumatic stress disorder, marital problems, sexual problems, sexual abuse, drug and alcohol problems and suicide.

I felt the number of appointments which I could offer was sometimes not adequate to sort out the complex problems with which I was confronted.

The NHS had many clinics to which I could refer people. When space was available, I referred patients for further help, but there was usually a delay as the NHS waiting lists were very long. As a result, I felt obliged to find other organisations within the community which offered help for specific problems. To deal with difficulties related to rent and housing and individuals who required guidance in parenting and childcare, I contacted Brent Social Services.

I was constantly passing on the telephone number of the Samaritans, particularly to those who were in desperate straits or had suicidal tendencies. Couples who were having relationship problems were referred to Marriage Guidance for counselling. But the waiting lists were so long that they often pleaded to have sessions with me at the surgery and I sometimes complied with their wishes. The Citizens Advice Bureau always dealt with problems related to Brent Council and could always direct people to the correct department to sort out their problems.

There were several teen-agers and young twenty year olds who had left school early and now found their lives unbearably dull and their jobs extremely boring. Being seriously angry and dissatisfied, they couldn't contemplate spending the rest of their lives in such tedium.

We looked at what sort of life they envisioned for themselves and the likelihood of succeeding in their ambitions. We discussed their education and their interests, changing jobs, apprenticeships (There weren't many) and Access Courses. As many had never learned to stick with any task long term, they found it difficult to move on. These were the times that I felt the service I was offering was totally inadequate. Many of these young people had never received the family support they so needed, especially for their hopes of better jobs and possibly further education. They required individual mentoring but the concept of mentoring students in difficulty had not yet developed in any school or institution within the community. At the time, no outside help was available. I did my best to help them boost their self-confidence and tried to guide them in the directions they desired, but was always aware that they required more consistent, individualised help than I could offer.

There were a few without any formal qualifications, who jumped at the opportunity to complete an Access Course as the first step towards entering further education. To observe their transformation from a despondent, hopeless individual to one with aspirations in the future was always a very rewarding experience.

It took a few years to compile a list of what help was available and which organisations provided it.

Although help was available through various agencies in the community, it was never immediately forthcoming. There were often long waiting lists here too. The problem was that, in Brent, the social services and the many agencies offering help suffered from insufficient funding, so their services were often oversubscribed. Inevitably, trying to access more help required an inordinate amount of patience on all sides as the process was so delayed.

As our work at the surgery revealed areas in which we felt we should become more specialised, on weekends, Jess and I constantly attended conferences which focussed on specific psychological problems. We wanted to improve our understanding of the difficulties involved in specific problems and how to manage them better.

As much of the work to improve the quality of the service I offered was performed outside of surgery hours, week after week, I found myself immersed in activities which forced me to work longer and longer hours. I was also rushing home from work to see private clients and on my free days, I saw private clients, as well.

I hadn't expected to have so many private clients, but, by word of mouth, my client list had increased considerably. I didn't feel under any undue stress or strain but realised that I had absolutely no time to pursue any enjoyable, leisure activities. Having to acknowledge that my life was totally consumed with work and work-related activities, I vowed to rectify the problem.

In order to regain some balance in my life, I decided to relinquish seeing private clients. It took some time to reduce the list but as I consistently refused to take any new clients, the list was slowly shrinking.

Just as I had finally succeeded in eliminating all of my private clients, the doctors made a shocking announcement.

THE MANCHESTER RULING

The year was 1998. At one of our monthly staff meetings, the doctors stated that they were very sorry, but they could no longer hire me. They didn't want to lose me, but they had no choice. Brent council had informed them that there was a new law, The Manchester Ruling, which stated that counsellors could no longer be hired in surgeries.

I was completely taken aback at this news but also astonished that there had been no announcements to that effect in either the British Psychological Society or the British Association of Counselling journals.

I rang both groups and was told that neither one had been informed that counsellors were to be withdrawn from surgeries. Nor had either one heard of the Manchester Ruling.

I approached the doctors again. What was the Manchester Ruling? When was it passed and what exactly did it say? For how much longer was I allowed to work? The doctors knew absolutely nothing about the Manchester ruling. They hadn't read it and were only reporting what the council officials in Brent had told them.

I rang various friends in the counselling and therapy field but to no avail. They had never heard of the Manchester Ruling either. As I could gather no information from anyone about the Manchester Ruling, I decided to ring Brent council as the councillors there seemed to be the only people who had any knowledge of this new legislation.

When I rang Brent Council, I spoke to a man who at first, seemed willing to answer all of my questions and confirmed that the Manchester ruling did state that counselling could no longer be provided in GP surgeries.

As I didn't have a copy of the ruling and didn't know where to obtain one, I asked if he would send me a copy.

He sounded horrified. "You don't really want a copy of this ruling. It's very long and full of legal jargon. You would have to be a lawyer to understand it."

I assured him that I did want a copy. My job was at stake. I wanted to understand the reason why I was being made redundant. Would he please send me a copy.

He protested once again that I wouldn't be able to understand it and that it would take hours to read all the difficult details. I insisted that I did want a copy and with great reluctance, he agreed to send me a copy in the post.

About forty-five minutes later, my phone rang. It was the same councillor I had spoken to, stating that he had spoken to his colleagues, and they had agreed that it was impossible to send me a copy of the Manchester Ruling.

I responded, saying, "Surely this is a document in the public domain. What reason would there be to prevent the council from sending me a copy?"

He never answered this question but kept repeating that it was the Council's decision that it was just impossible so he couldn't mail me a copy. In a state of frustration and fury, I ended the conversation.

For three days, I thought, at length, about my predicament. I felt defeated and didn't know which way to turn. I told myself to unwind, sleep on it, relax.

And it eventually worked. When I woke up on the fourth morning, for the very first time, I produced an idea which sounded as if it might be useful. If the legislation was called the Manchester Ruling, it must have originated in Manchester. I rang telephone enquiries to obtain the telephone number of the Manchester Health Authority.

I explained my situation in regard to the Manchester Ruling and met with a very perplexed response. The individual I spoke to had never heard of this legislation but would give me the number of a surgery to ring to see if they could clarify matters. I rang the surgery but received a similar response. They were sorry they couldn't help but gave me the name of another GP who might be helpful.

This was the first of many similar responses I received, day after day, as I was passed from one surgery to another. Any mention of the Manchester ruling always produced a totally blank response.

I spent three days on the phone, doing nothing but ringing people, waiting for return calls, and being passed on to different surgeries and sometimes different organisations and different people.

I was completely distraught, spending all my free time on the phone every day with no positive results of any kind. But I was so angry with the Brent Councillors for refusing to send me a document which was in the public domain that I felt impelled to continue until I, actually, had proof of what this document contained.

By the fourth day, I was shocked and surprised to find to find that I was talking to people who didn't know anything about the Manchester Ruling but, in fact, had heard of it. I allowed myself the first glimmer of hope.

By the fifth day, I, finally, spoke to someone who did know about the legislation. He offered to put me in touch with a person who had more expertise on the subject. When I rang his number, he was not in his office. His secretary would ask him to ring me after the weekend, when he was due to return. I took his number and prayed that I would not be waiting, in vain, for a return call, as I had so many other days. At least I had his number so I could contact him if he failed to ring me.

To my delight, on Monday morning, the phone rang. It was Mr Merce from the Manchester Health Authority. He said he knew all about the Manchester Ruling and would be pleased to answer my questions. (He was obviously in a different department from the one I had reached with my first phone call at the Manchester Health Authority).

I explained that I was about to lose my job because of this ruling. He was appalled!

"The Manchester Ruling has nothing to do with counsellors in surgeries. It related to a problematic case about a social worker. How could anyone draw the conclusion that counsellors should not work in surgeries because of this legislation? They can't possibly have read this document." When I asked if he could mail me a copy, mentioning that I understood that it was very long and full of legal jargon, he laughed preposterously. "Absolutely not! It is a very short document written in very clear, simple English."

He said he was pleased to help and would post me a copy of the legislation and reiterated that the Council could not justify firing me because of the Manchester Ruling.

In two days, I received a copy of the court proceedings and a copy of the Manchester Ruling. It was just as he had said, a document of three pages typed in clear and simple English, with absolutely no legal jargon involved at all.

MY REDUNDANCY

I sent a copy of the Manchester Ruling to all the doctors in the surgery with an accompanying note, explaining that the ruling in no way related to counsellors and that there were no grounds for firing me because of this legislation.

The doctors next meeting with the Brent councillors proved to be a stormy event. Not only were the doctors angry that the councillors had lied to them about the significance of the document, but they were also furious that they had refused to post me a copy of the Manchester Ruling. For a few months, we heard nothing more about Brent Council deciding that my job was to be eliminated, until the day that another notice arrived, stating a new reason why I couldn't maintain my job at the surgery.

Let me interject here, Brent Council was always in debt and was well-known for saving money by removing jobs they supported monetarily. Brent council paid 90% of my salary. Eliminating my job would produce a sizeable saving for their accounts.

I was informed that we had already lost a dietician and a social worker, thanks to Brent Council's decisions. I felt that my job was just next on the list.

To completely remove my job, Brent Council had concocted an entirely new scheme. I had been working in the Primary Care Services of the NHS for many years. The new notice from the Council specified that Brent Council could no longer support counsellors who worked in Primary Care.

The doctors did not dispute the point. But, in order to outsmart the Brent councillors, they produced a document which proved that I now worked in Secondary Care in the NHS.

It was just possible, technically, according to a strict interpretation of the rules, to make a case for this conclusion. Primary Care is the first point of contact for medical consultation between a patient and a GP. Medical specialists and other health care professionals who, typically, don't have initial contact with the patients, provide Secondary Care.

My list of patients were all referrals from the doctors. I was never their first point of contact.

This clever plan of action was not well received by the councillors. The final blow was that that they still refused to provide 90% of my salary, the sum to which they were previously committed. The doctors concerted campaign for nearly two years, to save my job, had all been in vain. Without any fuss or fanfare, my job was suddenly removed from Brent Council's list and I was made redundant.

MY RETIREMENT

Despite the fact that I had always believed that the Brent councillors would be victorious in the battle over my job, I was still shocked when I fully appreciated the fact that I would no longer be working at the job to which I was so devoted.

In the midst of my distress, the practice manager casually mentioned that it was understandable that my job was at stake. There was no evidence that counselling had ever helped anyone. I wasn't angry, I was just appalled at his ignorance.

"Are you contradicting the scientific evidence in the British Medical Journals and the American Counselling and Psychology Journals that prove how effective counselling can be?"

"Your assumptions are totally mistaken. I suggest you read the relevant research before you come to any conclusions about counselling." Uttering these comments, I walked away in disapproval, not waiting for a response.

Brent's decision not to pay 90% of my salary, had left the doctors in a dreadful dilemma. They wanted to continue a counselling service at the surgery. They paid 10% of my salary but couldn't afford to pay 100%.

They suggested that I could keep my job at the surgery, but I would have to charge the patients for their counselling sessions.

I understood why they were making this proposal and was grateful for their consideration of my position. But I was both delighted and distressed at their suggestion.

Charging the patients completely undermined my reasons for wanting to work for the NHS. I had always been critical of the fact that psychiatry was so expensive and mainly available to those who could afford it. Though less expensive, a similar criticism could be made of counselling and other types of therapy available privately.

The NHS had included psychiatric help in their services and more recently, had accepted counselling in surgeries, making free psychological help available to everyone, irrespective of income.

I wanted to offer psychological help to those who needed it and not just to those who could afford it. My response was highly emotional. How could I start charging patients who couldn't afford to pay? I thought of the man who couldn't attend a job interview because he didn't have the bus fare to travel there and the woman who had to make a choice for the week between buying milk for the baby and buying nappies.

These were people living on benefits who didn't waste money, but on the funds they were given, could never quite make ends meet.

I thought of one of the most complicated cases that I took on board. She was, actually, Jess's client. Jess arrived home from work one day looking very distraught.

During her fifty-minute session, her client had cried incessantly. She was pregnant. When she told her partner, he vanished without saying a word, taking all the money they had.

She had moved recently and knew no-one in the neighbourhood. She felt abandoned and alone and was very upset that she had nothing for the new baby and no money to buy anything.

Despite the fact that social services had promised to help her, she had received no money. The baby was already overdue. She was worried that she would come home from hospital with a new baby who would have no clothes, no nappies no food and no cot.

Jess rang social services but did not succeed in getting a definite commitment about when any money would arrive. The woman saw no way out of her situation, nor did Jess and I. The help she wanted might be available in the future, but it was simply not available now when she needed it. How could we desert this woman who had no-one to assist her and was in such a destitute state?

I, immediately, rang my daughter, Michèle. Did she still have the children's old pram? The grandchildren had recently outgrown it. I explained the woman's predicament and asked if she would like to offer the pram to her.

Michèle, also appalled at this woman's situation, immediately agreed to give her the pram. With Jess accompanying me, I drove to her house in south London to collect it, along with some brand new clothes, soft toys and baby clothes of different sizes, including some for new born babies which Michèle had freely offered.

Jess and I bought nappies and powdered formula for the baby and drove to her client's very tiny one-room flat, so tiny, that we could barely fit the pram in at the end of the bed.

Social Services did eventually come to Jess's client's aid but not before she delivered the baby. She was someone who had fallen through the cracks of all the helping agencies. Jess and I felt vindicated in our efforts to help her.

Despite being trained not to get over-involved with clients as it could alter the client-therapist relationship detrimentally, we felt, in this instance, we could only make a humane decision and not one based on boundaries in the relationship between client and counsellor.

When the case for following the rules laid down by our governing bodies was juxtaposed against alleviating the situation of a helpless individual in abject poverty, there seemed no moral justification for adhering to the boundaries.

Remembering the plight of Jess's client and many other unforgettable individuals only increased my resolve never to charge money for my services at the surgery.

The doctors' proposition that patients should pay for counselling was incompatible with my decision and what I believed were the principles of the NHS. I decided to resign my job at the surgery.

In the third week of December 1999, I officially departed from the job I had so much enjoyed, despite its many challenges. I was sixty-six and had hoped to work until I was seventy, but that was not to be.

In 1982, when I was hired, there were no jobs for psychologists or counsellors in doctors' surgeries. Within the NHS, no provision was made for the widespread existence of psychological problems. My post was experimental and was not included on the NHS list of available jobs. Because my job did not officially exist, there was no pension available for my seventeen years of service.

I was delighted when pensions for counsellors became available on the NHS, about one year after I left my job, but it was too late for me.

I returned to seeing private clients and because they offered such a wide variety of courses, I joined the U3A (University of the Third Age) in Hampstead. While I was happily immersed in engaging in new activities, my children suggested that I should write my autobiography.

I acceded to their request and somewhat reluctantly abandoned most of my new interests to focus on the writing. But I could not abandon my deep concern for the difficulties which beset the world which we all inhabit.

The prevalence of injustice on the grounds of race, religion, sex and age has, inevitably, propelled me to support equality for unfairly treated individuals and groups, including the LGBT communities.

I maintain that freedom of speech is an important right which must be upheld if we are to successfully advocate for those who suffer unwarranted discrimination or are denied access to the possibility of freedom of speech.

I have continually protested about a tax system which heavily contributes to an unequal distribution of wealth, in favour of the rich.

Climate change is already devastating people's lives by producing extreme weather events which produce homelessness and damage the accustomed methods of food production, thus creating the spread of world poverty.

We know that the use of fossil fuels results in the creation of excess CO_2 in the atmosphere and has accelerated the rate of climate change. But both governments and relevant businesses appear reluctant to commit to the rapid development of solar, wind and tidal power. These sources of renewable energy are our greatest assets in combatting environmental damage from fossil fuels.

Nuclear power is often proposed as a solution to the fossil fuel problem because it provides low carbon emissions even when the wind remains calm, and the sun deigns to shine.

But, despite low carbon emissions, nuclear energy continually produces dangerous radioactive waste which cannot be destroyed but must be stored.

No permanent sites for the storage of nuclear waste have ever been established in any country possessing nuclear weapons. Even if they were, they would not be permanently safe because they are still vulnerable to natural disasters which can cause the release of the dangerous radioactive materials into the atmosphere.

Many of us have voiced our concern about the outstanding problems of the day but we have not yet provided any long-term answers.

Viable solutions for a more healthy and harmonious future will depend on the resilience of the next generation. They have, in many ways, already demonstrated their profound understanding of the issues at stake.

I wish them every success and trust that their determination and fortitude can rectify the many contentious issues which confront them.

Milton Keynes UK
Ingram Content Group UK Ltd.
UKHW050946291223
435160UK00002B/2